Ordnance Survey

STREET ATLAS
West Kent

Contents

III Key to map symbols

IV-V Key to map pages

VI Administrative and post code boundaries

1 Street maps

190 Town plans of Ashford and Canterbury

191 Town plans of Dover and Folkestone

192 Index of hospitals, railway stations, schools, shopping centres, street names and universities

PHILIP'S

First edition published 1989
Third edition published 1994
First colour edition published 1997
Reprinted 1998 by

Ordnance Survey®   and   George Philip Ltd
Romsey Road,   an imprint of Reed Consumer Books Ltd
Maybush,   Michelin House, 81 Fulham Road,
Southampton SO16 4GU   London SW3 6RB
                                 and Auckland, Melbourne

ISBN 0-540-07366-0 (hardback)
ISBN 0-540-07367-9 (wire-o)

To the best of the Publishers´ knowledge, the information in this atlas
was correct at the time of going to press. No responsibility can be
accepted for any errors or their consequences.

The representation in this atlas of a road, track or path is no evidence
of the existence of a right of way.

**The mapping between pages 1 and 191 (inclusive) in this atlas is
derived from Ordnance Survey® OSCAR® and Land-Line® data,
and Landranger® mapping.**

Ordnance Survey, OSCAR, Land-Line and Landranger are registered
trade marks of Ordnance Survey, the National Mapping Agency of
Great Britain.

Printed and bound in Spain by Cayfosa

Motorway (with junction number)	
Primary routes (dual carriageway and single)	
A roads (dual carriageway and single)	
B roads (dual carriageway and single)	
Minor through road (dual carriageway and single)	
Minor roads	
Roads under construction	
Railways	
Tramway, miniature railway	
Rural track, private road or narrow road in urban area	
Gate or obstruction to traffic (restrictions may not apply at all times or to all vehicles)	
All paths, bridleways, byway open to all traffic, road used as a public path	
The representation in this atlas of a road, track or path is no evidence of the existence of a right of way	
29 **130** **Adjoining page indicators**	
Leeds Castle **Non-Roman antiquity**	
ROMAN FORT **Roman antiquity**	

Acad	**Academy**	
Cemy	**Cemetery**	
C Ctr	**Civic Centre**	
CH	**Club House**	
Coll	**College**	
Ex H	**Exhibition Hall**	
Ind Est	**Industrial Estate**	
Inst	**Institute**	
Ct	**Law Court**	
L Ctr	**Leisure Centre**	
LC	**Level Crossing**	
Liby	**Library**	
Mkt	**Market**	
Meml	**Memorial**	
Mon	**Monument**	
Mus	**Museum**	
Obsy	**Observatory**	
Pal	**Royal Palace**	
PH	**Public House**	
Resr	**Reservoir**	
Ret Pk	**Retail Park**	
Sch	**School**	
Sh Ctr	**Shopping Centre**	
Sta	**Station**	
TH	**Town Hall/House**	
Trad Est	**Trading Estate**	
Univ	**University**	
YH	**Youth Hostel**	

British Rail station	
D	**Docklands Light Railway station**
Private railway station	
Bus, coach station	
Ambulance station	
Coastguard station	
Fire station	
Police station	
Casualty entrance to hospital	
Church, place of worship	
H	**Hospital**
i	**Information centre**
P	**Parking**
PO	**Post Office**
West Kent College	**Important buildings, schools, colleges, universities and hospitals**
County boundaries	
River Medway	**Water name**
Stream	
River or canal (minor and major)	
Water	
Tidal water	
Woods	
Houses	

■ The dark grey border on the inside edge of some pages indicates that the mapping does not continue onto the adjacent page

■ The small numbers around the edges of the maps identify the 1 kilometre National Grid lines

The scale of the maps is 5.52 cm to 1 km (3½ inches to 1 mile)

0	¼	½	¾	1 mile
0	250m	500m	750m	1 Kilometre

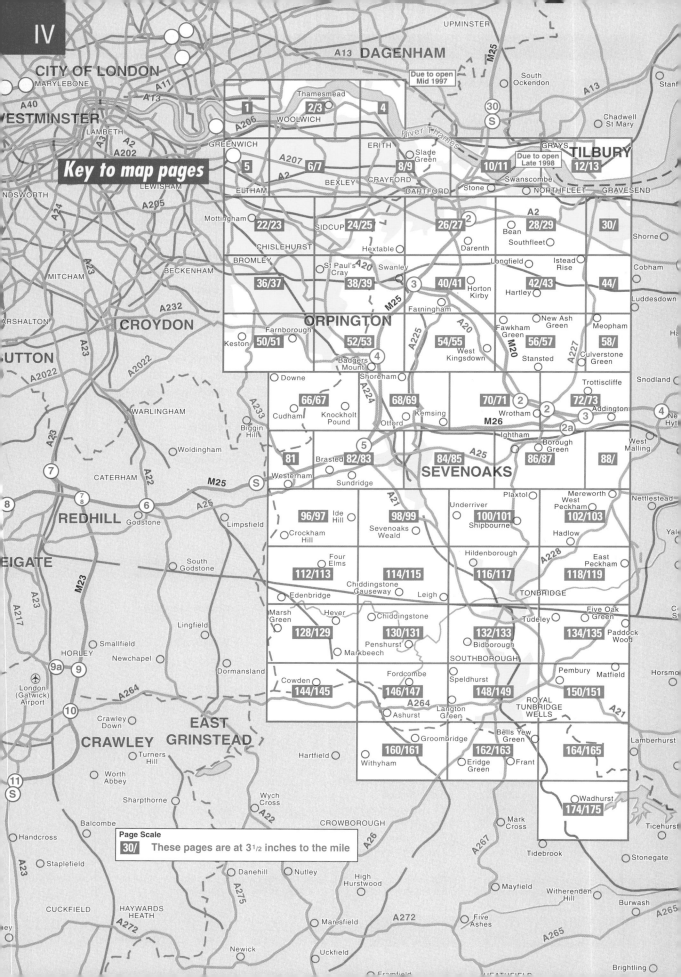

Key to map pages

IV

CITY OF LONDON

DAGENHAM

TILBURY

WESTMINSTER

CROYDON

ORPINGTON

SEVENOAKS

SUTTON

REDHILL

REIGATE

CRAWLEY

EAST GRINSTEAD

TONBRIDGE

ROYAL TUNBRIDGE WELLS

SOUTHBOROUGH

Due to open Mid 1997

Due to open Late 1998

1	2/3	4	
5	6/7	8/9	10/11	12/13
22/23	24/25	26/27	28/29	30/
36/37	38/39	40/41	42/43	44/
50/51	52/53	54/55	56/57	58/
66/67	68/69	70/71	72/73	
81	82/83	84/85	86/87	88/
96/97	98/99	100/101	102/103	
112/113	114/115	116/117	118/119	
128/129	130/131	132/133	134/135	
144/145	146/147	148/149	150/151	
160/161	162/163	164/165		
174/175				

Page Scale

30/ These pages are at 3½ inches to the mile

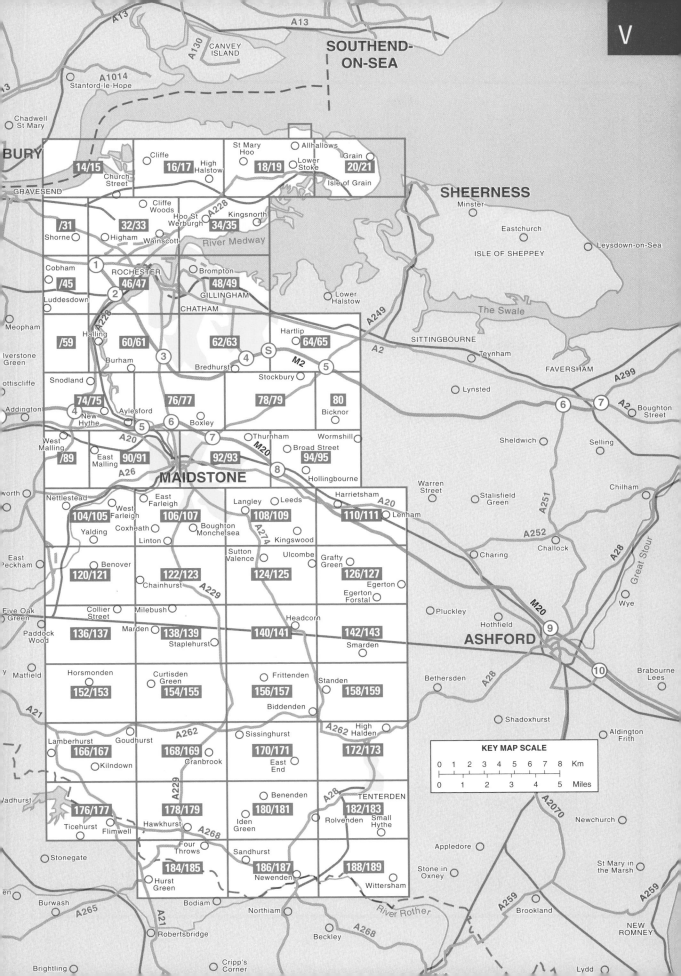

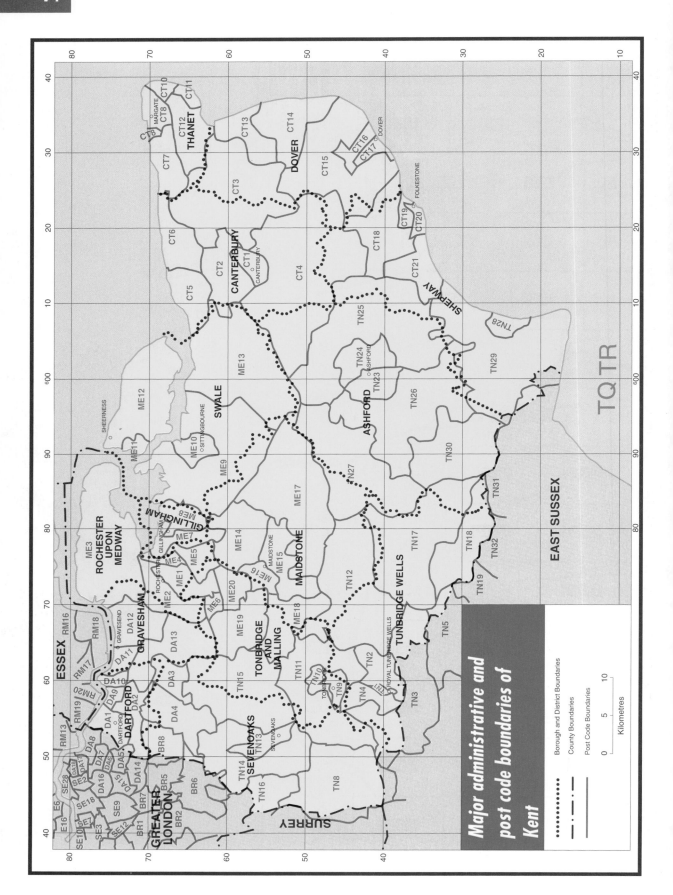

Major administrative and post code boundaries of Kent

Borough and District Boundaries
County Boundaries
Post Code Boundaries

Kilometres
0   5   10

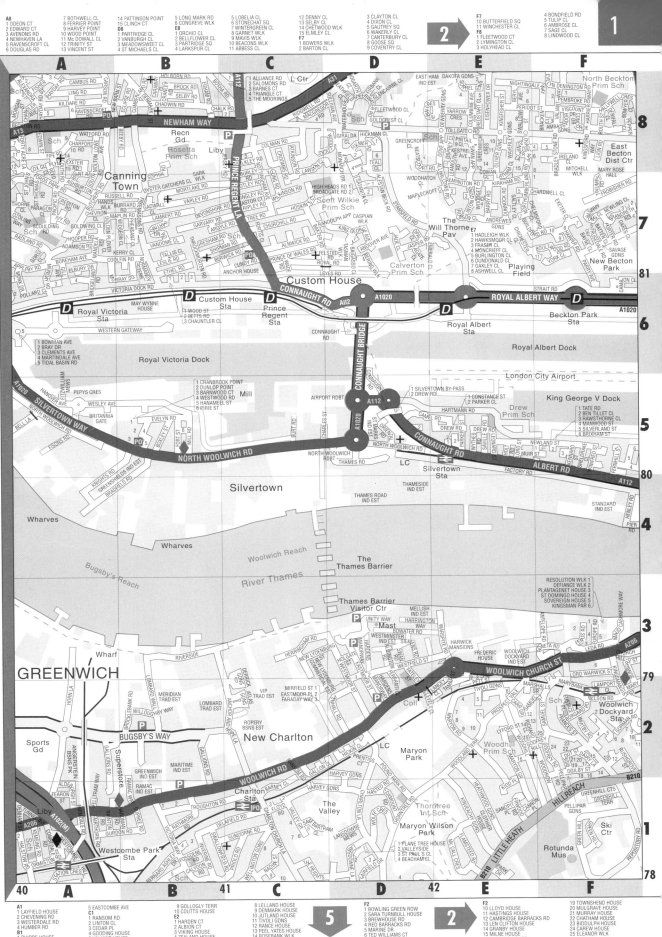

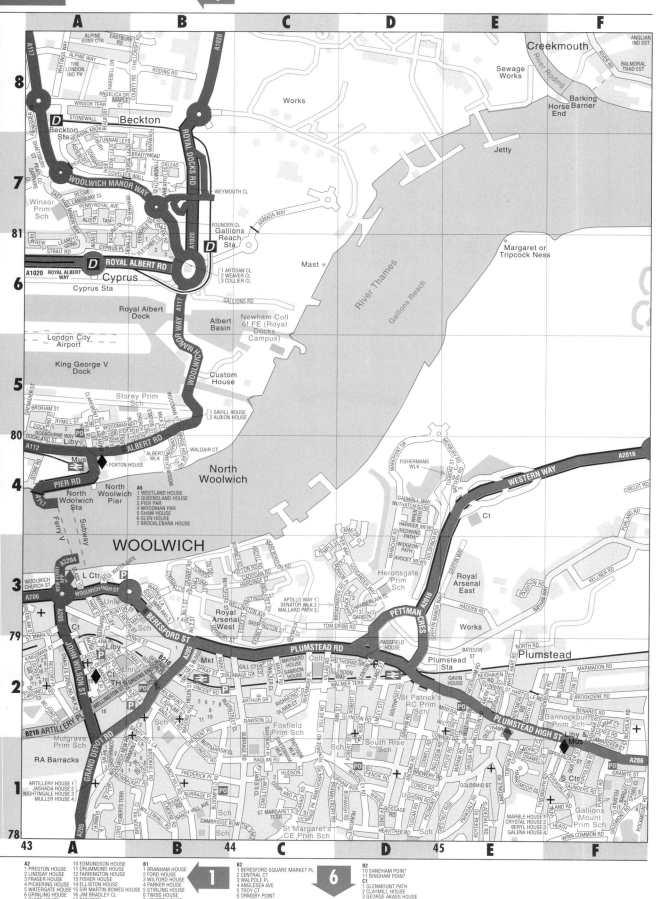

ANGLIAN
IND EST

Creekmouth

BALMORAL
TRAD EST

Sewage
Works

Horse
End

Barking
Barrier

Jetty

Works

Margaret or
Tripcock Ness

River Thames

Gallions Reach

Mast

WESTERN WAY   A2016

CIRCUIT RD

FISHERMANS
WLK

Ct

Royal
Arsenal
East

Royal Arsenal
West

Heronsgate
Prim Sch

PETTMAN CRES

Works

Plumstead

PLUMSTEAD RD

North
Woolwich

WOOLWICH

North
Woolwich
Sta

North
Woolwich
Pier

Plumstead
Sta

PLUMSTEAD HIGH ST   A206

Liby &
Mus

S Ctr

St Patrick's
RC Prim Sch

Foxfield
Prim Sch

South Rise
Sch

Bannockburn
Prim Sch

Gallions
Mount
Prim Sch

RA Barracks

B210 ARTILLERY PL

GRAND DEPOT RD

JOHN WILSON ST

St Margaret's
CE Prim Sch

Mulgrave
Prim Sch

Beckton

Beckton
Sta

WOOLWICH MANOR WAY

Winsor
Prim
Sch

ROYAL DOCKS RD

A1020

Gallions
Reach
Sta

Royal Albert
Dock

ROYAL ALBERT RD

Cyprus

Cyprus Sta

A1020
ROYAL ALBERT
WAY

London City
Airport

King George V
Dock

Albert
Basin

Newham Coll
of FE (Royal
Docks
Campus)

Custom
House

Storey Prim
Sch

ALBERT RD

PIER RD

A117

Ferry V

Subway

A2204

Woolwich
Church St

A206

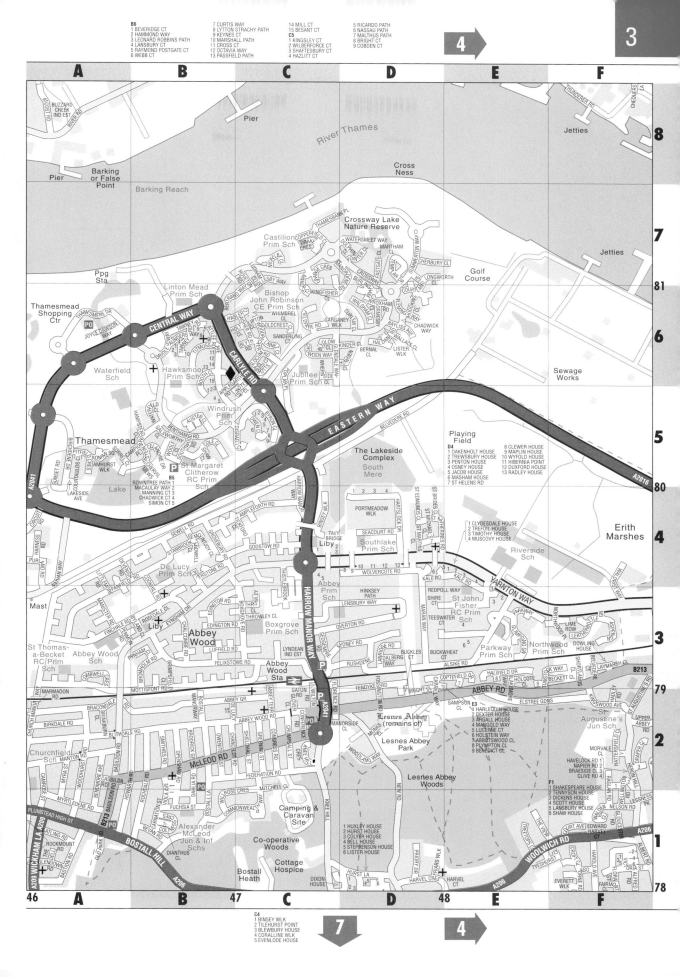

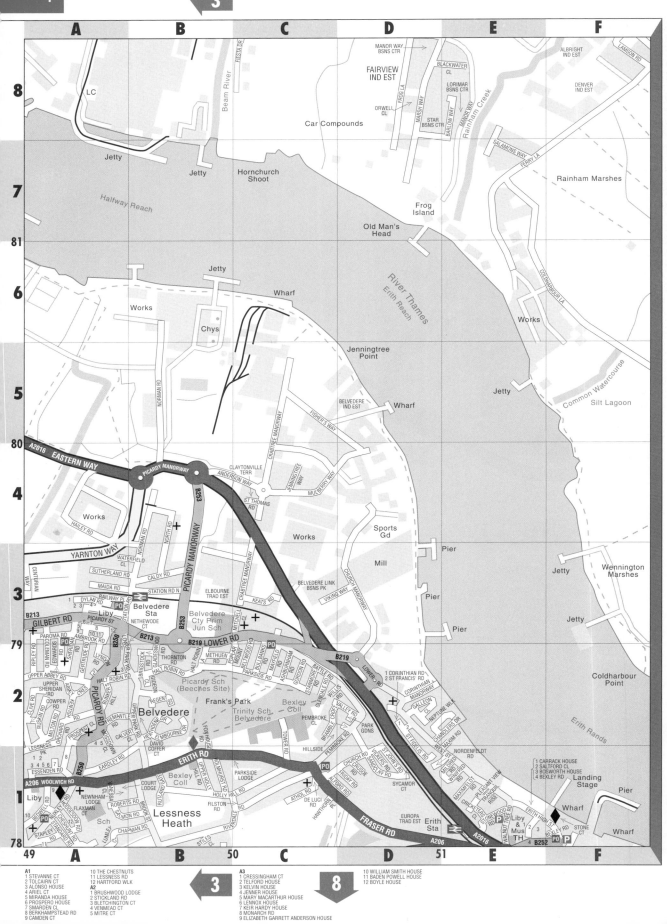

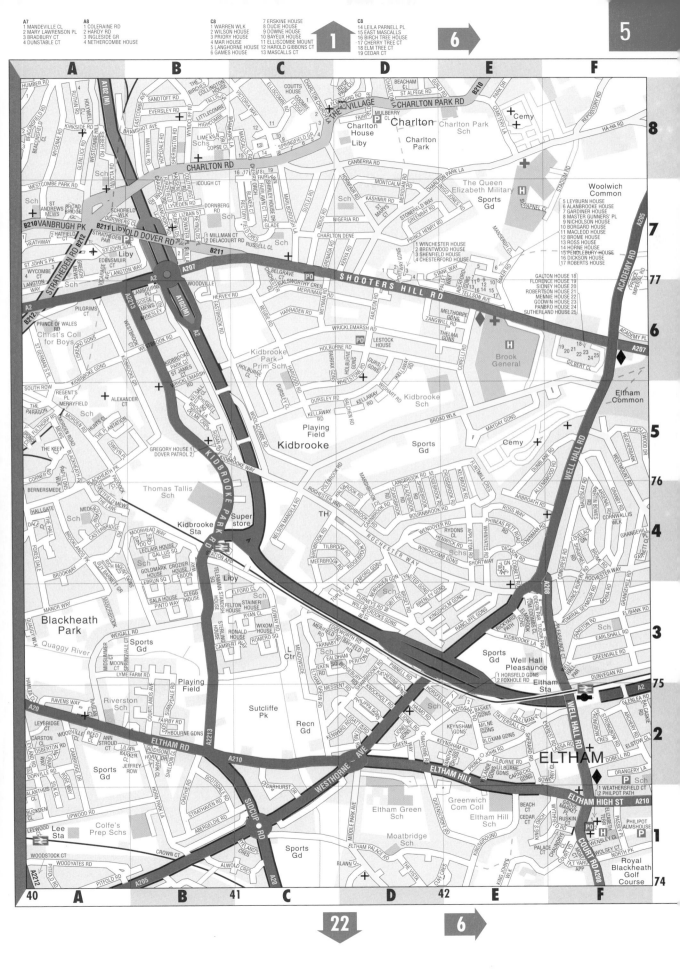

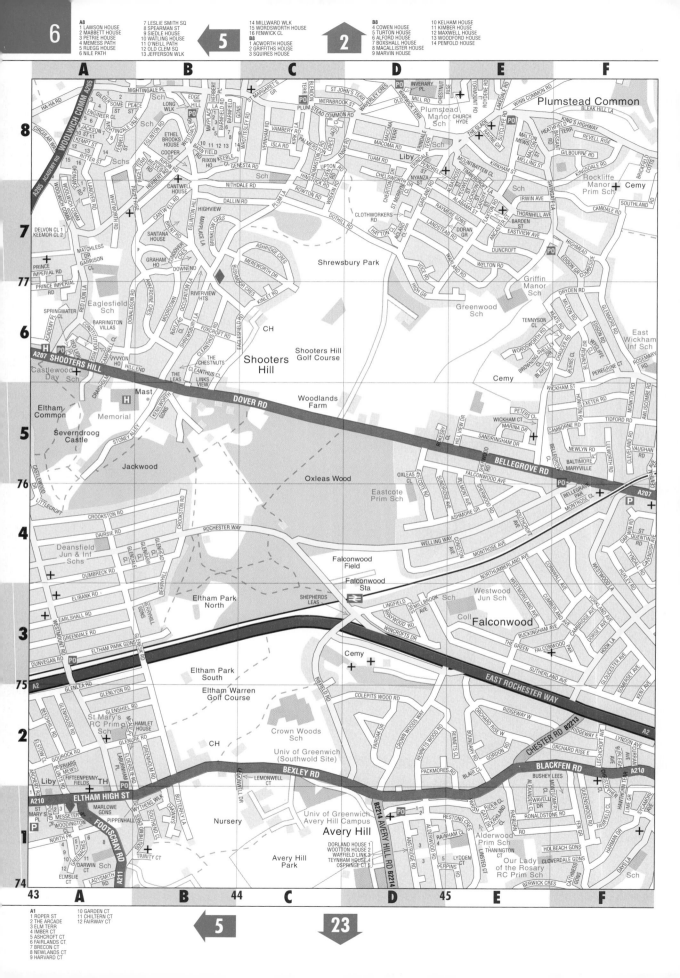

5

2

5

23

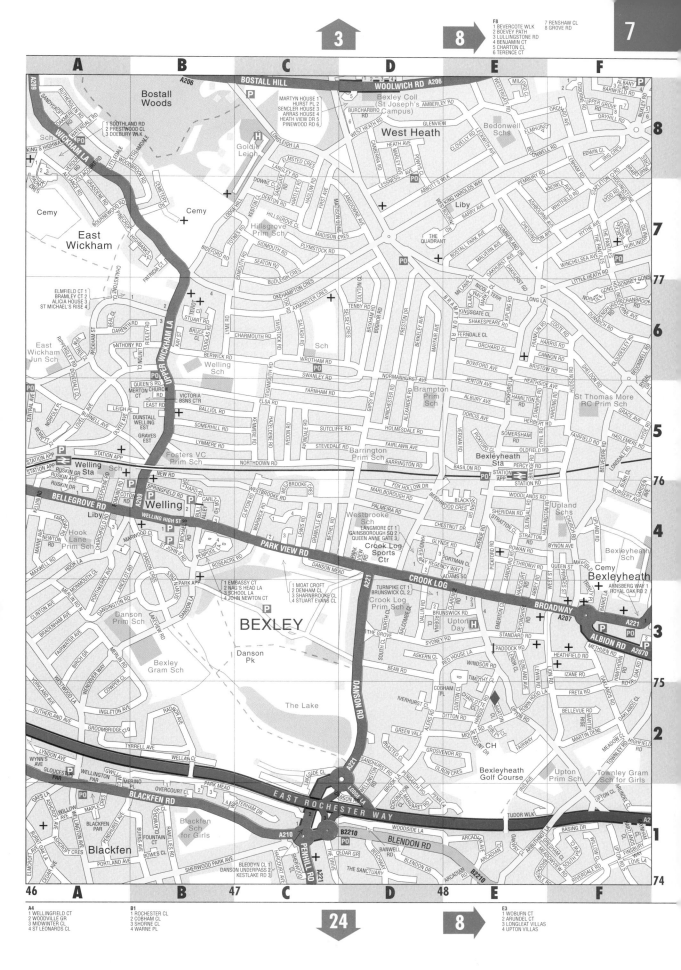

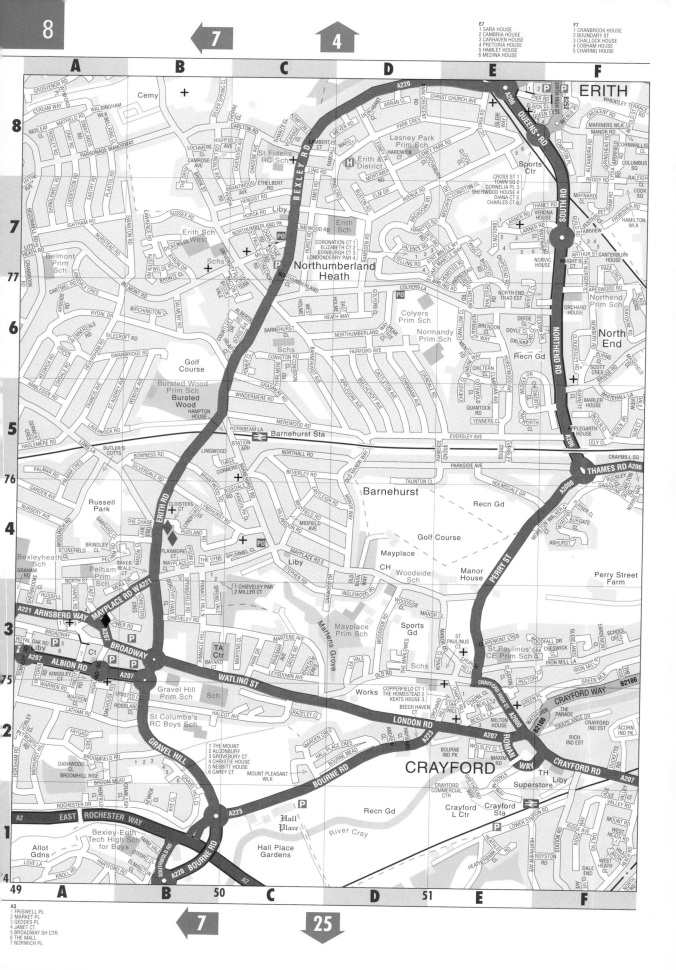

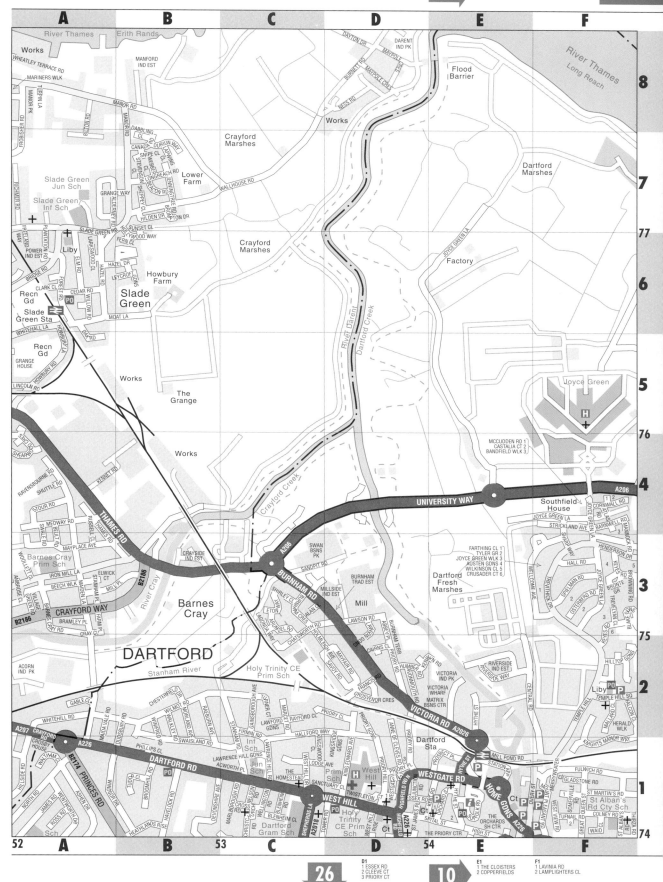

D1
1 ESSEX RD
2 CLEEVE CT
3 PRIORY CT

E1
1 THE CLOISTERS
2 COPPERFIELDS

F1
1 LAVINIA RD
2 LAMPLIGHTERS CL

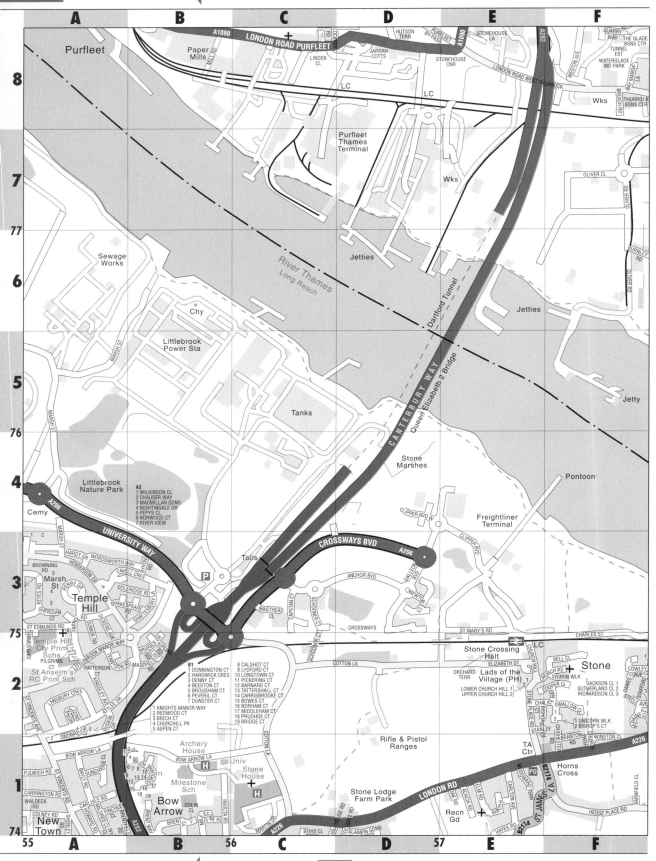

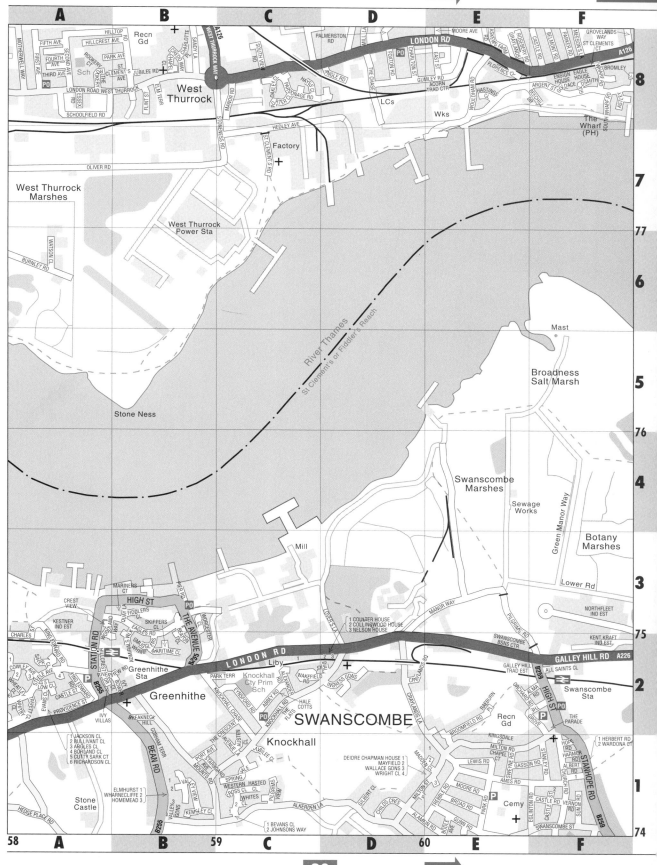

12

A B C D E F

8

7

77

6

5

76

4

3

75

2

1

74

28
12

MOTHERWELL WAY
FIFTH AVE
HILLTOP
HILLCREST AVE
Recn Gd
FIRST AVE
FOURTH AVE
SECOND AVE
THIRD AVE
PARK AVE
ROOKERY WAY
ST CLEMENT'S AVE
Sch
LONDON ROAD WEST THURROCK
PO
ESSEX RD
SCHOOLFIELD RD
FLINT TERR
ELM TERR
SANDY LA
CROD WAY
CR CHAPEL
JUBILEE RD
SOUTH VIEW
WEST THURROCK WAY
A126

West Thurrock

MANOR RD
STONENESS RD
ST CLEMENTS RD

West Thurrock Marshes

OLIVER RD
WATSON CL
BURNLEY RD

Factory

West Thurrock Power Sta

Stone Ness

River Thames
St Clements or Fiddler's Reach

PALMERSTON RD
FOXTON RD
CHARLTON ST
THE CHASE
HAYES RD
PARSONAGE RD
OAKLEY RD
ANGLE RD
GUMLEY RD
EAST ST
HEDLEY AVE

LONDON RD
MOORE AVE
ASKEW'S FARM LA
GRAYLANDS
CROSSKERY GRANGE
CASTLE RD
BELMONT RD
PARKER RD
MEESON'S LA
GROVELANDS WAY
ST CLEMENTS CT
A126

ACORN TRAD CTR
LCs
Wks
WOULDHAM RD
HASTINGS
FLORENCE CL
BEECHILL
ARGENT ST
DACE
ENSIGN HOUSE
EAGLE HOUSE
WHARF
BROMLEY RD
SMITH
SOUTH WHARF RD
ASTLEY
The Wharf (PH)

Broadness Salt Marsh

Mast

Swanscombe Marshes

Sewage Works

Green Manor Way

Botany Marshes

Lower Rd

Mill

MARINERS CT
CREST VIEW
HIGH ST
FIDDLERS
SKIPPERS CL
EAGLES RD
KESTNER IND EST
CHARLES
STATION RD
WOODLAND
QUAY LA
ADMIRALS WK
MARITIME CL
SMUGGLERS
BEATON
WORCESTER
THE AVENUE
B255
PERRY RD
PO
LONDON RD
Liby
COULTER HOUSE
COLLINGWOOD HOUSE
NELSON HOUSE
LOWER ST
MANOR WAY
PILGRIMS RD
NORTHFLEET IND EST
SWANSCOMBE BSNS CTR
KENT KRAFT IND EST

GALLEY HILL RD A226
GALLEY HILL TRAD EST
ALL SAINTS CL
B259
Swanscombe Sta

COWLEY
WHEAT
STEELE AVE
KING EDWARD RD
LOW CL
CASTLE VIEW
EVANS CL
WHITE
RIVERVIEW
B255
Greenhithe Sta
IVY VILLAS
PROVIDENCE ST
BREAKNECK HILL
CLARKE
KING EDWARD RD
Greenhithe

PARK TERR
Knockhall Cty Prim Sch
KNOCKHALL CHASE
EYNSFORD RD
ABBEY RD
KNOCKHALL RD
ALEXANDER RD
WAKEFIELD RD
HALE COTTS
FLATS
DIAL
INGRESS GDNS
CRAYLANDS LA
CRAYLANDS SQ

SWANSCOMBE
Knockhall

BROOMFIELD RD
KINGSDALE
MILTON RD
CHAPEL CT
LEWIS RD
DWEYNE RD
GASSON RD
STANLEY RD
ALBERT RD
CHURCH RD
ORCHARD RD
ALMA RD
RAEBURN
HIGH ST
Recn Gd
PO
THE PARADE
HERBERT RD
WARDONA CT
HOPE RD
HARMER RD

JACKSON CL
BULLIVANT CL
ARGLES CL
BORLAND CL
CUTTY SARK CT
RICHARDSON CL
BEAN RD
B255
THE CRESCENT
PORT AVE
STEDMAN
CROSS CL
VALLEY VIEW
MOUNTS RD
SPRING
WESTERN
HASTED
WHITES CL
PILGRIMS VIEW
JUBILEE RD
KEMSLEY CL

DEIDRE CHAPMAN HOUSE
MAYFIELD
WALLACE GDNS
WRIGHT CL
MADDEN CL
GILBERT RD
CHILDS CRES
ALAMEIN RD
BIDTLE RD
GUNN RD
MOORE RD
BROAD RD
TREBLE RD
PARK RD
AMES RD
LEWIS RD
Cemy
EGLINTON RD
CASTLE RD
VERNON RD
GINNS
SWANSCOMBE ST
STANHOPE RD
B259

ELMHURST
WHARNECLIFFE
HOMEMEAD
Stone Castle
HEDGE PLACE RD
GALLEY GDNS
ALKERDEN LA
BEVANS CL
JOHNSONS WAY

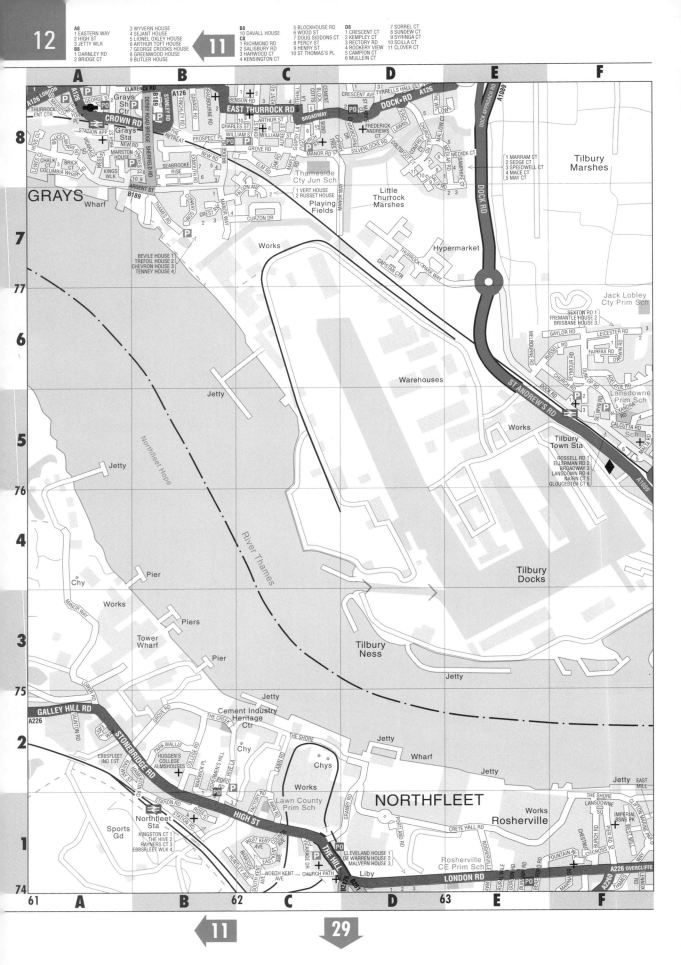

11

11
29

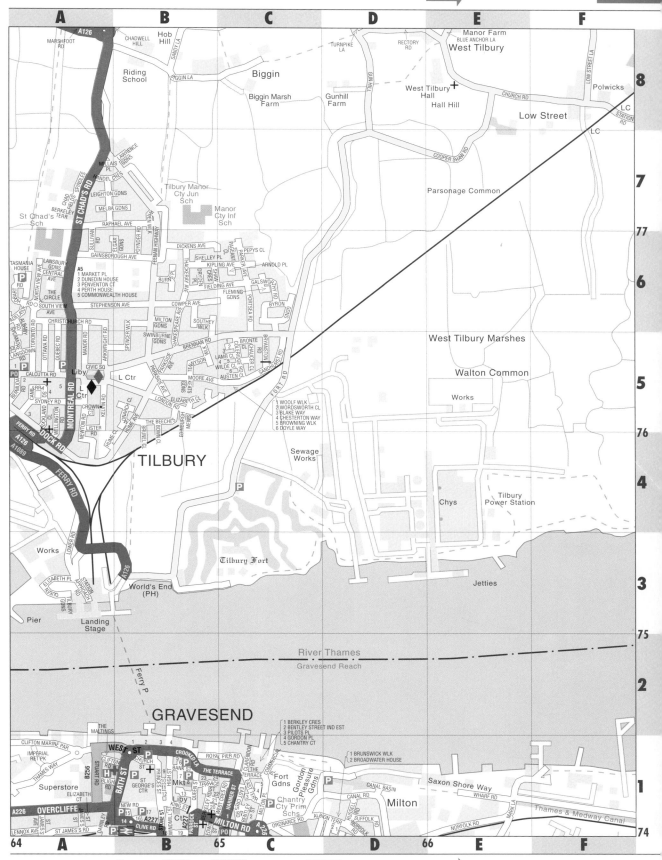

B1
1 CRAWLEY CT
2 REGENTS CT
3 MELBOURNE CT
4 TOWN PIER
5 BULL YD
6 HORN YD
7 NEW SWAN YD
8 MARKET ALLEY
9 CHURCH ALLEY
10 JURY ST
11 GLOBE YD
12 CHASE SQ
13 BREWHOUSE YD
14 BARRACK ROW
15 GARRICK ST
16 ANGLESEA PL
17 ANGLESEA CTR
18 RAILWAY PL
19 MANOR RD
20 WILFRED ST
21 BERNARD ST
22 THE TERRACE
23 ST ANDREWS CT
24 CROSS ST

13

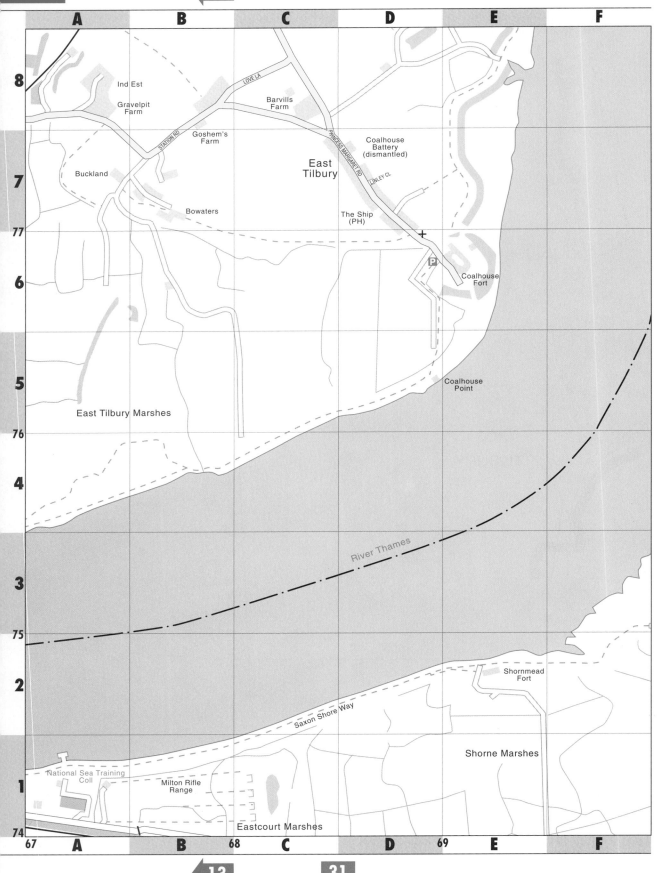

Ind Est

Gravelpit
Farm

LOVE LA

Barvills
Farm

STATION RD

Goshem's
Farm

PRINCESS MARGARET RD

Coalhouse
Battery
(dismantled)

Buckland

East
Tilbury

LINLEY CL

Bowaters

The Ship
(PH)

P

Coalhouse
Fort

Coalhouse
Point

East Tilbury Marshes

River Thames

Shornmead
Fort

Saxon Shore Way

Shorne Marshes

National Sea Training
Coll

Milton Rifle
Range

Eastcourt Marshes

River Thames
The Lower Hope

COASTGUARD
COTTS

Pier

Boatrick
House

Cliffe Creek

Saxon Shore Way

Cliffe Fort
(dis)

Jetties

Higham Creek

Conveyor

Depot

Royal
Albert
(PH)

CONCRETE
COTTS

Quarries
(dis)

SALT LA

Wks

West
Court

LC

Higham
Saltings

Higham
Marshes

Higham
Common

Barrow
Hill

Beckley
Hill

Oakleigh

Higham or
Church Street

CHURCH ST

15

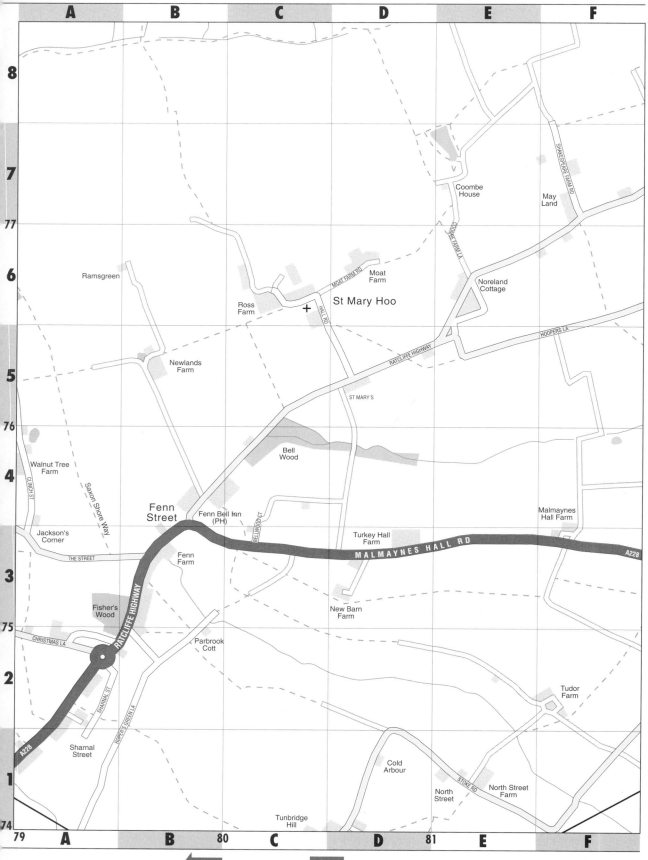

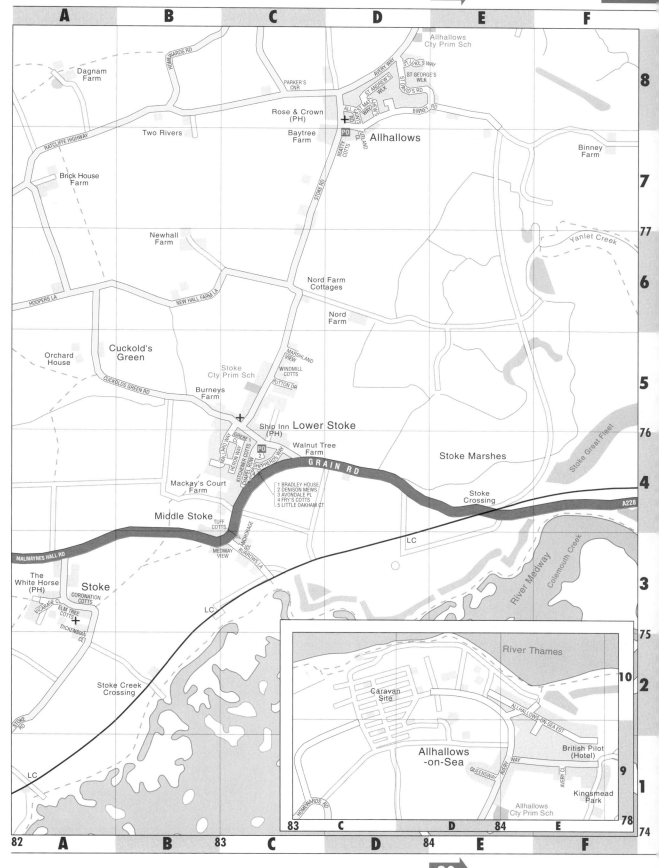

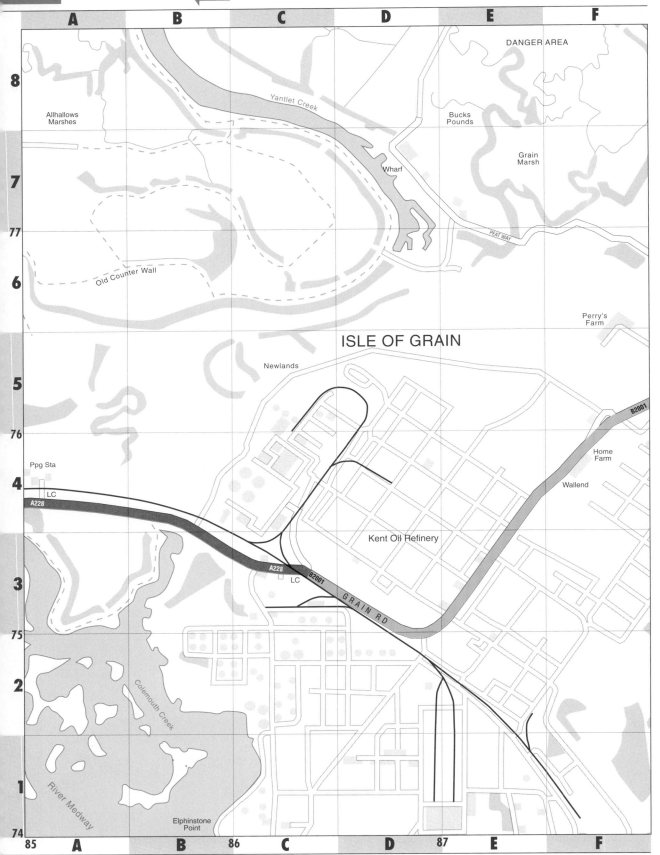

A B C D E F

8

Grain Spit

7

The Flats

River Thames

77

Works

Rosecourt Farm

P

B2001

Grain

St James' CE (VA) Sch

WEST LA

6

PARNELL RD

FRY CL

LEVETT CL

HIGH ST

GREAT TEAL CL

PINTAIL CL

PH

PO

MID BURGESS RD

ST JAMES RD

ST JAMES CL

SHELLDRAKE CL

CHAPEL RD

EDINBURGH RD

CORONATION RD

GRAYNE AVE

CORINTHIAN CT

PUFFIN RD

LAPWING RD

COASTGUARD COTTS

SEA VIEW

SMITHFIELD RD

GRAIN RD

Whitehouse Farm

5

Grain Tower

76

PORT VICTORIA RD

4

Smithfield Marshes

Garrison Point

LB Sta

GARRISON RD

SLIPWAY RD

BOATHOUSE RD

Chy

Grain Power Station

ANCHOR LA

Docks

STOREHOUSE WHARF

SHEERNESS

3

Jetty

SHEERNESS HARBOUR EST

GREAT BASIN RD

75

House Fleet

2

River Medway

Piers

Cockleshell Hard

Jetty

1

The Lappel

Horseshoe Point

74

88 A B 89 C D 90 E F

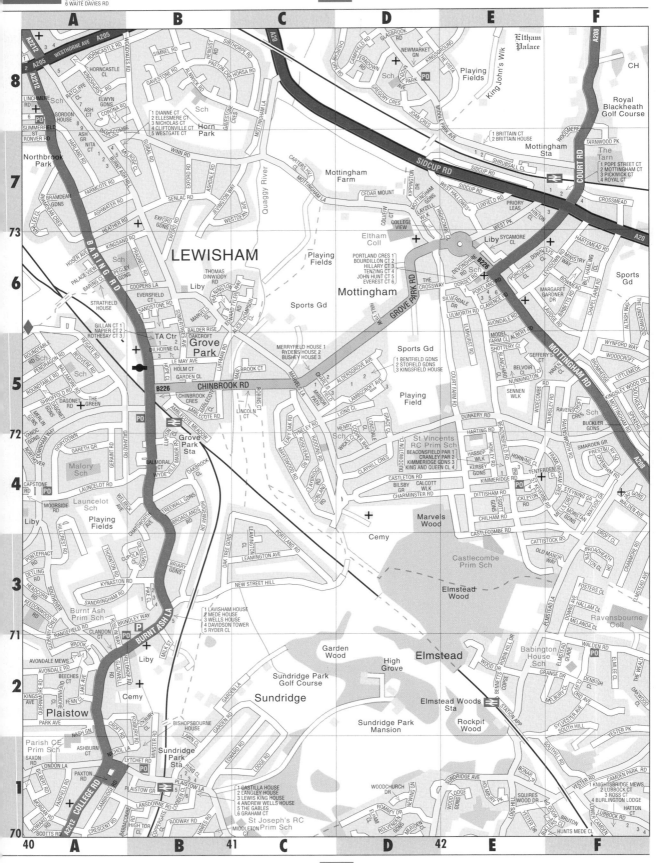

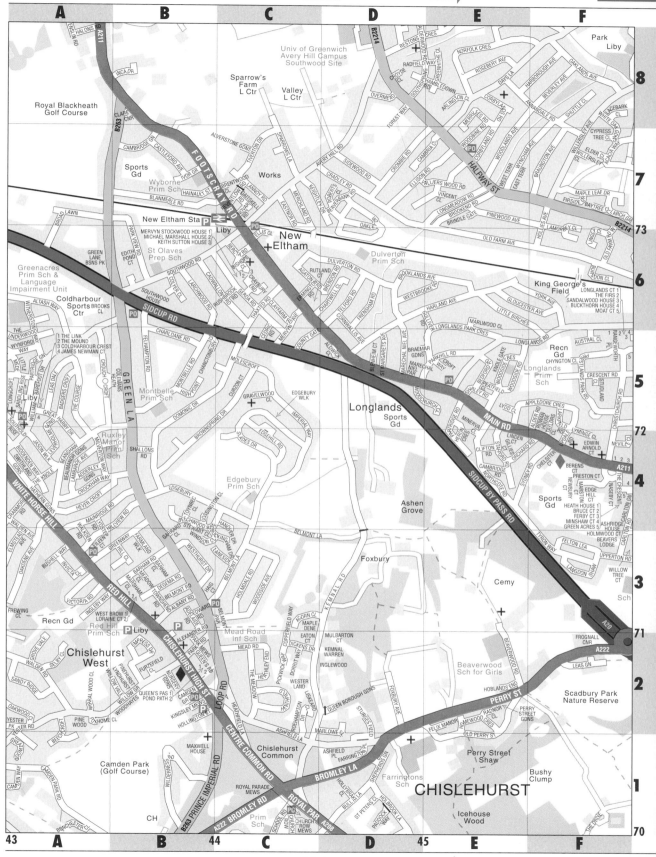

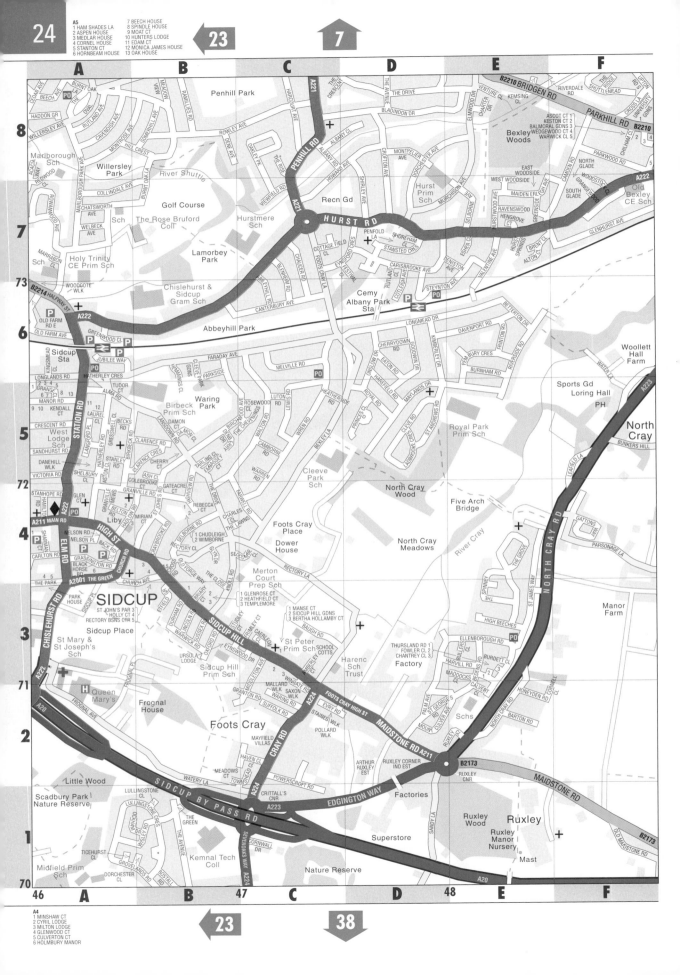

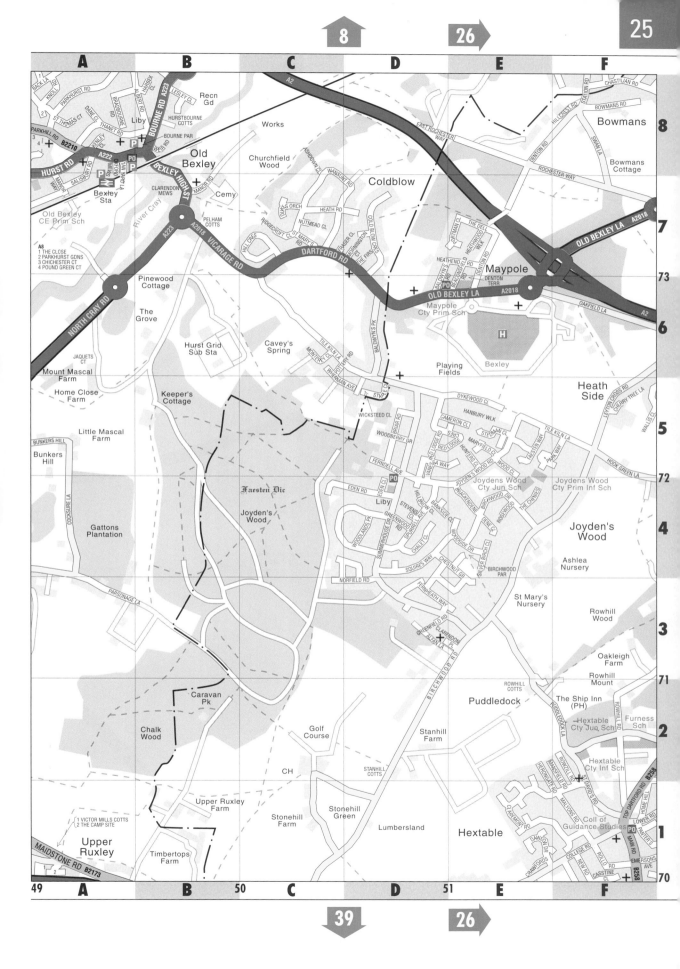

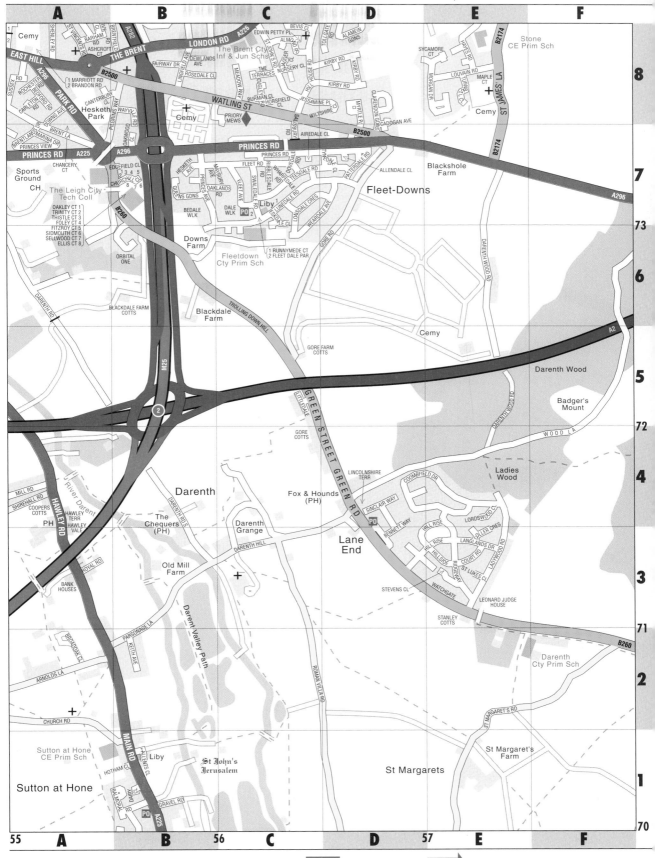

27
11

A B C D E F

8

7

73

6

5

72

4

71

3

2

1

70

B255
HEDGE PLACE RD
WOOD LA
A296
BEAN RD
A2
BEAN LA
IGHTHAM COTTS
HOPE COTTS
Bean House
ASHWOOD PL
DRUDGEON WAY
FOXWOOD
BEACON DR
BRAMBLE AVE
The Thrift
STONE WOOD
PAGE CL
SCHOOL LA
The Thrift
Stonewood
Works
A296
A2
CLAYWOOD LA
SANDY LA
Water Works
B259
Bean Farm
TURNER RD
Bean
NEW COTTS
HIGH ST
PO
The Royal Oak (PH)
Drudgeon Farm
BEAN HILL COTTS
Bean City Prim Sch
SOUTHFLEET RD
Shellbank
Lords Wood
SHELLBANK LA
Beacon Wood Country Park
Betsham
INGRESS TERR
Colyers Arms (PH)
BROOMHILLS
ORCHARD LEA
CRAYBURNE
STATION RD
B262
North End Farm
PARK CORNER RD
Manor House Farm
B259
Beacon House
B255
BETSHAM RD
SANDBANKS HILL
WESTWOOD RD
Manor Farm
B260
GREEN STREET GREEN RD
B262
The Ship (PH)
HIGHCROSS RD
Chambers Cottages
BANBURY VILLAS
Green Street Green
Malt House Farm
GILL'S RD
B260
Westwood
B255 WHITEHILL RD
Wheat Sheaf (PH)
HOOK GREEN RD
AXTANE

Manor Road Cty Inf Sch
MANOR RD
IRVING WLK
BOLEYN WAY
DURRANT WAY
LEONARD AVE
RECTORY RD
BETSHAM CL
ST MOUR WLK
ST PAUL'S CL
LORD DR
KEARY RD
BAXTER'S CL
ST PAUL'S
SOUTHFLEET RD
B259
Sch
The Sweyne Cty Prim Jun Sch

1 BUSHFIELD WLK
2 MITCHELL WLK
3 BUTCHER WLK
4 BRENDA TERR

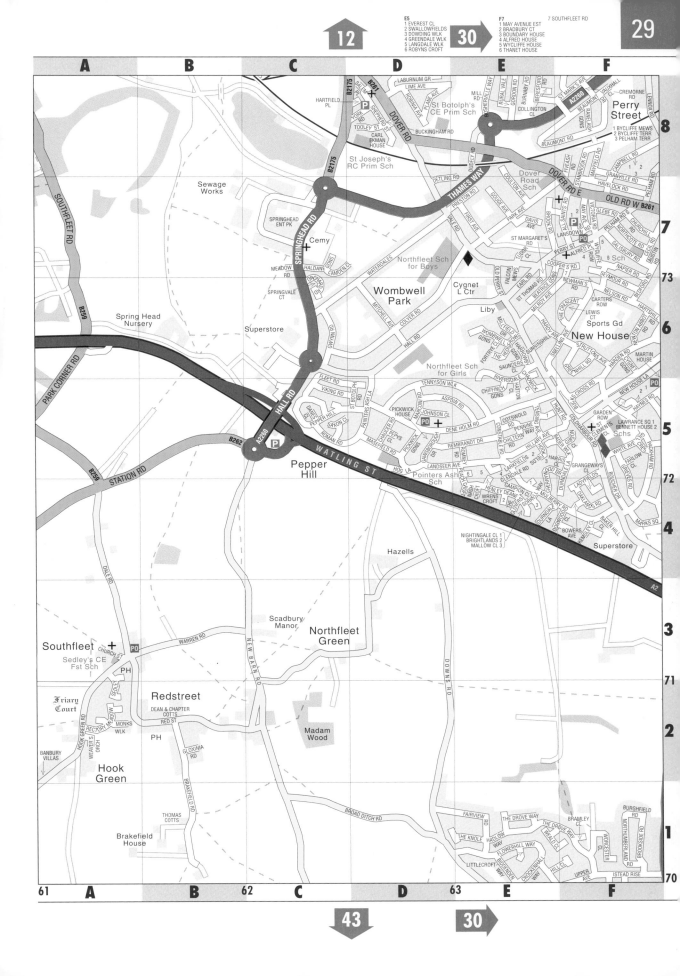

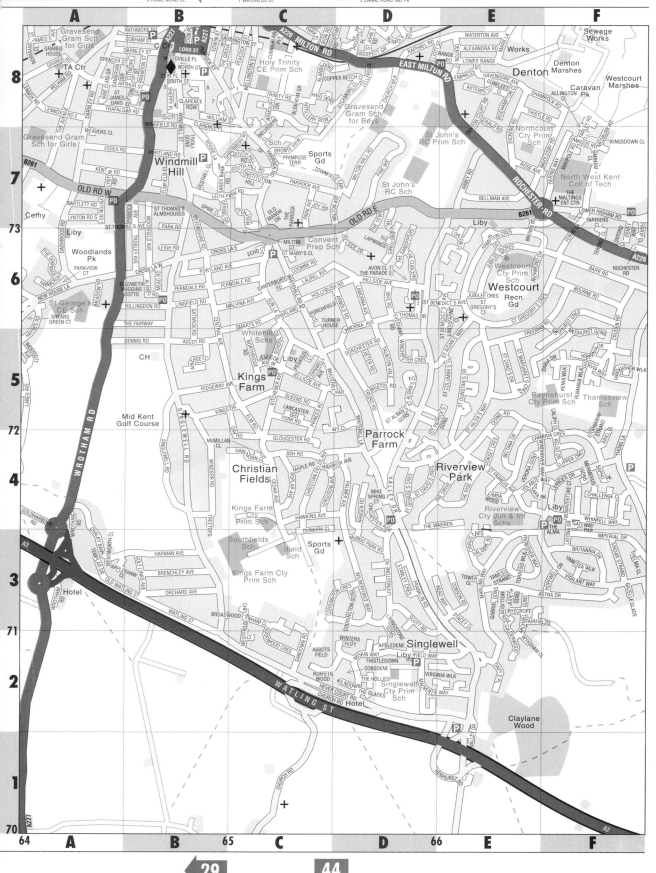

B8
1 CLAREMONT PL
2 LYDIA COTTS
3 VICTORIA AVE
4 WILLIAM HOUSE
5 PETER ST
6 HOME MEAD CL

B8
7 HOMEMEAD
8 GRAVESHAM CT
9 PRESENTATION HOUSE
10 ST ANDREW'S RD
C8
1 WATERLOO ST

C8
1 CHRIST CHURCH CRES
2 CHRIST CHURCH RD
3 ALBERT MURRY CL
D8
1 BRUNSWICK WLK
2 CANAL ROAD IND PK

29
13
29
44

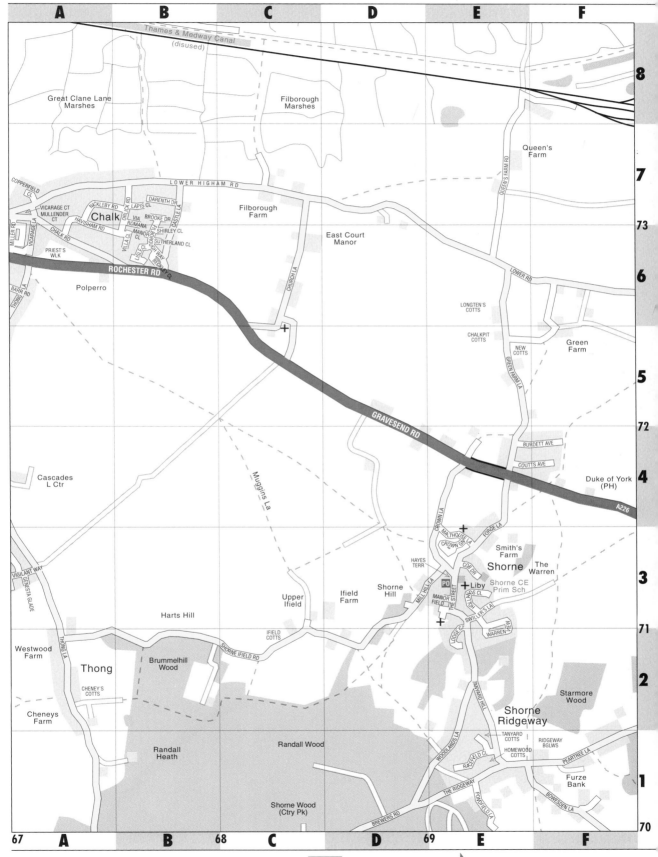

Thames & Medway Canal
(disused)

8

Great Clane Lane
Marshes

Filborough
Marshes

Queen's
Farm

7

LOWER HIGHAM RD

Filborough
Farm

QUEEN'S FARM RD

COPPERFIELD CL

VICARAGE CT
MULLENDER CT

NICKLEBY RD

DARENTH DR

LAPIS CL

ORLICK RD

CASTLE LA

BROOKE DR

Chalk

VIA
ROMANA

HAVISHAM RD

MANOR RD

SHIRLEY CL

WILLA CL

SUTHERLAND CL

LISLE CL

SHORTLANDS CL

BECKLEY CL

MILLER RD

VICARAGE LA

CHALK RD

73

East Court
Manor

LOWER RD

PRIEST'S
WLK

6

ROCHESTER RD

Polperro

CHURCH LA

LONGTEN'S
COTTS

BARR RD

THONG LA

CHALKPIT
COTTS

NEW
COTTS

Green
Farm

GREEN FARM LA

5

Cascades
L Ctr

Muggins La

72

GRAVESEND RD

BURDETT AVE

COUTTS AVE

Duke of York
(PH)

4

A226

VIGILANT WAY

GENESTA GLADE

CROWN LA

MALTHOUSE LA

FORGE LA

Smith's
Farm

The
Warren

Shorne

HAYES
TERR

CROWN GN

CG DR

COS CL

Shorne CE
Prim Sch

3

Upper
Ifield

Ifield
Farm

Shorne
Hill

MILL HILL LA

PO

Liby

MANOR
FIELD

THE STREET

SWILLER'S LA

Harts Hill

SHORNE IFIELD RD

IFIELD
COTTS

LODGE CT

WARREN VIEW

71

Westwood
Farm

THONG LA

Brummelhill
Wood

Thong

TANYARD HILL

Shorne
Ridgeway

Starmore
Wood

2

CHENEY'S
COTTS

TANYARD
COTTS

RIDGEWAY
BGLWS

Cheneys
Farm

HOMEWOOD
COTTS

PEARTREE LA

WOODLANDS LA

RUCKFIELD CL

Randall
Heath

Randall Wood

THE RIDGEWAY

Furze
Bank

POND FIELD LA

BOWESDEN LA

1

Shorne Wood
(Ctry Pk)

BREWERS RD

70

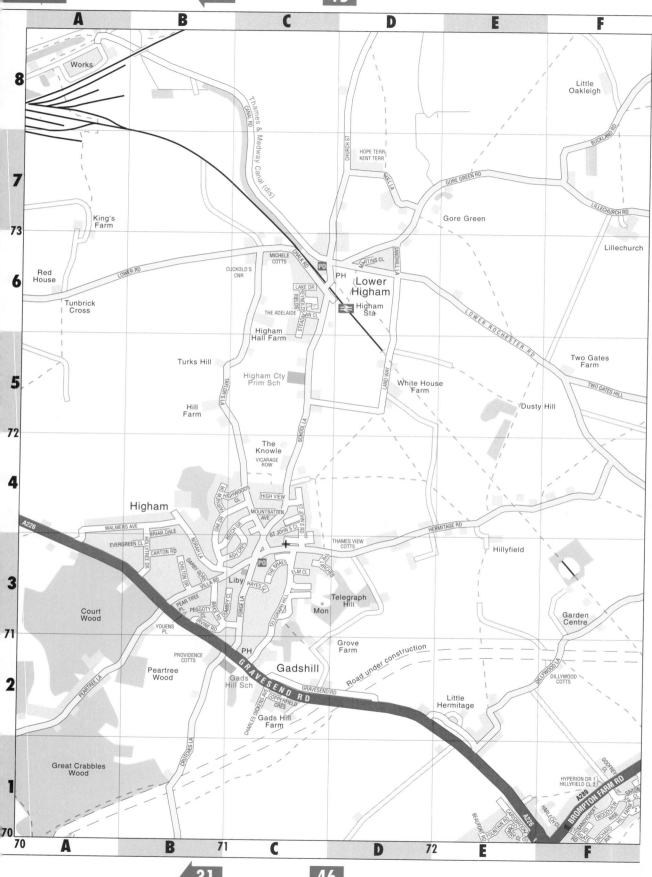

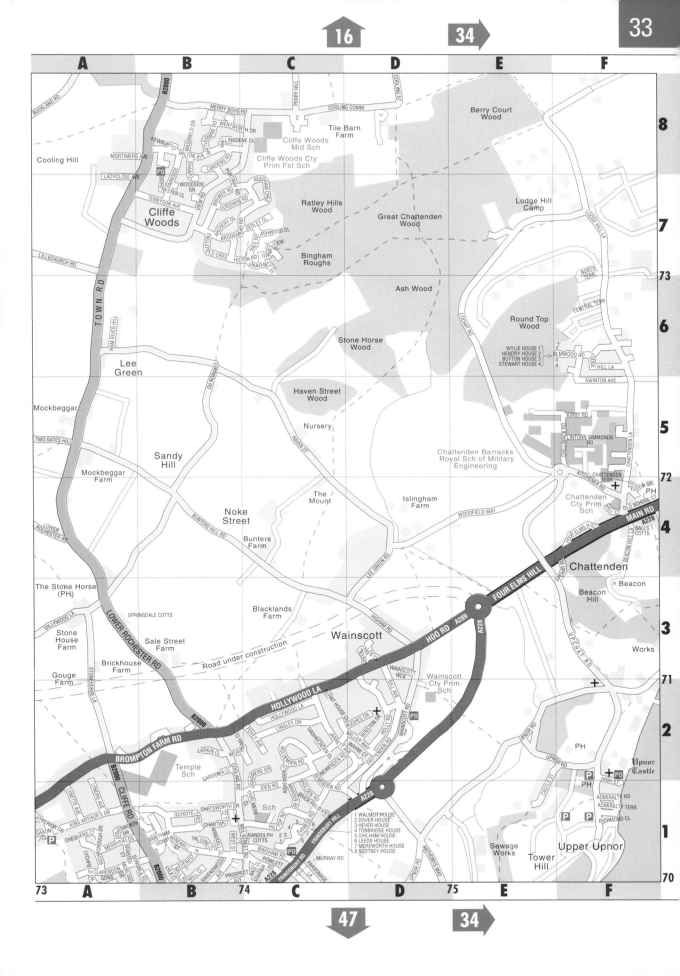

	A	B	C	D	E	F

8 Depot — Deangate Ridge Sports Gd

Deangate Wood — Deangate

CH

7 Deangate Ridge Golf Course — Tile Barn

73 Chattenden Farm — The Windmill (PH) — Mill Farm — Mast — STREET FARM COTTS

6 Sundown — BLACKMAN CL — WAT CL — FOURWENTS RD — BLACKMAN CL — KINGSHILL DR — BELL'S LA — GRANDSHIRE GDNS

PANKHURST RD — MOREMENT RD — MARLEY — ROCHESTER CRES — ST JOHNS RD — WALTERS RD

Stonebridge — LINTON DANN CL — VICGEON AVE — PIGEON AVE LING CL — ROBSON DR — WYTLE RD — WYLE RD — KNIGHTS — MISKIN RD — Hoo St Werburgh

RATCLIFFE HIGHWAY

5 Broad Street — HAIG VILLAS — Hundred of Hoo Sch — Hoo St Werburgh Cty Prim Sch — HTS RD — HERDSDOWN — GORDON RD — ST WERBURGH CT — POTTERY RD — KILLICK RD — TRUBRIDGE RD — NEWITT RD — COOMBE RD — PO — FLACK GDNS — PH — JENNIFER CT — Hoo St Werburgh

Hoo St Werburgh Mid Sch — MAIN RD — ST WERBURGH CRES — BROOKSIDE — CHURCH ST — P — BUTT LA — PO

72 A228 — MAIN RD — PO — HOO COMMON RD — ELM AVE — BROADWOOD RD — ARMYTAGE CL 1 — EVEREST MEWS 2 — EVEREST DR — Liby — WHITEHOUSE CL — ABBOTS COURT RD

4 CHURCH FARM RD — VICARAGE LA

Cockham Farm — Hoo Lodge

Hoo Marina Park — VICARAGE LA — Wks

3 MARBETTS LA — UPNOR RD — P — Saxon Shore Way — Cockham Wood — Gull Down Plantation — OAK CL — TEENDER RD — DAMSON DR — RAY CL — MARINE — BERRY — POPLAR CL

BRISSENDEN CL — PIER PL — Lower Upnor — WILLOW AVE — HAZEL AVE — MAPLE RD — BIRCH RD — OAK RD — LARCH CRES — CEDAR RD — ASTER RD — CHERRY RD — Hoo Marina

DAMSON DR — CYPRESS AVE 1 — CLOVER RD 2 — BEECH RD

71 Upnor Reach — RIVERSIDE NORTH RD — River Medway

Pier — RIVERSIDE WEST RD

2 St Mary's Island — ST MARY'S RD — Finsborough Ness — Short Reach — Hoo Salt Marsh

1 NORTH BASIN ONE RD — THE PINTAILS — MARINE VIEW — MARITIME WAY — RIVERSIDE EAST RD — Hoo Ness

70 DOCK HEAD RD — EIGHT DOCK EAST RD — NORTH SIDE THREE RD

| 76 | A | B | 77 | C | D | 78 | E | F |

A B C D E F

Roper's
Farm

Saxon Shore Way

ROPER'S GREEN LA

White Hall
Farm House

STOKE RD

8

Beluncle
Farm

BELUNCLE
VILLAS

ROPER'S LA

STOKE RD

7

STURDEE
COTTS

JACOB'S LA

ESHCOL RD

ALPHA CL
BETA RD
JETTY RD
MAIN RD
GAMMA RD

Works

73

Damhead Creek

6

Kingsnorth

Abbots
Court

5

Mast

Sewage
Works

Saxon Shore Way

Power
Station

72

4

Hoo Flats

Jetty

River Medway

Long Reach

3

71

Middle Creek

Pinup Reach

Darnet Ness

Darnet
Fort

Bishop Saltings

2

South Yantlet Creek

Hoo Fort

Folly Point

1

Gillingham Reach

Nor Marsh

70

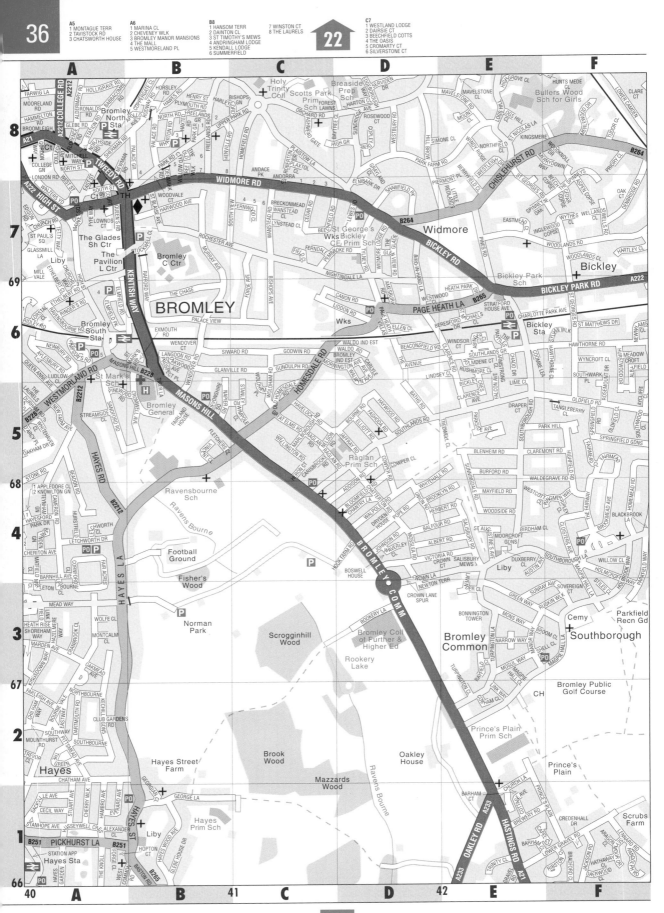

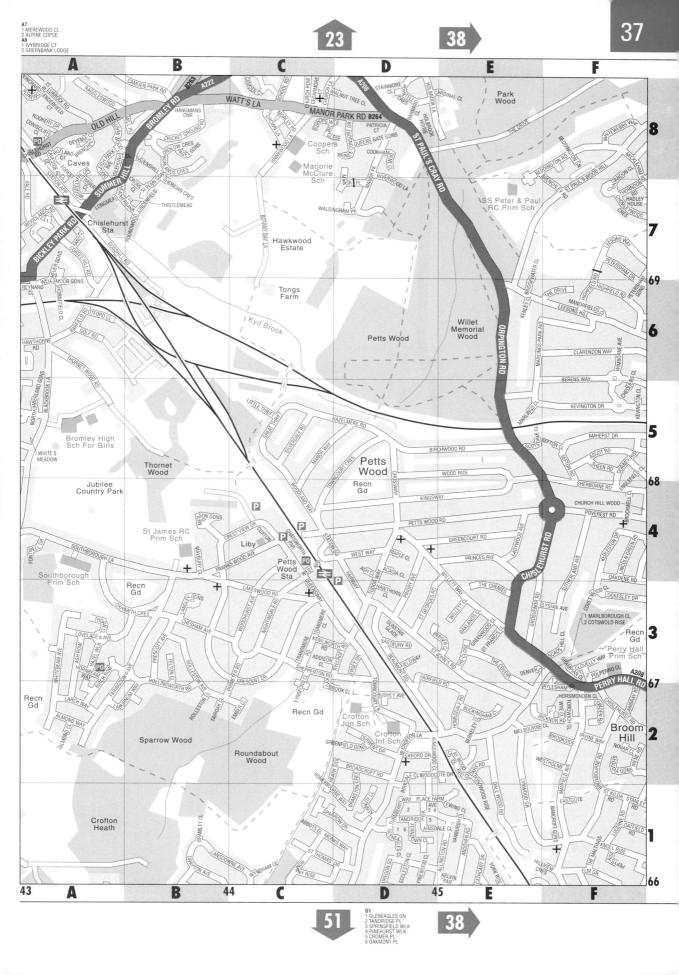

B6
1 SELWYN PL
2 LEIGH TERR
3 WOULDHAM TERR
← 37

C5
1 MOUNTFIELD WAY
2 HORTON TOWER
3 ELMSTONE TERR
4 TIDEBROOK CT
5 BELGRAVE CL
6 SANDWAY PATH
↑ 24

C5
7 HARBLEDOWN PL
8 BAPCHILD PL
9 ALKHAM TOWER

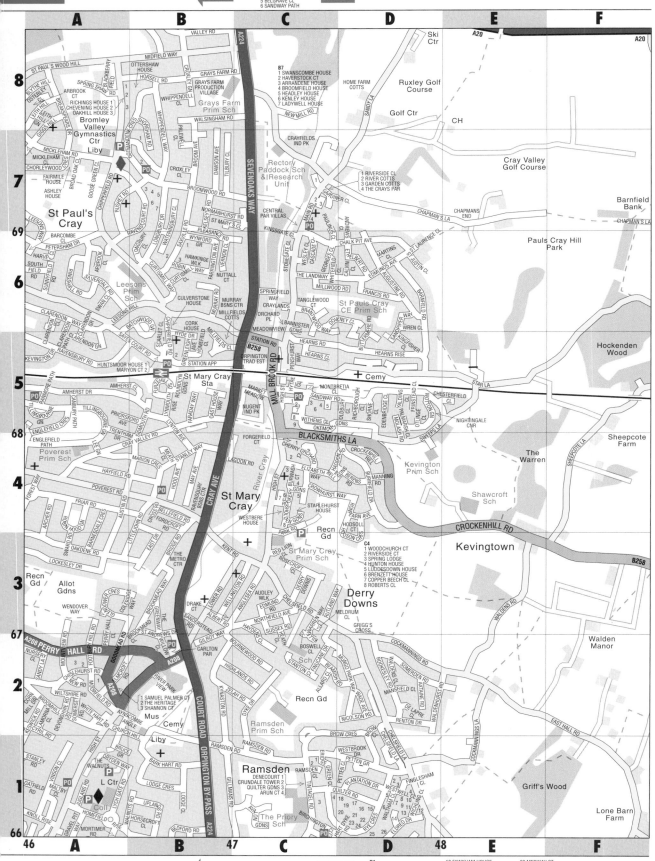

← 37
52 ↓

D1
1 BREDGAR HOUSE
2 WITTERSHAM HOUSE
3 CHALLOCK HOUSE
4 HOLLINGBOURNE TOWER
5 THURNHAM HOUSE
6 PECKHAM HOUSE
7 STOCKBURY HOUSE
8 EASTLING HOUSE
9 NEWINGTON HOUSE
10 FAWKHAM HOUSE
11 HOUGHAM HOUSE
12 BEKESBOURNE TOWER
13 LENHAM HOUSE
14 LAMBERHURST CL
15 LODDEN CT
16 KENNETT CT
17 EDEN CT
18 CUCKMERE CT
19 DARENTH CT
20 MEDWAY CT
21 MEON CT
22 STOUR CT
23 RAVENSBOURNE CT
24 ROTHER CT
25 RYE FIELD
26 BOX TREE WLK

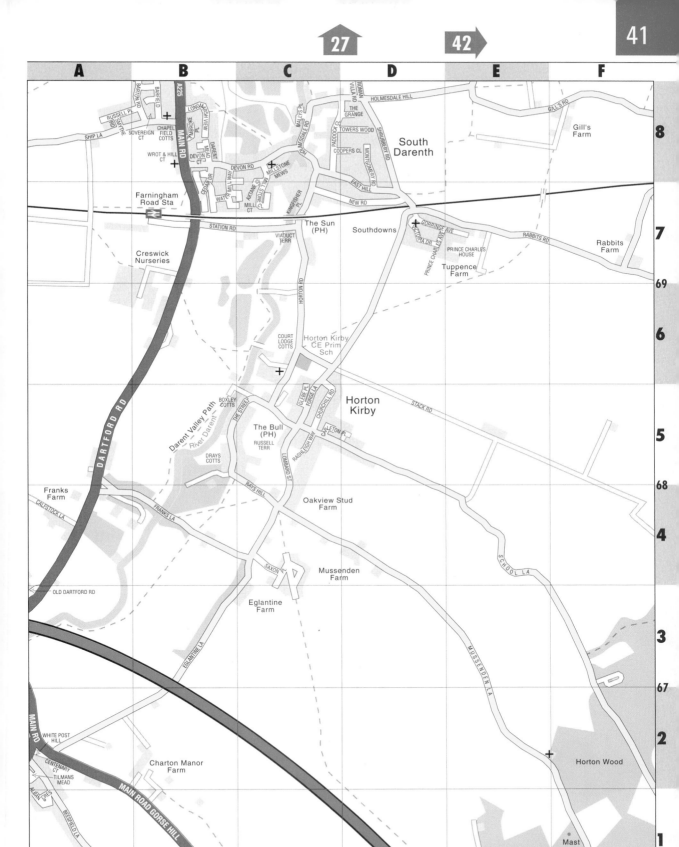

A B C D E F

8
South Darenth

7
69

6

5
68

4

3
67

2

1
66

A225

BARFIELD
RUSSELL PL
BARTON RD
SMITHE
SOVEREIGN CT
CHAPEL FIELD COTTS
LONG MARSH VIEW
MARSH VIEW
PEMBROKE PL
DARENT MEAD
CEDAR RD
WROT & HILL CT
DEVON CT
DEVON RD
WATER MILL WAY
MILL CT
AXTANE CL
SINGLIS TINS
MILLSTONE MEWS
KINGFISHER PL
SHIP LA
MAIN RD

ROMAN VILLA RD
MALLYS PL
HOLMESDALE RD
PADDOCK CL
TOWERS WOOD
THE GRANGE
HOLMESDALE HILL
SHRUBBERY RD
MONTGOMERY RD
COOPERS CL
EAST HILL
NEW RD
GILL'S RD
Gill's Farm

Farningham Road Sta
STATION RD
The Sun (PH)
VIADUCT TERR
Southdowns
CORRINGE AVE
VICTORIA DR
PRINCE CHARLES HOUSE
PRINCE CHARLES DR
Tuppence Farm
RABBITS RD
Rabbits Farm

Creswick Nurseries
HORTON RD

COURT LODGE COTTS
Horton Kirby CE Prim Sch

DARTFORD RD

Darent Valley Path
River Darent
BOXLEY COTTS
THE STREET
GLEBE PL
FORGE LA
CHURCHILL RD
Horton Kirby
STACK RD

The Bull (PH)
RUSSELL TERR
LOMBARD ST
RASHLEIGH WAY
CARLETON PL
DRAYS COTTS
RAYS HILL
Oakview Stud Farm

Franks Farm
CALFSTOCK LA
FRANKS LA
SCHOOL LA

OLD DARTFORD RD
SAXON LA
Mussenden Farm
Eglantine Farm
EGLANTINE LA

MAIN RD
WHITE POST HILL
CENTENARY CT
TILMANS MEAD
ALBIN CRES
BEESFIELD LA
Charton Manor Farm
MUSSENDEN LA
Horton Wood

MAIN ROAD GORSE HILL
A20
M20
Beesfield Farm
Mast

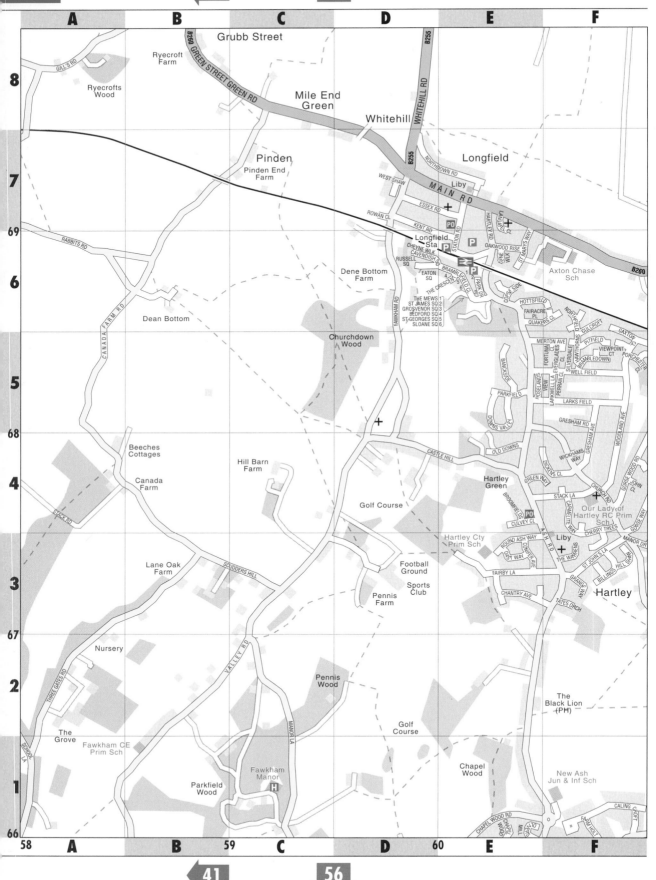

A B C D E F

8

Grubb Street

Ryecroft
Farm

Ryecrofts
Wood

GILL'S RD

Mile End
Green

Whitehill

B260 GREEN STREET GREEN RD

WHITEHILL RD

B255

B255

Longfield

7

Pinden

Pinden End
Farm

NORTHDOWN RD

WEST SHAW

MAIN RD

Liby

69

RABBITS RD

ROWAN CL

ESSEX RD

KENT RD

PO

HARTLEY RD

LANGAFEL CL

ST MARY'S WAY

OAKWOOD RISE

Axton Chase
Sch

B260

6

Dene Bottom
Farm

CANADA FARM RD

Dean Bottom

FAWKHAM RD

CHEYNE WLK
CAVENDISH SQ
RUSSELL SQ
EATON SQ
THE CRESCENT

Longfield
Sta

P

P

P

BRAMBLEFIELD CL

PARK DR

COPSE SIDE

HOTTSFIELD
FAIRACRE
PL
QUAKERS CL

NORTHFIELD

GILCROFT

CAXTON

Churchdown
Wood

THE MEWS 1
ST JAMES SQ 2
GROSVENOR SQ 3
BEDFORD SQ 4
ST GEORGES SQ 5
SLOANE SQ 6

MERTON AVE
FORTUNA
CL
HAWTHORNS
SILVERDALE
BRAMBLEDOWN
PITFIELD
VIEWPOINT
CT
PORCHESTER
CL

5

BACKSIDE

HOSELANDS
VIEW
LARKWELL LA
PERRAL CL
SWELL FIELD

LARKS FIELD

GRESHAM RD

WOODLAND AVE

GRESHAM AVE

68

Beeches
Cottages

PARKFIELD

DOWNS VALLEY

OLD DOWNS

WICKHAMS
WAY

4

Canada
Farm

STACK RD

Hill Barn
Farm

CASTLE HILL

GREEN WAY

INCKS CL

Hartley
Green

STACK LA

CHURCH RD

GORSE WOOD RD

JOHN CL

Our Lady of
Hartley RC Prim
Sch

GORSE WAY

MANOR DR

3

Lane Oak
Farm

SCUDDERS HILL

Golf Course

BROOMFIELDS

CULVEY CL

PO

Football
Ground

Sports
Club

Pennis
Farm

Hartley Cty
Prim Sch

ROUND ASH WAY

COXBY WAY

ASH RD

CARMELITE WAY

FAIRBY LA

THE WARRENS

CHERRY TREES

Liby

ST JOHN'S LA

GRANBY WAY

BILLINGS HILL LA

Hartley

CHANTRY AVE

TATES ORCH

67

Nursery

THREE GATES RD

VALLEY RD

2

The
Grove

Fawkham CE
Prim Sch

MANOR LA

Pennis
Wood

Golf
Course

The
Black Lion
(PH)

New Ash
Jun & Inf Sch

SCHOOL LA

Parkfield
Wood

Fawkham
Manor

H

Chapel
Wood

CALING CROFT

FARM HILL

1

CHAPEL WOOD RD

CHAPEL WOOD

66

58 A B 59 C D 60 E F

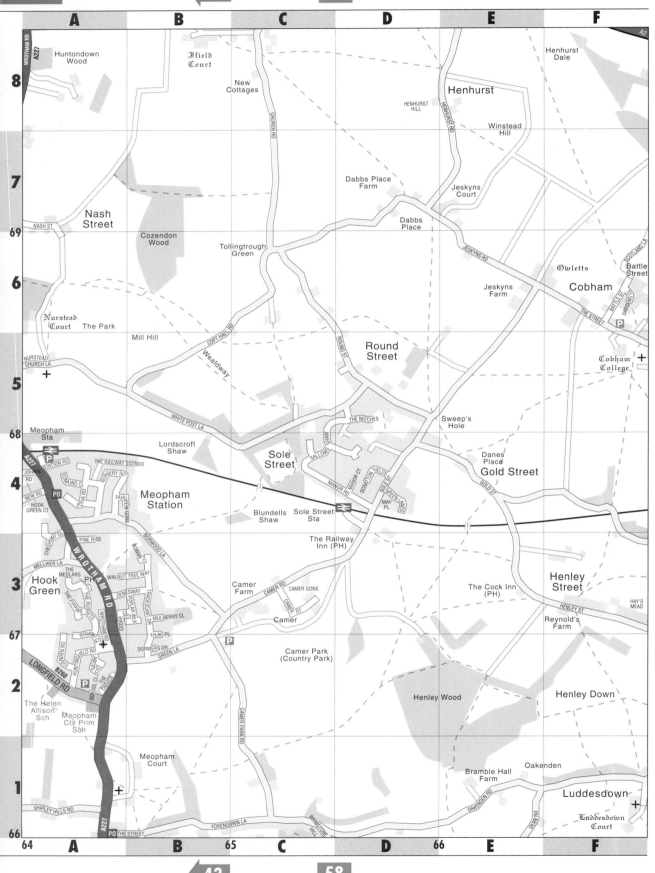

43
30

A B C D E F

8

7

69

6

5

68

4

3

67

2

1

66

64 A B 65 C D 66 E F

WROTHAM RD
A227
A2

Huntondown
Wood

Ifield
Court

New
Cottages

CHURCH RD

Henhurst
Dale

Henhurst

HENHURST
HILL

Winstead
Hill

HENHURST RD

Nash
Street

NASH ST

Cozendon
Wood

Tollingtrough
Green

Dabbs Place
Farm

Jeskyns
Court

Dabbs
Place

Jeskyns
Farm

JESKYNS RD

Owletts

SCOTLAND LA

Battle
Street

Cobham

Nurstead
Court

The Park

Mill Hill

Wealdway

COPT HALL RD

ROUND ST

Round
Street

Sweep's
Hole

THE STREET

BATTLE ST

SARBER'S RD

Cobham
College

NURSTEAD
CHURCH LA

WHITE POST LA

THE BEECHES

Danes
Place

Gold Street

GOLD ST

Meopham
Sta

Lordscroft
Shaw

Sole
Street

SALLOWS SHAW

MANOR CT

SCRATTON FIELDS

SOLE ST

GREEN LANDS

Meopham
Station

STATION RD

THE RAILWAY SIDINGS

NURSERY RD

EDMUND CL

SYLVIA RD

FAIRVIEW GDNS

Blundells
Shaw

Sole Street
Sta

MAY
PL

JOHN'S
RD

NEW RD

HOOK
GREEN CT

PO

PINE RISE

CHESTNUT CL

ROWAN CL

NORWOOD LA

The Railway
Inn (PH)

The Cock Inn
(PH)

HENLEY ST

Henley
Street

HAY'S
MEAD

WROTHAM RD

MELLIKER LA

THE
MEDLARS

PH

THE PIPPINS

THE RUSSETS

WALNUT TREE WAY

DENESWAY

POPLAR WLK

TRADESCANT DR

MULBERRY CL

LILAC PL

Camer
Farm

CAMER RD

CAMER GDNS

CAMER ST

Camer

Reynold's
Farm

Hook
Green

ARDEN RD

THE STRAND

HUNTINGFIELD RD

CEDAR

B260

SCHOOL CL

GREEN LA

DORMERS DR

P

Camer Park
(Country Park)

LONGFIELD RD

SOUTH CL

THE PARADE

CAMER PARK RD

The Helen
Allison
Sch

Meopham
Cty Prim
Sch

Henley Wood

Henley Down

Oakenden

Bramble Hall
Farm

OAKENDEN RD

DEAN RD

Luddesdown

Meopham
Court

SHIPLEY HILLS RD

A227

PO

THE STREET

FOXENDOWN LA

BRIMSTONE HILL

Luddesdown
Court

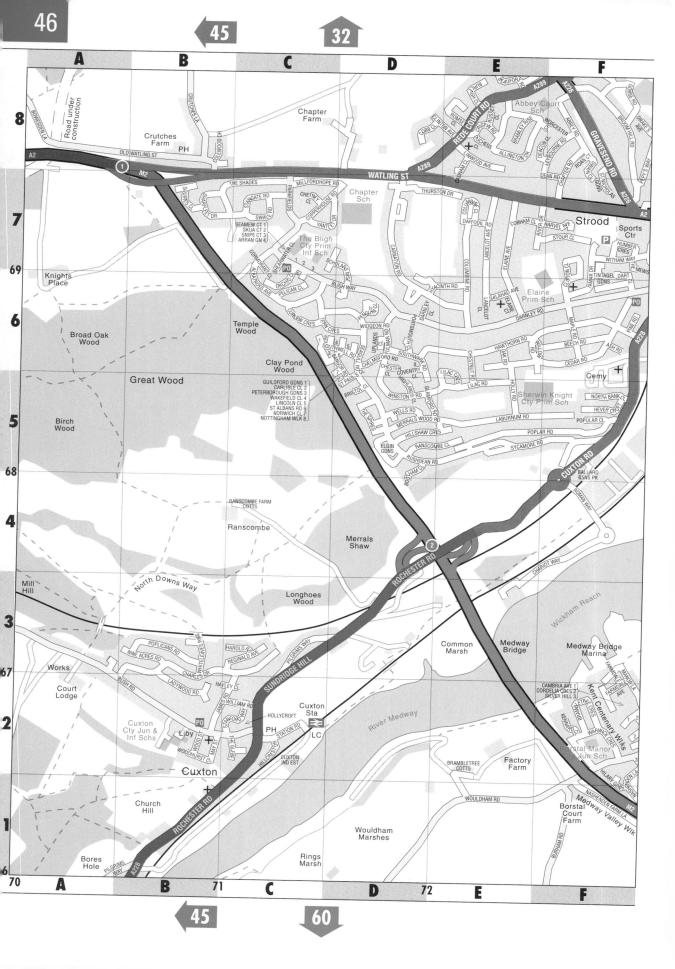

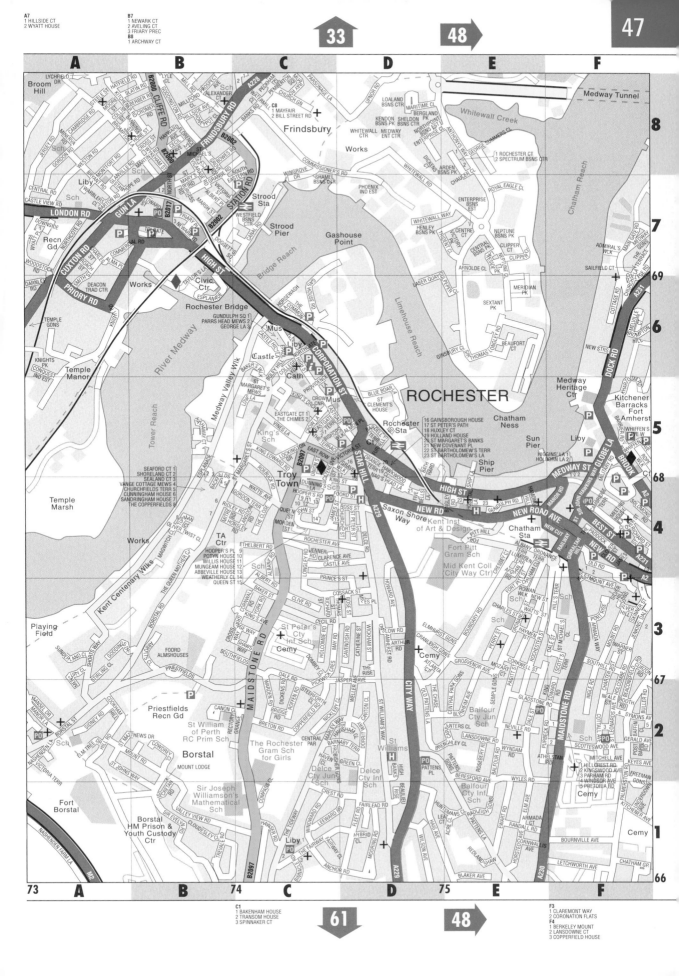

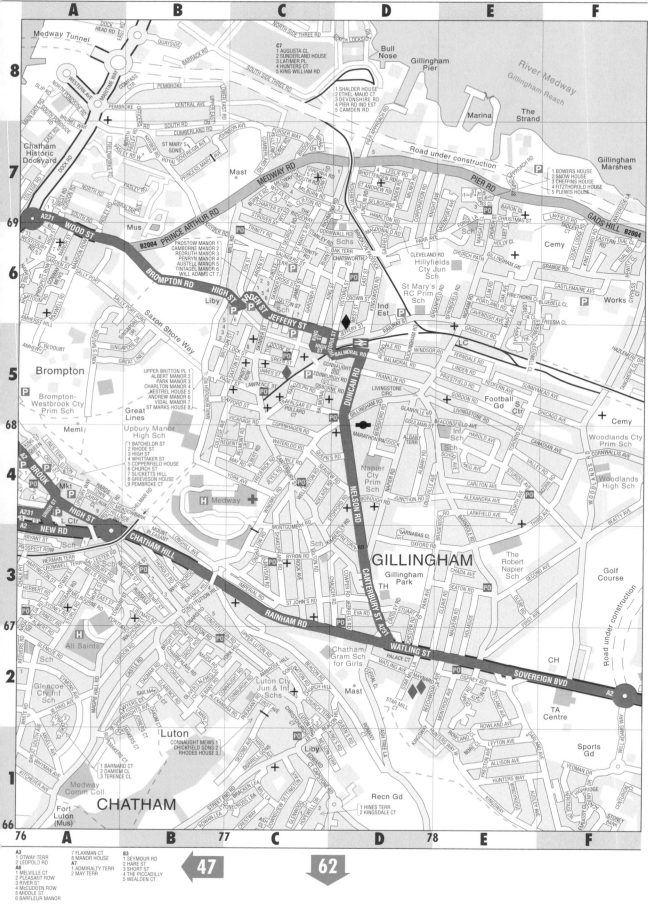

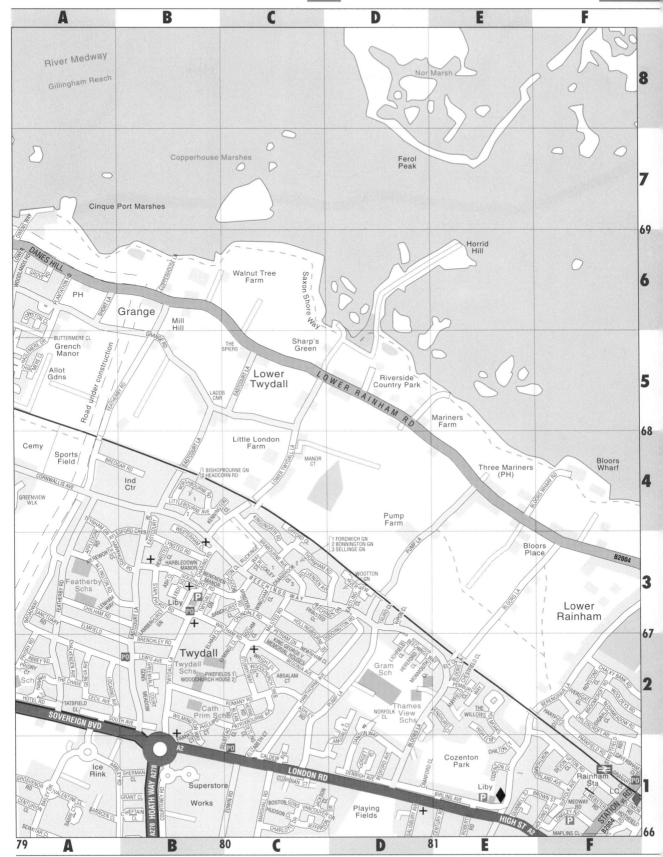

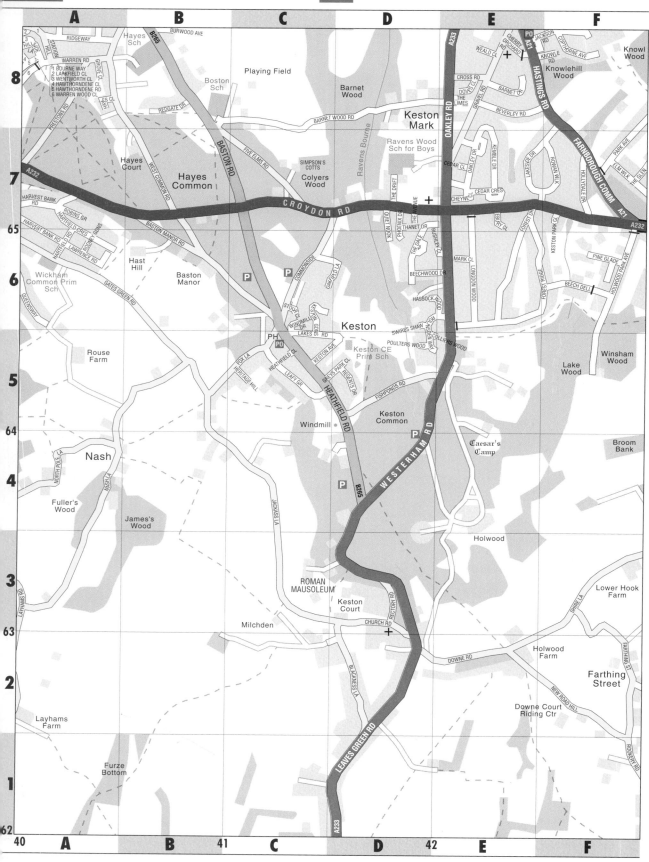

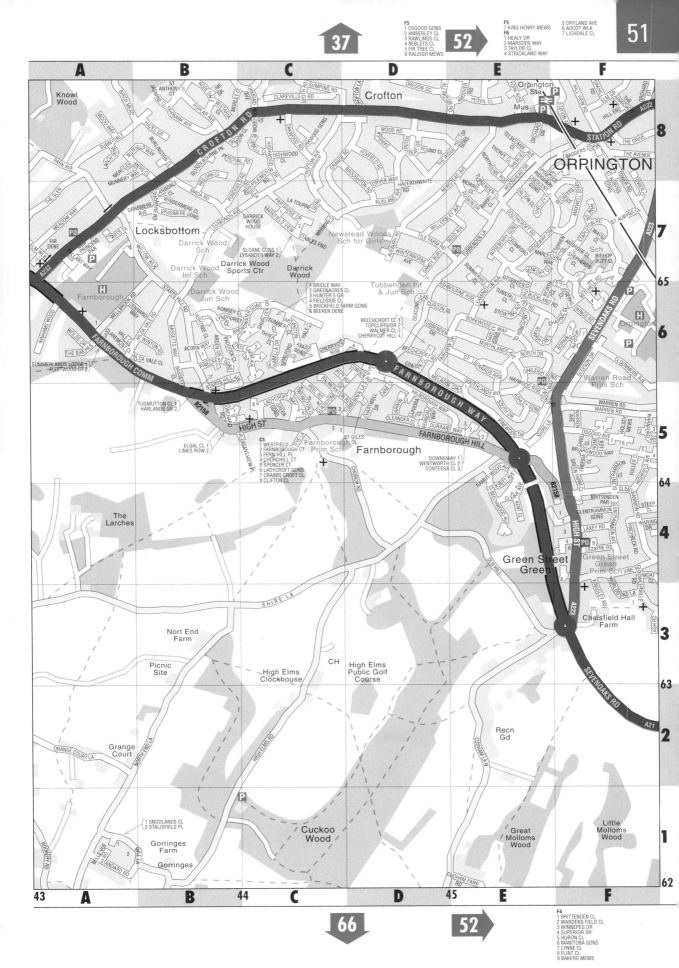

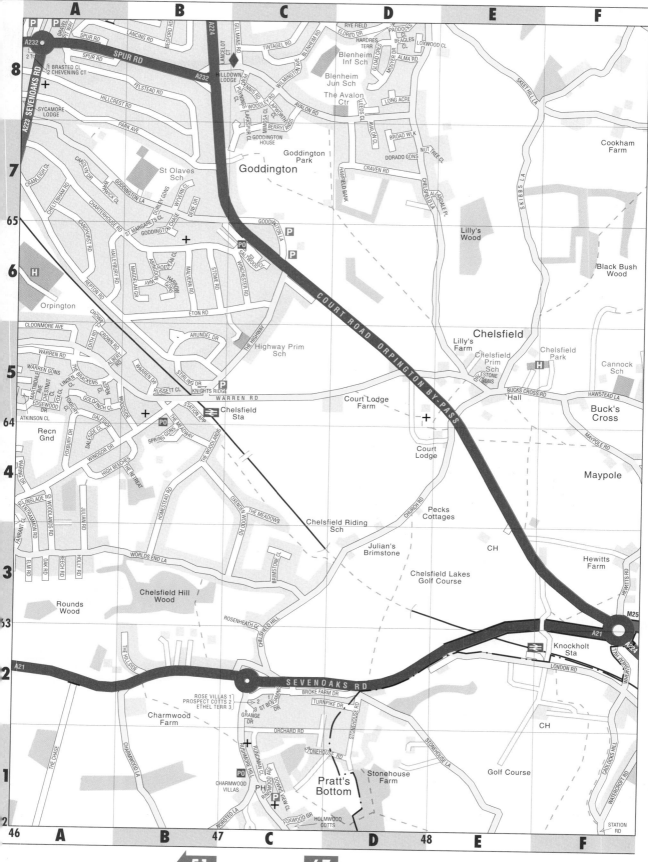

51
38

A   B   C   D   E   F

8

1 BRASTED CL
2 CHEVENING CT

SPUR RD

A232

SEVENOAKS RD

A23

7

65

6

H

Orpington

5

64

Recn
Gnd

4

63

3

Rounds
Wood

2

A21

SEVENOAKS RD

1

Charmwood
Farm

Pratt's
Bottom

2

46   A   47   B   C   47   D   48   E   F

Goddington

Goddington
Park

St Olaves
Sch

Highway Prim
Sch

Chelsfield
Sta

Court Lodge
Farm

Chelsfield Riding
Sch

Chelsfield Hill
Wood

Julian's
Brimstone

Chelsfield Lakes
Golf Course

Pecks
Cottages

Court
Lodge

COURT ROAD ORPINGTON BY-PASS

Chelsfield

Lilly's
Farm

Chelsfield
Prim Sch

Lilly's
Wood

Cookham
Farm

Black Bush
Wood

Chelsfield
Park

Cannock
Sch

Hall

Buck's
Cross

Maypole

Hewitts
Farm

M25
A21

Knockholt
Sta

Golf Course

Stonehouse
Farm

51
67

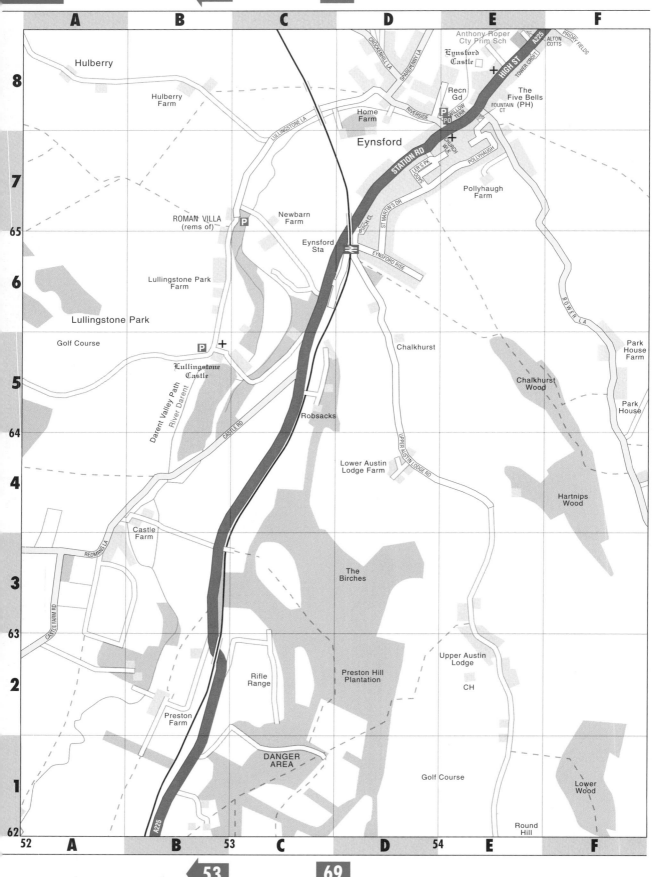

A   B   C   D   E   F

8

Hulberry

Hulberry
Farm

Anthony Roper
Cty Prim Sch

Eynsford
Castle

ALTON
COTTS

PRIORY FIELDS

Recn
Gd

The
Five Bells
(PH)

FOUNTAIN
CT

Home
Farm

RIVERSIDE

7

Eynsford

STATION RD

CHURCH WLK

POLLYHAUGH

Pollyhaugh
Farm

65

ROMAN VILLA
(rems of)

P

Newbarn
Farm

Eynsford
Sta

ST MARTIN'S DR

BIRCH CL

EYNSFORD RISE

6

Lullingstone Park
Farm

BOWER LA

5

Lullingstone Park

Golf Course

P

Lullingstone
Castle

Darent Valley Path
River Darent

CASTLE RD

Chalkhurst

Chalkhurst
Wood

Park
House
Farm

Park
House

64

Robsacks

UPPER AUSTIN LODGE RD

4

Lower Austin
Lodge Farm

Hartnips
Wood

Castle
Farm

REDMANS LA

3

The
Birches

CASTLE FARM RD

63

Upper Austin
Lodge

CH

2

Rifle
Range

Preston Hill
Plantation

Preston
Farm

DANGER
AREA

Golf Course

Lower
Wood

1

62

Round
Hill

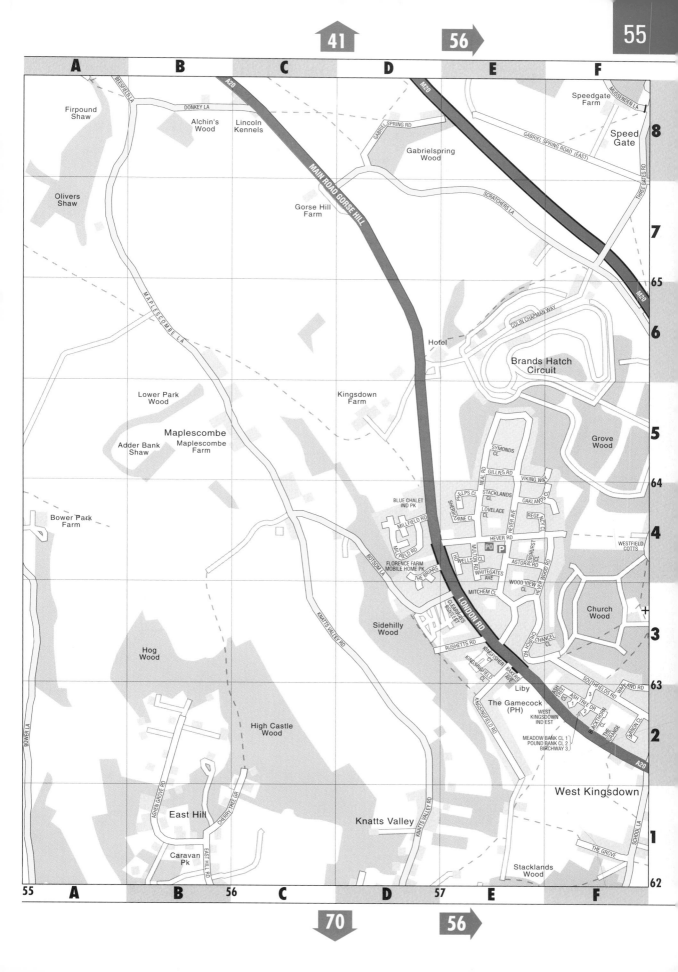

A B C D E F

8

7

65

6

5

64

4

63

3

2

1

62

BEESFIELD LA

Firpound
Shaw

DONKEY LA

Alchin's
Wood

Lincoln
Kennels

A20

Speedgate
Farm

MUSSENDEN LA

Speed
Gate

GABRIEL SPRING RD

Gabrielspring
Wood

M20

GABRIEL SPRING ROAD (EAST)

THREE GATES RD

Olivers
Shaw

MAIN ROAD GORSE HILL

Gorse Hill
Farm

SCRATCHERS LA

M20

MAPLESCOMBE LA

Hotel

COLIN CHAPMAN WAY

Brands Hatch
Circuit

Grove
Wood

Lower Park
Wood

Kingsdown
Farm

Maplescombe

Adder Bank
Shaw

Maplescombe
Farm

SYMONDS
CL

GILLIES RD

NEAL RD

VIKING WK

STACKLANDS
CL

OAKLANDS

HEVER AVE

REGE

Bower Park
Farm

BLUE CHALET
IND PK

PHELPS CL

SHELBRS

RNE CL

LOVELACE
CL

MILLFIELD RD

HEVER RD

PO P

ASHURST

WESTFIELD
COTTS

MILLFIELD RD

HEVER WOOD RD

MILLS

WELLS

ASTOR

FLORENCE FARM
MOBILE HOME PK

THE BRIARS

BOTSOM LA

WHITEGATES
AVE

WOOD VIEW
CL

HEVER WOOD RD

Church
Wood

MITCHEM CL

Sidehilly
Wood

LONDON RD

CLEARWAYS
BASKET

CHANCEL
CL

KNATTS VALLEY RD

Hog
Wood

RUSHETTS RD

BAKERS

KINGFISHER

KINGSFIELD
CL

Liby

The Gamecock
(PH)

SOUTHFIELDS RD

WAY

LAND RD

63

ASH TREE DR

3

WEST
KINGSDOWN
IND EST

THE GRANGE

BLACKTHORN

2

SEPTON CL

High Castle
Wood

BOWER LA

ASHEN GROVE RD

CHERRY TREE GR

EAST HILL RD

MEADOW BANK CL 1
POUND BANK CL 2
BIRCHWAY 3

KINGSFIELD RD

A20

West Kingsdown

East Hill

Caravan
Pk

Knatts Valley

KNATTS VALLEY RD

Stacklands
Wood

THE GROVE

SCHOOL LA

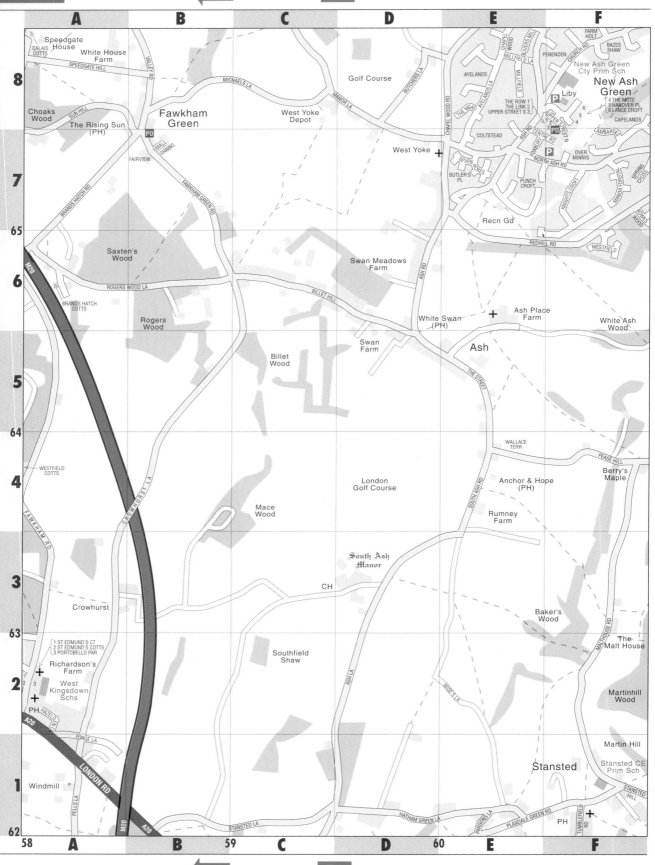

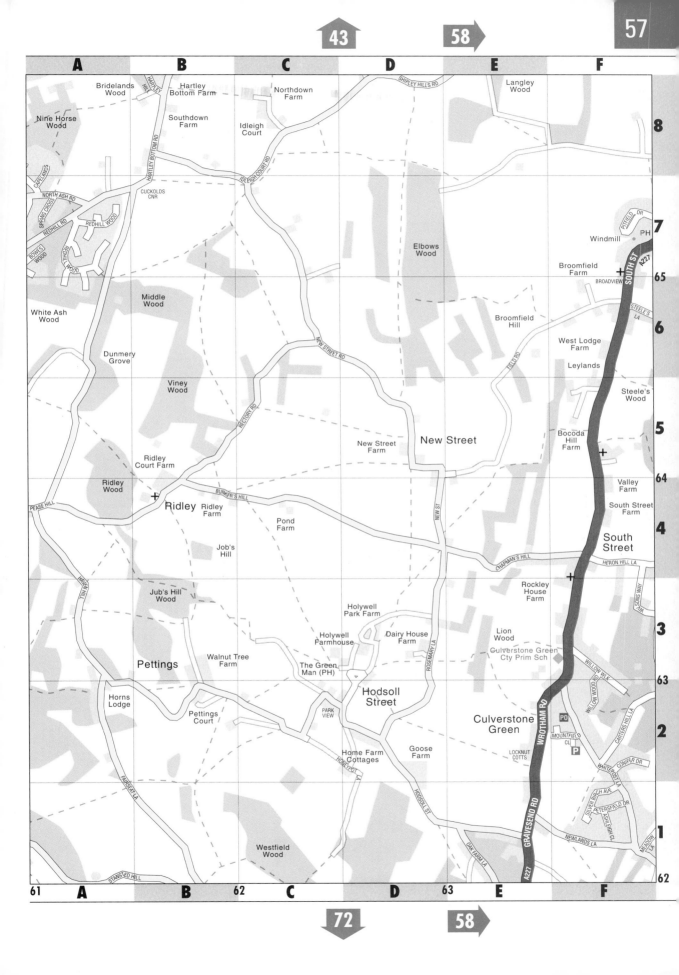

57
44

A · B · C · D · E · F

Meopham

Foxendown

L Ctr
Meopham Sch
Liby
Lomer Farm
MEADFIELD RD
ARNOLD AVE
HADLEY CL
OAKMEAD
BLENHEIM CL
WARWICK GDNS
GRENVILLE CL
CHENE WY
WROTHAM RD
A227
MILLERS WK
KENT TERR
CROCKETERS DR

The Larches

Brimstone Wood

DEAN RD

Dene Manor

Rid Ridge

Dunstan Wood

WELLINGTON COTTS

Meopham Green

STEELE'S LA

WHITEHILL RD

Wood Hill Farm

Dilmer Wood

Strawberry Hill

Rochester Forest

Nutfield Farm

Purvil Wood

Coomb Hill Farm

Waares Meadow Farm

HORN'S OAK RD

CHANDLER'S

Merry Hill

Priestwood

David Street

CHANDLER'S RD

Priestwood Green

PRIESTWOOD RD

DEAN LA

PLUG LA

Lenniker Wood

Ham Farm

Great Buckland Farm

LOCKYERS HILL

Haddocks Wood

Eastfield Farm

Luxon Wood

LUXON RD

Wealdway

Dean Mead

Lie Wood

Harvel

HERON HILL LA

LEAFY LA

Beechen Wood

Harvel Hike

WRANGLING LA

HOLLY HILL

ST FRANCIS RD

HORNFIELD COTTS

Harvel Hill Farm

Little Delmar Farm

Boughurst Street Farm

Holly Hill
P

PH
HARVEL ST
PO

Harvel House Farm

Upper Harvel

RIDGE LA

SCHOOL LA

RHODODENDRON AVE

Ridge Wood

VALLEY LA

HARVEL LA

Harvel Hike

WHITE HORSE LA

LEYWOOD RD

BEECHWOOD DR

MEADOW LA

BEECHWOOD GDNS

Sparrowhaugh Farm

SOUTHFIELD SHAW

HIGH VIEW

HARVEL RD

Swanswood Farm

Poundgate

Wealdway

Daniel Chambers

WHITE HORSE RD

57
73

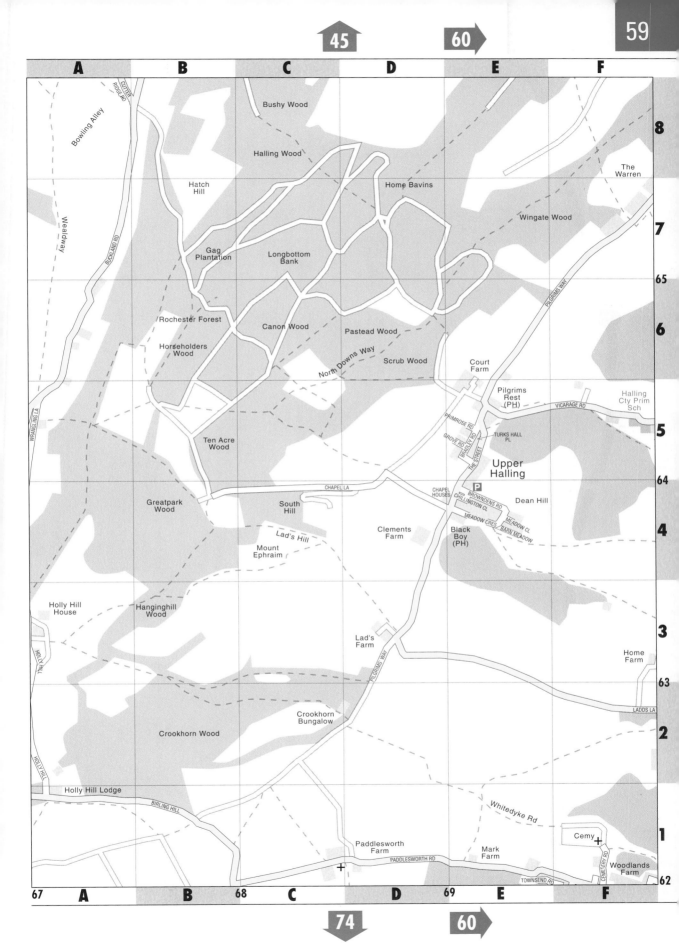

A B C D E F

8

7

65

6

5

64

4

3

63

2

1

62

Bowling Alley

CUTTER RIDGE RD

Wealdway

BUCKLAND RD

Bushy Wood

Halling Wood

Hatch Hill

Gag Plantation

Longbottom Bank

Home Bavins

The Warren

Wingate Wood

PILGRIMS WAY

Rochester Forest

Canon Wood

Pastead Wood

North Downs Way

Scrub Wood

Court Farm

Pilgrims Rest (PH)

VICARAGE RD

Halling Cty Prim Sch

Horseholders Wood

WRANGLING LA

Ten Acre Wood

PRIMROSE RD

GROVE RD

BRADLEY RD

THE STREET

TURKS HALL PL

Upper Halling

Greatpark Wood

CHAPEL LA

South Hill

CHAPEL HOUSES

BROWNDENS RD

CHILLINGTON CL

Dean Hill

Lad's Hill

Mount Ephraim

Clements Farm

MEADOW CRES

BARN MEADOW

MEADOW CL

Black Boy (PH)

Holly Hill House

Hanginghill Wood

Lad's Farm

PILGRIMS WAY

Home Farm

HOLLY HILL

LADDS LA

Crookhorn Wood

Crookhorn Bungalow

Holly Hill Lodge

BIRLING HILL

Whitedyke Rd

Cemy

Paddlesworth Farm

PADDLESWORTH RD

Mark Farm

CEMETERY RD

Woodlands Farm

TOWNSEND RD

67 A B 68 C D 69 E F

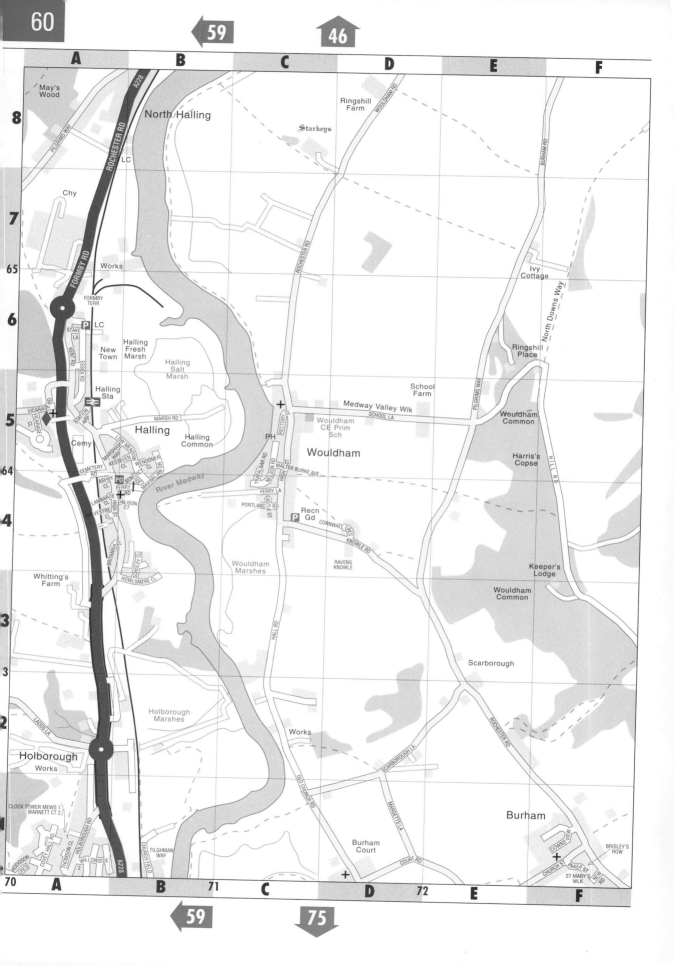

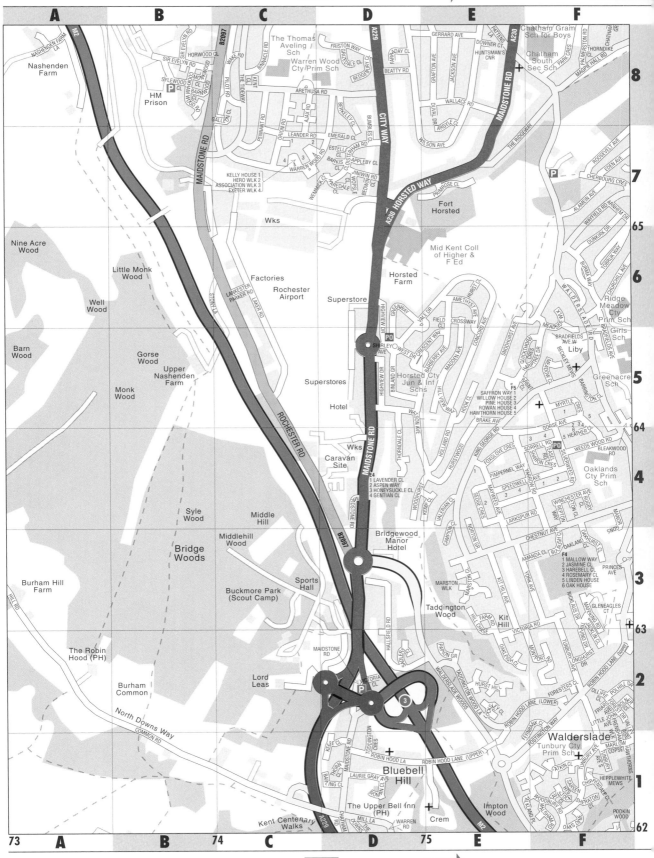

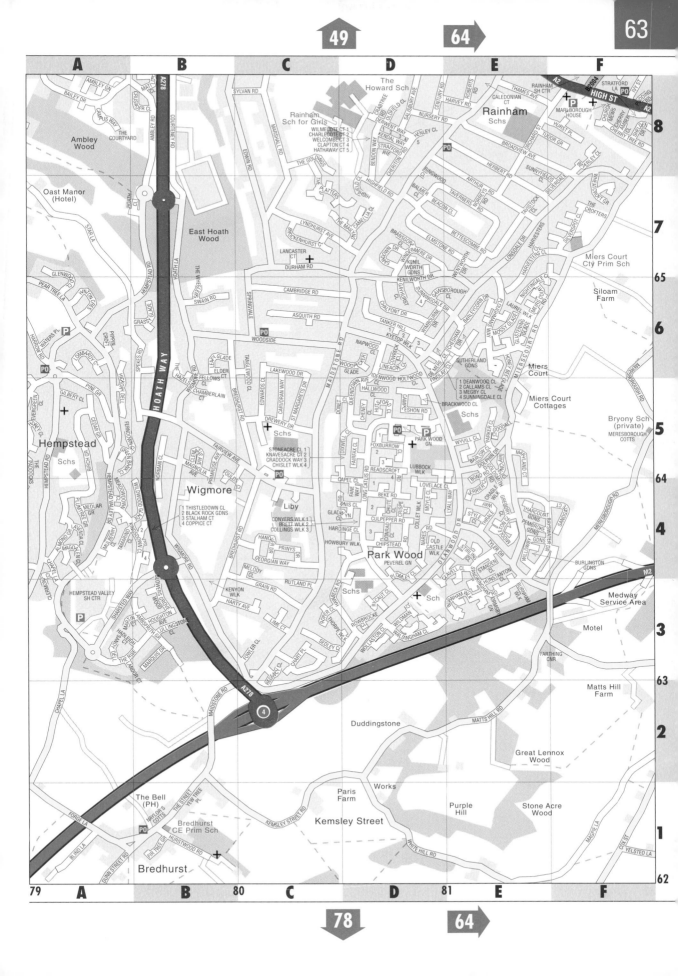

63

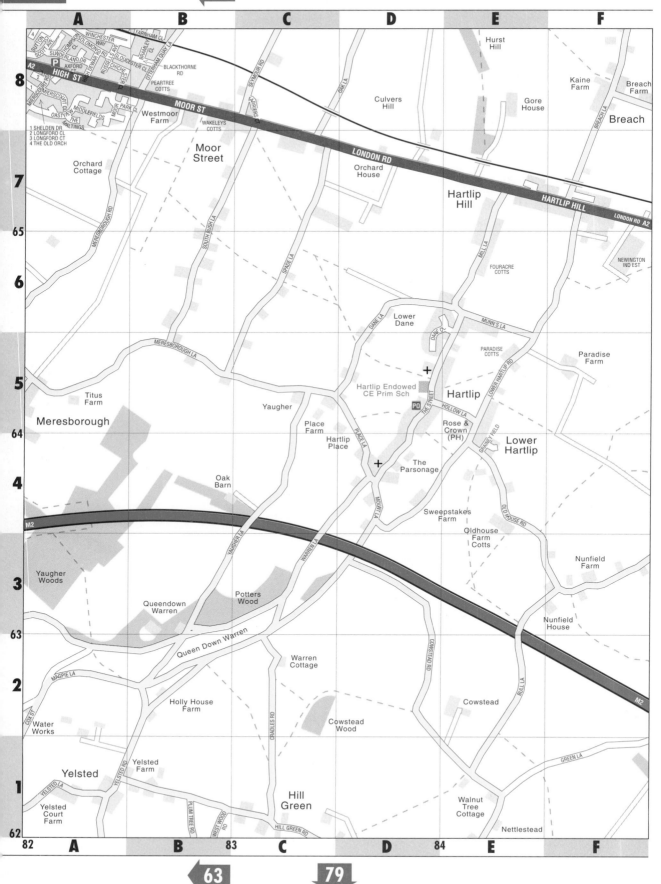

63   79

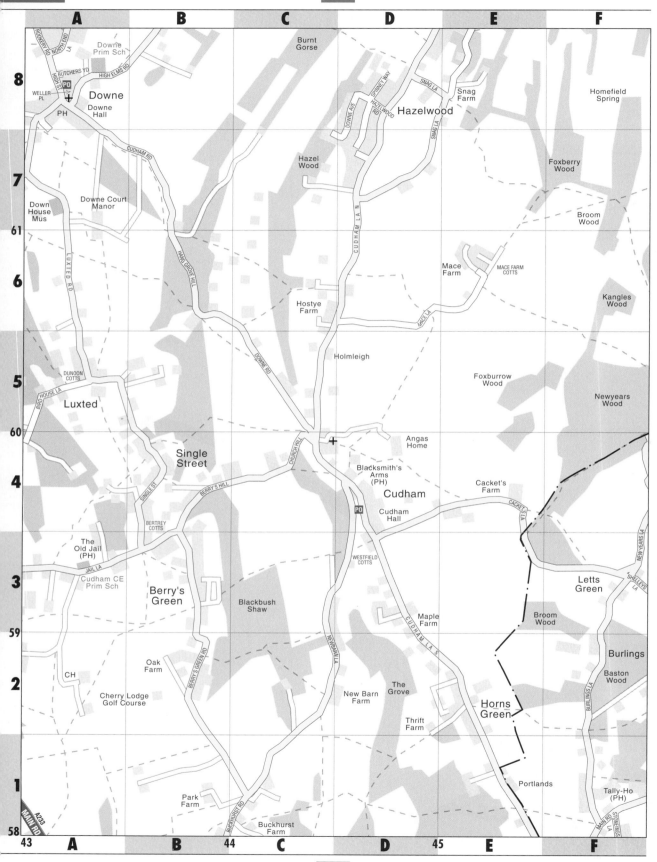

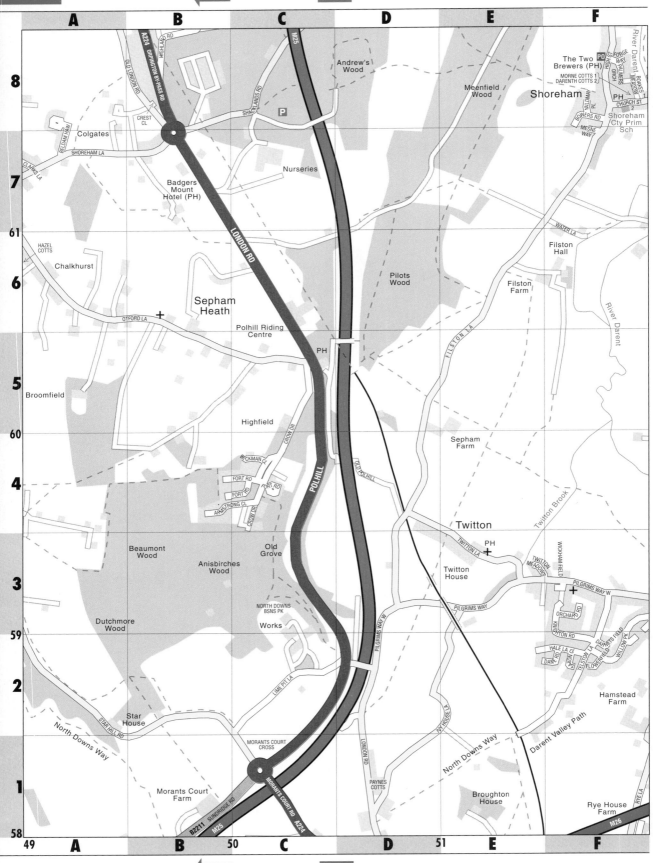

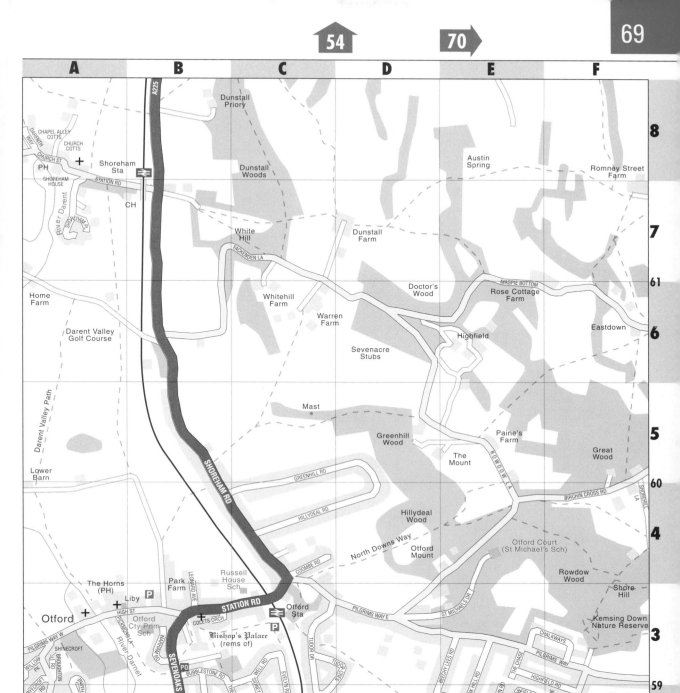

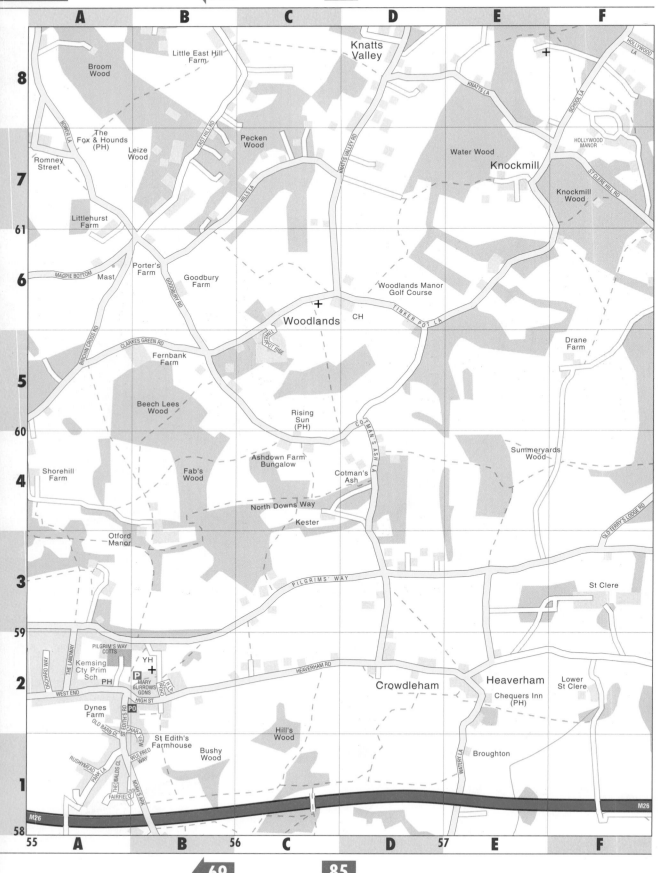

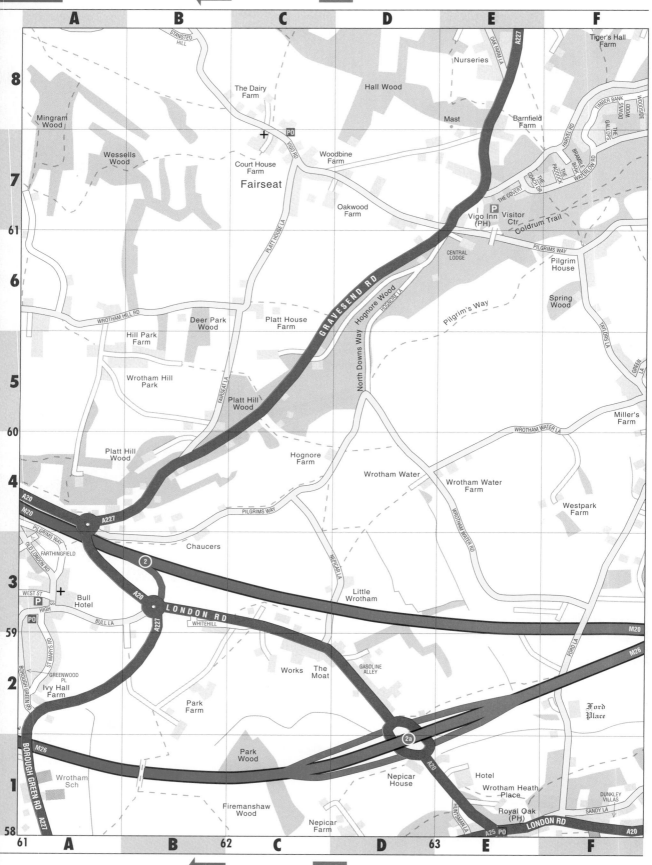

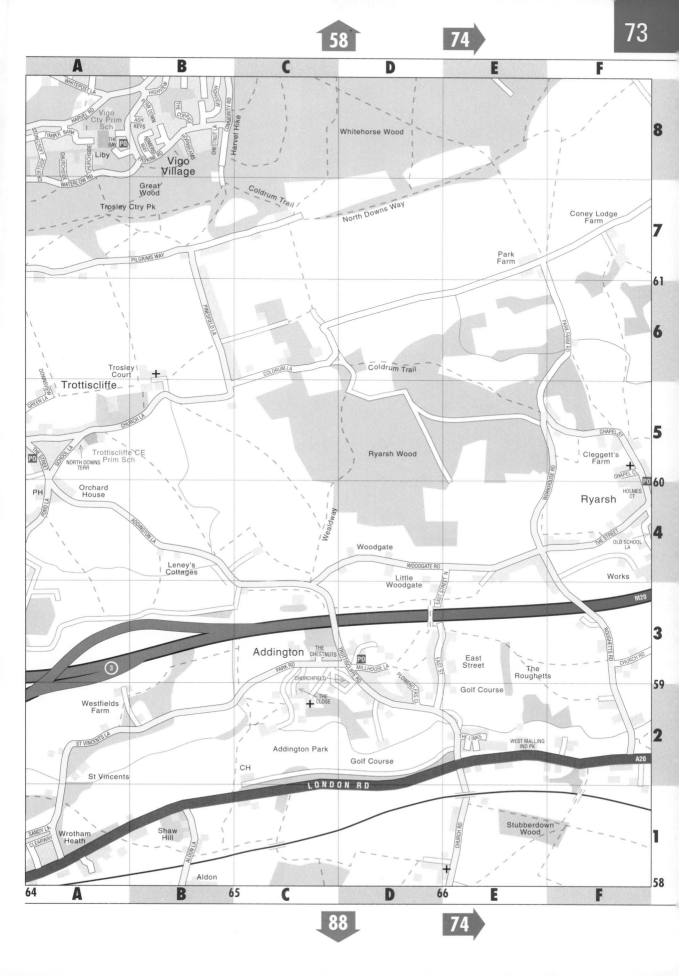

A B C D E F

8

7

61

6

5

60

4

59

3

2

1

58

WHITEPOST LA
HARVEL RD
HIGH VIEW
FERN DOWN
THE COPPICE
WHINGATE
COMMUNITY RD
Vigo Cty Prim Sch
ASH KEYS
ADMERS RD
HORNBEAMS
CHESTNUT LA
HARVEL HIKE
STONECROFT
TIMBER BANK
THE BAY
PO
CHURCHSIDE
CROFTSIDE
Liby
ERSKINE RD
Vigo Village
WATERLOW RD
CHURCHSIDE

Whitehorse Wood

Great Wood
Trosley Ctry Pk

Coldrum Trail

North Downs Way

Coney Lodge Farm

PILGRIMS WAY

Park Farm

PINESFIELD LA

PARK FARM RD

DOWNSVIEW

Trosley Court
Trottiscliffe
GREEN LA
CHURCH LA

COLDRUM LA

Coldrum Trail

CHAPEL ST

Cleggett's Farm
CHAPEL CL
PO
HOLMES CT

Ryarsh

Trottiscliffe CE Prim Sch
THE STREET
SCHOOL LA
NORTH DOWNS TERR
PO

Orchard House
PH
FORD LA

Ryarsh Wood

WORKHOUSE RD

THE STREET
OLD SCHOOL LA

ADDINGTON LA

Woodgate
WOODGATE RD

Works

Leney's Cottages

Wealdway

Little Woodgate

EAST STREET N

M20

ROUGHETTS RD
CHURCH RD

3

Addington
THE CHESTNUTS
PARK RD
CHURCHFIELD
THE CLOSE

TROTTISCLIFFE RD
PO
MILLHOUSE LA
PLOWENDERS CL

EAST ST

East Street

The Roughetts

Golf Course
59

Westfields Farm

ST VINCENTS LA

THE LINKS

Addington Park

WEST MALLING IND PK

A20

St Vincents

CH

Golf Course

LONDON RD

SANDY LA
CLEARWAY
Wrotham Heath

Shaw Hill

ALDON LA

Aldon

CHURCH RD

Stubberdown Wood

64 A 65 B C 66 D E F 58

73 59

A B C D E F

8

Walnut Tree Farm

Snodland CE Prim Sch

TOWNSEND RD
COOK RD
WOODLANDS AVE
CONSTITUTION HILL
BRADBOURNE RD
ROMAN RD
BIGLEY CL
TAYLOR RD

Birling Place Farm

Dyke Place

Stalks Wood

MIDSUMMER HL
GLOSSOP RD
RITCH
ST BENEDICT RD
FREELANDS RD
COT'S CL
DRYLAND RD
GODDEN RD
BIRLING RD
ROOKERY HILL
TAYLOR RD

STANGATE RD

DOWN CL
MORRIN CL
GORHAM CL
BIRLING RD
ST KATHERINE'S LA
ORCHARD RD
MEADOW WLK

LUCAS RD
THE GROVES
POUT RD

7

Langhold House

St Katherine's Cty Prim Sch

61

Parson's Corner

SNODLAND RD

Austen's Farm

TON JOYCE CL

Holmesdale Comm Sch

LEGGE LA

SANDY LA

HAYS RD

HOLBOROUGH RD
LYNTON RD

Holmesdale Sch (Farm Annex)

ANNIE RD
SOPER RD

6

Ley Farm

Birling Lodge

Birling

Liby

Sandhole

Golf Course

CH

CORONA TERR
MALLING RD
BROOK LA

PH
BULL RD
BIRLING PK
THE CLOSE

RYARSH RD

MASTERS LA

LAKESIDE
A228

5

Godfreys Farm

Clacketts Farm

Placee Farm

MALLING RD

The Vicarage

BIRLING RD

60

PH

Ryarsh Cty Prim Sch

Birling Ashes

LEYBOURNE WAY
WODEHOUSE
BROOK RD
LEYBOURNE WAY

4

Stables

Birling Wood

Birling Ashes

CASTLE WAY

Leybourne Lake

SPRINGFIELD RD
LUNSFORD LA
STEVENSON WAY
AUSTEN WAY
GIGHILL RD
CHAUCER WAY
PRIESTLEY DR

M20

Lunsford

4

Spider's Hall

HANOVER GN

Lunsford Hall

JEROME WAY
BRONTE CL
ORWELL CL
CARROLL GDNS
KEATS RD
BETJEMAN CL
CHAUCER WAY
RACKHAY WAY

3

CHURCH RD

BIRLING RD

PARK RD

Leybourne Pk

Castle Lake

WILLOW RD
PARTRIDGE AVE

M20

59

Audley House

Leybourne Castle

Leybourne CE (VA) Prim Sch

WATERSIDE CT

WILLOW WAY
WILLOWSIDE

LUNSFORD LA
SWALLOW RD
ORIOLE WAY
KINGFISHER RD

2

Sports Gd

A20

LITTLE MARKET ROW 1
EVERGREEN CL 2
BROADOAK 3

CASTLE WAY

RECTORY LA N
THE MEADWAY
BRIDGEWATER
THE CROFT
LITTLE CROFT

MALLARD WLK 2
SISKIN WLK 1
GRASMERE

MERLIN AVE
PLOVER RD

Leybourne

Nurseries

Wheatsheaf (PH)

GRANGE CL

Leybourne Wood

MAYFIELD
OXLEY SHAW LA
REDBANK
HIGHWAY

WREN CL
ODPECKER RD
NIGHTINGALE

1

SANDY LA

BROCKLEBS

TOWN HILL
TOWN HILL

LONDON RD

PUMP CL
MILLBROOK

ASHTON WAY

OLD ORCHARD LA
ROMANY
BARLEYCORN
WHEATFIELD
RECTORY LA S

GREBE CT 1
FALCON GN 2
BLATCHFORD CL 3
SHAFTESBURY CL 4
ADDISON CL 5
WALPOLE CL 6
COLUMBINE RD 7
COLUMBINE CL 8

HERON RD

A20

58

FARTHERWELL RD
NORMAN RD

RYARSH LA

NEVILL CT

A228

WINTERFIELD LA
DICKENS DR
MORRIS CL
HARDIE CL
TEMPLE WAY
CARNATION
ROSEMARY RD

LARKSPUR RD

67 A B 68 C D 69 E F

F4
1 SOUTHEY WAY
2 CRONIN CL
3 BLAKE DR
4 COLERIDGE CL
5 CHESTERTON RD
6 BROWNING CL
7 BARRIE DR
8 CHRISTIE DR

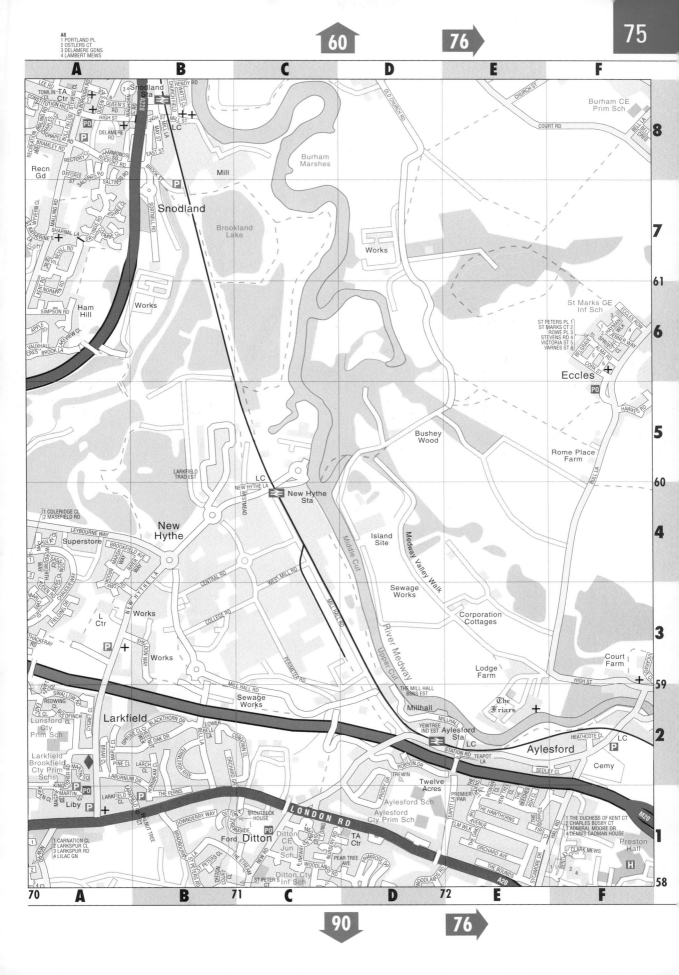

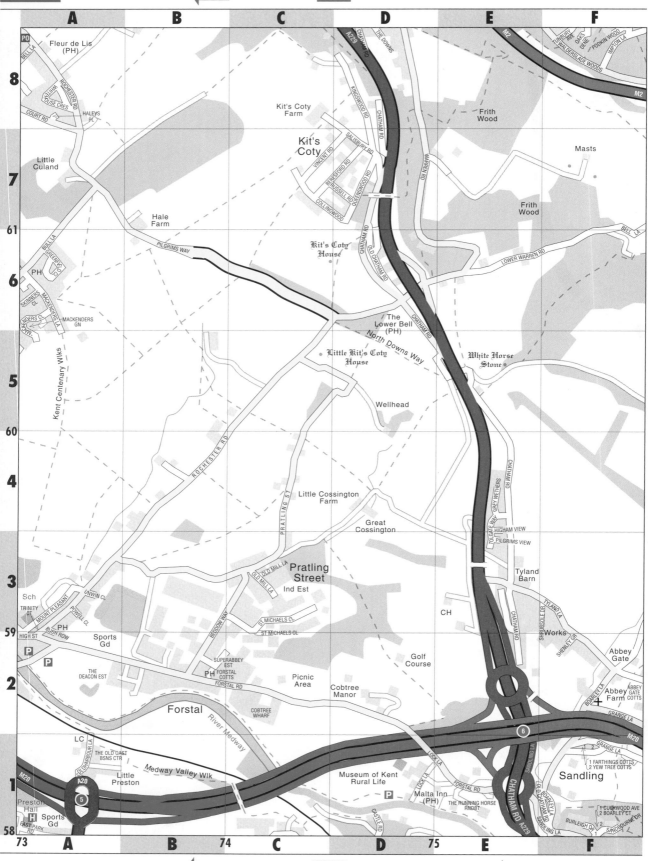

A   B   C   D   E   F

8

7

61

6

5

60

4

3

59

2

1

58

PO
Bell La
Fleur de Lis
(PH)

JOHN
ROCHESTER CL
HOUSE CRES
HALEYS
PL
COURT RD

Little
Culand

PH
BULL LA
GREENE'S CL
SKINNERS CL

MACKENDERS CL
MACKENDERS LA
MACKENDERS
GN
SANDERS CL

Kent Centenary Wlks

Hale Farm

PILGRIMS WAY

Kit's Coty
Farm

Kit's
Coty

KINGSWOOD RD
VINCENT RD
SALISBURY RD
BERESFORD RD
BRUSSELL RD
QUEENSWOOD RD
COLLINGWOOD

A229
CHATHAM RD
THE DOWNS

WARREN RD

Frith
Wood

Masts

Kit's Coty
House

CHATHAM RD
OLD CHATHAM RD

Frith
Wood

BELL LA
LOWER WARREN RD

The
Lower Bell
(PH)

North Downs Way

Little Kit's Coty
House

Wellhead

White Horse
Stone

ROCHESTER RD

PRATLING ST

Little Cossington
Farm

Great
Cossington

CHATHAM RD
GREY WETHERS
TO GAE WAY

HIGHER VIEW
PILGRIMS VIEW

Tyland
Barn

Pratling
Street
Ind Est

OLD MILL LA
BEDOW WAY
UNWIN CL
POWELL CL

ST MICHAELS CL
ST MICHAELS CL

CH

TYLAND DR
TYLAND LA
SHRUBSOLE DR
SHENLEY DR

CHATHAM RD

Works

Abbey
Gate

Sch
TRINITY
CT
MOUNT PLEASANT
PH
BUSH ROW
HIGH ST

Sports
Gd

SUPERABBEY
EST
FORSTAL
COTTS
PH
FORSTAL RD

THE
DEACON EST

Picnic
Area

Cobtree
Manor

Golf
Course

BOARLEY LA
Abbey
Farm
ABBEY
GATE
COTTS
GRANGE LA

Forstal

River Medway

COBTREE
WHARF

M20

6

M20

1 FARTHINGS COTTS
2 YEW TREE COTTS

GRANGE LA

Sandling

LC
THE OLD OAST
BSNS CTR

CARHARBOUR LA

Medway Valley Wlk

Little
Preston

Museum of Kent
Rural Life

P

LOCK LA
CASTLE RD

Malta Inn
(PH)

FORSTAL RD
THE RUNNING HORSE
RNDBT

CHATHAM RD A229
SANDLING LA
OLD CHATHAM RD
BOARLEY LA

1 CUCKWOOD AVE
2 BOARLEY CT

1 CUCKWOOD AVE

BURLEIGH DR
SANDBOURNE DR

M20

Preston
Hall
H
Sports
Gd
EAST PARK
RD

A20

5

73   A   B   74   C   D   75   E   F

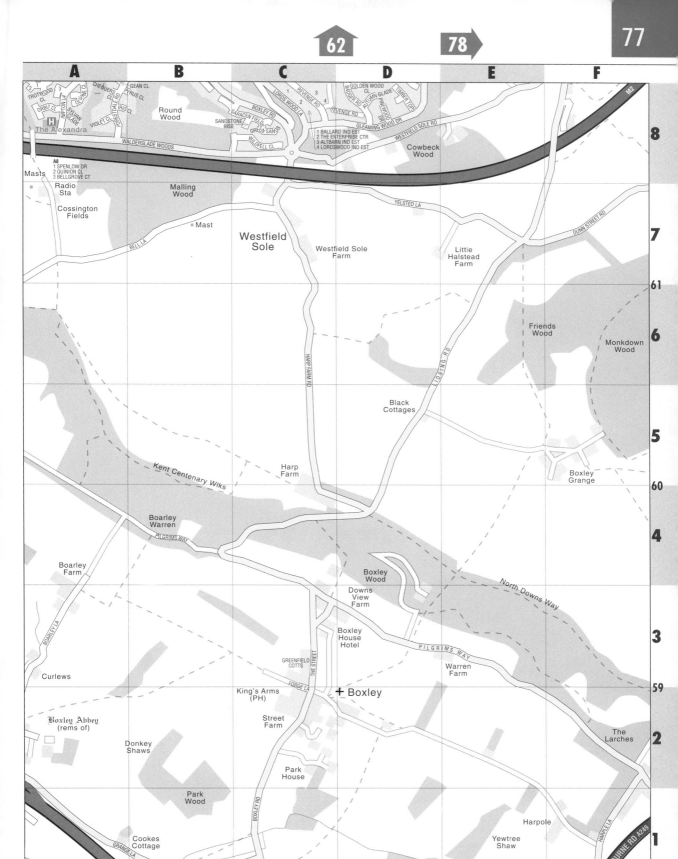

A B C D E F

8
7
61
6
5
60
4
3
59
2
1
58

Masts

A8
1 SPENLOW DR
2 QUINION CL
3 BELLGROVE CT

The Alexandra

Radio Sta

Cossington Fields

Round Wood

Malling Wood

WALDERSLADE WOODS

TROTWOOD CL
ORBIT CL
LINTON LA
CHEQUERS
GEAN CL
CYRUS CL
IRIS CL
SYLVAN GLADE
VIOLET CL
FIRESTDALE RD

BELL LA

Mast

Westfield Sole

Westfield Sole Farm

Little Halstead Farm

YELSTED LA

DUNN STREET RD

HARP FARM RD

LIDSING RD

Friends Wood

Monkdown Wood

Black Cottages

Boxley Grange

Harp Farm

Kent Centenary Wlks

Boarley Warren

PILGRIMS WAY

Boarley Farm

Boxley Wood

North Downs Way

Curlews

BOARLEY LA

Downs View Farm

Boxley House Hotel

THE STREET

Greenfield Cotts

FORGE LA

King's Arms (PH)

Street Farm

+ Boxley

Warren Farm

PILGRIMS WAY

The Larches

Boxley Abbey (rems of)

Donkey Shaws

Park House

BOXLEY RD

Park Wood

Harpole

Yewtree Shaw

HARPLE LA

SITTINGBOURNE RD A249

Cookes Cottage

GRANGE LA

M20

Harbourlands Farm

SANDY LA

Round Wood

SARACEN FIELD
SANDSTONE RISE
GREEN SANDS
WILDFELL CL

LORDS WOOD LA
BOXLEY RD
REVENGE RD
REVENGE RD
GLEAMING WOOD DR

GOLDEN WOOD CL
BADGER RD
AUTUMN GLADE
TIMBER TOP
PINEWOOD

WESTFIELD SOLE RD

Cowbeck Wood

1 BALLARD IND EST
2 THE ENTERPRISE CTR
3 ALTBARN IND EST
4 LORDSWOOD IND EST

M2

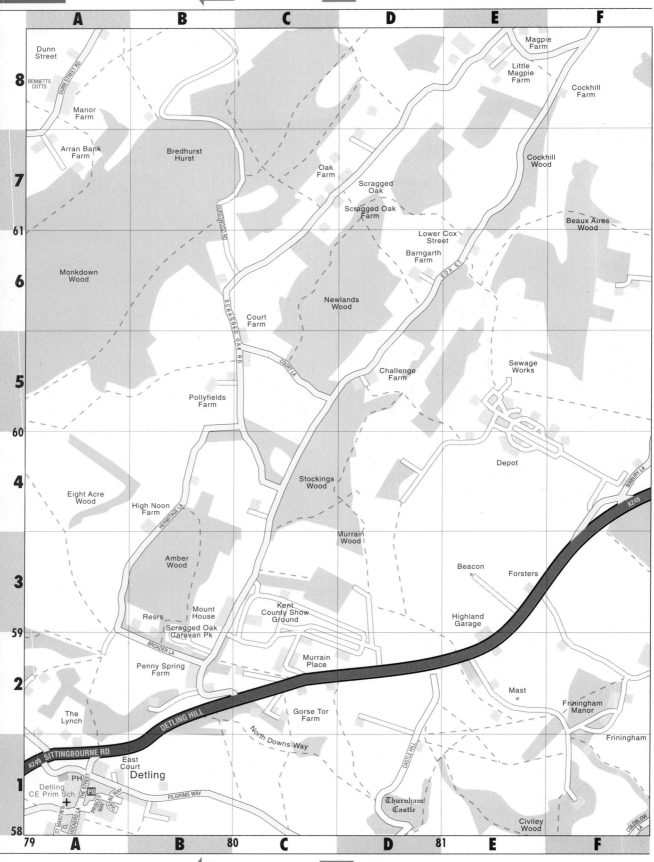

77
63

A B C D E F

8

7

61

6

5

60

4

3

59

2

1

58

79 A B 80 C D 81 E F

77
93

Dunn Street

BENNETTS COTTS

Manor Farm

Arran Bank Farm

DUNN STREET RD

Bredhurst Hurst

HURSTWOOD RD

Monkdown Wood

SCRAGGED OAK RD

Court Farm

COURT LA

Pollyfields Farm

Eight Acre Wood

High Noon Farm

HERMITAGE LA

Amber Wood

Resrs

Mount House

Scragged Oak Caravan Pk

BROADER LA

Penny Spring Farm

The Lynch

A249 SITTINGBOURNE RD

East Court

PH

Detling

Detling CE Prim Sch

PO

PRINCES WAY

HOCKERS LA

ST MARTIN'S CL

QUEENS WAY

PILGRIMS WAY

DETLING HILL

North Downs Way

Gorse Tor Farm

Murrain Place

Kent County Show Ground

Stockings Wood

Murrain Wood

Newlands Wood

Oak Farm

Scragged Oak

Scragged Oak Farm

Lower Cox Street

Barngarth Farm

COX ST

Challenge Farm

Magpie Farm

Little Magpie Farm

Cockhill Farm

Cockhill Wood

Beaux Aires Wood

Sewage Works

Depot

BINBURY LA

A249

Beacon

Forsters

Highland Garage

Mast

Friningham Manor

Friningham

CASTLE HILL

Thurnham Castle

Civiley Wood

COLDBLOW LA

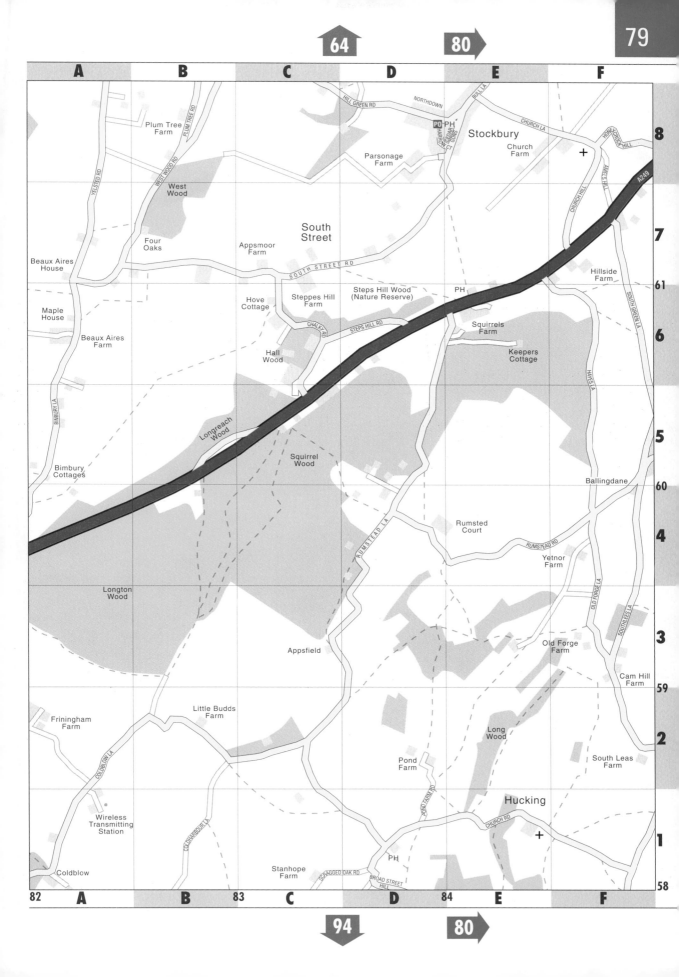

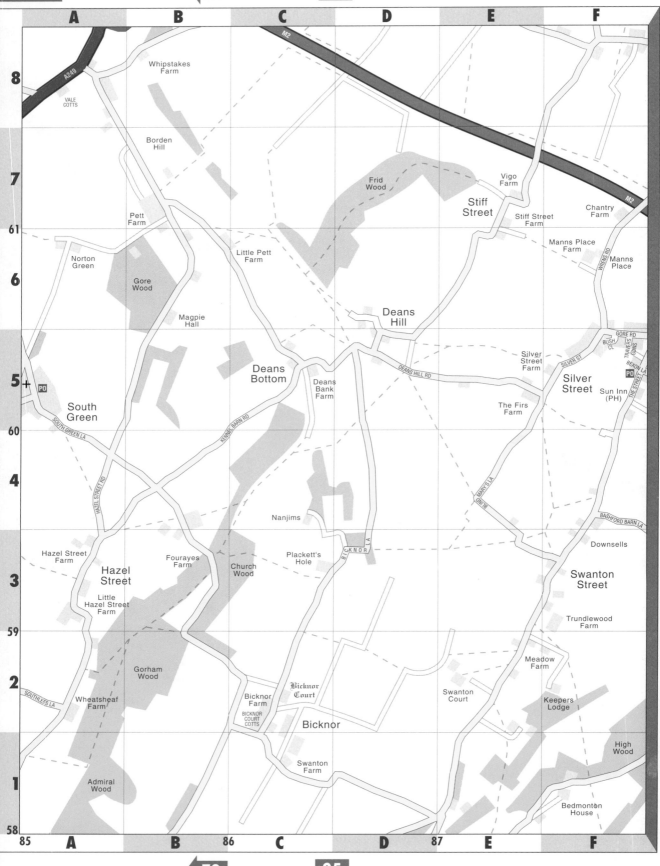

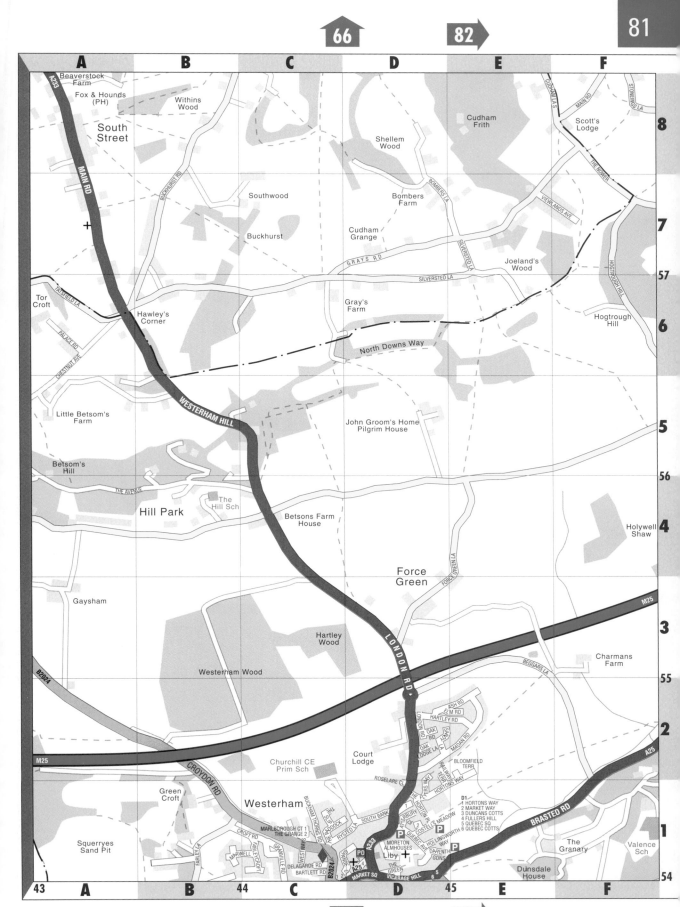

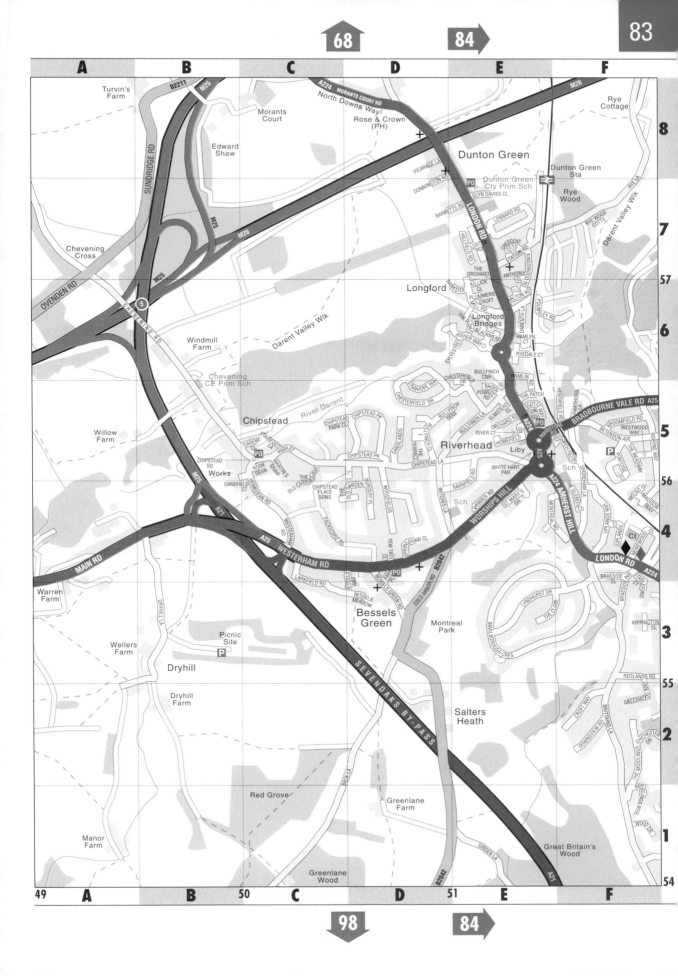

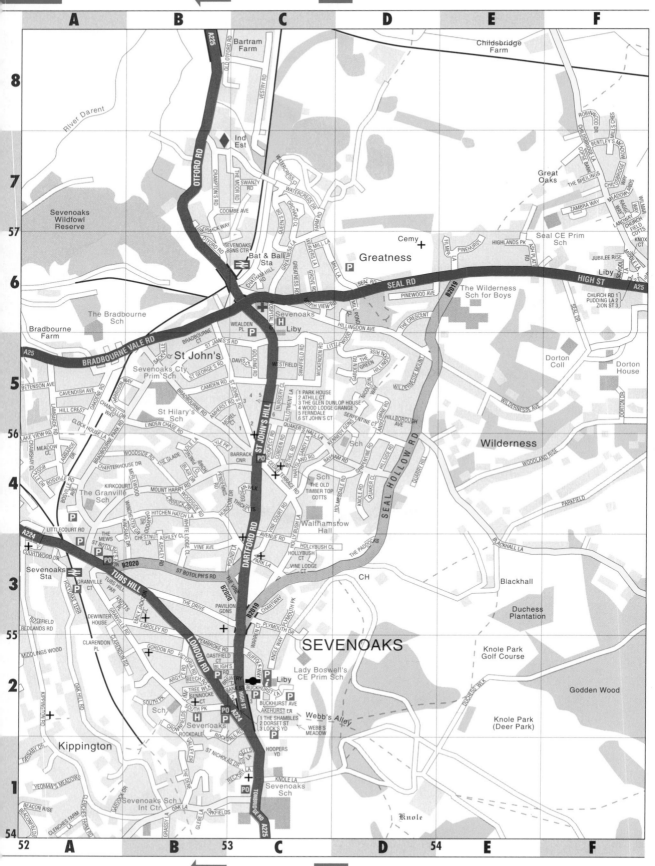

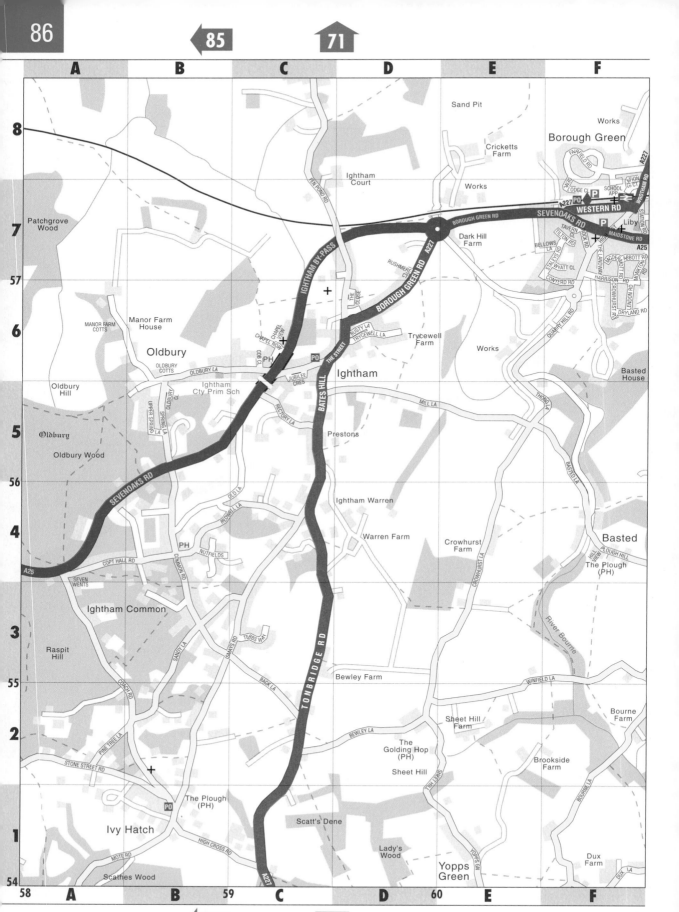

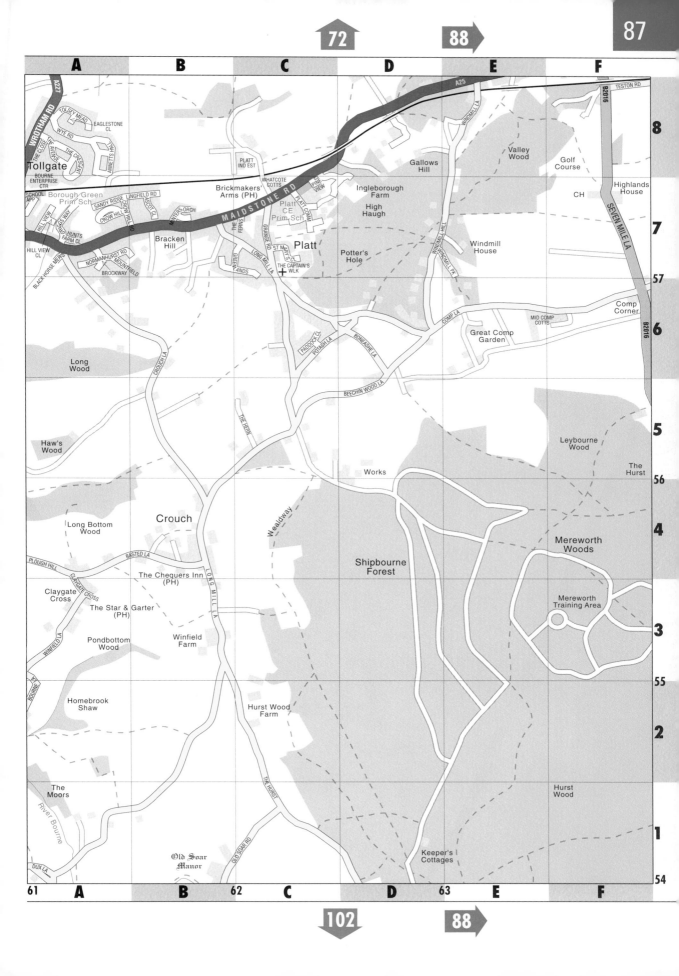

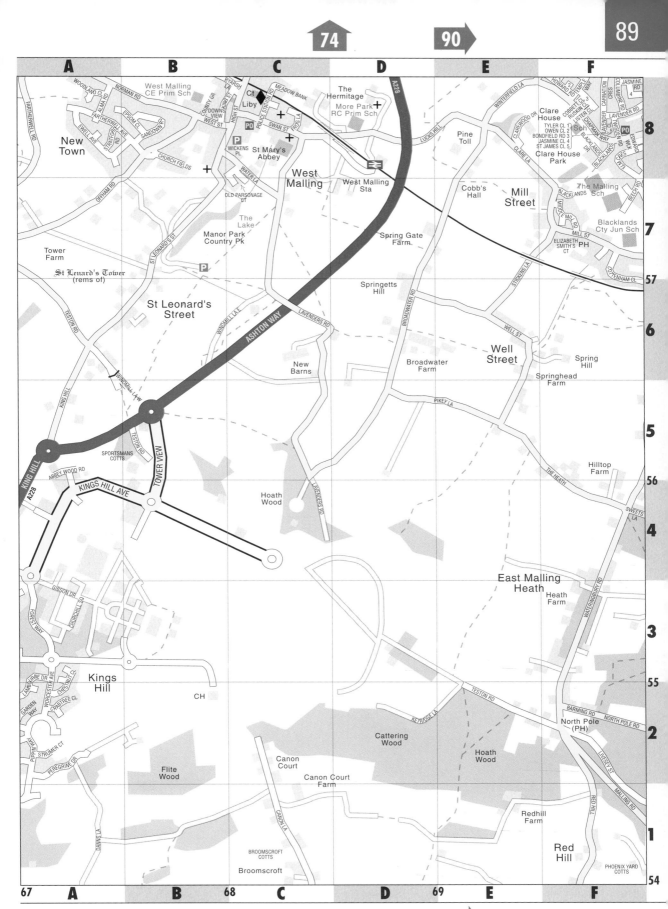

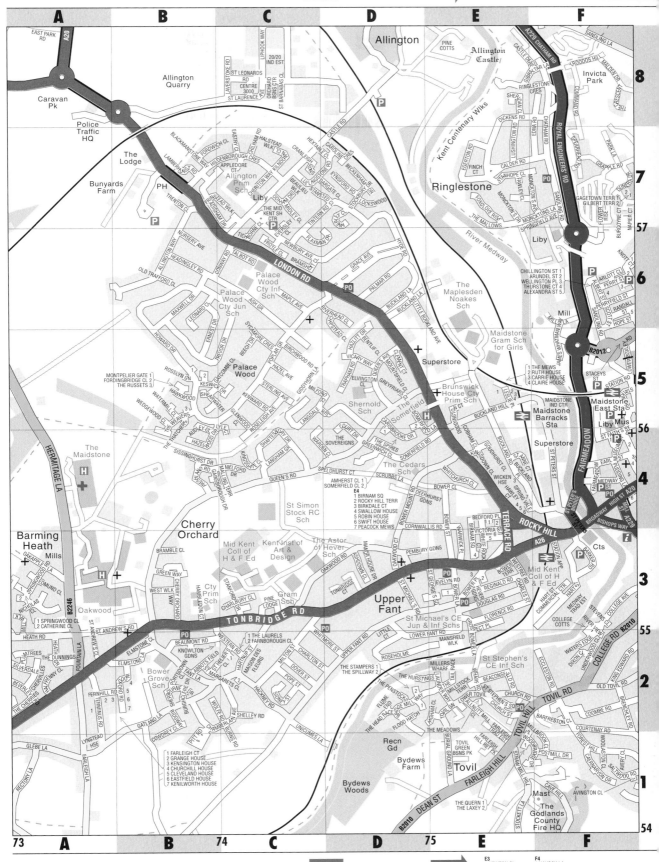

E3
1 NEWTON CL
2 ORCHARD PL
3 OLDCHURCH CT
4 RYECOURT CL
5 WHITE ROCK PL
6 VICTORIA CT

F4
1 HAVOCK LA
2 MARKET ST
3 MARKET COLONNADE
4 MARKET BLDGS
5 ROYAL STAR ARC
6 MIDDLE ROW

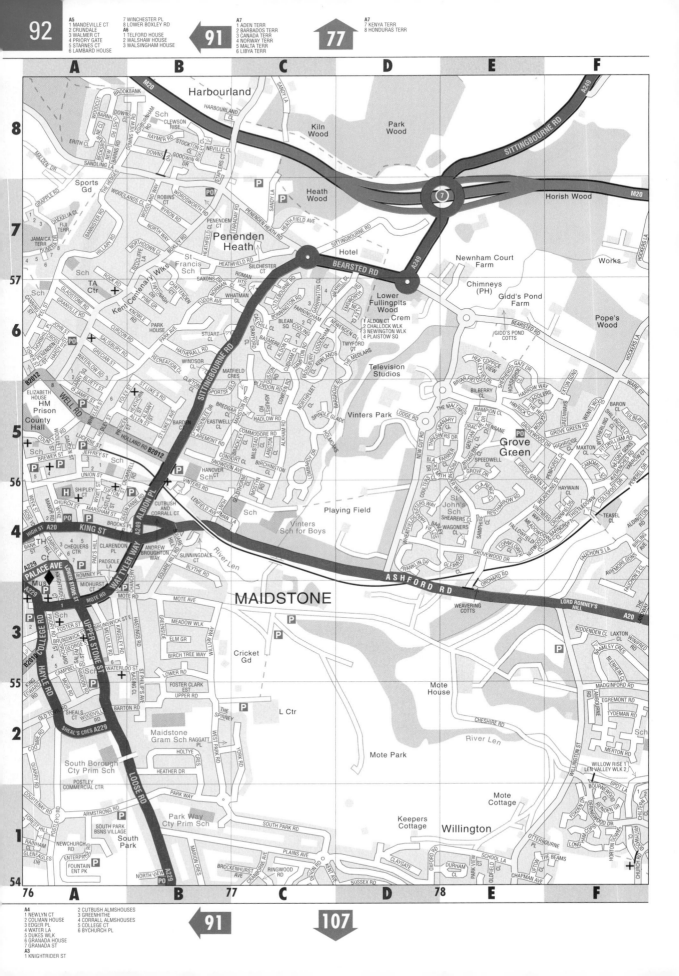

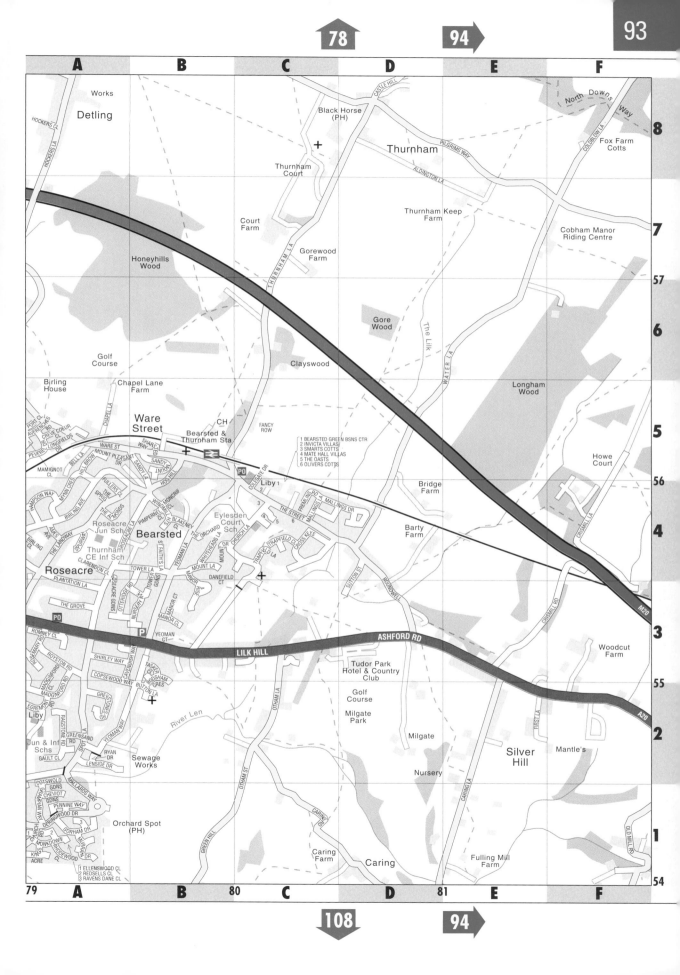

← 93
↑ 79

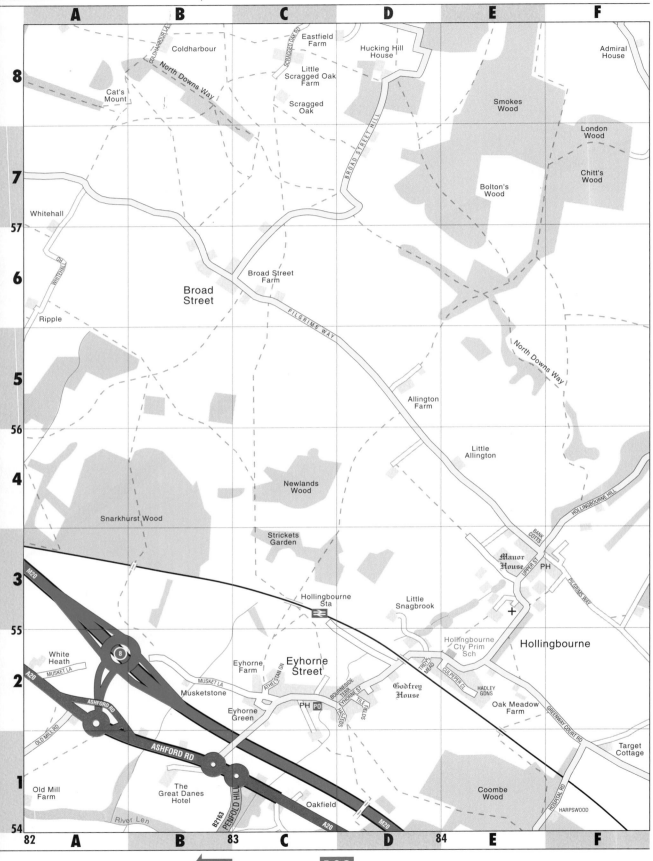

← 93
↓ 109

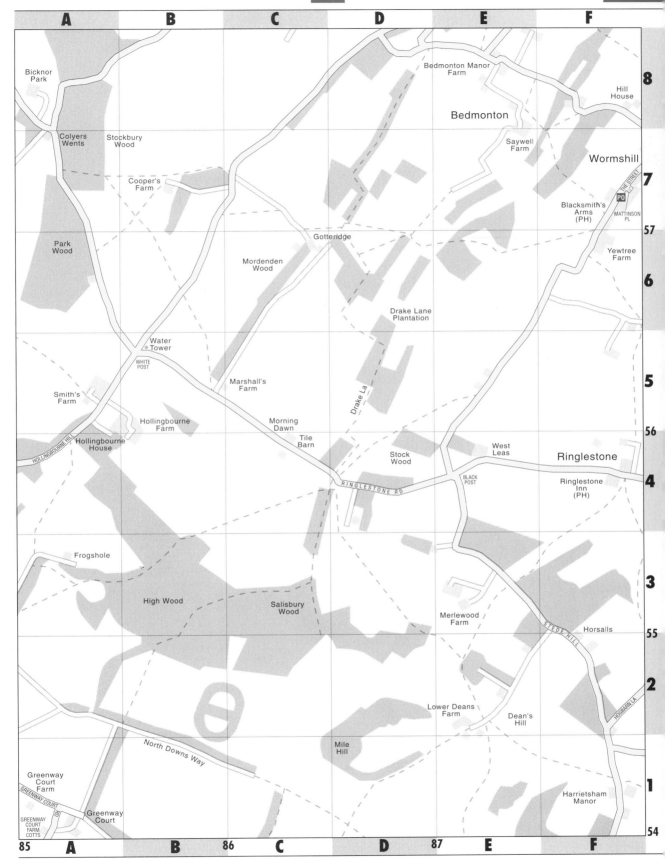

A   B   C   D   E   F

Valence Wood

Vines Gate

Great Wood

Sundridge   H

NEW RD   CHURCH RD

8

PIPERS LA

Foxwold

Brasted Chart

7

The Star (PH)

Quornden Wood

Penn Farm

PIPER'S GREEN RD

CHART LA

53

Stanhope wood

Round Wood

Quornden

6

Parson's Marsh

Great Norman Street Farm

Cordons Farm

Frenchstreet Farm

Phillippines

EMMETTS RD

NORMANS LA

The Chart

Emmetts Garden (National Trust)

5

Weardale

CREASEY'S ROW

Scords Wood

52

Fox & Hounds (PH)

PO

CAMBERWELL LA

MOUNT PLEASANT

Greensand Way

Ide Hill CE Prim Sch

Ide Hill

B2042

4

P

WHEATSHEAF HILL

HOSEY COMMON LA

Toy's Hill

Ide Hill

Hanging Bank

Castle Grove

GARDEN CL

SCORDS LA

Toy's Hill

Quinten Wood

The Guzzle

3

PUDDLEDOCK LA

Bardogs

TOY'S HILL

51

Puddlelock

Oakwood Lodge

2

Ties Wood

Tanhouse Wood

Round Wood

IDE HILL RD

Toy's Hill Wood

Tan House

Henden Manor

1

Obriss Farm

Boons Wood

B2042

50

97
83

A B C D E F

8

7

53

6

5

52

4

3

51

2

1

50

49 A 50 B C D 51 E F

Willow Wood

Hawks Wood

BACK LA

Greenlane Wood

Whitley

Dibden

DIBDEN LA

Mildridge Wood

A21

SEVENOAKS BY-PASS

Brook Place

Whitley Row

Whitley Forest

Mill Bank Wood

GOLDSMITH'S BOTTOM

OAK LA

The Woodman (PH)

Dust Wood

CHAPEL WLK

Apps Hollow

Hyde's Forest

Roundabout Wood

GRACIOUS LANE END

WHITE HOUSE LA

NIGHTINGALE LA

THE PANTYLES

Goathurst Common

York's Hill

Sheephill Wood

Pitfield Wood

RYCROFT LA

WHITE HOUSE RD

Bayley's Hill

Everlands

P

LADY AMHERST'S DR

Brockhill Wood

Stubbs Wood

B2042

Hanging Bank

Greensand Way

BAYLEY'S HILL

WICKHURST RD

Boarhill

Yorkshill Farm

Harbour Hook

Hatchlands Farm

Wickhurst Manor

Bowzell Farm

BOWZELL RD

Bowzell Wood

Scollops Farm

Old House Farm

B2042

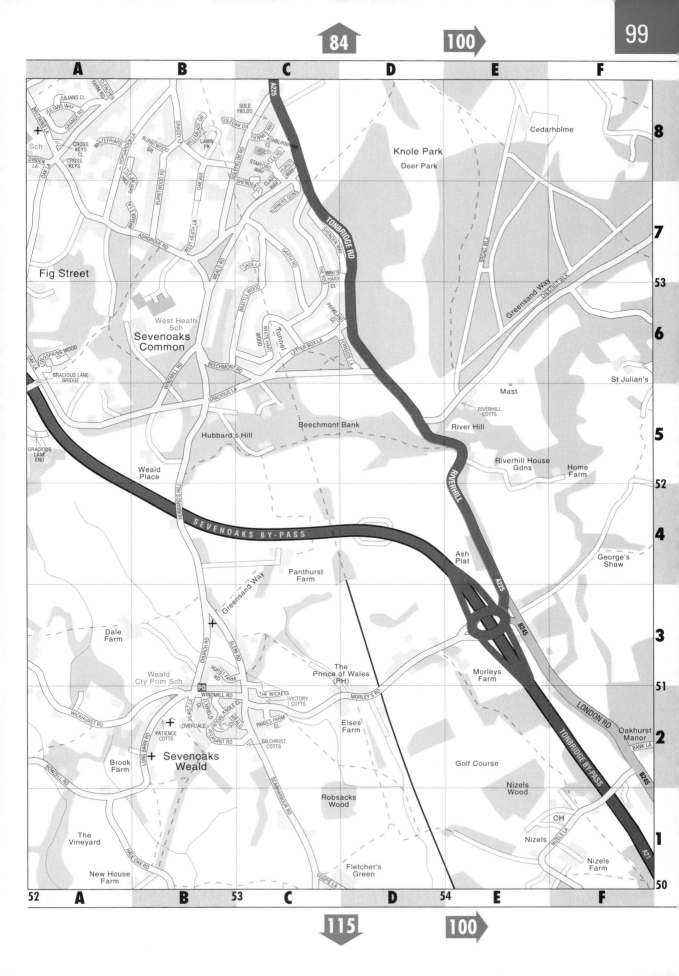

99
85

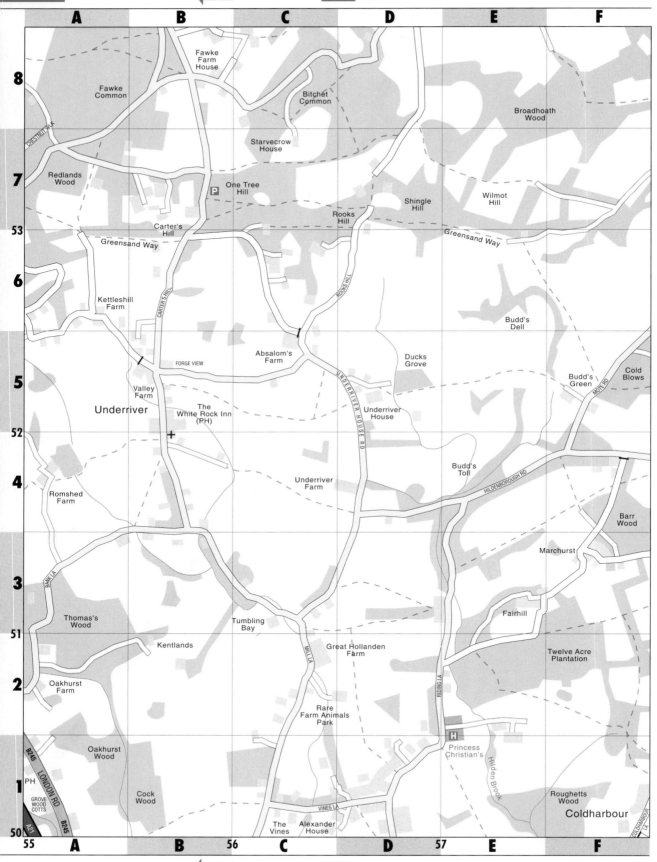

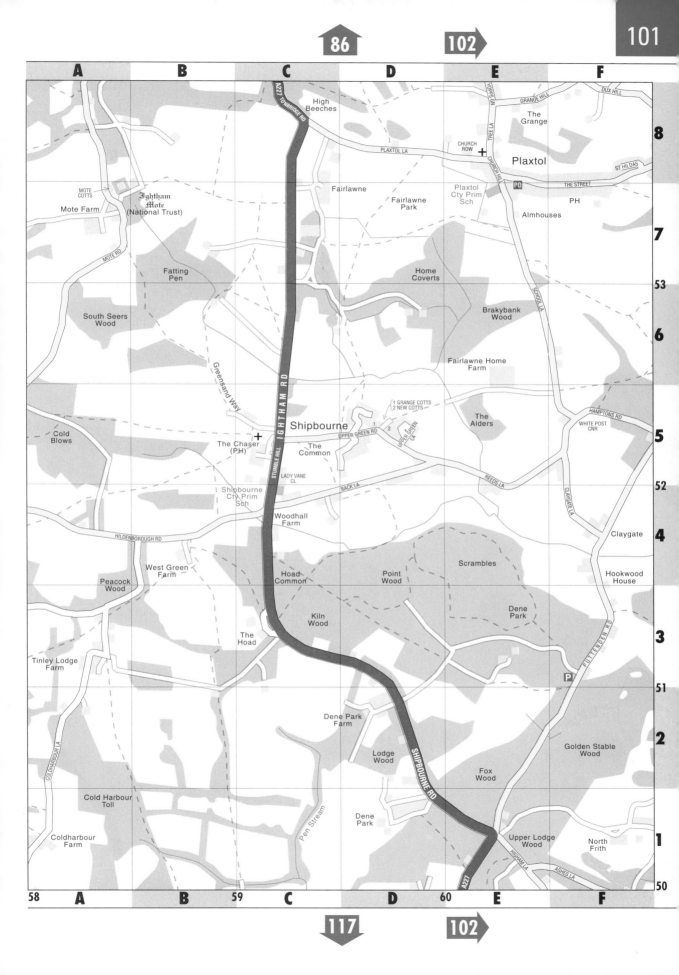

A   B   C   D   E   F

8

7

53

6

5

52

4

51

3

2

1

50

58   A   59   B   C   60   D   E   F

High
Beeches

GRANGE HILL

DUX HILL

The
Grange

TONBRIDGE RD
A227

PLAXTOL LA

CHURCH ROW

TREE LA

NO SCHOOL

CHURCH HILL

Plaxtol

ST HILDAS

Fairlawne

Fairlawne
Park

Plaxtol
Cty Prim
Sch

PO

THE STREET

PH

Almhouses

MOTE
COTTS

Ightham
Mote
(National Trust)

Mote Farm

MOTE RD

Fatting
Pen

Home
Coverts

SCHOOL LA

South Seers
Wood

Brakybank
Wood

Greensand Way

IGHTHAM RD

Fairlawne Home
Farm

Cold
Blows

Shipbourne

The Chaser
(P.H)

The
Common

STUMBLE HILL

UPPER GREEN RD

1 GRANGE COTTS
2 NEW COTTS

1

2

UPPER GREEN LA

The
Alders

HAMPTONS RD

WHITE POST
CNR

LADY VANE
CL

BACK LA

REEDS LA

CLAYGATE LA

Claygate

Shipbourne
Cty Prim
Sch

HILDENBOROUGH RD

Woodhall
Farm

West Green
Farm

Scrambles

Hookwood
House

Peacock
Wood

Hoad
Common

Point
Wood

Dene
Park

PUTTENDEN RD

Kiln
Wood

Tinley Lodge
Farm

The
Hoad

COLDHARBOUR LA

P

Dene Park
Farm

Golden Stable
Wood

Cold Harbour
Toll

Lodge
Wood

SHIPBOURNE RD

Fox
Wood

Pen Stream

Dene
Park

Coldharbour
Farm

Upper Lodge
Wood

North
Frith

HIGHAM LA

ASHES LA

A227

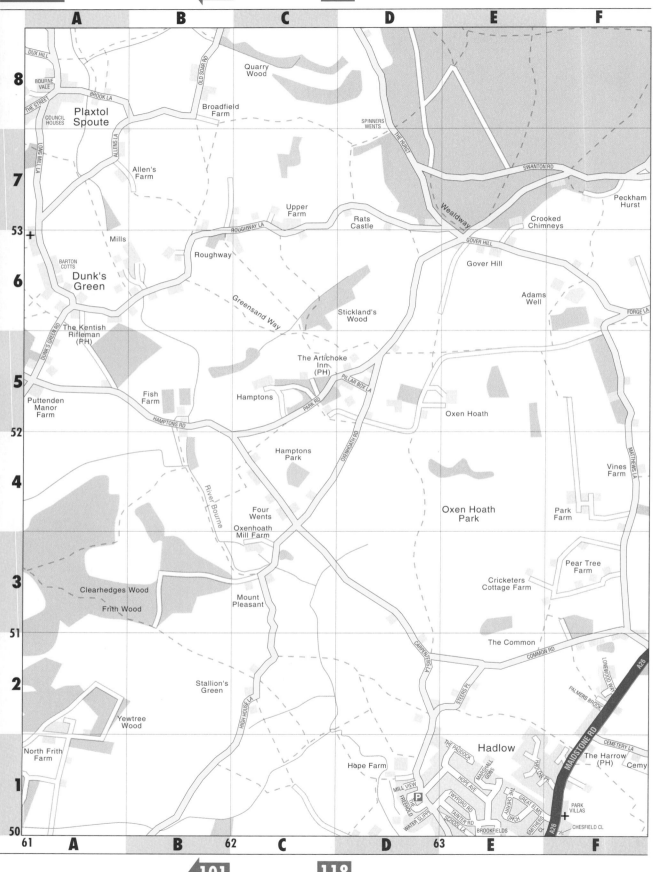

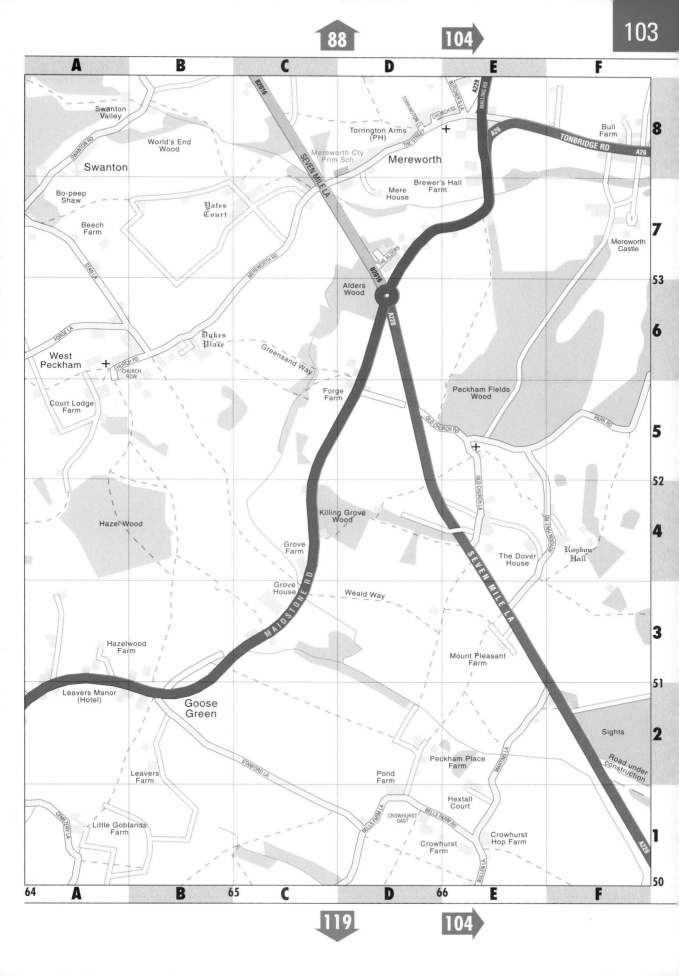

A B C D E F

8

Hermitage Farm

PAVILION LA
DANNS LA

Fuller's Corner

A26

Cemy

Manor Farm

OLD RD

CANON LA

RED HOUSE GDNS

MILL LA

UPPER MILL

LODGE CL

LOVE LA

TONBRIDGE RD

VINE CT

ALLINGTON GDNS

HANBURY CL

GLEBE MEADOW

COBBS CL

HILLSIDE CT

BOW TERR

WARDEN MILL CL

THE BRICKS

FIELDS LA

LENEY RD

PHOENIX DR

PO

P

Hotel

Wateringbury

RED HILL

THE ORPINES

A26

Sewage Works

7

PIZIEN WELL RD

Pizien Well

BOW RD

53

East Woods

PARK RD

NETTLESTEAD LA

Caravan Park

PHOENIX COTTS

WATERSIDE MEWS

PH

Wateringbury CE Prim Sch

LC

Wateringbury Sta

6

Rock Farm

Nettlestead

BRYANT CL

BISHOPS CL

KING'S COTTS

SCHOOL HILL

Bow Bridge

Waregrave's Wood

ROCK FARM COTTS

GIBBS HILL

BOW HILL

5

Birchetts Wood

Nettlestead Court Farm

Nettlestead Place

Bowhill Farm

HUNT ST

SMALL PROFITS

52

Bow Hill House

4

Diamond Place Farm

MAIDSTONE RD

River Medway

Kenward House

Hillside Cotts

3

Moat Wood

Green Farm

Kenward Farm

KENWARD RD

Greensand Way

51

Milbay's Wood

Hale Park Wood

FORGE COTTS

Court Lodge Farm

WARDE'S

THE NOOK

MEDWAY AVE

2

WELLS COTTS

Nettlestead Green

PH

Hook Wood

Beech Wood

STANDEN RD

Hampstead Marina

WALNUT CL

Yalding

HOPGARDEN OAST

OAST CT

YALDING HILL

Road under construction

A228

B2015

B2162

Cronks Farm

Yalding Sta

LC

HAMPSTEAD LA

Works

Caravan Park

Marina

River Beult

PH

HIGH ST

B2010

BARTON CL

1

A228

B2162

ACOTT FIELDS

Liby

50

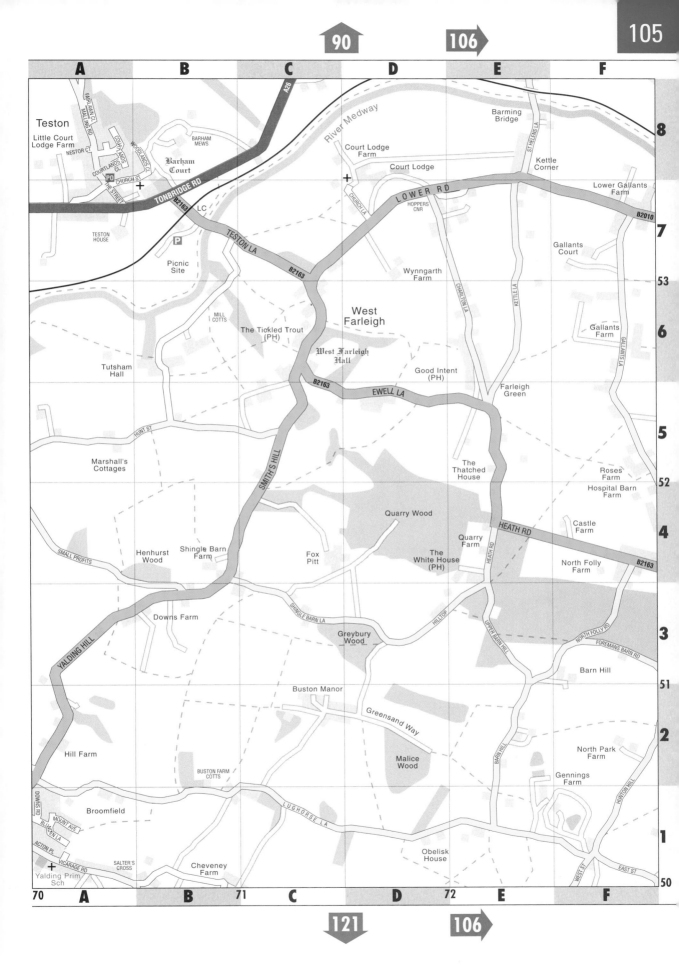

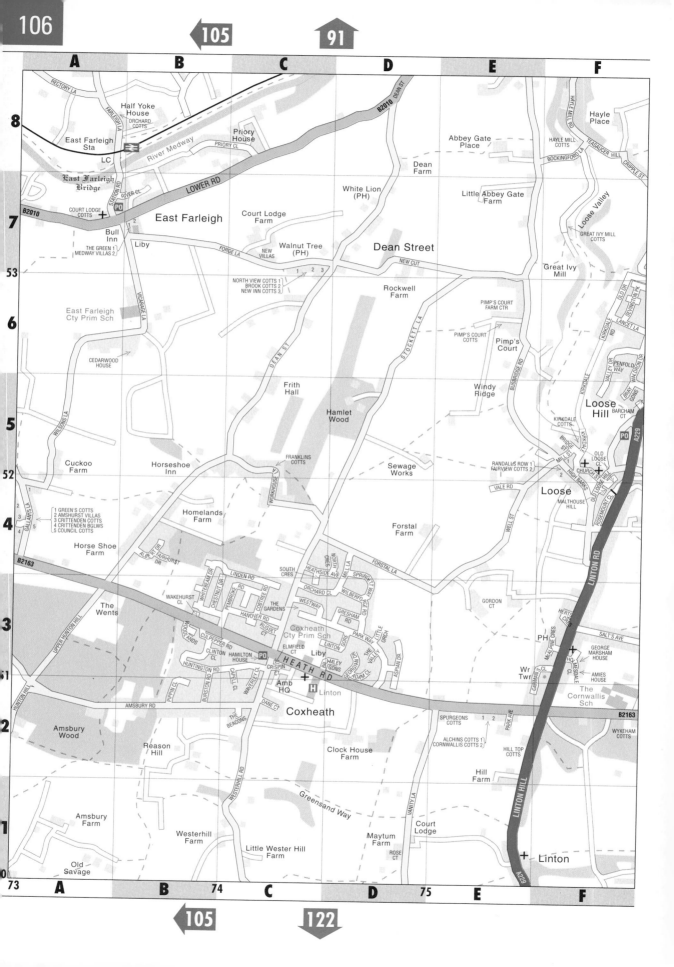

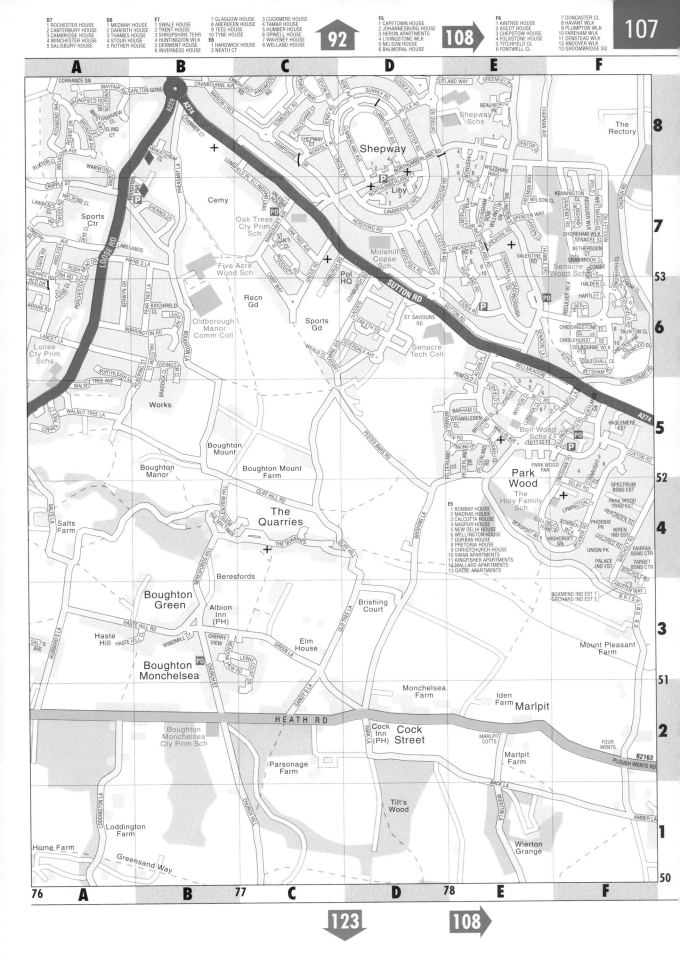

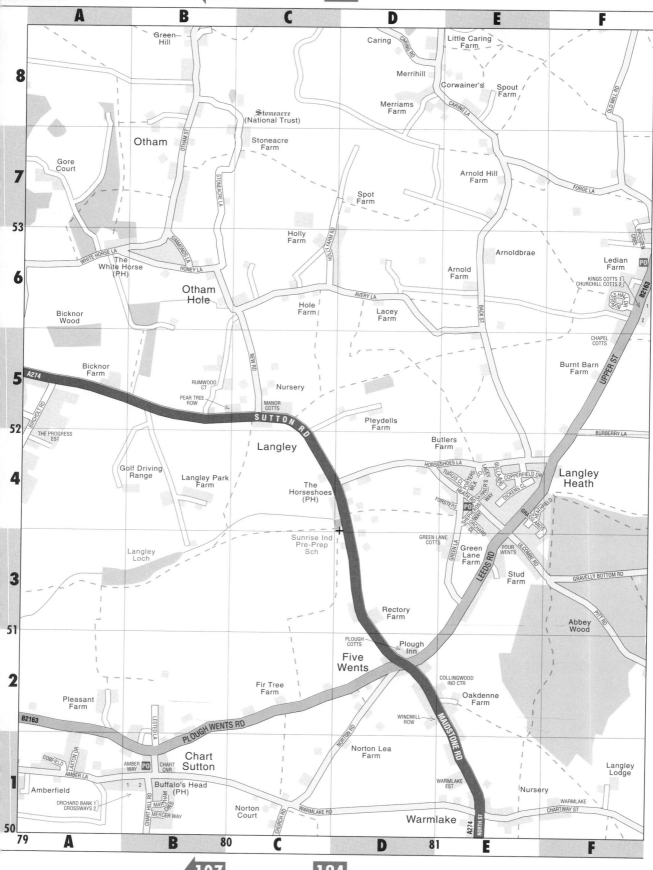

107
93

A B C D E F

8
7
53
6
5
52
4
3
51
2
1
50

Green-Hill
Otham
Stoneacre (National Trust)
Stoneacre Farm
Gore Court
OTHAM ST
STONEACRE LA
SUMMONDS LA
HONEY LA
WHITE HORSE LA
The White Horse (PH)
Otham Hole
Bicknor Wood
BIRCHOLT RD
Bicknor Farm
A274
THE PROGRESS EST
PEAR TREE ROW
RUMWOOD CT
MANOR COTTS
NEW RD
SUTTON RD
Nursery
Langley
Holly Farm
Hole Farm
HOLLY FARM RD
AVERY LA
Lacey Farm
Pleydells Farm
Golf Driving Range
Langley Park Farm
Langley Loch
The Horseshoes (PH)
Sunrise Ind Pre-Prep Sch
Caring
CARING RD
Little Caring Farm
Merrihill
Merriams Farm
CARING LA
Corwainer's
Spout Farm
Arnold Hill Farm
FORGE LA
Arnoldbrae
Arnold Farm
BACK ST
Spot Farm
Ledian Farm
OLD MILL RD
BROGDEN CRES
PO
B2163
KINGS COTTS 1
CHURCHILL COTTS 2
S HA DR
CHAPEL COTTS
UPPER ST
Burnt Barn Farm
BURBERRY LA
Butlers Farm
HORSESHOES LA
TURGIS CL
POTTERS WLK
SUTTING LA
COPPERFIELD DR
Langley Heath
HEATH RD
SKINNER'S WAY
DICKENS CL
FORSTERS
PO
SHEPPEYS WAY
ORCHARD CL
HEATHFIELD
GRASSLANDS
ULCOMBE RD
GREEN LA
Green Lane Farm
GREEN LANE COTTS
Stud Farm
FOUR WENTS
GRAVELLY BOTTOM RD
PITT RD
Abbey Wood
LEEDS RD
LACEY
Rectory Farm
Five Wents
PLOUGH COTTS
Plough Inn
Fir Tree Farm
Pleasant Farm
B2163
PLOUGH WENTS RD
LESTED LA
Chart Sutton
COBFIELD
LAXTON DR
AMBER LA
AMBER WAY
PO
CHART CNR
Buffalo's Head (PH)
CHART HILL RD
MARSHAM CRES
MERCER WAY
Amberfield
ORCHARD BANK 1
CROSSWAYS 2
Norton Court
NORTON RD
Norton Lea Farm
CHURCH RD
WARMLAKE RD
Collingwood Ind Ctr
COLLINGWOOD IND CTR
Oakdenne Farm
WINDMILL ROW
MAIDSTONE RD
WARMLAKE EST
Warmlake
NORTH ST
A274
CHARTWAY ST
WARMLAKE
Nursery
Langley Lodge

107
124

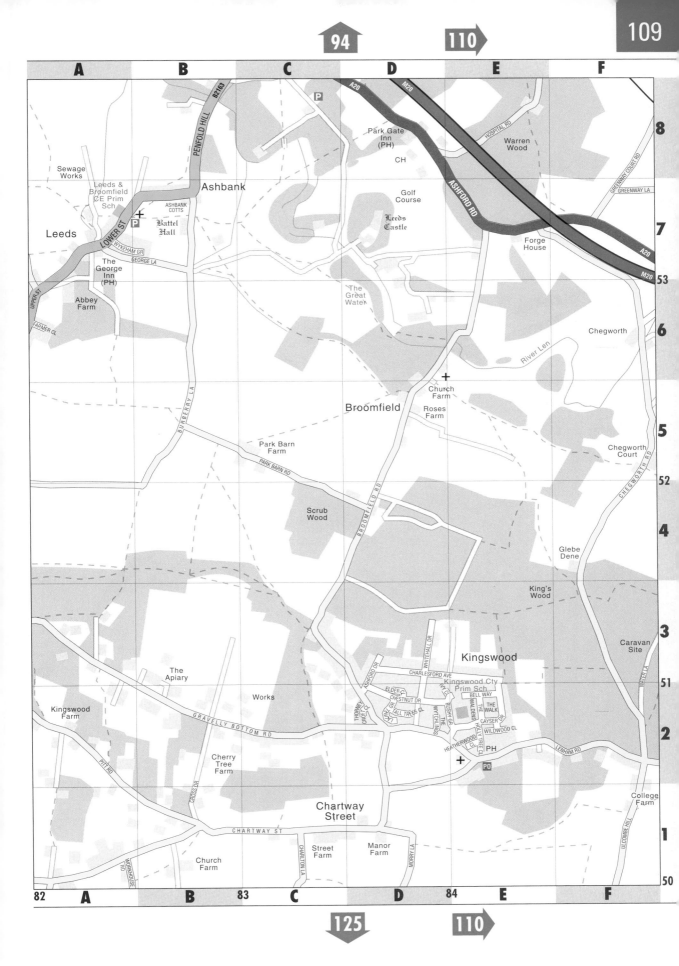

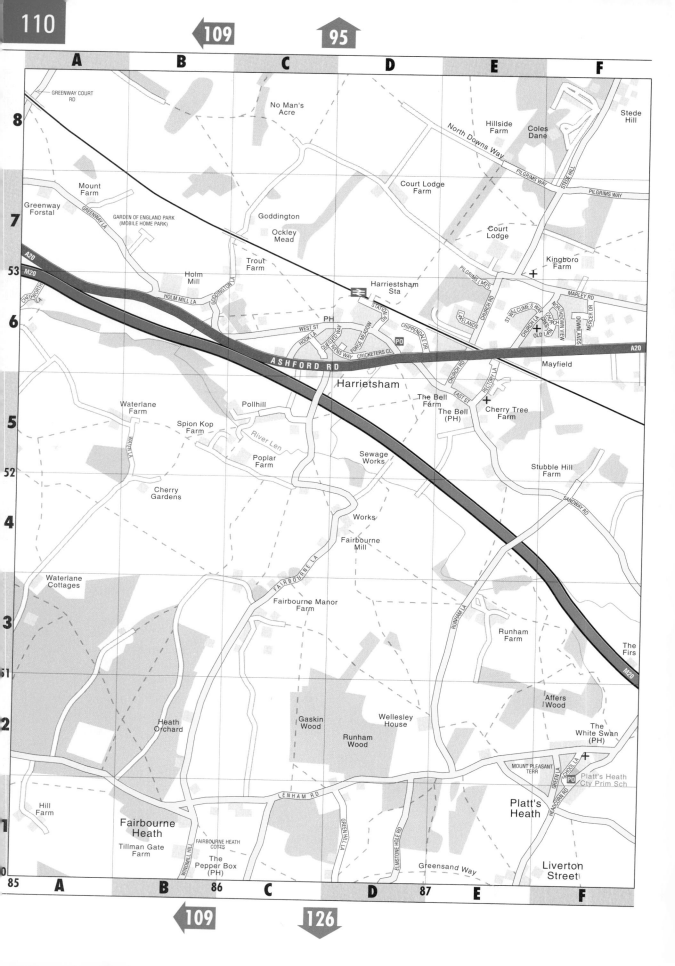

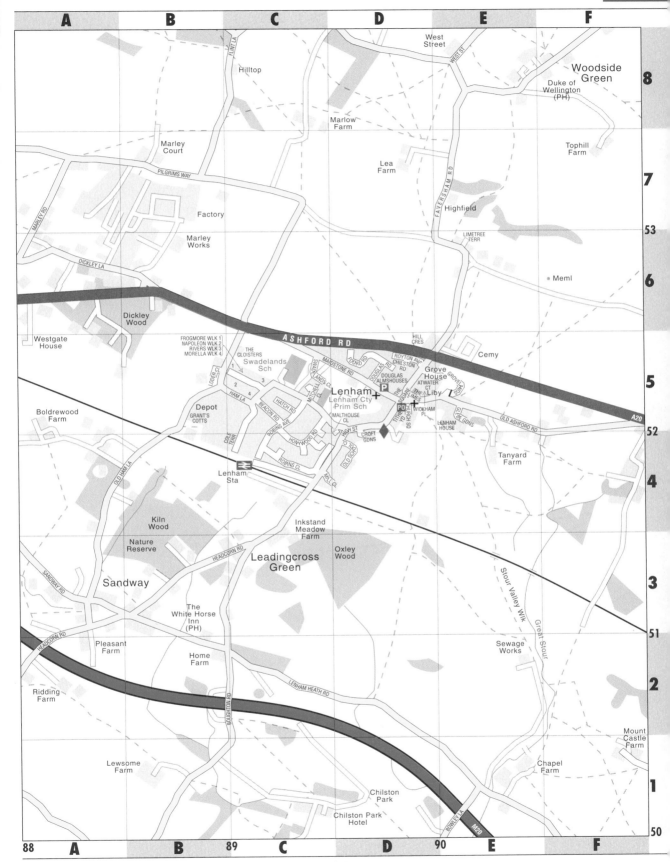

Woodside Green

West Street

Duke of Wellington (PH)

Hilltop

FLINT LA

Tophill Farm

Marlow Farm

Marley Court

PILGRIMS WAY

Lea Farm

FAVERSHAM RD

Highfield

MARLEY RD

Factory

LIMETREE TERR

Marley Works

DICKLEY LA

Meml

Dickley Wood

ASHFORD RD

HILL CRES

Westgate House

FROGMORE WLK 1
NAPOLEON WLK 2
RIVERS WLK 3
MORELLA WLK 4

THE CLOISTERS

ROYTON AVE
CHILSTON RD

Cemy

MAIDSTONE RD

Swadelands Sch

GROVELANDS

Grove House

Lenham Liby

ALDER CL

DOUGLAS RD

ATWATER CT

HAM LA

Boldrewood Farm

Depot

HATCH RD

GRANT'S COTTS

BEACON RD

MITCHELL CL

Lenham
Lenham Cty Prim Sch

DOUGLAS ALMSHOUSES

THE SQUARE
THE LIMES

GRACE GDNS

WICKHAM PL

OLD ASHFORD RD

A20

COLE TERR

ROBINS AVE

HONYWOOD RD

MALTHOUSE CL

Lenham House

OLD HAM LA

ROBINS CL

HIGH ST

CROFT GDNS

OS HOUSES

Tanyard Farm

Lenham Sta

MILL CL

OLD SCH C

TO 144

Kiln Wood

Inkstand Meadow Farm

HEADCORN RD

Nature Reserve

Stour Valley Wlk

Leadingcross Green

Oxley Wood

Great Stour

Sandway

SANDWAY RD

Sewage Works

The White Horse Inn (PH)

Pleasant Farm

Home Farm

HEADCORN RD

BOUGHTON RD

LENHAM HEATH RD

Ridding Farm

Mount Castle Farm

Lewsome Farm

M20

Chapel Farm

Chilston Park

BOXLEY LA

Chilston Park Hotel

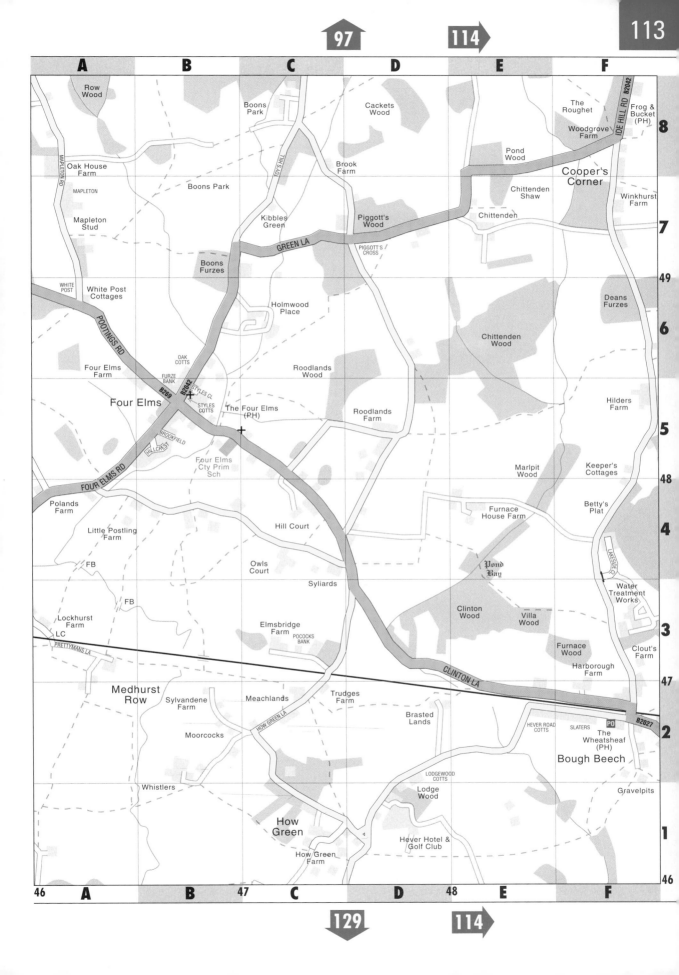

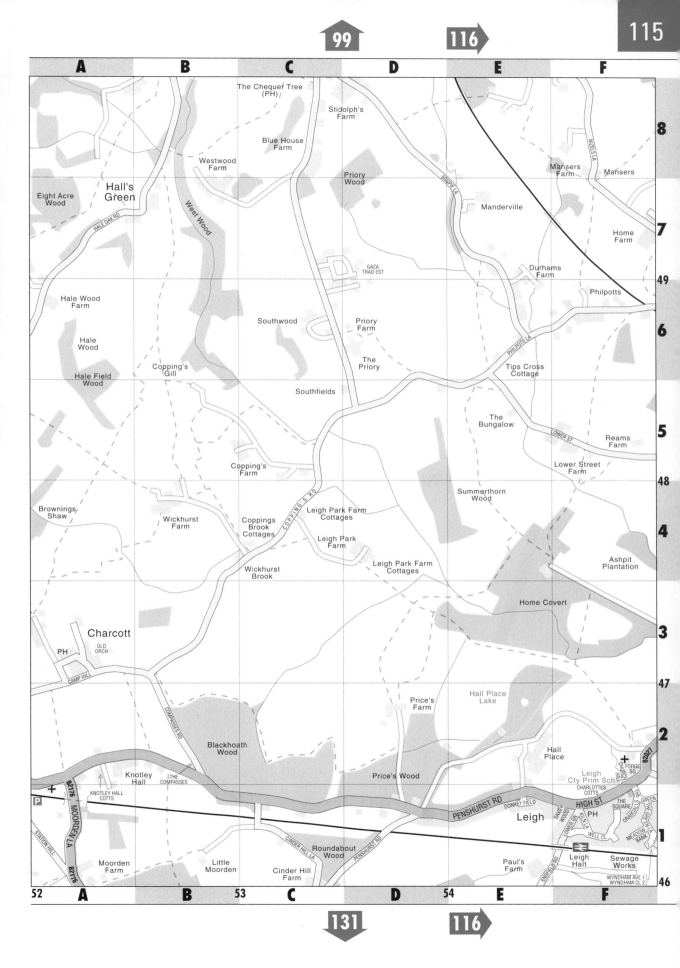

A B C D E F

8
7
49
6
5
48
4
3
47
2
1
46

The Chequer Tree (PH)

Stidolph's Farm

Blue House Farm

Westwood Farm

Hall's Green

West Wood

HALE OAK RD

Eight Acre Wood

Priory Wood

EGRPE LA

Mansers Farm

Mansers

Manderville

NIZELS LA

Home Farm

Hale Wood Farm

Southwood

Durhams Farm

Philpotts

Hale Wood

Priory Farm

The Priory

PHILPOTS LA

Tips Cross Cottage

Hale Field Wood

Copping's Gill

Southfields

The Bungalow

LOWER ST

Reams Farm

Copping's Farm

Lower Street Farm

Brownings Shaw

Wickhurst Farm

Coppings Brook Cottages

COPPING'S RD

Leigh Park Farm Cottages

Summerthorn Wood

Leigh Park Farm

Leigh Park Farm Cottages

Ashpit Plantation

Wickhurst Brook

Home Covert

Charcott

PH

OLD ORCH

CAMP HILL

Price's Farm

Hall Place Lake

COMPASSES RD

Blackhoath Wood

Price's Wood

Hall Place

B2027

Knotley Hall

THE COMPASSES

Leigh Cty Prim Sch

CHURCH HILL

FORGE SQ

CHARLOTTES COTTS

HIGH ST

Leigh

THE SQUARE

THE GREEN

B2176

MOORDEN LA

KNOTLEY HALL COTTS

PENSHURST RD

Donkey Field

SAXBY WOOD

KILN LA

PH

WELL CL

CRANDALLS

MEADOW BANK

STATION HILL

B2176

Moorden Farm

Little Moorden

CINDER HILL LA

Roundabout Wood

PENSHURST RD

Paul's Farm

LOWER GN

ENSFIELD RD

Leigh Halt

Sewage Works

Cinder Hill Farm

WYNDHAM AVE 1
WYNDHAM CL 2

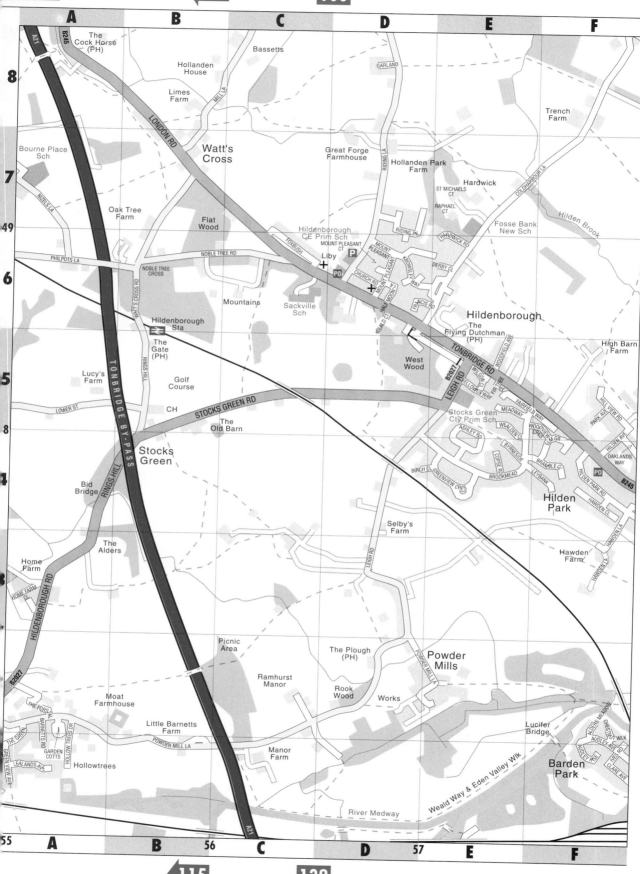

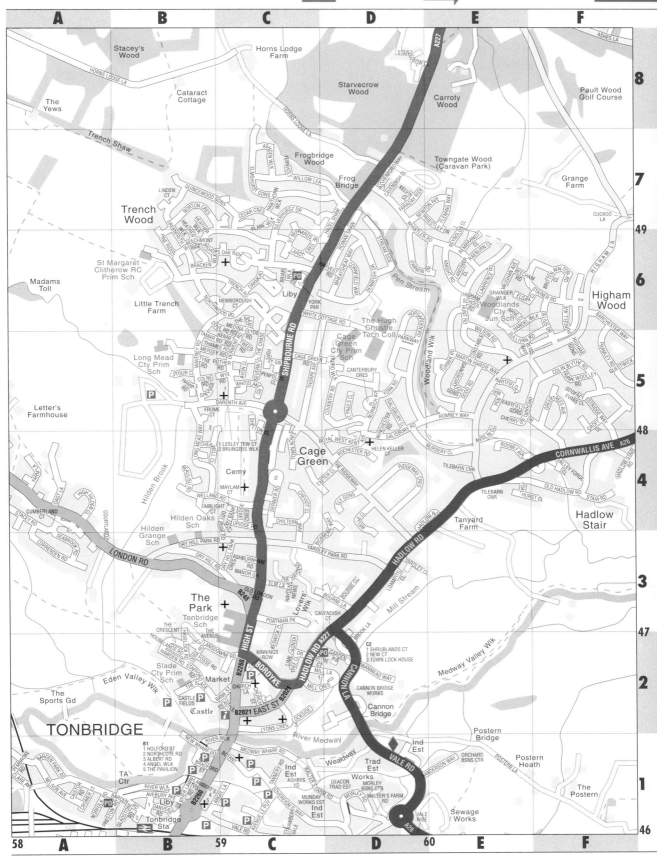

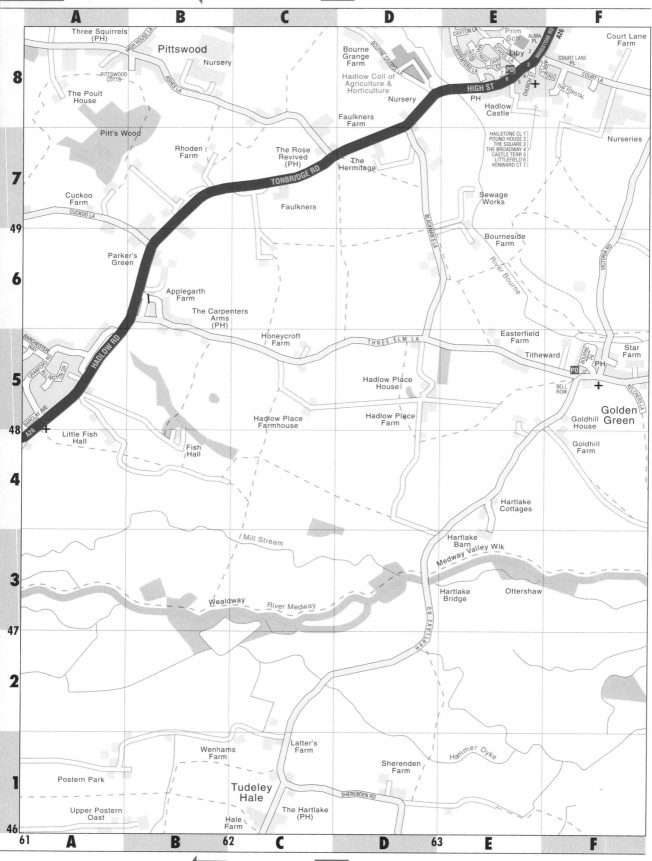

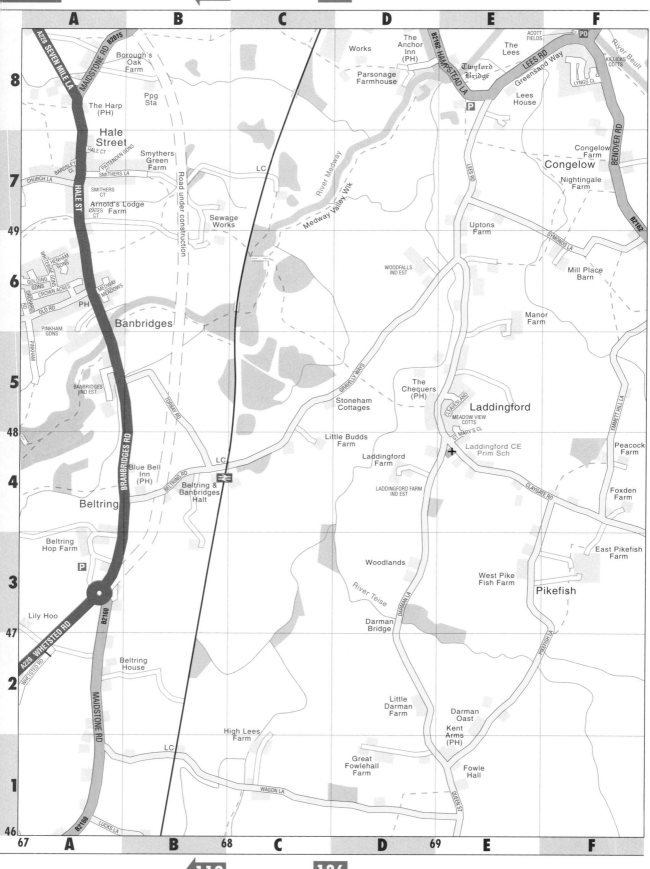

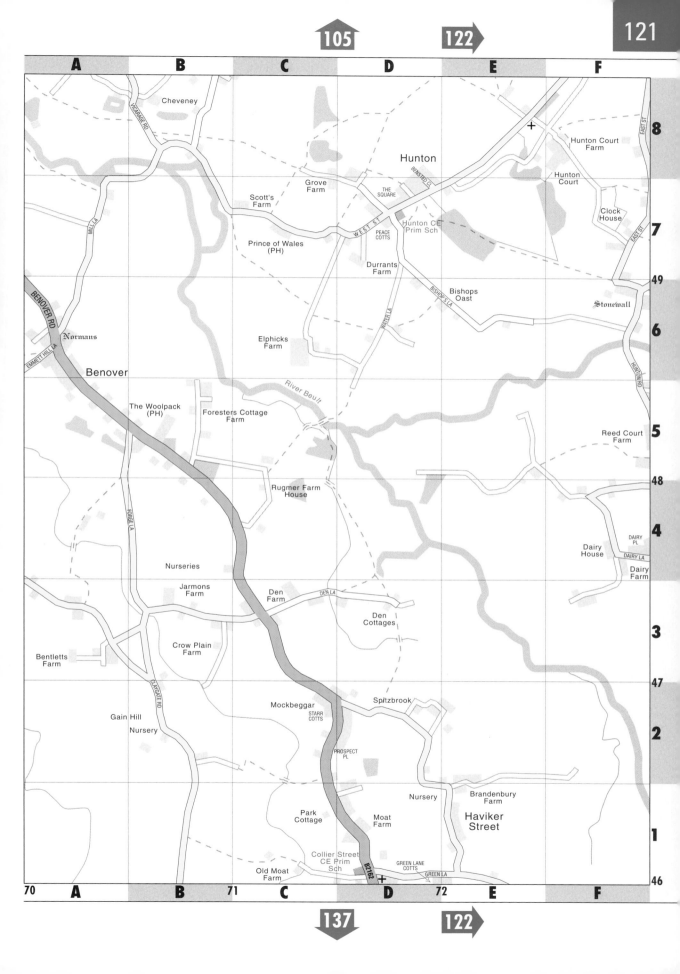

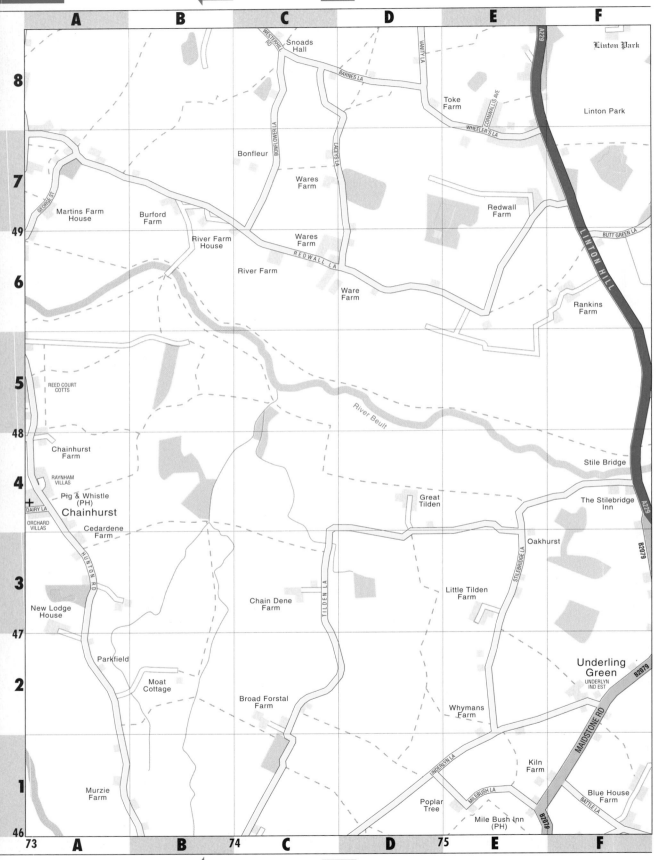

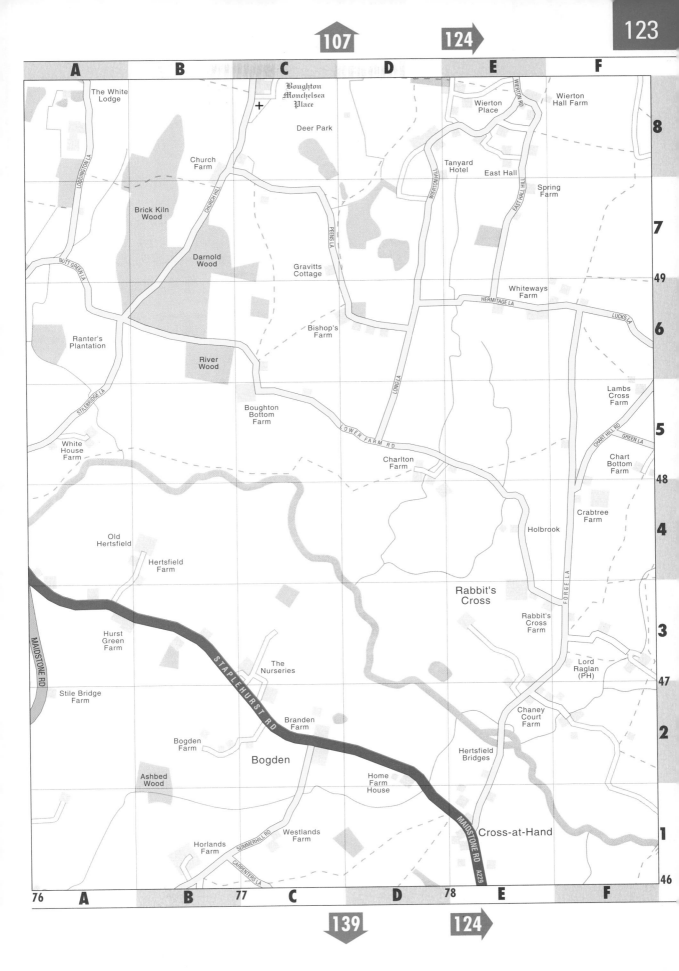

123 108

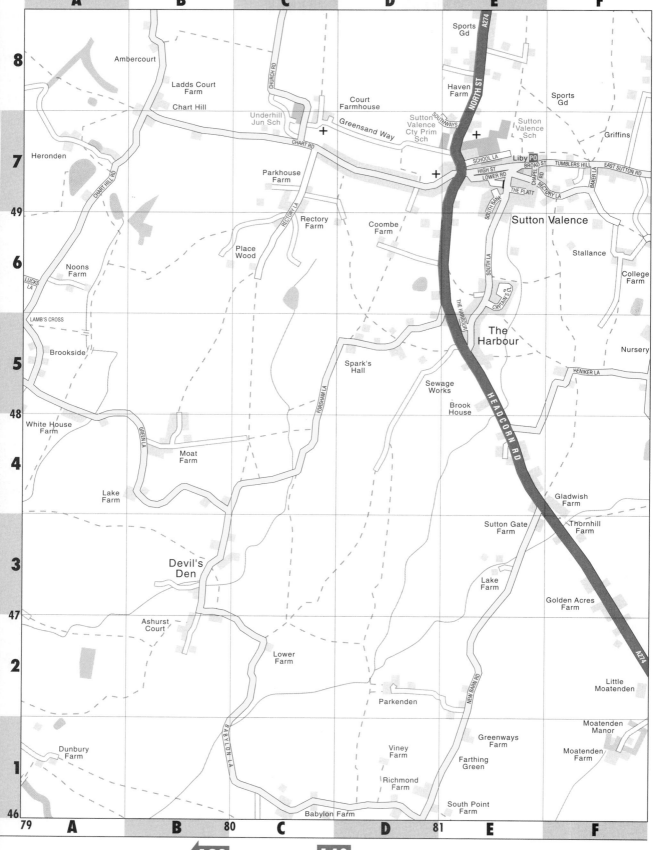

123 140

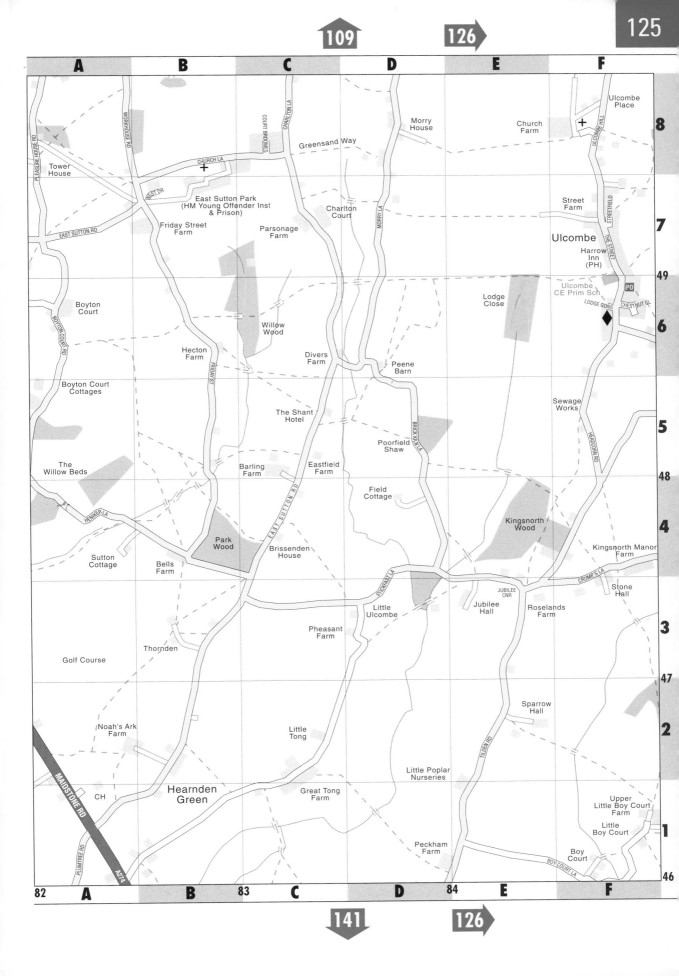

111

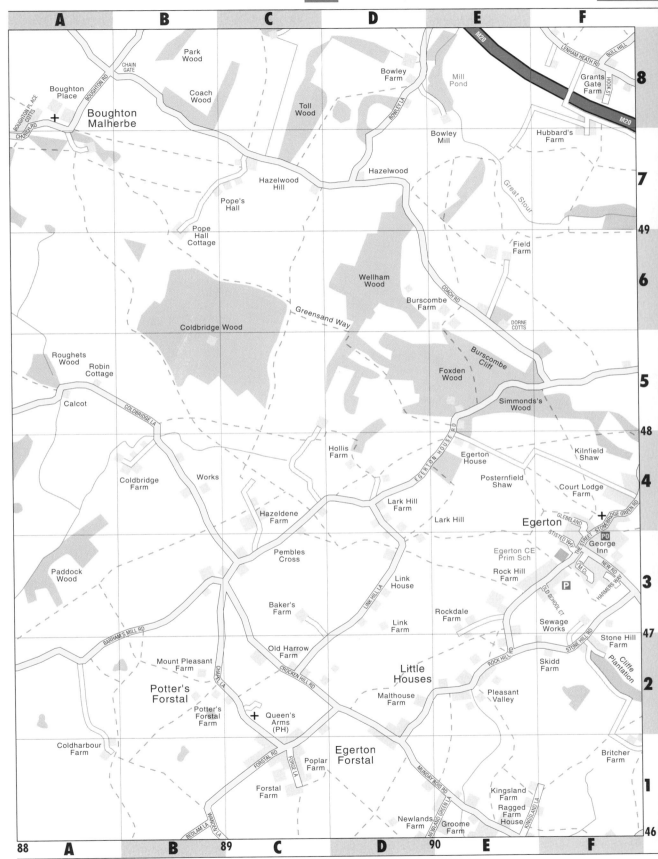

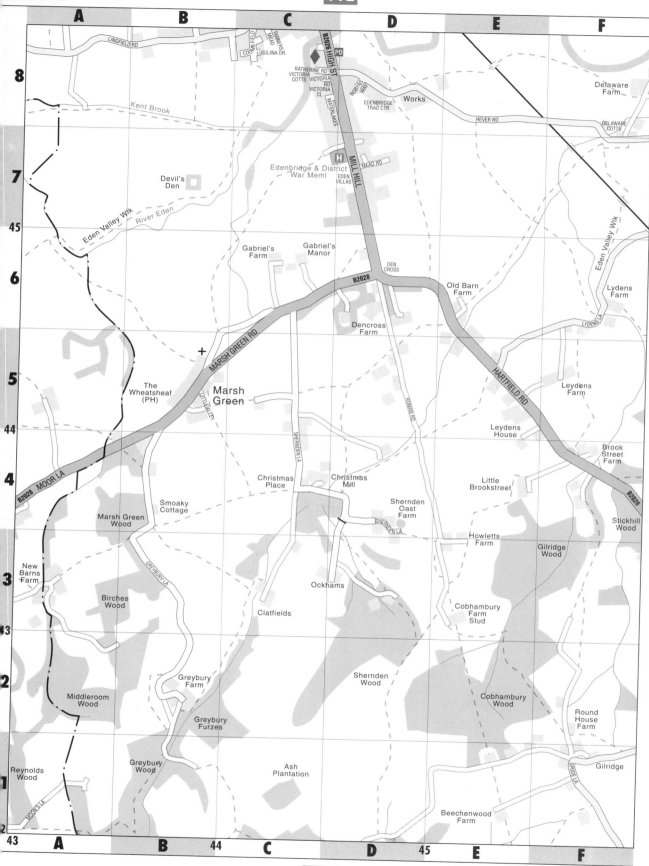

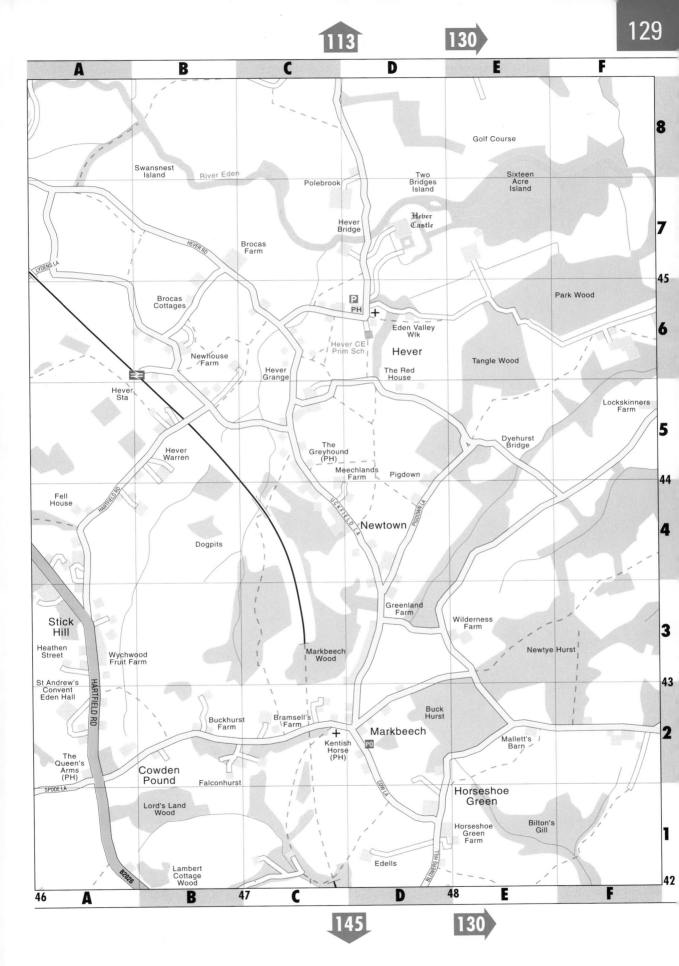

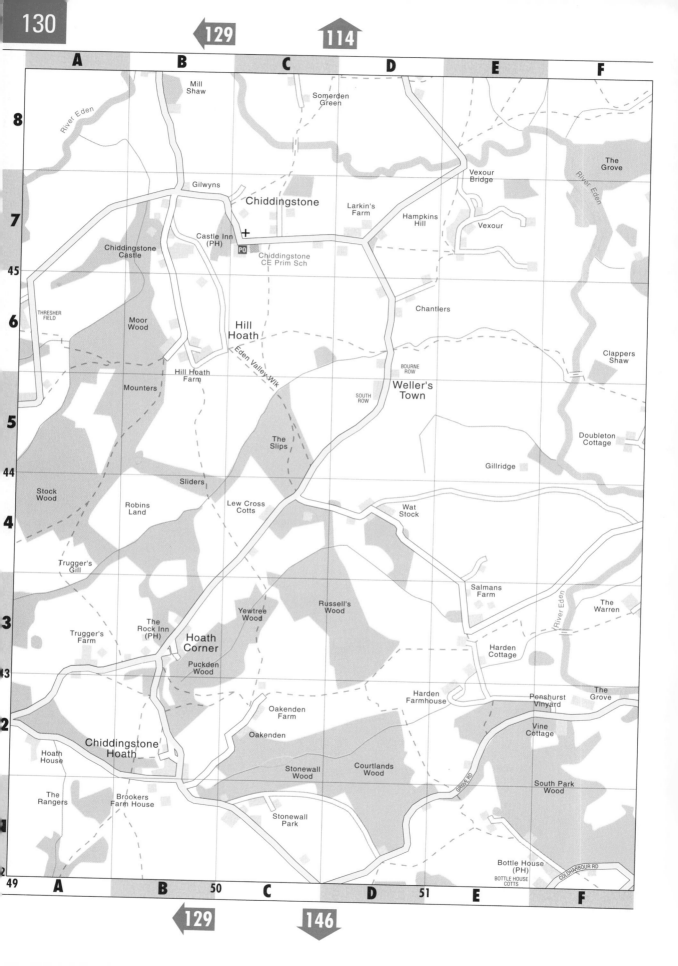

A   B   C   D   E   F

8

River Eden

The Grove

River Eden

Mill Shaw

Somerden Green

Vexour Bridge

7

Gilwyns

Chiddingstone

Larkin's Farm

Hampkins Hill

Vexour

Castle Inn (PH)

PO

Chiddingstone CE Prim Sch

45

Chiddingstone Castle

THRESHER FIELD

Chantlers

6

Moor Wood

Hill Hoath

Clappers Shaw

Hill Hoath Farm

Eden Valley Wlk

BOURNE ROW

Mounters

Weller's Town

SOUTH ROW

Doubleton Cottage

5

The Slips

Gillridge

44

Sliders

Stock Wood

Robins Land

Lew Cross Cotts

Wat Stock

4

Trugger's Gill

Salmans Farm

The Warren

River Eden

3

Trugger's Farm

The Rock Inn (PH)

Yewtree Wood

Russell's Wood

Hoath Corner

Harden Cottage

Puckden Wood

43

The Grove

Harden Farmhouse

Penshurst Vinyard

2

Oakenden Farm

Vine Cottage

Chiddingstone Hoath

Oakenden

Hoath House

Stonewall Wood

Courtlands Wood

South Park Wood

GROVE RD

The Rangers

Brookers Farm House

Stonewall Park

Bottle House (PH)

COLDHARBOUR RD

BOTTLE HOUSE COTTS

49   A   B   50   C   D   51   E   F

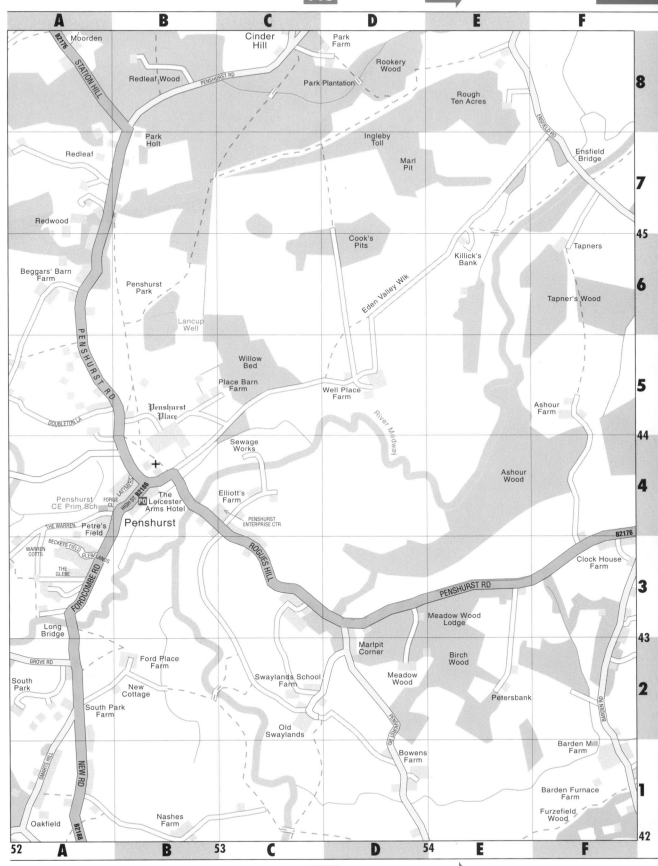

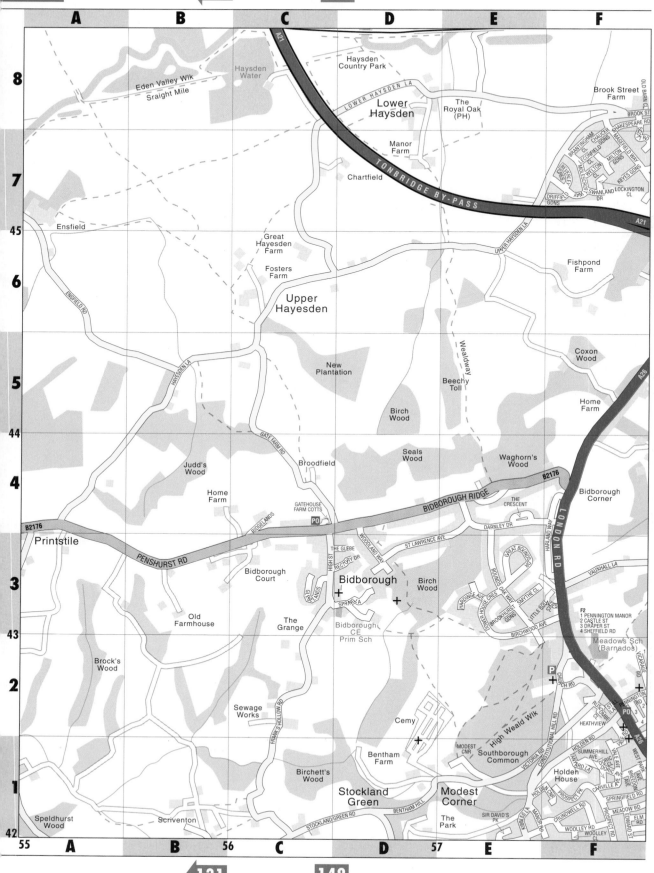

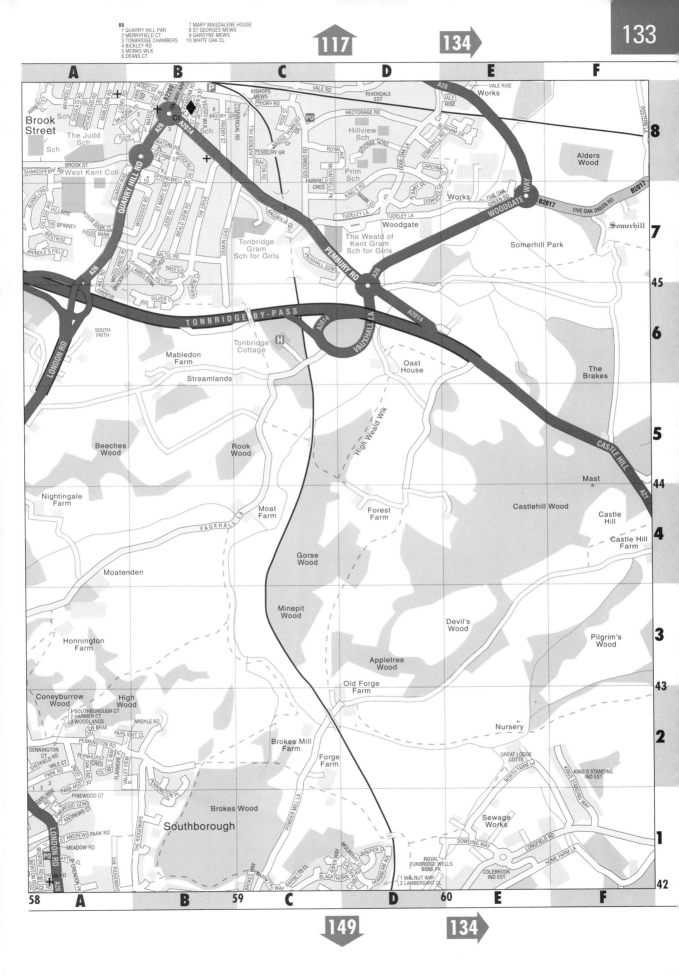

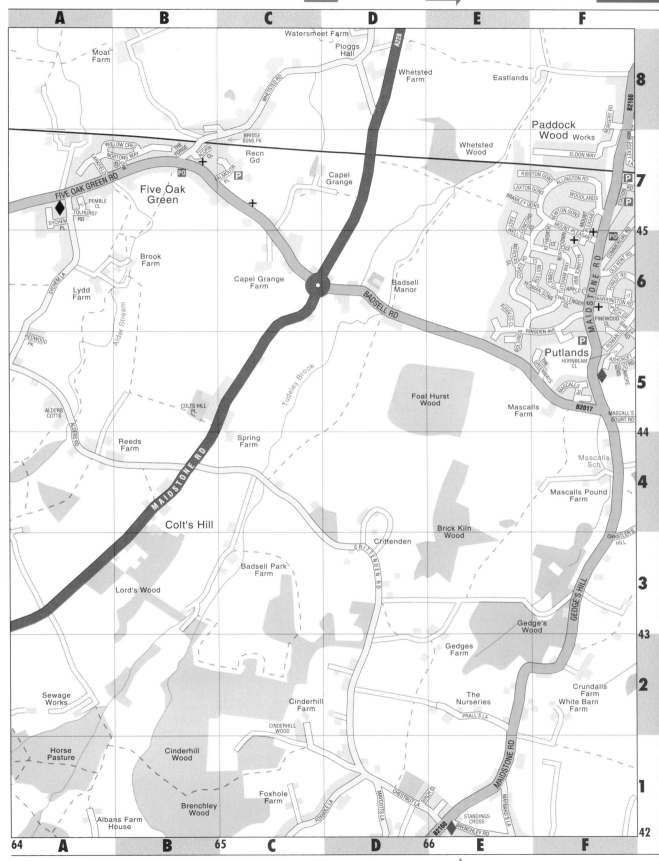

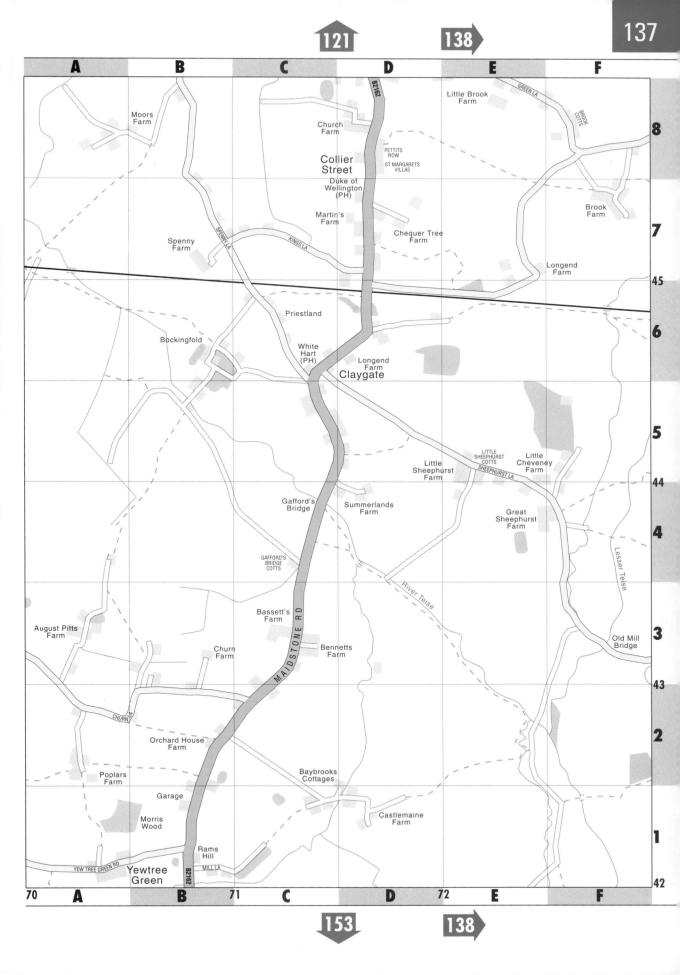

121
138
153
138

A B C D E F

8 7 45 6 5 44 4 3 43 2 1 42

Moors Farm

Little Brook Farm

GREEN LA

BROOK COTTS

Church Farm

Collier Street

PETTITS ROW
ST MARGARETS VILLAS

B2162

Brook Farm

Duke of Wellington (PH)

Martin's Farm

Chequer Tree Farm

Spenny Farm

SPENN LA

KINGS LA

Longend Farm

Priestland

Bockingfold

White Hart (PH)

Longend Farm

Claygate

Little Sheephurst Farm

LITTLE SHEEPHURST COTTS

SHEEPHURST LA

Little Cheveney Farm

Gafford's Bridge

Summerlands Farm

Great Sheephurst Farm

Lesser Teise

GAFFORD'S BRIDGE COTTS

River Teise

August Pitts Farm

Bassett's Farm

MAIDSTONE RD

Bennetts Farm

Old Mill Bridge

Churn Farm

CHURN LA

Orchard House Farm

Poplars Farm

Garage

Baybrooks Cottages

Morris Wood

Castlemaine Farm

Rams Hill

YEW TREE GREEN RD

Yewtree Green

B2162

MILL LA

70 71 72

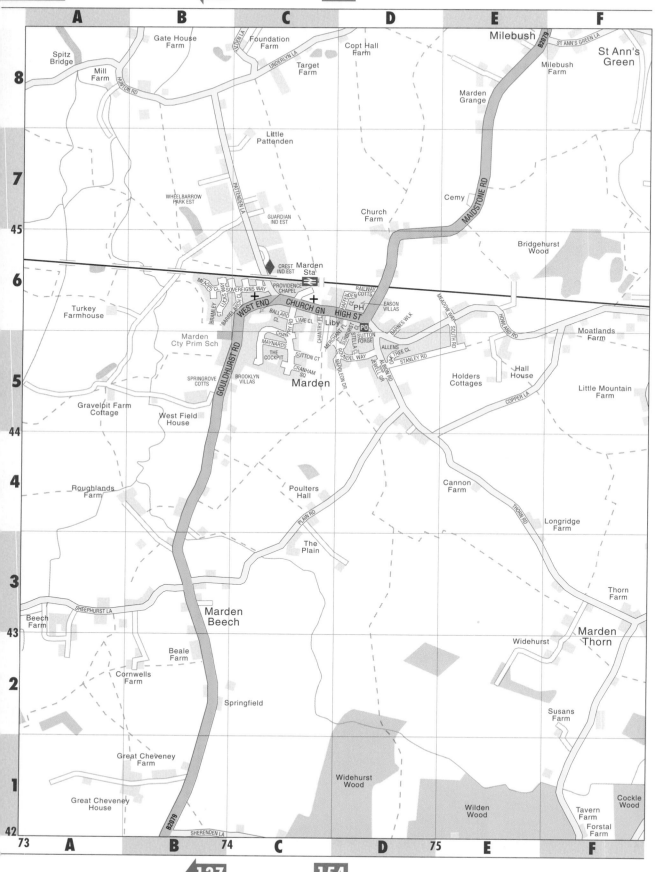

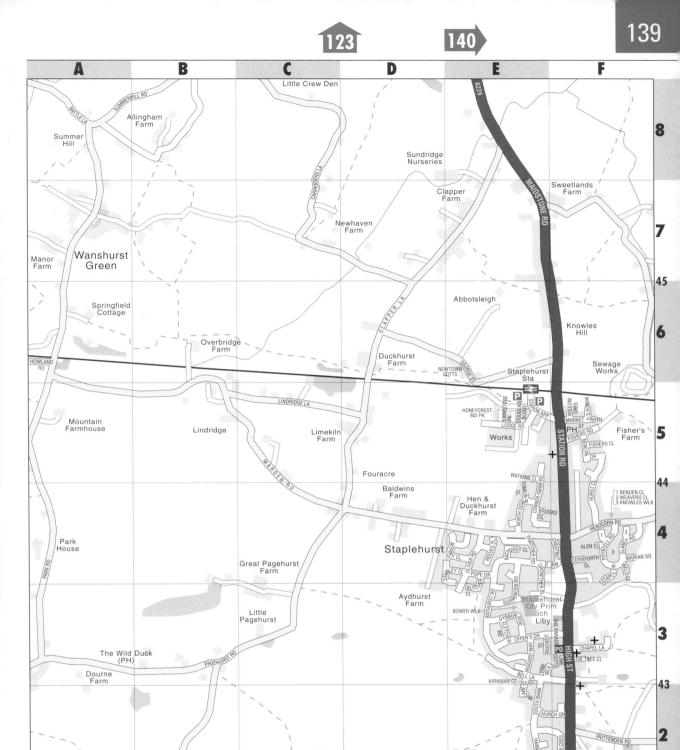

139
124

A   **B**   **C**   **D**   **E**   **F**

Forge Farm

NEW BARN RD

8

New Barn Farm

Four Oaks Wood

Bardingley

Hawkenbury

New Barn Wood

Four Oaks

Sweetlands Couchman Green

PLUMTREE RD

7

Newstead Farm

Hawkenbury Farm

Leighbridge Farm

FOUR OAKS RD

45

The Hare & Hounds (PH)

Boarden Farm

DRAY CORNER RD

Dray Corner Farm

6

Little Hawkenbury

HAWKENBURY RD

Hawkenbury Bridge

Turley Farm

Kelsham Farm

Sewage Farm

5

Slaney Place

River Beult

HEADCORN RD

44

Cottons Farm

Works

Spills Hill Farm

Place Farm

4

Crab Tree Farm

Sunny Mead

Chickenden Farm

Oak Tree Farm

CRADDOCKS LA

Spilsill Farm

3

Spilsill Court

Bailey Farm

Little Craddock

33

Exhurst Manor

2

FRITTENDEN RD

Folly Farm

Sinkhurst Green

Appleton Farm House

Nursery

PARK WOOD LA

Pullen Barn

Staplehurst Manor

1

Park Wood

Broadlake

STAPLEHURST RD

Sandhurst Bridge Farm

MILL LA

Maplehurst Farm

The Twins

Sandhurst Bridge

Great Hungerden Farm

SANDHURST CROSS

79   **A**   **B**   80   **C**   **D**   81   **E**   **F**

139
156

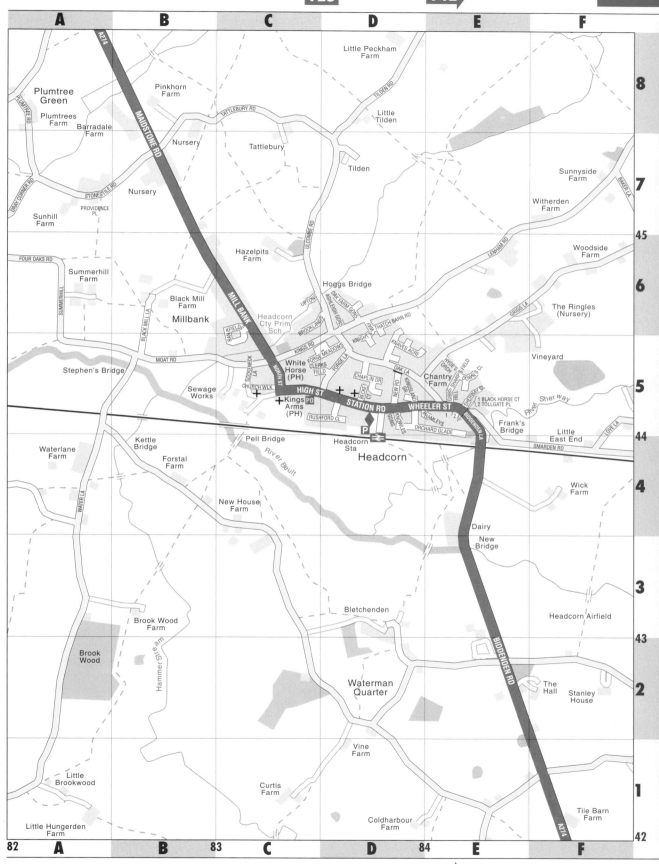

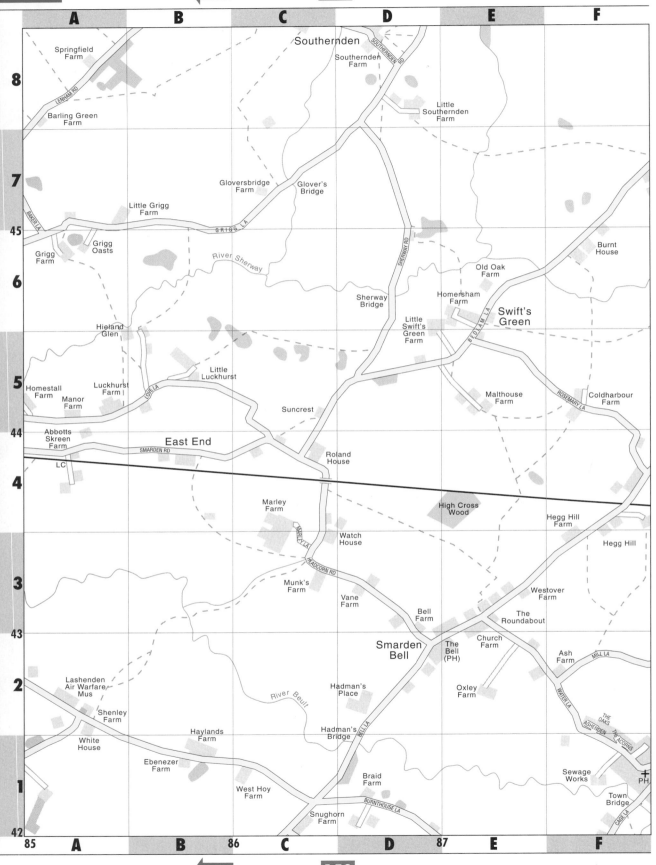

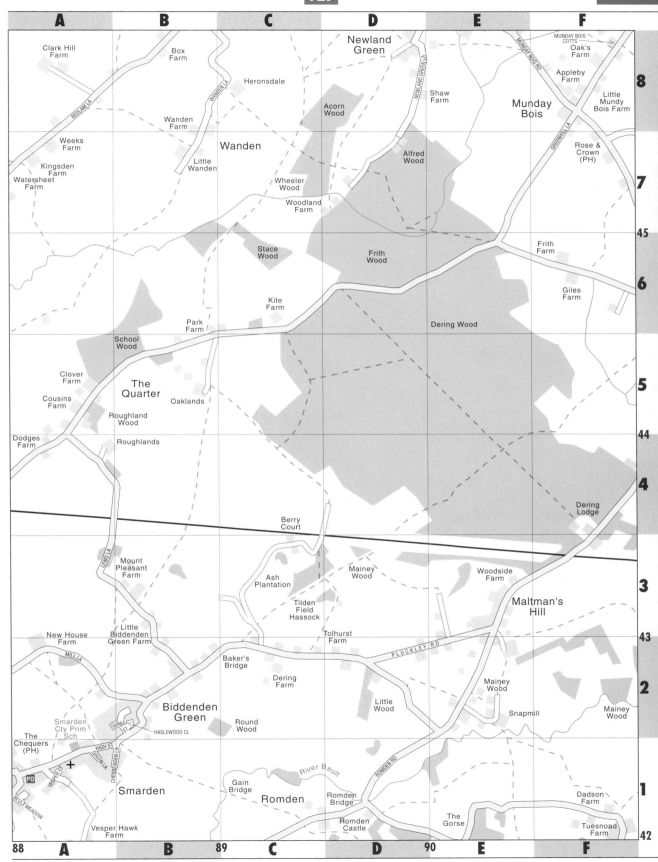

128

145
130

A   B   C   D   E   F

8

Birchcope
Shaw

Coldharbour   Westfield
House

COLDHARBOUR RD

Frienden
Gill   Cook's
Wood   Harts

Bassett's
Mill   Finch
Green

White
Post   Blacklands
Wood

7   BASSETTS LA   Frienden
Farm

Bassett's
Farm   Hartslands
Prinkham   Farm

SANDFIELD
RD

NUNNERY LA

WALTER'S GREEN RD

41

Top Hill
Wood

6   Walter's
Kent Water   Hobbs Hill   Green
Farm

Pilbeams   BRADLEY RD

CHAFFORD LA

Nore   Sussex Border Path
Farm

CH   Golf   Chafford
5   Course   Bridge   CHAFFORD
Tollhurst   COTTS
Farm

40

Salenhurst
Farm   Willett's
Stephnett's   Farm
Farm

4   Chafford
Blackham   River Medway   Park

WILLETTS LA
Carriers Pl   WILLETTS
COTTS   Cousins
Shaw

TEASLEY
MEAD

3   Ashurst
Pound   Wood   Stable
Farm   Teasley   Cottage
Mead

A264
39   +   ASHURST RD   A264
Highfields   ASHURST HILL   Manor Court
Park   Ashurst Bridge   Farm
MILLSTREAM   The
CL   Bald Faced Stag
2   Lodgefield   Ashurst   (PH)
Wood   Ashurst   Sta   Ashurst
Lodgefield
Farm   Jessup's
CLAYTON'S LA   Farm

Lords
Wood

1   Clay
Shaw
Old Woodland
Wood   Wealdway

Minepit
Wood

38
49   A   50   B   C   50   D   51   E   F

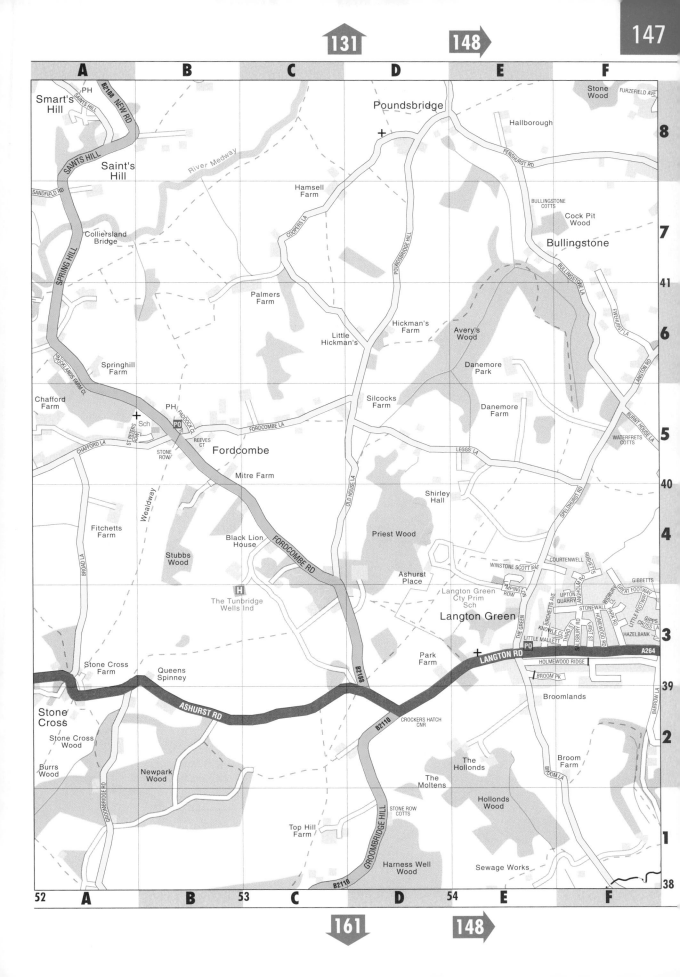

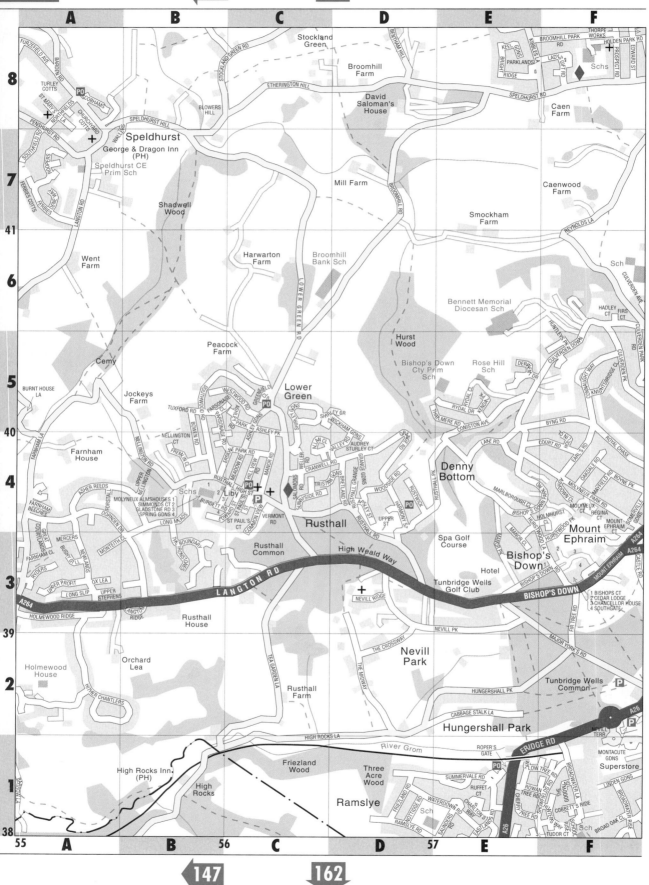

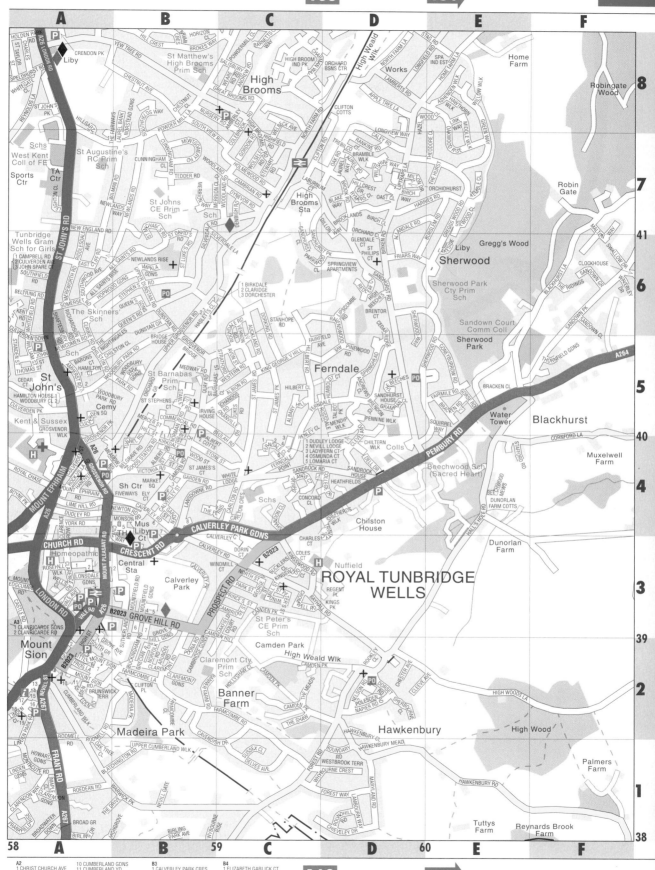

A2
1 CHRIST CHURCH AVE
2 CASTLE ST
3 WHITE BEAR PAS
4 WARWICK RD
5 BELGROVE
6 SPENCER MEWS
7 BERKELEY RD
8 CHAPEL PL
9 BEDFORD TERR
10 CUMBERLAND GDNS
11 CUMBERLAND YD
12 CUMBERLAND MEWS
13 MARKET ST
14 MARKET PL
15 COACH & HORSES PAS
16 SUSSEX MEWS
17 THE PANTILES
18 UNION SQ
19 REGENCY HALL

B3
1 CALVERLEY PARK CRES
2 MOUNT PLEASANT AVE
3 GREAT HALL ARC
4 MOUNTFIELD CT
5 THE MEWS
6 MEADOW HILL RD
7 GUILDFORD RD

B4
1 ELIZABETH GARLICK CT
2 CAMDEN CT
3 GROVER ST
4 SPENCER'S MEWS
5 MONSON WAY
6 CADOGAN GDNS
7 CATHERINE PL
8 LANSDOWNE SQ

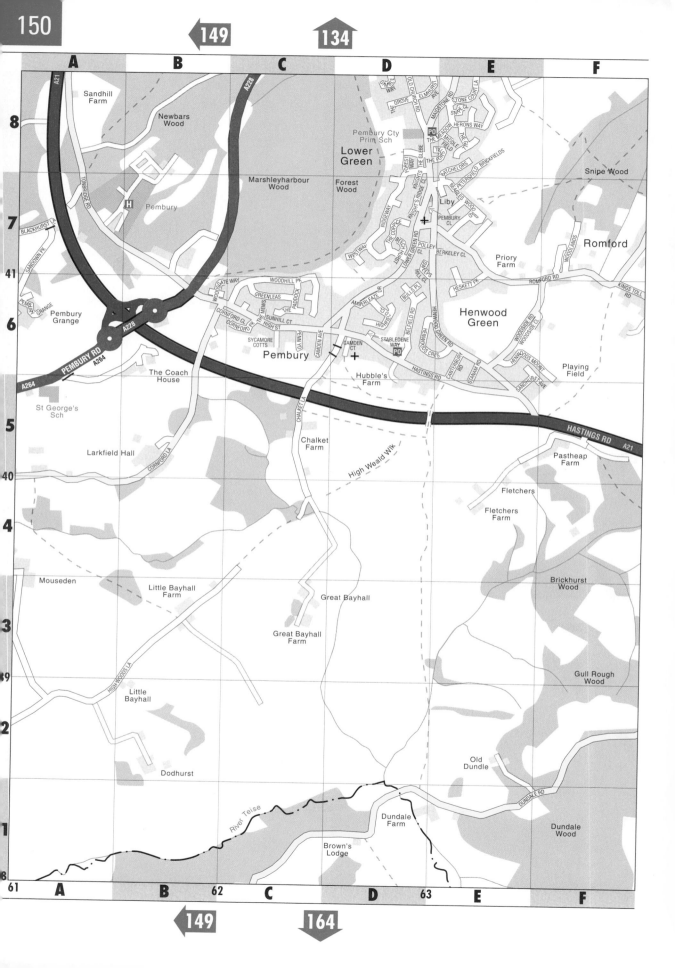

Matfield

Widmore Farm

Nature Reserve

The Wheelwrights Arms (PH)

Tutty's Farm

Three Towns Farm

Court Farm

Goshen Farm

Grove Cottage Farm

The Hopbine (PH)

Hayes View Farm

Friars Coach House

Lodge Farm

Porter's Wood

Petteridge

HUMPHREYS

Romford Manor

Wellgrove Farm

Matfield Grange

Egypt Farm

Kings Toll Farm

Becketts

CRYALS CT

Cryals Farm

Kingsmead

Becketts Grove Farm

SOPURST WOOD

Old Cryals

Kipping's Cross Farm

Kingsmead Farm

Kipping's Cross

Bassetts Farm

HASTINGS RD

B2160

Blue Boys Inn (PH)

COUNCIL COTTS

Beech Wood

Elmhurst Farm

Key's Green

Marlpit Wood

Hanger Wood

Old Farm

Beechers Lodge

Great Sandhurst Wood

Swan Farm

Brookland Wood

Little Dunks Farm

Little Sandhurst Wood

Three Horseshoe Farm

The Grange

Lamberhurst Quarter

Little Grange

Lindridge Place Farm

Lindridge Lodge Farm

A21

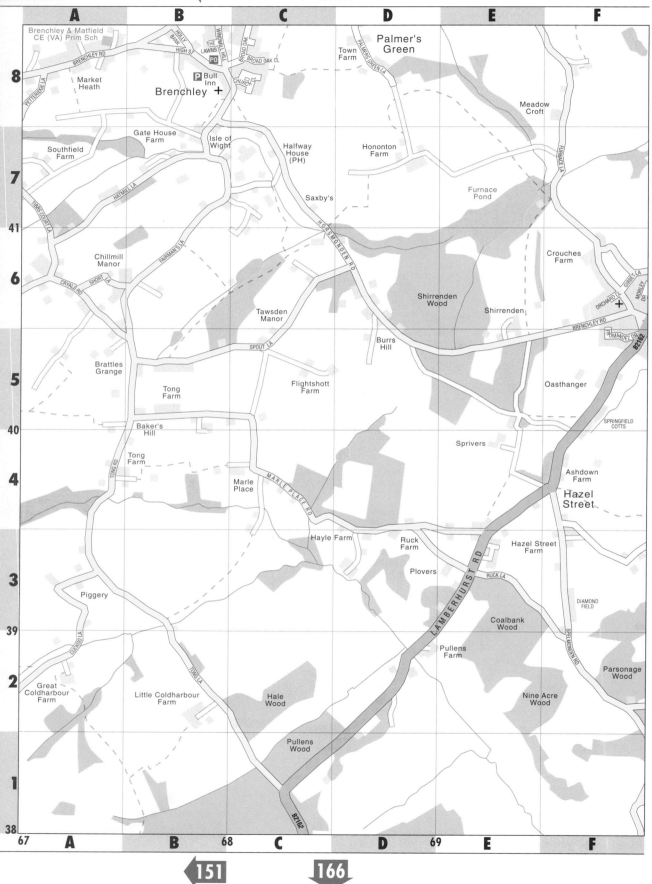

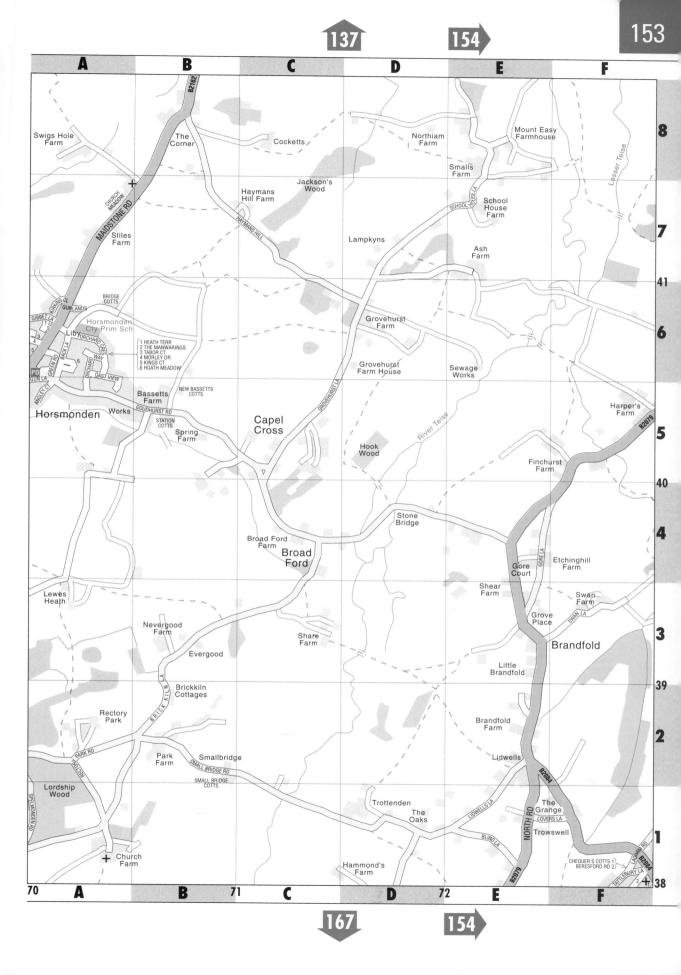

A B C D E F

8
7
41
6
5
40
4
3
39
2
1
38

Swigs Hole Farm
The Corner
B2162
Cocketts
Northiam Farm
Mount Easy Farmhouse
Lesser Teise
Smalls Farm
Jackson's Wood
Haymans Hill Farm
School House Farm
CHURCH MEADOW
MAIDSTONE RD
HAYMANS HILL
SCHOOL HOUSE LA
Stiles Farm
Lampkyns
Ash Farm
KIRKS CL
GIBBET LA
GUNLANDS
BRIDGE COTTS
Horsmonden Cty Prim Sch
Grovehurst Farm
Liby
1 HEATH TERR
2 THE MANWARINGS
3 TABOR CT
4 MORLEY DR
5 KINGS CT
6 HOATH MEADOW
GREEN RD
BACK LA
ORCHARD CRES
ORCHARD WAY
OAST VIEW
PO
GUN LA
ANGLEY CT
Bassetts Farm
NEW BASSETTS COTTS
Grovehurst Farm House
Sewage Works
Harper's Farm
B2079
Horsmonden
Works
GOUDHURST RD
STATION COTTS
Spring Farm
Capel Cross
GROVEHURST LA
Hook Wood
River Teise
Finchurst Farm
Lewes Heath
Broad Ford Farm
Stone Bridge
Gore Court
Etchinghill Farm
GORE LA
Swan Farm
Broad Ford
Shear Farm
Nevergood Farm
Share Farm
SWAN LA
Grove Place
Brandfold
Evergood
Little Brandfold
BRICK KILN LA
Brickkiln Cottages
Rectory Park
Brandfold Farm
PARK RD
RECTORY RD
Park Farm
Smallbridge
SMALL BRIDGE RD
Lidwells
B2084
SPELMONDEN RD
Lordship Wood
SMALL BRIDGE COTTS
Trottenden
The Oaks
LIDWELLS LA
The Grange
LOVERS LA
Trowswell
NORTH RD
LADHAM RD
B2084
Church Farm
BLIND LA
Hammond's Farm
B2079
CHEQUER'S COTTS 1
BERESFORD RD 2
TATTLEBURY LA

153
138

A   B   C   D   E   F

8

Nurseries

Love's
Farm

B2079

Tanner
House

Mount
Pleasant

7

ASH TREE
COTTS

Love's
Wood

Mab's
Wood

Huggins
Farm

SHERENDEN LA

Sherenden
Wood

Hobbs
Wood

FIVE OAK LA

SNOAD LA

Plain
Farm

Little
Harts Heath

Harts Heath
Farm

41

Dodges
Farm

Winchet
Hill

Pookhill
Wood

Hush Heath
Manor

Husheath
Farm

HUSHEATH HILL

6

SUMMERFIELD

Mallions
Farm

PO

+

5

B2079

Ladysden
Farm

Bethany
Sch

Curtisden
Green

Great Horden
Farm

Sewage
Works

HILL TOP

Little Horden
Farm

Blantyre House
(HM Prison)

40

Worms
Hill

4

Combourne
Farm

Little
Combourne
Cottages

Broadoak
Wood

ROUND GREEN
COTTS

Round
Green

3

Bockingfold
Farm

Bakers
Farm

Bakers
Corner

Spring
Wood

Footway
Cottages

Woodfield

JARVIS LA

39

LADHAM RD

Blue Barn
Farm

Colliers'
Green

Colliers' Green
CE Prim
Sch

2

Ladham
House

Fruit
Packing
Station

Knight's
Hole

Colliers'
Green
Farm

1

Ladham Farm
Cottages

Cherry
Gardens
Farm

MILE LA

Old Park
Wood

Lynx
Park

MEREBREDIS

Sewage
Works

B2084

38

73   A   B   74   C   D   75   E   F

153
168

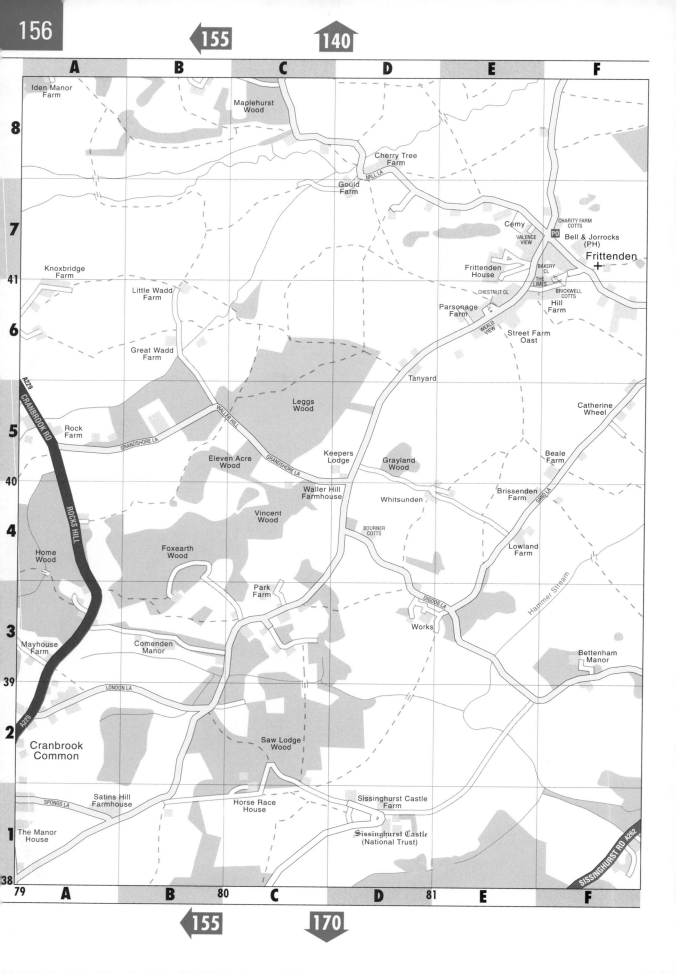

155
140

A B C D E F

8

7

41

6

5

40

4

3

39

2

1

38

Iden Manor
Farm

Maplehurst
Wood

Cherry Tree
Farm

MILL LA

Gould
Farm

Cemy

CHARITY FARM
COTTS

VALENCE
VIEW

P O

Bell & Jorrocks
(PH)

Frittenden

Knoxbridge
Farm

Frittenden
House

BAKERY
CL

THE
LIMES

CHESTNUT CL

BRICKWELL
COTTS

Little Wadd
Farm

Parsonage
Farm

WEALD
VIEW

Hill
Farm

Street Farm
Oast

Great Wadd
Farm

Tanyard

Catherine
Wheel

A229

CRANBROOK RD

WALLER HILL

Leggs
Wood

Rock
Farm

GRANDSHORE LA

GRANDSHORE LA

Keepers
Lodge

Grayland
Wood

Beale
Farm

Eleven Acre
Wood

Waller Hill
Farmhouse

Whitsunden

Brissenden
Farm

SAND LA

ROCKS HILL

Vincent
Wood

BOURNER
COTTS

Lowland
Farm

Home
Wood

Foxearth
Wood

Park
Farm

DIGDOG LA

Works

Hammer Stream

Mayhouse
Farm

Comenden
Manor

Bettenham
Manor

LONDON LA

A229

Cranbrook
Common

Saw Lodge
Wood

SPONGS LA

Satins Hill
Farmhouse

Horse Race
House

Sissinghurst Castle
Farm

The Manor
House

Sissinghurst Castle
(National Trust)

SISSINGHURST RD A262

79 A 80 B C 81 D E F

155
170

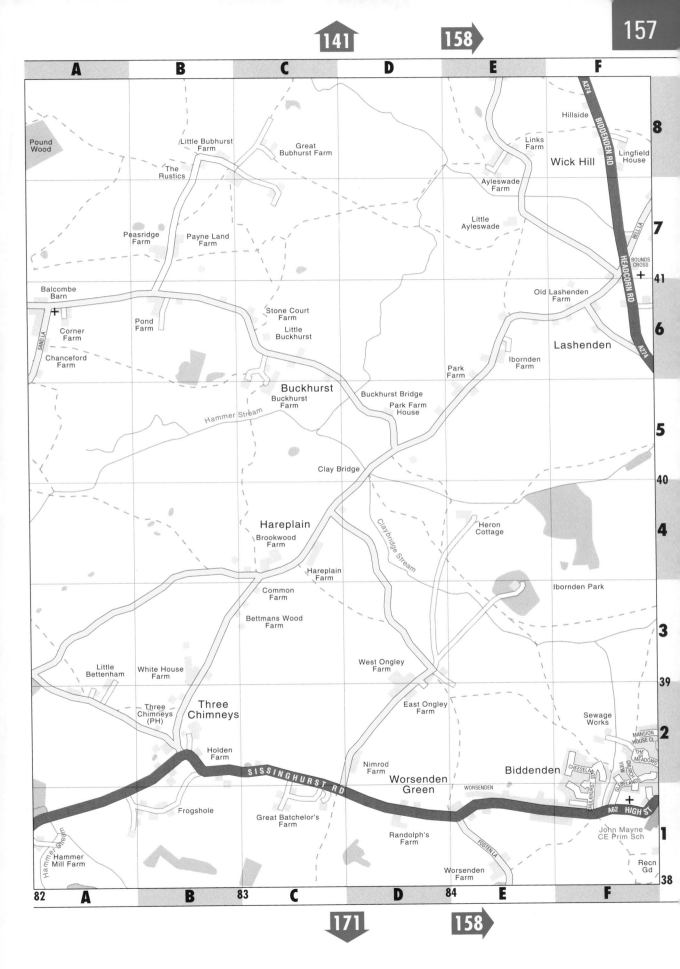

157
142

8

Hill View
Oak Acre
BELL LA
Stanlash

Barnden Farm
Obeden Farm
Snughorne House

SNUGHORNE LA

BURNTHOUSE LA
BIDDENDEN RD
Grigsby Farm
Walford House
CAGE LA
BETHERSDEN RD

Thorn Farm
Bardleden Farm

THE CUT

7

Limes Farmhouse
Lime Kiln Farm
Tilden Farm
Gilham Land Farm

Monk's Hill
SMARDEN BSNS EST

Tylden

41

Lashenden Farm
Priory Farm
Monks Hill Farm
Roberts Farm
Gilham Farm

6

Standen Wood
SMARDEN RD
Kelsham

Chart Hills Golf Course
Vane Court Farm

A274

Cackle Hill
Vane Court
Deadman's Wood
Great Omenden Farm
Great Omenden Cottages

5

WEEKS LA
Standen
Ponds Farm

HEADCORN RD

40

Standen

Newcastle Farm
Forstal Farm
Little Omenden Farm

4

Apsley
Gorse Farm
POOK LA
Omenden Barn
Wagstaff

3

Curteis' Corner
COT LA

NORTH ST

39

Elmstone
River Hall

2

MANSION HOUSE CL
SHUTTLE CL
SAWYERS SQ
CLOTH HALL
GDNS
TEASELS
A274
THE WEAVERS
PO
HIGH ST
A262
P

HIGH HALDEN RD
Guy House
Sweet Meadow Farm

1

John Mayne CE Prim Sch
TENTERDEN RD
A262
Whitfield Farm
Stede Quarter
HIGH HALDEN RD

Washenden Manor
Podkin Farm

85   **A**   **B**   **86**   **C**   **D**   **87**   **E**   **F**

157
172

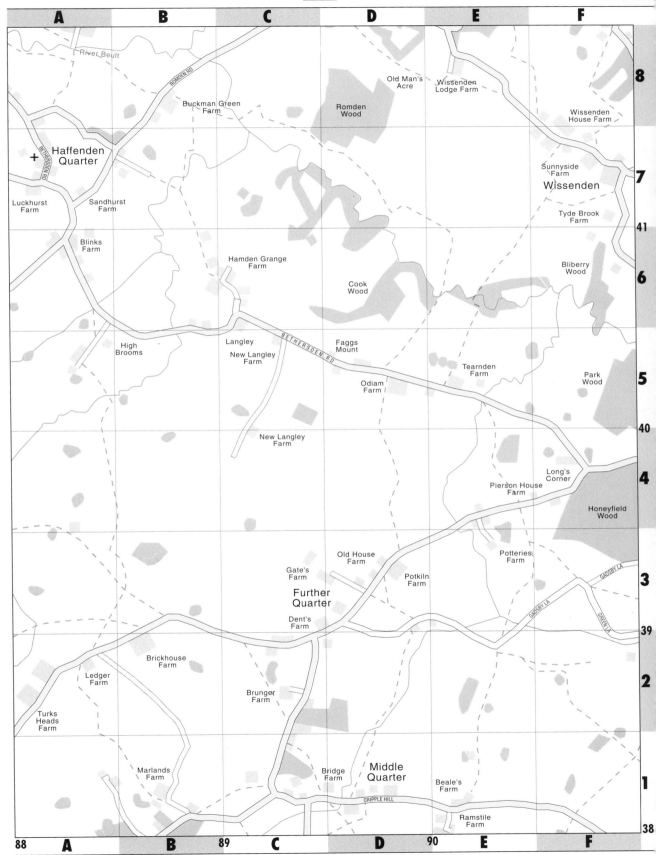

A B C D E F

8

Old Man's Acre
Wissenden Lodge Farm
Romden Wood
Wissenden House Farm

Buckman Green Farm
ROMDEN RD
River Beult

Haffenden Quarter

7

Sunnyside Farm
Wissenden
41

Luckhurst Farm
Sandhurst Farm
BETHERSDEN RD

Tyde Brook Farm

Blinks Farm

6

Hamden Grange Farm
Cook Wood
Bliberry Wood

High Brooms
Langley
New Langley Farm
BETHERSDEN RD
Faggs Mount
Tearnden Farm
Park Wood

5

Odiam Farm
40

New Langley Farm

4

Long's Corner
Pierson House Farm
Honeyfield Wood

Old House Farm
Potteries Farm

Gate's Farm
Potkiln Farm

3

Further Quarter
Dent's Farm
GADSBY LA
GREEN LA

Brickhouse Farm

39

Ledger Farm
Brunger Farm

2

Turks Heads Farm

Marlands Farm
Bridge Farm
Middle Quarter
Beale's Farm

1

CRIPPLE HILL
Ramstile Farm

38

88 A B 89 C D 90 E F

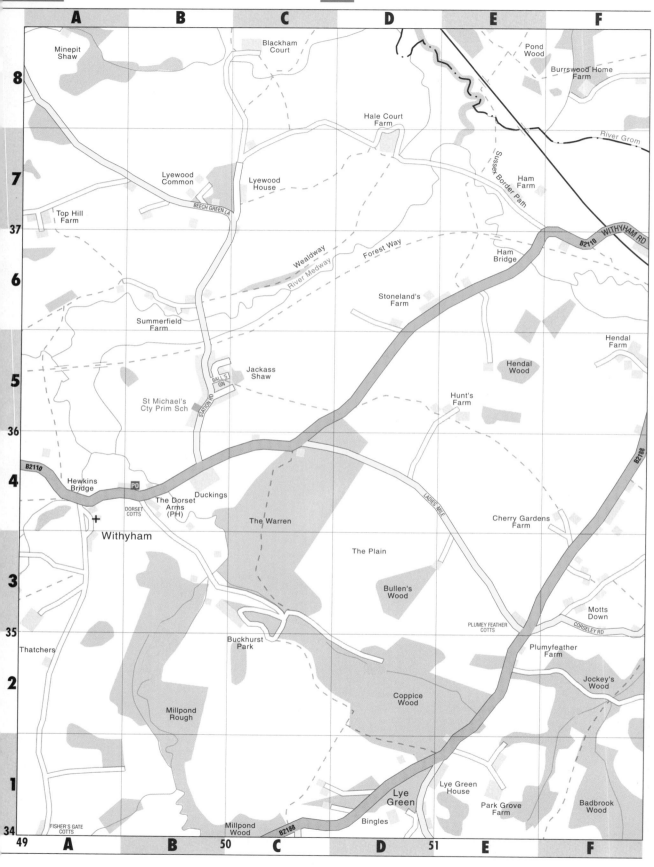

A   B   C   D   E   F

8   Minepit
    Shaw

    Blackham
    Court

    Pond
    Wood

    Burrswood Home
    Farm

    River Grom

    Hale Court
    Farm

7   Lyewood
    Common

    Lyewood
    House

    Sussex Border Path

    Ham
    Farm

    Top Hill
    Farm

    BEECH GREEN LA

37

    B2110   WITHYHAM RD

6   Wealdway

    River Medway   Forest Way

    Ham
    Bridge

    Stoneland's
    Farm

    Summerfield
    Farm

    Hendal
    Farm

5   Jackass
               Shaw

    BALL'S
    GN

    Hendal
    Wood

    St Michael's
    Cty Prim Sch

    STATION RD

    Hunt's
    Farm

36

4   B2110

    Hewkins
    Bridge   Duckings

    PO

    DORSET
    COTTS

    The Dorset
    Arms
    (PH)

    The Warren

    LADIES MILE

    Cherry Gardens
    Farm

    B2188

    +

    Withyham

    The Plain

3   Bullen's
                     Wood

    Motts
    Down

    PLUMEY FEATHER
    COTTS

    CORSELEY RD

35

    Buckhurst
    Park

    Plumyfeather
    Farm

2   Thatchers

    Millpond
    Rough

    Coppice
    Wood

    Jockey's
    Wood

1   Lye Green
                          House

    Lye
    Green

    Park Grove
    Farm

    Badbrook
    Wood

    Bingles

34 FISHER'S GATE
    COTTS

    Millpond
    Wood

    B2188

49   A   B   50   C   D   51   E   F

147

162

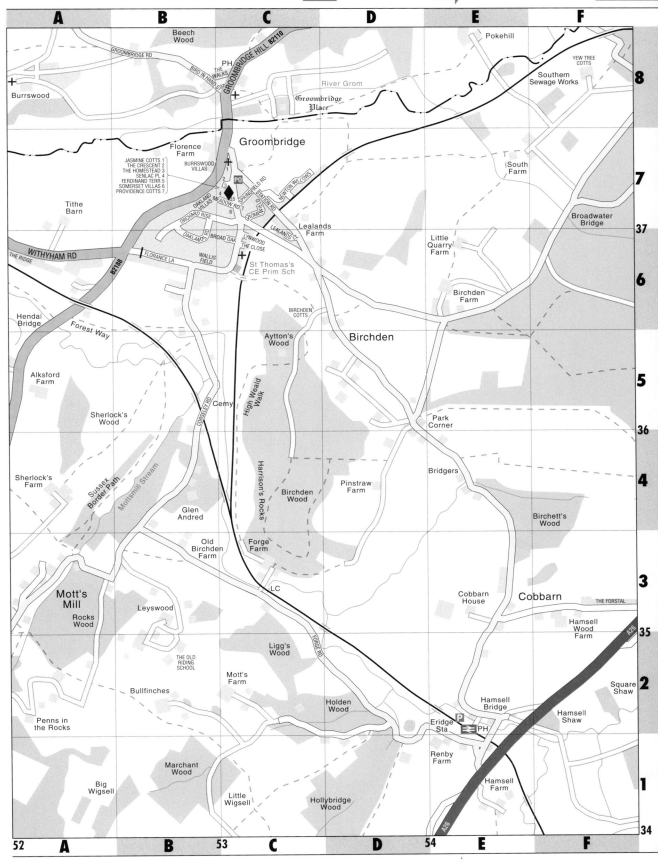

A   B   C   D   E   F

Beech Wood

GROOMBRIDGE RD

GROOMBRIDGE HILL B2110

Pokehill

YEW TREE COTTS

8

Burrswood

River Grom

Southern Sewage Works

PH
THE WALKS
BIRD IN HAND ST

Groombridge Place

Florence Farm

Groombridge

South Farm

7

Jasmine Cotts 1
The Crescent 2
The Homestead 3
Senlac Pl 4
Ferdinand Terr 5
Somerset Villas 6
Providence Cotts 7

BURRSWOOD VILLAS
1
2
3
4
5
6
7

PO

NEWTON WILLOWS

SPRINGFIELD RD
STATION RD
GROMEW

Tithe Barn

OAKLAND VILLAS
MEADOW RD

Lealands C'
Lealands Farm

Little Quarry Farm

Broadwater Bridge

37

ORCHARD RISE
OAKLANDS RD   BROAD OAK
LYNWOOD
THE CLOSE

Birchden Farm

6

WITHYHAM RD
THE RIDGE
B2188

FLORANCE LA
WALLIS FIELD

St Thomas's CE Prim Sch

Hendal Bridge

Forest Way

BIRCHDEN COTTS

Birchden

Aytton's Wood

5

Alksford Farm

Sherlock's Wood

CORSELEY RD
Cemy

High Weald Walk

Park Corner

36

Sherlock's Farm

Sussex Border Path
Mottsmill Stream

Glen Andred

Harrison's Rocks

Birchden Wood

Pinstraw Farm

Bridgers

Birchett's Wood

4

Old Birchden Farm

Forge Farm

3

Mott's Mill

Leyswood

LC

Cobbarn House

Cobbarn

THE FORSTAL

A26

Rocks Wood

THE OLD RIDING SCHOOL

Ligg's Wood

FORGE RD

Hamsell Wood Farm

35

Bullfinches

Mott's Farm

Holden Wood

Hamsell Bridge

Square Shaw

2

Penns in the Rocks

P
Eridge Sta
PH

Hamsell Shaw

Renby Farm

Marchant Wood

Little Wigsell

Hollybridge Wood

Hamsell Farm

1

Big Wigsell

A26

34

52   A   B   53   C   D   54   E   F

A   B   C   D   E   F

8   Coker's Down   Sunninglye Farmhouse

Rushlye Down

Coneyburrow Wood   Furnace Wood

7   Oxpasture Wood   River Teise   Tollslye   The Bothy

37

6   Rushlye Farmhouse   Hollow Wood   Jews Wood   Great Coppice Wood   Bayham Lake

Abbots Down

Highfield   Diamonds

5   MIDDLE RD   Forest Lodge   Upper Sluice Wood   LITTLE BAYHAM COTTS

B2169

36   Burnt Wood   B2169

Little Bayham

4   Higham Wood   Higham Farm   Bartley Mill Wood

Verridge Wood   Bartley Mill   Wickhurst Farmhouse

Churchfield Wood   Bartley House

3   Little Shoesmiths

35   Sewers Bridge   Brookland Wood

Grigg's Wood   Shoesmith's Wood   Brick Kiln Wood

2   Camden Wood   Great Shoesmith Farm

Henley Wood   Sussex Border Path   Hewley Wood

1   Down Wood   WHITEGATES LA   Sewage Works

61   A   B   62   C   D   63   E   F

A21

A   B   C   D   E   F

8

Sandhurst

Clay Hill
Cottages

Maynards
Farm

Tongs Wood

Rear Wood

Clayhill Wood

Uzzards

7

Stubb's Wood

Snagg's
Well

Ellis
Wood

Owl
House

Cooksbroom
Wood

Garden House

Owlet
Farm

37

CLAY HILL RD

Mount
Pleasant

Bayham
Abbey

MOUNT PLEASANT

6

MOUNT PLEASANT LA

River Teise

Hoathly
Farm

Timberlog
Wood

Bayham Abbey
(rems of)

Furnace
Mill

5

Stumlets
Wood

Floshet
Wood

BULL LANE
COTTS

36

Sluice
Wood

Win
Bridge

Elephant's Head
(PH)

Furnace
Farm

4

B2169

Apps's
Wood

Hook
Green

Hook Green
Farm

STONE
COTTS

FURNACE LA

Copthall
Farm

Skent's
Wood

3

Rowland
Wood

FREE HEATH RD

35

Buss's
Green

Owl's Castle
Farm

Toll
Wood

Stiver's
Wood

Yew Tree Green
Farm

NEILLS RD

Maitlands

HOGHOLE LA

2

B2100

Crowhurst
House

Broadwell
Wood

SWEETINGS LA

Buckland
Hill

Free
Heath

Buckland Hill
Farm

Markwicks

SLEEPERS STILE RD

Monk's
Park

Hunter's Hall
Farm

B2100

34

64   A   B   65   C   D   66   E   F

165 152

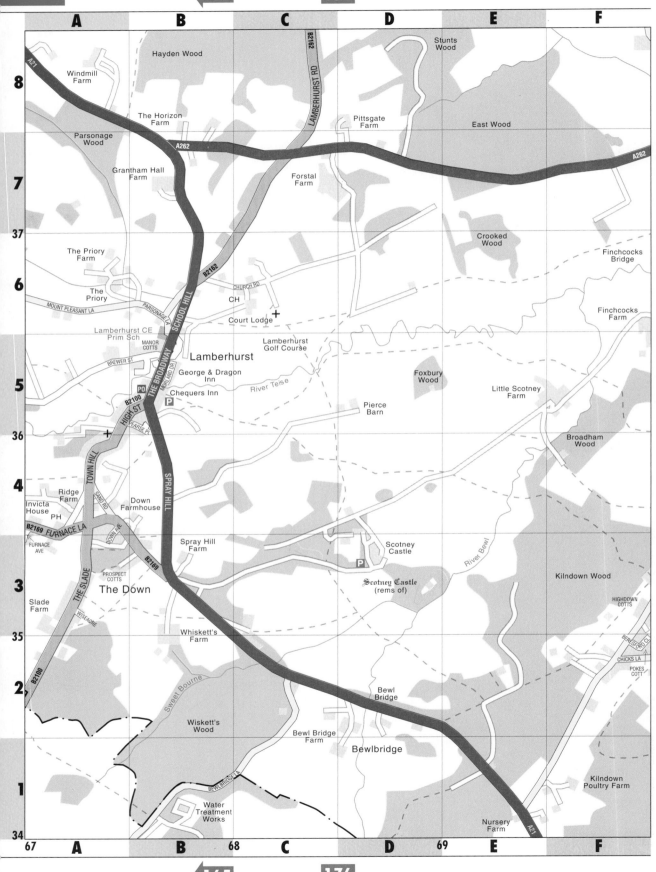

165 176

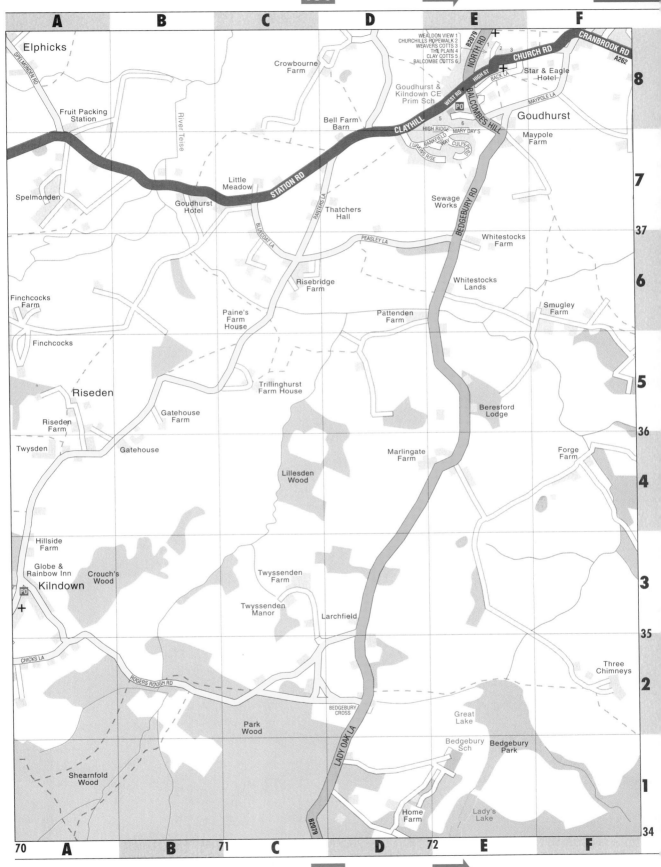

Elphicks

Crowbourne
Farm

WEALDON VIEW 1
CHURCHILLS ROPEWALK 2
WEAVERS COTTS 3
THE PLAIN 4
CLAY COTTS 5
BALCOMBE COTTS 6

Fruit Packing
Station

Goudhurst &
Kilndown CE
Prim Sch

Star & Eagle
Hotel

River Teise

CLAYHILL

Goudhurst

8

Bell Farm
Barn

HIGH RIDGE

Maypole
Farm

Spelmonden

MARY DAY'S

Goudhurst
Hotel

Little
Meadow

STATION RD

Thatchers
Hall

Sewage
Works

7

BLUEGOAT LA

RANTERS LA

PEASLEY LA

BEDGEBURY RD

Whitestocks
Farm

37

Risebridge
Farm

Whitestocks
Lands

6

Finchcocks
Farm

Paine's
Farm House

Pattenden
Farm

Smugley
Farm

Finchcocks

Trillinghurst
Farm House

5

Riseden

Gatehouse
Farm

Beresford
Lodge

Riseden
Farm

36

Twysden

Gatehouse

Marlingate
Farm

Forge
Farm

Lillesden
Wood

4

Hillside
Farm

Globe &
Rainbow Inn

Twyssenden
Farm

Kilndown

Crouch's
Wood

3

Twyssenden
Manor

Larchfield

35

CHICKS LA

Three
Chimneys

ROGERS ROUGH RD

BEDGEBURY
CROSS

2

Park
Wood

LADY OAK LA

Great
Lake

Bedgebury
Sch

Bedgebury
Park

Shearnfold
Wood

1

B2079

Home
Farm

Lady's
Lake

34

70   A   B   71   C   D   72   E   F

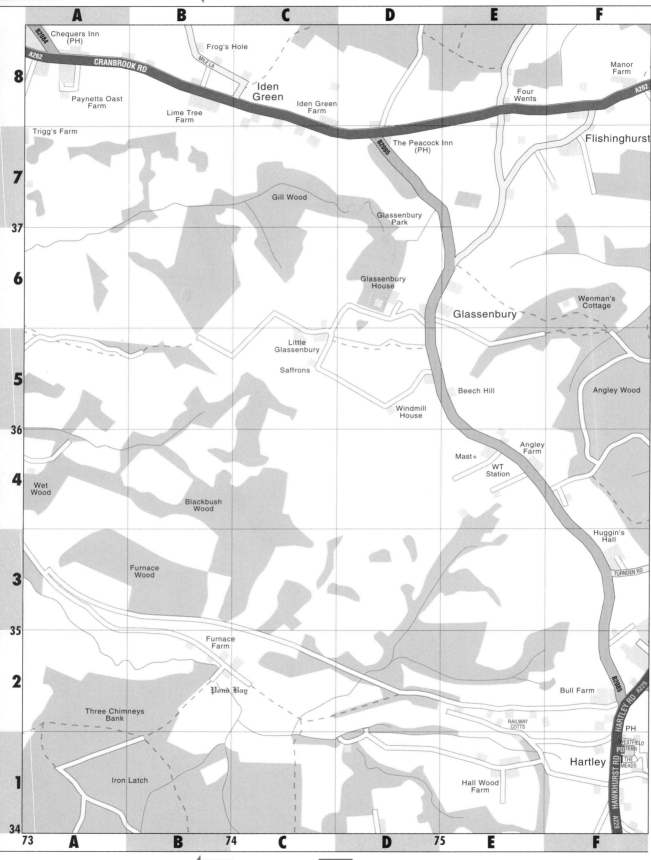

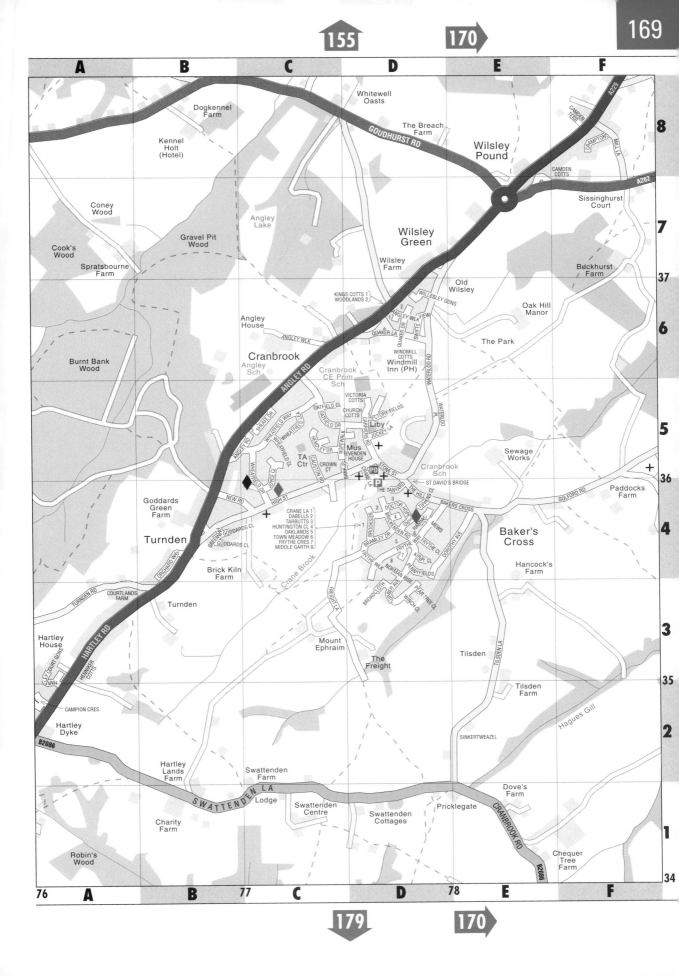

169
156

A B C D E F

8

Skinner Clvs
Cleavers Cl
COMMON RD
Sewage
Works
MILK HOUSE COTTS
BROAD VIEW
PH
REEDS COTTS
HOP POCKET CL
Roundshill
Park Wood
A262
THE NIGHTINGALES
Hammer Stream

Sissinghurst
Cty Prim Sch
SISSINGHURST RD
Copden
Wood

A262
THE STREET
PO
Plummer's
Barn
Roundshill

Sissinghurst
CHAPEL LA

7
Branden
Crane Brook
Milestone
Wood

37
Lake
Chad
High Tilt
Farm
CRANBROOK RD

6
Golford
Lodge
Sabah House
Farm
High
Tilt

Golford
Stream
Farm
Middleton
Farm
Chittenden
Wood

5
GOLFORD RD
Tollgate
Farm

36
Cemy
Coursehorn

4
Coursehorne
Farm
Golf
Course
Old Cloth
Hall
CH
Hemsted
Forest
Dockenden

3
Farningham
Oast
Farningham
Wood

35
Little
Coursehorne
Church
Wood

2
Chittenden
Farm
ADMIRALS WLK
Tottenden
Wood
Eaton
Farm
Goddard's
Green
GODDARD'S GREEN
COTTS

1
Crabtree
Farm
Park
Wood
BEACH
CT
WALKHURST RD

34
Sewage
Works
NEW POND RD
MEADOWS

79 A B 80 C D 81 E F

171
158

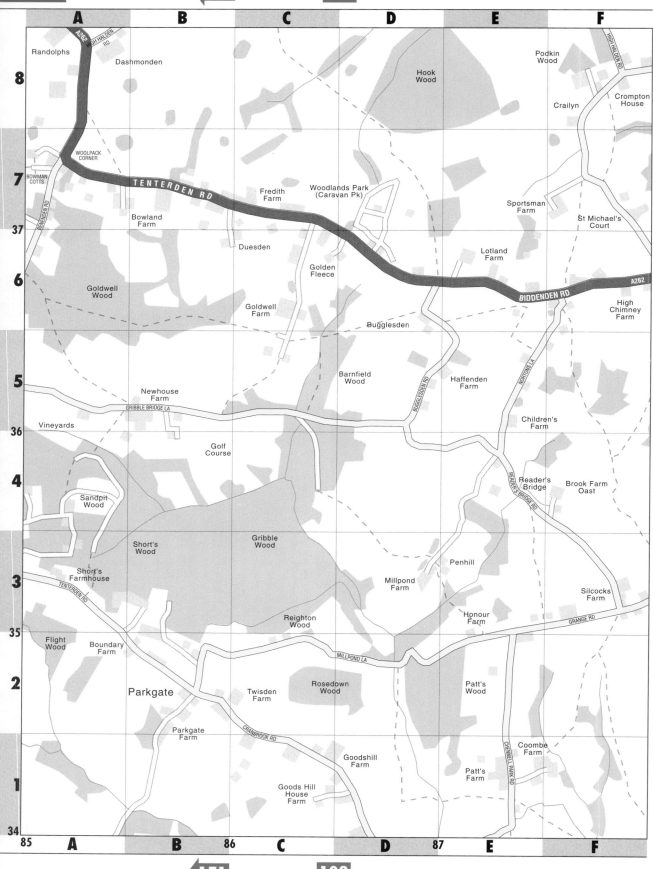

171
182

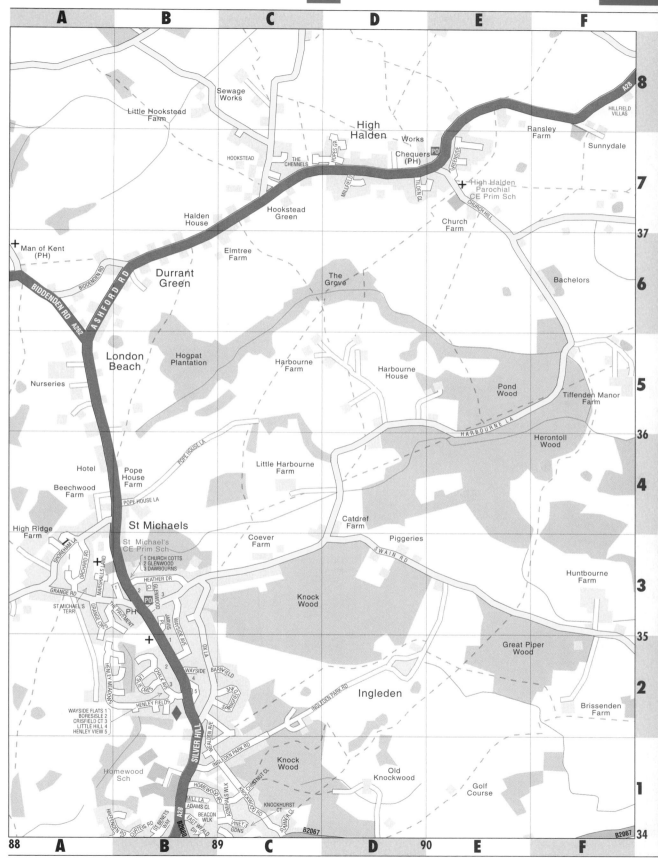

164

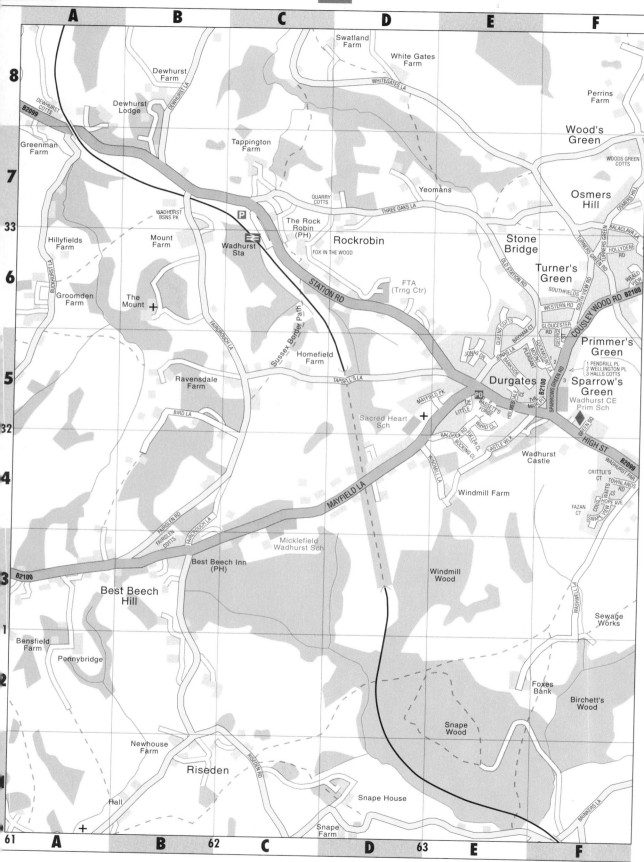

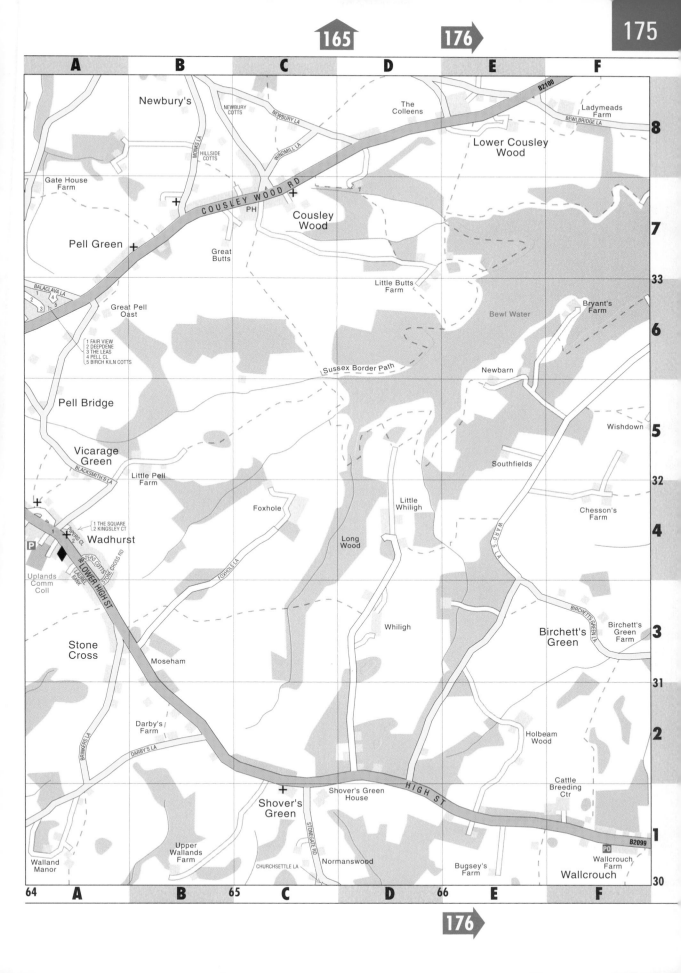

A B C D E F

Newbury's
NEWBURY COTTS
NEWBURY LA
The Colleens
B2100
Ladymeads Farm
BEWLBRIDGE LA
8
MONKS LA
HILLSIDE COTTS
WINDMILL LA
Lower Cousley Wood
Gate House Farm
COUSLEY WOOD RD
PH
Cousley Wood
7
Pell Green
Great Butts
Little Butts Farm
33
Bryant's Farm
BALACLAVA LA
1
4
5
2
3
Great Pell Oast
Bewl Water
6
1 FAIR VIEW
2 DEEPDENE
3 THE LEAS
4 PELL CL
5 BIRCH KILN COTTS
Sussex Border Path
Newbarn
Pell Bridge
Wishdown
5
Vicarage Green
BLACKSMITH'S LA
Little Pell Farm
Southfields
32
Foxhole
Little Whiligh
Chesson's Farm
1 THE SQUARE
2 KINGSLEY CT
Long Wood
WARD'S LA
4
P
Wadhurst
COOPERS CL
WATERS COTTS
STONE CROSS RD
FOXHOLE LA
LOWER HIGH ST
LAUREL BANK
Uplands Comm Coll
Whiligh
Birchett's Green
BIRCHETT'S GREEN LA
Birchett's Green Farm
3
Stone Cross
Moseham
31
Darby's Farm
Holbeam Wood
2
DARBY'S LA
BRINKERS LA
Shover's Green House
HIGH ST
Cattle Breeding Ctr
Shover's Green
STONEGATE RD
Normanswood
Bugsey's Farm
PO
B2099
Wallcrouch Farm
1
Walland Manor
Upper Wallands Farm
CHURCHSETTLE LA
Wallcrouch
30

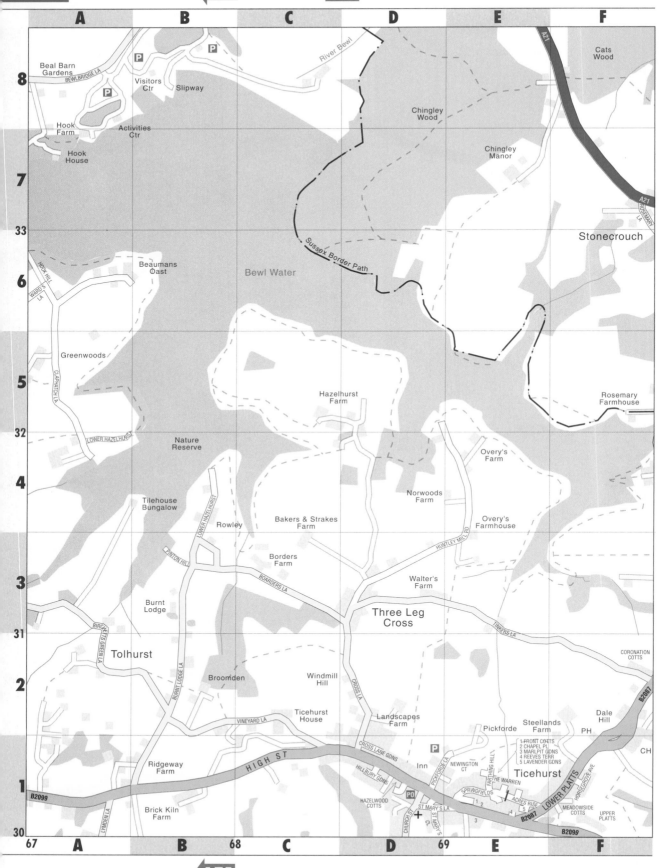

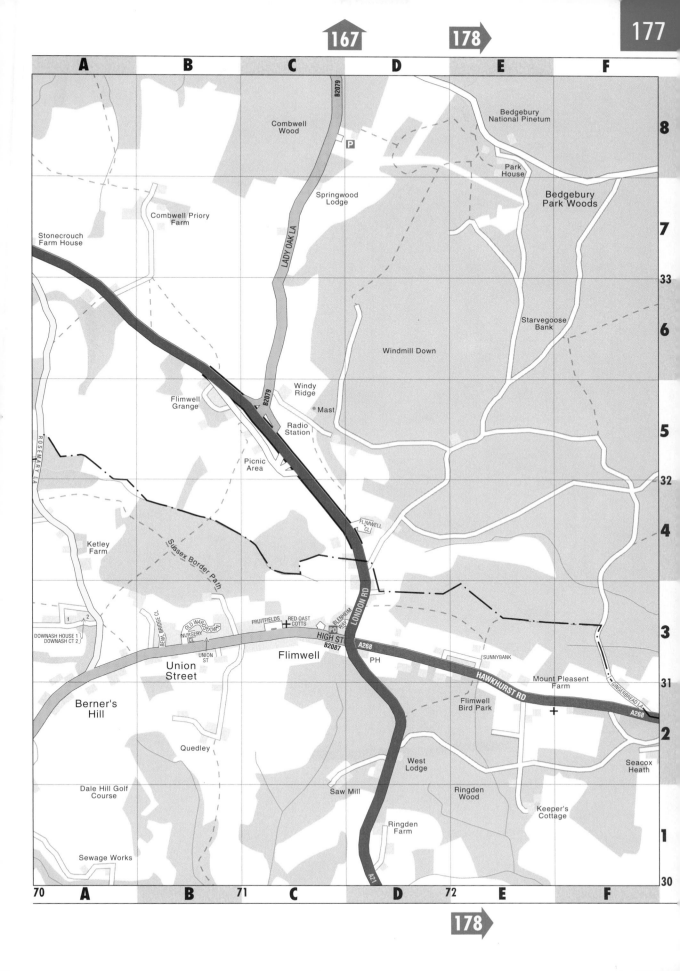

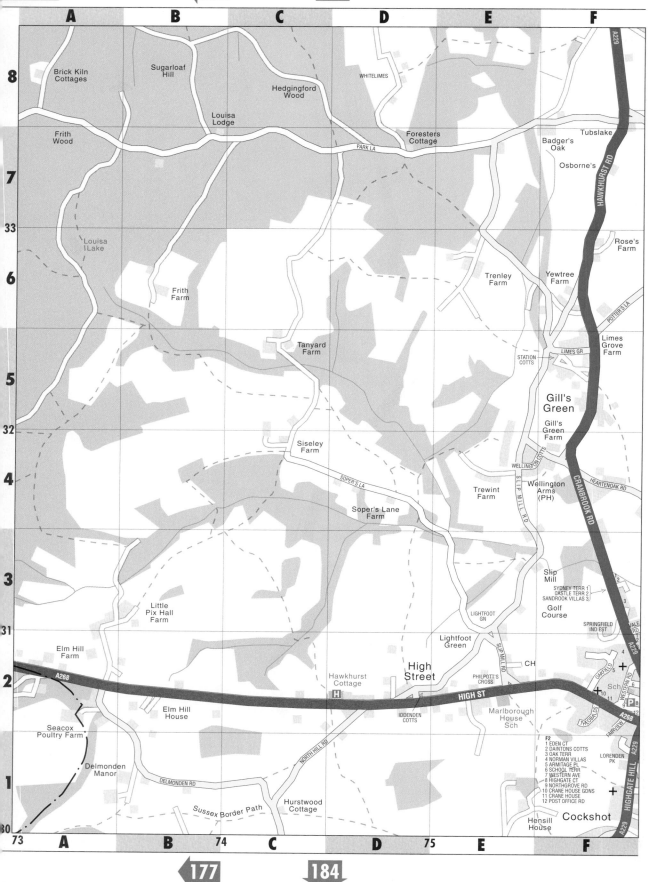

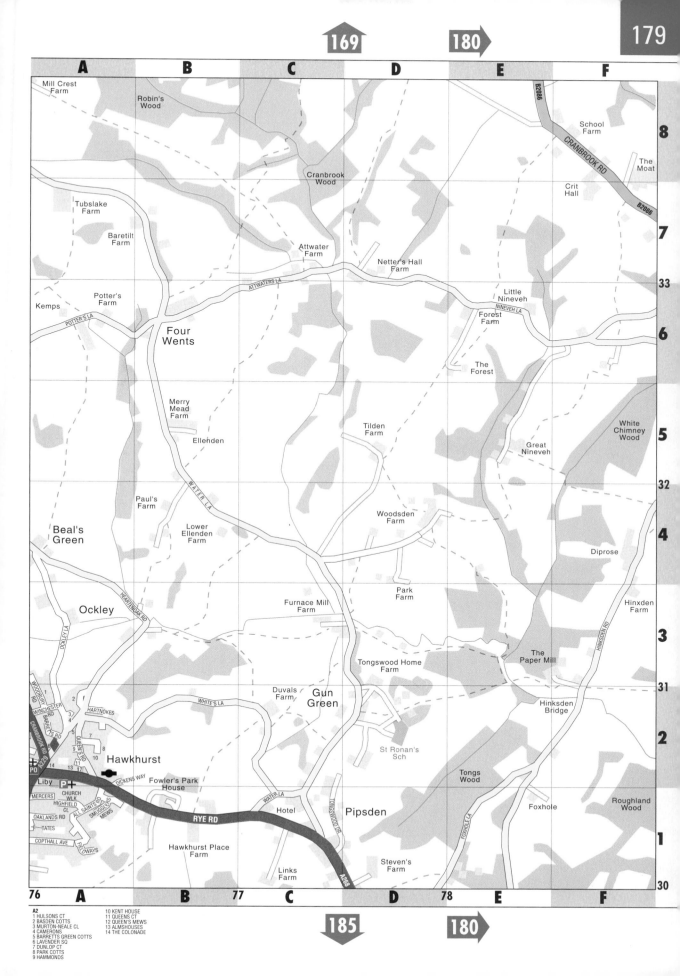

Mill Crest Farm

Robin's Wood

Cranbrook Wood

School Farm

B2086

CRANBROOK RD

Crit Hall

The Moat

B2086

Tubslake Farm

Baretilt Farm

Attwater Farm

Netter's Hall Farm

ATTWATERS LA

Little Nineveh

NINEVEH LA

Kemps

Potter's Farm

POTTER'S LA

Four Wents

Forest Farm

The Forest

Merry Mead Farm

Ellenden

Tilden Farm

Great Nineveh

White Chimney Wood

Beal's Green

Paul's Farm

WATER LA

Lower Ellenden Farm

Woodsden Farm

Diprose

Park Farm

Hinxden Farm

Ockley

HEARTENOAK RD

OCKLEY LA

Furnace Mill Farm

The Paper Mill

HINKSDEN RD

Tongswood Home Farm

WHITE'S LA

Duvals Farm

Gun Green

Hinksden Bridge

WOODBURY RD

WINCHESTER RD

BARRETTS RD

HARTNOKES

QUEEN'S RD

Hawkhurst

CRANBROOK RD

PO

Liby

P

CHURCH WLK

MERCERS

HIGHFIELD CL

ALL SAINTS'S

SMUGGLERS MEWS

DICKENS WAY

Fowler's Park House

St Ronan's Sch

Tongs Wood

OAKLANDS RD

TATES

COPTHALL AVE

FIELDWAYS

RYE RD

Hotel

WATER LA

TONGSWOOD DR

Pipsden

FOXHOLE LA

Foxhole

Roughland Wood

Hawkhurst Place Farm

Links Farm

A268

Steven's Farm

Tongs Wood

76 A   B   77 C   D   78 E   F

A2
1 HULSONS CT
2 BASDEN COTTS
3 MURTON-NEALE CL
4 CAMERONS
5 BARRETTS GREEN COTTS
6 LAVENDER SQ
7 DUNLOP CT
8 PARK COTTS
9 HAMMONDS
10 KENT HOUSE
11 QUEENS CT
12 QUEEN'S MEWS
13 ALMSHOUSES
14 THE COLONADE

8
33
7
6
5
32
4
3
31
2
1
30

179
170

A   **B**   **C**   **D**   **E**   **F**

8

New House

Coggers

Benenden Sch

Walkhurst Farm

Apple Pie Farm

Mount's Farm House

New Pond

Sewage Works

7

CRANBROOK RD

MOUNTS HILL

WALKHURST RD

WALKHURST COTTS

B2086

1 CHERRYFIELDS
2 BARRACK ROW

33

NINEVEH LA

BABBS LA

PO

THE STREET

KINGSFORD COTTS

Babbes Farm

FUGGLES CT

The Green

PH

ROTTVINMERE CL

LEYBOURNE DELL

1 CHURCHILL HOUSE
2 KENNEDY HOUSE

6

NINEVEH LA

Collingwood Grange

ORCHARD CT

Benenden CE Prim Sch

Benenden

PULLINGTON COTTS

NEW POND RD

BENENDEN RD

B2086

Scullsgate House

Pullington Farm

5

HINKSDEN RD

Iden Green Farm

Stream Farm

Frame Farm

Ramsden Farm

32

CROUHEBOUR RD

CLAREMONT PL

RAMSDEN LA

Sarnden

CHAPEL LA

Royal Oak (PH)

4

Yewtree Farm

PO

OAKFIELD COTTS

Sewage Works

Iden Green

Broom Hill

Reed Wood

Moor Wood

Nurseries

VYVYAN COTTS

MEDWAY COTTS

WOODCOCK LA

3

MILL ST

Depot

The Woodcock (PH)

Standen Wood

Dingleden

31

Eaglesden

STANDEN ST

Trafford Farm

2

Campion House

DINGLEDEN LA

SPONDEN LA

Mount Wood

Wandle Mill

Old Standen

Standen Street

Springhill Farm

Cattsford

1

Bankside Farm

HOPEHOUSE LA

SANDHURST LA

30

79   **A**   **B**   80   **C**   **D**   81   **E**   **F**

179
186

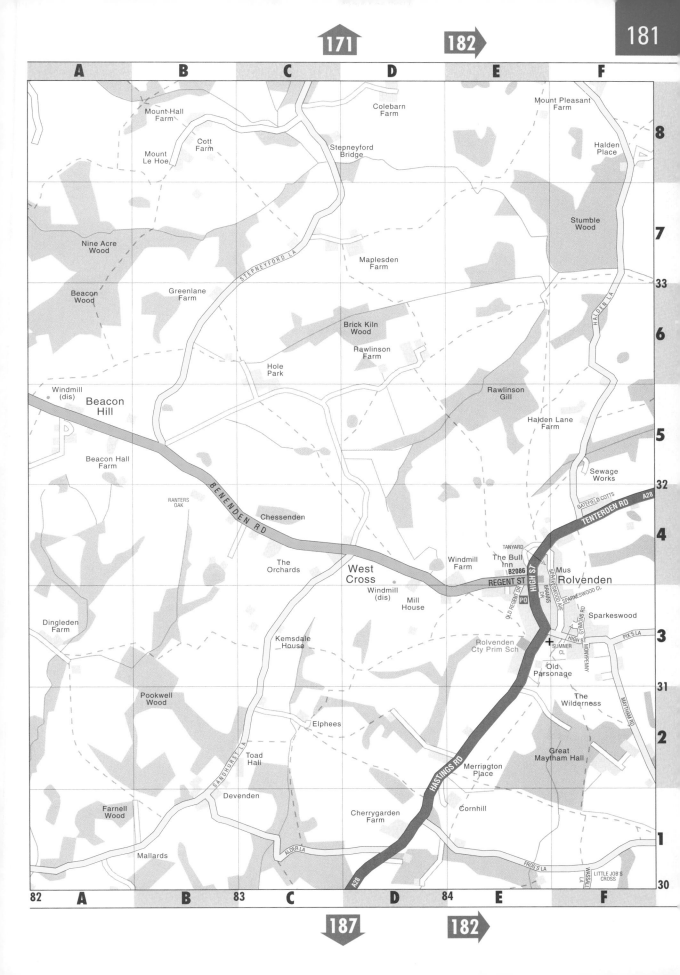

171
182

A B C D E F

8

7

33

6

5

32

4

3

31

2

1

30

Mount Hall
Farm

Colebarn
Farm

Mount Pleasant
Farm

Cott
Farm

Stepneyford
Bridge

Halden
Place

Mount
Le Hoe

Stumble
Wood

Nine Acre
Wood

Maplesden
Farm

Greenlane
Farm

STEPNEYFORD LA

HALDEN LA

Beacon
Wood

Brick Kiln
Wood

Rawlinson
Farm

Hole
Park

Rawlinson
Gill

Windmill
(dis)

Beacon
Hill

Halden Lane
Farm

Beacon Hall
Farm

Sewage
Works

BENENDEN RD

GATEFIELD COTTS

A28

RANTERS
OAK

TENTERDEN RD

Chessenden

TANYARD

The Bull
Inn

Mus

Rolvenden

The
Orchards

Windmill
Farm

B2086

HIGH ST

SPARKESWOOD AVE

West
Cross

REGENT ST

OLD REGENT DR

PO

BRAINS DR

SPARKESWOOD CL

Sparkeswood

Windmill
(dis)

Mill
House

OLD SANDHURST

HIGH ST

PIX'S LA

Kemsdale
House

Rolvenden
Cty Prim Sch

SUMNER
CL

MONYPENNY

Dingleden
Farm

Old
Parsonage

MAYTHAM RD

Pookwell
Wood

The
Wilderness

Elphees

SANDHURST LA

Great
Maytham Hall

Toad
Hall

Merrington
Place

HASTINGS RD

Devenden

Cornhill

Farnell
Wood

Cherrygarden
Farm

ALDER LA

Mallards

A28

FROG'S LA

WASSALL LA

LITTLE JOB'S
CROSS

82 A 83 B C 84 D E F

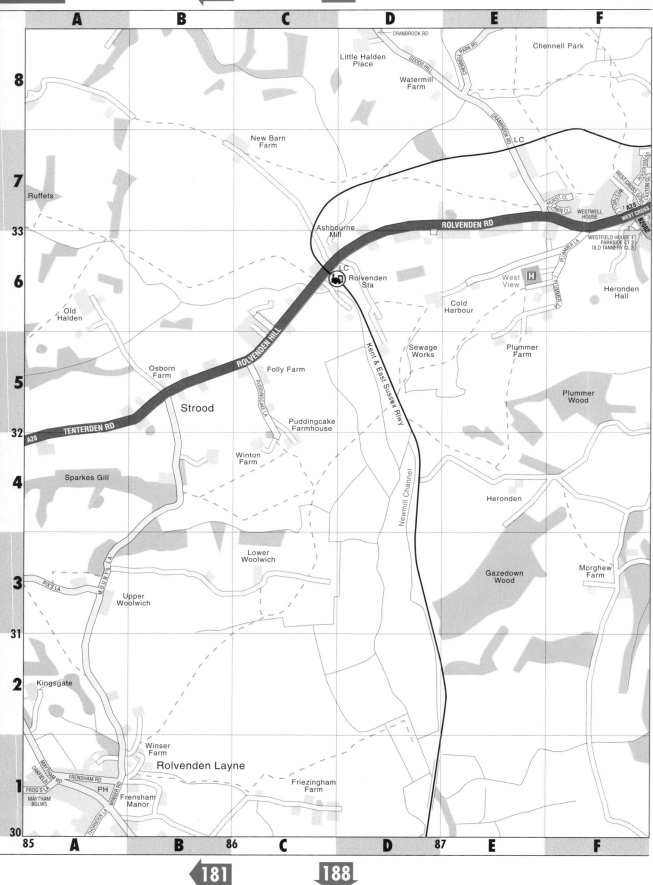

173

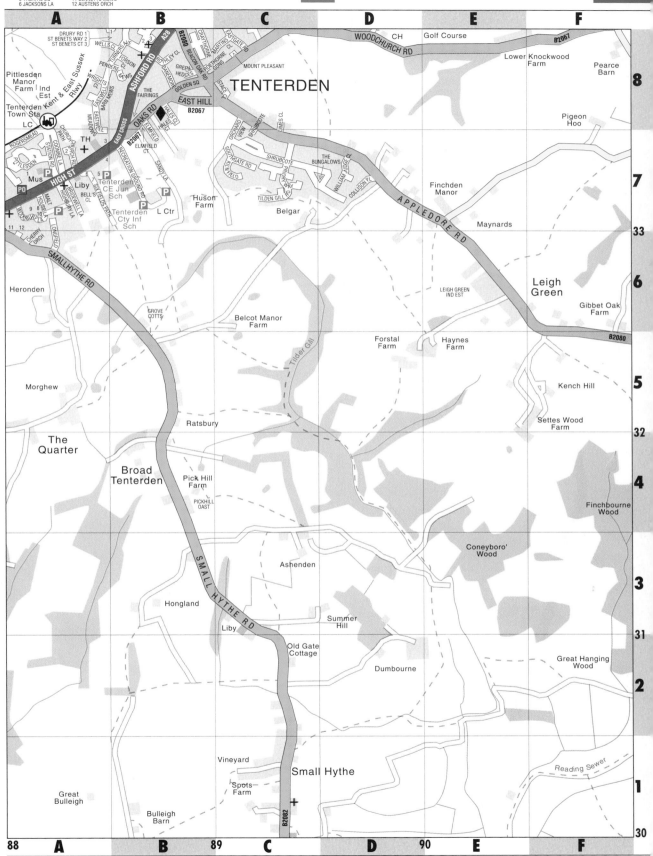

A7
1 PITTLESDEN PL
2 ST MILDRED'S CL
3 EASTWELL
4 SAYERS LA
5 THEATRE SQ
6 JACKSONS LA
7 BELLS LA
8 BURGESS ROW
9 MAYOR'S PL
10 CEDAR CT
11 BENNETTS MEWS
12 AUSTENS ORCH

WOODCHURCH RD
CH
Golf Course
B2067
Lower Knockwood Farm
Pearce Barn

DRURY RD 1
St BENETS WAY 2
St BENETS CT 3
WELLS CL
CRAYTHORNE
EASTGATE RD
MARTINS CL
MOUNT PLEASANT
Pigeon Hoo

Pittlesden Manor Farm Ind Est
PENDERED
WRIGHT'S
BARN MEWS
EASTWELL MEADOWS
ROWLEY CL
BEACON OAK RD
GREEN HEDGES
GOLDEN SQ
STACE Y
TENTERDEN

Tenterden Town Sta
LC
ASHFORD RD
A28
B2080
THE FAIRINGS
Finchden Manor

East Cross
OAKS RD
EAST HILL
B2067
ELMFIELD
HALES
Maynards

ROGERSMEAD
STATION RD
COOMBE LA
CHURCH RD
CHURCH PATH
TH
ELMFIELD CT
SANDY LA
ORCHARD VIEW
SHRUBCOTE
SOUTHGATE RD
SHRUBCOTE
PRIORY WAY
HINES CL
THE BUNGALOWS
COLLISON PL
WILLIAM JUDGE CL
APPLEDORE RD

PITTLESDEN
HIGH ST
MALT HOUSE LA
WOODBURY
PO
Mus
Liby
BELL'S CL
BRIDEWELL LA
HIGHBURY LA
SIX FIELDS PATH
RECREATION GROUND RD
Tenterden CE Jun Sch
P
Tenterden Cty Inf Sch
P
L Ctr
P
KILN FIELD
TILDEN GILL
Huson Farm
Belgar
33

11 12
CHERRY ORCH
LONGFIELD
SMALLHYTHE RD
Leigh Green
6

Heronden
GROVE COTTS
Belcot Manor Farm
Tilder Gill
Forstal Farm
LEIGH GREEN IND EST
Haynes Farm
Gibbet Oak Farm

Morghew
Ratsbury
Kench Hill
5

The Quarter
Broad Tenterden
Pick Hill Farm
PICKHILL OAST
Settes Wood Farm
32

Finchbourne Wood
4

SMALL HYTHE RD
Ashenden
Coneyboro' Wood
3

Hongland
Liby
Summer Hill
Old Gate Cottage
Dumbourne
Great Hanging Wood
31

Reading Sewer
2

Vineyard
Small Hythe
B2082
1

Great Bulleigh
Spots Farm
Bulleigh Barn
30

88   A   B   89   C   D   90   E   F

189

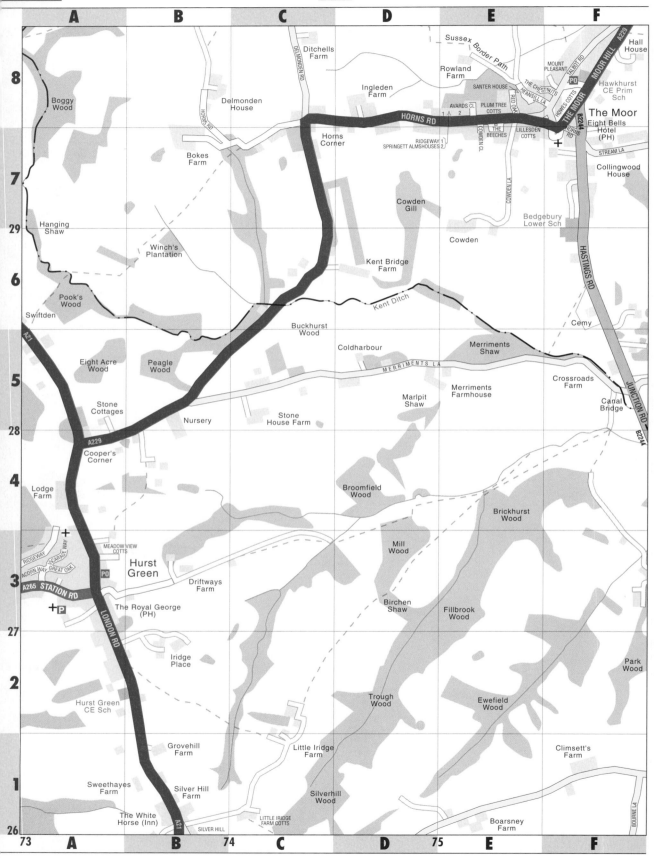

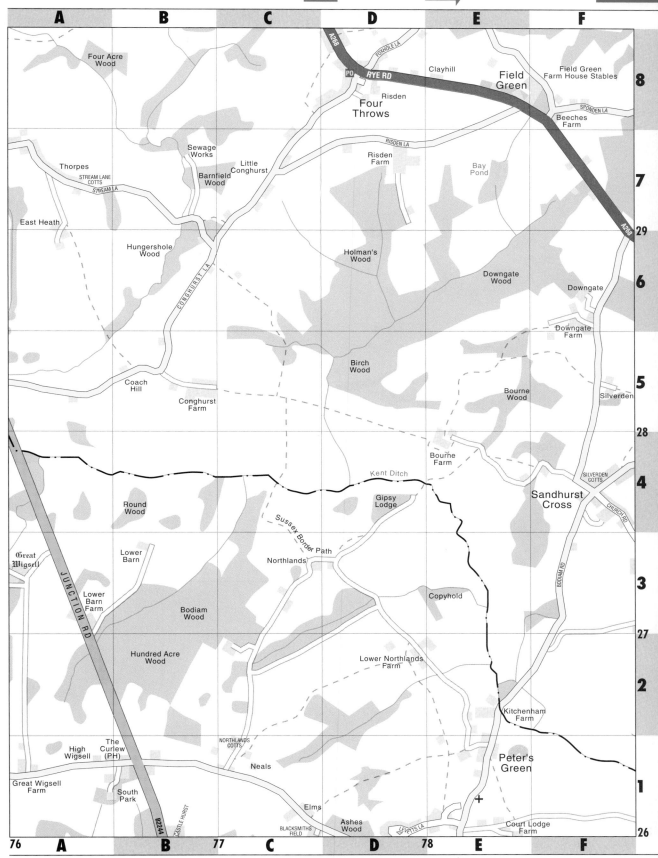

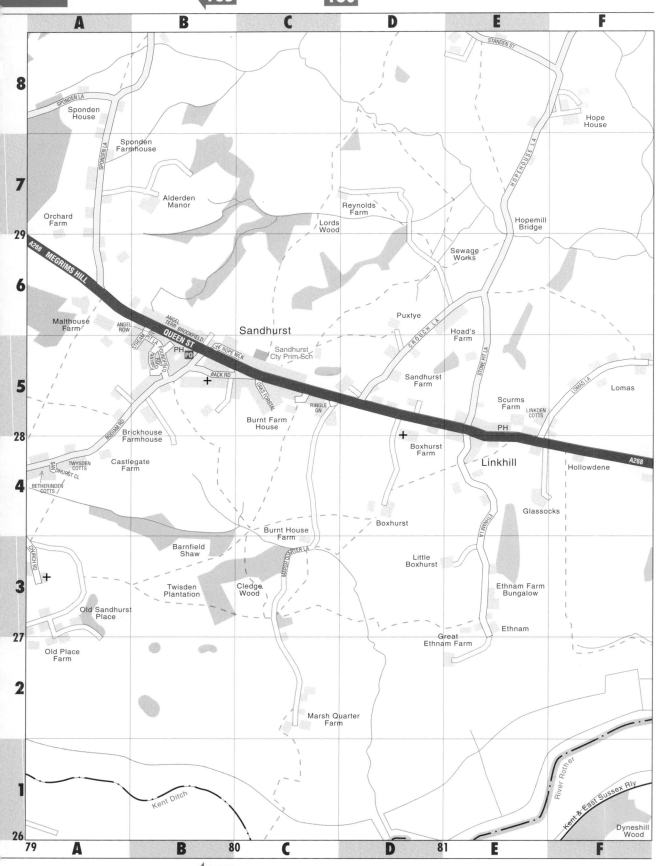

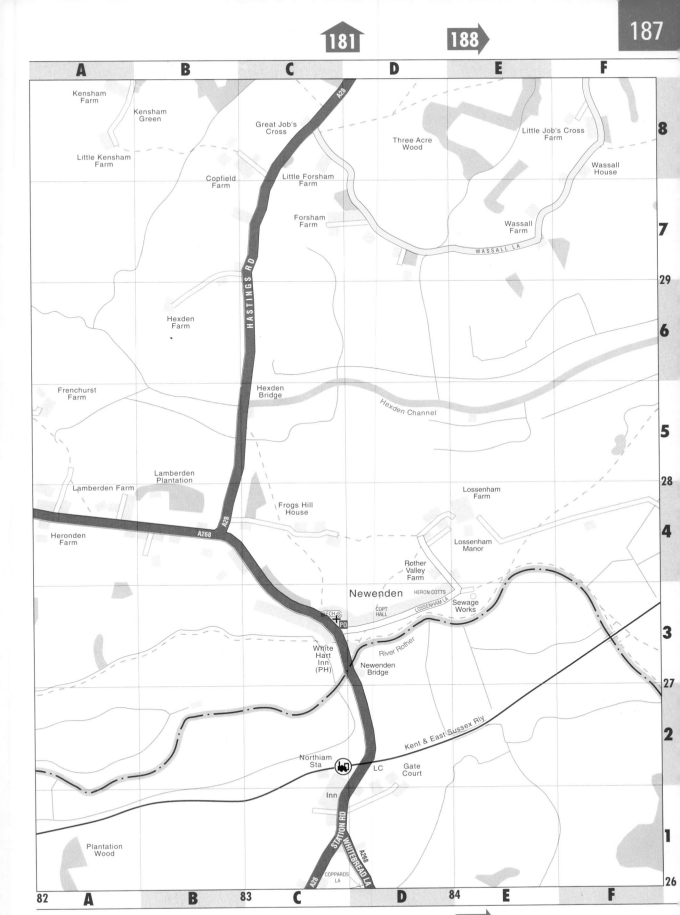

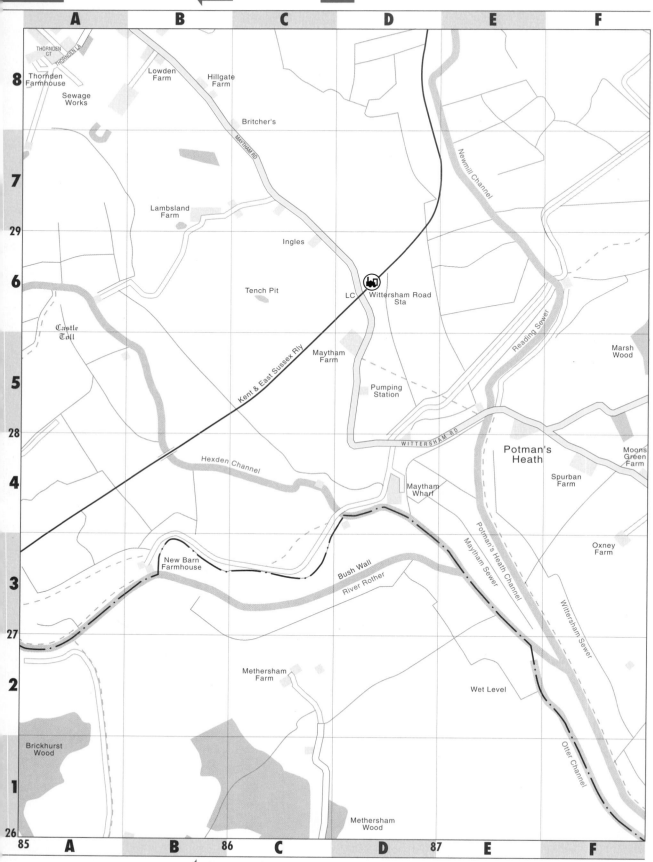

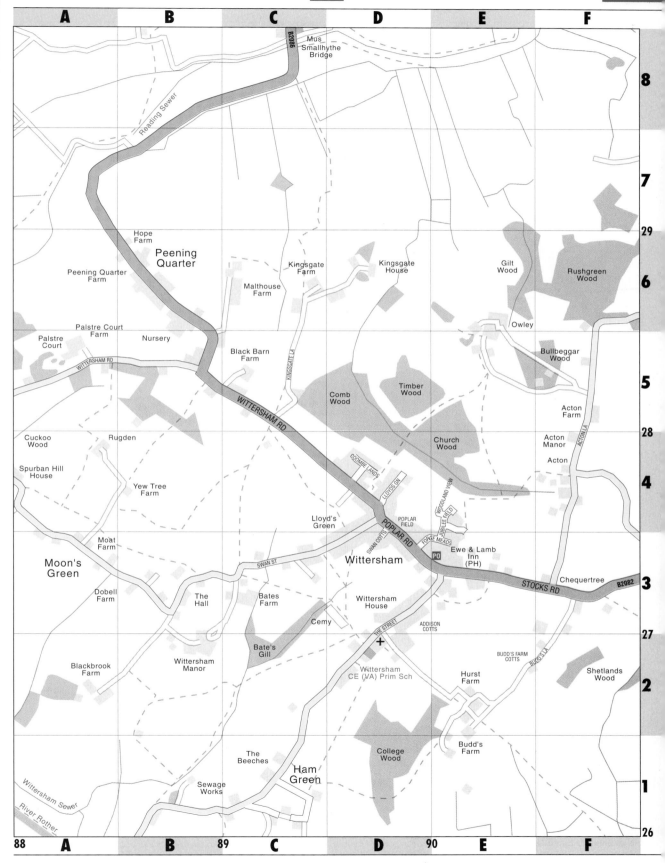

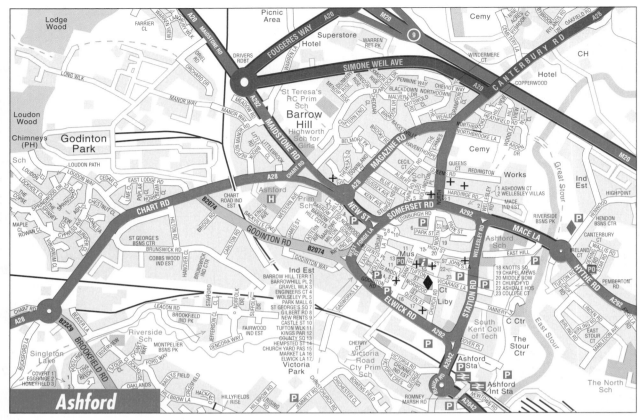

Ashford

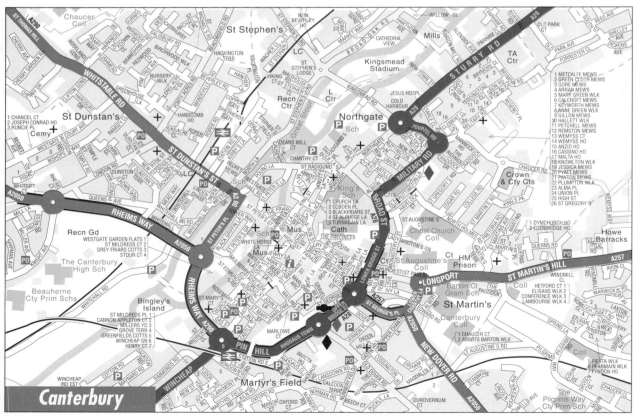

Canterbury

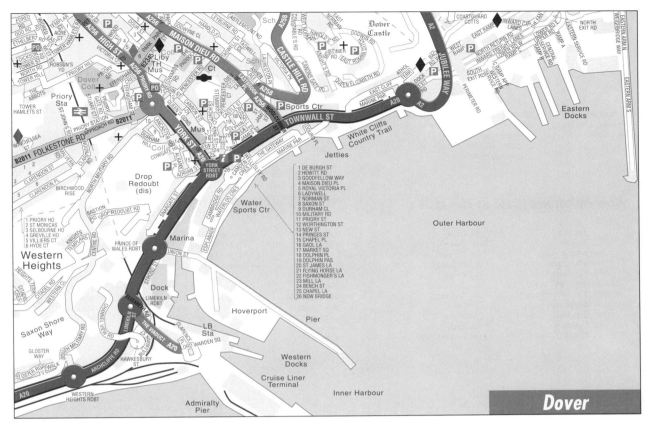

Dover

Index (Dover):
1 DE BURGH ST
2 HEWITT RD
3 GOODFELLOW WAY
4 MAISON DIEU PL
5 ROYAL VICTORIA PL
6 LADYWELL
7 NORMAN ST
8 SAXON ST
9 DURHAM CL
10 MILITARY RD
11 PRIORY ST
12 WORTHINGTON ST
13 NEW ST
14 PRINCES ST
15 CHAPEL PL
16 GAOL LA
17 MARKET SQ
18 DOLPHIN PL
19 DOLPHIN PAS
20 ST JAMES LA
21 FLYING HORSE LA
22 FISHMONGER'S LA
23 MILL LA
24 BENCH ST
25 CHAPEL LA
26 NEW BRIDGE

1 PRIORY HO
2 ST MONICAS
3 SELBOURNE HO
4 GREVILLE HO
5 VILLIERS CT
6 HYDE CL

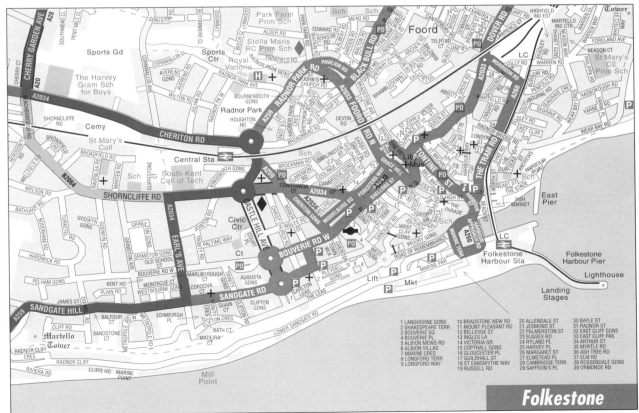

Folkestone

Index (Folkestone):
1 LANGHORNE GDNS
2 SHAKESPEARE TERR
3 BOUVERIE SQ
4 BOUVERIE PL
5 ALBION MEWS RD
6 ALBION VILLAS
7 MARINE CRES
8 LONGFORD TERR
9 LONGFORD WAY
10 BRADSTONE NEW RD
11 MOUNT PLEASANT RD
12 BELLEVUE ST
13 INGLES LA
14 VICTORIA GR
15 COPTHALL GDNS
16 GLOUCESTER PL
17 GUILDHALL ST
18 ST EANSWYTHE WAY
19 RUSSELL RD
20 ALLENDALE ST
21 JESMOND ST
22 PALMERSTON ST
23 SUSSEX RD
24 RYLAND PL
25 HARVEY PL
26 MARGARET ST
27 ELMSTEAD PL
28 CAMBRIDGE TERR
29 SAFFRON'S PL
30 BAYLE ST
31 RADNOR ST
32 EAST CLIFF GDNS
33 EAST CLIFF PAS
34 ARTHUR ST
35 MYRTLE RD
36 ASH TREE RD
37 ELM RD
38 ROSSENDALE GDNS
39 ORMONDE RD

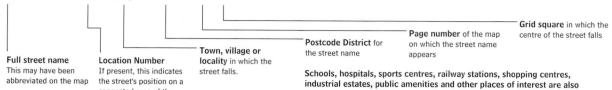

Index

Street names are listed alphabetically and show the locality, the Postcode District, the page number and a reference to the square in which the name falls on the map page

Roberts Cl. 8 Orpington BR5 .... 38 C4

Full street name
This may have been abbreviated on the map

Location Number
If present, this indicates the street's position on a congested area of the map instead of the name

Town, village or locality in which the street falls.

Postcode District for the street name

Page number of the map on which the street name appears

Grid square in which the centre of the street falls

Schools, hospitals, sports centres, railway stations, shopping centres, industrial estates, public amenities and other places of interest are also listed. These are highlighted in magenta

Abbreviations used in the index

App **Approach**	Cl **Close**	Espl **Esplanade**	Orch **Orchard**	Sq **Square**
Arc **Arcade**	Comm **Common**	Est **Estate**	Par **Parade**	Strs **Stairs**
Ave **Avenue**	Cnr **Corner**	Gdns **Gardens**	Pk **Park**	Stps **Steps**
Bvd **Boulevard**	Cotts **Cottages**	Gn **Green**	Pas **Passage**	St **Street, Saint**
Bldgs **Buildings**	Ct **Court**	Gr **Grove**	Pl **Place**	Terr **Terrace**
Bsns Pk **Business Park**	Ctyd **Courtyard**	Hts **Heights**	Prec **Precinct**	Trad Est **Trading Estate**
Bsns Ctr **Business Centre**	Cres **Crescent**	Ind Est **Industrial Estate**	Prom **Promenade**	Wlk **Walk**
Bglws **Bungalows**	Dr **Drive**	Intc **Interchange**	Ret Pk **Retail Park**	W **West**
Cswy **Causeway**	Dro **Drove**	Junc **Junction**	Rd **Road**	Yd **Yard**
Ctr **Centre**	E **East**	La **Lane**	Rdbt **Roundabout**	
Cir **Circus**	Emb **Embankment**	N **North**	S **South**	

20/20 Ind Est. ME16 .... 91 C8
Abbess Cl. 11 E6 .... 1 E8
Abbeville House. ME1 .... 47 C4
Abbey Court Sch. ME2 .... 46 E8
Abbey Cres. DA17 .... 4 C1
Abbey Gate Cotts. ME20 .... 76 F2
Abbey Gr. SE2 .... 3 B2
Abbey Pl. DA1 .... 9 D2
Abbey Prim Sch. SE2 .... 3 C3
Abbey Rd. Bexley DA6 & DA7 .... 7 E3
Abbey Rd. Erith DA17 .... 3 E3
Abbey Rd. Gillingham ME8 ...... 49 A2
Abbey Rd. Gravesend DA12 ...... 30 E7
Abbey Rd. Rochester ME2 .... 46 F8
Abbey Rd. Swanscombe DA9 ... 11 C2
Abbey Terr. SE2 .... 3 C2
Abbey Wood Rd. Kings Hill ME19 89 A5
Abbey Wood Rd. Woolwich SE2 .... 3 C2
Abbey Wood Sta. SE2 .... 3 A3
Abbey Wood Sta. SE2 .... 3 C3
Abbeyhill Rd. DA15 .... 24 C6
Abbots Cl. BR5 .... 37 C1
Abbots Court Rd. ME3 .... 34 F5
Abbots Field. Gravesend DA12 .. 30 C2
Abbots Field. Maidstone ME16 .. 91 B2
Abbotswood Cl. 7 DA17 .... 3 E3
Abbott Rd. TN15 .... 86 F7
Abbott's Wlk. DA7 .... 7 D7
Abbotts Cl. Rochester ME1 ...... 47 B3
Abbotts Cl. Swanley BR8 .... 40 A5
Abbotts Cl. Woolwich SE28 .... 3 C6
Aberdeen House. 8 ME15 ...... 107 E7
Aberford Gdns. SE18 .... 5 E6
Abergeldie Rd. SE12 .... 5 B1
Abery St. SE18 .... 2 E2
Abigail Cres. ME5 .... 62 A1
Abingdon Rd. ME16 .... 90 F2
Abingdon Way. BR6 .... 52 B6
Abinger Cl. BR1 .... 36 E6
Abinger Dr. ME5 .... 62 D2
Absalam Ct. ME8 .... 49 C2
Acacia Cl. BR5 .... 37 D4
Acacia Rd. Dartford DA1 .... 26 D7
Acacia Rd. Stone DA9 .... 10 E1
Acacia Way. DA15 .... 23 F7
Acacia Wlk. BR8 .... 39 D7
Academy Dr. ME7 .... 48 F1
Academy Pl. SE18 .... 6 A6
Academy Rd. SE18 .... 5 F7
Acer Ave. TN2 .... 163 C8
Achilles Rd. ME5 .... 62 C2
Acland Cl. SE18 .... 6 D7
Acorn Cl. Chislehurst BR7 .... 23 C3
Acorn Cl. Five Oak Green TN12 .. 135 B7
Acorn Gr. ME20 .... 90 D8
Acorn Ind Pk. DA1 .... 9 A2
Acorn Pl. ME15 .... 107 E6
Acorn Rd. ME4 .... 48 F4
Acorn Trad Ctr. RM16 .... 11 E8
Acorn Way. Hurst Green TN19 .. 184 A3
Acorn Way. Orpington BR6 ...... 51 B6
Acorns The. TN27 .... 142 F1
Acott Fields. ME18 .... 120 F8

Acre Cl. ME4 .... 47 E1
Acres Rise. TN5 .... 176 E1
Acton La. TN30 .... 189 F4
Acton Pl. ME18 .... 105 A1
Acworth House. 1 SE18 .... 6 B8
Acworth Pl. DA1 .... 9 C1
Adam Cl. ME17 .... 106 D3
Adams Cl. ME8 .... 63 A6
Adams Sq. DA6 .... 7 E4
Adamson Rd. E16 .... 1 A7
Adbert Dr. ME15 .... 106 B4
Adcot Wlk. 6 BR6 .... 51 F6
Adderley Gdns. SE9 .... 23 A4
Addington La. ME19 .... 73 B4
Addison Cl. East Malling ME19 .. 74 F1
Addison Cl. Orpington BR5 ...... 37 C3
Addison Cotts. TN30 .... 189 D3
Addison Dr. SE12 .... 5 B2
Addison Rd. BR2 .... 36 D4
Addlestead Rd. TN12 .... 119 E6
Adelaide Rd. Chislehurst BR7 .. 23 B3
Adelaide Rd. Gillingham ME7 .... 48 C4
Adelaide Rd. Tilbury RM18 ...... 12 F5
Adelaide The. ME3 .... 32 C6
Aden Terr. 1 ME14 .... 92 A7
Adisham Dr. ME15 .... 91 B7
Admaston Rd. SE18 .... 6 C8
Admers Way. DA13 .... 73 B8
Admiral Moore Dr. 8 ME20 .... 75 F1
Admiral Seymour Rd. SE9 .... 5 F3
Admiral's Wlk. ME4 .... 47 F7
Admirals Wlk. Chatham ME5 ... 62 B3
Admirals Wlk.
  Goddard's Green TN17 .... 170 D2
Admirals Wlk. Gillingham ME7 .. 48 A7
Admirals Wlk. Tenterden TN30 .. 173 C1
Admiralty Rd. ME2 .... 33 F1
Admiralty Terr. 1
  Gillingham ME4 .... 48 A7
Admiralty Terr. Upper Upton ME2 33 F1
Afghan Rd. ME4 .... 47 E4
Agate Cl. E16 .... 1 D7
Agaton Rd. BR7 & SE9 .... 23 C6
Agnes Cl. E6 .... 2 A6
Ainsdale Cl. BR6 .... 37 D1
Aintree Cl. DA12 .... 30 B5
Aintree House. 1 ME15 .... 107 E7
Aintree Rd. ME5 .... 62 C3
Airedale Cl. DA2 .... 27 C7
Airport Rdbt. E16 .... 1 D5
Aisher Rd. SE28 .... 3 C6
Aisher Way. TN13 .... 83 E6
Ajax Rd. ME1 .... 61 C8
Akehurst La. TN15 .... 84 C2
Alabama St. SE18 .... 6 E7
Alamein Ave. ME5 .... 61 F7
Alamein Gdns. DA2 .... 27 D8
Alamein Rd. DA10 .... 11 D1
Alan Cl. DA1 .... 9 C3
Alanbrooke. DA12 .... 30 C8
Alanbrooke House. SE18 .... 5 E7
Alanthus Cl. SE12 .... 5 A1
Alban Cres. DA4 .... 41 A1

Albany Cl. Sidcup DA5 .... 24 D8
Albany Cl. Tonbridge TN9 ...... 133 D7
Albany Hill. TN2 .... 149 C5
Albany Park Sta. DA14 .... 24 D6
Albany Rd. Chatham ME4 .... 48 B2
Albany Rd. Chislehurst BR7 ..... 23 B3
Albany Rd. Erith DA17 .... 7 F8
Albany Rd. Gillingham ME7 ..... 48 D4
Albany Rd. Rochester ME1 ...... 47 C4
Albany Rd. Sidcup DA5 .... 24 C8
Albany Rd. Tilbury RM18 .... 13 A6
Albany St. ME14 .... 92 B5
Albany Terr. Chatham ME4 ...... 47 E4
Albany Terr. Gillingham ME7 ... 48 D4
Albatross Ave. ME2 .... 46 C6
Albatross St. SE18 .... 6 E7
Albemarle Rd. ME5 .... 62 C2
Albert Cotts. TN11 .... 149 B4
Albert Manor. ME7 .... 48 B5
Albert Murry Cl. 4 DA12 .... 30 C8
Albert Pl. ME2 .... 47 B7
Albert Rd. Bromley BR2 .... 36 D4
Albert Rd. Chatham ME4 .... 48 A3
Albert Rd. Chislehurst SE9 ...... 22 E5
Albert Rd. Erith DA17 .... 3 F1
Albert Rd. Gillingham ME7 ...... 48 C4
Albert Rd. Newham E16 .... 1 F5
Albert Rd.
  Orpington,Chelsfield BR6 .... 52 A5
Albert Rd.
  Orpington,St Mary Cray BR5 .. 38 B3
Albert Rd. Rochester ME1 .... 47 C3
Albert Rd. Sidcup DA5 .... 25 B8
Albert Rd. Swanscombe DA10 .. 11 F1
Albert Rd. 3 Tonbridge TN9 ... 117 B1
Albert St. Maidstone ME14 ...... 91 F6
Albert St.
  Royal Tunbridge Wells TN1 .. 149 B4
Albert Wlk. E16 .... 2 C5
Alberta Rd. DA7 .... 8 C6
Albion Cl. 2 SE7 .... 1 E2
Albion House. E16 .... 2 B5
Albion Pl. Maidstone ME14 ...... 92 B4
Albion Pl. Newington ME9 .... 65 B6
Albion Rd. Bexley DA6 .... 8 A3
Albion Rd. Chatham ME5 .... 62 B2
Albion Rd. Gravesend DA12 .... 30 C8
Albion Rd. Marden TN12 .... 138 D5
Albion Rd.
  Royal Tunbridge Wells TN1 .. 149 C5
Albion Terr. DA12 .... 13 D1
Albion Way. TN8 .... 112 C4
Albright Ind Est. RM13 .... 4 F8
Albury Ave. DA7 .... 7 E5
Albury Cl. ME5 .... 62 D2
Albyfield. BR1 .... 36 F6
Alchins Cotts. ME17 .... 106 E2
Alconbury. DA6 .... 8 B2
Aldeburgh St. SE18 .... 1 A1
Alder Cl. TN2 .... 133 D1
Alder La. TN17 .... 181 C1
Alder Rd. DA14 .... 23 F5

Alder Way. BR8 .... 39 D7
Aldermary Rd. BR1 .... 36 A8
Alderney Rd. DA8 .... 9 A7
Alders Cotts. TN11 .... 135 A5
Alders Meadow. TN9 .... 116 F2
Alders Rd. TN11 & TN12 .... 134 E6
Alders The. ME18 .... 103 D7
Aldershot Rd. ME5 .... 62 A7
Aldersgrove Ave. SE12 & SE9 .. 22 D5
Alderwood Rd. SE9 .... 6 D1
Aldington Cl. ME5 .... 62 B5
Aldington La. ME14 .... 93 D8
Aldington Rd. Greenwich SE18 .. 1 D3
Aldington Rd. Maidstone ME14 .. 92 F4
Aldon Cl. ME14 .... 92 C6
Aldon Ct. ME14 .... 92 C6
Aldon La. ME19 .... 88 C8
Aldwick Cl. BR7 .... 23 D5
Alen Sq. TN12 .... 139 F4
Alers Rd. DA6 .... 7 D2
Alestan Beck Rd. E16 .... 1 D7
Alexander Cl. Hayes BR2 .... 36 A1
Alexander Cl. Sidcup DA15 .... 6 E1
Alexander Ct. Greenwich SE3 .... 5 B5
Alexander Ct. Rochester ME2 .. 47 B8
Alexander McLeod Inf Sch. SE2 . 3 B1
Alexander McLeod Jun Sch. SE2 3 B1
Alexander Rd. Bexley DA5 .... 7 D5
Alexander Rd. Chislehurst BR7 .. 23 B3
Alexander Rd. Swanscombe DA9 11 C2
Alexandra Ave. ME7 .... 48 E4
Alexandra Cl. BR8 .... 39 E7
Alexandra Glen. ME5 .... 62 A1
Alexandra Hospl The. ME5 ...... 77 A8
Alexandra Rd. Chatham ME4 .... 48 B2
Alexandra Rd. Erith DA8 .... 8 F8
Alexandra Rd. Gravesend DA12 .. 30 B6
Alexandra Rd. Tilbury RM18 .... 12 F5
Alexandra Rd. Tonbridge TN9 .. 133 B8
Alexandra St. Maidstone ME14 .. 91 F6
Alexandra St. Newham E16 .... 1 A8
Alfan La. DA2 .... 25 D3
Alford House. 8 SE18 .... 6 B8
Alford Rd. DA8 .... 4 C1
Alfred Cl. ME4 .... 48 B2
Alfred House. 4 DA11 .... 29 F7
Alfred Pl. DA11 .... 29 F7
Alfred Rd. Erith DA17 .... 3 F1
Alfred Rd. Gravesend DA11 ...... 30 B6
Alfred Rd. Hawley DA2 .... 26 F4
Alfred St. RM17 .... 12 C8
Alice Thompson Cl. SE12 .... 22 C6
Alicia House. DA16 .... 7 B6
Alison Cl. E6 .... 2 A7
Alkerden La. DA9 & DA10 .... 11 C1
Alkham Rd. ME14 .... 92 C5
Alkham Tower. 9 ME5 .... 38 C5
All Saints' CE Prim Sch.
  Chatham ME4 .... 48 A3
All Saints CE Prim Sch.
  Maidstone ME15 .... 92 A3
All Saints Cl. DA10 .... 11 F2

All Saints Hospl. ME4 .... 48 A2
All Saints Rd. Allhallows ME3 .. 19 D8
All Saints Rd. Hawkhurst TN18 . 179 A1
All Saints' Rd. Northfleet DA11 .. 29 F7
All Saints Rd.
  Royal Tunbridge Wells TN4 .. 149 B6
All Saints Rise. TN4 .... 149 A6
Allan Cl. TN4 .... 148 C4
Allandale Pl. BR6 .... 52 D7
Allandale Rd. TN2 .... 149 D7
Allard Cl. BR5 .... 38 C2
Allen Cl. ME5 .... 62 C6
Allen St. ME14 .... 92 B5
Allendale Cl. DA2 .... 27 D7
Allens. TN12 .... 138 D5
Allens La. TN15 .... 102 A7
Allenswood Rd. SE9 .... 5 F5
Allhallows Cty Prim Sch. ME3 . 19 D8
Allhallows Rd. E6 .... 1 E7
Allhallows-on-Sea Est. ME3 .. 19 E10
Alliance Rd. Newham E16 .... 1 C8
Alliance Rd. Woolwich SE18 ...... 7 A7
Alliance Way. TN12 .... 135 F6
Allington Cl. DA12 .... 30 F7
Allington Dr. Rochester ME2 .... 46 E8
Allington Dr. Tonbridge TN10 .. 118 A5
Allington Gdns. ME18 .... 104 E7
Allington Prim Sch. ME16 .... 91 C7
Allington Rd. Gillingham ME8 .. 49 A3
Allington Rd. Orpington BR6 .... 37 E1
Allington Rd.
  Paddock Wood TN12 .... 135 F7
Allington Way. ME16 .... 91 B6
Allison Ave. ME7 .... 48 E1
Allnutt Mill Cl. ME15 .... 91 E2
Allotment La. TN13 .... 84 C5
Allsworth Cl. ME9 .... 65 B6
Alma Pl. Hadlow TN11 .... 118 E8
Alma Rd. Eccles ME20 .... 75 F6
Alma Rd. New Town ME19 .... 89 A8
Alma Rd. Orpington BR5 & BR6 . 52 D8
Alma Rd. Sidcup DA14 .... 24 A5
Alma Rd. Swanscombe DA10 ... 11 F2
Almon Pl. ME1 .... 47 D5
Almond Cl. BR2 .... 37 A2
Almond Dr. BR8 .... 39 D7
Almond Gr. ME7 .... 63 A4
Almond Rd. DA2 .... 27 C8
Almond Way. BR2 .... 37 A2
Almonds The. ME14 .... 93 A4
Alms Row. TN16 .... 82 B3
Almshouses. 13 TN18 .... 179 A2
Alnwick Rd. Eltham SE12 .... 22 B8
Alnwick Rd. Newham E16 .... 1 C7
Alonso House. 3 DA17 .... 4 A1
Alpha Cl. ME3 .... 35 D7
Alpine Bsns Ctr. SE6 .... 2 A8
Alpine Copse. 2 BR1 .... 37 A7
Alpine Way. E6 .... 2 A8
Alsike Rd. DA18 .... 3 E3
Altash Way. SE9 .... 23 A6
Altbarn Ind Est. ME5 .... 77 C8

Alton Cl. DA5 .... 24 E7
Alton Cotts. DA4 .... 54 E8
Alverstone Gdns. SE9 .... 23 C7
Alwold Cres. SE12 .... 5 C1
Amanda Cl. ME5 .... 61 F3
Amar Ct. SE18 .... 2 F2
Amardeep Ct. SE18 .... 2 F1
Ambassador Gdns. E6 .... 1 F8
Amber La. ME17 .... 108 A1
Amber Way. ME17 .... 108 B1
Amberleaze Dr. TN2 .... 150 D6
Amberley Cl. 2 Orpington BR6 .. 51 F5
Amberley Cl. Tonbridge TN9 .. 133 A8
Amberley Ct.
  Royal Tunbridge Wells TN4 .. 149 C8
Amberley Ct. Sidcup DA14 .... 24 C3
Amberley Rd. SE2 .... 7 D8
Amblecote Cl. SE12 .... 22 B5
Amblecote Meadow. SE12 .... 22 B5
Amblecote Rd. SE12 .... 22 B5
Ambleside Rd. DA7 .... 8 A5
Ambley Gn. ME7 .... 63 A8
Ambley Rd. ME7 .... 63 B8
Ambrook Rd. DA17 .... 4 A3
Ambrose Cl. Crayford DA1 ... 9 A3
Ambrose Cl. 6 Newham E6 .. 1 F8
Ambrose Cl. Orpington BR6 .. 51 F7
Ambrose Hill. ME4 & ME5 ... 48 C2
Amels Hill. ME9 .... 79 F8
Ames Ave. ME14 .... 93 A4
Ames Rd. DA10 .... 11 E1
Amesbury Rd. BR1 .... 36 D6
Amethyst Ave. ME5 .... 61 E6
Amherst Cl. Maidstone ME16 .. 91 D4
Amherst Cl. Orpington BR5 .. 38 A5
Amherst Cty Jun Sch. TN13 .. 83 E4
Amherst Dr. BR5 .... 38 A5
Amherst Hill. Chatham ME4 .. 48 A6
Amherst Hill. Sevenoaks TN13 .. 83 F4
Amherst Rd. Rochester ME1 .. 47 D3
Amherst Rd.
  Royal Tunbridge Wells TN4 .. 149 A5
Amherst Rd. Sevenoaks TN13 .. 84 B5
Amherst Redoubt. ME4 ...... 48 A5
Amhurst Bank Rd. TN11 & TN2 134 F4
Amhurst Wlk. SE28 .... 3 A5
Amies House. ME15 .... 106 F3
Amsbury Rd. ME17 .... 106 B2
Amshurst Villas. ME15 ..... 106 A4
Ancaster St. SE18 .... 6 E7
Anchor and Hope La. SE7 ... 1 C2
Anchor Bvd. DA9 .... 10 D3
Anchor House. E16 .... 1 C7
Anchor La. ME12 .... 21 F3
Anchor Rd. ME1 .... 47 C1
Anchorage Cl. ME3 .... 19 C3
Ancona Rd. SE18 .... 2 D1
Andace Pk. BR1 .... 36 C8
Anderson Way. DA17 .... 4 B4
Andorra Ct. BR1 .... 36 C8
Andover Ave. E16 .... 1 D7
Andover Rd. BR6 .... 37 E1
Andover Wlk. 12 ME15 ..... 107 F6
Andrew Broughton Way. ME14 92 B4
Andrew Cl. DA1 .... 8 D2
Andrew Manor. ME7 .... 48 C6
Andrew Rd. TN4 .... 149 C8
Andrew Wells House. BR1 .. 22 B1
Andrewes Gdns. E6 .... 1 E7
Andrews Cl.
  Royal Tunbridge Wells TN2 .. 149 D5
Andrews Cl. St Paul's Cray BR5 .. 38 D6
Andringham Lodge. 4 BR1 .. 36 B8
Andwell Cl. SE2 .... 3 B4
Anerley Cl. ME16 .... 91 D7
Angel La. TN9 .... 117 B1
Angel Row. TN18 .... 186 B5
Angel Terr. TN18 .... 186 B6
Angel Wlk. 4 TN9 .... 117 B1
Angelica Dr. E6 .... 2 A8
Angersteln Bsns Pk. SE10 .. 1 A2
Angle Rd. RM16 .... 11 D8
Anglesea Ave. 4 SE18 ..... 2 B2
Anglesea Ct. 17 DA11 ...... 13 B1
Anglesea Pl. 16 DA11 ...... 13 B1
Anglesea Rd. Orpington BR5 .. 38 C3
Anglesea Rd. Woolwich SE18 .. 2 B2
Anglesey Ave. ME15 ...... 107 A7
Anglesey Cl. ME7 .... 62 B7
Anglesey St. SE18 .... 2 C3
Angley Ct. TN12 .... 153 A5
Angley Rd. TN17 .... 169 C6
Angley Sch. TN17 .... 169 C5
Angley Wlk. Cranbrook TN17 169 C6
Angley Wlk. Wilsley Green TN17 169 D6
Anglian Ind Est. E6 .... 2 F8
Ankerdine Cres. SE18 ...... 6 B6
Ann St. SE18 .... 2 D2
Ann Stroud Ct. SE12 .... 5 A2
Annandale Rd. DA15 .... 23 F8
Anne of Cleves Rd. DA1 .... 9 D1
Annesley Rd. SE3 .... 5 B6
Annetts Hall. TN15 .... 87 A8
Annex The. BR8 .... 40 B6
Annie Rd. ME6 .... 74 F6
Ansell Ave. ME4 .... 48 A1
Anson Cl. ME5 .... 62 C6
Anson Rd. ME18 & ME19 ... 88 E2
Anstridge Rd. SE9 .... 6 D1
Antelope Rd. SE18 .... 1 F3
Anthony Cl. TN13 .... 83 E7
Anthony Rd. DA16 .... 7 A6
Anthony Roper Cty Prim Sch.
  DA4 .... 54 E8
Anthonys La. BR8 .... 40 A8
Anthonys Way. ME2 .... 47 E8
Aperfield Rd. DA8 .... 8 F8

Apollo Ave. BR1 .... 36 B8
Apollo House. ME5 .... 62 A6
Apollo Way. SE18 .... 2 D3
Apple Cl. ME6 .... 75 A6
Apple Ct. TN12 .... 135 F6
Apple Tree Cl. ME16 .... 90 F2
Apple Tree La. TN1 & TN4 .. 149 D8
Appleby Cl. ME1 .... 61 D7
Appleby Rd. E16 .... 1 A7
Appledore Ave. DA7 .... 8 D5
Appledore Ct. BR2 .... 36 A4
Appledore Cres. DA15 ..... 23 F5
Appledore Ct. ME16 .... 91 C7
Appledore Rd. Gillingham ME8 .. 49 A3
Appledore Rd. Tenterden TN30 183 E7
Applegarth Dr. DA1 .... 26 F6
Applegarth House. DA8 ..... 8 F5
Applegarth Rd. SE28 .... 3 B5
Appleshaw Cl. DA11 .... 30 A3
Appleton Rd. SE9 .... 5 E4
Appletons. TN11 .... 118 E8
Appold St. DA8 .... 8 F8
Approach The. BR6 .... 51 F8
April Cl. BR6 .... 51 F5
Apsledene. DA12 .... 30 D2
Apsley St. TN4 .... 148 D4
Aragon Cl. BR2 .... 36 F1
Arbroath Rd. SE9 .... 5 E4
Arbrook Cl. BR5 .... 38 A6
Arbrook Ct. BR5 .... 38 A8
Arbuthnot La. DA5 .... 7 E1
Arcade The. 2 SE9 .... 6 A1
Arcadia Rd. DA13 .... 43 F8
Arcadian Cl. DA5 .... 7 E1
Arcadian Ct. DA5 .... 7 E1
Arcadian Rd. DA5 .... 7 E1
Archer Rd. Chatham ME5 ... 62 B6
Archer Rd. Orpington BR5 .. 38 A4
Archer Way. BR8 .... 40 A7
Archery Cl. ME3 .... 33 B7
Archery House Hospl. DA2 .. 10 B1
Archery Rd. SE9 .... 5 F2
Archway Ct. 1 ME2 .... 47 B8
Arden Bsns Pk. ME2 .... 47 E8
Arden Cty Jun Sch. ME7 ... 48 D6
Arden Gr. BR6 .... 51 B6
Arden St. ME7 .... 48 C6
Ardenlee Dr. ME15 .... 92 B5
Arethusa Rd. ME1 .... 61 C8
Argall House. 3 DA18 ...... 3 E3
Argent St. RM17 .... 12 B7
Argles Ct. DA9 .... 11 A2
Argyle Cl. ME1 .... 61 E8
Argyle Rd. Newham E16 ..... 1 B7
Argyle Rd.
  Royal Tunbridge Wells TN4 .. 133 A2
Argyle Rd. Sevenoaks TN13 .. 84 B2
Argyll Rd. SE18 .... 2 C3
Ariel Cl. DA12 .... 30 F4
Ariel Ct. 4 DA17 .... 4 A1
Arkwright Rd. RM18 .... 13 A5
Arlington Cl. DA15 .... 23 E8
Arlott Cl. ME14 .... 91 F6
Armada Ct. ME4 .... 47 E1
Armada Way. Chatham ME4 .. 47 F3
Armada Way. Newham E6 ... 2 C7
Armitage Pl. 5 TN18 ..... 178 F2
Armoury Dr. ME7 .... 30 C8
Armstrong Cl. Bromley BR1 .. 36 E6
Armstrong Cl. Newham E6 ... 1 F7
Armstrong Cl.
  Shepham Heath TN14 .... 68 B4
Armstrong Rd. ME15 .... 92 A1
Armytage Cl. ME3 .... 34 E4
Arne Cl. TN10 .... 117 E6
Arne Gr. BR6 .... 51 F7
Arnhem Dr. ME5 .... 61 F7
Arnold Ave. DA13 .... 58 B8
Arnold Pl. RM18 .... 13 C6
Arnold Rd. DA12 .... 30 D6
Arnolde Ct. ME2 .... 47 E7
Arnolds La. DA2 & DA4 .... 27 A2
Arnott Cl. SE28 .... 3 C5
Arnsberg Way. DA7 .... 8 A3
Arnside Rd. DA7 .... 8 A6
Arran Cl. DA8 .... 8 D8
Arran Gn. ME2 .... 46 C7
Arran Rd. ME15 .... 107 A6
Arrandene House. 3 BR5 .. 38 B7
Arras House. SE2 .... 7 D8
Arsenal Rd. SE9 .... 5 F4
Artemis Cl. DA12 .... 30 E8
Arthur Gr. SE18 .... 2 C2
Arthur Rd. Gillingham ME8 .. 63 E7
Arthur Rd. Rochester ME1 .. 47 D3
Arthur Ruxley Est. DA14 ... 24 D2
Arthur St. Erith DA8 .... 8 F7
Arthur St. Gravesend DA11 .. 30 A8
Arthur St. Grays RM17 ..... 12 C8
Arthur Toft House. 6 RM17 .. 12 B8
Artillery House. SE18 ...... 2 A1
Artillery Pl. SE18 .... 2 A2
Artillery Row. DA12 ...... 30 C8
Artington Cl. BR6 .... 51 C6
Artisan Cl. E16 .... 2 B6
Arun Ct. BR5 .... 38 C1
Arundel Cl. Chatham ME5 .. 62 D1
Arundel Cl. Sidcup DA5 .... 7 F1
Arundel Cl. Tonbridge TN9 .. 133 A8
Arundel Ct. 2 DA6 .... 7 E3
Arundel Dr. BR6 .... 52 B5
Arundel Rd. Dartford DA1 .. 9 C3
Arundel Rd.
  Royal Tunbridge Wells TN1 .. 149 B2
Arundel Ct. ME14 .... 91 F6
Ascot Cl. Borough Green TN15 .. 87 B7
Ascot Ct. Chatham ME5 .... 62 C2
Ascot Ct. Sidcup DA5 ...... 24 F8

Ascot House. 2 ME15 .... 107 F6
Ascot Rd. Gravesend DA12 .. 30 B5
Ascot Rd. Orpington BR5 ... 37 F5
Ash Cl. Aylesford ME20 .... 75 E1
Ash Cl. Chatham ME5 ...... 48 C1
Ash Cl. Edenbridge TN8 ... 112 B1
Ash Cl. Gillingham ME8 .... 49 B3
Ash Cl. Orpington BR5 ..... 37 D4
Ash Cl.
  Royal Tunbridge Wells TN2 .. 163 D7
Ash Cl. Sidcup DA14 ...... 24 B5
Ash Cl. Swanley BR8 ...... 39 D7
Ash Cres. ME3 .... 32 C3
Ash Ct. SE12 .... 22 A8
Ash Gr. Lewisham SE12 .... 22 A7
Ash Gr. Maidstone ME16 ... 91 C6
Ash Keys. DA13 .... 73 B8
Ash La. TN5 .... 56 D2
Ash Platt Rd. TN15 .... 84 E6
Ash Rd. Ash TN15 .... 56 D6
Ash Rd. Dartford DA1 ..... 26 D7
Ash Rd. Gravesend DA12 .. 30 C4
Ash Rd. Hartley DA3 ...... 42 F3
Ash Rd. Hawley DA2 ...... 26 F4
Ash Rd. Orpington BR6 .... 51 F3
Ash Rd. Rochester ME2 ... 46 F6
Ash Rd. Westerham TN16 .. 81 E2
Ash Row. BR2 .... 37 A3
Ash Tree Cl. TN15 .... 55 F2
Ash Tree Cotts. TN12 .... 154 B7
Ash Tree Dr. TN15 .... 55 F2
Ash Tree La. ME5 .... 48 D1
Ashbank Cotts. ME17 .... 109 B7
Ashbee Cl. ME6 .... 75 A7
Ashbourne Ave. DA7 .... 7 E7
Ashbourne Rise. BR6 ...... 51 E6
Ashburn Ct. BR1 .... 22 A1
Ashburnham Cl. TN13 ..... 99 C8
Ashburnham Rd. Erith DA17 .. 4 C2
Ashburnham Rd.
  Maidstone ME14 .... 92 B8
Ashburnham Rd.
  Tonbridge TN10 .... 117 C3
Ashburton Rd. E16 .... 1 A7
Ashby Cl. ME2 .... 60 A4
Ashbys Yd. TN9 .... 117 C1
Ashcombe Dr. TN8 ...... 112 B4
Ashcroft Ave. DA15 .... 7 A1
Ashcroft Cres. DA15 ...... 7 A1
Ashcroft Ct. Dartford DA1 .. 27 A8
Ashcroft Ct. 5 Eltham SE9 .. 6 A1
Ashcroft Rd. TN12 ...... 136 A5
Ashdale Rd. SE12 .... 22 B7
Ashden Wlk. TN10 .... 117 C7
Ashdown Cl. Coldblow DA5 .. 25 C8
Ashdown Cl. Maidstone ME16 91 D3
Ashdown Cl.
  Royal Tunbridge Wells TN4 .. 148 F4
Ashen. E6 .... 2 A7
Ashen Dr. DA1 .... 9 A1
Ashen Grove Rd. DA4 ...... 55 B1
Ashenden Cl. ME2 .... 33 C2
Ashenden Rd. ME2 .... 33 C2
Ashenden Wlk. TN2 ...... 149 E8
Asher Reeds. TN3 .... 148 A8
Ashes La. TN11 .... 118 B8
Ashfield La. BR7 .... 23 C1
Ashfield Pl. BR7 .... 23 D1
Ashford Dr. ME17 .... 109 D3
Ashford Rd.
  Durrant Green TN26 & TN30 173 A6
Ashford Rd. Harrietsham ME17 110 C6
Ashford Rd.
  Maidstone,Grove Green
  ME14 & ME15 .... 92 D4
Ashford Rd.
  Maidstone,Silver Hill ME14 .. 93 D3
Ashford Rd. Tenterden TN30 .. 183 B8
Ashgrove Rd. TN13 .... 99 B7
Ashlar Pl. SE18 .... 2 B2
Ashleigh Cl. DA13 .... 57 F1
Ashleigh Gdns. TN27 .... 141 D6
Ashley Cl. TN13 .... 84 B3
Ashley Gdns. Orpington BR6 .. 51 E5
Ashley Gdns. Rusthall TN4 148 C5
Ashley House. BR5 .... 38 A7
Ashley Park Cl. TN4 ..... 148 C5
Ashley Pk. TN4 .... 148 C5
Ashley Rd. Gillingham ME8 .. 49 C2
Ashley Rd. Hildenborough TN11 .. 116 E5
Ashley Rd. Sevenoaks TN13 .. 84 B3
Ashmead Cl. ME5 .... 62 C3
Ashmead Gate. BR1 .... 36 C8
Ashmere Ave. BR3 .... 6 E4
Ashridge House. DA14 .... 23 F4
Ashton Way. ME19 .... 89 C6
Ashtree Cl. BR6 .... 51 B6
Ashurst Cl. DA8 .... 8 F4
Ashurst Hill. TN3 .... 146 D2
Ashurst Rd. Maidstone ME14 .. 92 C5
Ashurst Rd. Stone Cross TN3 147 B2
Ashurst Sta. TN3 .... 146 D2
Ashwater Rd. SE12 .... 22 A7
Ashwell Cl. 8 E6 .... 1 E7
Ashwood Cl. ME3 .... 33 C7
Ashwood Pl. DA2 .... 28 B5
Askern Cl. DA6 .... 7 D3
Askews Farm Rd. RM16 ... 11 E8
Askham Lodge. 8 SE12 ... 22 A8
Aspdin Rd. DA11 .... 29 E5
Aspen Cl. Orpington BR6 .. 52 A5
Aspen Cl. Swanley BR8 .... 39 D8
Aspen Copse. BR1 .... 36 F7
Aspen Ct. DA1 .... 10 A2
Aspen Gn. DA18 .... 3 F3
Aspen House. 2 DA15 ..... 24 A5
Aspen Way. 2 Chatham ME5 61 E4

Aspen Way.
  Royal Tunbridge Wells TN2 .. 133 C1
Aspian Dr. ME17 .... 106 D3
Asquith Rd. ME8 .... 63 C6
Association Wlk. ME1 ..... 61 C7
Aster Rd. ME3 .... 34 E3
Astley. RM17 .... 11 F8
Astley St. ME14 .... 92 A4
Aston Cl. Chatham ME5 .... 62 A2
Aston Cl. Sidcup DA14 .... 24 A5
Astor Ct. E16 .... 1 C7
Astor of Hever Sch The. ME16 .. 91 C3
Astor Rd. TN15 .... 55 E4
Astra Dr. DA12 .... 30 F3
Atcost Rd. IG11 .... 3 A8
Athelstan Gn. ME17 .... 94 C2
Athelstan Rd. ME4 .... 47 F2
Athill Ct. TN13 .... 84 C5
Athol Rd. DA8 .... 4 C1
Atkinson Cl. BR6 .... 52 A5
Atkinson Rd. E16 .... 1 C8
Atlanta Ct. ME1 .... 47 D3
Atlas Gdns. SE7 .... 1 C2
Atlas Rd. DA1 .... 9 F4
Atterbury Rd. TN16 .... 81 D1
Attlee Dr. DA1 .... 10 A2
Attlee Rd. SE28 .... 3 B6
Attwaters La. TN18 ...... 179 C6
Atwater Ct. ME17 .... 111 D5
Auckland Rd. RM18 .... 13 A5
Auckland Rd. TN1 .... 149 C5
Auden Rd. ME20 .... 75 A3
Audley Ave. Gillingham ME7 .. 48 E1
Audley Ave. Tonbridge TN9 .. 116 F2
Audley Cl. ME16 .... 91 B5
Audley Rise. TN9 .... 116 F1
Audley Wlk. BR5 .... 38 C3
Audrey Sturley Ct. TN4 ... 148 D4
Augusta Ct. 1 ME7 .... 48 C7
Augustine Ct. SE18 .... 2 D3
Augustine Rd. St Paul's Cray BR5 38 D6
Austell Manor. ME7 .... 48 C6
Austen Cl. Swanscombe DA9 .. 11 C1
Austen Cl. Tilbury RM18 ... 13 C5
Austen Cl. Woolwich SE28 .. 3 B5
Austen Gdns. DA1 .... 9 F3
Austen Rd. DA8 .... 8 B7
Austen Way. ME20 .... 74 F4
Austens Orch. 12 TN30 .. 183 A7
Austin Ave. BR1 & BR2 .... 36 E4
Austin Cl. ME5 & ME7 ..... 48 E2
Austin Rd. Gravesend DA11 .. 29 F7
Austin Rd. Orpington BR5 .. 38 A4
Austral Ct. DA15 .... 23 F5
Autumn Glade. ME14 ...... 77 D8
Avalon Cl. BR6 .... 52 D7
Avalon Ctr The. BR6 ...... 52 D8
Avalon Gdns. BR5 .... 38 C1
Avalon Rd. BR5 & BR6 .... 52 C8
Avard Gdns. BR6 .... 51 C6
Avards Cl. TN18 .... 184 E8
Avebury Ave. TN9 .... 117 B1
Avebury Rd. BR6 .... 51 D7
Aveling Cl. ME3 .... 34 D6
Aveling Ct. 2 ME7 .... 47 B7
Avenons Rd. 3 E16 .... 1 A8
Avenue La. DA9 .... 11 C1
Avenue Le Puy. TN9 ..... 117 C1
Avenue Rd. Bexley DA7 & DA6 .. 7 E4
Avenue Rd. Erith DA8 ...... 8 D7
Avenue Rd. Erith DA8 ...... 8 D7
Avenue Rd. Sevenoaks TN13 .. 84 C3
Avenue The. Aylesford ME20 .. 75 E1
Avenue The. Borough Green TN15 87 A8
Avenue The. Bromley BR1 .. 36 D6
Avenue The. Gravesend DA11 .. 30 B8
Avenue The. Hill Park TN16 .. 81 A4
Avenue The. Keston Mark BR2 .. 50 D7
Avenue The. Orpington BR6 .. 51 F8
Avenue The. Sidcup DA8 ... 24 D8
Avenue The. St Paul's Cray BR5 .. 24 B1
Avenue The. Swanscombe DA9 .. 11 B2
Avenue The. Tonbridge TN9 .. 117 B2
Averenches Rd. ME14 ..... 92 F5
Avery Cl. Allhallows-on-Sea ME3 .. 19 E9
Avery Cl. Maidstone ME15 .. 91 F1
Avery Hill Rd. SE9 .... 23 D7
Avery La. ME15 .... 108 D6
Avery Way. ME3 .... 19 D8
Aviemore Gdns. ME14 ..... 92 F4
Avington Cl. ME15 .... 91 F1
Avocet Mews. SE28 .... 2 D3
Avocet Wlk. ME5 .... 62 D2
Avon Cl. Gravesend DA12 .. 30 D6
Avon Cl. Tonbridge TN10 .. 117 C5
Avon St. TN1 .... 149 C5
Avondale Mews. BR1 ...... 22 A2
Avondale Pl. ME3 .... 19 C4
Avondale Rd. Bromley BR1 .. 22 A2
Avondale Rd. Chislehurst SE9 .. 22 E6
Avondale Rd. Gillingham ME7 .. 48 D5
Avonmouth Rd. DA1 .... 9 D2
Awliscombe Rd. DA16 ...... 6 F5
Axford Ct. ME8 .... 64 A8
Axminster Cres. DA16 ...... 7 C6
Axtaine Rd. BR5 .... 38 D2
Axtane. DA13 .... 28 F1
Axtane Cl. DA4 .... 41 C8
Axton Chase Sch. DA3 .... 42 F6
Aycliffe Cl. BR1 .... 36 F5
Ayelands. DA3 .... 56 E8
Ayelands La. DA3 .... 56 E8
Aylesbury Rd. BR2 .... 36 A6
Aylesbury Cres. ME8 .... 49 B4
Aylesford Cty Prim Sch. ME20 .. 75 D1
Aylesford Rd. ME20 .... 75 D1
Aylesford Sta. ME20 ...... 75 E2

Aylesham Rd. BR6 .... 37 F2
Aynscombe Angle. BR6 .... 38 A2
Azalea Dr. BR8 .... 39 E5

Babb's La. TN17 .... 180 A6
Babbacombe Rd. BR1 ...... 22 B1
Babington House Sch. BR7 .. 22 F2
Babylon La. ME17 & TN12 .. 124 B1
Back La. Godden Green TN15 .. 85 A2
Back La. Goudhurst TN17 .. 167 E8
Back La. Horsmonden TN12 .. 153 A6
Back La. Ightham Common TN15 .. 86 C2
Back La. Marlpit ME17 ... 107 C1
Back La. Sevenoaks TN13 & TN14 83 C2
Back La. Shipbourne TN11 .. 101 D4
Back La. Sidcup DA5 ...... 25 A8
Back Rd. Sandhurst TN18 .. 186 B5
Back Rd. Sidcup DA14 ..... 24 A4
Back St. ME17 .... 108 E6
Backfields. ME1 .... 47 B4
Baden Powell House. 11 DA17 .. 4 A3
Baden Powell Rd. TN13 .... 83 E5
Baden Rd. ME7 .... 48 D7
Bader Cres. ME5 .... 62 A7
Bader Rd. ME5 .... 62 C1
Badgers Copse. BR6 .... 51 F8
Badgers Croft. SE9 .... 23 A5
Badgers Rd. TN14 .... 53 B1
Badgers Rise. TN14 .... 53 A1
Badlow Cl. DA8 .... 8 E7
Badsell Park Farm. TN12 .. 135 C3
Badsell Rd. TN12 .... 135 D6
Baffin Cl. ME4 .... 47 F2
Bailey Dr. ME7 .... 49 A1
Bakenham House. 1 ME1 .. 47 C1
Baker Beall Ct. DA7 .... 8 A4
Baker Hill Cl. DA11 .... 29 F4
Baker La. Headcorn TN27 .. 141 F7
Baker La. Sutton Valence ME17 .. 124 F7
Baker Rd. SE18 .... 5 E6
Baker St. Burham ME1 ..... 60 F1
Baker St. Rochester ME1 .. 47 C3
Baker's Wlk. ME1 .... 47 C6
Bakers Ave. TN15 .... 55 E3
Bakers Cross. TN17 ...... 169 E4
Bakers Mews. 9 BR6 ...... 51 F4
Bakery Cl. TN17 .... 156 E7
Balaclava La. TN5 .... 175 A6
Balcaskie Rd. SE9 .... 5 F2
Balchen Rd. SE3 .... 5 D5
Balcombe Cl. DA6 .... 7 D3
Balcombe Cotts. TN17 .... 167 E8
Balcombes Hill. TN17 .... 167 E8
Balder Rise. SE12 .... 22 B6
Baldock Rd. TN5 .... 174 E4
Baldwin's Pk. DA5 .... 25 D6
Baldwyn's Rd. DA5 .... 25 D6
Balfour Cty Inf Sch. ME4 .. 47 E1
Balfour Cty Jun Sch. ME4 .. 47 E2
Balfour Rd. Bromley BR2 .. 36 D4
Balfour Rd. Chatham ME4 .. 47 E2
Balgowan St. SE18 .... 2 F2
Ball's Gn. TN7 .... 160 B5
Ballamore Rd. BR1 .... 22 A5
Ballard Bsns Pk. ME2 ..... 46 F5
Ballard Ct. TN12 .... 138 C6
Ballard Ind Est. ME5 ..... 77 C8
Ballard Way. TN12 ...... 136 B7
Ballens Rd. ME5 .... 62 C3
Balliol Rd. DA16 .... 7 B5
Balls Cotts. ME3 .... 33 F4
Balmer Cl. ME8 .... 63 D7
Balmoral Cl. SE12 .... 22 B4
Balmoral Gdns. DA5 .... 24 E7
Balmoral House. 6 ME15 .. 107 F5
Balmoral Rd. Gillingham ME7 .. 48 D5
Balmoral Rd. Sutton at Hone DA4 27 B1
Balmoral Trad Est. E6 ...... 2 F8
Baltic Rd. TN9 .... 133 B7
Baltimore Pl. DA16 .... 6 F5
Banbridges Ind Est. TN12 .. 120 A5
Banbury Villas. DA13 ..... 28 F1
Banchory Rd. SE3 .... 5 B8
Banckside. DA3 .... 42 E5
Bancroft Gdns. BR6 .... 37 F1
Bancroft Rd. TN15 .... 71 F3
Bandfield Wlk. DA1 .... 9 B1
Bangor Rd. ME2 .... 46 D6
Bank Cotts. ME17 .... 94 E3
Bank Houses. DA2 .... 27 A3
Bank La. TN11 & TN15 ... 100 A3
Bank St. Chatham ME4 .... 48 B3
Bank St. Cranbrook TN17 .. 169 C5
Bank St. Gravesend DA11 .. 13 B1
Bank St. Maidstone ME14 & ME15 92 A4
Bank St. Sevenoaks TN13 .. 84 C2
Bank St. Tonbridge TN9 .. 117 C2
Bankfield Way. TN17 ..... 167 E7
Bankfields. TN27 .... 141 C5
Banks La. DA6 .... 7 F3
Banks Rd. ME2 .... 47 C8
Bankside. Chatham ME5 .... 62 B8
Bankside. Northfleet DA11 .. 12 C1
Bankside. Sevenoaks TN13 .. 83 E6
Bankside. Sparrow's Green TN5 174 E5
Bankside Cl. DA2 .... 25 D4
Banky Meadow. ME16 ...... 90 F3
Banner Farm Rd. TN2 .... 149 B2
Banning St. ME2 .... 47 B8
Bannister Gdns. BR5 ...... 38 C6
Bannister Rd. ME14 .... 92 A7
Bannockburn Prim Sch. SE18 .. 2 F2
Bannockburn Rd. SE18 ..... 2 F2
Banwell Rd. DA5 .... 7 D1

Bapchild Pl. 8 BR5 .... 38 C5
Barbados Terr. 2 ME14 .... 92 A7
Barberry Ave. ME5 .... 61 E5
Barcham Ct. ME15 .... 106 F5
Barchester Way. TN10 .... 117 F6
Barclay Ave. TN10 .... 118 A5
Barcombe Cl. BR5 & BR7 .... 38 A6
Bardell Terr. ME1 .... 47 D5
Barden Ct. ME14 .... 92 B5
Barden Park Rd. TN9 .... 117 A1
Barden Rd. Printstile TN3 .... 131 F2
Barden Rd. Tonbridge TN9 .... 117 B1
Barden St. SE18 .... 6 E7
Bardsley Cl. TN12 .... 120 A7
Barfield. DA4 .... 41 B8
Barfield Rd. BR1 & BR7 .... 37 A6
Barfleur Manor. 6 ME4 .... 48 A6
Barfreston Cl. ME15 .... 91 F2
Bargate Cl. SE18 .... 2 F1
Barge House Rd. E16 .... 2 B4
Bargrove Rd. ME14 .... 92 C5
Barham Cl. Chislehurst BR7 .... 23 B3
Barham Cl. Gravesend DA12 .... 30 F7
Barham Cl. Keston Mark BR2 .... 36 E1
Barham Cl. Park Wood ME15 .... 107 E5
Barham Ct. BR2 .... 36 E1
Barham Mews. ME18 .... 105 B8
Barham Rd. Chislehurst BR7 .... 23 B3
Barham Rd. Dartford DA1 .... 27 A8
Barham's Mill Rd. TN27 .... 127 B3
Baring Cl. SE12 .... 22 A6
Baring Prim Sch. SE12 .... 22 A8
Baring Rd. SE12 .... 22 A6
Bark Hart Rd. BR6 .... 38 B1
Barker Rd. ME16 .... 91 F3
Barking Rd. E16 .... 1 A8
Barkis Cl. ME1 .... 61 D7
Barley Fields. ME14 .... 92 D4
Barleycorn. ME19 .... 74 E1
Barleycorn Dr. ME8 .... 63 E6
Barleymow Cl. ME5 .... 62 C7
Barling Cl. ME5 .... 61 D1
Barlow Cl. ME8 .... 63 E5
Barlow Way. RM13 & RM9 .... 4 E8
Barming Cty Prim Sch. ME16 .... 90 F2
Barming Rd. ME19 .... 89 F2
Barming Sta. ME16 .... 90 F6
Barn End Ctr. DA2 .... 26 C5
Barn End Dr. DA2 .... 26 C5
Barn End La. DA2 .... 26 C4
Barn Hill. ME15 .... 105 E2
Barn Meadow. ME2 .... 59 E4
Barnaby Terr. ME1 .... 47 D2
Barnard Cl. Chislehurst BR7 .... 37 D8
Barnard Cl. Woolwich SE18 .... 2 A3
Barnard Ct. Chatham ME4 .... 48 A2
Barnard Ct. 10 Dartford DA2 .... 10 B1
Barncroft Cl. ME14 .... 92 F4
Barncroft Dr. ME7 .... 62 F4
Barned Ct. ME16 .... 90 F2
Barnehurst Ave. DA7 & DA8 .... 8 C6
Barnehurst Cl. DA8 .... 8 C6
Barnehurst Inf Sch. DA8 .... 8 C6
Barnehurst Jun Sch. DA8 .... 8 C6
Barnehurst Rd. DA7 .... 8 C5
Barnehurst Sta. DA7 .... 8 C5
Barnes Cray Prim Sch. DA1 .... 9 A3
Barnes Cray Rd. DA1 .... 9 A3
Barnes Ct. E16 .... 1 C8
Barnes La. ME17 .... 122 D8
Barnes Wlk. TN12 .... 138 D6
Barnesdale Cres. BR5 .... 38 A4
Barnet Dr. BR2 .... 50 E8
Barnet Wood Rd. BR2 .... 50 C8
Barnett Cl. DA8 .... 8 F5
Barnetts Cl. TN2 & TN4 .... 133 C1
Barnetts Rd. TN11 .... 116 A2
Barnetts Way. TN4 .... 133 C1
Barney Cl. SE7 .... 1 C1
Barnfield. Chatham ME5 .... 62 A8
Barnfield. Royal Tunbridge Wells TN2 .... 162 F7
Barnfield. St Michaels TN30 .... 173 C2
Barnfield Cl. Crockenhill BR8 .... 39 C2
Barnfield Cl. New Barn DA3 .... 43 D6
Barnfield Cl. Stone DA9 .... 10 F1
Barnfield Cres. TN14 .... 69 E2
Barnfield Gdns. SE18 .... 6 B8
Barnfield Rd. Erith DA17 .... 7 F8
Barnfield Rd. Sevenoaks TN13 .... 83 E4
Barnfield Rd. St Paul's Cray BR5 .... 38 D6
Barnfield Rd. Woolwich SE18 .... 6 B8
Barnhill Ave. BR2 .... 36 A4
Barnhurst Rd. ME14 .... 92 A8
Barnsole Cty Inf Sch. ME7 .... 48 E4
Barnsole Cty Jun Sch. ME7 .... 48 E4
Barnsole Rd. ME7 .... 48 E3
Barnwell Rd. DA1 .... 9 F4
Barnwood Cl. ME1 .... 61 B8
Barnwood Ct. E16 .... 1 B5
Baron Cl. Gillingham ME7 .... 48 E7
Baron Cl. Maidstone ME14 .... 92 F5
Barons Ct. TN4 .... 149 A5
Barr Rd. DA12 .... 30 F6
Barrack Cnr. TN13 .... 84 C4
Barrack Rd. ME4 .... 48 B8
Barrack Row. Benenden TN17 .... 180 D6
Barrack Row. 14 Gravesend DA11 .... 13 B1
Barrel Arch Cl. TN12 .... 138 C6
Barretts Green Cotts. 5 TN18 .... 179 A2
Barretts Rd. Hawkhurst TN18 .... 179 A2
Barretts Rd. Sevenoaks TN13 .... 83 E7
Barrie Dr. 7 ME20 .... 74 F4
Barrier Rd. ME4 .... 47 F5
Barrington Cl. ME5 .... 61 F5
Barrington Prim Sch. DA16 .... 7 D5
Barrington Rd. DA16 .... 7 D5
Barrington Villas. SE18 .... 6 A6
Barrow La. TN3 .... 147 F1
Barrowfields. ME5 .... 62 D1
Barry Ave. DA7 .... 7 E7
Barry Cl. BR6 .... 51 E7
Barry Rd. E6 .... 1 E7
Barth Rd. SE18 .... 2 E2
Bartholomew Way. BR8 .... 39 E6
Bartlett Cl. ME5 .... 62 C1
Bartlett Rd. Gravesend DA11 .... 30 A7
Bartlett Rd. Westerham TN16 .... 81 C1
Bartley Mill. TN3 .... 164 E4
Barton Cl. Bexley DA6 .... 7 E2
Barton Cl. 2 Newham E6 .... 1 F7
Barton Cl. Yalding ME18 .... 104 F1
Barton Cotts. TN11 .... 102 A6
Barton Rd. Maidstone ME15 .... 92 A2
Barton Rd. Rochester ME2 .... 47 A7
Barton Rd. Sidcup DA14 .... 24 E2
Barton Rd. Sutton at Hone DA4 .... 41 B8
Basden Cotts. 2 TN18 .... 179 A2
Baseing Cl. E6 .... 2 A6
Bashford Barn La. ME9 .... 80 F4
Basi Cl. ME2 .... 33 C1
Basildon Rd. SE2 .... 3 A1
Basilon Rd. DA7 .... 7 E5
Basing Cl. ME15 .... 92 B3
Basing Dr. DA5 .... 7 F1
Basket Gdns. SE9 .... 5 E2
Basmere Cl. ME14 .... 92 C6
Bassant Rd. SE18 .... 6 F8
Bassett's Forge. TN5 .... 174 E5
Bassetts Cl. BR6 .... 51 B6
Bassetts La. TN11 & TN8 .... 146 C7
Bassetts Way. BR6 .... 51 B6
Basted La. Basted TN15 .... 86 F5
Basted La. Crouch TN15 .... 87 B4
Bastion Rd. SE18 & SE2 .... 3 A1
Baston Manor Rd. BR2 & BR4 .... 50 B6
Baston Rd. BR2 .... 50 B7
Bat & Ball Sta. TN14 .... 84 C6
Batchelor St. ME4 .... 48 A4
Batchelors. TN2 .... 150 E8
Batchwood Gn. BR5 .... 38 B6
Bates Cl. ME20 .... 75 A3
Bates Hill. TN15 .... 86 C5
Bateson St. SE18 .... 2 E2
Bath Hard. ME1 .... 47 D5
Bath Rd. DA1 .... 26 B8
Bath St. DA11 .... 13 B1
Baths Rd. BR1 & BR2 .... 36 D5
Bathurst Cl. TN12 .... 139 E4
Bathurst Rd. TN12 .... 139 E3
Bathway. 17 SE18 .... 2 A2
Batt's Rd. DA12 & DA13 .... 45 A4
Batten Cl. E6 .... 1 F7
Battery Rd. SE28 .... 2 E4
Battle La. TN12 .... 139 A8
Battle Rd. DA8 & DA17 .... 4 C2
Battle St. DA12 .... 44 F6
Battlefields. TN15 .... 71 F3
Battlesmere Rd. ME3 .... 33 B8
Baugh Rd. DA14 .... 24 C3
Baxter Rd. E16 .... 1 C7
Bay Cl. ME3 .... 34 E3
Bay Manor La. RM16 .... 10 F8
Bay The. DA13 .... 73 A8
Bayard Ct. DA7 .... 8 B3
Bayeux House. 10 SE7 .... 5 C8
Bayfield Rd. SE9 .... 5 D3
Bayhall Rd. TN2 .... 149 C3
Bayham Abbey (rems of). TN3 .... 165 B5
Bayham Ct. TN5 .... 174 E6
Bayham Rd. Royal Tunbridge Wells TN2 & TN3 .... 163 C7
Bayham Rd. Sevenoaks TN13 .... 84 D4
Bayley's Hill. TN14 .... 98 E3
Bayliss Ave. SE28 .... 3 D6
Bayly Rd. DA1 .... 10 A1
Bayne Cl. E6 .... 1 F7
Baynham Cl. DA5 .... 7 F1
Bayswater Dr. ME8 .... 63 E4
Baytree Cl. Bromley BR1 .... 36 D8
Baytree Cl. Sidcup DA15 .... 23 F7
Baywell. ME19 & ME20 .... 74 E2
Bazes Shaw. DA3 .... 56 F8
Beach Ct. Eltham SE9 .... 5 E1
Beach Ct. Goddard's Green TN17 .... 170 D1
Beacham Cl. SE7 .... 5 D8
Beacon Cl. ME8 .... 63 D7
Beacon Dr. DA2 .... 28 C5
Beacon Hill. ME5 .... 48 D2
Beacon Hill La. ME3 .... 33 F4
Beacon Oak Rd. TN30 .... 183 B8
Beacon Rd. Chatham ME5 .... 48 C2
Beacon Rd. Erith DA8 .... 9 B7
Beacon Rd. Lenham ME17 .... 111 C5
Beacon Rise. TN13 .... 84 A1
Beacon Wlk. TN30 .... 173 B1
Beacon Wood Cty Pk. DA2 .... 28 B4
Beaconfields. TN13 .... 84 A1
Beacons The. ME17 .... 106 C2
Beacons Wlk. 10 E6 .... 1 E8
Beaconsfield Ave. ME7 .... 48 E5
Beaconsfield Cl. SE3 .... 5 A8
Beaconsfield Par. SE9 .... 22 E4
Beaconsfield Rd. Bromley BR1 .... 36 D6
Beaconsfield Rd. Chatham ME4 .... 47 F3
Beaconsfield Rd. Chislehurst SE9 .... 22 E4
Beaconsfield Rd. Greenwich SE3 .... 5 A7
Beaconsfield Rd. Maidstone ME15 .... 91 E2
Beaconsfield Rd. Maypole DA5 .... 25 E6
Beadon Rd. BR2 .... 36 A4
Beagles Cl. BR5 .... 52 D8
Beagles Wood Rd. TN2 .... 150 E7
Beal Cl. DA16 .... 7 A6
Beamish Rd. BR5 .... 38 C2
Beams The. ME15 .... 92 F1
Bean Cty Prim Sch. DA2 .... 28 C4
Bean Hill Cotts. DA2 .... 28 C4
Bean La. DA2 .... 28 B6
Bean Rd. Bexley DA6 .... 7 D3
Bean Rd. Swanscombe DA9 .... 28 B8
Beanshaw. BR7 & SE9 .... 23 A4
Bearsted Cl. ME8 .... 49 B3
Bearsted Green Bsns Ctr. ME14 .... 93 C4
Bearsted Rd. ME14 .... 92 E6
Bearsted & Thurnham Sta. ME14 .... 93 B5
Beaton Cl. DA9 .... 11 B2
Beatrice Gdns. DA11 .... 29 E6
Beatty Ave. ME7 .... 48 F4
Beatty Cotts. ME3 .... 19 D7
Beatty Rd. ME1 .... 61 D8
Beaufighter Rd. ME19 .... 88 E3
Beaufort. E6 .... 2 A8
Beaufort Ct. ME2 .... 47 E6
Beaufort Rd. ME2 .... 46 E8
Beaufort Wlk. ME15 .... 107 E4
Beaulieu Rd. TN10 .... 117 B4
Beaulieu Rise. ME1 .... 47 D1
Beaulieu Wlk. ME16 .... 91 C7
Beaumanor Gdns. SE9 .... 23 A4
Beaumont Dr. DA11 .... 29 F8
Beaumont Rd. Maidstone ME16 .... 91 B2
Beaumont Rd. Northfleet DA11 .... 29 E8
Beaumont Rd. Orpington BR5 & BR6 .... 37 D3
Beauworth Pk. ME15 .... 107 E8
Beaverbank Rd. SE9 .... 23 D7
Beavers Lodge. DA14 .... 23 F3
Beaverwood Rd. BR7 .... 23 E2
Beaverwood Sch for Girls. BR7 .... 23 E2
Bebbington Rd. SE18 .... 2 E2
Beblets Cl. 4 BR6 .... 51 F5
Beckenham Dr. ME16 .... 91 D7
Beckenham La. BR1 & BR2 .... 36 A7
Becket Ct. TN27 .... 141 D5
Beckets Field. TN11 .... 131 A3
Beckett Cl. DA17 .... 3 F3
Becketts Cl. BR6 .... 51 F7
Beckford Dr. BR5 & BR6 .... 37 D2
Beckley Cl. DA12 .... 31 B6
Beckley Mews. ME5 .... 61 F5
Beckman Cl. TN14 .... 68 C4
Becks Rd. DA14 .... 24 A5
Becksbourne Cl. ME14 .... 92 A8
Beckton Park Sta. E16 .... 1 F6
Beckton Rd. E16 .... 1 A8
Beckton Sch. E16 .... 1 D8
Beckton Sta. E6 .... 2 A8
Becton Pl. DA8 .... 8 C6
Bedale Wlk. DA1 .... 27 B7
Beddington Gn. BR5 .... 37 F8
Beddington Rd. BR5 .... 37 F8
Beddow Way. ME20 .... 76 B3
Bedens Rd. DA14 .... 24 E3
Bedford Ave. ME8 .... 49 D1
Bedford Pl. ME16 .... 91 E4
Bedford Rd. Dartford DA1 .... 27 A8
Bedford Rd. Northfleet DA11 .... 29 F6
Bedford Rd. Orpington BR6 .... 38 B1
Bedford Rd. Royal Tunbridge Wells TN4 .... 133 A1
Bedford Rd. Sidcup DA15 .... 23 E5
Bedford Sq. DA3 .... 42 E6
Bedford Terr. 9 TN1 .... 149 A2
Bedgebury Cl. Chatham ME1 .... 61 D8
Bedgebury Cl. Maidstone ME14 .... 92 C6
Bedgebury Cross. TN17 .... 167 D2
Bedgebury Lower Sch. TN18 .... 184 F7
Bedgebury National Pinetum. TN17 .... 177 E8
Bedgebury Rd. Eltham SE9 .... 5 D3
Bedgebury Rd. Goudhurst TN17 .... 167 E7
Bedgebury Sch. TN17 .... 167 E1
Bedivere Rd. BR1 .... 22 A5
Bedlam La. TN27 .... 142 E6
Bedonwell Jun Sch. DA17 .... 7 E8
Bedonwell Prim Inf Sch. SE2 .... 7 E8
Bedonwell Rd. Bexley DA7 .... 7 F6
Bedonwell Rd. Erith DA7 & DA17 .... 7 E8
Bedwell Rd. DA17 .... 4 A1
Bedwin Cl. ME1 .... 61 D7
Beeby Rd. E16 .... 1 B8
Beech Ave. Sidcup DA15 .... 24 A8
Beech Ave. Swanley BR8 .... 39 F5
Beech Copse. BR1 .... 36 F7
Beech Ct. DA1 .... 10 A1
Beech Dell. BR2 & BR6 .... 50 F6
Beech Dr. ME16 .... 91 C5
Beech Gr. ME3 .... 32 C4
Beech Green La. Blackham TN7 .... 145 F1
Beech Green La. Withyham TN7 .... 160 B7
Beech Haven Ct. DA1 .... 8 D2
Beech House. 7 DA15 .... 24 A5
Beech Hurst. TN2 .... 150 D7
Beech La. TN12 .... 151 C4
Beech Rd. Dartford DA1 .... 26 D7
Beech Rd. East Malling ME19 .... 89 F7
Beech Rd. Herne Pound ME18 .... 88 D2
Beech Rd. Hoo St Werburgh ME3 .... 34 E3
Beech Rd. Newenden TN18 .... 187 C3
Beech Rd. Orpington BR6 .... 52 A3
Beech Rd. Rochester ME2 .... 46 F6
Beech Rd. Sevenoaks TN13 .... 84 B2
Beech St. TN1 .... 149 B4
Beech Wlk. DA1 .... 9 A3
Beecham Rd. TN10 .... 117 E6
Beechcroft. BR7 .... 23 A1
Beechcroft Ave. DA7 .... 8 D5
Beechcroft Cl. BR6 .... 51 D6
Beechcroft Rd. BR6 .... 51 D6
Beechen Bank Rd. ME5 .... 62 A1
Beechenlea La. BR8 .... 40 B6
Beeches Ct. BR1 .... 22 A2
Beeches The. Aylesford ME20 .... 75 E1
Beeches The. Chatham ME5 .... 62 A4
Beeches The. Royal Tunbridge Wells TN2 .... 149 D5
Beeches The. Sole Street DA12 .... 44 D5
Beeches The. The Moor TN18 .... 184 E7
Beeches The. Tilbury RM18 .... 13 B5
Beechfield Cotts. 3 BR1 .... 36 C7
Beechfield Rd. Bromley BR1 .... 36 C7
Beechfield Rd. Erith DA8 .... 8 E7
Beechhill Rd. SE9 .... 6 A2
Beechill Dr. RM17 .... 11 F8
Beechin Wood La. TN15 .... 87 D5
Beeching Rd. ME5 .... 62 B3
Beechings Gn. ME8 .... 49 C3
Beechings Way. ME8 .... 49 C3
Beechlands Cl. DA3 .... 43 A4
Beechmont Rd. TN13 .... 99 B6
Beechmont Rise. TN10 .... 117 B6
Beechmore Dr. ME5 .... 62 A2
Beechway. DA5 .... 7 D1
Beechwood Ave. Chatham ME5 .... 48 D2
Beechwood Ave. Orpington BR6 .... 51 E4
Beechwood Cres. DA7 .... 7 E4
Beechwood Dr. Keston BR2 .... 50 D6
Beechwood Dr. Vigo Village DA13 .... 58 A1
Beechwood Gdns. DA13 .... 58 A1
Beechwood Mews. TN2 .... 149 E4
Beechwood Rd. ME16 .... 90 F3
Beechwood Rise. BR7 .... 23 B4
Beechwood Sch (Sacred Heart). TN2 .... 149 E4
Beechy Lees Rd. TN14 .... 69 E3
Beeken Dene. BR6 .... 51 C6
Beesfield La. DA4 .... 41 A1
Beeston Ct. DA1 .... 10 B1
Begbie Rd. SE3 .... 5 C6
Beggars La. TN16 .... 81 E3
Begonia Ave. ME8 .... 49 C2
Beke Rd. ME8 .... 63 D4
Bekesbourne Tower. 12 BR5 .... 38 D1
Beldam Haw. TN14 .... 68 A8
Belfield Rd. TN2 .... 150 D6
Belford Gr. SE18 .... 2 A2
Belgrave Cl. 5 BR5 .... 38 C5
Belgrave Ct. SE7 .... 5 C7
Belgrave Rd. TN1 .... 149 B4
Belgrave St. ME20 .... 75 F6
Belgrove. 5 TN1 .... 149 A2
Bell Cl. DA9 .... 10 F2
Bell Cres. ME1 .... 75 F8
Bell Gdns. BR5 .... 38 C4
Bell House. SE2 .... 3 D1
Bell La. Burham ME1 .... 75 F8
Bell La. Larkfield ME20 .... 75 B2
Bell La. Lashenden TN27 .... 158 B8
Bell La. Maidstone ME14 .... 93 A5
Bell La. Newham E16 .... 1 A5
Bell La. Staplehurst TN12 .... 139 E3
Bell La. Westfield Sole ME14 .... 77 B7
Bell Rd. ME15 .... 107 E5
Bell Row. TN11 .... 118 F5
Bell Water Gate. SE18 .... 2 A3
Bell Way. ME17 .... 109 E2
Bell Wood Cty Inf Sch. ME15 .... 107 E5
Bell Wood Cty Jun Sch. ME15 .... 107 E5
Bell's Cl. TN30 .... 183 A7
Bell's La. ME3 .... 34 E6
Belle Vue Rd. BR6 .... 51 A1
Bellefield Rd. BR5 .... 38 B4
Bellegrave Par. DA16 .... 6 F4
Bellegrove Cl. DA16 .... 6 F5
Bellegrove Rd. DA16 .... 6 E5
Bellevue Rd. DA6 .... 7 F2
Bellflower Cl. 2 E6 .... 1 E8
Bellgrove Ct. ME5 .... 77 A8
Bellman Ave. DA12 .... 30 E7
Bellmeadow. ME15 .... 107 E6
Bellows La. TN15 .... 86 F7
Bellring Cl. DA17 .... 8 A8
Bells Farm La. TN11 & TN12 .... 119 C8
Bells Farm Rd. TN12 .... 103 D1
Bells La. 7 TN30 .... 183 A7
Bellwood Ct. ME3 .... 18 C3
Belmont Ave. DA16 .... 6 E4
Belmont Cl. ME16 .... 90 F2
Belmont La. BR7 .... 23 C3
Belmont Par. BR7 .... 23 C3
Belmont Prim Sch. DA7 .... 8 A7
Belmont Rd. Chislehurst BR7 .... 23 B3
Belmont Rd. Erith DA8 .... 8 B6
Belmont Rd. Gillingham ME7 .... 48 C4
Belmont Rd. Grays RM17 .... 11 F8
Belnor Ave. ME9 .... 65 F8
Belson Rd. SE18 .... 1 F2
Beltana Dr. DA12 .... 30 E4
Belton Rd. DA14 .... 24 A4
Beltring & Banbridges Halt. TN12 .... 120 B4
Beltring Hop Farm. TN12 .... 120 A3
Beltring Rd. Beltring TN12 .... 120 B4
Beltring Rd. Royal Tunbridge Wells TN4 .... 149 A6
Beltwood Rd. DA17 .... 4 C2
Beluncle Villas. ME3 .... 35 C7
Belvedere Cl. DA12 .... 30 C7
Belvedere Ct. DA17 .... 3 F3
Belvedere Cty Prim Jun Sch. DA17 .... 4 B3
Belvedere Ind Est. DA17 .... 4 D5
Belvedere Link Bsns Pk. DA17 .... 4 C3
Belvedere Rd. Bexley DA7 .... 7 F5
Belvedere Rd. Erith SE28 .... 3 D5
Belvedere Sta. DA17 .... 4 B3
Belvoir Cl. SE9 .... 22 E5
Ben Tillet Cl. E16 .... 1 F5
Benares Rd. SE18 & SE2 .... 2 F2
Benden Cl. TN12 .... 139 F4
Bendmore Ave. SE2 .... 3 A2
Bendon Way. ME8 .... 63 D8
Benedict Cl. 9 Erith DA17 .... 3 E3
Benedict Cl. Halling ME2 .... 60 B4
Benedict Cl. Orpington BR6 .... 51 E7
Benenden CE Prim Sch. TN17 .... 180 D6
Benenden Gn. BR2 .... 36 A4
Benenden Hospl. TN17 .... 171 C3
Benenden Manor. ME8 .... 49 B3
Benenden Rd. Benenden TN17 .... 181 B4
Benenden Rd. Fosten Green TN17 & TN27 .... 171 F5
Benenden Rd. Rochester ME2 .... 33 C1
Benenden Sch. TN17 .... 180 C8
Beneneden Rd. TN27 .... 172 A7
Benhall Mill Rd. TN2 & TN3 .... 163 D8
Benjamin Ct. 4 DA17 .... 7 F8
Benn House. 7 SE7 .... 1 C1
Bennett Cl. DA16 .... 7 A5
Bennett House. DA11 .... 29 F5
Bennett Memorial Diocesan Sch. TN4 .... 148 E6
Bennett Way. DA2 .... 27 D3
Bennetts Ave. TN15 .... 71 C7
Bennetts Copse. BR7 .... 22 E2
Bennetts Cotts. ME7 .... 78 A8
Bennetts Mews. 11 TN30 .... 183 A7
Benover Rd. ME18 .... 120 F7
Benson Rd. RM17 .... 12 C8
Bensted Cl. ME15 .... 121 D7
Bentfield Gdns. SE9 .... 22 D5
Bentham Hill. TN3 & TN4 .... 132 D1
Bentham Rd. SE28 .... 3 B5
Bentley Cl. Aylesford ME20 .... 75 F1
Bentley Cl. Chatham ME5 .... 62 D2
Bentley Cl. New Barn DA3 .... 43 C7
Bentley St. DA11 .... 13 C1
Bentley Street Ind Est. DA11 .... 13 C1
Bentley's Meadow. TN15 .... 84 F7
Bentlif Cl. ME16 .... 91 D5
Berber Rd. ME2 .... 47 B8
Bercta Rd. SE9 .... 23 C6
Berengrave La. ME8 .... 49 F2
Berens Ct. DA14 .... 23 F4
Berens Rd. BR5 .... 38 D4
Berens Way. BR5 & BR7 .... 37 F6
Beresford Ave. ME4 .... 47 E2
Beresford Cl. TN17 .... 166 F2
Beresford Dr. BR1 .... 36 E6
Beresford Rd. Gillingham ME7 .... 48 D4
Beresford Rd. Goudhurst TN17 .... 153 F1
Beresford Rd. Kit's Coty ME20 .... 76 D7
Beresford Rd. Northfleet DA11 .... 29 E8
Beresford Square Market Pl. 1 SE18 .... 2 B2
Beresford St. SE18 .... 2 B3
Beresfords Hill. ME17 .... 107 B4
Berger Cl. BR5 .... 37 E3
Bergland Pk. ME2 .... 47 D8
Bering Wlk. E16 .... 1 D7
Berkeley Ave. DA16 .... 7 D6
Berkeley Cl. Chatham ME1 .... 61 D8
Berkeley Cl. Orpington BR5 & BR6 .... 37 E2
Berkeley Cl. Pembury TN2 .... 150 E7
Berkeley Cres. DA1 .... 26 F7
Berkeley Ct. 6 BR8 .... 39 E6
Berkeley Mount. 1 ME4 .... 47 F4
Berkeley Rd. Gravesend DA11 .... 13 B1
Berkeley Rd. 7 Royal Tunbridge Wells TN1 .... 149 A2
Berkeley Terr. RM18 .... 13 A7
Berkhampstead Rd. 8 DA17 .... 4 A1
Berkley Cres. DA11 .... 13 C1
Berkshire Cl. ME5 .... 62 C8
Bermuda Rd. RM18 .... 13 A5
Bernal Cl. SE28 .... 3 D6
Bernard Ashley Dr. SE7 .... 1 B1
Bernard St. 21 DA11 .... 13 B1
Bernersmede. SE3 .... 5 A4
Berry Rd. ME3 .... 34 E3
Berry's Green Rd. TN16 .... 66 B2
Berry's Hill. TN14 & TN16 .... 66 B4
Berryfield Cl. BR1 .... 36 E7
Berryhill. SE9 .... 6 B3
Berryhill Gdns. SE9 .... 6 B3
Berrylands. Hartley DA3 .... 43 A3
Berrylands. Orpington BR6 .... 52 C7
Bert Reilly House. 1 SE18 .... 2 D1
Bertha Hollamby Ct. DA14 .... 24 C3
Bertrand Way. SE28 .... 3 C6
Bertrey Cotts. TN16 .... 66 B3
Berwick Cres. DA15 .... 6 E1
Berwick Rd. Bexley DA16 .... 7 B6
Berwick Rd. Newham E16 .... 1 C7
Berwick Way. TN14 .... 84 B7
Berwyn Gr. ME15 .... 107 A6
Beryl Ave. E6 .... 1 E8
Beryl House. SE18 .... 2 F1
Besant Ct. 15 SE28 .... 3 B6
Bessels Green Rd. TN13 .... 83 D3
Bessels Meadow. TN13 .... 83 D3
Bessels Way. TN13 .... 83 D4
Bessie Lansbury Cl. E6 .... 2 A7
Best St. ME4 .... 47 F4
Beta Rd. ME3 .... 35 D7
Betenson Ave. TN13 .... 83 F5
Bethany Sch. TN17 .... 154 B5
Bethel Rd. Bexley DA16 .... 7 C4
Bethel Rd. Sevenoaks TN13 .... 84 C4
Betherinden Cotts. TN18 .... 186 A4
Bethersden Ct. ME15 .... 107 F7
Bethersden Rd. TN27 & TN26 .... 159 C5
Betjeman Cl. ME20 .... 74 F3
Betony Gdns. ME14 .... 92 F5

Betsham Rd. Betsham DA13 ...... 28 D3
Betsham Rd. Erith DA8 .... 8 F7
Betsham Rd. Maidstone ME15 .. 107 F6
Betsham Rd. Swanscombe DA10 . 28 E8
Betterton Dr. DA14 .... 24 E6
Bettescombe Rd. ME8 .... 63 E7
Betts Rd. E16 .... 1 B6
Beulah Rd. TN1 .... 149 C4
Beult Meadow. TN27 .... 143 A1
Beult Rd. DA1 .... 9 A3
Bevan Pl. BR8 .... 39 F5
Bevan Rd. SE2 .... 3 B1
Bevans Cl. DA9 .... 11 C1
Bevercote Wlk. ◼1 DA17 .... 7 F8
Beveridge Rd. ◼1 SE28 .... 3 B6
Beverley Ave. DA15 .... 23 F8
Beverley Cl. ME8 .... 63 F8
Beverley Cres. TN9 .... 132 F7
Beverley Rd. Bexley DA7 .... 8 C5
Beverley Rd. Keston Mark BR2 .. 50 E8
Beverley Rd. Maidstone ME16 .. 90 F2
Bevile House. RM17 .... 12 B7
Bevis Cl. DA2 .... 27 C8
Bewl Bridge Cl. TN5 .... 177 B3
Bewl Water. TN5 .... 176 C6
Bewlbridge La.
  Bewlbridge TN3 & TN5 .... 166 B1
Bewlbridge La.
  Lower Cousley Wood TN5 ..... 175 F8
Bewley La. TN15 .... 86 D2
Bexley Cl. DA1 .... 8 E2
Bexley Coll. Erith DA17 .... 4 B1
Bexley Coll. Erith DA17 .... 4 C2
Bexley Coll (St Joseph's Campus).
  SE2 .... 7 D8
Bexley Gram Sch. DA16 .... 7 B3
Bexley High St. DA5 .... 25 B7
Bexley Hospl. DA5 .... 25 E6
Bexley La. Crayford DA1 .... 8 E2
Bexley La. Sidcup DA14 .... 24 C5
Bexley Rd. Eltham SE9 .... 6 C2
Bexley Rd. Erith DA8 .... 4 F1
Bexley Rd.
  Erith,Northumberland Heath DA8 .. 8 C8
Bexley Sta. DA5 .... 25 A7
Bexley-Erith
  Tech High Sch for Boys. DA5 .. 8 B1
Bexleyheath Golf Course. DA6 .. 7 E2
Bexleyheath Sch. DA7 .... 7 F4
Bexleyheath Sta. DA7 .... 7 E5
Bexon La. ME9 .... 80 F5
Bickley Cres. ME1 .... 36 E5
Bickley Park Rd. BR1 & BR7 ..... 36 F6
Bickley Park Sch. BR1 .... 36 E6
Bickley Rd. Bromley BR1 .... 36 E7
Bickley Rd. ◼4 Tonbridge TN9 .. 133 B8
Bickley Sta. BR1 .... 36 E6
Bickmore Way. TN9 .... 117 D3
Bicknor Court Cotts. ME9 .... 80 C2
Bicknor La. ME9 .... 80 D3
Bicknor Rd. Orpington BR6 .... 37 F2
Bicknor Rd. Park Wood ME15 .. 107 F4
Bidborough CE Prim Sch.
  TN4 .... 132 D3
Bidborough Ridge. TN4 .... 132 E4
Biddenden Cl. ME15 .... 92 F3
Biddenden La. TN27 .... 141 E5
Biddenden Rd.
  Durrant Green TN26 .... 173 A6
Biddenden Rd. Headcorn TN27 .. 141 E2
Biddenden Rd.
  London Beach TN26 & TN27 .. 172 E6
Biddenden Rd. Tylden TN27 .... 158 F8
Biddenden Way. Eltham SE9 ..... 23 A4
Biddenden Way.
  Istead Rise DA13 .... 29 E1
Biddulph House. ◼23 SE18 .... 1 F2
Bideford Rd. DA16 .... 7 B7
Biggin La. RM17 .... 13 B8
Bignell Rd. SE18 .... 2 B1
Bilberry Cl. ME14 .... 92 E5
Bill Hamling Cl. SE9 .... 22 F6
Bill Street Rd. ME2 .... 33 C1
Billet Hill. TN15 .... 56 C6
Billings. DA3 .... 42 F3
Bilsby Gr. SE9 .... 22 D4
Bilsington Cl. ME5 .... 62 B5
Bilton Rd. DA8 .... 9 A8
Binbury La. ME14 .... 79 A5
Bines The. TN12 .... 136 A5
Bingham Point. ◼11 SE18 .... 2 B2
Bingham Rd. ME2 .... 33 C1
Bingley Cl. ME6 .... 74 F8
Bingley Rd. Chatham ME1 .... 47 E4
Bingley Rd. Newham E16 .... 1 C7
Binland Gr. ME5 .... 61 D5
Binnacle Rd. ME1 .... 61 C8
Binney Rd. ME3 .... 19 D8
Binsey Wlk. ◼1 SE2 .... 3 C4
Birbeck Prim Sch. DA14 .... 24 B5
Birbetts Rd. SE9 .... 22 F6
Birch Cl. Eynsford DA4 .... 54 D7
Birch Cl. Hildenborough TN11 .. 116 D4
Birch Cl. Matfield TN12 .... 135 D3
Birch Cl. New Barn DA3 .... 43 C7
Birch Cl.
  Royal Tunbridge Wells TN1 ... 149 D7
Birch Cl. Sevenoaks TN13 .... 84 B4
Birch Cres. ME20 .... 90 D8
Birch Dr. ME5 .... 62 D1
Birch Gr. Bexley DA16 .... 7 A3
Birch Gr. Gillingham ME7 .... 63 A5
Birch Kiln Cotts. TN5 .... 175 A6
Birch Mead. BR2 & BR6 .... 51 A8
Birch Pl. ME3 .... 10 E1
Birch Rd. Hoo St Werburgh ME3 .. 34 E3
Birch Rd. Paddock Wood TN12 .. 136 A6
Birch Row. BR2 .... 37 A3

Birch Tree House. ◼16 SE7 .... 5 C8
Birch Tree Way. ME15 .... 92 B3
Birch Way. TN1 & TN2 .... 149 D7
Birchden Cotts. TN3 .... 161 C6
Birchdene Dr. SE28 .... 3 A3
Birches The. Greenwich SE7 ...... 5 B8
Birches The. Orpington BR6 ...... 51 A6
Birches The. Swanley BR8 .... 39 E7
Birches The. Tonbridge TN9 .... 133 B7
Birchetts Ave. TN3 .... 147 E3
Birchetts Green La. TN5 .... 176 A2
Birchfield Cl. ME15 .... 107 B6
Birchfields. ME5 .... 62 A3
Birchin Cross Rd. TN15 & TN14 .. 70 A5
Birchington Cl. Bexley DA7 .... 8 B6
Birchington Cl. Maidstone ME14 .. 92 C5
Birchington Cl. Orpington BR5 .. 38 C1
Bircholt Rd. ME15 .... 107 F4
Birchway. TN15 .... 55 F2
Birchwood Ave. Bidborough TN4 132 E3
Birchwood Ave. Sidcup DA14 .... 24 B5
Birchwood Cty Prim Sch. BR8 .. 39 D8
Birchwood Dr. DA2 .... 25 E4
Birchwood La. TN14 .... 67 F4
Birchwood Par. DA2 .... 25 E4
Birchwood Park Ave. BR8 .... 39 F6
Birchwood Rd.
  Joyden's Wood DA2 .... 25 D3
Birchwood Rd. Maidstone ME16 . 91 C5
Birchwood Rd. Orpington BR5 .. 37 E5
Birchwood Terr. BR8 .... 39 C8
Bird House La. BR6 .... 66 A5
Bird in Hand St. TN3 .... 161 B8
Bird La. TN5 .... 174 B5
Bird-in-Hand La. BR1 .... 36 D7
Birdbrook Rd. SE3 & SE9 .... 5 C4
Birdham Cl. BR1 .... 36 E4
Birkbeck Rd. DA14 .... 24 A5
Birkdale. TN4 .... 149 B6
Birkdale Cl. BR6 .... 37 D2
Birkdale Cl. ◼3 ME16 .... 91 E4
Birkdale Rd. SE2 .... 3 A2
Birken Rd. TN1 & TN2 .... 149 D6
Birkhall Cl. ME5 .... 62 A5
Birling Ave. Gillingham ME8 ..... 49 E1
Birling Ave. Maidstone ME14 .... 93 A4
Birling Cl. ME14 .... 93 A4
Birling Dr. TN2 .... 149 A1
Birling Hill. DA13 & ME6 .... 59 B1
Birling Park Ave. TN2 .... 163 B8
Birling Rd. ME19 .... 74 C5
Birling Rd. Erith DA8 .... 4 B1
Birling Rd. Leybourne ME19 ..... 74 C3
Birling Rd.
  Royal Tunbridge Wells TN2 ... 163 B8
Birling Rd. Ryarsh ME19 .... 74 A5
Birling Rd. Snodland ME6 .... 74 F7
Birling Rd. Snodland ME6 .... 74 F8
Birnam Sq. ◼1 ME16 .... 91 E4
Birtrick Dr. DA13 .... 43 F4
Bishop Butt Cl. BR6 .... 51 F7
Bishop John Robinson CE Prim Sch.
  SE28 .... 3 C6
Bishop's Down. TN4 .... 148 F3
Bishop's Down Cty Prim Sch.
  TN4 .... 148 E5
Bishop's Down Park Rd. TN4 .. 148 F4
Bishop's Down Rd. TN4 .... 148 F3
Bishop's La. ME15 .... 121 D6
Bishopbourne Gn. ME8 .... 49 B4
Bishops Ave. BR1 .... 36 C6
Bishops Cl. Eltham SE9 .... 23 C5
Bishops Cl. Nettlestead ME18 .. 104 D6
Bishops Ct.
  Royal Tunbridge Wells TN4 ... 148 F3
Bishops Cl. Stone DA9 .... 10 F2
Bishops Gn. BR1 .... 36 C8
Bishops Mews. TN9 .... 133 C8
Bishops Oak Ride. TN10 .... 117 C6
Bishops Way. ME15 .... 91 F4
Bishops Wlk. Chislehurst BR7 .. 37 C8
Bishops Wlk. Rochester ME1 .... 47 C5
Bishopsbourne House. BR1 ..... 22 E1
Black Eagle Cl. TN16 .... 96 C8
Black Horse Ct. TN27 .... 141 E5
Black Horse Mews. TN15 .... 87 A7
Black Horse Rd. DA14 .... 24 A4
Black Mill La. TN27 .... 141 B6
Black Post. ME17 .... 95 E4
Black Rock Gdns. ME7 .... 63 B4
Blackberry Field. BR5 .... 38 A8
Blackbrook La. BR1 & BR2 .... 37 A5
Blackdale Farm Cotts. DA1 ..... 27 B6
Blackfen Par. DA16 .... 7 A1
Blackfen Rd. DA15 .... 7 B1
Blackhall La. TN15 .... 84 E4
Blackheath Bluecoat CE Sec Sch.
  SE3 .... 5 B7
Blackheath High Sch. SE3 .... 5 A7
Blackheath High Sch
  GPDST (Jun Dept). SE3 .... 5 A5
Blackheath Pk. SE3 .... 5 B5
Blackhurst La. TN2 .... 149 F6
Blacklands. East Malling ME19 .. 89 F8
Blacklands. Mill Street ME19 .. 89 F7
Blacklands Cty Jun Sch. ME19 .. 89 F7
Blacklands Dr. ME19 .... 89 F8
Blackman Cl. ME3 .... 34 D7
Blackman's La. TN11 .... 118 D6
Blackmans Cl. DA1 .... 26 C7
Blackmanstone Way. ME16 ..... 91 B7
Blackmead. TN13 .... 83 E6
Blackness. BR2 .... 50 D2
Blacksmith Dr. ME14 .... 92 D5
Blacksmith's La. TN5 .... 175 A5
Blacksmiths Field. TN32 .... 185 C1
Blacksmiths La. BR5 .... 38 C4

Blacksole. TN15 .... 71 F3
Blacksole. TN15 .... 71 F3
Blackthorn Ave. Chatham ME5 .. 62 A3
Blackthorn Ave.Royal Tunbridge Wells .
  TN2 & TN4 .... 133 C1
Blackthorn Cl. TN15 .... 55 F2
Blackthorn Dr. ME20 .... 75 B2
Blackthorn Gr. DA7 .... 7 E4
Blackthorne Rd. ME8 .... 64 B8
Blackwater Cl. RM13 .... 4 E8
Bladindon Dr. DA5 .... 24 D8
Blair Cl. DA15 .... 6 E2
Blair Dr. TN13 .... 84 B4
Blake Cl. DA16 .... 6 E6
Blake Dr. ◼3 ME20 .... 74 F4
Blake Gdns. DA1 .... 9 F3
Blake Way.
  Royal Tunbridge Wells TN1 ... 149 D7
Blake Way. Tilbury RM18 .... 13 C3
Blakemore Way. DA17 .... 3 E3
Blakeney Cl. ME14 .... 93 B4
Blaker Ave. ME1 .... 47 E1
Blaker Ct. SE7 .... 5 C7
Blanchard Cl. SE9 .... 22 E5
Bland St. SE18 .... 5 D3
Blanmerle Rd. SE9 .... 23 B7
Blann Cl. SE9 .... 5 D1
Blatchford Cl. ME19 .... 74 F1
Blatchington Rd. TN1 .... 149 B1
Bleak Hill La. SE18 .... 6 F8
Bleakwood Rd. ME5 .... 61 F4
Blean Rd. ME8 .... 49 C2
Blean Sq. ME14 .... 92 C6
Bleddyn Cl. DA15 .... 7 C1
Bledlow Cl. SE28 .... 3 C6
Blendon Dr. DA5 .... 7 D1
Blendon Rd. Maidstone ME14 .. 92 C5
Blendon Rd. Sidcup DA5 .... 7 D1
Blendon Terr. SE18 .... 6 C8
Blenheim Ave. ME1 & ME4 ...... 47 E2
Blenheim Cl. Dartford DA1 .... 9 C1
Blenheim Cl. Maidstone ME15 .. 92 F3
Blenheim Cl. Meopham DA13 ... 58 B8
Blenheim Ct. DA15 .... 23 D5
Blenheim Dr. DA16 .... 6 F6
Blenheim Gr. DA12 .... 30 C8
Blenheim Inf Sch. BR6 .... 52 C8
Blenheim Jun Sch. BR6 .... 52 C8
Blenheim Rd. Bromley BR1 & BR2 36 E5
Blenheim Rd. Dartford DA1 .... 9 C1
Blenheim Rd.
  Orpington BR5 & BR6 .... 52 C8
Blenheim Rd. Sidcup DA15 ...... 24 C7
Blenheim Way. TN5 .... 177 C3
Bletchington Ct. ◼3 DA17 .... 4 A2
Blewbury House. ◼3 SE2 .... 3 C4
Bligh Cty Prim Inf Sch The.
  ME2 .... 46 C7
Bligh Rd. DA11 .... 13 A1
Bligh Way. ME2 .... 46 D6
Bligh's Rd. TN13 .... 84 B2
Blind La. Bredhurst ME7 .... 63 A1
Blind La. Goudhurst TN17 .... 153 E1
Blind La. Lidsing ME7 .... 62 F1
Blind Mary's La. ME9 .... 80 E4
Bliss Way. TN10 .... 117 E5
Blithdale Rd. SE2 .... 3 A2
Blockhouse Rd. ◼5 RM17 .... 12 C8
Blockmakers Ct. ME4 .... 48 B1
Bloomfield Rd. Bromley BR2 .... 36 D4
Bloomfield Rd. Woolwich SE18 .. 2 B1
Bloomfield Terr. TN16 .... 81 E2
Bloors La. Gillingham ME8 .... 49 D1
Bloors La. Gillingham ME8 .... 49 E3
Bloors Wharf Rd. ME7 .... 49 F4
Blowers Grove Wood. ME7 ..... 63 B3
Blowers Hill. Cowden TN8 ...... 145 D8
Blowers Hill. Speldhurst TN3 .. 148 B8
Bloxam Gdns. SE9 .... 5 E2
Blue Anchor La. RM18 .... 13 E8
Blue Boar La. ME1 .... 47 D5
Blue Chalet Ind Pk. TN15 .... 55 D4
Bluebell Cl. Gillingham ME7 .... 48 F6
Bluebell Cl. Orpington BR6 ...... 51 C8
Blueberry La. TN14 .... 67 C4
Bluecoat La. TN17 .... 167 C6
Bluett St. ME14 .... 92 A5
Blunden La. ME18 .... 105 A1
Blunts Rd. SE9 .... 6 A2
Blyth Rd. SE28 .... 3 C6
Blythe Hill. BR5 .... 38 A8
Blythe Rd. ME15 .... 92 B4
Boakes Meadow. TN14 .... 68 F8
Boarders La. TN5 .... 176 C3
Boarley Ct. ME14 .... 76 F1
Boarley La. ME14 .... 76 F2
Boathouse Rd. ME12 .... 21 F3
Bobbing Hill. ME9 .... 65 F5
Bocking Cl. TN5 .... 174 E4
Bockingford La. ME15 .... 106 F8
Bodiam Cl. ME8 .... 49 C3
Bodiam Rd. TN18 & TN32 ...... 185 F3
Bodle Ave. DA10 .... 11 E1
Bodsham Cres. ME15 .... 93 B3
Boevey Path. ◼2 SE2 .... 7 F8
Bognor Rd. DA16 .... 7 D6
Boley Hill. ME1 .... 47 C6
Boleyn Rd. TN14 .... 69 E2
Boleyn Way. DA10 .... 28 E8
Bolner Cl. ME5 .... 61 F2
Bombay House. ◼1 ME15 .... 107 E5
Bombers La. TN16 .... 81 D7
Bonar Pl. BR7 .... 22 E1
Bonaventure Ct. DA12 .... 30 F4
Bonchester Cl. BR7 .... 23 A1
Bond Cl. TN14 .... 67 D4
Bond Rd. ME8 .... 63 E5
Bond St. RM17 .... 12 C8

Bondfield Rd. East Malling ME19 89 F8
Bondfield Rd. ◼4 Newham E6 .... 1 F8
Boneashe La. TN15 .... 87 D6
Boneta Rd. SE18 .... 1 F3
Bonflower La. ME17 .... 122 C7
Bonney Way. BR8 .... 39 E6
Bonnington Gn. ME8 .... 49 C3
Bonnington Rd. ME14 .... 92 C6
Bonnington Tower. BR2 .... 36 E3
Booth Cl. SE28 .... 3 B6
Booth Rd. ME4 .... 47 F2
Bootham Cl. ME4 .... 46 D5
Borden CE Cty Prim Sch. ME9 . 65 F3
Bordyke. TN9 .... 117 C2
Boreham Ave. E16 .... 1 A7
Boresisle. TN30 .... 173 B2
Borgard House. SE18 .... 5 E7
Borgard Rd. SE18 .... 1 F2
Borkwood Pk. BR6 .... 51 F6
Borkwood Way. BR6 .... 51 E6
Borland Cl. DA9 .... 11 A2
Borough Green Prim Sch. TN15 87 A7
Borough Green Rd.
  Borough Green TN15 .... 86 E7
Borough Green Rd.
  Ightham TN15 .... 86 D6
Borough Green Rd.
  Wrotham TN15 .... 72 A1
Borough Green Rd.
  Wrotham TN15 .... 72 A2
Borough Green & Wrotham Sta.
  TN15 .... 86 F7
Borough Rd. ME7 .... 48 D4
Borstal HM Prison &
  Youth Custody Ctr. ME1 .... 47 B1
Borstal Manor Cty Jun Sch.
  ME1 .... 46 F7
Borstal Rd. ME1 .... 47 B3
Borstal St. ME1 .... 47 A2
Bostall Hill. SE2 .... 3 B1
Bostall La. SE2 .... 3 B1
Bostall Manorway. SE2 .... 3 B1
Bostall Park Ave. DA7 .... 7 F7
Bostall Rd. BR5 .... 24 B1
Boston Gdns. ME8 .... 49 C1
Boston Rd. ME5 .... 62 C2
Boston Sch. BR2 .... 50 B8
Bosville Ave. TN13 .... 84 A4
Bosville Dr. TN13 .... 84 A4
Bosville Rd. TN13 .... 84 A4
Boswell Cl. BR5 .... 38 C3
Boswell House. BR2 .... 36 D4
Bosworth House. DA8 .... 4 E1
Botany. TN9 .... 117 C1
Botany Bay La. BR7 .... 37 C7
Botha Rd. E13 .... 1 C8
Bothwell Cl. ◼7 E16 .... 1 A8
Botsom La. TN15 .... 55 D4
Bott Rd. DA2 .... 26 F4
Bottle House Cotts. TN11 ...... 130 F1
Bottlescrew Hill. ME17 .... 107 B4
Boucher Dr. DA11 .... 29 E4
Boughton Cl. ME8 .... 49 B3
Boughton La. ME15 .... 107 B6
Boughton Monchelsea
  Cty Prim Sch. ME17 .... 107 B2
Boughton Par. ME15 .... 107 A2
Boughton Place Cotts. ME17 .. 127 A8
Boughton Rd.
  Boughton Malherbe ME17 .... 111 B2
Boughton Rd. Woolwich SE28 ... 2 E3
Boultwood Rd. E6 .... 1 F7
Boundary House. ◼3 DA11 .... 29 F7
Boundary Rd.
  Chatham ME1 & ME4 .... 47 E3
Boundary Rd.
  Royal Tunbridge Wells TN2 .. 149 D1
Boundary Rd. Sidcup DA15 .... 6 E2
Boundary St. ◼2 DA8 .... 8 F7
Boundary The. TN3 & TN4 ..... 148 B3
Bounds Cross. TN27 .... 157 F7
Bounds Oak Way. TN4 .... 132 S3
Bounds The. ME20 .... 75 E1
Bourdillon Rd. SE9 .... 22 E6
Bourne Cl. TN9 .... 117 D3
Bourne Ent Ctr. TN15 .... 87 A7
Bourne Grange La. TN11 .... 118 D8
Bourne Ind Pk. DA1 .... 8 E2
Bourne La. Silver Hill TN32 ... 184 F1
Bourne La. Tonbridge TN9 ..... 117 D3
Bourne La. Yopps Green TN15 .. 86 F1
Bourne Mead. DA5 .... 8 D2
Bourne Par. DA5 .... 25 B8
Bourne Pk. TN11 .... 118 F8
Bourne Place Sch. TN11 .... 116 A7
Bourne Rd. Bexley DA1 & DA5 ... 8 D2
Bourne Rd. Bromley BR2 .... 36 D5
Bourne Rd. Gravesend DA12 ... 30 F6
Bourne Rd. Sidcup DA5 .... 25 B8
Bourne Row. TN8 .... 130 D6
Bourne Vale. Hayes BR2 .... 36 A2
Bourne Vale.
  Plaxtol Spoute TN15 .... 102 A8
Bourne Way. Hayes BR2 .... 50 A8
Bourne Way. Swanley BR8 .... 39 C6
Bourner Cotts. TN17 .... 156 D4
Bourneside Terr. ME17 .... 94 D2
Bournewood Cl. ME15 .... 92 F1
Bournewood Rd.
  Bexley SE18 & SE2 .... 7 A7
Bournewood Rd. Orpington BR5 38 C2
Bournville Ave. ME4 .... 47 F1
Bow Arrow La. DA2 .... 10 B1
Bow Hill. ME18 .... 104 D5
Bow Rd. ME18 .... 104 E7
Bow Terr. ME18 .... 104 D5
Bowater Pl. SE3 .... 5 B7

Bowater Rd. SE18 .... 1 D3
Bowen Rd. TN4 .... 148 B4
Bower Cl. ME16 .... 91 E4
Bower Gr. ME5 .... 62 C1
Bower La. Eynsford DA4 .... 54 F6
Bower La. Maidstone ME16 ..... 91 E2
Bower La. Maidstone ME16 ..... 91 E3
Bower Mount Rd. ME16 .... 91 D4
Bower Pl. ME16 .... 91 E3
Bower Rd. BR8 .... 26 A2
Bower St. ME16 .... 91 E3
Bower Terr. ME16 .... 91 E3
Bower Wlk. TN12 .... 139 E3
Bowers Ave. DA11 .... 29 F4
Bowers House. ME7 .... 48 E7
Bowers Rd. TN14 .... 68 F8
Bowers Wlk. ◼1 E6 .... 1 F7
Bowes Cl. DA15 .... 7 B1
Bowes Rd. ME2 .... 47 B8
Bowes Wood. DA3 .... 56 F7
Bowesden La.
  Shorne Ridgeway DA12 .... 31 F1
Bowesden La.
  Shorne Ridgeway ME2 .... 46 A8
Bowford Ave. DA7 .... 7 E6
Bowley La. ME17 .... 127 D8
Bowling Green Row. ◼1 SE18 ... 1 F2
Bowls Pl. TN12 .... 136 A7
Bowman Ave. E16 .... 1 A6
Bowman Cl. ME5 .... 62 C5
Bowman Cotts. TN27 .... 172 A7
Bowmans Rd. DA1 .... 25 F8
Bowmead. SE9 .... 22 F6
Bown Cl. RM18 .... 13 B5
Bowness Rd. DA7 .... 8 B5
Bowyer Cl. E6 .... 1 F8
Bowzell Rd. TN14 .... 99 A2
Box Tree Wlk. ◼28 BR5 .... 38 D1
Boxgrove Prim Sch. SE2 .... 3 C3
Boxgrove Rd. SE2 .... 3 C3
Boxley Cl. ME14 .... 92 B8
Boxley Cotts. DA4 .... 41 C5
Boxley Rd. Chatham ME5 .... 62 B2
Boxley Rd. Maidstone ME14 .... 92 B7
Boxley St. E16 .... 1 B5
Boxmend Ind Est. ME15 .... 107 F3
Boxshall House. ◼7 SE18 .... 6 B8
Boy Court La. TN27 .... 125 F1
Boyard Rd. SE18 .... 2 B1
Boyces Hill. ME9 .... 65 D6
Boyle House. ◼12 DA17 .... 4 A3
Boyne Pk. TN4 .... 148 F4
Boyton Court Rd. ME17 .... 125 A6
Brabourne Ave. ME8 .... 49 C3
Brabourne Cres. DA7 .... 7 F8
Bracken Cl.
  Royal Tunbridge Wells TN2 .. 149 E5
Bracken Hill. ME1 .... 62 A1
Bracken Lea. ME5 .... 48 C1
Bracken Rd. TN2 .... 149 E5
Bracken Wlk. TN10 .... 117 B6
Brackendene. DA2 & DA5 .... 25 E4
Brackens The. BR6 .... 52 A5
Brackley Cl. ME14 .... 92 C5
Brackwood Cl. ME8 .... 63 D5
Bracondale Ave. DA13 .... 43 F8
Bracondale Rd. SE2 .... 3 A2
Bradbourne Ct. TN13 .... 84 B6
Bradbourne La. ME19 .... 75 B1
Bradbourne Park Rd. TN13 ..... 84 A4
Bradbourne Rd. Grays RM17 ... 12 B8
Bradbourne Rd.
  Sevenoaks TN13 & TN14 ...... 84 B5
Bradbourne Rd. Sidcup DA5 .... 25 A8
Bradbourne Sch The. TN14 ..... 84 A6
Bradbourne Vale Rd.
  TN13 & TN14 .... 84 A5
Bradbury Ct. ◼3 Greenwich SE3 .. 5 A7
Bradbury Ct. ◼2 Northfleet DA11 29 F7
Braddick Cl. ME15 .... 107 B6
Bradenham Ave. DA16 .... 7 A3
Bradfield Rd. E16 .... 1 B4
Bradfields Ave. ME5 .... 61 F5
Bradfields Ave W. ME5 .... 61 F5
Bradfields Sch. ME5 .... 62 A6
Bradford Cl. BR2 .... 36 F1
Bradford St. TN9 .... 117 B1
Bradley House. ME3 .... 19 C4
Bradley Rd. Upper Halling ME2 .. 59 E1
Bradley Rd. White Post TN3 ... 146 D5
Bradley Stone Rd. E6 .... 1 F8
Bradymead. E6 .... 2 B7
Braemar Ave. DA7 .... 8 C3
Braemar Gdns. DA15 .... 23 D5
Braes The. ME3 .... 32 C3
Braeside Ave. TN13 .... 83 F3
Braeside Cl. TN13 .... 83 F4
Braeside Cres. DA7 .... 8 C3
Braesyde Cl. DA17 .... 3 F2
Brake Ave. ME5 .... 61 E5
Brakefield Rd. DA13 .... 29 B1
Bramble Ave. DA2 .... 28 C5
Bramble Cl. Hilden Park TN11 .. 116 F4
Bramble Cl. Maidstone ME16 ... 91 B3
Bramble Croft. DA8 .... 4 C2
Bramble La. TN3 .... 99 B7
Bramble Reed La. TN12 .... 151 B7
Bramble Wlk. TN1 .... 149 D2
Bramblebury Rd. SE18 .... 2 C1
Brambledown. Chatham ME5 ... 62 B8
Brambledown. Hartley DA3 ..... 42 F5
Bramblefield Cl. DA3 .... 42 E6

Brambletree Cotts. ME1 46 E2
Brambletree Cres. ME1 46 F2
Bramdean Cres. SE12 22 A7
Bramdean Gdns. SE12 22 A7
Bramhope La. SE7 5 B8
Bramley Cl. Gillingham ME8 64 B8
Bramley Cl. Istead Rise DA13 29 F1
Bramley Cl. Orpington BR6 37 B1
Bramley Cl. Swanley BR8 39 E5
Bramley Cres. ME15 92 F3
Bramley Ct. Bexley DA16 7 B6
Bramley Ct. Marden TN12 138 B6
Bramley Dr. TN17 169 D4
Bramley Gdns. Coxheath ME17 106 C3
Bramley Gdns.
Paddock Wood TN12 135 E7
Bramley Pl. DA1 9 A3
Bramley Rd. East Peckham TN12 119 F6
Bramley Rd. Snodland ME6 75 A8
Bramley Rise. ME2 46 E8
Bramleys. TN27 141 D5
Brampton Prim Sch. DA16 7 D5
Brampton Rd. DA7 7 E6
Bramshot Ave. SE3 & SE7 5 B8
Bramshott Cl. ME16 91 C6
Branbridges Rd. TN12 120 B4
Brandon Rd. DA1 27 A8
Brandon St. DA11 30 B8
Brandreth Rd. E6 1 F7
Brands Hatch Circuit. DA3 55 F6
Brands Hatch Cotts. TN15 56 A6
Brands Hatch Rd. TN15 56 A7
Branham House. 1 SE18 2 B1
Branns Dr. TN17 181 E3
Bransell Cl. BR8 39 C3
Bransgore Cl. ME8 63 D7
Branston Cres. BR5 37 D1
Branstone Ct. RM16 10 B8
Brantingham Cl. TN9 132 F7
Branton Rd. DA9 10 F1
Brantwood Ave. DA8 8 C7
Brantwood Rd. DA7 8 B4
Brantwood Way. BR5 38 C6
Brasenose Rd. ME7 48 E4
Brassey Dr. ME20 90 D8
Brasted Cl. Bexley DA6 7 D2
Brasted Cl. Orpington BR6 52 A8
Brasted Ct. Brasted TN14 82 D2
Brasted Ct. Rochester ME2 33 A1
Brasted Hill. TN14 82 A7
Brasted Hill Rd. TN14 & TN16 82 C5
Brasted La. TN14 67 A1
Brasted Rd. Erith DA8 8 E7
Brasted Rd. Westerham TN16 81 E1
Brattle Farm Mus. TN12 139 D1
Brattle Wood. TN13 99 C6
Braundton Ave. DA15 23 F7
Bray Dr. E16 1 A6
Bray Gdns. ME15 106 F5
Braywood Rd. SE9 6 D3
Breach La. ME9 64 F8
Breach Rd. RM16 10 F8
Breakneck Hill. DA9 11 B2
Breakspears Dr. BR5 38 A8
Breaside Prep Sch. BR1 36 D8
Breckonmead. BR1 36 C7
Brecon Ct. 7 SE9 6 A1
Bredgar Cl. ME14 92 C5
Bredgar House. 1 BR5 38 D1
Bredgar Rd. ME8 49 B4
Bredhurst CE Prim Sch. ME7 63 B1
Bredhurst Rd. Gillingham ME8 63 B4
Bredhurst Rd. Gillingham ME8 63 C5
Breedon Ave. TN4 132 F1
Bremner Cl. BR8 40 A5
Brenchley Ave. DA11 30 B3
Brenchley Cl. Chatham ME1 47 D2
Brenchley Cl. Chislehurst BR7 37 A8
Brenchley Cl. Hayes BR2 36 A4
Brenchley & Matfield
CE (VA) Prim Sch. TN12 152 A8
Brenchley Rd. Gillingham ME8 49 B2
Brenchley Rd.
Horsmonden. TN12 152 F6
Brenchley Rd. Maidstone ME15 91 F2
Brenchley Rd. Matfield TN12 151 F8
Brenchley Rd. St Paul's Cray BR5 37 F7
Brenda Terr. DA10 28 E8
Brendon Ave. ME5 62 A3
Brendon Cl. Erith DA8 8 E6
Brendon Cl.
Royal Tunbridge Wells TN2 149 D5
Brendon Rd. BR7 23 D6
Brenley Gdns. SE9 5 D3
Brennan Rd. RM18 13 B5
Brent Cl. Chatham ME5 61 E5
Brent Cl. Dartford DA2 10 B1
Brent Cl. Sidcup DA5 24 E7
Brent Cty Prim Inf Sch The.
DA2 27 C8
Brent Cty Prim Jun Sch The.
DA2 27 C8
Brent La. DA1 27 A7
Brent Rd. Newham E16 1 A8
Brent Rd. Woolwich SE18 6 B7
Brent The. Dartford DA1 & DA2 27 B8
Brent The. Tonbridge TN10 117 C6
Brent Way. DA2 10 B1
Brentfield Rd. DA1 27 B8
Brentlands Dr. DA1 27 A7
Brentor Ct. TN2 149 D6
Brentwood Cl. SE9 23 C7
Brentwood House. SE18 5 D7
Brenzett Cl. ME5 62 B5
Brenzett House. 6 BR5 38 C4
Bretland Rd. TN4 148 D4
Breton Rd. ME1 47 C2
Brett Wlk. ME8 63 D4
Brewer Rd. ME3 33 B7
Brewer St. Lamberhurst TN3 166 A5
Brewer St. Maidstone ME14 92 A5
Brewers Field. DA2 26 C4
Brewers Rd. DA12 45 C8
Brewery La. TN13 84 C2
Brewery Rd. Keston Mark BR2 36 E1
Brewery Rd. Woolwich SE18 2 D1
Brewhouse Rd. 3 SE18 1 F2
Brewhouse Yd. 13 DA11 13 B1
Brian Cres. TN4 149 B8
Briar Cl. Larkfield ME20 75 A2
Briar Cl. 8 Marlpit Hill TN8 112 D3
Briar Dale. ME3 32 B4
Briar Fields. ME14 92 E5
Briar Rd. DA5 25 D5
Briar Wlk. TN10 117 C6
Briars The. TN15 55 D4
Briars Way. DA3 43 A4
Briarswood Way. BR6 51 F5
Briary Ct. DA14 24 B3
Briary Gdns. BR1 22 B3
Brice Rd. ME3 32 B3
Brick Ct. RM17 12 A8
Brick Field View. ME2 33 C1
Brick Kiln La. Broad Ford TN12 153 B2
Brick Kiln La. Ulcombe ME17 125 D5
Brickenden Rd. TN17 169 D4
Brickfield Cotts. SE18 6 F8
Brickfield Farm Gdns. BR6 51 C6
Brickfields. Pembury TN2 150 E8
Brickfields. West Malling ME19 74 B1
Brickwell Cotts. TN17 156 F6
Brickworks Cl. TN9 133 B7
Bridewell La. TN30 183 A7
Bridge Bsns Pk. TN12 135 C7
Bridge Cl. TN9 133 C8
Bridge Cotts. TN12 153 A6
Bridge Ct. 14 Dartford DA2 10 B1
Bridge Ct. 2 Grays RM17 12 B8
Bridge House. TN4 149 B5
Bridge Mill Way. ME15 91 D2
Bridge Rd. Bexley DA7 7 E5
Bridge Rd. Erith DA8 8 F6
Bridge Rd. Gillingham ME7 48 C7
Bridge Rd. Grays RM17 12 B8
Bridge Rd. Orpington BR5 38 B3
Bridge Rd. Rochester ME1 47 C2
Bridge St. ME15 106 F5
Bridgeland Rd. E16 1 A6
Bridgen Rd. DA5 24 E8
Bridges Dr. DA1 10 B2
Bridgewater Cl. BR5 & BR7 37 E6
Bridgewater Pl. ME19 & ME20 74 E2
Bridle Way. BR6 51 C6
Brier Cl. ME5 62 C8
Bright Cl. DA17 3 D2
Bright Ct. 8 SE28 3 C5
Bright Rd. ME4 48 B2
Bright Ridge. TN4 148 E8
Brightlands. DA11 29 E4
Brigstock Rd. DA17 4 B2
Brimpsfield Cl. SE2 3 B3
Brimstone Cl. BR6 52 C3
Brimstone Hill. DA13 58 D8
Brindle Gate. DA15 23 E7
Brindle Way. ME5 62 C1
Brindle's Field. TN9 133 A7
Brindley Cl. DA7 8 A4
Brindley Way. BR1 22 B3
Brinkburn Cl. SE2 3 A2
Brinkers La. TN5 175 A2
Brinklow Cres. SE18 6 B7
Brionne Gdns. TN9 133 D8
Brisbane House. RM18 12 F6
Brisbane Rd. ME4 48 A3
Briset Prim Sch. SE9 5 D3
Briset Rd. SE9 5 D3
Brishing Cl. ME15 107 E5
Brishing La. ME17 107 D4
Brishing Rd. ME15 & ME17 107 F3
Brisley's Row. ME1 60 F1
Brissenden Cl. ME2 34 A3
Bristol Cl. ME2 46 D5
Bristol Rd. DA12 30 D5
Bristow Rd. DA7 7 E6
Britannia Bsns Pk. ME20 90 E7
Britannia Cl. ME2 60 A4
Britannia Dr. DA12 30 F3
Britannia Gate. E16 1 A5
Brittain Ct. SE9 22 E7
Brittain House. SE9 22 E7
Brittains La. TN13 83 F2
Britten Cl. TN10 117 F6
Brittenden Cl. 1 BR6 51 F4
Brittenden Par. BR6 51 F4
Britton St. ME7 48 B5
Brixham Rd. DA16 7 D6
Brixham St. E16 2 A5
Broad Bridge Cl. SE3 5 A7
Broad Ditch Rd. DA13 29 D1
Broad Gr. TN2 149 A1
Broad La. Heath Side DA2 26 B4
Broad La. Stone Cross TN3 147 A4
Broad Lawn. SE9 23 A7
Broad Oak. Brenchley TN12 152 C8
Broad Oak. Groombridge TN3 161 C6
Broad Oak Cl. Brenchley TN12 152 C8
Broad Oak Cl.
Royal Tunbridge Wells TN2 148 F1
Broad Oak Cl. St Paul's Cray BR5 38 A7
Broad Rd. DA10 11 E1
Broad St. ME17 124 E7
Broad Street Hill. ME14 & ME17 94 D7
Broad View. TN17 170 A8
Broad Wlk.
Eltham SE18 & SE3 & SE9 5 E5
Broad Wlk.
Greenwich SE18 & SE3 & SE9 5 E5
Broad Wlk. Orpington BR6 52 D7
Broad Wlk. Sevenoaks TN15 99 E7
Broadcloth. TN17 169 D3
Broadcroft. TN2 162 F8
Broadcroft Rd. BR5 37 D2
Broader La. ME14 78 B2
Broadfield Rd. ME15 107 A8
Broadgate Rd. E16 1 D7
Broadheath Dr. BR7 22 F3
Broadhoath. TN15 85 E1
Broadlands Dr. ME5 62 B4
Broadlands Rd. BR1 22 B4
Broadmead. TN2 162 F8
Broadmead Ave. TN2 162 F8
Broadoak. ME19 74 E2
Broadoak Ave. ME15 107 A8
Broadoak Cl. DA2 & DA4 27 A2
Broadoak Rd. DA8 8 D7
Broadview. DA13 57 F6
Broadview Ave. ME8 63 E8
Broadwater Ct. TN2 162 E8
Broadwater Down. TN2 162 F8
Broadwater Down Cty Prim Sch.
TN2 162 F8
Broadwater Gdns. BR6 51 C6
Broadwater House. DA12 13 D1
Broadwater La.
Royal Tunbridge Wells TN2 & TN4 148 F1
Broadwater La.
Royal Tunbridge Wells TN2 162 F8
Broadwater Rd. Well Street ME19 89 D6
Broadwater Rd. Woolwich SE18 2 D3
Broadwater Rise. TN2 148 F1
Broadway. Bexley DA6 7 F3
Broadway. Bexley DA6 & DA7 8 A3
Broadway. Crockenhill BR8 39 C3
Broadway. Gillingham ME8 49 A3
Broadway. Grays RM17 12 C8
Broadway. Maidstone ME16 91 F4
Broadway. Tilbury RM18 12 F5
Broadway Sh Ctr. 5 DA6 8 A3
Broadway The. Hadlow TN11 118 E8
Broadway The.
Lamberhurst TN3 166 B5
Broadwood. DA11 30 B3
Broadwood Rd. ME3 34 A4
Brock Rd. E13 1 B8
Brockenhurst Ave. ME15 92 C1
Brockenhurst Cl. ME8 63 C7
Brocklebank House. 7 E16 2 A5
Brocklebank Rd. SE7 1 B2
Brockway. TN15 87 A7
Brockwell Cl. BR5 37 F4
Brodrick Gr. SE2 3 B2
Brogden Cres. ME17 108 F7
Broke Farm Dr. BR6 52 C2
Brokes Way. TN4 149 B8
Brome House. SE18 5 E6
Brome Rd. SE9 5 F4
Bromhedge. SE9 22 F5
Bromholm Rd. SE2 3 B3
Bromley. RM17 11 F8
Bromley Cl. Chatham ME5 62 B4
Bromley Cl. Newington ME9 65 A5
Bromley Col
of Further & Higher Ed. BR2 36 D3
Bromley Comm. BR2 36 D3
Bromley General Hospl. BR1 36 B5
Bromley High Sch for Girls.
BR1 37 A5
Bromley Ind Est. BR1 36 D6
Bromley La. BR7 23 D1
Bromley Manor Mansions. 3
BR1 36 A6
Bromley North Sta. BR1 36 A8
Bromley Public Golf Course.
BR2 36 E2
Bromley Rd. BR7 37 B8
Bromley South Sta. BR2 36 A6
Bromley Valley Gymnastics Ctr.
BR5 38 A7
Brompton Dr. DA8 9 B7
Brompton Farm Rd. ME2 33 A2
Brompton Hill. ME4 47 F6
Brompton La. ME2 47 A8
Brompton Rd. ME7 48 B6
Brompton-Westbrook
Cty Prim Sch. ME7 48 A5
Bronington Cl. ME5 62 A5
Bronte Cl. Erith DA8 8 B7
Bronte Cl. Lunsford ME20 74 F3
Bronte Cl. Tilbury RM18 13 C5
Bronte Gr. DA1 9 F3
Bronte Sch. DA12 30 C7
Bronte View. DA12 30 C7
Brook. ME4 48 A4
Brook Cotts. Collier Street TN12 137 F8
Brook Cotts. Dean Street ME15 106 C7
Brook Ct. 10 TN8 112 D3
Brook General Hospl. SE18 5 E6
Brook Hill Cl. SE18 2 B1
Brook La. Bexley DA5 7 D2
Brook La. Bromley BR1 22 A2
Brook La. Greenwich SE3 5 B5
Brook La. Plaxtol Spoute TN15 102 A8
Brook La. Snodland ME6 75 A6
Brook La. Tonbridge TN9 117 D2
Brook Rd. Lunsford ME20 74 F4
Brook Rd. Northfleet DA11 29 E7
Brook Rd.
Royal Tunbridge Wells TN1 149 D7
Brook Rd. Swanley BR8 39 D7
Brook St. Erith DA8 8 B7
Brook St. Snodland ME6 75 B8
Brook St. Tonbridge TN9 133 A8
Brook Vale. DA8 8 B6
Brookbank. ME14 92 A8
Brookdale Rd. DA5 7 E1
Brookdene Rd. SE18 & SE2 2 F2
Brooke Dr. DA12 31 B7
Brookend Rd. DA15 23 E7
Brookes Pl. ME9 65 B6
Brookfield. Four Elms TN8 113 B5
Brookfield. Kemsing TN14 69 E2
Brookfield. Sandhurst TN18 186 B5
Brookfield Ave. ME20 75 A4
Brookfields. TN11 102 E1
Brookhill Rd. SE18 2 B1
Brookhurst Gdns. TN4 132 E3
Brooklands. Dartford DA1 26 E7
Brooklands. Headcorn TN27 141 C6
Brooklands.
Royal Tunbridge Wells TN1 149 D7
Brooklands Ave. DA15 23 D6
Brooklands Farm Cl. TN3 147 A6
Brooklands Pk. SE3 5 A4
Brooklands Prim Sch. SE3 5 A4
Brooklands Rd. ME20 75 A4
Brooklyn Paddock. ME7 48 D6
Brooklyn Rd. BR2 36 D4
Brooklyn Villas. TN12 138 C5
Brookmead. TN11 116 E4
Brookmead Ave. BR1 & BR2 36 F4
Brookmead Cl. BR6 38 B3
Brookmead Rd. ME3 33 B7
Brookmead Way. BR5 & BR6 38 B3
Brooks Cl. Eltham SE9 23 A6
Brooks Cl. Staplehurst TN12 139 E4
Brooks Pl. ME14 92 A4
Brookside. Cranbrook TN17 169 D4
Brookside. Hoo St Werburgh ME3 34 E5
Brookside. Orpington BR6 37 F2
Brookside Rd. DA13 29 F1
Brookway. SE3 5 A4
Broom Ave. BR5 38 B7
Broom Cl. BR2 36 E3
Broom Hill Rd. ME2 46 F8
Broom La. TN3 147 E2
Broom Mead. DA6 8 A2
Broom Pk. TN3 147 E3
Broomcroft Rd. ME8 49 F2
Broomfield House. 4 BR5 38 B7
Broomfield Rd. Bexley DA6 8 A2
Broomfield Rd.
Broomfield ME17 109 D4
Broomfield Rd. Sevenoaks TN13 83 F5
Broomfield Rd.
Swanscombe DA10 11 E2
Broomfields. DA3 42 E4
Broomhill Bank Sch. TN3 148 C6
Broomhill Park Rd. TN4 148 F8
Broomhill Rd. Dartford DA1 9 B1
Broomhill Rd. Orpington BR6 38 A2
Broomhill Rd.
Royal Tunbridge Wells TN3 148 D7
Broomhill Rise. DA6 8 A2
Broomhills. DA13 28 E4
Broomleigh. BR1 36 A8
Broomscroft Cotts. ME18 89 C1
Broomshaw Rd. ME16 90 F3
Broomwood Rd. BR5 38 B7
Brougham Ct. 2 DA2 10 B1
Broughton Rd. Orpington BR6 51 D8
Broughton Rd. Otford TN14 69 A3
Brow Cl. BR5 38 D2
Brow Cres. BR5 38 D2
Brown Rd. DA12 30 E7
Brown St. ME8 49 F1
Browndens Rd. ME2 59 E4
Brownelow Copse. ME5 62 B1
Brownhill Cl. ME5 62 A4
Browning Cl. Bexley DA16 6 E6
Browning Cl. 6 Lunsford ME20 74 F4
Browning Rd. DA1 9 F3
Browning Wlk. RM18 13 C5
Brownings. TN8 112 C4
Brownspring Dr. SE9 23 B5
Broxbourne Rd. BR6 37 F2
Bruce Cl. DA16 7 B6
Bruce Ct. DA15 23 F4
Bruce Gr. BR6 38 A1
Bruces Wharf Rd. RM17 12 A8
Brucks The. ME18 104 E7
Brummel Cl. DA7 8 C4
Brunel Cl. RM18 13 B4
Brunel Way. ME4 48 A7
Brungers Wlk. TN10 117 B5
Brunswick Cl. DA6 7 D3
Brunswick House Cty Prim Sch.
ME16 91 E5
Brunswick Rd. DA6 7 E3
Brunswick St. ME15 92 A3
Brunswick St E. ME15 92 A3
Brunswick Terr. TN1 149 A2
Brunswick Wlk. 1 DA12 30 D8
Brushwood Lodge. 1 DA17 4 A2
Bruton Cl. BR7 22 F1
Bryanston Rd. RM18 13 C5
Bryant Cl. ME18 104 D6
Bryant Rd. ME2 47 A7
Bryant St. ME4 48 A3
Bryony Sch (private). ME8 63 F5
Bubblestone Rd. TN14 69 B3
Buckden Cl. SE12 5 A1
Buckham Thorns Rd. TN16 81 C1
Buckhole Farm Rd. ME23 17 C4
Buckhurst Ave. TN15 84 C2
Buckhurst La. Rockrobin TN5 174 A6
Buckhurst La.
Sevenoaks TN13 & TN15 84 C2
Buckhurst Rd. TN16 81 B7
Buckingham Ave. DA16 6 E3
Buckingham Cl. BR5 37 E2
Buckingham Dr. BR7 23 C3
Buckingham Rd. Gillingham ME7 48 D5
Buckingham Rd. Northfleet DA11 29 D8
Buckingham Rd.
Royal Tunbridge Wells TN1 149 B2
Buckingham Row. ME15 107 E7
Buckland Cl. ME5 62 A2
Buckland Hill. ME16 91 E5
Buckland La. ME16 91 D6
Buckland Pl. ME16 91 E4
Buckland Rd. Cliffe Woods ME3 33 A8
Buckland Rd.
Lower Luddesdown DA13 59 A7
Buckland Rd. Maidstone ME16 91 E4
Buckland Rd. Orpington BR6 51 E6
Buckler Gdns. SE9 22 F5
Bucklers Cl. TN2 149 C3
Buckles Ct. SE2 3 D2
Buckley Cl. DA1 8 F5
Buckmore Park (Scout Camp).
ME5 61 C3
Bucks Cross Rd. Chelsfield BR6 52 F5
Bucks Cross Rd. Northfleet DA11 29 F5
Buckthorn House. DA15 23 F5
Buckwheat Ct. SE2 3 D3
Budd's Farm Cotts. TN30 189 F2
Budd's La. TN30 189 F2
Budgin's Hill. BR6 & TN14 67 C8
Budleigh Cres. DA16 7 C6
Bugglesden Rd. TN27 172 D5
Bugsby's Way. SE10 & SE7 1 A2
Bull Alley. DA16 7 B4
Bull Fields. ME6 75 A8
Bull Hill. ME17 127 F8
Bull La. Chislehurst BR7 23 D1
Bull La. Eccles ME20 75 F5
Bull La. Lower Higham ME3 32 D7
Bull La. Stockbury ME9 64 E2
Bull La. Wrotham TN15 72 A3
Bull Lane Cotts. TN3 165 C4
Bull Orch. ME16 90 F1
Bull Rd. ME19 74 C5
Bull Yd. 5 DA11 13 B1
Bullbanks Rd. DA17 4 C2
Bulldog Rd. ME5 62 B2
Bullen La. TN12 119 E7
Buller Rd. ME4 47 F2
Bullers Cl. DA14 24 E3
Bullers Wood Dr. BR7 22 F1
Bullers Wood Sch for Girls.
BR7 36 F8
Bullfinch Cl.
Paddock Wood TN12 136 A5
Bullfinch Cl. Sevenoaks TN13 83 D5
Bullfinch Cnr. TN13 83 E5
Bullfinch Dene. TN13 83 D5
Bullfinch La. TN13 83 E5
Bullingstone Cotts. TN3 147 E7
Bullingstone La. TN3 147 F7
Bullion Cl. TN12 135 F6
Bullivant Cl. DA9 11 A2
Bulls Pl. TN2 150 D6
Bulrush Cl. ME5 61 F3
Bumbles Cl. ME1 61 D7
Bungalows The. TN30 183 D7
Bunker's Hill. Erith DA17 4 A2
Bunker's Hill. Ridley TN15 57 B4
Bunkers Hill. DA14 24 F5
Bunny La. TN3 162 E5
Bunters Hill Rd. ME3 33 B4
Bunton St. SE18 2 A3
Burberry La. ME17 109 B5
Burch Rd. DA11 12 F1
Burcharbro Rd. SE2 7 D8
Burdett Ave. DA12 31 F4
Burdett Cl. DA14 24 E3
Burdett Rd. TN4 148 B4
Burford Rd. BR1 36 E5
Burgate Cl. DA1 8 F4
Burgess Hall Dr. ME17 108 F6
Burgess Rd. ME2 47 B7
Burgess Row. 8 TN30 183 A7
Burghclere Dr. ME16 91 B2
Burghfield Rd. DA13 29 F1
Burgoyne Ct. ME14 91 F7
Burham CE Prim Sch. ME1 75 F8
Burham Rd. ME1 60 E8
Burial Ground La. ME15 91 E1
Burleigh Ave. DA15 6 F2
Burleigh Cl. ME2 46 E8
Burleigh Dr. ME14 76 F1
Burley Rd. E16 1 C8
Burlings La. TN14 66 F2
Burlington Cl. 5 Newham E6 1 E7
Burlington Cl. Orpington BR6 51 B8
Burlington Gdns. ME8 63 E4
Burlington Lodge. BR7 22 F1
Burma Way. ME5 61 F6
Burman Cl. DA2 27 C8
Burmarsh Cl. ME5 62 B5
Burn's Rd. ME7 48 C7
Burnaby Rd. DA11 12 E1
Burnell Ave. DA16 7 A5
Burnett Rd. DA8 9 D8
Burnham Cres. DA1 9 C3
Burnham Rd. Dartford DA1 9 C3
Burnham Rd. Sidcup DA14 24 E6
Burnham Terr. DA1 9 D2
Burnham Trad Est. DA1 9 D3
Burnham Wlk. ME8 63 E3
Burnley Rd. RM16 11 A6
Burns Ave. DA15 7 B1
Burns Cl. Bexley DA16 6 F6
Burns Cl. Erith DA8 8 F6
Burns Cres. TN9 133 A7
Burns Pl. RM18 13 B6
Burns Rd. ME16 91 C2

Burnt Ash Hill. SE12 .... 22 A7
Burnt Ash La. BR1 & SE12 .... 22 B3
Burnt Ash Prim Sch. BR1 ...... 22 A3
Burnt House Cl. ME2 .... 33 C2
Burnt House La. Dartford DA1 .. 26 F5
Burnt House La. Hawley DA2 .. 26 F4
Burnt House La. Speldhurst TN3 148 A5
Burnt Lodge La. TN5 .... 176 B2
Burnt Oak Jun Mix Sch. DA15 .. 24 A7
Burnt Oak La. Sidcup DA15 ...... 7 A1
Burnt Oak La. Sidcup DA15 .... 24 B7
Burnt Oak Terr. ME7 .... 48 D6
Burntash Rd. ME20 .... 90 F8
Burnthouse La. TN27 .... 142 D1
Burntwood Gr. TN13 .... 99 B8
Burntwood Rd. TN13 .... 99 B7
Burr Bank Terr. DA2 .... 26 C4
Burr Cl. DA7 .... 7 F4
Burrage Gr. SE18 .... 2 C2
Burrage Pl. SE18 .... 2 B1
Burrage Rd. SE18 .... 2 C1
Burrard Rd. E16 .... 1 B7
Burrfield Dr. BR5 .... 38 D4
Burrows La. ME3 .... 19 C3
Burrswood Villas. TN3 .... 161 B7
Bursdon Cl. DA15 .... 23 F6
Burslem Rd. TN2 .... 149 E7
Bursted Wood Prim Sch. DA7 .... 8 B5
Burston Rd. ME17 .... 106 B2
Burt Rd. E16 .... 1 C5
Burwash Cl. BR5 .... 38 C4
Burwash Rd. SE18 .... 2 D1
Burwood Ave. BR2 .... 50 B8
Busbridge Rd. Loose ME15 .... 106 E6
Busbridge Rd. Snodland ME6 .. 74 E7
Bush Cl. ME9 .... 80 F5
Bush Rd. Cuxton ME2 .... 46 B2
Bush Rd. East Peckham TN12 .. 119 E8
Bush Row. ME20 .... 76 A3
Bushell Way. BR7 .... 23 A3
Bushey Ave. BR5 .... 37 D2
Bushey House. SE12 .... 22 C5
Bushey Lees. ME6 .... 6 F1
Bushfield Wlk. DA10 .... 28 E8
Bushmeadow Rd. ME8 .... 49 F2
Bushmoor Cres. SE18 .... 6 B1
Bushy Gill. TN3 .... 148 A3
Bushy Gr. ME17 .... 109 D2
Buston Farm Cotts. ME18 .... 105 B2
Busty La. TN15 .... 86 D6
Butcher Cl. TN12 .... 139 E3
Butcher Wlk. DA10 .... 28 E8
Butcher's La. ME19 .... 88 D1
Butchers La. TN15 .... 56 D8
Butchers Rd. E16 .... 1 A7
Butchers Yd. BR6 .... 66 A8
Butler House. ME17 RM17 .... 12 B8
Butler's Cotts. DA7 .... 8 A5
Butler's Pl. DA3 .... 56 E7
Butt Green La. ME17 .... 123 A7
Butt Law Cl. ME3 .... 34 E5
Butterfield Sq. E6 .... 1 F7
Butterfly Ave. DA1 .... 26 F6
Butterfly La. SE9 .... 6 B1
Buttermarsh Cl. SE18 .... 2 B1
Buttermere Cl. ME7 .... 49 A5
Buttermere Rd. BR5 .... 38 D5
Button Dr. ME3 .... 19 C5
Button House. ME3 .... 33 F6
Button La. ME15 .... 93 B2
Button St. BR8 .... 40 C5
Butts The. TN14 .... 69 B2
Buttway La. ME3 .... 16 A6
Buxton Cl. Chatham ME5 .... 62 D1
Buxton Cl. Maidstone ME15 .. 107 A8
Buxton Rd. DA8 .... 8 D7
Buzzard Creek Ind Est. IG11 .... 3 A8
Bychurch Pl. ME15 .... 92 A3
Bycliffe Mews. DA11 .... 29 F8
Bycliffe Terr. DA11 .... 29 F8
Byland Cl. SE2 .... 3 B3
Byng Rd. TN4 .... 148 F5
Bynon Ave. DA7 .... 7 F4
Byrneside. TN11 .... 116 E4
Byron Cl. SE28 .... 3 C5
Byron Cty Prim Sch. ME7 ...... 48 C3
Byron Dr. DA7 .... 8 B7
Byron Gdns. RM18 .... 13 C6
Byron Rd. Dartford DA1 .... 10 B3
Byron Rd. Gillingham ME7 ...... 48 C3
Byron Rd. Maidstone ME14 .... 92 B7

Cabbage Stalk La. TN4 .... 148 E2
Cacket's La. TN14 .... 66 E4
Cade La. TN13 .... 99 C7
Cadlocks Hill. TN14 .... 52 F1
Cadnam Cl. ME2 .... 46 E8
Cadogan Ave. DA2 .... 27 D8
Cadogan Gdns. TN1 .... 149 B4
Cadogan Rd. SE18 .... 2 C3
Cadwallon Rd. SE9 .... 23 C6
Caerleon Cl. DA14 .... 24 C3
Caernarvon Dr. ME15 .... 91 F1
Cage Green Cty Prim Sch.
  TN10 .... 117 D5
Cage Green Rd. TN10 .... 117 C5
Cage La. TN27 .... 142 F1
Cairns Cl. DA1 .... 9 D2
Caistor Rd. TN9 .... 117 A1
Caithness Gdns. DA15 .... 6 F1
Calais Cotts. DA3 .... 56 A8
Calcott Wlk. SE9 .... 22 D4
Calcutta House. ME15 .... 107 E5
Calcutta Rd. RM18 .... 13 A5
Calder Rd. ME4 .... 91 E7
Calderwood. DA12 .... 30 E2
Calderwood St. SE18 .... 2 A2
Caldew Ave. ME8 .... 49 C1

Caldy Rd. DA17 .... 4 B3
Caledonian Ct. ME8 .... 63 E8
Calehill Rd. ME14 .... 92 C6
Caley Rd. TN1 .... 149 D7
Calfstock La. DA4 .... 40 F5
Caling Croft. DA3 .... 42 F1
Caliph Cl. DA12 .... 30 F5
Callams Cl. ME8 .... 63 D6
Callaways La. ME9 .... 65 B6
Callshot Dr. DA2 .... 10 B1
Calverley Ct. TN2 .... 149 C3
Calverley Park Cres.
  TN1 & TN2 .... 149 B3
Calverley Park Gdns.
  TN1 & TN2 .... 149 C4
Calverley Pk. TN1 & TN2 .... 149 B3
Calverley Rd. TN1 & TN2 .... 149 B3
Calverley St. TN1 .... 149 B4
Calvert Cl. DA17 .... 4 B2
Calvert Cl. Sidcup DA14 .... 24 E2
Calverton Prim Sch. E16 .... 1 C7
Calvin Cl. BR5 .... 38 D6
Calydon Rd. SE7 .... 1 B1
Cambert Way. SE3 .... 5 B3
Camberwell La. TN14 .... 97 F4
Camborne Manor. ME7 .... 48 C6
Camborne Rd. Bexley DA16 ...... 6 F5
Camborne Rd. Sidcup DA14 .... 24 C5
Cambray Rd. BR6 .... 37 F2
Cambria Ave. ME1 .... 46 F2
Cambria Cl. DA15 .... 23 E7
Cambria Cres. DA12 .... 30 F4
Cambria House. DA8 .... 8 E7
Cambrian Gr. DA11 .... 30 A8
Cambrian Rd. TN4 .... 149 C7
Cambridge Ave. DA16 .... 6 F3
Cambridge Barracks Rd.
  SE18 .... 1 F2
Cambridge Cres. ME15 .... 107 D7
Cambridge Dr. SE12 .... 5 A2
Cambridge Gdns. ME8 .... 149 B2
Cambridge Gn. SE9 .... 23 B7
Cambridge House. ME15 ...... 107 D7
Cambridge Rd. Bromley BR1 .... 22 A1
Cambridge Rd. Gillingham ME8 .. 63 C6
Cambridge Rd. Rochester ME2 .. 47 C8
Cambridge Rd. Sidcup DA14 .... 23 E4
Cambridge Row. SE18 .... 2 B1
Cambridge St. TN2 .... 149 C3
Cambridge Terr. ME4 .... 47 F4
Cambus Rd. E16 .... 1 A8
Camdale Rd. SE18 .... 6 F7
Camden Ave. TN2 .... 150 C4
Camden Cl. Chatham ME5 ...... 62 B5
Camden Cl. Chislehurst BR7 .... 37 C8
Camden Cl. Northfleet DA11 .... 29 C7
Camden Cotts. TN17 .... 169 F8
Camden Cl. Erith DA17 .... 4 A1
Camden Ct. Pembury TN2 .... 150 D6
Camden Ct.
  Royal Tunbridge Wells TN1 .. 149 B4
Camden Gr. BR7 .... 23 B2
Camden Hill. TN2 .... 149 B3
Camden Park (Golf Course).
  BR7 .... 23 B1
Camden Park Rd. BR7 .... 23 A1
Camden Pk. TN2 .... 149 C2
Camden Rd. Gillingham ME7 .... 48 D7
Camden Rd.
  Royal Tunbridge Wells TN1 .. 149 B4
Camden Rd. Sevenoaks TN13 .. 84 B5
Camden Rd. Sidcup DA5 .... 24 F8
Camden St. ME14 .... 92 A5
Camden Terr. TN17 .... 169 F8
Camden Way. BR7 .... 23 A1
Camel Rd. E16 .... 1 D5
Camellia Cl. ME8 .... 63 D7
Camelot Cl. SE18 .... 2 D4
Camer Gdns. DA13 .... 44 C3
Camer Park (Ctry Pk). DA13 .. 44 C2
Camer Park Rd. DA13 .... 44 C2
Camer Rd. DA13 .... 44 C3
Camer St. DA13 .... 44 C3
Cameron Cl. Chatham ME5 .... 62 B8
Cameron Cl. Joyden's Wood DA5 25 E5
Cameron Rd. BR2 .... 36 A4
Camerons. TN18 .... 179 A2
Camomile Dr. ME14 .... 92 F5
Camp Site The. BR8 .... 25 A1
Camp Way. ME15 .... 107 C6
Campbell Cl. SE18 .... 6 A6
Campbell Rd. Gravesend DA11 .. 29 E8
Campbell Rd. Maidstone ME15 .. 92 A3
Campbell Rd.
  Royal Tunbridge Wells TN4 .. 149 A6
Campfield Rd. SE9 .... 22 D8
Campion Cl. Chatham ME5 ...... 61 E3
Campion Cl. Newham E6 .... 1 F6
Campion Cl. Northfleet DA11 .... 29 E4
Campion Cres. TN17 .... 169 A2
Campion Ct. RM17 .... 12 D8
Campion Pl. SE28 .... 3 B5
Campleshon Rd. ME8 .... 63 D5
Campus Way. ME7 .... 63 A8
Camrose Ave. DA8 .... 8 B8
Camrose St. SE2 .... 3 A2
Canada Farm Rd. DA4 .... 42 A6
Canada Rd. DA8 .... 9 B7
Canada Terr. ME4 .... 92 A7
Canadian Ave. ME7 .... 48 F4
Canal Basin. DA12 .... 13 D1
Canal Rd. Gravesend DA12 .... 13 D1
Canal Rd. Lower Higham ME3 .. 32 C6
Canal Rd. Rochester ME2 ...... 47 C7
Canal Road Ind Pk. DA12 .... 30 D8
Canberra Rd. Erith DA7 .... 7 D8
Canberra Rd. Greenwich SE7 .... 5 D8

Canberra Sq. RM18 .... 13 A5
Canbury Path. BR5 .... 38 A5
Canning St. ME4 .... 92 A6
Cannock Sch. BR6 .... 52 F5
Cannon Bridge Works. TN9 .. 117 D2
Cannon La. TN9 .... 117 D2
Cannon Pl. SE7 .... 1 E1
Cannon Rd. DA7 .... 7 F6
Canon Cl. ME1 .... 47 B2
Canon La. ME18 .... 89 C1
Canon Rd. BR1 .... 36 D6
Cansiron La. TN7 & TN8 ...... 144 E2
Canterbury Ave. DA14 & DA15 .. 24 C6
Canterbury Cl. Dartford DA1 .... 27 A8
Canterbury Cl. Newham E6 ...... 1 F7
Canterbury Cres. TN10 .... 117 D5
Canterbury House. Erith DA8 .... 8 F7
Canterbury House.
  Maidstone ME15 .... 107 D7
Canterbury Rd. Gravesend DA12 .. 30 C6
Canterbury Rd. Pembury TN2 .. 150 E6
Canterbury St. ME7 .... 48 C4
Canterbury Way. RM16 & DA1 .. 10 D5
Cantwell House. SE18 .... 6 B7
Cantwell Rd. SE18 .... 6 B7
Capel Cl. Gillingham ME8 ...... 63 D4
Capel Cl. Keston Mark BR2 .... 36 E1
Capel Cty Prim Sch. TN12 .... 134 F7
Capel Pl. DA2 .... 26 C4
Capelands. DA3 .... 57 A8
Capell Cl. ME17 .... 106 C3
Capetown House. ME15 .... 107 F5
Capstan Ctr. RM17 .... 12 E7
Capstan Ctr. RM17 .... 10 C3
Capstan Farm Country Pk.
  ME7 .... 62 D5
Capstone Rd. Chatham ME5 .... 62 B1
Capstone Rd. Gillingham ME7 .. 62 F6
Capstone Rd. Lewisham BR1 .... 22 A4
Captain's Cl. ME17 .... 124 E6
Captain's Wlk The. TN15 ...... 87 C7
Caraway Cl. E13 .... 1 B8
Cardens Rd. ME3 .... 33 B8
Cardiff St. SE18 .... 6 E7
Cardinal Cl. Chislehurst BR7 .... 37 D8
Cardinal Cl. Tonbridge TN9 .... 133 B8
Cardwell Prim Sch. SE18 .... 1 F2
Cardwell Rd. SE18 .... 2 A2
Carew House. SE18 .... 1 F2
Carey Ct. DA6 .... 8 B3
Carhaven House. DA8 .... 8 E7
Caring La. ME15 .... 93 E1
Caring Rd. ME15 .... 93 C1
Carisbrooke Ave. DA5 .... 24 D7
Carisbrooke Ct. ME16 .... 91 D4
Carisbrooke Dr. ME16 .... 91 D4
Carisbrooke Rd. Bromley BR2 .. 36 C5
Carisbrooke Rd. Rochester ME2 32 E1
Carl Ekman House. DA11 ...... 29 D8
Carleton Pl. DA4 .... 41 C5
Carleton Rd. DA1 .... 27 A8
Carlisle Cl. ME2 .... 46 C6
Carlisle Rd. DA1 .... 10 A1
Carlton Ave. Gillingham ME7 .. 48 E4
Carlton Ave. Stone DA9 .... 10 E1
Carlton Cres. Chatham ME5 .... 62 D8
Carlton Cres.
  Royal Tunbridge Wells TN2 .. 149 C4
Carlton Gdns. ME15 .... 107 B8
Carlton Par. BR5 .... 38 B2
Carlton Rd. Bexley DA5 .... 7 B4
Carlton Rd. Erith DA8 .... 8 C8
Carlton Rd.
  Royal Tunbridge Wells TN2 .. 149 C4
Carlton Rd. Sidcup DA14 ...... 23 F3
Carlyle Ave. ME1 .... 36 D6
Carlyle Rd. SE28 .... 3 C6
Carman's Cl. ME15 & ME17 .. 106 F3
Carmelite Way. DA3 .... 42 F4
Carnation Cl. ME19 & ME20 .. 75 A1
Carnation Cres. ME19 .... 74 F1
Carnation Rd. ME2 .... 46 D7
Carnation St. SE2 .... 3 B1
Carnbrook Rd. SE3 .... 5 D4
Carnecke Gdns. SE9 .... 5 E2
Caroline Cres. ME16 .... 91 D7
Carolyn Dr. BR6 .... 52 A7
Carpeaux Cl. ME4 .... 48 A4
Carpenters Cl. ME4 .... 48 A4
Carpenters La. Hadlow TN11 .. 102 D2
Carpenters La.
  Staplehurst TN12 .... 139 C8
Carpinus Cl. ME5 .... 62 B1
Carr Gr. SE18 .... 1 E2
Carrack House. DA8 .... 4 E1
Carriage Mus. ME15 .... 92 A3
Carriageway The. TN14 .... 82 D3
Carrick Dr. TN13 .... 84 B4
Carrie House. ME16 .... 91 E5
Carriers Pl. TN3 .... 146 B3
Carriers Rd. TN17 .... 169 D5
Carrill Way. DA17 .... 3 D3
Carrington Rd. DA1 .... 10 A1
Carroll Gdns. ME20 .... 74 F3
Carronade Pl. SE28 .... 2 C3
Carsington Gdns. DA1 .... 26 C6
Carson Rd. E16 .... 1 A8
Carston Cl. SE12 & SE13 ...... 5 A2
Carter's Hill. TN15 .... 100 B6
Carters Hill Cl. SE9 .... 22 C7
Carters Hill La. DA13 .... 57 F2
Carters Row. DA11 .... 29 F6
Cartmel Rd. DA7 .... 8 A6
Carton Cl. ME1 .... 47 A4
Carton Rd. ME3 .... 32 B3
Carville Ave. TN4 .... 132 F1
Carvoran Way. ME8 .... 63 C5

Cascade Cl. BR5 .... 38 C6
Cascades L Ctr. DA12 .... 31 A4
Caspian Wlk. E16 .... 1 D7
Cassida Rd. SE2 .... 3 A2
Casstine Ct. BR8 .... 25 F1
Castalia Ct. DA1 .... 9 F4
Casterbridge Rd. SE3 .... 5 A4
Castile Rd. SE18 .... 2 A2
Castilion Prim Sch. SE28 .... 3 C7
Castilla House. BR1 .... 22 B1
Castle Ave. ME1 .... 47 C4
Castle Dene. ME14 .... 91 F8
Castle Dr. TN14 .... 69 E2
Castle Farm Rd. TN14 .... 54 A3
Castle Fields. TN9 .... 117 B2
Castle Hill. Hartley DA3 .... 42 E4
Castle Hill. Rochester ME1 .... 47 C6
Castle Hill. Thurnham ME14 .. 78 D1
Castle Hill. Tonbridge TN11 .. 133 F5
Castle Hurst. TN32 .... 185 B1
Castle La. DA12 .... 31 B6
Castle Rd. Chatham ME4 .... 48 B2
Castle Rd. Eynsford DA4 .... 54 C5
Castle Rd. Grays RM17 .... 11 F8
Castle Rd. Maidstone ME16 .... 91 D7
Castle Rd.
  Royal Tunbridge Wells TN4 .. 149 A3
Castle Rd. Swanscombe DA10 .. 11 F1
Castle St. 2 Royal Tunbridge Wells,
  Mount Sion TN1 .... 149 A2
Castle St. Stone DA9 .... 11 A2
Castle St. Swanscombe DA10 .. 11 F1
Castle St. Tonbridge TN9 ...... 117 C2
Castle St. Upper Upton ME2 .. 33 E1
Castle St. Wouldham ME1 ...... 60 C4
Castle Terr. Hadlow TN11 .... 118 E8
Castle Terr. Hawkhurst TN18 .. 178 F3
Castle View Rd. ME2 .... 47 A7
Castle Way. ME19 .... 74 D2
Castle Wlk. TN5 .... 174 E4
Castlecombe Prim Sch. SE9 .... 22 E3
Castlecombe Rd. SE9 .... 22 E3
Castlefields. DA13 .... 43 F8
Castleford Ave. SE9 .... 23 B7
Castlemaine Ave. ME7 .... 48 F6
Castleton Ave. DA7 .... 8 D5
Castleton Rd. SE12 & SE9 .... 22 D4
Castlewood Day Hospl. SE18 .... 6 A6
Castlewood Dr. SE9 .... 5 F5
Cates Ct. TN12 .... 120 A7
Cathcart Dr. BR6 .... 37 E1
Catherine Cl. ME16 .... 91 A3
Catherine Pl. TN1 .... 149 B4
Catherine St. ME1 .... 47 D3
Catkin Cl. ME5 .... 61 F1
Catlyn Cl. ME19 .... 90 A8
Catterick Rd. ME5 .... 62 D2
Cattistock Rd. SE9 .... 22 F3
Catts Pl. TN12 .... 136 C4
Causton Rd. TN17 .... 169 C5
Cave Hill. ME15 .... 91 F1
Cavell Cres. DA1 .... 10 B3
Cavendish Ave. Bexley DA16 .... 6 F4
Cavendish Ave. Erith DA8 ...... 8 C8
Cavendish Ave. Gillingham ME7 .. 48 E6
Cavendish Ave. Sevenoaks TN13 84 A1
Cavendish Ave. Sidcup DA15 .. 24 A8
Cavendish Cl. TN10 .... 117 D7
Cavendish Ct. TN9 .... 117 D3
Cavendish Dr. TN2 .... 149 B1
Cavendish Rd. ME1 .... 47 D3
Cavendish Sq. DA3 .... 42 D6
Cavendish Way. ME15 .... 93 B3
Caverley Rd. TN1 .... 149 B4
Caversham Cl. ME8 .... 49 F1
Caveside Cl. BR7 .... 37 A8
Caxton Cl. Hartley DA3 .... 42 E4
Caxton Cl. Tenterden TN30 .. 182 F7
Caxton La. TN11 .... 118 E8
Cayser Dr. ME17 .... 109 E2
Cazeneuve St. ME1 .... 47 C5
Cecil Ave. Gillingham ME8 .... 49 A2
Cecil Ave. Rochester ME2 ...... 47 B8
Cecil Rd. Gravesend DA11 .... 29 F7
Cecil Rd. Rochester ME1 ...... 47 C3
Cecil Road Cty Prim Sch. DA11 29 F7
Cecil Way. BR2 .... 36 A1
Cedar Ave. Gravesend DA12 .. 30 C4
Cedar Ave. Sidcup DA15 ...... 24 A8
Cedar Cl. Bromley BR1 .... 36 F4
Cedar Cl. Keston Mark BR2 .. 50 E7
Cedar Cl. Meopham Station DA13 44 A3
Cedar Cl. Swanley BR8 .... 39 C7
Cedar Copse. BR1 .... 36 F7
Cedar Cres. Keston Mark BR2 .. 50 E7
Cedar Cres. Tonbridge TN10 .. 117 C7
Cedar Ct. Eltham SE9 .... 5 E1
Cedar Ct. Greenwich SE7 .... 5 C8
Cedar Ct.
  Royal Tunbridge Wells TN4 .. 149 A5
Cedar Ct. Tenterden TN30 .... 183 A7
Cedar Dr. Edenbridge TN8 .... 112 D2
Cedar Dr. Maidstone ME16 .... 90 E2
Cedar Dr. Sutton at Hone DA4 .. 41 B7
Cedar Gdns. ME9 .... 79 D8
Cedar Gr. Gillingham ME7 .... 63 A5
Cedar Gr. Sidcup DA5 .... 7 D1
Cedar Lodge. TN4 .... 148 F3
Cedar Mount. SE9 .... 22 D7
Cedar Pl. SE7 .... 1 C1
Cedar Rd. Bromley BR1 .... 36 C7
Cedar Rd. Dartford DA1 .... 26 D7
Cedar Rd. Erith DA8 .... 9 A6
Cedar Rd. Hoo St Werburgh ME3 34 E3
Cedar Rd. Rochester ME2 ...... 46 F6
Cedar Ridge. TN2 .... 149 D5

Cedar Terrace Rd. TN13 .... 84 C4
Cedarhurst Dr. SE9 .... 5 C2
Cedarmore Ct. BR7 .... 37 C8
Cedars Sch The. Maidstone ME16 91 D4
Cedars Sch The. Rochester ME1 47 C4
Cedars The. TN12 .... 136 A7
Cedarwood House. ME15 ...... 106 B6
Cedric Rd. SE9 .... 23 C5
Celandine Dr. SE28 .... 3 B5
Celestine Cl. ME5 .... 62 A1
Cement Block Cotts. RM17 .... 12 C8
Cement Industry Heritage Ctr.
  DA11 .... 12 B2
Cemetery La. Hadlow TN11 .. 103 A1
Cemetery La. Woolwich SE7 .... 5 E8
Cemetery Rd. Halling ME7 .... 60 A4
Cemetery Rd. Snodland ME6 .. 59 F1
Cemetery Rd. Woolwich SE2 .... 7 B7
Centenary Ct. DA4 .... 41 A2
Central Ave. Bexley DA16 .... 7 A5
Central Ave. Gillingham ME4 .. 48 B8
Central Ave. Gravesend DA12 .. 30 B5
Central Ave. Tilbury RM18 .... 13 A6
Central Bsns Pk. ME2 .... 47 E7
Central Cl. SE28 .... 2 B2
Central Lodge. TN15 .... 72 E6
Central Par. ME1 .... 47 D2
Central Par Villas. BR5 .... 38 C7
Central Park Gdns. ME1 .... 47 E2
Central Rd. Dartford DA1 .... 9 E2
Central Rd. New Hythe ME20 .. 75 B4
Central Rd. Rochester ME2 .... 47 A7
Central Sta. TN1 .... 149 A3
Central Terr. ME4 .... 33 F6
Central Way. SE28 .... 3 B6
Centre 2000. ME1 .... 91 C8
Centre Common Rd. BR7 ...... 23 C1
Centre Ct. ME2 .... 47 E7
Centre Rd. DA3 .... 56 E7
Centurion Way. DA18 .... 4 A3
Centurion Cl. ME7 .... 48 F1
Century Rd. ME8 .... 63 D8
Ceres Rd. SE18 .... 2 F2
Cerne Rd. DA12 .... 30 E5
Cervia Way. DA12 .... 30 F5
Chada Ave. ME7 .... 48 E3
Chadd Dr. BR1 .... 36 E6
Chadfields. RM18 .... 13 A7
Chadwell Hill. RM17 .... 13 A8
Chadwick Cl. DA11 .... 29 E5
Chadwick Ct. SE28 .... 3 B5
Chadwick Way. SE28 .... 3 D6
Chadwin Rd. E13 .... 1 B8
Chaffey House. SE7 .... 1 C1
Chaffinch Cl. ME5 .... 62 A7
Chaffinch Way. TN12 .... 136 A5
Chafford Cotts. TN3 .... 146 F5
Chafford La. TN3 .... 146 F5
Chain Gate. TN27 .... 127 A8
Chalcombe Rd. SE2 .... 3 B3
Chalet Cl. DA2 .... 25 D4
Chalfont Dr. ME8 .... 63 D6
Chalice Way. DA9 .... 10 F2
Chalk Ave. TN30 .... 173 B2
Chalk Ct. RM17 .... 12 A8
Chalk Pit Ave. BR5 .... 38 D6
Chalk Pit Hill. ME4 .... 48 A3
Chalk Rd. Chalk DA12 .... 31 A6
Chalk Rd. Lower Higham ME3 .. 32 C6
Chalk Rd. Newham E13 .... 1 C8
Chalkenden Ave. ME8 .... 49 A2
Chalket La. TN2 .... 150 C5
Chalkpit Cotts. DA12 .... 31 E5
Chalkstone Cl. DA16 .... 7 A6
Chalkways. TN14 .... 69 F3
Chalky Bank. DA11 .... 30 A3
Chalky Rd. ME9 .... 79 C6
Challenge Cl. DA12 .... 30 F4
Challenger Cl. TN12 .... 135 F6
Challock House. Erith DA8 ...... 8 F7
Challock House.
  Orpington BR5 .... 38 D1
Challock Wlk. ME14 .... 92 C5
Chamberlain Ave. ME16 .... 91 C2
Chamberlain Cl. SE18 .... 2 D3
Chamberlain Rd. ME8 .... 63 B5
Chamberlain Rd. ME4 .... 48 B2
Chancel Cl. TN15 .... 55 E3
Chancellor House. TN4 .... 148 F3
Chancellor Way. TN13 .... 84 A5
Chancelot Rd. SE2 .... 3 B2
Chancery Ct. DA1 .... 27 A7
Chancery La. ME15 .... 92 B3
Chancery Rd. ME3 .... 16 B5
Chanctonbury Cl. SE9 .... 23 B5
Chandler Ave. E16 .... 1 A8
Chandler's Hill. DA13 .... 58 C5
Chandler's Rd. DA13 .... 58 C5
Chandlers Dr. DA8 .... 4 E2
Chandos Rd. TN1 .... 149 C5
Chantler's Hill. TN12 .... 136 A4
Chantlers Mead. TN8 .... 145 A5
Chantrey Cl. DA14 .... 24 E3
Chantry Ave. DA3 .... 42 E3
Chantry Cl. DA1 .... 13 C1
Chantry Cty Prim Schs. DA12 .. 13 C1
Chantry La. BR2 .... 36 D4
Chantry Pl. TN12 .... 138 C6
Chantry Rd. TN12 .... 138 C6
Chapel Alley Cotts. TN14 ...... 69 A8
Chapel Cl. Crayford DA1 .... 8 E2
Chapel Cl. Ryarsh ME19 .... 73 F5
Chapel Cl. West Thurrock RM16 .. 11 B8
Chapel Cotts. ME17 .... 108 F5
Chapel Ct. DA10 .... 11 E1

Chapel Farm Rd. SE9 22 F6
Chapel Field Cotts. DA4 41 B8
Chapel Hill. DA1 8 E2
Chapel Houses. ME2 59 E4
Chapel La. Gillingham,Hempstead ME7 63 A4
Chapel La. Gillingham,Lidsing ME7 63 A2
Chapel La. Iden Green TN17 180 C4
Chapel La. Maidstone ME14 93 A5
Chapel La. Potter's Forstal TN27 127 B2
Chapel La. Sissinghurst TN17 170 B7
Chapel La. Staplehurst TN12 139 F3
Chapel La. Upper Halling ME2 59 C4
Chapel Pl. 8 Royal Tunbridge Wells TN1 149 A2
Chapel Pl. Ticehurst TN5 176 E1
Chapel Rd. Bexley DA7 8 A3
Chapel Rd. Grain ME3 21 B5
Chapel Rd. Snodland ME6 75 A8
Chapel Rd. Sutton Valence ME17 124 E7
Chapel Row. Ightham TN15 86 C6
Chapel Row. Lower Stoke ME3 19 C4
Chapel St. East Malling ME19 90 A6
Chapel St. Ryarsh ME19 73 F5
Chapel View. TN15 86 C6
Chapel Wlk. TN14 98 B5
Chapel Wood. DA3 56 E8
Chapel Wood Rd. DA3 56 E8
Chaplin Dr. TN27 141 D5
Chapman Ave. ME15 107 F8
Chapman Rd. DA17 4 B1
Chapman Way. East Malling ME19 89 F8
Chapman Way. Royal Tunbridge Wells TN4 149 C8
Chapman's Hill. DA13 & TN15 57 E4
Chapman's La. Hockenden BR8 39 A7
Chapman's La. St Paul's Cray BR5 38 D7
Chapmans End. BR5 38 E7
Chapmans Rd. TN14 82 E3
Chapter Rd. ME2 46 F8
Chapter Sch. ME2 46 E8
Chardwell Cl. E6 1 F7
Charford Rd. E16 1 A8
Charing Cl. BR6 51 F6
Charing House. 5 DA8 8 F7
Charing Rd. ME8 49 B3
Chariot Way. ME2 46 F4
Charity Farm Cotts. TN17 156 F7
Charlbury Cl. ME16 91 C3
Charldane Rd. SE9 23 B5
Charlecote Ct. ME8 63 D8
Charles Busby Ct. 2 ME20 75 F1
Charles Cl. Sidcup DA14 24 B4
Charles Cl. Snodland ME6 75 A8
Charles Ct. Erith DA8 8 E8
Charles Ct. Royal Tunbridge Wells TN2 149 C3
Charles Dickens Ave. ME2 32 C2
Charles Dr. ME2 46 B2
Charles Grinling Wlk. SE18 2 A2
Charles Rd. TN14 53 B1
Charles St. Chatham ME4 47 E3
Charles St. Grays RM17 12 C8
Charles St. Maidstone ME16 91 E3
Charles St. Newham E16 1 C5
Charles St. Rochester ME2 47 A7
Charles St. Royal Tunbridge Wells TN4 149 A8
Charles St. Stone DA9 10 F2
Charlesfield. SE12 22 C5
Charlesford Ave. ME17 109 D3
Charlieville Rd. DA8 8 C7
Charlotte Cl. Bexley DA6 7 E2
Charlotte Cl. Chatham ME5 62 B6
Charlotte Dr. ME8 49 C1
Charlotte Park Ave. BR1 36 E6
Charlotte Pl. RM16 11 B8
Charlottes Cotts. TN11 115 F1
Charlton Church La. SE7 1 C1
Charlton Dene. SE7 5 D7
Charlton La. Chartway Street ME17 125 C8
Charlton La. Greenwich SE7 1 D1
Charlton La. West Farleigh ME15 105 E6
Charlton Manor. ME7 48 B5
Charlton Manor Prim Sch. SE7 5 D7
Charlton Park La. SE7 5 E8
Charlton Park Rd. SE7 5 D8
Charlton Park Sch. SE7 5 E8
Charlton Rd. SE3 & SE7 5 B8
Charlton St. Grays RM16 11 D8
Charlton St. Maidstone ME16 91 C2
Charlton's Way. TN4 148 E1
Charminster Rd. SE12 & SE9 22 D4
Charmouth Rd. DA16 7 C6
Charmwood La. BR6 52 B1
Charmwood Villas. BR6 52 C1
Charne The. TN14 69 A2
Charnock. BR8 39 E5
Chart Cnr. ME17 108 B1
Chart Hill Rd. ME17 124 A7
Chart Hills Golf Course. TN27 158 A5
Chart La. TN16 97 B7
Chart Pl. ME8 63 C3
Chart Rd. ME17 124 C7
Chart View. TN15 70 B2
Charter Dr. DA5 24 E8
Charter St. Chatham ME4 47 F2
Charter St. Gillingham ME7 48 C7
Charterhouse Dr. TN13 84 A4
Charterhouse Rd. BR6 52 A6
Charton Cl. 5 DA17 7 F8
Chartway. TN13 & TN15 84 C3
Chartway St. ME17 109 C1
Chartwell Cl. Rochester ME2 33 B1
Chartwell Cl. Sidcup BR7 23 D6
Chartwell Dr. BR6 51 D5
Chartwell (National Trust). TN16 96 F4
Chase Sq. 12 DA11 13 B1
Chase The. Bexley DA7 8 B4
Chase The. Bromley BR1 36 B6
Chase The. Chatham ME1 47 D2
Chase The. Gillingham ME8 49 A2
Chase The. Kemsing TN14 69 E3
Chase The. Pratt's Bottom BR6 & TN14 52 A1
Chase The. Tonbridge TN10 117 C5
Chase The. West Thurrock RM16 11 D8
Chastilian Rd. DA1 26 A8
Chatham Ave. BR2 36 A2
Chatham Gr. ME4 47 F1
Chatham Gram Sch for Boys. ME4 61 F8
Chatham Gram Sch for Girls. ME5 48 C2
Chatham Hill. ME4 48 B3
Chatham Hill Rd. TN14 84 C6
Chatham Historic Dockyard. ME4 48 A7
Chatham House. 22 SE18 1 F2
Chatham Rd. Chatham ME20 76 D8
Chatham Rd. Kit's Coty ME20 76 D6
Chatham Rd. Kit's Coty ME20 76 D7
Chatham Rd. Maidstone ME14 76 E1
Chatham Rd. Sandling ME14 76 E3
Chatham Rd. Sandling ME14 76 E4
Chatham Ski Ctr. ME7 62 E6
Chatham South Sec Sch. ME4 61 F8
Chatham St. SE18 2 B3
Chatham Sta. ME4 47 E4
Chatsworth Ave. Bromley BR1 22 B4
Chatsworth Ave. Sidcup DA15 24 A7
Chatsworth Dr. ME2 33 B1
Chatsworth House. 3 BR2 36 A5
Chatsworth Inf Sch. DA15 24 A7
Chatsworth Par. BR5 37 C4
Chatsworth Rd. Dartford DA1 9 C3
Chatsworth Rd. Gillingham ME7 48 C6
Chattenden Barracks Royal Sch of Military Engineering. ME3 33 F5
Chattenden Ct. ME14 92 B6
Chattenden Cty Prim Sch. ME3 33 F4
Chattenden La. ME3 33 F5
Chattenden Terr. ME3 33 F4
Chatterton Rd. BR2 36 D4
Chaucer Cl. Rochester ME2 47 E8
Chaucer Cl. Tilbury RM18 13 C5
Chaucer Gdns. TN9 132 F7
Chaucer Ind Pk. TN15 85 D8
Chaucer Pk. DA1 26 F8
Chaucer Rd. Bexley DA16 6 F6
Chaucer Rd. Gillingham ME7 48 D3
Chaucer Rd. Northfleet DA11 29 D5
Chaucer Rd. Sidcup DA15 24 C7
Chaucer Way. ME20 75 A3
Chaundrye Cl. SE9 5 F1
Chauntler Cl. E16 1 B6
Chauser Way. 2 DA1 10 A3
Chave Rd. DA1 26 E5
Cheeselands. TN27 157 F2
Cheffins House. ME7 48 E7
Chegwell Dr. ME5 62 B4
Chegworth La. ME17 110 A6
Chegworth Rd. ME17 109 F5
Chelmar Rd. ME7 48 B4
Chelmsford Cl. E6 1 F7
Chelmsford Rd. ME2 46 D6
Chelsfield Hill. BR6 52 C2
Chelsfield La. Badgers Mount BR6 & TN14 53 B2
Chelsfield La. Chelsfield BR5 & BR6 52 D7
Chelsfield La. Orpington BR5 38 D2
Chelsfield Lakes Golf Course. BR6 52 E3
Chelsfield Park Hospl. BR6 52 F5
Chelsfield Prim Sch. BR6 52 E5
Chelsfield Rd. BR5 38 C3
Chelsfield Sta. BR6 52 B5
Chelsiter Ct. DA14 23 F4
Chelsworth Dr. SE18 6 D8
Cheltenham Cl. Gravesend DA12 30 C3
Cheltenham Cl. Maidstone ME15 107 F6
Cheltenham Rd. BR6 52 A7
Cheney Cl. ME8 63 D5
Cheney's Cotts. DA12 31 A2
Chenies Cl. TN2 163 A8
Chenies The. Joyden's Wood DA2 25 E4
Chenies The. Orpington BR5 & BR6 37 E3
Chennell Park Rd. TN30 172 E1
Chennels The. TN26 173 C7
Chepstow House. 3 ME15 107 F6
Chequer's Cotts. TN17 153 F1
Chequers Cl. Chatham ME5 77 A8
Chequers Cl. Istead Rise DA13 43 F7
Chequers Cl. St Paul's Cray BR5 37 F5
Chequers Ctr. ME15 92 A4
Chequers Hill Cotts. TN8 114 A2
Chequers La. RM9 3 F8
Cherbourg Cres. ME5 61 F7
Cherbury Cl. SE28 3 E6
Cheriton Ave. BR2 36 A4
Cheriton Ct. 7 SE12 22 A8
Cheriton Dr. SE18 6 D8
Cheriton Rd. ME8 63 D8
Cheriton Way. ME16 91 C7
Cherries The. ME16 91 A2
Cherry Amber Cl. ME8 63 F8
Cherry Ave. BR8 39 D5
Cherry Ct. DA14 24 B5
Cherry Gr. TN10 117 E5
Cherry Hill Ct. ME9 65 B6
Cherry Lodge Golf Course. TN16 66 A2
Cherry Orch. Ditton ME19 90 C8
Cherry Orch. Greenwich SE7 5 C8
Cherry Orch. Tenterden TN30 183 A6
Cherry Orch The. TN11 102 E1
Cherry Orchard Cl. BR5 38 C4
Cherry Orchard Inf Sch. SE7 5 C7
Cherry Orchard Rd. BR2 50 E8
Cherry Orchard Way. ME16 91 B3
Cherry Rd. ME3 34 E3
Cherry Tree Cl. RM17 12 C8
Cherry Tree Ct. 17 SE7 5 C8
Cherry Tree Gr. DA4 55 B1
Cherry Tree La. DA2 25 F5
Cherry Tree Rd. Gillingham ME8 63 F8
Cherry Tree Rd. Royal Tunbridge Wells TN2 148 E1
Cherry Trees. DA3 42 F4
Cherry View. ME17 107 B3
Cherry Wlk. BR2 36 A1
Cherrycot Hill. BR6 51 D6
Cherrycot Rise. BR6 51 C6
Cherrydown Rd. DA14 24 D6
Cherryfields. TN17 180 D6
Cherrywood Dr. DA11 29 E5
Chervil Mews. SE28 3 B5
Chervilles. ME16 91 A2
Cherwell Cl. TN10 117 B4
Chesfield Cl. TN11 102 F1
Chesham Ave. BR2 & BR5 37 B3
Chesham Dr. ME8 63 E6
Cheshire Rd. Maidstone,Shepway ME15 107 E7
Cheshire Rd. Maidstone,Willington ME15 92 E2
Cheshunt Cl. DA13 44 A3
Cheshunt Rd. DA17 4 A1
Chessenden La. TN27 143 A1
Chessington Ave. DA7 7 E7
Chester Ave. TN2 149 D2
Chester Cl. ME2 46 D6
Chester Rd. Gillingham ME7 48 D2
Chester Rd. Sidcup DA15 6 E2
Chesterfield Cl. BR5 38 D5
Chesterfield Dr. Dartford DA1 9 B2
Chesterfield Dr. Sevenoaks TN13 83 D5
Chesterfield Dr. Sevenoaks TN13 83 E5
Chesterford House. SE18 5 D7
Chesterton Rd. 5 ME20 74 F4
Chesterton Way. RM18 13 C5
Chestfield Cl. ME8 49 E2
Chestnut Ave. Chatham ME5 61 F3
Chestnut Ave. Hill Park TN16 81 A6
Chestnut Ave. Royal Tunbridge Wells TN4 149 B8
Chestnut Ave. Staplehurst TN12 139 F4
Chestnut Cl. Edenbridge TN8 112 B2
Chestnut Cl. Frittenden TN17 156 E6
Chestnut Cl. Kings Hill ME19 89 A2
Chestnut Cl. Northfleet DA11 12 F1
Chestnut Cl. Orpington BR6 52 A5
Chestnut Cl. Royal Tunbridge Wells TN4 149 B8
Chestnut Cl. Tenterden TN30 173 C1
Chestnut Cl. Ulcombe ME17 125 F6
Chestnut Dr. Bexley DA7 7 E4
Chestnut Dr. Coxheath ME17 106 B3
Chestnut Dr. Kingswood ME17 109 D2
Chestnut Gr. DA2 25 E4
Chestnut La. Matfield TN12 135 D1
Chestnut La. Sevenoaks TN13 84 B3
Chestnut La. Vigo Village DA13 73 B8
Chestnut Pl. TN8 145 A5
Chestnut Rd. Dartford DA1 26 D7
Chestnut Rd. Rochester ME2 46 E6
Chestnut Rise. SE18 2 E1
Chestnut St. ME9 65 E4
Chestnut Wlk. Larkfield ME20 75 B2
Chestnut Wlk. Sevenoaks TN15 99 F6
Chestnut Wlk. Tonbridge TN9 116 F2
Chestnut Wood La. ME9 65 E3
Chestnuts The. Addington ME19 73 C3
Chestnuts The. 10 Erith DA17 4 A1
Chestnuts The. The Moor TN18 184 F8
Chestnuts The. Woolwich SE18 6 B6
Cheswick Cl. DA1 8 F3
Chesworth Cl. DA8 8 E5
Chetney Cl. ME2 46 C7
Chetwood Wlk. 14 E6 1 E8
Cheveney Wlk. 2 BR2 36 A6
Chevening CE Prim Sch. TN13 83 B5
Chevening Cl. ME5 62 A5
Chevening Ct. BR6 52 A8
Chevening House. BR5 38 A8
Chevening La. TN14 67 E3
Chevening Rd. 2 Greenwich SE10 1 A1
Chevening Rd. Sevenoaks TN13 & TN14 83 B6
Chevening Rd. Sundridge TN14 82 F4
Chevenings The. DA14 24 C5
Cheviot Cl. Erith DA7 8 E5
Cheviot Cl. Tonbridge TN9 117 C4
Cheviot Gdns. ME15 93 A1
Chevron Cl. E16 1 A7
Chevron House. RM17 12 B7
Cheyne Cl. BR2 50 E7
Cheyne Wlk. Longfield DA3 42 D6
Cheyne Wlk. Meopham DA13 58 A8
Chicago Ave. ME7 48 F5
Chichester Cl. Gillingham ME8 64 A8
Chichester Cl. Greenwich SE3 5 C6
Chichester Cl. Newham E6 1 E7
Chichester Ct. 3 DA5 25 A8
Chichester Dr. TN13 83 F2
Chichester Rd. Stone DA9 10 F1
Chichester Rd. Tonbridge TN9 133 A8
Chichester Rise. DA12 30 D4
Chickfield Gdns. ME5 48 C2
Chicks La. TN17 167 A2
Chiddingstone Ave. DA7 7 F7
Chiddingstone Castle. TN8 130 B7
Chiddingstone CE Prim Sch. TN8 130 C7
Chiddingstone Cl. ME15 107 F6
Chidley Cross Rd. TN12 119 E6
Chieftain Cl. ME7 49 B1
Chieveley Dr. TN2 149 D1
Chieveley Par. DA7 8 B4
Chieveley Rd. DA7 8 B3
Chiffinch Gdns. DA11 29 E5
Childs Cres. DA10 11 D1
Childs Way. TN15 71 F3
Childsbridge La. TN14 & TN15 84 F7
Childsbridge Way. TN15 84 F7
Childscroft Rd. ME8 49 F2
Chilham Cl. Chatham ME4 47 E3
Chilham Cl. Sidcup DA5 24 F8
Chilham House. ME2 33 C1
Chilham Rd. Chislehurst SE9 22 E4
Chilham Rd. Gillingham ME8 49 A3
Chilham Rd. Maidstone ME16 91 C7
Chilham Way. BR2 36 A2
Chillington Cl. ME2 59 E4
Chillington St. ME14 91 F6
Chilliwack Rd. ME3 33 F5
Chilston Cl. TN4 149 A5
Chilston Rd. Lenham ME17 111 D5
Chilston Rd. Royal Tunbridge Wells TN4 149 A5
Chiltern Cl. Erith DA7 8 E6
Chiltern Cl. Maidstone ME15 92 F1
Chiltern Ct. 11 SE9 6 A1
Chiltern Rd. DA11 29 E5
Chiltern Way. TN9 117 C4
Chiltern Wlk. TN2 149 D4
Chilton Ct. ME8 49 E1
Chilton Dr. ME3 32 B3
Chimes The. ME1 47 C5
Chinbrook Cres. SE12 22 B5
Chinbrook Rd. SE12 22 B5
Chippendale Cl. ME5 61 F1
Chippendale Dr. ME17 110 D6
Chipperfield Rd. BR5 38 A7
Chipstead Cl. ME16 91 D6
Chipstead La. TN13 83 D5
Chipstead Park Cl. TN13 83 C5
Chipstead Pk. TN13 83 D5
Chipstead Place Gdns. TN13 83 D5
Chipstead Rd. Erith DA8 8 E7
Chipstead Rd. Gillingham ME8 63 D4
Chipstead Sq. TN13 83 C5
Chislehurst CE Prim Sch. BR7 23 C1
Chislehurst Cl. ME15 107 F6
Chislehurst High St. BR7 23 B2
Chislehurst Rd. Bromley BR1 & BR7 36 E8
Chislehurst Rd. Orpington,Broom Hill BR6 38 A2
Chislehurst Rd.Orpington,Petts Wood BR5 & BR6 & BR7 37 E4
Chislehurst Rd. Sidcup DA14 24 A3
Chislehurst & Sidcup Gram Sch. DA15 24 B6
Chislehurst Sta. BR7 37 A7
Chislet Wlk. ME8 63 D5
Chiswell Sq. SE3 5 B5
Chorleywood Cres. BR5 38 A7
Christ Church Ave. Erith DA8 8 E8
Christ Church Ave. 1 Royal Tunbridge Wells TN1 149 A2
Christ Church CE Sch. SE18 6 A6
Christ Church Cres. 2 DA12 30 C8
Christ Church Rd. 3 DA12 30 C8
Christ's Coll for Boys. SE3 5 A6
Christchurch Ct. ME5 48 C2
Christchurch House. 9 ME15 107 E5
Christchurch Rd. Dartford DA1 9 C1
Christchurch Rd. Sidcup DA15 23 F5
Christchurch Rd. Tilbury RM18 13 A6
Christen Way. ME15 & ME17 107 F3
Christian Fields Ave. DA12 30 C4
Christie Cl. ME5 62 B6
Christie Dr. 8 ME20 74 F4
Christie House. DA6 8 B2
Christies Ave. TN14 53 B1
Christmas La. ME23 17 F3
Christmas St. ME7 48 E7
Christopher Cl. DA15 6 F2
Chudleigh. DA14 24 B4
Chulkhurst. TN27 157 F1
Church Alley. 9 DA11 13 B1
Church Ave. DA14 24 B3
Church Cl. Brenchley TN12 152 C8
Church Cl. Cliffe ME3 16 B6
Church Cl. Mereworth ME18 103 D8
Church Cotts. Cranbrook TN17 169 D5
Church Cotts. Crockenhill BR8 39 D2
Church Cotts. Shoreham TN14 69 A8
Church Cotts. St Michaels TN30 173 B3
Church Cres. ME17 110 F6
Church Farm Cl. Crockenhill BR8 39 D3
Church Farm Cl. Hoo St Werburgh ME3 34 E4
Church Field. Dartford DA1 26 D6
Church Field. Edenbridge TN8 112 D1
Church Field. Snodland ME6 60 B1
Church Field Cotts. TN15 84 F7
Church Fields. New Town ME19 89 B8
Church Fields. Sevenoaks TN13 83 F5
Church Gn. Marden TN12 138 C6
Church Gn. Rochester ME2 47 C8
Church Gn. Staplehurst TN12 139 E2
Church Hill. Boughton Monchelsea ME17 123 B7
Church Hill. Chatham ME5 48 C2
Church Hill. Crayford DA1 8 E3
Church Hill. Cudham TN14 66 C4
Church Hill. Dartford DA1 26 D6
Church Hill. High Halden TN26 173 E7
Church Hill. Leigh TN11 115 F2
Church Hill. Orpington BR6 38 A2
Church Hill. Plaxtol TN15 101 E8
Church Hill. Stockbury ME9 79 F7
Church Hill. Stone DA9 10 E2
Church Hill. Woolwich SE18 1 F3
Church Hill Wood. BR5 37 F4
Church Hyde. SE18 6 E8
Church La. Capel TN11 134 F6
Church La. Chalk DA12 31 C6
Church La. Chartway Street ME17 125 B8
Church La. Chatham ME4 47 F6
Church La. Chislehurst BR7 37 C8
Church La. East Peckham TN12 119 F7
Church La. Frant TN3 163 B4
Church La. Harrietsham ME17 110 E6
Church La. Kemsing TN15 70 B2
Church La. Keston Mark BR2 36 E1
Church La. Maidstone ME14 93 B4
Church La. Newington ME9 65 B6
Church La. Stockbury ME9 79 E8
Church La. Tonbridge TN9 117 C2
Church La. Trottiscliffe ME19 73 B5
Church La. West Farleigh ME15 105 D7
Church Manor Way. SE18 & SE2 3 A2
Church Manorway. DA8 4 D3
Church Meadow. TN12 153 A7
Church Mews. ME8 63 F8
Church Path. Gillingham ME7 48 E6
Church Path. Northfleet DA11 12 C1
Church Path. Stone DA9 10 F1
Church Rd. Bexley, DA7 & DA6 7 F4
Church Rd. Bexley,Welling DA16 7 B5
Church Rd. Brasted TN16 82 B3
Church Rd. Bromley BR1 & BR2 36 A7
Church Rd. Chart Sutton ME17 124 C8
Church Rd. Chelsfield BR6 52 D4
Church Rd. Crockenhill BR8 39 D2
Church Rd. Erith DA8 4 D1
Church Rd. Goudhurst TN17 167 F8
Church Rd. Grafty Green ME17 126 F7
Church Rd. Gravesend DA12 30 C2
Church Rd. Harrietsham ME17 110 E6
Church Rd. Hartley DA3 43 A2
Church Rd. Henhurst DA13 44 C8
Church Rd. Hildenborough TN11 116 D6
Church Rd. Hucking ME17 79 E1
Church Rd. Keston BR2 50 D3
Church Rd. Lamberhurst TN3 166 C6
Church Rd. Low Street RM18 13 E8
Church Rd. Maidstone,Shepway ME15 107 F7
Church Rd. Maidstone,Tovil ME15 91 E2
Church Rd. Offham ME18 88 D8
Church Rd. Orpington BR6 51 D5
Church Rd. Paddock Wood TN12 136 B6
Church Rd. Royal Tunbridge Wells TN1 & TN4 149 A3
Church Rd. Royal Tunbridge Wells, Southborough TN4 132 F2
Church Rd. Ryarsh ME19 74 A3
Church Rd. Sandhurst Cross TN18 185 F4
Church Rd. Seal TN15 84 F6
Church Rd. Sevenoaks Weald TN14 99 B3
Church Rd. Sidcup DA14 24 A4
Church Rd. Stone DA9 10 F2
Church Rd. Stone Street TN15 85 E3
Church Rd. Sundridge TN14 82 E2
Church Rd. Sutton at Hone DA4 26 F1
Church Rd. Sutton at Hone DA4 27 A2
Church Rd. Swanley Village BR8 40 D8
Church Rd. Swanscombe DA10 11 F1
Church Rd. Tenterden TN30 183 A7
Church Rd. Tilbury RM18 12 F6
Church Rd. West Kingsdown TN15 55 E3
Church Rd. West Peckham ME18 103 A6
Church Row. Chislehurst BR7 37 C8
Church Row. Plaxtol TN15 101 E8
Church Row. West Peckham ME18 103 B6
Church Row Mews. BR7 23 C1
Church Sq. ME17 111 D5
Church St. Boughton Monchelsea ME17 107 B2
Church St. Burham ME1 60 F1
Church St. Chatham ME4 48 A4
Church St. Cliffe ME3 16 B5
Church St. Cowden TN8 145 B5
Church St. Edenbridge TN8 112 D1
Church St. Gillingham ME7 48 E6
Church St. Gravesend DA11 13 B1
Church St. Grays RM17 12 C8
Church St. Hadlow TN11 118 E8
Church St. Hoo St Werburgh ME3 34 E5
Church St. Loose ME15 106 F5
Church St. Lower Higham ME3 32 D7
Church St. Maidstone ME14 92 A4
Church St. Maidstone,Tovil ME15 91 E2
Church St. Newham E16 2 B5
Church St. Rochester ME1 47 D4
Church St. Seal TN15 85 A7
Church St. Shoreham TN14 69 A8
Church St. Southfleet DA13 29 A3
Church St. Teston ME18 105 A8
Church St. Ticehurst TN5 176 D1
Church St. Tonbridge TN9 117 C2
Church Terr. ME5 48 C2
Church View. Biddenden TN27 157 F2

Church View. Swanley BR8 .... 39 D6
Church Wlk. Dartford DA1 .... 26 D5
Church Wlk. East Malling ME19 ... 90 A7
Church Wlk. Eynsford DA4 .... 54 E7
Church Wlk. Gravesend DA12 ...... 30 D8
Church Wlk. Hawkhurst TN18 .... 179 A1
Church Wlk. Headcorn TN27 ..... 141 C5
Churchbury Rd. SE9 .... 22 C8
Churchfield. ME19 .... 73 D3
Churchfield Rd. DA16 .... 7 A4
Churchfield Sch. SE2 .... 3 A2
Churchfields Terr. ME1 .... 47 B4
Churchill Ave. ME5 .... 62 A7
Churchill CE Prim Sch. TN16 .... 81 C2
Churchill Cl. DA1 .... 27 B7
Churchill Cotts. ME17 .... 108 F6
Churchill Ct. BR6 .... 51 C5
Churchill House.
  Benenden TN17 .... 180 E6
Churchill House.
  Maidstone ME16 .... 91 B2
Churchill Pk. DA1 .... 10 A2
Churchill Rd. Gravesend DA11 .... 29 F7
Churchill Rd. Grays RM17 .... 12 D8
Churchill Rd. Horton Kirby DA4 .. 41 C5
Churchill Rd. Newham E16 .... 1 C7
Churchill Sq. ME19 .... 89 A3
Churchill Way. BR1 .... 36 A7
Churchills Ropewalk. TN17 .... 167 E8
Churchsettle La. TN5 .... 175 C1
Churchside. DA13 .... 73 A8
Churchyard Cotts. TN3 .... 148 A8
Churn La. TN12 .... 137 A2
Chute Cl. ME8 .... 63 D4
Chyngton Cl. DA15 .... 23 F5
Cimba Wood. DA12 .... 30 E4
Cinder Hill La. TN11 .... 115 C1
Cinderhill Wood. TN12 .... 135 C2
Cinnabar Cl. ME5 .... 62 A1
Circle The. RM18 .... 13 A6
Circuit Rd. SE28 .... 1 C7
Circular Way. SE18 .... 6 A8
Cirrus Cres. DA12 .... 30 E3
City Way. ME1 .... 47 D2
Civic Sq. RM18 .... 13 A5
Civic Way. TN1 .... 149 A3
Clacket La. TN16 .... 96 A8
Claire House. ME16 .... 91 E5
Clandon Ct. BR1 .... 22 A2
Clandon Rd. ME5 .... 62 D2
Clanricarde Gdns. ① TN1 ...... 149 A3
Clanricarde Rd. ② TN1 .... 149 A3
Claphatch La. TN5 .... 176 A5
Clapper La. TN12 .... 139 D6
Clapton Ct. ME8 .... 63 D8
Clara Pl. SE18 .... 2 A2
Clare Ave. TN9 .... 116 F1
Clare Cnr. SE9 .... 23 B8
Clare Ct. BR7 .... 36 F8
Clare La. ME19 .... 89 E8
Clare Way. Bexley DA6 .... 7 E6
Clare Way. Sevenoaks TN13 ..... 99 C8
Claremont Cl. Newham E16 .... 2 A5
Claremont Cl. Orpington BR6 ... 51 A6
Claremont Cres. DA1 .... 8 E3
Claremont Cty Prim Sch. TN2 149 B2
Claremont Gdns. TN1 & TN2 .. 149 B2
Claremont Pl. ①
  Gravesend DA11 .... 30 B8
Claremont Pl. Iden Green TN17 180 C4
Claremont Rd. Bromley BR1 ...... 36 F5
Claremont Rd. Hextable BR8 ..... 25 E1
Claremont Rd. Maidstone ME14 . 92 B5
Claremont Rd.
  Royal Tunbridge Wells TN1 ...... 149 B2
Claremont St. E16 .... 2 A4
Claremont Way. ① ME4 .... 47 F3
Clarence Ave.
  Bromley BR1 & BR2 .... 36 E5
Clarence Ave. Rochester ME1 ... 47 C4
Clarence Cres. DA14 .... 24 B5
Clarence Ct. ME14 .... 92 E4
Clarence Pl. DA11 .... 30 B7
Clarence Rd. Bexley DA6 .... 7 E3
Clarence Rd. Bromley BR1 & BR2 36 E4
Clarence Rd. Chatham ME4 ...... 48 B2
Clarence Rd. Chislehurst SE9 ... 22 E6
Clarence Rd. ② Grays RM17 .... 12 A8
Clarence Rd.
  Royal Tunbridge Wells
  TN1 & TN4 .... 149 A3
Clarence Rd. Sidcup DA14 .... 24 B5
Clarence Row. Gravesend DA11 . 30 B8
Clarence Row.
  Royal Tunbridge Wells TN1 ...... 149 A3
Clarendon Cl. Maidstone ME14 . 93 A4
Clarendon Cl. St Paul's Cray BR5 38 A6
Clarendon Gdns. Dartford DA2 .. 27 D8
Clarendon Gdns. Rochester ME2 33 A1
Clarendon Gdns.
  Royal Tunbridge Wells TN2 .... 149 A1
Clarendon Gn. BR5 .... 38 A5
Clarendon Gr. BR5 .... 38 A5
Clarendon Mews. DA5 .... 25 B7
Clarendon Path. BR5 .... 38 A6
Clarendon Pl.
  Joyden's Wood DA2 .... 25 E3
Clarendon Pl. Maidstone ME14 . 92 A4
Clarendon Pl. Sevenoaks TN13 .. 84 A2
Clarendon Pl. Gravesend DA11 .. 13 C1
Clarendon Rd. Sevenoaks TN13 . 84 A1
Clarendon Way.
  Royal Tunbridge Wells TN2 .... 149 A1
Clarendon Way.
  St Paul's Cray BR5 & BR7 .... 37 F6
Clareville Rd. BR5 & BR6 .... 51 C8
Clarewood Dr. ME19 .... 89 E8
Claridge. TN4 .... 149 B6
Claridge Cl. ME7 .... 62 F4

Clark Cl. DA8 .... 9 A6
Clark Mews. ME20 .... 75 F1
Clarkbourne Dr. RM17 .... 12 D8
Clarkes Green Rd. TN15 .... 70 B5
Clarks La. TN14 .... 67 F7
Claston Cl. DA1 .... 8 E3
Clavadal Rd. TN12 .... 136 A7
Clavell Cl. ME8 .... 63 E4
Clay Cotts. TN17 .... 167 E8
Clay Hill Rd. TN3 .... 165 D6
Clay Wood Cl. BR6 .... 37 E2
Claybridge Rd. SE12 .... 22 C4
Clayfarm Rd. SE9 .... 23 C6
Claygate. ME15 .... 92 D1
Claygate Cross. TN15 .... 87 A3
Claygate La. TN11 .... 101 F4
Claygate Rd. TN12 .... 121 B2
Clayhill. TN17 .... 167 D8
Clayhill Cres. SE12 & SE9 .... 22 D4
Claymill House. ② SE18 .... 2 C1
Clayton Cl. ③ E6 .... 1 F7
Clayton Croft Rd. DA2 .... 26 A6
Clayton's La. TN3 .... 146 E2
Claytonville Terr. DA17 .... 4 C4
Claywood La. DA13 & DA2 .... 28 D5
Clayworth Cl. DA15 .... 7 B1
Cleanthus Cl. SE18 .... 6 B6
Cleanthus Rd. SE18 .... 6 B6
Clearway. TN15 .... 73 A1
Clearways Bsns Est. TN15 .... 55 E3
Cleave Ave. BR6 .... 51 E4
Cleave Rd. ME7 .... 48 E3
Cleavers. TN17 .... 170 A8
Cleavers Cl. TN17 .... 170 A8
Cleavesland. ME14 .... 120 E5
Cleeve Ave. TN2 .... 149 D2
Cleeve Ct. ② DA1 .... 9 D1
Cleeve Park Gdns. DA14 .... 24 B6
Cleeve Park Sch. DA14 .... 24 C5
Clegg House. SE3 .... 5 B3
Clematis Ave. ME8 .... 63 B5
Clement Cl. ME16 .... 91 D5
Clement St. BR8 .... 26 E2
Clements Ave. E16 .... 1 A6
Clenches Farm La. TN13 .... 84 A1
Clenches Farm Rd. TN13 .... 84 A1
Clendon Way. SE18 .... 2 C2
Clerks Field. TN27 .... 141 D5
Clermont Cl. ME7 .... 63 A4
Cleve Rd. DA14 .... 24 D5
Cleveland. TN2 .... 149 D4
Cleveland House.
  Maidstone ME16 .... 91 B2
Cleveland House.
  Northfleet DA11 .... 12 D1
Cleveland Rd. Bexley DA16 .... 6 F5
Cleveland Rd. Gillingham ME7 ... 48 D6
Clevely Cl. SE7 .... 1 D2
Cleves Rd. TN14 .... 69 E2
Clewer House. ⑧ SE2 .... 3 D4
Clewson Rise. ME14 .... 92 B8
Cliff Hill. ME17 .... 107 D4
Cliff Hill Rd. ME17 .... 107 C4
Cliffe Rd. ME2 .... 33 A1
Cliffe Woods Cty Prim Fst Sch.
  ME3 .... 33 C8
Cliffe Woods Mid Sch. ME3 ...... 33 C8
Clifford Ave. BR7 .... 22 F8
Clifton Cl. Maidstone ME14 ...... 92 B5
Clifton Cl. ⑧ Orpington BR6 .... 51 C5
Clifton Cl. Rochester ME2 .... 46 F7
Clifton Cotts. TN1 .... 149 D8
Clifton Gr. DA11 .... 30 B8
Clifton Marine Par. DA11 .... 12 F1
Clifton Pl. TN1 .... 149 B2
Clifton Rd. Bexley DA16 .... 7 C4
Clifton Rd. Gillingham ME7 ...... 48 E7
Clifton Rd. Gravesend DA11 ..... 13 A1
Clifton Rd.
  Royal Tunbridge Wells TN1 ...... 149 C7
Clifton Rd. Sidcup DA14 .... 23 E4
Cliftonville Ct. SE12 .... 22 A7
Clinch Ct. ⑮ E16 .... 1 A8
Clinch St. ME3 .... 18 A4
Clinton Ave. Bexley DA16 .... 7 A3
Clinton Ave. Rochester ME2 ..... 46 F7
Clinton Cl. ME17 .... 106 B3
Clinton La. TN8 .... 113 C3
Clipper Bvd. DA9 .... 10 E3
Clipper Bvd W. DA9 .... 10 D4
Clipper Cl. ME2 .... 47 E7
Clipper Cres. DA12 .... 30 F4
Clipper Ct. ME2 .... 47 E7
Clive Ave. DA1 .... 8 F1
Clive House. ME20 .... 90 F8
Clive Rd. Erith DA17 .... 4 A2
Clive Rd. Gravesend DA11 .... 13 B1
Clive Rd. Rochester ME1 .... 47 C3
Clock House. SE3 .... 84 A4
Clock Tower Mews. ME6 .... 60 A1
Clockhouse. TN2 .... 149 F6
Cloisterham Rd. ME1 .... 61 D7
Cloisters Ave. BR1 & BR2 .... 36 F4
Cloisters Ct. DA7 .... 8 B4
Cloisters The. ① Dartford DA1 ... 9 E1
Cloisters The. Lenham ME17 .. 111 C5
Cloonmore Ave. BR6 .... 51 F6
Close The. Addington ME19 ...... 73 C2
Close The. Birling ME19 .... 74 B5
Close The. Borough Green TN15 .. 87 A8
Close The. Bough Beech TN8 .. 114 A2
Close The. Groombridge TN3 .. 161 C6
Close The. Ightham TN15 .... 86 D6
Close The. New Barn DA3 .... 43 B7
Close The. Orpington BR5 .... 37 E3
Close The. Rochester ME1 .... 47 C4
Close The. Sevenoaks TN13 ...... 83 E3
Close The. Sidcup DA14 .... 24 B3

Close The. ①
Sidcup,Old Bexley DA5 .... 25 A8
Close The. Wilmington DA2 ...... 26 D5
Cloth Hall Gdns. TN27 .... 158 A2
Clothier House. SE7 .... 1 E1
Clothworkers Rd. SE18 .... 6 D7
Cloudesley Cl. ME1 .... 47 B1
Cloudesley Rd. Bexley DA7 .... 7 F6
Cloudesley Rd. Erith DA8 .... 9 A8
Clovelly Rd. DA7 .... 7 E8
Clovelly Way. BR6 .... 37 F3
Clover Bank View. ME5 .... 62 B6
Clover Rd. ME3 .... 34 E3
Clover St. ME4 .... 47 F4
Clover Wlk. ⑬ TN8 .... 112 D3
Cloverdale Gdns. DA15 .... 6 F1
Clovers The. DA11 .... 29 E4
Club Gardens Rd. BR2 .... 36 A2
Clyde Rd. TN10 .... 117 C6
Clydesdale House. DA18 .... 3 E4
Clydon Cl. DA8 .... 8 E8
Coach Dr The. DA13 .... 72 E7
Coach & Horses Pas. ⑬ TN2 .. 149 A2
Coach Rd. Egerton TN27 .... 127 E6
Coach Rd. Ightham Common TN15 86 B2
Coalhouse Fort. RM18 .... 14 E6
Coastguard Cotts. Cliffe ME3 ... 15 C8
Coastguard Cotts. Grain ME3 ... 21 B5
Coates Hill Rd. BR1 .... 37 A7
Cob Cl. TN15 .... 86 C6
Cob Dr. DA12 .... 31 E3
Cobb Cl. ME2 .... 46 D8
Cobbett Cl. ME19 .... 89 F8
Cobbett Rd. SE9 .... 5 E4
Cobblestones. ME7 .... 62 F5
Cobbs Cl. Paddock Wood TN12 . 135 F6
Cobbs Cl. Wateringbury ME18 .. 104 E7
Cobden Ct. ⑨ SE28 .... 3 C5
Cobden Rd. Orpington BR6 .... 51 D6
Cobden Rd. Sevenoaks TN13 .... 84 C4
Cobdown Cl. ME20 .... 75 C2
Cobfield. ME17 .... 108 A1
Cobham Cl. Bromley BR2 .... 36 E2
Cobham Cl. Maidstone ME16 .... 91 E4
Cobham Cl. Rochester ME2 .... 46 E7
Cobham Cl. ② Sidcup DA16 .... 7 B1
Cobham Cty Prim Sch. DA12 ... 45 A3
Cobham Hall. DA12 .... 45 C6
Cobham House. ④ DA8 .... 8 F7
Cobham Pl. DA6 .... 7 D2
Cobham St. DA11 .... 30 B8
Cobham Terr. DA9 .... 11 B1
Cobhambury Rd. DA12 & DA13 .. 45 B4
Cobhams. TN3 .... 148 A8
Cobland Rd. SE12 .... 22 C4
Cobsdene. DA12 .... 30 D2
Cobtree Cl. ME5 .... 62 C8
Cobtree Rd. ME17 .... 106 C3
Cobtree Wharf. ME20 .... 76 C2
Cockerhurst Rd. TN14 .... 53 E2
Cockmannings La. BR5 .... 38 E1
Cockmannings Rd. BR5 .... 38 D2
Cockmount La. TN5 .... 174 F5
Cockpit The. TN12 .... 138 C5
Cocksett Ave. BR6 .... 51 E4
Cocksure La. DA14 .... 25 A4
Codrington Cres. DA12 .... 30 D3
Codrington Gdns. DA12 .... 30 D3
Cogate Rd. TN12 .... 135 E6
Colchester Cl. ME5 .... 62 A7
Cold Arbor Rd. TN13 .... 83 D3
Cold Blow Cres. DA5 .... 25 D7
Cold Harbour La. ME9 .... 65 F6
Coldblow La. ME14 .... 79 A2
Coldbridge La. TN27 .... 127 B5
Coldharbour Crest. SE9 .... 23 A5
Coldharbour La. Aylesford ME20 76 A1
Coldharbour La.
  Hildenborough TN11 .... 116 E7
Coldharbour La. Hucking ME14 . 79 B1
Coldharbour La. Rainham RM13 .. 4 F6
Coldharbour Rd.
  Iden Green TN17 .... 180 B4
Coldharbour Rd. Northfleet DA11 29 F5
Coldharbour Rd.
  White Post TN11 .... 146 E8
Coldharbour Sports Ctr. SE9 .... 23 A6
Coldred Rd. ME15 .... 107 F4
Coldrum La. ME19 .... 73 C6
Cole Cl. SE28 .... 3 B5
Cole Terr. ME17 .... 111 C4
Colebrook Ind Est. TN2 .... 133 E1
Colebrook Rd. TN4 .... 149 C8
Colebrooke Ct. DA14 .... 24 B4
Colegate Dr. ME14 .... 93 C4
Coleman Rd. DA17 .... 4 A2
Colemans Heath. SE9 .... 23 B5
Colepits Wood Rd. SE9 .... 6 D2
Coleraine Rd. ① SE3 .... 5 A8
Coleridge Cl. ④ ME20 .... 74 F4
Coleridge Rd. Dartford DA1 ..... 10 B3
Coleridge Rd. Tilbury RM18 .... 13 C5
Coleridge Way. BR6 .... 38 A3
Coles Ct. TN2 .... 149 C3
Coles La. TN16 .... 82 C4
Coleshall Cl. ME15 .... 107 F6
Colets Orch. TN14 .... 69 B3
Colewood Dr. ME2 .... 46 B8
Colfe's Prep Sch. SE12 .... 5 B1
Colin Blythe Rd. TN10 .... 117 F5
Colin Chapman Way. DA3 .... 55 E6
Colin Cl. DA2 .... 10 E1
Coll of Guidance Studies. BR8 .. 25 F1
College Ave. Gillingham ME7 .... 48 B4
College Ave. Maidstone ME15 ... 91 F4
College Ave. Tonbridge TN9 .... 133 A7

College Cotts. ME16 .... 91 F3
College Ct. ⑤ ME15 .... 92 A3
College Dr. TN2 .... 149 D4
College Gn. BR1 .... 36 A8
College Rd. Bromley BR1 .... 22 A1
College Rd. Chatham ME4 .... 48 A7
College Rd. Hextable BR8 .... 25 F1
College Rd. Maidstone ME15 .... 91 F2
College Rd. New Hythe ME20 .... 75 B3
College Rd. Northfleet DA11 .... 12 B2
College View. SE9 .... 22 D7
College Yd. ME1 .... 47 C6
Coller Cres. DA2 .... 27 E3
Collet Cl. ME17 .... 69 E2
Collet Wlk. ME8 .... 63 D4
Collier Cl. E16 .... 2 B6
Collier Street CE Prim Sch.
  TN12 .... 121 D1
Colliers' Green CE Prim Sch.
  TN17 .... 154 F2
Colliers Wood. BR2 .... 50 D5
Collindale Ave. Erith DA8 .... 8 B8
Collindale Ave. Sidcup DA15 .... 24 A7
Collings Wlk. ME8 .... 63 D4
Collington Cl. DA11 .... 29 E8
Collington House. SE7 .... 5 B8
Collington Terr. ME15 .... 107 E4
Collingwood House. DA9 .... 11 D2
Collingwood Ind Ctr. ME17 .... 108 C2
Collingwood Rd. ME20 .... 76 C7
Collis St. ME2 .... 47 A8
Collison Pl. ME2 .... 183 D7
Colman House. ② ME14 .... 92 A4
Colman Rd. E16 .... 1 C8
Colne Rd. TN10 .... 117 B5
Colney Rd. DA1 .... 9 F1
Colonade The. ⑭ TN18 .... 179 A2
Colonel's Way. TN4 .... 133 A2
Coltness Cres. SE2 .... 3 B1
Colts Hill Pl. TN12 .... 135 B5
Coltsfoot Ct. RM17 .... 12 D8
Coltsfoot Dr. ME14 .... 92 F4
Coltstead. DA3 .... 56 E7
Columbia Wharf Rd. RM17 ...... 12 A8
Columbine Ave. E6 .... 1 E8
Columbine Cl. East Malling ME19 74 F1
Columbine Cl. Rochester ME2 .. 46 E7
Columbine Rd. East Malling ME19 89 F8
Columbine Rd. Rochester ME2 .. 46 E7
Columbus Ct. SE28 .... 8 F8
Colveiw Ct. SE9 .... 22 D7
Colyer Cl. SE9 .... 23 B6
Colyer House. SE2 .... 3 D1
Colyer Rd. DA11 .... 29 D6
Colyers Cl. DA8 .... 8 D6
Colyers La. DA8 .... 8 D6
Colyers Prim Sch. DA7 .... 8 D6
Colyton Cl. DA16 .... 7 D6
Combe Bank Cotts. TN14 .... 82 D5
Combe Bank Sch. TN14 .... 82 E4
Combedale Rd. SE10 .... 1 A1
Combeside. SE18 .... 6 F7
Combwell Cres. SE2 .... 3 A3
Comfrey Cl. RM17 .... 12 D8
Command Rd. ME14 .... 91 F8
Commercial Pl. DA11 .... 13 C1
Commercial Rd.
  Paddock Wood TN12 .... 135 F6
Commercial Rd. Rochester ME2 . 47 A7
Commercial Rd.
  Royal Tunbridge Wells TN1 ..... 149 B5
Commercial Rd. Tonbridge TN9 133 C8
Commissioner's Rd. ME2 .... 47 B8
Commodore Rd. ME4 .... 92 C5
Common La. Cliffe ME3 .... 16 C5
Common La. Heath Side DA2 .... 26 B5
Common Rd. Burham ME1 .... 61 B1
Common Rd. Cliffe Woods ME3 . 33 B6
Common Rd. Hadlow TN11 .... 102 C2
Common Rd.
  Ightham Common TN15 .... 86 B4
Common Rd. Sissinghurst TN17 170 A8
Common The. ME1 .... 47 C6
Common View. TN4 .... 148 C4
Common Wall. ME3 .... 16 D6
Commonside. BR2 .... 50 B4
Commonwealth House. ⑤
  RM18 .... 13 A5
Commonwealth Way. SE2 .... 3 C1
Commority Rd. DA13 .... 73 B8
Comp La. TN15 .... 87 E6
Compass Cl. ME1 .... 47 C1
Compass Ctr. ME4 .... 48 B8
Compasses Rd. TN11 .... 115 B2
Compasses The. TN11 .... 115 B2
Compton Cl. ME5 .... 62 D2
Compton Pl. DA8 .... 8 F8
Concord Ave. ME5 .... 61 E5
Concord Cl. Paddock Wood TN12 135 E7
Concord Cl.
  Royal Tunbridge Wells TN2 .... 149 C4
Concorde Dr. E6 .... 1 F8
Concrete Cotts. ME3 .... 15 E4
Condover Cres. SE18 .... 6 B7
Conduit Rd. SE18 .... 2 B1
Coneyburrow Rd. TN2 .... 149 E5
Conference Rd. SE2 .... 3 C2
Conghurst La. TN18 .... 185 B6
Congleton Gr. SE18 .... 2 C1
Congo Rd. SE18 .... 2 C1
Congress Rd. SE2 .... 3 C2
Congreve Rd. SE9 .... 5 F4
Congreve Wlk. ⑥ E16 .... 1 D8
Conifer Ave. DA13 .... 42 E3
Conifer Cl. BR6 .... 51 D6
Conifer Dr. Chatham ME5 .... 62 D1
Conifer Dr.
  Culverstone Green DA13 .... 57 D2

Conifer Way. BR8 .... 39 C8
Coniscliffe Cl. BR7 .... 37 A8
Coniston Ave. Bexley DA16 .... 6 E4
Coniston Ave.
  Royal Tunbridge Wells TN4 ..... 148 E5
Coniston Cl. Bexley DA7 .... 8 C6
Coniston Cl. Dartford DA1 .... 26 B7
Coniston Cl. Erith DA8 .... 8 E7
Coniston Cl. Gillingham ME7 .... 49 A6
Coniston Rd. DA7 .... 8 C6
Connaught Br. E16 .... 1 D6
Connaught Cl. ME15 .... 107 F4
Connaught Mews. Chatham ME4 48 C2
Connaught Mews. Woolwich SE18 2 B1
Connaught Rd. Chatham ME4 ... 48 C2
Connaught Rd. Gillingham ME7 .. 48 D5
Connaught Rd.
  Newham,Custom House E16 ..... 1 C6
Connaught Rd.
  Newham,Silvertown E16 .... 1 D5
Connaught Rd. Woolwich SE18 .. 2 B1
Connaught Way. TN4 .... 148 F5
Conquest Ind Est. ME2 .... 47 A6
Conrad Cl. ME8 .... 63 D4
Consort Cl. ME14 .... 92 B5
Constable Rd. Northfleet DA11 . 29 E5
Constable Rd. Tonbridge TN10 . 117 C5
Constance St. E16 .... 1 E5
Constitution Hill. Chatham ME4 . 48 B3
Constitution Hill.
  Gravesend DA12 .... 30 C7
Constitution Hill. Snodland ME6 75 A8
Constitution Rd. ME4 .... 48 C2
Constitution Rise. ME4 .... 6 A6
Constitutional Hill Rd. TN4 .... 132 F1
Consul Gdns. BR8 .... 26 A1
Contessa Cl. BR6 .... 51 E5
Convalescent La. TN17 .... 155 F2
Convent Prep Sch. DA12 .... 30 C6
Conway Cl. ME2 .... 32 E1
Conway Gdns. RM17 .... 12 B7
Conway Inf & Jun Sch. SE18 .... 2 E2
Conway Mews. ME7 .... 48 A6
Conway Rd. Maidstone ME16 ... 91 C6
Conway Rd. Woolwich SE18 ...... 2 E2
Conyerd Rd. TN15 .... 86 F6
Conyers Wlk. ME8 .... 63 D4
Cooden Cl. BR1 .... 22 B1
Cook Cl. ME5 .... 62 C6
Cook Sq. DA8 .... 8 F7
Cookham Dene Cl. BR7 .... 37 D8
Cookham Hill. ME1 .... 47 A2
Cookham Rd. BR8 .... 39 A8
Cookham Wood Rd. ME1 .... 61 B8
Cookhill Rd. SE2 .... 3 B3
Coolfin Rd. E16 .... 1 B7
Cooling Cl. ME14 .... 92 C6
Cooling Comm. ME3 .... 33 D8
Cooling Rd. Cliffe ME3 .... 16 C4
Cooling Rd. Cooling ME3 .... 16 C5
Cooling Rd. High Halstow ME23 . 17 C3
Cooling Rd. Rochester ME2 ...... 33 B2
Cooling St. ME3 .... 16 D1
Coomb Field. TN8 .... 128 C8
Coombe Ave. TN14 .... 84 B7
Coombe Bank Sch. TN14 .... 82 F6
Coombe Cl. Chatham ME5 .... 62 B3
Coombe Cl. Snodland ME6 .... 75 A7
Coombe Farm La. ME3 .... 18 E6
Coombe La. TN30 .... 183 A7
Coombe Lands. TN30 .... 189 D4
Coombe Lea. BR1 .... 36 E6
Coombe Lodge. SE7 .... 5 C8
Coombe Rd. Gravesend DA12 ... 30 C6
Coombe Rd.
  Hoo St Werburgh ME3 .... 34 E5
Coombe Rd. Maidstone ME15 ... 91 F2
Coombe Rd. Otford TN14 .... 69 C4
Coombfield Dr. DA2 .... 27 D4
Cooper Cl. DA9 .... 10 F2
Cooper Ct. SE18 .... 6 B8
Cooper Rd. Chatham ME5 .... 62 B3
Cooper Rd. Snodland ME6 .... 74 F6
Cooper Shaw Rd. RM18 .... 13 E7
Cooper's Rd. DA11 .... 29 F7
Coopers Cl. DA4 .... 41 D8
Coopers Cotts. DA2 .... 27 A4
Coopers La. Lewisham SE12 .... 22 B6
Coopers La.
  Poundsbridge TN11 & TN3 .... 147 C2
Coopers Lane Prim Sch. SE12 22 B6
Coopers Sch. BR7 .... 37 C8
Coote Rd. DA7 .... 7 F6
Copenhagen Rd. ME7 .... 48 C4
Copley Dene. BR1 .... 36 D8
Coppards La. TN31 .... 187 D1
Copper Beech Cl.
  Gravesend DA12 .... 30 D8
Copper Beech Cl. ⑦
  Orpington BR5 .... 38 C4
Copper La. TN12 .... 138 E5
Copper Tree Ct. ME15 .... 107 A5
Copper Tree Wlk. ME5 .... 62 C1
Copperfield Cl. Chalk DA12 ..... 31 A7
Copperfield Cl. Erith SE28 .... 3 C7
Copperfield Cres. ME2 .... 32 C2
Copperfield Dr. DA1 .... 8 E2
Copperfield Dr. ME17 .... 108 C4
Copperfield House. ME4 .... 48 A4
Copperfield Rd. ME1 .... 47 C2
Copperfield Way. BR7 .... 23 C2
Copperfields. ② Dartford DA1 ... 9 E1
Copperfields. Kemsing TN15 .... 69 F2
Copperfields Cl. TN15 .... 69 F2
Copperfields Orch. TN15 .... 69 F2
Copperfields The. ME1 .... 47 B4

Copperfields Wlk. TN15 .... 69 F2
Coppergate. ME7 .... 62 F5
Coppergate Cl. BR1 .... 36 B8
Copperhouse La. ME7 .... 49 B6
Copperhouse Rd. ME2 .... 46 C7
Coppice Ct. ME7 .... 63 B4
Coppice Rd. ME5 .... 62 C2
Coppice The. Aylesford ME20 .... 75 E1
Coppice The. Bitchet Green TN15 85 D1
Coppice The. Pembury TN2 .... 150 D7
Coppice The. Vigo Village DA13 .. 73 B8
Coppice View. ME14 .... 92 E6
Copping's Rd. TN11 .... 115 C4
Copse Bank. TN15 .... 84 F7
Copse Cl. SE7 .... 5 B8
Copse Rd. TN11 .... 116 E4
Copse Side. DA3 .... 42 E6
Copse The. ME3 .... 34 E3
Copsehill. ME20 .... 74 E2
Copsewood Way. ME15 .... 93 A3
Copt Hall. TN18 .... 187 D3
Copt Hall Rd.
  Ightham Common TN15 .... 86 A4
Copt Hall Rd. Sole Street DA13 .. 44 B5
Coptefield Dr. DA17 .... 3 E3
Copthall Ave. TN18 .... 179 A1
Copthorne Ave. BR2 .... 50 F8
Coralline Wlk. 4 SE2 .... 3 C4
Corbyland Rd. DA15 .... 23 E7
Corbylands Rd. DA15 .... 23 E8
Cordelia Cres. ME1 .... 46 F2
Corelli Rd. SE18 & SE3 .... 5 E6
Corinthian Ct. ME3 .... 21 B5
Corinthian Manorway. DA8 ...... 4 D2
Corinthian Rd. DA8 .... 4 D2
Cork House. BR5 .... 38 B6
Cork La. TN12 .... 155 D8
Cork St. ME20 .... 75 F6
Corkwell St. ME4 .... 47 E3
Cormorant Cl. ME2 .... 46 C7
Corn Mill Dr. BR6 .... 38 A2
Cornel House. 4 DA15 .... 24 A5
Cornelia Pl. DA8 .... 8 E8
Cornell Cl. DA14 .... 24 E2
Corner Farm Rd. TN12 .... 139 E4
Corner Gn. SE3 .... 5 A5
Cornfield Way. TN10 .... 117 D6
Cornflower Cl. ME14 .... 92 E4
Cornford Cl. Hayes BR2 .... 36 A4
Cornford Cl. Pembury TN2 .... 150 B6
Cornford La. TN2 .... 150 B5
Cornford Pk. TN2 .... 150 C6
Cornforth Cl. TN12 .... 139 F4
Cornwall Ave. DA16 .... 6 F4
Cornwall Cl. ME15 .... 107 E7
Cornwall Cres. ME1 .... 60 D4
Cornwall Dr. BR5 .... 24 C1
Cornwall Rd. Dartford DA1 ...... 9 F4
Cornwall Rd. Gillingham ME7 .. 48 D6
Cornwall Rd. Rochester ME1 .... 47 C3
Cornwallis Ave. Chatham ME4 .... 47 E1
Cornwallis Ave. Gillingham ME8 .. 49 A4
Cornwallis Ave. Linton ME17 .. 122 E8
Cornwallis Ave. Sidcup DA15 .. 23 D6
Cornwallis Ave. Tonbridge TN10 117 F4
Cornwallis Cl. 8 F8
Cornwallis Cotts. ME17 .... 106 E2
Cornwallis Rd. Maidstone ME16 .. 91 D4
Cornwallis Rd. Woolwich SE18 .... 2 B3
Cornwallis Sch The. ME15 .... 106 F2
Cornwallis Wlk. SE9 .... 5 F4
Cornwell Ave. DA12 .... 30 C5
Corona Rd. SE12 .... 22 A8
Corona Terr. ME6 .... 74 F6
Coronation Rd. DA5 .... 7 E1
Coronation Cotts.
  Berner's Hill TN5 .... 176 F2
Coronation Cotts. Stoke ME3 .... 19 A3
Coronation Ct. DA8 .... 8 D7
Coronation Flats. 2 ME4 .... 47 F3
Coronation Rd. Chatham ME5 .. 48 C2
Coronation Rd. Grain ME3 ...... 21 B5
Corporation Rd. ME7 .... 48 D7
Corporation St. ME1 .... 47 C6
Corral Cl. ME5 .... 48 D2
Corrall Almshouses. 4 ME15 .. 92 A3
Corrance Gn. ME15 .... 107 A8
Correnden Rd. TN11 .... 117 A3
Corseley Rd. TN3 .... 161 B5
Cossack St. ME1 .... 47 D3
Cossington Rd. ME5 .... 62 B1
Costells Meadow. TN16 ...... 81 D1
Cot La. TN27 .... 158 B3
Cotleigh Ave. DA5 .... 24 D6
Cotman Way. TN12 .... 119 E6
Cotman's Ash La. TN15 ...... 70 D4
Cotmandene Cres. BR5 ...... 38 A7
Coton Rd. DA16 .... 7 A4
Cotswold Cl. DA7 .... 8 E5
Cotswold Gdns. ME15 .... 93 A2
Cotswold Rd. DA11 .... 29 E5
Cotswold Rise. BR6 .... 37 F3
Cottage Ave. BR2 .... 36 E1
Cottage Field Cl. DA5 & DA14 .. 24 C7
Cottage Rd. ME4 .... 47 F6
Cottall Ave. ME4 .... 47 F2
Cottenham Cl. ME19 .... 89 F7
Cotton La. DA9 .... 10 D2
Coulman St. ME7 .... 48 D5
Coulter House. DA9 .... 11 C2
Coulters Cl. ME14 .... 92 D5
Coulton Ave. DA11 .... 29 E7
Council Ave. DA11 .... 12 C1
Council Cotts. Coxheath ME15 .. 106 A4
Council Cotts. Key's Green TN12 151 C4

Council Houses. TN15 .... 102 A8
Countess of Thanet's Almshouses.
  TN8 .... 144 F3
County Gate. BR7 .... 23 C5
County Gr. ME19 .... 89 B8
County Rd. Maidstone ME14 .. 92 A5
County Rd. Newham E6 .... 2 B8
Coupland Pl. SE18 .... 2 C1
Course The. SE9 .... 23 A5
Court Ave. DA17 .... 3 F1
Court Broomes. ME17 .... 125 C8
Court Cres. BR8 .... 39 E5
Court Dr. ME16 .... 91 D4
Court Farm Rd. SE9 .... 22 E5
Court La. Detling ME14 .... 78 C5
Court La. Hadlow TN11 .... 119 B7
Court Lane Pl. TN11 .... 118 F8
Court Lodge. DA17 .... 4 A1
Court Lodge Cotts.
  East Farleigh ME15 .... 106 A7
Court Lodge Cotts.
  Horton Kirby DA4 .... 41 C6
Court Lodge Rd. ME7 .... 48 F6
Court Meadow. Gillingham ME8 .. 49 B2
Court Meadow. Wrotham TN15 .. 71 F3
Court Rd. Burham ME1 .... 75 E8
Court Rd. Eltham SE9 .... 22 F7
Court Rd. Lane End DA2 .... 27 E3
Court Rd.
  Royal Tunbridge Wells TN4 .. 148 F4
Court Road (Orpington By-Pass).
  Chelsfield BR6 & TN14 .... 52 D5
Court Road (Orpington By-Pass).
  Orpington BR5 & BR6 .... 38 B2
Court St. BR1 .... 36 A7
Court Yd. SE9 .... 5 F1
Courtaulds Cl. SE28 .... 3 A5
Courtenay Rd. ME15 .... 91 F2
Courtenay Rd. ME8 .... 63 B8
Courtenwell. TN3 .... 147 E4
Courtfield Ave. ME5 .... 62 B3
Courthope. TN12 .... 136 A6
Courthope Ave. TN5 .... 174 F4
Courtland Gr. SE28 .... 3 D6
Courtlands. Hilden Park TN11 .. 117 A3
Courtlands. Teston ME18 .... 105 A8
Courtlands Ave. SE12 .... 5 B2
Courtlands Cl. ME18 .... 105 A8
Courtlands Farm. TN17 .... 169 A3
Courtleet Dr. DA8 .... 8 B6
Courtwood Dr. TN13 .... 84 A3
Courtyard Gdns. TN15 .... 71 F3
Courtyard The. ME7 .... 63 A8
Cousley Wood Rd. TN5 .... 175 C7
Couthurst Rd. SE3 .... 5 B7
Coutts Ave. DA12 .... 31 E4
Coutts House. SE7 .... 5 C8
Covelees Wall. E6 .... 2 A7
Coventry Cl. 9 Newham E6 ...... 1 F7
Coventry Cl. Rochester ME2 .. 46 D6
Coventry Rd. TN10 .... 117 D5
Coverdale Ave. ME5 .... 107 D6
Coverdale Cl. ME5 .... 62 B7
Covert The. Chatham ME5 ...... 62 B7
Covert The. Orpington BR5 & BR6 37 E3
Covert The. Vigo Village DA13 .. 72 E7
Covet Wood Cl. BR5 .... 37 F3
Covey Hall Rd. ME6 .... 60 A1
Cow La. TN8 .... 120 D1
Cow Leaze. E6 .... 2 A7
Cowan Cl. E6 .... 1 B8
Cowbeck Cl. ME8 .... 63 D6
Cowden Cl. TN18 .... 184 E8
Cowden Cross. TN8 .... 145 C7
Cowden La. TN18 .... 184 E7
Cowden Mews. TN8 .... 145 A5
Cowden Rd. Maidstone ME14 .. 92 C5
Cowden Rd. Orpington BR6 .. 37 F2
Cowden Sta. TN8 .... 145 D8
Cowdrey Cl. Maidstone ME16 .. 91 B2
Cowdrey Cl. Rochester ME1 .. 47 B2
Cowdrey Ct. DA1 .... 26 B8
Cowen House. 4 SE18 .... 6 B8
Cowley Ave. DA9 .... 11 A2
Cowper Ave. RM18 .... 13 B6
Cowper Cl. Bexley DA16 .... 7 A2
Cowper Cl. Bromley BR2 .... 36 D5
Cowper Rd. Bromley BR2 .... 36 D5
Cowper Rd. Erith DA17 .... 4 A2
Cowper Rd. Gillingham ME7 .. 48 D3
Cowstead Rd. ME9 .... 64 D2
Cox St. ME14 .... 78 E6
Cox's Cl. ME5 .... 62 A2
Coxheath Cty Prim Sch. ME17 106 C3
Coxmount Rd. SE7 .... 1 D1
Coxwell Rd. SE18 .... 2 D1
Cozenton Cl. ME8 .... 49 E1
Crabbs Croft Cl. 7 BR6 .... 51 C5
Crabtree Cl. ME18 & ME19 ...... 89 A2
Crabtree Manorway. Erith DA17 .. 4 C5
Crabtree Manorway. Erith DA17 .. 4 C5
Crabtree Rd. ME8 .... 63 D8
Craddock Way. ME8 .... 63 D5
Cradducks La. TN12 .... 140 B4
Cradles Rd. ME9 .... 64 C2
Cradley Rd. SE9 .... 23 D7
Cragie Wlk. ME8 .... 63 E4
Craigerne Rd. SE3 & SE7 ...... 5 B7
Craigholm. SE18 .... 6 A6
Craigton Rd. SE9 .... 5 F3
Crampton's Rd. TN14 .... 84 B7
Cramptons. TN17 .... 169 F8
Cranborne Ave. ME15 .... 92 C1
Cranborne Ave. ME15 .... 107 B8
Cranbrook CE Prim Sch. TN17 169 D5
Cranbrook Cl. Gillingham ME8 .. 49 C3
Cranbrook Cl. Hayes BR2 .... 36 A3
Cranbrook Cl. Maidstone ME15 107 F7

Cranbrook House. 1 DA8 .... 8 F7
Cranbrook Point. E16 .... 1 B5
Cranbrook Rd. Benenden TN17 179 F8
Cranbrook Rd. Erith DA7 .... 7 F6
Cranbrook Rd.
  Fosten Green TN27 & TN17 .. 171 C6
Cranbrook Rd. Gill's Green TN18 178 F4
Cranbrook Rd. Goudhurst TN17 168 A8
Cranbrook Rd.
  Knox Bridge TN12 & TN17 .. 155 F7
Cranbrook Rd.
  Parkgate TN27 & TN30 .... 172 C1
Cranbrook Rd. Tenterden TN30 182 E7
Cranbrook Sch. TN17 .... 169 D5
Crandalls. TN11 .... 115 F1
Crandfield Dr. DA1 .... 26 E7
Crane House. 11 TN18 .... 178 F4
Crane House Gdns. 10 TN18 .. 178 F2
Crane La. Cranbrook TN17 .. 169 D4
Crane La. Cranbrook TN17 .. 169 D5
Cranford Cl. ME8 .... 49 D1
Cranford Rd. Dartford DA1 ...... 26 E7
Cranford Rd. Tonbridge TN10 .. 118 A5
Cranham Sq. TN12 .... 138 C5
Cranleigh Cl. Bexley DA5 ...... 8 B1
Cranleigh Cl. Orpington BR6 .. 52 A7
Cranleigh Dr. BR8 .... 39 E5
Cranleigh Gdns. Chatham ME1 .. 47 D3
Cranleigh Gdns. Maidstone ME16 91 C1
Cranley Par. SE9 .... 22 E4
Cranley Rd. E13 .... 1 B8
Cranmer Ct. ME15 .... 107 B8
Cranmer Rd. TN13 .... 83 E4
Cranmore Rd. BR7 & SE9 ...... 22 F3
Cranwell Rd. TN4 .... 148 C4
Crathie Rd. SE12 .... 5 B1
Craven Rd. BR6 .... 52 D7
Crawfords. BR5 .... 25 E1
Crawley Ct. 1 DA11 .... 13 B1
Crawshay Cl. TN13 .... 84 A4
Cray Ave. BR5 .... 38 B4
Cray Cl. DA1 .... 9 A3
Cray Cl. Crockenhill BR8 .... 39 C3
Cray Rd. Erith DA17 .... 8 A8
Cray Rd. Sidcup DA14 .... 24 C2
Cray Valley Golf Course. BR5 .. 38 E7
Cray Valley Rd. BR5 .... 38 B4
Craybrooke Rd. DA14 .... 24 B4
Crayburne. DA11 .... 28 F4
Craybury End. SE9 .... 23 C6
Craydene Rd. DA8 .... 8 F6
Crayfields Ind Pk. BR5 .... 38 C7
Crayford Cl. ME14 .... 92 C6
Crayford Commercial Ctr. DA1 .. 8 E1
Crayford High St. DA1 .... 8 E2
Crayford Ind Est. DA1 .... 8 F2
Crayford L Ctr. DA1 .... 8 E1
Crayford Rd. DA1 .... 8 F2
Crayford Sta. DA1 .... 8 E1
Crayford Way. DA1 .... 9 A3
Craylands. BR5 .... 38 C6
Craylands La. DA10 .... 11 D2
Craylands Sq. DA10 .... 11 D2
Craymill Sq. DA1 .... 8 F5
Crays Par The. BR5 .... 38 C7
Crayside Ind Est. DA1 .... 9 B3
Craythorne. TN30 .... 183 B8
Creasey's Row. TN14 .... 97 E5
Credenhall Dr. BR2 .... 36 F1
Crediton Rd. E16 .... 1 A7
Credo Way. RM16 .... 11 B8
Creek The. DA11 .... 12 B2
Cremorne Rd. DA11 .... 29 F8
Crendon Pk. TN4 .... 149 A8
Crescent Ave. RM17 .... 12 D8
Crescent Cotts. TN13 .... 83 E7
Crescent Ct. 1 RM17 .... 12 D8
Crescent Dr. BR5 .... 37 C3
Crescent Gdns. BR8 .... 39 C7
Crescent Rd. Bromley BR1 ...... 22 A1
Crescent Rd. Erith DA8 .... 8 F3
Crescent Rd. Royal Tunbridge Wells
  TN1 & TN2 .... 149 B3
Crescent Rd. Sidcup DA15 .. 23 F5
Crescent Rd. Woolwich SE18 .... 2 B2
Crescent The. Bexley DA5 ...... 24 C8
Crescent The. Bidborough TN4 . 132 E4
Crescent The.
  Borough Green TN15 .... 87 A8
Crescent The. Groombridge TN3 161 C2
Crescent The. Longfield DA3 .. 42 E6
Crescent The. Maidstone ME14 .. 91 F8
Crescent The. Northfleet DA11 .. 29 F6
Crescent The. Sevenoaks TN13 .. 84 D6
Crescent The. Sidcup DA14 .... 23 F4
Crescent The. Swanscombe DA9 11 C2
Crescent The. Tonbridge TN9 .. 117 B3
Crescent Way. Chatham ME5 .. 61 D5
Crescent Way. Orpington BR6 .. 51 E5
Cressey Ct. ME4 .... 47 E4
Cressingham Ct. 1 DA17 ...... 4 A3
Crest Ave. RM17 .... 12 B7
Crest Cl. TN14 .... 68 B8
Crest Ind Est. TN12 .... 138 C6
Crest Rd. ME1 .... 47 C1
Crest View. DA9 .... 11 A3
Crest View Dr. BR5 .... 37 C4
Crestway. ME5 .... 62 B8
Crete Hall Rd. DA11 .... 12 E1
Creton St. SE18 .... 2 A3
Creve Coeur Cl. ME14 .... 93 A5
Cricket Ground Rd. BR7 .... 37 B8
Cricketers Cl. Erith DA8 .... 4 E1
Cricketers Cl.
  Harrietsham ME17 .... 110 D6
Cricketers Dr. DA13 .... 58 A7
Cripple Hill. TN26 .... 159 D1
Cripple St. ME15 .... 107 A7
Crisfield Ct. TN30 .... 173 B2

Crismill La. ME14 .... 93 F4
Crismill Rd. ME14 .... 93 F3
Crispe Rd. ME3 .... 63 D4
Crispin Ct. ME17 .... 106 C3
Crispin Rd. ME2 .... 46 E8
Crittall's Cnr. DA14 .... 24 C1
Crittenden Bglws. ME15 .... 106 A4
Crittenden Cotts. ME15 .... 106 A4
Crittenden Rd. TN12 .... 135 D3
Crittle's Ct. TN5 .... 174 F4
Crocken Hill Rd. TN27 .... 127 C2
Crockenhall Way. DA13 .... 29 E1
Crockenhill Cty Prim Sch. BR8 39 C3
Crockenhill Hill. BR5 .... 38 D4
Crockenhill Rd. BR5 & BR8 .. 38 E4
Crockers Hatch Cnr. TN3 .... 147 D2
Crockham Hill CE Prim Sch.
  TN8 .... 96 C2
Crockham Way. SE9 .... 23 A4
Croft Cl. Chatham ME5 .... 62 C1
Croft Cl. Chislehurst BR7 .... 22 F3
Croft Cl. Erith DA17 .... 3 F1
Croft Cl. Tonbridge TN10 .... 117 F5
Croft Cl. TN8 .... 112 C1
Croft Gdns. ME17 .... 111 D4
Croft La. TN8 .... 112 C1
Croft Rd. Bromley BR1 .... 22 A2
Croft Rd. Westerham TN16 .. 81 C1
Croft The. Leybourne ME20 .. 74 E2
Croft The. Swanley BR8 .... 39 C6
Croft Way. Sevenoaks TN13 .. 83 F2
Croft Way. Sidcup DA15 .... 23 E5
Crofters The. ME8 .... 63 F7
Crofton Ave. Orpington BR6 .. 51 C8
Crofton Ave. Sidcup DA5 ...... 24 D8
Crofton Inf Sch. BR5 .... 37 D2
Crofton Jun Sch. BR5 .... 37 D2
Crofton La. BR5 & BR6 .... 37 D2
Crofton Rd. BR6 .... 51 B8
Croftside. DA13 .... 73 A8
Cromarty Ct. 5 BR1 .... 36 C7
Crombie Rd. DA15 .... 23 D7
Cromer Pl. 5 BR6 .... 37 D1
Cromer Rd. ME2 .... 47 B8
Cromer St. TN9 .... 117 A1
Cromford Cl. BR6 .... 51 E7
Cromford Rd. DA1 .... 37 B7
Cromlix Cl. BR7 .... 37 B2
Cromwell Ave. BR2 .... 36 B5
Cromwell Rd. Maidstone ME14 .. 92 B5
Cromwell Rd.
  Royal Tunbridge Wells TN2 .. 149 C3
Cromwell Terr. ME4 .... 48 A3
Cronin Cl. 2 ME20 .... 74 F4
Crook Log. DA6 .... 7 D3
Crook Log Prim Sch. DA6 ...... 7 D3
Crook Log Sports Ctr. DA16 .... 7 D4
Crook Rd. TN12 .... 136 D1
Crooked La. DA1 .... 13 B1
Crookston Rd. SE9 .... 6 A4
Croombs Rd. E16 .... 1 C8
Crosby House. 3 DA9 .... 9 A1
Crosley Rd. ME7 .... 48 D3
Cross Ct. 11 SE28 .... 3 B6
Cross Dr. ME17 .... 109 B1
Cross Keys. Maidstone ME14 .. 93 C4
Cross Keys. Sevenoaks TN13 .. 99 A8
Cross Keys Cl. TN13 .... 99 A8
Cross La. Sidcup DA5 .... 24 F8
Cross La. Ticehurst TN5 .... 176 D2
Cross La E. DA12 .... 30 B6
Cross La W. DA11 .... 30 B6
Cross Lane Gdns. TN5 .... 176 D1
Cross Rd. Dartford DA1 .... 9 C1
Cross Rd. Hawley DA2 .... 26 B8
Cross Rd. Keston Mark BR2 .. 50 E8
Cross Rd. Northfleet DA11 ...... 12 F1
Cross Rd. Orpington BR5 .... 38 B4
Cross Rd. Sidcup DA14 .... 24 B4
Cross St. Chatham ME4 .... 48 A4
Cross St. Erith DA8 .... 8 E8
Cross St. Gillingham ME7 .. 48 C6
Cross St. 24 Gravesend DA11 .. 13 B1
Cross St. Maidstone ME14 ...... 92 A6
Cross St. Rochester ME2 .... 47 B8
Cross Way. ME1 .... 47 C5
Crossbrook Rd. SE3 .... 5 E4
Crossmead. SE9 .... 22 F7
Crossway. Chatham ME5 .... 61 E6
Crossway. Erith SE28 .... 3 C5
Crossway. Orpington BR5 .... 37 D4
Crossway The. Chislehurst SE9 .. 22 D6
Crossway The.
  Royal Tunbridge Wells TN4 .. 148 D2
Crossways. Chart Sutton ME17 .. 108 B1
Crossways. Dartford DA9 .... 10 C3
Crossways Bvd. DA9 .... 10 C3
Crouch Croft. SE9 .... 23 A5
Crouch House Cotts. TN8 .... 112 B2
Crouch House Rd. TN8 .... 112 B2
Crouch La. Crouch TN15 .... 87 B6
Crouch La. Linkhill TN18 .... 186 D6
Crow Cnr. ME1 .... 47 C5
Crow Dr. TN14 .... 68 C4
Crow Hill. TN15 .... 87 A7
Crow Hill Rd. TN15 .... 87 A7
Crow La. ME1 .... 47 C5
Crowden Way. SE28 .... 3 C6
Crowhurst La.
  West Kingsdown TN15 .... 56 B4
Crowhurst Oast. TN12 .... 103 D1
Crowhurst Rd. TN15 .... 86 F6
Crowhurst Way. BR5 .... 38 C4
Crown Acres. TN12 .... 120 A6
Crown Cl. BR6 .... 52 A6
Crown Ct. Bromley BR1 .... 36 E4
Crown Ct. Cranbrook TN17 .. 169 C5

Crown Ct. Eltham SE12 .... 5 B1
Crown Ct. Tilbury RM18 .... 13 A5
Crown Gn. DA12 .... 31 E3
Crown La. Bromley BR2 .... 36 D4
Crown La. Chislehurst BR7 .. 37 C8
Crown La. Shorne DA12 .... 31 E4
Crown Lane Spur. BR2 .... 36 D3
Crown Rd. Grays RM17 .... 12 A8
Crown Rd. Marlpit Hill TN8 .. 112 D4
Crown Rd. Orpington BR6 .. 52 A5
Crown Rd. Shoreham TN14 .. 53 F1
Crown St. ME7 .... 48 D6
Crown Woods Sch. SE9 ...... 6 C2
Crown Woods Way. SE9 ...... 6 D2
Crownfields. Maidstone ME14 .. 92 F4
Crownfields. Sevenoaks TN13 .. 84 B2
Crowther Cl. TN12 .... 139 E4
Croxley Cl. BR5 .... 38 B7
Croxley Gn. BR5 .... 38 B8
Croyde Cl. SE9 .... 23 D8
Croydon Cl. ME5 .... 62 C4
Croydon Rd.
  Keston Mark BR2 & BR4 & BR6 .. 50 C7
Croydon Rd. Westerham TN16 .. 81 B2
Crozier House. SE3 .... 5 B4
Cruden Rd. DA12 .... 30 F6
Crump's La. ME17 .... 126 B4
Crumpsall St. SE2 .... 3 C2
Crundale. 2 ME14 .... 92 A5
Crundale Rd. ME8 .... 49 C3
Crundale Tower. BR5 .... 38 C1
Crundwell Rd. TN4 .... 132 F1
Crusader Cl. ME7 .... 63 B8
Crusader Ct. DA1 .... 9 F3
Crusoe Rd. DA8 .... 4 D1
Crutches La. ME2 .... 32 B1
Cryals Ct. TN12 .... 151 E5
Cryals Rd. TN12 .... 151 D5
Crystal House. SE18 .... 2 F1
Cuckmere Ct. 18 BR5 .... 38 C1
Cuckmere House. 3 ME15 .. 107 B8
Cuckold's Cnr. ME3 .... 32 C6
Cuckolds Cnr. DA3 .... 57 B7
Cuckolds Green Rd. ME3 .. 19 B5
Cuckoo La. Lamberhurst Quarter
  TN12 & TN3 .... 152 A2
Cuckoo La.
  Tonbridge TN10 & TN11 ...... 118 A7
Cuckoowood Ave. ME14 ...... 76 C3
Cudham CE Prim Sch. TN16 .. 66 A3
Cudham Cl. ME14 .... 92 C6
Cudham La N. TN14 & BR6 .. 66 D7
Cudham La S. TN14 & TN16 .. 66 D2
Cudham Park Rd. TN14 .... 51 E1
Cudham Rd. BR6 .... 66 B7
Cuff Cres. SE9 .... 5 D1
Cugley Rd. DA2 .... 27 C8
Culcroft. DA3 .... 42 F6
Culpeper Cl. Hollingbourne ME17 94 E2
Culpeper Cl. Rochester ME2 .. 47 E6
Culpepers. TN17 .... 167 C8
Culpepper Cl. Coxheath ME17 .. 106 B3
Culpepper Rd. Gillingham ME8 .. 63 D4
Culverden Ave. TN4 .... 149 A6
Culverden Down. TN4 .... 148 F5
Culverden Park Rd. TN4 .... 148 F5
Culverden Pk. TN4 .... 148 F5
Culverden Sq. TN1 & TN4 ...... 149 A5
Culverden St. TN1 .... 149 A4
Culverstone Green Cty Prim Sch.
  DA13 .... 57 F3
Culverstone House. BR5 .... 38 B6
Culverton Ct. 5 DA14 .... 24 A4
Culvey Cl. DA3 .... 42 E4
Cumberland Ave.
  Gravesend DA12 .... 30 C8
Cumberland Ave.
  Maidstone ME15 .... 107 D8
Cumberland Cl. TN11 .... 117 A4
Cumberland Dr. Dartford DA1 .. 26 F8
Cumberland Dr. Erith DA7 ...... 7 E7
Cumberland Gdns. 10 TN1 .. 149 A2
Cumberland Mews. 12 TN1 .. 149 A2
Cumberland Rd.
  Gillingham ME4 & ME7 .... 48 B7
Cumberland Rd. Gillingham ME7 48 C7
Cumberland Rd. Newham E13 .. 1 B8
Cumberland Sch. E16 .... 1 A8
Cumberland Wlk. TN1 .... 149 A2
Cumberland Yd. 11 TN1 .... 149 A2
Cumbrian Ave. DA7 .... 8 E5
Cundy Rd. E16 .... 1 B6
Cunningham Cl. TN4 .... 149 B7
Cunningham Cres. ME5 ...... 62 A8
Cunningham House. ME1 .. 47 B4
Cunningham Rd. TN4 .... 149 B7
Cupola Cl. BR1 .... 22 B3
Curlew Cl. SE28 .... 3 C6
Curlew Cres. ME2 .... 46 C6
Curlews The. DA12 .... 30 D6
Curran Ave. DA15 .... 6 F2
Currie Rd. TN4 .... 149 A5
Curteis Rd. TN30 .... 173 B1
Curtis Way. 7 SE28 .... 3 B6
Curtismill Cl. BR5 .... 38 B6
Curtismill Way. BR5 .... 38 B6
Curzon Cl. BR6 .... 51 D6
Curzon Cl. SE9 .... 23 C5
Curzon Dr. RM17 .... 12 C7
Curzon Rd. Chatham ME4 ...... 47 F4
Curzon Rd. Maidstone ME14 .. 92 A6
Custom House Sta. E16 .... 1 B6
Cut The. TN27 .... 158 E8
Cutbush Almshouses. 9 ME2 92 A3
Cutbush Cl. ME15 .... 92 B4
Cutbush and Corrall Ct. ME14 .. 92 B4
Cutmore St. DA11 .... 30 B8
Cutter Ridge Rd. DA13 .... 45 A1

Cutty Sark Ct. DA9 ...... 11 A2
Cuxton. BR5 ...... 37 C4
Cuxton Cl. DA6 ...... 7 E2
Cuxton Cty Inf Sch. ME2 ...... 46 B2
Cuxton Cty Jun Sch. ME2 ...... 46 B2
Cuxton Ind Est. ME2 ...... 46 C2
Cuxton Rd. Park Wood ME15 ... 107 F5
Cuxton Rd. Rochester ME2 ...... 46 F5
Cuxton Sta. ME2 ...... 46 C2
Cyclamen Cl. BR8 ...... 39 D5
Cygnet Cl. ME20 ...... 75 A2
Cygnet Gdns. DA11 ...... 29 F6
Cygnet L Ctr. DA11 ...... 29 E6
Cygnet Rd. ME5 ...... 62 C2
Cypress Ave. ME3 ...... 34 E3
Cypress Ct. ME7 ...... 48 F6
Cypress Gr. TN2 ...... 163 C8
Cypress Rd. ME2 ...... 33 C1
Cypress Tree Cl. DA15 ...... 23 F7
Cyprus Pl. E6 ...... 2 A6
Cyprus Sta. E6 ...... 2 A6
Cyril Lodge. 2 DA14 ...... 24 A4
Cyril Rd. Bexley DA7 ...... 7 E5
Cyril Rd. Orpington BR6 ...... 38 A2

D'arcy Pl. BR2 ...... 36 A5
Dabbling Cl. DA8 ...... 9 B7
Dabells. TN17 ...... 169 D4
Daerwood Cl. BR2 ...... 36 F1
Daffodil Rd. ME2 ...... 46 E7
Dagmar Rd. ME4 ...... 48 B2
Dagonet Gdns. BR1 ...... 22 A5
Dagonet Rd. BR1 ...... 22 A5
Dahlia Dr. BR8 ...... 39 F7
Dahlia Rd. SE2 ...... 3 B2
Dainton Cl. 2 BR1 ...... 36 B8
Daintons Cotts. 2 TN18 ... 178 F2
Dairsie Cl. 2 BR1 ...... 36 C7
Dairsie Rd. SE9 ...... 6 A4
Dairy Cl. DA4 ...... 27 B1
Dairy La. Chainhurst TN12 ... 121 F4
Dairy La. Crockham Hill TN8 ... 96 B1
Dairy La. Woolwich SE18 ...... 1 F2
Dairy Pl. TN12 ...... 121 F4
Dakota Gdns. E6 ...... 1 E8
Dalberg Way. SE2 ...... 3 D3
Dale Cl. Crayford DA1 ...... 8 F1
Dale Cl. Greenwich SE3 ...... 5 A4
Dale End. ME4 ...... 48 C2
Dale Rd. Crayford DA1 ...... 8 F1
Dale Rd. Rochester ME1 ...... 47 C3
Dale Rd. Southfleet DA13 ...... 29 A4
Dale Rd. Swanley BR8 ...... 39 C6
Dale St. Chatham ME4 ...... 47 E2
Dale St.
  Royal Tunbridge Wells TN1 ...... 149 B4
Dale The. BR2 ...... 50 D6
Dale View. DA8 ...... 8 F5
Dale Wlk. DA2 ...... 27 C7
Daleside. ME4 ...... 52 A5
Daleside Cl. BR6 ...... 52 A4
Dalison Cl. ME2 ...... 60 A4
Dallin Rd. Bexley DA6 ...... 7 D3
Dallin Rd. Woolwich SE18 ...... 6 B7
Dalmeny Rd. DA7 & DA8 ...... 8 B6
Dalton Cl. BR6 ...... 51 E7
Dalton St. ME7 ...... 48 C6
Daltons BR6 & BR8 ...... 53 C7
Damiem Cl. ME4 ...... 48 A2
Damigos Rd. DA12 ...... 30 F7
Damon Cl. DA14 ...... 24 B5
Damon Cl. DA14 ...... 24 B5
Damon Dr. ME3 ...... 34 E3
Damson Ct. BR8 ...... 39 D5
Damson Dr. ME7 ...... 48 E7
Danaway Cotts. ME9 ...... 65 C3
Dando Cres. SE3 ...... 5 B4
Dandridge Cl. SE10 ...... 1 A1
Dane Cl. Chatham ME5 ...... 62 C2
Dane Cl. Hartlip ME9 ...... 64 D6
Dane Cl. Orpington BR6 ...... 51 D5
Dane Cl. Sidcup DA5 ...... 25 A8
Dane Cl. ME17 ...... 106 C2
Dane La. ME9 ...... 64 D6
Dane Rd. TN14 ...... 68 F2
Danecourt Sch The. ME8 ...... 49 A2
Danefield Ct. Maidstone ME14 ... 93 B4
Danefield Ct. Sevenoaks TN13 ... 83 C4
Danehill Wlk. DA14 ...... 24 A5
Danemore. TN30 ...... 183 B8
Danes Cl. DA11 ...... 29 C5
Danes Hill. ME7 ...... 49 A6
Danescombe. SE12 ...... 22 A7
Danns La. ME18 ...... 89 A1
Dansington Rd. DA16 ...... 7 A3
Danson Cres. DA16 ...... 7 B4
Danson La. DA16 ...... 7 B3
Danson Mead. DA16 ...... 7 C4
Danson Prim Sch. DA16 ...... 7 A3
Danson Rd. Bexley DA6 ...... 7 D2
Danson Rd. Sidcup DA5 ...... 7 D1
Danson Underpass. DA5 ...... 7 C1
Danson Way. ME8 ...... 49 D2
Danvers Rd. TN9 ...... 117 B1
Darby Gdns. ME3 ...... 32 B3
Darby's La. TN5 ...... 175 B2
Darent Cl. TN13 ...... 83 C5
Darent Ind Pk. DA8 ...... 9 D8
Darent Mead. DA4 ...... 41 B8
Darent Valley Golf Course.
  TN14 ...... 69 A6
Darenth Ave. TN10 ...... 117 C5
Darenth Cotts. TN14 ...... 68 F8
Darenth Ct. 19 BR5 ...... 38 D1
Darenth Cty Prim Sch. DA2 ... 27 E2
Darenth Dr. DA12 ...... 31 B7
Darenth Gdns. TN16 ...... 81 D1
Darenth Hill. DA2 & DA4 ...... 27 C3

Darenth House. 2 ME15 ...... 107 D8
Darenth La. TN13 ...... 83 E6
Darenth Rd. Bexley DA16 ...... 7 A6
Darenth Rd. Dartford DA1 ...... 26 F7
Darenth Rd S. DA2 ...... 27 B4
Darenth Rise. ME5 ...... 62 B3
Darenth Way. TN14 ...... 69 A8
Darenth Wood Rd. Dartford DA2 27 E6
Darenth Wood Rd. Lane End DA2 27 E6
Dargate Cl. ME16 ...... 91 D7
Dargets Rd. ME5 ...... 62 A3
Daria Dr. DA12 ...... 30 F5
Darland Ave. ME7 ...... 48 E1
Darlton Cl. DA1 ...... 8 F4
Darman La. TN12 ...... 120 D3
Darnets Field. TN14 ...... 68 F2
Darnley Cl. ME2 ...... 46 D6
Darnley Dr. TN4 ...... 132 E4
Darnley Rd. Gravesend DA11 ... 30 A8
Darnley Rd. 1 Grays RM17 ... 12 B8
Darnley Rd. Rochester ME2 ... 46 E6
Darnley St. DA11 ...... 30 B8
Darns Hill. BR8 ...... 39 C2
Darrick Wood House. BR6 ...... 51 C7
Darrick Wood Inf Sch. BR6 ... 51 C7
Darrick Wood Jun Sch. BR6 ... 51 B6
Darrick Wood Rd. BR6 ...... 51 D8
Darrick Wood Sch. BR6 ...... 51 C7
Darrick Wood Sports Ctr. BR6 51 E8
Dart Cl. ME2 ...... 46 F7
Dartford Golf Club. DA1 ...... 26 B6
Dartford Gram Sch. DA1 ...... 9 C1
Dartford Gram Sch for Girls.
  DA1 ...... 26 C8
Dartford Rd. Coldblow DA5 ... 25 C7
Dartford Rd. Dartford DA1 ...... 9 B1
Dartford Rd. Farningham DA4 ... 41 A5
Dartford Rd. Sevenoaks TN13 ... 84 C3
Dartford Sta. DA1 ...... 9 E1
Dartford Trad Pk. DA1 ...... 26 F6
Dartmouth Rd. BR2 ...... 36 A2
Darwin Cl. BR6 ...... 51 D5
Darwin Cl. SE9 ...... 6 A1
Darwin Dr. TN10 ...... 117 D6
Darwin Rd. Bexley DA16 ...... 6 F4
Darwin Rd. Tilbury RM18 ...... 12 F6
Dashmonden Cl. ME2 ...... 33 C2
Dashwood Cl. DA6 ...... 8 A2
Dashwood Rd. DA11 ...... 30 A6
Davall House. 10 RM17 ...... 12 B8
Davenport Ave. ME7 ...... 48 E7
Davenport Rd. DA14 ...... 24 E6
David Coffer Ct. DA17 ...... 4 B2
David Saloman's House. TN3 148 D8
Davidson Tower. BR1 ...... 22 B3
Davis Ave. DA11 ...... 29 E7
Davis Cl. TN13 ...... 84 C5
Davy's Pl. DA12 ...... 30 E2
Dawbourns. TN30 ...... 173 B3
Dawes Cl. DA9 ...... 10 F2
Dawes St. ME7 ...... 48 C5
Dawson Ave. BR5 ...... 38 B7
Dawson Cl. SE18 ...... 2 C2
Dawson Dr. BR8 ...... 25 E1
Days La. DA15 ...... 23 E8
Days Lane Prim Sch. DA15 ...... 7 E5
Dayton Dr. DA8 ...... 9 D8
De Lapre Cl. BR5 ...... 38 D2
De Luci Rd. DA8 ...... 4 C1
De Lucy Prim Sch. SE2 ...... 3 B1
De Lucy St. SE2 ...... 3 B2
De Mere Cl. ME8 ...... 63 D6
De Warren House. DA11 ...... 12 D1
Deacon Cl. ME2 ...... 46 E8
Deacon Est The. ME20 ...... 76 A2
Deacon Trad Ctr. ME2 ...... 47 A6
Deacon Trad Est. TN9 ...... 117 D1
Deacons Leas. BR6 ...... 51 D6
Deakin Leas. TN11 & TN9 ... 133 B7
Dean & Chapter Cotts. DA13 ... 29 B2
Dean La. DA13 ...... 58 C5
Dean Rd. Luddesdown DA13 ... 58 E8
Dean Rd. Rochester ME2 ...... 46 F8
Dean St. ME15 ...... 106 C6
Dean Wood Cty Prim Inf Sch.
  ME8 ...... 63 D3
Dean Wood Cty Prim Jun Sch.
  ME8 ...... 63 D4
Deanery Rd. TN8 ...... 96 C2
Deangate Ridge Sports Ground.
  ME3 ...... 34 D8
Deans Ct. 6 TN9 ...... 133 B8
Deans Hill Rd. ME9 ...... 80 D5
Deansfield Inf Sch. SE9 ...... 6 A4
Deansfield Jun Sch. SE9 ...... 6 A4
Deanwood Cl. ME8 ...... 63 D6
Deanwood Dr. ME8 ...... 63 E4
Debrabant Cl. DA8 ...... 8 D8
Decoy Hill Rd. ME23 ...... 17 F6
Deepdene. TN5 ...... 175 A6
Deepdene Rd. DA16 ...... 7 A4
Deerhurst Cl. DA3 ...... 43 C6
Deerhurst Gdns. ME16 ...... 91 D4
Deerleap La. TN14 ...... 67 E6
Defiance Wlk. SE18 ...... 1 F3
Defiant Cl. ME5 ...... 62 B6
Defoe Cl. Chatham ME5 ...... 62 B6
Defoe Cl. Erith DA8 ...... 8 F6
Degema Rd. BR7 ...... 23 B3
Deirdre Chapman House. DA10 11 E1
Delacourt Rd. SE3 ...... 5 B7
Delafield Rd. SE7 ...... 1 C1
Delagarde Rd. TN16 ...... 81 C1
Delamere Gdns. 3 ME6 ...... 75 A8
Delamere Rd. ME6 ...... 75 A8
Delaware Cotts. TN8 ...... 128 F8
Delce Cty Inf Sch. ME1 ...... 47 D2
Delce Cty Jun Sch. ME1 ...... 47 C2

Delce Rd. ME1 ...... 47 D4
Delius Dr. TN10 ...... 117 F6
Dell Dr. TN2 ...... 149 D4
Dell The. Maypole DA5 ...... 25 E7
Dell The. Woolwich SE2 ...... 3 A1
Delme Cres. SE3 ...... 5 B5
Delmonden Rd. TN18 ...... 178 B1
Delves Ave. TN2 ...... 149 C1
Delvon Cl. SE18 ...... 6 A7
Den Cross. TN8 ...... 128 D6
Den La. TN12 ...... 121 C3
Denbeigh Dr. TN10 ...... 117 D6
Denberry Dr. DA14 ...... 24 B5
Denbigh Ave. ME8 ...... 49 D1
Denbigh Cl. BR7 ...... 22 F2
Denbigh Rd. TN4 ...... 149 C7
Denbridge Rd. BR1 & BR7 ... 36 F7
Dene Ave. DA15 ...... 24 B8
Dene Cl. DA2 ...... 25 E4
Dene Dr. New Barn DA3 ...... 43 B7
Dene Dr. Orpington BR6 ...... 52 B7
Dene Holm Rd. DA11 ...... 29 E5
Dene Lodge Cl. TN15 ...... 86 F7
Dene Rd. DA1 ...... 26 F8
Dene The. TN13 ...... 84 B1
Dene Way. TN3 ...... 148 A7
Dene Wlk. DA3 ...... 42 E6
Denecourt. ME5 ...... 38 C1
Denesway. DA13 ...... 44 B3
Denham Rd. ME9 ...... 65 B7
Denham St. SE10 ...... 1 A1
Denison Mews. ME3 ...... 19 C4
Deniston Ave. DA5 ...... 24 E7
Denmark House. 9 SE7 ...... 1 E2
Denmark Rd. ME1 ...... 36 B8
Denmark St. E13 ...... 1 B8
Dennard Way. BR6 ...... 51 A6
Dennettsland Rd. TN8 ...... 96 C1
Dennington Rd. TN13 ...... 133 A2
Dennis Cadman House. 4
  ME20 ...... 75 F1
Dennis Rd. DA11 ...... 30 B5
Dennis Willocks Cl. ME9 ...... 65 B6
Denny Cl. 12 E6 ...... 1 E8
Denny Ct. 1 DA2 ...... 10 B1
Denstead Wlk. 11 ME15 ...... 107 F6
Denton Cl. ME15 ...... 107 E8
Denton Court Rd. DA12 ...... 30 E8
Denton Rd. Bexley DA16 ...... 7 C7
Denton Rd. Dartford DA1 ...... 25 E8
Denton Rd. Maypole DA5 ...... 25 E7
Denton St. DA12 ...... 30 E8
Denton Terr. DA5 ...... 25 E6
Denver Cl. BR6 ...... 37 E3
Denver Ind Est. RM13 ...... 4 F8
Denver Rd. DA1 ...... 26 A8
Derby Cl. TN1 ...... 116 E6
Derby Rd. Chatham ME5 ...... 48 E2
Derby Rd. Gillingham ME5 ...... 48 E2
Derby Rd. Grays RM17 ...... 12 B8
Derby Rd. Maidstone ME15 ... 107 C8
Derby Road Bridge. RM17 ... 12 B8
Derifall Cl. E6 ...... 1 F8
Dering Way. DA12 ...... 30 F7
Deringwood Dr. ME15 ...... 92 F1
Dernier Rd. TN10 & TN9 ... 117 C4
Derrick Gdns. SE7 ...... 1 C2
Derry Downs. BR5 ...... 38 C3
Derwent Cl. DA1 ...... 26 B7
Derwent Cres. DA7 ...... 8 A5
Derwent Dr. Orpington BR5 ... 37 D2
Derwent Dr.
  Royal Tunbridge Wells TN4 ... 148 E5
Derwent House. 5 ME15 ...... 107 E7
Derwent Lodge Sch. TN1 ... 149 B4
Derwent Rd. TN10 ...... 117 C5
Derwent Way. ME8 ...... 63 D8
Detling CE Prim Sch. ME14 ... 78 A1
Detling Cl. ME8 ...... 49 C2
Detling Hill. ME14 ...... 78 B2
Detling Rd. Bromley BR1 ...... 22 A3
Detling Rd. Erith DA8 ...... 8 D7
Detling Rd. Northfleet DA11 ... 29 D7
Devalls Cl. E6 ...... 2 A6
Devema Cl. BR7 ...... 37 A8
Devenish Rd. SE2 ...... 3 A4
Devon Cl. Chatham ME5 ...... 62 C7
Devon Cl. Gillingham ME8 ... 49 F1
Devon Cl. DA4 ...... 41 B8
Devon Rd. Maidstone ME15 ... 107 C8
Devon Rd. Sutton at Hone DA4 ... 41 C8
Devonshire Ave. DA1 ...... 9 B1
Devonshire Cl. TN2 ...... 162 F8
Devonshire Rd. Bexley DA6 ... 7 E3
Devonshire Rd. Chislehurst SE9 . 22 E6
Devonshire Rd. Gillingham ME7 . 48 D7
Devonshire Rd. Gravesend DA12 30 B6
Devonshire Rd. Newham E16 ... 1 B7
Devonshire Rd. Orpington BR6 ... 38 A2
Devonshire Sq. BR2 ...... 36 B5
Dewberry Gdns. E6 ...... 1 E8
Dewhurst Cotts. TN5 ...... 174 A1
Dewhurst La. TN5 ...... 174 B8
DeWinter House. TN13 ...... 84 A3
Dewlands Ave. DA2 ...... 27 B8
Dexter House. 2 DA18 ...... 3 E3
Dhekelia Cl. ME14 ...... 92 A7
Dial Cl. Gillingham ME7 ...... 48 F6
Dial Cl. Swanscombe DA9 ...... 11 D2
Dial Rd. ME7 ...... 48 F6
Diameter Rd. BR5 ...... 37 C3
Diamond Field. TN12 ...... 152 F3
Diana Cl. DA8 ...... 8 E8
Dianne Ct. SE12 ...... 22 A7
Dianthus Cl. SE2 ...... 3 B1
Dibden La. TN13 & TN14 ... 98 E8
Dickens Ave. Dartford DA1 ... 10 A3
Dickens Ave. Tilbury RM18 ... 13 B6

Dickens Cl. Erith DA8 ...... 8 B7
Dickens Cl. Hartley DA3 ...... 42 F4
Dickens Cl. Langley Heath ME17 108 E4
Dickens Cl. ME2 ...... 47 D8
Dickens Dr. Chislehurst BR7 ... 23 C2
Dickens Dr. East Malling ME19 ... 74 F1
Dickens House. 3 DA17 ...... 3 F1
Dickens Rd. Gravesend DA12 ... 30 E7
Dickens Rd. Maidstone ME14 ... 91 E3
Dickens Rd. Rochester ME1 ... 47 C2
Dickens Way. TN18 ...... 179 A2
Dickensian Cl. ME3 ...... 19 A2
Dickley La. ME17 ...... 111 A6
Dickson House. SE18 ...... 5 E6
Dickson Rd. SE9 ...... 5 E4
Digdog La. TN17 ...... 156 D3
Dignals Cl. ME8 ...... 49 F2
Dilhorne Cl. SE12 ...... 22 B5
Dillon Way. TN1 ...... 149 D6
Dillywood Cotts. ME3 ...... 32 F2
Dillywood La. ME3 ...... 32 F2
Dimmock Cl. TN12 ...... 136 B7
Dingleden La. TN17 ...... 180 F2
Dippers Cl. TN15 ...... 69 F2
Dislingbury Rd. TN11 ...... 134 C4
Disraeli Cl. Park Wood ME15 ... 107 E5
Disraeli Cl. Woolwich SE28 ...... 3 C5
Dittisham Rd. SE9 ...... 22 E4
Ditton CE Jun Sch. ME20 ...... 75 C1
Ditton Court Cl. ME19 ...... 75 B1
Ditton Cty Inf Sch. ME20 ...... 75 C1
Ditton Pl. ME19 & ME20 ...... 75 B1
Ditton Rd. DA6 ...... 7 E2
Dixon Cl. Maidstone ME15 ... 91 F2
Dixon Cl. 4 Newham E6 ...... 1 F7
Dixon House. SE2 ...... 3 C1
Dixwell Cl. ME8 ...... 63 D5
Dobell Rd. SE9 ...... 5 F2
Dobson Rd. DA12 ...... 30 E3
Dock Approach Rd. RM17 ... 12 E8
Dock Head Rd. ME4 ...... 48 A8
Dock Rd. Chatham ME4 ...... 47 F6
Dock Rd. Gillingham ME4 ...... 48 A7
Dock Rd. Grays RM17 ...... 12 D8
Dock Rd. Grays RM17 ...... 12 E7
Dock Rd. Tilbury RM18 ...... 13 A4
Dockland St. Newham E16 ...... 2 A4
Dockland St. Newham E16 ...... 2 A5
Doctor Hope's Rd. TN17 ... 169 D4
Dodd Rd. TN10 ...... 117 F5
Doddington Cl. ME16 ...... 91 E5
Doddington Rd. ME8 ...... 49 D3
Doebury Wlk. SE18 ...... 7 A8
Dog Cotts. RH19 ...... 144 B1
Doggett's Sq. ME2 ...... 47 C7
Doggetts Row. ME3 ...... 21 B6
Dogwood Cl. Chatham ME5 ... 62 D1
Dogwood Cl. Northfleet DA11 ... 29 F4
Dolphin Cl. SE28 ...... 3 D7
Dolphin Dr. ME8 ...... 63 C5
Dombey Cl. Higham ME3 ...... 32 C3
Dombey Cl. Rochester ME1 ... 47 C3
Domonic Dr. SE9 ...... 23 B5
Donaldson Rd. SE18 ...... 6 A6
Doncaster Ct. 7 ME15 ...... 107 F6
Donet Cl. ME8 ...... 63 C5
Dongola Rd. E13 ...... 1 B8
Donkey Field. TN11 ...... 115 E1
Donkey La. ME18 ...... 55 B8
Donnington Rd. TN13 ...... 83 D8
Doon Brae. TN4 ...... 133 A2
Dorado Gdns. BR6 ...... 52 D7
Doran Gr. SE9 ...... 6 E7
Dorchester Ave. DA5 ...... 24 D8
Dorchester Cl. Cliffe Woods ME3 33 B7
Dorchester Cl. Dartford DA1 ... 26 F7
Dorchester Cl. St Paul's Cray BR5 24 B1
Dorchester Rd. DA12 ...... 30 D5
Dorcis Ave. DA7 ...... 7 E5
Doric Ave. TN4 ...... 132 F1
Doric Cl. TN4 ...... 132 F1
Dorin Ct. TN2 ...... 149 C3
Doris Ave. DA7 ...... 8 C6
Dorking Rd. TN1 ...... 149 C6
Dorland House. SE9 ...... 6 D1
Dormers. DA13 ...... 44 B2
Dornberg Cl. SE3 ...... 5 A7
Dornberg Rd. SE3 ...... 5 B7
Dornden Dr. TN3 ...... 148 A4
Dornden Gdns. ME5 ...... 62 B2
Dorne Cotts. TN27 ...... 127 E6
Dorney Rise. BR5 ...... 37 F5
Dorothy Ave. TN17 ...... 169 E4
Dorothy Evans Cl. DA7 ...... 8 B3
Dorrit Way. Chislehurst BR7 ... 23 C2
Dorrit Way. Rochester ME1 ... 47 D2
Dorset Ave. DA16 ...... 6 F3
Dorset Cotts. TN7 ...... 160 B4
Dorset Cres. DA12 ...... 30 E4
Dorset Rd. Chislehurst SE9 ... 22 E6
Dorset Rd.
  Royal Tunbridge Wells TN2 ... 149 D2
Dorset Road Inf Sch. SE9 ... 22 E6
Dorset Sq. ME8 ...... 49 D1
Dorset St. TN13 ...... 84 C2
Dorset Way. ME15 ...... 107 C8
Dorton Coll. TN15 ...... 84 F5
Dorton Dr. TN15 ...... 84 F5
Dorton House
  (Royal London Society
  Sch for the Blind). TN15 ... 84 F5
Dorville Rd. SE12 & SE13 ...... 5 A2
Dothill Rd. SE18 ...... 6 C7
Dotterel Cl. ME5 ...... 62 D2
Doubleton La. TN11 ...... 131 A5
Doug Siddons Ct. 7 RM17 ... 12 C8

Douglas Almshouses. ME17 ... 111 D5
Douglas Bldgs. TN12 ...... 139 E5
Douglas Rd. Bexley DA16 ...... 7 B6
Douglas Rd. Lenham ME17 ... 111 D5
Douglas Rd. Maidstone ME16 ... 91 E3
Douglas Rd. 6 Newham E16 ... 1 A8
Douglas Rd. Rochester ME1 ... 47 C2
Douglas Rd. Tonbridge TN9 ... 133 A8
Dove App. E6 ...... 1 E8
Dove Cl. ME5 ...... 62 B6
Dove Rd. TN10 ...... 117 C6
Dovedale Cl. DA16 ...... 7 A5
Dovedale Rd. DA2 ...... 27 C7
Doveney Cl. BR5 ...... 38 D6
Dover House. ME2 ...... 33 C1
Dover Patrol. SE3 ...... 5 C5
Dover Rd. Northfleet DA11 ... 29 D8
Dover Rd. Woolwich SE18 ...... 6 C5
Dover Rd E. DA11 ...... 29 E7
Dover Road Cty Prim Jun Sch.
  DA11 ...... 29 E7
Dover St. ME16 ...... 91 E4
Doves Cl. BR2 ...... 50 E8
Dowding Way. TN2 ...... 133 E1
Dowding Wlk. 3 DA11 ...... 29 E5
Dower House Cres. TN4 ...... 132 E3
Dowgate Cl. TN9 ...... 133 D7
Dowlerville Rd. BR6 ...... 51 F4
Dowling Cl. ME6 ...... 74 E7
Dowling House. DA17 ...... 3 F3
Down Ave. TN3 ...... 166 A4
Down House. BR6 ...... 66 A7
Down La. TN3 ...... 163 C1
Down's Cl. TN27 ...... 141 E5
Downage The. DA11 ...... 30 A6
Downash Ct. TN5 ...... 177 A3
Downash House. TN5 ...... 177 A3
Downbank Ave. DA7 ...... 8 D5
Downderry Way. ME19 ...... 75 B1
Downe Ave. TN14 ...... 66 B8
Downe Cl. DA16 ...... 7 C7
Downe House. 9 SE7 ...... 5 C8
Downe Prim Sch. BR6 ...... 66 A8
Downe Rd. Cudham BR6 & TN14 ... 66 C5
Downe Rd. Farthing Street BR2 ... 50 C2
Downend. SE18 ...... 6 B7
Downer Ct. ME4 ...... 61 E8
Downham Way. BR1 & SE12 ... 22 A4
Downings. E6 ...... 2 A7
Downlands. ME17 ...... 110 F6
Downleys Cl. SE9 ...... 22 F6
Downman Rd. SE9 ...... 5 E4
Downs Ave. Chislehurst BR7 ... 22 F3
Downs Ave. Dartford DA1 ...... 27 A8
Downs Cl. ME14 ...... 92 B8
Downs Cl. Istead Rise DA13 ... 29 D3
Downs Rd. Maidstone ME5 ... 92 B8
Downs Rd. Yalding ME18 ... 105 A1
Downs The. ME5 ...... 61 D1
Downs Valley. DA3 ...... 42 E5
Downs View. Burham ME1 ...... 60 F1
Downs View. West Malling ME19 89 B8
Downs View Cl. BR6 ...... 52 C1
Downs View Rd. ME14 ...... 92 B8
Downs Wood. DA13 ...... 72 F8
Downside. ME2 ...... 47 A7
Downsview. Chatham ME5 ...... 62 C8
Downsview. Trottiscliffe ME19 ... 73 A5
Downsview Cl. BR8 ...... 39 F6
Downsview Cty Prim Sch. BR8 40 A6
Downsview Rd. TN13 ...... 83 F2
Downsway. BR6 ...... 51 E5
Doyle Cl. DA8 ...... 8 E6
Doyle Way. RM18 ...... 13 C5
Drage Rd. TN12 ...... 119 E6
Drake Cl. BR5 ...... 38 B3
Drake's Ave. ME2 ...... 46 F8
Draper Cl. DA17 ...... 3 F2
Draper St. 3 TN4 ...... 132 F2
Drawell Cl. SE18 ...... 2 E1
Dray Corner Rd. TN27 ...... 140 F7
Dray Ct. TN11 ...... 118 E8
Drays Cotts. DA4 ...... 41 B5
Drayton Ave. BR6 ...... 37 B1
Drayton Rd. TN9 ...... 133 C8
Drayton Prim Sch. E16 ...... 1 E5
Drew Rd. Newham E16 ...... 1 D5
Drew Rd. Newham E16 ...... 1 E5
Drewery Dr. ME8 ...... 63 C5
Driffield Gdns. TN9 ...... 132 F7
Drift The. BR2 ...... 50 D7
Drive The. Bexley DA5 ...... 24 D8
Drive The. Chislehurst BR7 ... 37 E8
Drive The. Erith DA8 ...... 8 B8
Drive The. Gravesend DA12 ... 30 E4
Drive The. New Barn DA3 ...... 43 B6
Drive The. Orpington BR6 ...... 51 F8
Drive The.
  Royal Tunbridge Wells TN2 ... 149 B1
Drive The. Sevenoaks TN13 ... 84 B3
Drive The. Sidcup DA14 ...... 24 B4
Drive The. St Paul's Cray BR7 ... 37 F6
Drove Way The. DA13 ...... 29 C1
Drudgeon Way. DA2 ...... 28 C5
Drummond Cl. DA8 ...... 8 E6
Drummond House. 11 SE18 ...... 2 A2
Drury Rd. TN30 ...... 183 B8
Dry Bank Ct. TN10 ...... 117 C4
Dry Bank Rd. TN10 ...... 117 C4
Dry Hill Park Cres. TN10 ... 117 C3
Dry Hill Park Rd. TN10 ... 117 B3
Dry Hill Rd. TN10 ...... 117 B3
Dryden House. BR2 ...... 36 D4

Dryden Pl. RM18 .... 13 B6
Dryden Rd. DA16 .... 6 F6
Dryden Way. BR6 .... 38 A1
Dryhill La. TN14 .... 83 B3
Dryhill Rd. DA17 .... 7 F8
Dryland Ave. 5 BR6 .... 51 F6
Dryland Rd. Borough Green TN15 .. 86 F6
Dryland Rd. Snodland ME6 .... 74 F8
Duchess Cl. ME2 .... 46 E8
Duchess of Kent Ct The. 1
ME20 .... 75 F1
Duchess of Kent Dr. ME5 .... 62 B3
Duchess' Wlk. TN15 .... 84 E2
Ducie House. 8 SE7 .... 5 C8
Ducketts Rd. DA1 .... 8 F2
Duddington Cl. SE9 .... 22 D4
Dudely Rd. DA11 .... 29 E8
Dudley Lodge. TN2 .... 149 C4
Dudley Rd. TN1 .... 149 A4
Dudsbury Rd. DA1 .... 9 B2
Dukes Meadow. TN11 .... 114 F2
Dukes Meadow Dr. ME7 .... 62 F6
Dukes Orch. DA5 .... 25 C7
Dukes Rd. TN1 .... 149 C5
Dukes Wlk. ME15 .... 92 A4
Dulverton Prim Sch. DA15 .... 23 D6
Dulverton Rd. SE9 .... 23 D6
Dumbreck Rd. SE9 .... 6 A4
Dunblane Rd. SE9 .... 5 E5
Duncan Rd. ME7 .... 48 D5
Duncans Cotts. 3 TN16 .... 81 D1
Duncroft. SE18 .... 6 E7
Dundale Rd. TN12 & TN3 .... 151 A3
Dundonald Cl. 6 E6 .... 1 E7
Dunedin House. 2 RM18 .... 13 A5
Dunera Dr. ME14 .... 92 A7
Dunk's Green Rd. TN11 .... 102 A5
Dunkery Rd. SE12 & SE9 .... 22 E5
Dunkin Rd. DA1 .... 10 A3
Dunkirk Cl. DA12 .... 30 C3
Dunkirk Dr. ME5 .... 61 F6
Dunkley Villas. TN15 .... 72 F1
Dunlop Cl. TN18 .... 179 A2
Dunlop Point. E16 .... 1 A5
Dunlop Rd. RM18 .... 12 F6
Dunn Street Rd. ME7 .... 78 A8
Dunning's La. ME1 .... 47 C4
Dunnings The. ME16 .... 91 A2
Dunnock Rd. E6 .... 1 E7
Dunnose Ct. RM16 .... 10 B8
Dunoon Cotts. BR6 .... 66 A5
Dunorlan Farm Cotts. TN2 .... 149 E4
Dunstable Ct. 4 SE3 .... 5 A7
Dunstall Welling Est. DA16 .... 7 B5
Dunstan Glade. BR5 .... 37 D3
Dunstan Gr. TN4 .... 149 B6
Dunstan Rd. TN4 .... 149 B6
Dunster Ct. 4 DA2 .... 10 B1
Dunton Green Cty Prim Sch.
TN13 .... 83 E7
Dunton Green Sta. TN13 .... 83 E7
Dunvegan Rd. SE9 .... 5 F3
Dunwich Rd. DA7 .... 7 F6
Dupree Rd. SE7 .... 1 B1
Durant Rd. BR8 .... 26 A2
Durban House. 7 ME15 .... 107 E5
Durham Cl. ME15 .... 92 E1
Durham Rd. Bromley BR2 .... 36 A5
Durham Rd. Gillingham ME8 .... 63 C7
Durham Rd. Sidcup DA14 .... 24 B3
Durham Rise. SE18 .... 2 D1
Duriun Way. DA8 .... 9 B7
Durley Gdns. BR6 .... 52 B7
Durndale La. Northfleet DA11 ...... 29 E5
Durndale La. Northfleet DA11 ...... 29 F5
Durrant Way. Orpington BR6 .... 51 D5
Durrant Way. Swanscombe DA10 .. 28 E8
Durrell Gdns. ME5 .... 48 C1
Dursley Cl. SE3 .... 5 C5
Dursley Gdns. SE3 .... 5 D6
Dursley Rd. SE3 .... 5 C5
Duval Dr. ME1 .... 61 E8
Duvard's Pl. ME9 .... 65 F1
Dux Hill. TN15 .... 101 F8
Dux La. TN15 .... 86 F1
Duxberry Rd. BR2 .... 36 E4
Duxford House. 12 SE2 .... 3 D4
Dyke Dr. BR5 .... 38 C2
Dykewood Cl. DA5 .... 25 E5
Dylan Rd. DA17 .... 4 A3
Dymchurch Cl. BR6 .... 51 E6
Dyneley Rd. SE12 .... 22 C5
Dynes Rd. TN14 & TN15 .... 69 E2
Dynevor Rd. TN4 .... 149 C7

Eagle Cl. ME20 .... 75 A2
Eagle House. RM17 .... 11 F8
Eagle Way. DA11 .... 12 A2
Eagles Rd. DA9 .... 11 B2
Eaglesfield Rd. SE18 .... 6 B6
Eaglesfield Sch. SE18 .... 6 A6
Eaglestone Cl. TN15 .... 87 A8
Ealdham Prim Sch. SE9 .... 5 C3
Ealdham Sq. SE9 .... 5 C3
Ealing Cl. ME5 .... 62 C4
Eardemont Cl. DA1 .... 8 F3
Eardley Point. 9 SE18 .... 2 B1
Eardley Rd. Erith DA17 .... 8 A1
Eardley Rd. Sevenoaks TN13 .... 84 B3
Earl Cl. ME5 .... 62 B4
Earl Rd. DA11 .... 29 E6
Earl Rise. SE18 .... 2 D2
Earl St. ME14 .... 91 F4
Earl's Rd. TN4 .... 148 F4
Earlshall Rd. SE9 .... 6 A3

Eason Villas. TN12 .... 138 D6
East Becton District Ctr. E16 ...... 1 F8
East Borough Cty Prim Sch.
ME14 .... 92 B5
East Cliff Rd. TN4 .... 149 A6
East Crescent Rd. DA11 .... 13 C1
East Cross. TN30 .... 183 B3
East Dr. BR5 .... 38 B3
East Farleigh Cty Prim Sch.
ME15 .... 106 B6
East Farleigh Sta. TN16 .... 106 B8
East Hall Hill. ME17 .... 123 E7
East Hall Rd. BR5 .... 38 F2
East Ham Ind Est. E16 .... 1 E8
East Ham Manor Way. E6 .... 2 A7
East Hill. Dartford DA1 .... 26 F8
East Hill. South Darenth DA4 ...... 41 D7
East Hill. Tenterden TN30 .... 183 B8
East Hill Dr. DA1 .... 26 F8
East Hill Rd. TN15 .... 70 B7
East Holme. DA8 .... 8 D6
East Kent Ave. ME12 .... 12 C1
East Malling Research Sta
(Horticultural). ME19 .... 90 C6
East Malling Sta. ME19 .... 90 A6
East Mascalls. 15 SE7 .... 5 C8
East Mill. DA11 .... 12 F1
East Milton Rd. DA12 .... 30 D8
East Park Rd. ME20 .... 91 A8
East Peckham Cty Prim Sch.
TN12 .... 119 F6
East Rd. Bexley DA16 .... 7 B5
East Rd. Chatham ME4 .... 48 A7
East Rd. Gillingham ME4 .... 48 A8
East Rochester Way.
Coldblow DA1 .... 25 D8
East Rochester Way. Sidcup SE9 .. 7 C1
East Row. ME1 .... 47 C5
East St. Addington ME19 .... 73 D3
East St. Bexley DA7 .... 8 A3
East St. Bromley BR1 .... 36 A7
East St. Chatham ME4 .... 48 A3
East St. Gillingham ME7 .... 48 D6
East St. Grays RM16 .... 11 E8
East St. Harrietsham ME17 .... 110 E5
East St. Hunton ME15 .... 121 F7
East St. Snodland ME6 .... 75 B8
East St. Tonbridge TN9 .... 117 C2
East Street N. ME19 .... 73 D3
East Sutton Park
(HM Young Offender Inst &
Prison). ME17 .... 125 B7
East Sutton Rd.
Hearnden Green ME17 .... 125 C4
East Sutton Rd.
Sutton Valence ME17 .... 125 A7
East Terr. Gravesend DA11 .... 13 C1
East Terr. Sidcup DA15 .... 23 E7
East Thurrock Rd. RM17 .... 12 C8
East Weald Dr. TN30 .... 173 B1
East Wickham Inf Sch. DA16 .... 6 F6
East Wickham Jun Sch. DA16 ...... 7 A4
East Woodside. DA5 .... 24 E7
Eastbrook Rd. SE3 .... 5 B6
Eastbury Rd. Newham E6 .... 2 A8
Eastbury Rd. Orpington BR5 .... 37 D3
Eastcombe Ave. SE7 .... 5 B8
Eastcote. BR6 .... 37 F1
Eastcote Prim Sch. DA16 .... 6 D4
Eastcote Rd. DA16 .... 6 D5
Eastcourt La. ME8 .... 49 B4
Eastcourt La. Gillingham ME8 ...... 49 B3
Eastcourt La.
Gillingham,Lower Twydall
ME7 & ME8 .... 49 B4
Easterfields. ME16 & ME19 .... 90 C5
Eastern Rd. ME7 .... 48 F6
Eastern Way. Erith SE28 .... 3 D5
Eastern Way. 1 Grays RM17 .... 12 A8
Eastfield Gdns. TN10 .... 117 E5
Eastfield House. ME16 .... 91 B2
Eastgate. ME1 .... 47 D5
Eastgate Cl. SE28 .... 3 D7
Eastgate Ct. ME1 .... 47 C5
Eastgate Rd. TN30 .... 183 C8
Eastgate Terr. ME1 .... 47 C5
Eastlands Cl. TN2 & TN4 .... 162 E8
Eastlands Rd. TN4 .... 148 E1
Eastleigh Rd. DA7 .... 8 C4
Eastling Cl. ME8 .... 49 D3
Eastling House. 8 BR5 .... 38 D1
Eastmead Cl. BR1 .... 36 E7
Eastmoor Pl. SE18 & SE7 .... 1 D3
Eastmoor St. SE7 .... 1 D3
Eastnor Rd. SE9 .... 23 C7
Eastry Cl. ME16 .... 91 C7
Eastry Rd. DA8 .... 8 A7
Eastview Ave. SE18 .... 6 E7
Eastway. BR2 .... 36 A2
Eastwell. 3 SE3 .... 183 A7
Eastwell Barn Mews. TN30 .... 183 A8
Eastwell Cl. Maidstone ME14 ..... 92 C5
Eastwell Cl.
Paddock Wood TN12 .... 135 E6
Eastwell Meadows. TN30 .... 183 A8
Eaton Ct. BR7 .... 23 C2
Eaton Rd. DA14 .... 24 D6
Eaton Sq. DA3 .... 42 D6
Ebbsfleet Ind Est. DA11 .... 12 B2
Ebbsfleet Wlk. DA11 .... 12 B1
Ebdon Way. SE3 .... 5 B4
Ebury Cl. BR2 .... 50 E7
Ebury Ct. BR2 .... 50 E7
Eccles Row. ME20 .... 75 F6
Eccleston Cl. BR6 .... 37 D1
Eccleston Rd. ME15 .... 91 F2
Echo Ct. ME15 .... 107 F6
Echo Rd. DA12 .... 30 C6
Eclipse Rd. E13 .... 1 B8

Edam Ct. 11 DA14 .... 24 A5
Eddington Cl. ME15 .... 107 B6
Eden Ave. ME5 .... 62 A7
Eden Cl. DA5 .... 25 C4
Eden Ct. 1 Hawkhurst TN18 ...... 178 F2
Eden Ct. 17 Orpington BR5 .... 38 D1
Eden Pl. DA11 .... 30 B8
Eden Rd. High Halstow ME23 ...... 17 E4
Eden Rd. Joyden's Wood DA5 ...... 25 C4
Eden Rd.
Royal Tunbridge Wells TN1 ..... 149 A2
Eden Valley Sch. TN8 .... 112 C2
Eden Villas. TN8 .... 128 D7
Edenbridge Cty Prim Sch.
TN8 .... 112 D1
Edenbridge & District
War Meml Hospl. TN8 .... 128 D7
Edenbridge Golf & Country Club.
TN8 .... 112 A2
Edenbridge Rd. TN8 & TN7 ...... 145 E2
Edenbridge Sta. TN8 .... 112 C3
Edenbridge Town Sta. TN8 ...... 112 D1
Edenbridge Trad Ctr. TN8 .... 128 D8
Edendale Rd. DA7 .... 8 D5
Edensmuir Ct. SE3 .... 5 A7
Edgar Cl. BR8 .... 39 F6
Edgar Rd. TN14 .... 69 E2
Edge Hill. SE18 .... 6 B8
Edge Hill Ct. DA14 .... 23 F4
Edgeborough Way. BR1 .... 36 D8
Edgebury. BR7 & SE9 .... 23 B4
Edgebury Prim Sch. BR7 .... 23 C4
Edgebury Wlk. BR7 .... 23 C5
Edgefield Cl. DA1 .... 27 B7
Edgehill Gdns. DA13 .... 43 F8
Edgehill Rd. BR7 .... 23 C4
Edger Pl. 3 ME15 .... 92 A4
Edgewood Dr. BR6 .... 52 A5
Edgeworth Rd. SE9 .... 5 D3
Edgington Way. DA14 .... 24 D1
Edinburgh Ct. DA8 .... 8 D7
Edinburgh Mews. RM18 .... 13 B5
Edinburgh Rd. Chatham ME4 ...... 48 A2
Edinburgh Rd. Gillingham ME7 .... 48 D5
Edinburgh Rd. Grain ME3 .... 21 B5
Edinburgh Sq. Maidstone ME15 . 107 C7
Edinburgh Sq. Maidstone ME15 . 107 D6
Edington Rd. SE2 .... 3 B3
Edison Gr. SE18 .... 6 F7
Edison Rd. Bexley DA16 .... 6 F6
Edison Rd. Bromley BR2 .... 36 A7
Edith Pond Ct. SE9 .... 23 B6
Edith Rd. BR6 .... 52 A5
Ediva Rd. DA13 .... 44 A4
Edmund Cl. Maidstone ME16 ...... 91 A3
Edmund Cl.
Meopham Station DA13 .... 44 A4
Edmund Rd. Bexley DA16 .... 7 A4
Edmund Rd. Orpington BR5 .... 38 C3
Edmunds Ave. BR5 .... 38 D6
Edmundson House. 10 SE18 .... 2 A2
Edna Rd. ME14 .... 91 F8
Edward Cl. Chatham ME5 .... 48 C1
Edward Ct. 2 Newham E16 .... 1 A8
Edward Harvey Ct. TN4 .... 3 F1
Edward Rd. Bromley BR1 .... 22 C1
Edward Rd. Chislehurst BR7 .... 23 B3
Edward Rd. Chatham ME4 .... 48 A3
Edward St. Rochester ME2 .... 47 B7
Edward St.
Royal Tunbridge Wells TN4 ..... 132 F1
Edward St. Rusthall TN4 .... 148 C4
Edward Tyler Rd. SE12 .... 22 C6
Edward Wlk. ME19 .... 89 F8
Edwards Cl. ME8 .... 63 C5
Edwards Gdns. BR8 .... 39 D5
Edwards Rd. DA17 .... 4 A2
Edwin Arnold Ct. DA15 .... 23 F4
Edwin Cl. DA7 .... 7 F8
Edwin Petty Pl. DA2 .... 27 C8
Edwin Rd. Gillingham ME8 .... 63 C8
Edwin Rd. Wilmington DA2 .... 26 C5
Edwin St. Gravesend DA11 .... 30 B8
Edwin St. Newham E16 .... 1 A8
Edwina Pl. ME9 .... 65 C7
Egdean Wlk. TN13 .... 84 C4
Egerton Ave. BR8 .... 39 F8
Egerton CE Prim Sch. TN27 ...... 127 F3
Egerton Cl. DA1 .... 26 B7
Egerton House Rd. TN27 .... 127 E4
Egerton Rd. ME14 .... 91 E7
Eggpie La. TN11 .... 115 E7
Egham Rd. E13 .... 1 B8
Eglantine La. DA4 .... 41 B3
Eglinton Hill. SE18 .... 6 B7
Eglinton Inf Sch. SE18 .... 6 A8
Eglinton Jun Mix Sch. SE18 .... 6 A8
Eglinton Rd. Swanscombe DA10 .. 11 F1
Eglinton Rd. Woolwich SE18 .... 6 B8
Egremont Rd. ME15 .... 92 F2
Eight Dock East Rd. ME4 .... 34 A1
Eileen Ct. BR7 .... 23 A3
Eisenhower Dr. E6 .... 1 E8
Elaine Ave. ME2 .... 46 E6
Elaine Ct. ME2 .... 46 E6
Elaine Prim Sch. ME2 .... 46 E6
Elbourne Trad Est. DA17 .... 4 B3
Elbury Dr. E16 .... 1 A7
Elder Cl. Hoo St Werburgh ME3 ... 34 E3
Elder Cl. Kingswood ME17 .... 109 D2
Elder Cl. Sidcup DA15 .... 23 F7
Elder Ct. SE8 .... 63 B6
Elderslie Rd. SE9 .... 6 A2
Eldon St. ME4 .... 48 A4
Eldon Way. TN12 .... 135 F7
Eldred Dr. BR5 .... 52 D8
Eleanor Wlk. 25 SE18 .... 1 F2

Elford Cl. SE9 .... 5 C3
Elgal Cl. BR6 .... 51 B5
Elgar Cl. TN10 .... 117 E6
Elgar Rd. RM18 .... 13 B6
Elgin Gdns. ME2 .... 46 D5
Elham Cl. Bromley BR1 .... 22 C1
Elham Cl. Gillingham ME8 .... 49 B3
Elibank Rd. SE9 .... 6 A3
Eling Ct. ME15 .... 107 A8
Eliot Rd. DA1 .... 10 B2
Elizabeth Cl. RM18 .... 13 B5
Elizabeth Ct. Chatham ME5 .... 62 A7
Elizabeth Ct. Erith DA8 .... 8 D7
Elizabeth Ct. Gillingham ME8 ..... 49 C1
Elizabeth Ct. Gravesend DA11 .... 13 A1
Elizabeth Garlick Ct. 1 TN1 ..... 149 B4
Elizabeth Garrett Anderson House.
9 DA17 .... 4 A3
Elizabeth House. ME14 .... 92 A6
Elizabeth Huggins Cotts. DA11 ... 30 B6
Elizabeth Pl. DA4 .... 40 E3
Elizabeth Raybould Ctr
(Univ of Greenwich)The. DA2 . 10 B1
Elizabeth Smith's Ct. ME19 .... 89 F7
Elizabeth St. DA9 .... 10 E2
Elizabeth Terr. SE9 .... 5 F1
Elizabeth Way. BR5 .... 38 C4
Ellen Cl. BR1 .... 36 D6
Ellen Wilkinson Prim Sch. E16 ..... 1 A8
Ellen's Pl. ME9 .... 65 C6
Ellenborough Rd. DA14 .... 24 E3
Ellenswood Cl. ME15 .... 93 A1
Ellerman Rd. RM18 .... 12 F5
Ellerslie. DA12 .... 30 D8
Ellesmere Ct. SE12 .... 22 A7
Ellingham Leas. ME15 .... 107 C2
Elliott Rd. BR2 .... 36 D5
Elliott St. DA12 .... 30 D8
Elliotts La. TN14 & TN16 .... 82 C3
Ellis Cl. DA1 .... 27 B7
Ellis Ct. DA1 .... 27 B7
Ellis Way. DA1 .... 26 F6
Elliscombe Mount. 11 SE7 .... 5 C8
Elliscombe Rd. SE7 .... 5 C8
Ellison Rd. DA15 .... 23 D7
Elliston House. 14 SE18 .... 2 A2
Elm Ave. Chatham ME4 .... 47 F1
Elm Ave. Chattenden ME3 .... 34 A4
Elm Cl. Dartford DA1 .... 26 C7
Elm Cl. Egerton TN27 .... 127 F3
Elm Cl. Higham ME3 .... 32 C3
Elm Cotts. BR8 .... 40 B8
Elm Court Ind Est. ME7 .... 62 E3
Elm Cres. ME19 .... 89 F8
Elm Gr. Erith DA8 .... 8 D7
Elm Gr. Hildenborough ME11 .... 116 F5
Elm Gr. Maidstone ME15 .... 92 B3
Elm Gr. Orpington BR6 .... 37 F1
Elm La. TN10 & TN9 .... 117 C3
Elm Rd. Dartford DA1 .... 26 D7
Elm Rd. Gillingham ME7 .... 48 C6
Elm Rd. Grays RM17 .... 12 C8
Elm Rd. Gravesend DA12 .... 30 C5
Elm Rd. Hoo St Werburgh ME3 ... 34 E3
Elm Rd. Orpington BR6 .... 52 A3
Elm Rd.
Royal Tunbridge Wells TN4 ..... 132 F1
Elm Rd. Sidcup DA14 .... 24 A4
Elm Rd. Stone DA9 .... 10 E1
Elm Rd. Westerham TN16 .... 81 D2
Elm Terr. SE9 .... 6 A1
Elm Terr. West Thurrock RM16 ... 11 B8
Elm Tree Cotts. ME3 .... 19 A3
Elm Tree Ct. ME1 .... 47 A2
Elm Tree Dr. ME4 .... 48 B3
Elm Wlk. Aylesford ME20 .... 75 E1
Elm Wlk. Orpington BR6 .... 50 F7
Elmbank Dr. BR1 .... 36 D7
Elmbourne Dr. DA17 .... 4 B2
Elmbrook Gdns. SE9 .... 5 E3
Elmcroft Ave. DA15 .... 7 A1
Elmcroft Rd. BR6 .... 38 A2
Elmdene Rd. SE18 .... 2 B1
Elmfield. Gillingham ME8 .... 49 A3
Elmfield. Tenterden TN30 .... 183 B8
Elmfield Cl. Gravesend DA11 ...... 30 B7
Elmfield Cl. Coxheath ME17 ...... 106 C3
Elmfield Cl. Tenterden TN30 ..... 183 B8
Elmfield Pk. BR1 .... 36 A6
Elmfield Rd. BR1 .... 36 A6
Elmhurst. Erith DA17 .... 7 B8
Elmhurst. Swanscombe DA9 .... 11 B1
Elmhurst Ave. TN2 .... 150 D8
Elmhurst Gdns. ME1 .... 47 E3
Elmhurst Rd. SE9 .... 22 E5
Elmington Cl. DA5 .... 8 B1
Elmlee Cl. BR7 .... 22 F2
Elmley Cl. 15 E6 .... 1 E8
Elmley St. SE18 .... 2 D2
Elmshurst Gdns. TN10 .... 117 C5
Elmslie Ct. SE9 .... 6 A1
Elmstead Ave. BR7 .... 22 F3
Elmstead Cl. TN13 .... 83 E5
Elmstead Glade. BR7 .... 22 F2
Elmstead La. BR7 & SE9 .... 22 F3
Elmstead Rd. DA8 .... 8 E6
Elmstead Woods Sta. BR7 .... 22 E2
Elmsted Cres. DA16 .... 7 C8
Elmstone Cl. ME16 .... 91 B2
Elmstone Hole Rd. ME17 .... 126 D8
Elmstone La. ME16 .... 91 B2
Elmstone Rd. ME8 .... 63 D7
Elmstone Terr. 3 BR5 .... 38 C5

Elmtree Cotts. TN14 .... 67 E8
Elmwood Dr. DA5 .... 24 E8
Elmwood Rd. ME3 .... 33 F6
Elphick's Pl. TN2 .... 163 B8
Elrick Cl. DA8 .... 8 E8
Elsa Rd. DA16 .... 7 C5
Elsinore House. 7 SE7 .... 1 E2
Elstow Cl. Eltham SE9 .... 5 F2
Elstow Cl. Eltham SE9 .... 6 A2
Elstree Gdns. DA17 .... 3 E2
Eltham CE Prim Sch. SE9 .... 5 F2
Eltham Coll. SE9 .... 22 D6
Eltham Green Rd. SE9 .... 5 C3
Eltham Green Sch. SE9 .... 5 D1
Eltham High St. SE9 .... 5 F1
Eltham Hill. SE9 .... 5 E2
Eltham Hill Sch. SE9 .... 5 E1
Eltham & Mottingham Hospl
(General). SE9 .... 5 F1
Eltham Palace. SE9 .... 22 E8
Eltham Palace Rd. SE12 & SE9 .... 5 D1
Eltham Park Gdns. SE9 .... 6 A3
Eltham Rd. SE12 & SE9 .... 5 B2
Eltham Sta. SE9 .... 5 F2
Eltham Warren Golf Course. SE9 .. 6 B2
Elvington Cl. ME16 .... 91 D5
Elwick Cl. DA1 .... 9 A3
Elwill Way. DA13 .... 43 F8
Elwyn Gdns. SE12 .... 22 A8
Ely Cl. Erith DA8 .... 8 F5
Ely Cl. Gillingham ME8 .... 49 B2
Ely Ct. TN2 .... 149 B4
Ely Gdns. TN10 & TN9 .... 117 D4
Elysian Ave. BR5 .... 37 F3
Embassey Ct. DA14 .... 24 B5
Embassy Cl. ME7 .... 48 F1
Embassy Ct. DA16 .... 7 B4
Ember Cl. BR5 .... 37 C2
Emerald Cl. Chatham ME1 .... 61 D7
Emerald Cl. Newham E16 .... 1 E7
Emersons Ave. BR8 .... 25 F1
Emerton Cl. DA6 .... 7 E3
Emes Rd. DA8 .... 8 C7
Emily Jackson Cl. TN13 .... 84 B3
Emily Rd. ME5 .... 62 B6
Emmett Hill La. ME15 .... 120 F5
Emmetts Garden (NT). TN14 ...... 97 C6
Emmetts Rd. TN14 & TN16 .... 97 C6
Empress Dr. BR7 .... 23 B2
Empress Rd. DA12 .... 30 E8
Emsworth Gr. ME14 .... 92 D6
Enderfield Ct. BR7 .... 37 A8
Engineer Cl. SE18 .... 6 A8
Englefield Cl. BR5 .... 37 F5
Englefield Cres.
Cliffe Woods ME3 .... 33 B7
Englefield Cres. Orpington BR5 ... 38 A5
Englefield Path. BR5 .... 38 A5
English Martyrs' RC Prim Sch.
ME2 .... 47 B8
Ennerdale Rd. DA7 .... 8 A6
Ennis Rd. SE18 .... 6 C8
Ensfield Rd. Leigh TN11 .... 115 E1
Ensfield Rd.
Upper Hayesden TN11 & TN3 .. 132 A6
Ensign House. RM17 .... 11 F8
Enslin Rd. SE9 .... 23 A8
Enterprise Bsns Est. ME2 .... 47 E7
Enterprise Cl. ME2 .... 47 D8
Enterprise Ctr The. ME5 .... 77 C8
Enterprise Rd. ME15 .... 92 A1
Enterprise Way. TN8 .... 112 C3
Epaul La. ME1 .... 47 C6
Epsom Cl. Bexley DA7 .... 8 B4
Epsom Cl. Maidstone ME15 ...... 107 F6
Epsom Cl. New Town ME19 .... 89 B8
Epstein Rd. SE28 .... 3 B5
Erica Ct. BR8 .... 39 E5
Eridge Green Cl. BR5 .... 38 C1
Eridge Rd. TN2 & TN4 .... 148 F1
Eridge Sta. TN3 .... 161 E2
Erindale. SE18 .... 6 D8
Erindale Terr. SE18 .... 6 D8
Erith Cl. ME14 .... 92 A8
Erith & District Hospl. DA8 .... 8 D8
Erith High St. Erith DA8 .... 4 E1
Erith High St. Erith DA8 .... 8 F8
Erith Rd. Bexley DA7 .... 8 B4
Erith Rd. Erith DA17 .... 4 B1
Erith Sch. DA8 .... 8 D7
Erith Sch West. DA8 .... 8 B7
Erith Sta. DA8 .... 4 E1
Ermington Rd. BR7 & SE9 .... 23 C6
Ernest Dr. ME16 .... 91 B5
Ernest Rd. ME4 .... 48 A3
Erskine House. 7 SE7 .... 5 C8
Erskine Park Rd. TN4 .... 148 C4
Erskine Rd. DA13 .... 73 B8
Erwood Rd. SE7 .... 1 E1
Escott Gdns. SE9 .... 22 E4
Escreet Gr. SE18 .... 2 A2
Eshcol Rd. ME3 .... 35 C6
Esher Cl. DA5 .... 24 E7
Eskdale Cl. DA2 .... 27 C7
Eskdale Rd. DA7 .... 8 A6
Esplanade. ME1 .... 47 B5
Essenden Rd. DA17 .... 4 A1
Essex Cl. TN2 .... 162 F8
Essex Rd. 1 Dartford DA1 .... 9 D1
Essex Rd. Gravesend DA11 .... 30 A7
Essex Rd. Halling ME2 .... 60 A6
Essex Rd. Longfield DA3 .... 42 D7
Essex Rd. Maidstone ME15 ...... 107 E6
Essex Rd. West Thurrock RM16 ... 11 A8
Essex St. SE18 .... 2 C3
Estelle Cl. ME1 .... 61 D7
Estridge Way. TN10 .... 117 F5
Etfield Gr. DA14 .... 24 B3

Ethel Brooks House. SE18 .... 6 B8
Ethel Rd. E16 .... 1 B7
Ethel Terr. BR6 .... 52 C2
Ethel-Maud Ct. ME7 .... 48 D7
Ethelbert Cl. BR1 .... 36 A6
Ethelbert Rd. Bromley BR1 & BR2 36 A6
Ethelbert Rd. Erith DA8 .... 8 C7
Ethelbert Rd. Rochester ME1 ...... 47 C4
Ethelbert Rd. St Paul's Cray BR5 . 38 D6
Ethelbery Rd. DA2 .... 26 E3
Etherington Hill. TN3 .... 148 C8
Ethnam La. TN18 .... 186 E4
Ethronvi Rd. DA7 .... 7 E4
Eton Cl. ME5 .... 61 F4
Eton Rd. BR6 .... 52 B6
Eton Way. DA8 .... 9 C3
Europa Trad Est. DA8 .... 4 D1
Europe Rd. SE18 .... 1 F3
Euroway. ME20 .... 90 E8
Eustace Pl. SE18 .... 1 F2
Eva Rd. ME7 .... 48 D3
Evans Cl. DA9 .... 11 A2
Evelyn Denington Rd. E6 .... 1 F8
Evelyn Rd. Maidstone ME16 ...... 91 E3
Evelyn Rd. Newham E16 .... 1 B5
Evelyn Rd. Otford TN14 .... 69 C2
Evenden House. TN17 .... 169 D5
Evenden Rd. DA13 .... 44 A2
Evenlode House. 5 SE2 .... 3 C4
Everard Ave. BR2 .... 36 A1
Everest Cl. 1 DA11 .... 29 E5
Everest Cl. SE9 .... 22 E6
Everest Dr. ME3 .... 34 E4
Everest La. ME3 .... 33 B1
Everest Mews. ME3 .... 34 E4
Everest Pl. BR8 .... 39 D5
Everest Rd. SE9 .... 5 F2
Everett Wlk. DA17 .... 3 F1
Everglades Cl. DA3 .... 42 F5
Everglades The. ME7 .... 62 F6
Evergreen Cl. Gillingham ME7 ... 63 A5
Evergreen Cl. Higham ME3 ...... 32 B3
Evergreen Cl. Leybourne ME19 ... 74 E2
Eversfield Ct. SE12 .... 22 B6
Eversley Ave. DA7 & DA8 .... 8 E2
Eversley Cl. ME16 .... 91 C6
Eversley Cross. DA7 .... 8 E5
Eversley Rd. SE7 .... 5 B8
Evesham Rd. DA12 .... 30 D6
Evry Rd. DA14 .... 24 C2
Ewart Rd. ME4 .... 47 E1
Ewehurst La. TN3 .... 147 F6
Ewell Ave. ME19 .... 89 A8
Ewell La. ME15 .... 105 D5
Ewins Cl. TN12 .... 136 A6
Exedown Rd. TN15 .... 71 C4
Exeter Cl. Newham E6 .... 1 F7
Exeter Cl. Tonbridge TN10 & TN9 117 D4
Exeter Rd. Bexley DA16 .... 6 F5
Exeter Rd. Gravesend DA12 ...... 30 D5
Exeter Rd. Newham E16 .... 1 A8
Exeter Wlk. ME1 .... 61 C7
Exford Gdns. SE12 .... 22 B7
Exford Rd. SE12 .... 22 B7
Exmouth Rd. Bexley DA16 ...... 7 C7
Exmouth Rd. Bromley BR2 ...... 36 B6
Exmouth Rd. Gillingham ME7 ... 48 C7
Exmouth Rd. Grays RM17 ...... 12 B8
Exton Cl. ME5 .... 62 C2
Exton Gdns. ME14 .... 92 F5
Eyhorne St. ME17 .... 94 D2
Eylesden Court Sch. ME14 ...... 93 B4
Eynsford Castle. DA4 .... 54 E8
Eynsford Cl. BR5 .... 37 C3
Eynsford Cres. DA5 .... 24 D7
Eynsford Rd. Crockenhill BR8 .. 39 E3
Eynsford Rd. Eynsford DA4 ...... 40 F1
Eynsford Rd. Maidstone ME16 ... 91 D7
Eynsford Rd. Swanscombe DA9 .. 11 C2
Eynsford Rise. DA4 .... 54 D6
Eynsford Sta. DA4 .... 54 D6
Eynsham Dr. SE2 .... 3 B3
Eynswood Dr. DA14 .... 24 C3

F Ave. SE18 .... 2 B3
Fackenden La. TN14 .... 69 C7
Factory Rd. Newham E16 .... 1 E5
Factory Rd. Northfleet DA11 ...... 12 C1
Faesten Way. DA5 .... 25 E5
Fagus Cl. ME5 .... 62 B1
Fair Acres. BR2 .... 36 A4
Fair View. TN5 .... 175 A6
Fair View Jun & Inf Schs. ME8 63 C5
Fairacre Pl. DA3 .... 42 E6
Fairbank Ave. BR6 .... 51 B8
Fairbourne Heath Cotts. ME17 110 B1
Fairbourne La. ME17 .... 110 C4
Fairby La. DA3 .... 42 E3
Fairby Rd. SE12 .... 5 B2
Faircrouch La. TN5 .... 174 B5
Fairfax Bsns Ctr. ME15 .... 107 F4
Fairfax Cl. ME8 .... 63 D5
Fairfax Gdns. SE3 .... 5 C3
Fairfax Rd. RM18 .... 12 F6
Fairfield Ave. TN1 & TN2 ...... 149 C5
Fairfield Cl. Kemsing TN15 ...... 70 A1
Fairfield Cl. Sidcup DA15 ...... 6 F1
Fairfield Cres. TN9 .... 133 C8
Fairfield Gr. SE7 .... 5 D8
Fairfield Rd. Bexley DA7 ...... 7 F5
Fairfield Rd. Borough Green TN15 86 F8
Fairfield Rd. Bromley BR1 ...... 22 A1
Fairfield Rd. Orpington BR5 ...... 37 D3
Fairfield Way. TN11 .... 116 F5
Fairfields. DA12 .... 30 E3
Fairford Ave. DA7 .... 8 D6
Fairglen Cotts. TN5 .... 174 B4
Fairglen Rd. TN5 .... 174 B4

Fairhurst Dr. ME15 .... 106 B4
Fairings The. TN30 .... 183 B8
Fairland House. BR2 .... 36 B5
Fairlands Ct. 6 SE9 .... 6 A1
Fairlawn. SE7 .... 5 C8
Fairlawn Ave. DA16 .... 7 D5
Fairlawn Cl. ME18 .... 105 A8
Fairlawn Cl. SE7 .... 5 C7
Fairlead Rd. ME1 .... 47 D1
Fairlight Cl. TN4 .... 133 A2
Fairlight Cross. DA3 .... 43 C6
Fairlight Ct. TN10 .... 117 B4
Fairman's La. TN12 .... 152 B6
Fairmead. ME1 .... 36 F5
Fairmead Cl. BR1 .... 36 F5
Fairmead Rd. TN8 .... 112 C5
Fairmeadow. ME14 .... 91 F4
Fairmile House. BR5 .... 38 A7
Fairmile Rd. TN2 .... 149 E5
Fairmont Cl. DA17 .... 3 F1
Fairoak Cl. BR5 .... 37 B2
Fairoak Dr. SE9 .... 6 D2
Fairseat Cl. Fairseat TN15 ...... 72 B5
Fairseat La. Stansted TN15 ...... 57 A1
Fairthorn Rd. SE10 & SE7 ...... 1 A1
Fairtrough Rd. BR6 .... 67 B7
Fairview. Erith DA8 .... 8 F7
Fairview. Fawkham Green DA3 .. 56 B7
Fairview. Hawkhurst TN18 ...... 178 F2
Fairview Ave. ME8 .... 63 B5
Fairview Cl. TN9 .... 133 B7
Fairview Cotts. ME15 .... 106 F5
Fairview Dr. Higham ME3 ...... 32 B4
Fairview Dr. Orpington BR6 ..... 51 D6
Fairview Gdns. DA13 .... 44 A4
Fairview Ind Est. RM9 .... 4 D8
Fairview Rd. DA13 .... 29 E1
Fairwater Ave. DA16 .... 7 A3
Fairway. Bexley DA6 .... 7 E2
Fairway. Orpington BR5 .... 37 D4
Fairway Cl. ME1 .... 47 C1
Fairway Ct. 12 SE9 .... 6 A1
Fairway Dr. DA2 .... 27 B8
Fairway The. Bromley BR1 & BR2 36 F4
Fairway The. Gravesend DA11 ... 30 B6
Fairway The. Rochester ME1 .... 47 C1
Fairways The. TN4 .... 149 A2
Falcon Ave. Bromley BR1 ...... 36 E5
Falcon Ave. Grays RM17 ...... 12 C7
Falcon Cl. DA1 .... 9 F2
Falcon Gn. ME20 .... 74 F1
Falcon Mews. DA11 .... 29 E7
Falconwood Ave. DA16 .... 6 E5
Falconwood Par. DA16 .... 6 E5
Falconwood Sta. SE9 .... 6 D3
Falkland Pl. ME5 .... 61 E1
Fallowfield. ME5 .... 62 B8
Fallowfield Cl. ME14 .... 92 E4
Falmouth Pl. TN12 .... 135 C7
Fanconi Rd. ME5 .... 62 B3
Fancy Row. ME14 .... 93 C5
Fane Way. ME8 .... 63 D4
Fant La. ME16 .... 91 B2
Faraday Ave. DA14 .... 24 B6
Faraday Rd. Bexley DA16 ...... 7 A4
Faraday Rd. Maidstone ME14 ... 92 C7
Faraday Ride. TN10 .... 117 D7
Faraday Way. Greenwich SE18 .. 1 D3
Faraday Way. Orpington BR5 ... 38 B5
Fareham Wlk. 10 ME15 .... 107 F6
Faringdon Ave. BR2 .... 37 A3
Farjeon Rd. SE18 & SE3 .... 5 D6
Farleigh Ave. BR2 .... 36 A2
Farleigh Ct. ME14 .... 91 A2
Farleigh Hill. ME15 .... 91 E1
Farleigh Hill Ret Pk. ME15 ...... 91 E1
Farleigh La. ME16 .... 91 A1
Farleigh Trad Est. ME15 ...... 91 E1
Farley Cl. ME5 .... 62 D2
Farley La. TN16 .... 96 B8
Farley Rd. DA12 .... 30 F7
Farleycroft. TN16 .... 81 C1
Farlow Cl. DA11 .... 29 F5
Farm Ave. BR8 .... 39 C6
Farm Holt. DA3 .... 42 F1
Farm La. TN11 .... 117 A4
Farm Pl. DA1 .... 9 A3
Farm Rd. Chatham ME5 .... 61 E3
Farm Rd. Sevenoaks TN14 ...... 84 C7
Farm Vale. DA5 .... 8 B1
Farmcombe Cl. TN1 .... 149 B2
Farmcombe La. TN1 .... 149 B2
Farmcombe Rd. TN1 & TN2 ... 149 C2
Farmcote Rd. SE12 .... 22 A7
Farmcroft. DA11 .... 30 A6
Farmdale. ME1 .... 46 F3
Farmdale Ave. ME1 .... 46 F2
Farmdale Rd. SE10 .... 1 A1
Farmer Cl. ME17 .... 109 A6
Farmland Wlk. BR7 .... 23 B3
Farmstead Dr. TN8 .... 112 D3
Farnaby Dr. TN13 .... 84 A1
Farnaby Rd. SE9 .... 5 C3
Farnborough Cl. ME16 .... 91 C2
Farnborough Comm.
    Keston Mark BR2 & BR6 ...... 50 F7
Farnborough Comm.
    Orpington BR6 .... 51 A6
Farnborough Ct. 2 BR6 .... 51 C5
Farnborough Hill. BR6 .... 51 E5
Farnborough Hospl. BR6 ...... 51 A6
Farnborough Prim Sch. BR6 .. 51 C5
Farnborough Way. BR6 .... 51 D5
Farne Cl. ME5 .... 107 A6
Farnham Beeches. TN3 .... 148 A4
Farnham Cl. Gillingham ME8 ... 64 A8
Farnham Cl. Langton Green TN3 148 A3
Farnham La. TN3 .... 148 A4

Farnham Rd. DA16 .... 7 C5
Farningham Cl. ME14 .... 92 C6
Farningham Hill Rd. DA4 ...... 40 D3
Farningham Road Sta. DA4 ... 41 B7
Farnol Rd. DA1 .... 10 A3
Faro Cl. BR1 .... 37 A7
Farraday Cl. ME1 .... 61 D8
Farrant Cl. BR6 .... 52 A3
Farrier Cl. ME1 .... 92 E5
Farriers Cl. DA12 .... 30 F7
Farriers Ct. ME8 .... 64 C8
Farrington Ave. BR5 .... 38 B6
Farrington House. 12 SE18 ...... 2 A2
Farrington Pl. BR7 .... 23 D1
Farringtons Sch. BR7 .... 23 D1
Fartherwell Ave. ME19 .... 89 A8
Fartherwell Rd. ME19 .... 89 A8
Farthing Cl. DA1 .... 9 F3
Farthing Cnr. ME9 .... 63 E3
Farthing Hill. TN5 .... 176 E1
Farthing St. BR6 .... 50 F2
Farthingfield. TN15 .... 72 A3
Farthings Cotts. ME14 .... 76 F1
Farwell Rd. DA14 .... 24 C4
Farwig La. BR1 .... 36 A8
Fashoda Rd. BR2 .... 36 D5
Fauchon's Cl. ME14 .... 92 F3
Fauchon's La. ME14 .... 92 F4
Faversham Rd. ME17 .... 111 E7
Fawkham Ave. DA3 .... 43 C6
Fawkham CE Prim Sch. DA3 .. 42 B1
Fawkham Green Rd. TN15 ...... 56 B7
Fawkham House. 10 BR5 ...... 38 D1
Fawkham Manor Hospl. DA3 ... 42 C1
Fawkham Rd. Longfield DA3 ... 42 D6
Fawkham Rd.
    West Kingsdown TN15 ...... 56 A4
Fawley Cl. ME14 .... 91 E7
Faygate Cres. DA6 .... 8 A2
Fazan Ct. TN5 .... 174 F4
Fearon St. SE18 .... 1 A1
Featherby Cty Prim Inf Sch.
    ME8 .... 49 A3
Featherby Jun Sch. ME8 ...... 49 A3
Featherby Rd.
    Gillingham,Lower Twydall ME7 49 A5
Featherby Rd.
    Gillingham,Twydall ME8 ...... 49 A3
Federation Rd. SE2 .... 3 C2
Feenan Highway. RM18 ...... 13 B6
Felderland Cl. ME17 .... 107 E5
Felderland Dr. ME17 .... 107 E5
Felderland Rd. ME17 .... 107 E5
Feldspar Ct. ME5 .... 62 A1
Felhampton Rd. SE9 .... 23 B5
Felix Manor. BR7 .... 23 E2
Felixstowe Ct. E6 .... 2 B3
Fell Mead. TN12 .... 119 F6
Fellowes Way. TN11 .... 116 E5
Fellows Cl. ME8 .... 63 B6
Felltram Way. SE7 .... 1 A1
Felspar Ct. SE18 .... 2 F1
Felstead Rd. ME6 .... 52 B8
Felsted Rd. E16 .... 1 D7
Felton Cl. BR5 .... 37 B3
Felton House. SE9 .... 5 C3
Felton Lea. DA14 .... 23 F3
Fen Gr. DA15 .... 6 F1
Fen Meadow. TN15 .... 71 C1
Fen Pond Rd. TN15 .... 86 C7
Fendyke Rd. SE2 .... 3 D3
Fenn Cl. BR1 .... 22 A2
Fennell St. SE18 .... 6 A8
Fens Way. BR8 .... 26 A2
Fenton Cl. BR7 .... 22 F3
Fenwick Cl. 16 SE18 .... 6 A8
Ferbies. TN3 .... 148 A7
Ferbies Cotts. TN3 .... 148 A7
Ferby Ct. DA15 .... 23 F4
Ferdinand Terr. TN3 .... 161 C7
Ferguson Ave. DA12 .... 30 C4
Fern Cl. DA8 .... 9 B6
Fern Down. DA13 .... 73 B8
Fern Hill Pl. 3 BR6 .... 51 C5
Fernbank Cl. ME5 .... 61 F2
Ferndale. Bromley BR1 .... 36 C7
Ferndale.
    Royal Tunbridge Wells TN2 149 D5
Ferndale. Sevenoaks TN13 ...... 84 C5
Ferndale Cl. Bexley DA7 ...... 7 E6
Ferndale Cl.
    Royal Tunbridge Wells TN2 149 C4
Ferndale Point. TN2 .... 149 C4
Ferndale Rd. Gillingham ME7 ... 48 E5
Ferndale Rd. Gravesend DA12 ... 30 B6
Ferndale St. E6 .... 2 B7
Ferndale Way. BR6 .... 51 D5
Ferndell Ave. DA5 .... 25 D5
Ferndene. DA3 .... 43 D6
Ferndown Cl. Gillingham ME7 ... 63 A5
Ferndown Cl. Orpington BR6 ... 37 D1
Ferndown Rd. SE9 .... 22 D8
Fernheath Way. DA2 .... 25 D3
Fernhill Rd. ME16 .... 91 A2
Fernhill St. E16 .... 1 F5
Fernholt. TN10 .... 117 C7
Fernhurst Cres. TN4 .... 133 A2
Fernleigh Rise. ME20 .... 75 B2
Ferns The. Larkfield ME20 ...... 75 B1
Ferns The. Platt TN15 .... 87 C7
Ferns The.
    Royal Tunbridge Wells TN1 149 C4
Fernside La. TN13 .... 99 D6
Fernwood Cl. BR1 .... 36 C7
Ferranti Cl. SE18 .... 1 D3
Ferrier Cl. ME8 .... 63 E4
Ferrier Point. 8 E16 .... 1 A8
Ferry La. Rainham RM13 ...... 4 E7

Ferry La. Wouldham ME1 ...... 60 C4
Ferry Rd. Halling ME2 .... 60 B4
Ferry Rd. Tilbury RM18 ...... 13 A4
Festival Ave. DA3 .... 43 D6
Festival Cl. Erith DA8 .... 8 F7
Festival Cl. Sidcup DA5 .... 24 D7
Ffinch Cl. ME20 .... 90 D8
Fiddlers Cl. DA9 .... 11 B3
Field Cl. Bromley BR1 .... 36 C7
Field Cl. Chatham ME5 .... 61 E6
Field Dr. TN8 .... 112 D3
Field Rd. DA13 & TN15 ...... 57 E6
Fieldfare Rd. SE28 .... 3 C6
Fielding Ave. RM18 .... 13 B6
Fielding Dr. ME20 .... 75 A3
Fields La. ME18 .... 104 E7
Fieldside. BR6 .... 51 C6
Fieldway. BR5 .... 37 D3
Fieldways. TN8 .... 179 A1
Fieldworks Rd. ME4 & ME7 ...... 48 A7
Fiennes Way. TN13 .... 99 C8
Fiesta Dr. RM9 .... 4 C8
Fife Rd. E16 .... 1 A8
Fifteenpenny Fields. SE9 ...... 6 A2
Filborough Way. DA12 .... 31 B6
Filmer La. TN13 & TN14 & TN15 .. 84 E6
Filston La. TN13 & TN14 ...... 68 E5
Filston Rd. DA8 .... 4 C1
Finch Ct. ME14 .... 91 E7
Finchale Rd. SE2 .... 3 A3
Finchley Cl. DA1 .... 10 A1
Finchley Rd. RM17 .... 12 B8
Findlay Cl. ME8 .... 63 D6
Finglesham Ct. BR5 .... 38 D1
Finglesham Ct. ME15 .... 107 C8
Finsbury Way. DA5 .... 7 F1
Fintonagh Dr. ME14 .... 92 B6
Finucane Dr. BR5 .... 38 C2
Fir Dene. BR6 .... 50 D4
Fir Tree Cl. Hildenborough TN11 116 E5
Fir Tree Cl. 5 Orpington BR6 ... 51 F5
Fir Tree Cl. Staplehurst TN12 ... 139 F3
Fir Tree Gr. Bredhurst ME7 ...... 63 B1
Fir Tree Gr. Chatham ME5 ...... 62 D1
Fir Tree Rd. TN4 .... 148 F3
Firbank Cl. E16 .... 1 D8
Fircroft Way. TN8 .... 112 C3
Firecrest Cl. DA3 .... 43 B6
Firethorn Cl. ME7 .... 48 E6
Firmin Rd. DA1 .... 9 C2
Firmingers Rd. BR6 .... 53 C5
Firs Cl. ME20 .... 75 E1
Firs Ct. TN4 .... 148 F6
Firs The. Coldblow DA5 .... 25 D7
Firs The. Sidcup DA15 .... 23 F5
Firside Gr. DA15 .... 23 F7
First Ave. Bexley DA7 .... 7 C7
First Ave. Chatham ME4 .... 48 C2
First Ave. Gillingham ME7 ...... 48 E3
First Ave. Northfleet DA11 ...... 29 E7
First Ave. West Thurrock RM16 ... 11 A8
First La. ME15 .... 93 E2
First St. TN10 .... 147 F3
Fisher House. 13 SE18 .... 2 A1
Fisher Rd. ME5 .... 62 B7
Fisher St. Maidstone ME14 ...... 92 A6
Fisher St. Newham E16 .... 1 A8
Fisher's Gate Cotts. TN7 ...... 160 A1
Fisher's Way. DA17 .... 4 C5
Fishermans Wlk. SE28 .... 2 E4
Fishermen's Hill. DA11 .... 12 B2
Fishers Cl. TN12 .... 139 F5
Fishers Rd. TN12 .... 139 F5
Fishponds Rd. BR2 .... 50 D5
Fisons Rd. E16 .... 1 A5
Fitzroy Ct. DA1 .... 27 B7
Fitzthorold House. ME7 .... 48 E7
Fitzwilliam Mews. E16 .... 1 A5
Fitzwilliam Rd. ME14 .... 92 F5
Five Acre Wood Sch. ME15 ... 107 B2
Five Bells La. ME1 .... 47 D4
Five Elms Rd. BR2 .... 50 C7
Five Oak Green Rd.
    Five Oak Green TN11 & TN12 .. 134 D6
Five Oak Green Rd.
    Tonbridge TN9 .... 133 F7
Five Oak La. TN12 .... 139 B1
Fiveways. TN11 .... 149 A4
Fiveways L Ctr. ME4 .... 48 A4
Flack Gdns. ME3 .... 34 E5
Flamingo Cl. ME5 .... 62 A7
Flamsted Rd. SE7 .... 1 E1
Flats The. DA9 .... 11 C2
Flaxman Ct. Erith DA17 ...... 4 A1
Flaxman Ct. 7 Gillingham ME7 . 48 A6
Flaxman Dr. ME16 .... 91 C6
Flaxmore Cl. DA7 .... 8 B4
Flaxmore Pl. TN4 .... 133 A2
Flaxton Rd. SE18 .... 6 E7
Fleet Ave. DA2 .... 27 C8
Fleet Dale Par. DA2 .... 27 C8
Fleet Rd. Dartford DA2 .... 27 C7
Fleet Rd. Northfleet DA11 ...... 29 C6
Fleetdown Cty Prim Sch. DA2 . 27 C6
Fleetwood Cl. E16 .... 1 D8
Fleetwood Cl. 1 Newham E6 .. 1 F8
Fleetwood Cl. Orpington BR6 .. 51 E6
Fleming Gdns. RM18 .... 13 C6
Fleming Way. Erith SE28 ...... 3 D6
Fleming Way. Tonbridge TN10 .. 117 E7
Fletcher Rd. TN12 .... 139 E3
Fletchers Cl. BR2 .... 36 B5
Fletching Rd. SE7 .... 5 D8

Flimwell Bird Pk. TN19 ...... 177 E2
Flimwell Cl. TN5 .... 177 D4
Flint Cl. 8 BR6 .... 51 F4
Flint Gn. ME5 .... 62 C3
Flint La. ME17 .... 111 C8
Flint St. RM16 .... 11 B8
Flintmill Cres. SE3 & SE9 ...... 5 E5
Floats The. TN13 .... 83 E6
Flood Hatch. ME15 .... 91 D2
Flora St. DA17 .... 3 F1
Florance La. TN3 .... 161 B6
Florence Cl. RM17 & RM16 ...... 11 E8
Florence Cotts. TN3 .... 148 C5
Florence Farm Mobile Home Pk.
    TN15 .... 55 D4
Florence House. SE18 .... 5 F6
Florence Rd. Bromley BR1 ...... 36 A8
Florence Rd. Erith SE2 .... 3 C2
Florence Rd. Maidstone ME16 ... 91 E3
Florence Rd. Erith DA8 .... 47 B8
Flower Rise. ME14 .... 91 F7
Flowerfield. TN14 .... 68 F2
Flowerhill Way. DA13 .... 29 E1
Floyd Rd. SE7 .... 1 C1
Flume End. ME16 .... 91 D2
Flyers Way The. TN16 .... 81 D1
Foalhurst Cl. TN10 .... 117 E4
Foley Ct. DA1 .... 27 B7
Foley St. ME14 .... 92 A5
Folkstone House. 4 ME15 ...... 107 F6
Fontwell Cl. 6 ME15 .... 107 F6
Fontwell Dr. BR2 .... 37 A4
Foord Almshouses. ME1 ...... 47 B3
Foord Rd. ME17 .... 111 D5
Foord St. ME1 .... 47 D4
Footbury Hill Rd. BR6 .... 38 A2
Foots Cray High St. DA14 ...... 24 D2
Foots Cray La. DA5 & DA14 .... 24 C7
Footscray Rd. BR7 & SE9 ...... 23 C7
Force Green La. TN16 .... 81 E4
Ford House. 2 SE18 .... 2 B1
Ford La. Trottiscliffe ME19 ...... 73 A4
Ford La. Wrotham Heath TN15 ... 72 F2
Ford Rd. DA11 .... 12 B2
Fordcombe CE Prim Sch. TN3 147 B5
Fordcombe Cl. ME15 .... 107 F7
Fordcombe La. TN3 .... 147 C5
Fordcombe Rd. Fordcombe TN3 147 C4
Fordcombe Rd. Penshurst TN11 131 A3
Fordcroft Rd. BR5 .... 38 B4
Forde Ave. BR1 .... 36 C6
Fordingbridge Cl. ME16 ...... 91 B5
Fords Park Rd. E16 .... 1 A7
Fordwich Cl. Maidstone ME16 ... 91 B7
Fordwich Cl. Orpington BR6 .... 37 F2
Fordwich Gn. ME8 .... 49 C3
Foreland St. SE18 .... 2 D2
Foremans Barn Rd. ME15 ...... 105 F3
Forest Cl. BR7 .... 37 A8
Forest Dr. Chatham ME5 ...... 61 F2
Forest Dr. Keston Mark BR2 .. 50 E7
Forest Gr. TN10 .... 117 C5
Forest Hill. ME15 .... 91 F1
Forest Lawns. BR1 .... 36 C8
Forest Rd. Erith DA8 .... 9 A6
Forest Rd. Paddock Wood TN12 . 136 A6
Forest Rd.
    Royal Tunbridge Wells,Hawkenbury
    TN2 .... 149 C1
Forest Rd.
    Royal Tunbridge Wells,
    Rumbers Hill TN2 .... 163 A8
Forest Ridge. BR2 .... 50 F6
Forest Way. Kings Hill ME19 ... 89 A3
Forest Way. Orpington BR5 .... 38 A4
Forest Way. Pembury TN2 ...... 150 D8
Forest Way.
    Royal Tunbridge Wells TN2 149 D1
Forest Way. Sidcup SE9 ...... 23 D8
Forestdale Rd. ME5 .... 77 A8
Foresters Cl. ME5 .... 61 F2
Foresters Cres. DA7 .... 8 B3
Forge Cl. Hayes BR2 .... 36 A1
Forge Cl. Penshurst TN11 ...... 131 B4
Forge Cotts. ME18 .... 104 C2
Forge Croft. TN8 .... 112 D1
Forge La. Benover ME18 ...... 121 B4
Forge La. Boxley ME14 .... 77 C2
Forge La. Bredhurst ME7 ...... 63 A1
Forge La. Dean Street ME15 ... 106 C7
Forge La. Egerton Forstal TN27 127 C1
Forge La. Gillingham ME7 ...... 48 E7
Forge La. Gravesend DA12 .... 30 F6
Forge La. Headcorn TN27 ...... 141 D5
Forge La. High Halstow ME23 ... 17 E3
Forge La. Higham ME3 .... 32 C3
Forge La. Horton Kirby DA4 .... 41 C5
Forge La. Leeds ME17 .... 108 F7
Forge La. Rabbit's Cross TN12 . 123 F3
Forge La. Shorne DA12 .... 31 E3
Forge La. West Kingsdown TN15 . 56 A1
Forge La. West Peckham ME18 . 103 E4
Forge Lane Cty Inf Sch. ME7 ... 48 E6
Forge Meadow. ME17 .... 110 D6
Forge Meadows. TN27 .... 141 D5
Forge Meads. TN30 .... 189 E3
Forge Rd.
    Groombridge TN3 & TN6 ...... 161 C2
Forge Rd.
    Royal Tunbridge Wells TN4 133 C2
Forge Sq. E14 .... 115 F2
Forge The. TN12 .... 135 B7
Forge View. TN15 .... 100 B5
Forge Way. Paddock Wood TN12 136 A7
Forge Way. Shoreham TN14 ... 68 F8

Forgefield Ct. BR5 .... 38 C4
Formby Rd. ME2 .... 60 A7
Formby Terr. ME7 .... 60 A6
Forsham La. ME17 .... 124 C5
Forson Cl. TN30 .... 183 B8
Forstal Cl. BR2 .... 36 A6
Forstal Cotts. ME20 .... 76 B2
Forstal La. ME17 .... 106 D4
Forstal Rd. Egerton Forstal TN27 127 C1
Forstal Rd. Forstal ME20 ..... 76 C2
Forstal The. Cobbarn TN3 ... 161 F3
Forstal The. Hadlow TN11 ... 118 F8
Forstal The. Pembury TN2 ... 150 E8
Forstall. TN3 .... 148 A4
Forstall The. TN11 .... 116 A2
Forsters. ME17 .... 108 E4
Fort Luton (Mus.) ME4 .... 48 A1
Fort Pitt Gram Sch. ME1 ...... 47 E4
Fort Pitt Hill. ME1 & ME4 ..... 47 E4
Fort Pitt St. ME4 .... 47 E3
Fort Rd. Shepham Heath TN14 .. 68 C4
Fort St. Newham E16 .... 1 B5
Fort St. Rochester ME1 .... 47 D4
Fortis Cl. E16 .... 1 C7
Fortrye Cl. DA11 .... 29 E6
Fortuna Cl. DA3 .... 42 F5
Forty Acre La. E16 .... 1 A8
Fossdene Prim Sch. SE7 .... 1 B1
Fossdene Rd. SE7 .... 1 B1
Fosse Bank. TN9 .... 133 A7
Fosse Bank Cl. TN9 .... 133 A7
Fosse Bank New Sch. TN11 .. 116 E7
Fosse Rd. TN9 .... 117 B2
Fossington Rd. DA17 .... 3 D2
Fosten La. TN27 .... 171 E7
Foster Clark Est. ME15 .... 92 B2
Foster St. ME15 .... 92 A3
Fosters Cl. BR7 .... 22 F3
Fosters VC Prim Sch. DA16 .... 7 B5
Fostington Way. ME5 .... 61 F1
Foulds Cl. ME8 .... 63 B5
Founder Cl. E6 .... 2 B7
Fountain Ct. Eynsford DA4 .... 54 E8
Fountain Cl. Sidcup DA15 ...... 7 B1
Fountain Ent Pk. ME15 .... 92 A1
Fountain La. ME2 .... 91 A2
Fountain Rd. ME2 .... 32 E1
Fountain Wlk. DA11 .... 12 F1
Four Acres. ME19 .... 90 B5
Four Elms Cty Prim Sch. TN8 113 B5
Four Elms Hill. ME3 .... 33 E4
Four Elms Rd. TN8 .... 112 D4
Four Oaks Rd. TN12 & TN27 .. 140 E7
Four Wents. Langley Heath ME17 108 E3
Four Wents. Marlpit ME17 ... 107 F2
Fouracre Cotts. ME9 .... 64 F6
Fourth Ave. Gillingham ME8 .. 48 E4
Fourth Ave. West Thurrock RM16 .. 11 A8
Fourwents Rd. ME3 .... 34 D7
Fowey Cl. ME5 .... 62 C5
Fowler Cl. Newham E16 .... 1 A8
Fowler Cl. Sidcup DA14 .... 24 E3
Fox Cl. Newham E16 .... 1 A8
Fox Cl. Orpington BR6 .... 52 A5
Fox Hollow Dr. DA16 .... 7 D4
Fox House Rd. DA17 .... 4 B1
Fox In The Wood. TN5 .... 174 C6
Fox La. BR2 .... 50 C5
Fox St. ME7 .... 48 C6
Foxburrow Rd. ME8 .... 63 D5
Foxbury. DA3 .... 56 E7
Foxbury Ave. BR7 .... 23 D2
Foxbury Cl. Bromley BR1 ...... 22 B2
Foxbury Cl. Orpington BR6 .... 52 A5
Foxbury Dr. BR6 .... 52 A4
Foxbury Rd. BR1 .... 22 B2
Foxbush. TN11 .... 116 C6
Foxcroft Rd. SE18 .... 6 B6
Foxden Dr. ME15 .... 92 F1
Foxendown La. DA13 .... 44 B1
Foxes Dale. SE3 .... 5 A4
Foxfield Prim Sch. SE18 .... 2 C2
Foxfield Rd. BR6 .... 51 D8
Foxglove Cl. TN8 .... 112 D3
Foxglove Cres. ME5 .... 61 E4
Foxglove Rise. ME14 .... 91 E7
Foxhole La. Four Throws TN18 .. 179 E1
Foxhole La. Matfield TN12 ... 151 C8
Foxhole La. Waterman TN5 .. 175 B4
Foxhole Rd. SE9 .... 5 E2
Foxhome Cl. BR7 .... 23 A2
Foxton House. E16 .... 2 A4
Foxton Rd. RM16 .... 11 D8
Foxwood Gr. BR6 .... 52 C1
Foxwood Rd. DA2 .... 28 B5
Foxwood Way. DA3 .... 43 D7
Framley Rd. TN10 .... 117 F5
Framlingham Cres. SE9 .... 22 F4
Frances St. SE18 .... 1 F2
Francis Ave. DA7 .... 8 A5
Francis Dr. ME5 .... 62 A2
Francis La. ME15 .... 107 F5
Francis Rd. Dartford DA1 .... 9 D2
Francis Rd. Hildenborough TN11 116 D6
Francis Rd. St Paul's Cray BR5 38 D6
Frank Burton Cl. SE7 .... 1 B1
Frank Woolley Rd. TN10 ..... 117 F5
Frankapps Cl. ME9 .... 65 B6
Frankfield Rise. TN2 .... 149 A1
Franklin Dr. ME14 .... 92 D4
Franklin Rd. Bexley DA7 .... 7 E6
Franklin Rd. Gillingham ME7 .. 48 D5
Franklin Rd. Gravesend DA12 .. 30 D3

Franklins Cotts. ME15 .... 106 C5
Franks Ct. ME8 .... 49 B2
Franks La. DA4 .... 41 B4
Franks Wood Ave. BR2 & BR5 .. 37 C4
Frant CE Prim Sch. TN3 ...... 163 B4
Frant Field. TN3 .... 163 B4
Frant Rd. TN2 & TN3 .... 163 A7
Frant Sta. TN3 .... 163 F5
Fraser Cl. Coldblow DA5 .... 25 C7
Fraser Cl. Newham Reg E6 .... 1 E7
Fraser House. SE18 .... 2 A2
Fraser Rd. DA8 .... 4 D1
Frederic House. SE7 .... 1 E3
Frederick Andrews Ct. RM17 .. 12 D8
Frederick Pl. SE18 .... 2 B1
Frederick Rd. ME7 .... 48 C4
Free Heath Rd. TN3 & TN5 ... 165 C3
Freehold. TN12 .... 119 F6
Freehold The. TN11 .... 102 D1
Freeland Way. DA8 .... 9 A6
Freelands Gr. BR1 .... 36 B8
Freelands Rd. Bromley BR1 ... 36 B8
Freelands Rd. Snodland ME6 .. 74 F8
Freeman Gdns. ME4 .... 47 F2
Freeman Rd. DA12 .... 30 E5
Freeman Way. ME15 .... 107 E7
Freemasons Rd. E16 .... 1 B7
Freesia Cl. Gillingham ME7 .... 48 F6
Freesia Cl. Orpington BR6 .... 51 F5
Freight La. TN17 .... 169 C3
Fremantle House. RM18 .... 12 F6
Fremantle Rd. DA17 .... 4 A2
Fremlin Cl. TN4 .... 148 B4
Fremlins Rd. ME14 .... 93 C4
Frensham Rd.
    Rolvenden Layne TN17 ..... 182 A1
Frensham Rd. Sidcup DA15 ... 23 D6
Frensham Wlk. ME5 .... 61 F1
Freshland Rd. ME5 .... 91 B4
Freshwater Rd. ME5 .... 62 B7
Freta Rd. DA7 .... 7 F2
Frewing Cl. TN3 .... 23 A3
Friar Rd. BR5 .... 38 A4
Friars Cl. ME5 .... 61 F2
Friars Mews. SE9 .... 6 A2
Friars Way. TN2 .... 149 D6
Friars Wlk. SE2 .... 3 D1
Friary Pl. ME2 .... 47 B7
Friary Prec. ME2 .... 47 B7
Friday Rd. DA8 .... 4 D1
Friday St. ME17 .... 125 B6
Friezland Rd. TN4 .... 148 D1
Friezley La. TN17 .... 155 C1
Frimley Ct. DA14 .... 24 C3
Frindsbury Hill. ME2 .... 33 C1
Frindsbury Rd. ME2 .... 47 B8
Frinstead Cl. BR5 .... 38 D5
Frinstead Wlk. ME16 .... 91 B7
Frinsted Cl. ME8 .... 49 C3
Frinsted Rd. DA8 .... 8 D7
Frinton Rd. DA14 .... 24 E6
Friston Way. ME1 .... 61 D8
Friswell Pl. DA7 .... 8 A3
Frithwood Cl. ME15 .... 92 F1
Frittenden Rd. Rochester ME2 .. 33 D2
Frittenden Rd. Staplehurst TN12 140 B2
Frobisher Gdns. ME1 .... 47 C2
Frobisher Rd. Erith DA8 .... 9 A7
Frobisher Rd. Newham E6 ...... 2 A7
Frobisher Way. DA12 .... 30 E3
Frog La. Rainham RM9 .... 4 D8
Frog La.
    Royal Tunbridge Wells TN1 .. 149 A2
Frog La. West Malling ME19 .. 89 C8
Frog's La. TN17 .... 181 E1
Froghole La. TN16 & TN8 .... 96 D2
Frogmore Wlk. ME17 .... 111 C5
Frognal Ave. DA14 .... 24 A2
Frognal Pl. DA14 .... 24 A3
Frognall Cnr. BR7 .... 23 F2
Frogs Hole La. TN17 .... 171 E3
Froissart Rd. SE9 .... 5 E2
Fromandez Dr. TN12 .... 152 F5
Frome Ct. TN10 .... 117 B5
Front Cotts. TN5 .... 176 E1
Frost Cres. ME5 .... 62 A7
Froyle Pl. ME16 .... 91 C6
Fruitfields. TN5 .... 177 C3
Fry Cl. ME3 .... 21 A6
Fry's Cotts. ME3 .... 19 C4
Fuchsia St. SE2 .... 3 B1
Fuggles Cl. TN12 .... 135 E6
Fuggles Cl. TN17 .... 180 D6
Fulbert Dr. ME14 .... 92 F5
Fuller Cl. Durgates TN5 ...... 174 E5
Fuller Cl. Orpington BR6 ...... 51 F5
Fullers Cl. ME14 .... 93 A4
Fullers Hill. TN16 .... 81 D1
Fulmar Rd. ME2 .... 46 D6
Fulmer Rd. E16 .... 1 D8
Fulthorp Rd. SE3 .... 5 A5
Fulwich Rd. DA1 .... 9 F1
Furfield Cl. ME17 .... 107 E5
Furnace Ave. TN3 .... 166 A3
Furnace La. Hook Green TN3 .. 165 E4
Furnace La. Horsmonden TN12 152 F7
Furner Cl. DA1 .... 8 F4
Furness Sch. BR8 .... 25 F2
Furnival Ct. TN2 .... 162 F8
Furrell's Rd. ME1 .... 47 D5
Furze Bank. TN8 .... 113 B5
Furzefield Ave. TN3 .... 148 A8
Furzefield Cl. BR7 .... 23 B2

Furzefield Rd. SE3 & SE7 .... 5 B7
Furzehill Sq. BR5 .... 38 B5
Fyfe Way. BR1 .... 36 A7

Gable Cl. DA1 .... 9 A2
Gables Cl. SE12 .... 22 A7
Gables The. Bromley BR1 ..... 22 B1
Gables The. New Barn DA3 ... 43 C6
Gabriel Gdns. DA12 .... 30 E3
Gabriel Spring Road (East).
    DA3 .... 55 F8
Gabriel's Hill. ME14 & ME15 .. 92 A4
Gabrielspring Rd. DA4 .... 55 D8
Gads Hill. ME7 .... 48 F6
Gads Hill Sch. ME2 .... 32 C2
Gadsby La. TN27 .... 159 F3
Gadwall Way. SE28 .... 2 D7
Gafford's Bridge Cotts. TN12 .. 137 C4
Gagetown Terr. ME14 .... 91 F7
Gainsborough Ave. Dartford DA1 .. 9 C2
Gainsborough Ave. Tilbury RM18 13 B6
Gainsborough Cl. ME8 .... 63 D6
Gainsborough Dr.
    Maidstone ME16 .... 91 B4
Gainsborough Dr.
    Northfleet DA11 .... 29 D5
Gainsborough Gdns. TN10 ... 117 C5
Gainsborough House. ME1 ... 47 D5
Gainsborough Sq. DA7 .... 7 D4
Gaitskell Rd. SE9 .... 23 C7
Galahad Ave. ME2 .... 46 E6
Galahad Rd. BR1 .... 22 A4
Galena Cl. ME5 .... 62 A1
Galena Rd. SE18 .... 2 F1
Gallants La. ME15 .... 105 F6
Galleon Bvd. DA9 .... 10 D3
Galleon Cl. Chatham ME1 ..... 61 C8
Galleon Cl. Erith DA8 .... 4 D2
Galley Hill Rd. DA11 .... 11 F2
Galley Hill Trad Est. DA10 ..... 11 E2
Gallions Mount Prim Sch. SE18 .. 2 F1
Gallions Rd. Greenwich SE7 .... 1 A2
Gallions Rd. Newham E16 ...... 2 C6
Gallions Reach Sta. E16 .... 2 B6
Gallop The. DA13 .... 72 F7
Gallosson Rd. SE18 .... 2 E2
Gallus Sq. SE3 .... 5 B4
Galsworthy Cl. SE28 .... 3 B5
Galsworthy Cres. SE3 .... 5 C6
Galsworthy Rd. RM18 .... 13 C6
Galton House. SE18 .... 5 F6
Games House. SE7 .... 5 C8
Gamma Rd. ME4 .... 35 D7
Gandy's La. ME17 .... 107 C2
Garden Ave. DA7 .... 8 A4
Garden Cl. Lewisham SE12 ... 22 B5
Garden Cl. Maidstone ME15 .. 107 E7
Garden Cl. Toy's Hill TN16 .... 97 C3
Garden Cotts. Leigh TN11 ... 116 A2
Garden Cotts. St Paul's Cray BR5 38 C7
Garden Cl. SE9 .... 6 A1
Garden La. BR1 .... 22 B2
Garden of England Pk
    (Mobile Home Pk). ME17 .. 110 B7
Garden Pl. DA2 .... 26 D5
Garden Rd. Bromley BR1 ...... 22 B2
Garden Rd.
    Royal Tunbridge Wells TN1 .. 149 B4
Garden Rd. Sevenoaks TN13 .. 84 D5
Garden Rd. Tonbridge TN9 ... 117 D2
Garden Row. DA11 .... 29 F5
Garden St. Gillingham ME7 ... 48 A6
Garden St.
    Royal Tunbridge Wells TN1 .. 149 B4
Garden Terr. TN15 .... 85 A6
Garden Way. ME18 .... 88 F2
Gardenia Cl. ME2 .... 33 B2
Gardens The. ME17 .... 106 C3
Gardiner Cl. BR5 .... 38 C7
Gardiner House. SE18 .... 5 F7
Gardiner St. ME7 .... 48 C6
Gardyne Mews. TN9 .... 133 B8
Gareth Gr. BR1 .... 22 A4
Garfield Rd. ME7 .... 48 D6
Gargany Wlk. SE28 .... 3 D6
Garibaldi St. SE18 .... 2 E2
Garland Rd. SE18 .... 6 D7
Garlands. TN11 .... 116 D8
Garlinge Rd. TN4 .... 133 A1
Garnet Rd. DA11 .... 29 F5
Garnett Cl. SE9 .... 5 F4
Garrard Cl. Bexley DA7 .... 8 A4
Garrick Dr. SE28 .... 2 D3
Garrick St. ME15 .... 13 B1
Garrington Cl. ME14 .... 92 C6
Garrison Cl. SE18 .... 6 A7
Garrison Rd. ME12 .... 21 F3
Garrolds Cl. BR8 .... 39 D7
Garrow. DA3 .... 43 B6
Garside Cl. SE28 .... 2 D3
Garth Rd. SE12 .... 22 A8
Garvary Rd. E16 .... 1 B7
Garvock Dr. TN13 .... 84 A1
Gas House Rd. ME1 .... 47 C6
Gascoyne Dr. DA1 .... 8 F4
Gasson Rd. SE28 .... 10 E1
Gassons Rd. ME6 .... 74 E8
Gatcombe Cl. Chatham ME5 .. 62 A5
Gatcombe Cl. Maidstone ME16 91 B5
Gate Farm Rd. TN3 & TN4 .. 132 C4
Gateacre Ct. DA14 .... 24 B4
Gatefield Cotts. TN17 .... 181 D4
Gatehouse Farm Cotts. TN4 .. 132 C4
Gates Green Rd. BR2 & BR4 .. 50 A6

Gateway Par. DA12 .... 30 F4
Gatland La. ME16 .... 91 B2
Gatling Rd. SE18 & SE2 .... 3 A1
Gaton Rd. SE2 .... 3 C3
Gattons Way. DA14 .... 24 F4
Gatwick Farm Cotts. RH19 .. 144 A4
Gatwick Rd. DA12 .... 30 B6
Gault Cl. ME15 .... 93 A2
Gautrey Sq. E6 .... 1 F7
Gavestone Cres. SE12 .... 22 B8
Gavestone Rd. SE12 .... 22 B8
Gavin House. SE18 .... 2 E2
Gaylor Rd. RM18 .... 12 F6
Gaza Trad Est. TN11 .... 115 D7
Gazelle Glade. DA12 .... 30 F3
Gean Cl. ME5 .... 77 A8
Geddes Pl. DA7 .... 8 A3
Gedge's Hill. TN12 .... 135 F3
Geffery's Ct. SE9 .... 22 E5
General Gordon Pl. SE18 .... 2 B2
Genesta Glade. DA12 .... 31 A3
Genesta Rd. SE18 .... 6 C8
Geneva Ave. ME8 .... 49 A2
Gentian Cl. Chatham ME5 .... 61 E4
Gentian Cl. Maidstone ME14 .. 92 E5
George Akass House. SE18 ..... 2 C1
George Crooks House. RM17 12 B8
George La. Hayes BR2 .... 36 B1
George La. Leeds ME17 ...... 109 B7
George La. Rochester ME1 .... 47 C6
George Marsham House.
    ME15 .... 106 F3
George St. Chainhurst ME15 .. 122 A7
George St. Grays RM17 .... 12 A8
George St. Maidstone ME15 ... 92 A3
George St.
    Royal Tunbridge Wells TN2 .. 149 C3
George St. Sparrow's Green TN5 174 F5
George St. Staplehurst TN12 .. 139 E6
George St. Tonbridge TN9 ... 133 B8
George Summers Cl. ME2 ..... 47 E8
Georges Cl. BR5 .... 38 C6
Georgian Cl. BR2 .... 36 B1
Georgian Dr. ME17 .... 106 D3
Georgian Way. ME8 .... 63 C4
Geraint Rd. BR1 .... 22 A4
Gerald Ave. ME4 .... 47 F2
Gerald Rd. DA12 .... 30 E8
Gerda Rd. SE9 .... 23 C6
Gerdview Dr. DA2 .... 26 C4
Gerrard Ave. ME1 .... 61 E8
Gertrude Rd. DA17 .... 4 A2
Gibbet La. TN12 .... 152 F6
Gibbetts. TN3 .... 147 F3
Gibbs Hill. Headcorn TN27 .. 141 E5
Gibbs Hill. Nettlestead ME18 .. 104 B5
Gibraltar Ave. ME4 .... 48 B7
Gibraltar Hill. ME4 .... 47 F4
Gibraltar La. ME14 .... 91 F8
Gibson Cl. DA11 .... 29 E5
Gibson Dr. ME19 .... 88 F4
Gidd's Pond Cotts. ME14 ..... 92 E6
Giddyhorn La. ME16 .... 91 C5
Gideon Cl. DA17 .... 4 B2
Gifford Cl. ME8 .... 49 C3
Giggs Hill. BR5 .... 38 A8
Gighill Rd. ME20 .... 74 F4
Gilbert Cl. Eltham SE18 .... 5 F6
Gilbert Cl. Gillingham ME7 ... 63 A5
Gilbert Cl. Swanscombe DA10 .. 11 D1
Gilbert Rd. Bromley BR1 ...... 22 A1
Gilbert Rd. Erith DA17 .... 4 A3
Gilbert Terr. ME14 .... 91 F7
Gilbourne Rd. SE18 .... 6 F8
Gilchrist Cotts. TN14 .... 99 C2
Gildenhill Rd. BR8 .... 26 C1
Gildersome St. SE18 .... 6 A8
Gill Ave. Newham E16 .... 1 A7
Gill Ave. Rochester ME2 ...... 33 D2
Gill Cres. DA11 .... 29 F5
Gill Ct. SE18 .... 2 C2
Gill The. TN2 .... 150 E8
Gill's Rd. Green Street Green DA2 28 B1
Gill's Rd. South Darenth DA4 .. 41 F8
Gillan Ct. SE12 .... 22 B5
Gilletts La. ME19 .... 90 A6
Gillies Cl. DA14 .... 23 E4
Gillies Rd. TN15 .... 55 E5
Gillingham Gn. ME7 .... 48 E6
Gillingham Rd. ME7 .... 48 D5
Gillingham Sta. ME7 .... 48 D5
Gillmans Rd. BR5 & BR6 ...... 38 B1
Gilroy Way. BR5 .... 38 B2
Gimble Way. TN2 .... 134 D1
Gingerbread La. TN18 .... 177 F2
Ginsbury Cl. ME2 .... 47 E6
Gipps Cross La. TN3 .... 147 F3
Gipsy La. RM17 .... 12 C8
Gipsy Rd. DA16 .... 7 D5
Giralda Cl. E16 .... 1 D8
Glade Bsns Ctr The. RM16 ... 10 F8
Glade The. Bromley BR1 ...... 36 D7
Glade The. Chatham ME5 ..... 62 A2
Glade The. Greenwich SE7 ..... 5 C7
Glade The. Sevenoaks TN13 .. 84 B4
Glades Sh Ctr The. BR1 .... 36 A7
Glades The. DA12 .... 30 D2
Gladeswood Rd. DA17 .... 4 B2
Gladstone Rd. Chatham ME4 .. 47 E2
Gladstone Rd. Dartford DA1 .... 9 F1
Gladstone Rd. Maidstone ME14 92 A6
Gladstone Rd. Orpington BR6 .. 51 C5
Gladstone Rd. Rusthall TN4 .. 148 B4
Gladstone Rd. Tonbridge TN9 .. 117 B1
Gladwell Rd. BR1 .... 22 A2
Gladwyn Cl. ME8 .... 63 D4
Glamford Rd. ME2 .... 46 D5

Glamis Cl. ME5 .... 62 A5
Glanville Rd. Bromley BR2 ... 36 B6
Glanville Rd. Gillingham ME4 .. 48 D5
Glanville Rd. Rochester ME2 .. 47 A8
Glasbrook Rd. SE9 .... 22 D8
Glasgow House. ME15 .... 107 E7
Glass Yd. SE18 .... 2 A3
Glassmill La. BR2 .... 36 A7
Gleaming Wood Dr. ME5 ..... 77 D8
Gleaners Cl. ME14 .... 92 E4
Glebe Cl. TN27 .... 143 B2
Glebe Cotts. TN16 .... 82 B4
Glebe Gdns. ME17 .... 111 E5
Glebe House. SE18 .... 2 A2
Glebe House Dr. BR2 .... 36 B1
Glebe La. Maidstone ME16 ... 91 A1
Glebe La. Sevenoaks TN13 .... 84 B1
Glebe Meadow. ME18 .... 104 E7
Glebe Pl. DA4 .... 41 C5
Glebe Rd. Bromley BR1 .... 36 A8
Glebe Rd. Gillingham ME7 .... 48 E3
Glebe Rd. Gravesend DA11 ... 29 F7
Glebe Rd. Sevenoaks Weald TN14 99 B3
Glebe The. Bidborough TN4 . 132 C3
Glebe The. Chislehurst BR7 ... 37 C8
Glebe The. Cuxton ME2 ...... 46 C2
Glebe The. Pembury TN2 .... 150 D8
Glebe The. Penshurst TN11 .. 131 A3
Glebe Way. DA8 .... 8 E8
Glebefield The. TN13 .... 83 F4
Glebeland. TN27 .... 127 F4
Glebelands.
    Bidborough TN3 & TN4 ..... 132 C3
Glebelands. Biddenden TN27 . 157 F1
Glebelands. Crayford DA1 .... 8 F3
Glebelands. Penshurst TN11 .. 131 A3
Gleeson Dr. BR6 .... 51 F6
Glen Ct. DA14 .... 24 A4
Glen Dunlop House The. TN13 84 C5
Glen House. E16 .... 2 A5
Glen The. BR6 .... 51 A7
Glen View. DA12 .... 30 C7
Glen View Rd. BR1 .... 36 D7
Glenalvon Way. SE7 .... 1 E2
Glenbarr Cl. SE9 .... 6 B4
Glencairne Cl. E16 .... 1 D8
Glencoe Cty Inf Sch. ME4 ..... 48 A8
Glencoe Cty Prim Sch. ME4 .. 48 A2
Glencoe Rd. ME4 .... 48 A2
Glendale. BR8 .... 39 F4
Glendale Cl. SE9 .... 6 A4
Glendale Cl. TN1 .... 149 D6
Glendale Rd. Erith DA8 .... 4 C2
Glendale Rd. Northfleet DA11 .. 29 E5
Glendale Way. SE28 .... 3 C6
Glendower Cres. BR5 & BR6 .. 38 A3
Glendown Rd. SE2 .... 3 A1
Gleneagles Cl. BR6 .... 37 D1
Gleneagles Cl. ME5 .... 61 F2
Gleneagles Dr. ME15 .... 92 A1
Gleneagles Gn. BR6 .... 37 D1
Glenesk Rd. SE9 .... 6 B3
Glengall Rd. DA7 .... 7 E4
Glenhead Cl. SE9 .... 6 B4
Glenhouse Rd. SE9 .... 6 A2
Glenhurst Ave. DA5 .... 24 F7
Glenister St. E16 .... 2 A5
Glenlea Rd. SE9 .... 6 A3
Glenluce Rd. SE3 .... 5 A8
Glenlyon Rd. SE9 .... 6 A2
Glenmore Pk. TN2 .... 162 F8
Glenmore Rd. DA16 .... 6 F6
Glenmount Path. SE18 .... 2 C1
Glenrosa Gdns. DA12 .... 30 F3
Glenrose Cl. DA14 .... 24 B3
Glenshiel Rd. SE9 .... 6 A2
Glentammon Ave. BR6 .... 51 F4
Glentammon Cl. BR6 .... 51 F5
Glentammon Gdns. BR6 ...... 51 F4
Glentammon Rd. BR6 .... 51 F4
Glenure Rd. SE9 .... 6 A2
Glenview. SE2 .... 7 D8
Glenwood. TN30 .... 173 B3
Glenwood Cl. Chatham ME5 .. 48 C1
Glenwood Cl. Gillingham ME7 .. 63 A7
Glenwood Cl. Maidstone ME16 .. 91 C5
Glenwood Cl. St Michaels TN30 173 B3
Glenwood Ct. DA14 .... 24 A4
Glimpsing Gn. DA18 .... 3 E3
Glistening Glade. ME8 .... 63 E6
Gload Cres. BR5 .... 52 D8
Globe La. ME4 .... 47 F5
Globe Yd. DA11 .... 13 B1
Gloucester Ave. Bexley DA16 ... 6 F3
Gloucester Ave. Sidcup DA15 .. 23 E8
Gloucester Cl. ME8 .... 64 A8
Gloucester Cl. RM18 .... 12 F5
Gloucester Par. DA15 .... 7 A2
Gloucester Rd. Dartford DA1 .. 26 B8
Gloucester Rd. Erith DA17 ...... 3 F1
Gloucester Rd. Gravesend DA12 30 C4
Gloucester Rd. Maidstone ME15 107 D8
Gloucester Rd.
    Sparrow's Green TN5 .... 174 F6
Glover Cl. SE2 .... 3 C2
Gloxinia Rd. DA13 .... 29 B2
Glyn Davies Cl. TN13 .... 83 E7
Glyn Dr. DA14 .... 24 B4
Glynde Rd. DA7 .... 7 E4
Glyndebourne Pk. BR6 .... 51 B8
Glyndon Rd. SE18 .... 2 C1
Goad Ave. ME5 .... 62 B3
Goddard's Green Cotts. TN17 170 F1
Goddards Cl. TN17 .... 169 B4
Godden Rd. ME6 .... 74 F8
Goddings Dr. ME1 .... 47 A3
Goddington Chase. BR6 ...... 52 B6
Goddington House. BR6 ...... 52 C7

Goddington La.
Harrietsham ME17 .... 110 B6
Goddington La. Orpington BR6 ... 52 A7
Goddington Rd. ME2 .... 47 B8
Godfrey Cl. ME2 .... 32 F1
Godfrey Evans Cl. TN10 ...... 117 F5
Godfrey Hill. SE18 .... 1 E2
Godfrey Rd. SE18 .... 1 F2
Godstow Rd. SE2 .... 3 C4
Godwin House. SE18 .... 5 F6
Godwin Rd. BR1 & BR2 .... 36 C6
Gold St. DA12 .... 44 E4
Goldace. RM17 .... 11 F8
Goldcrest Cl. Newham E16 ..... 1 D8
Goldcrest Cl. Woolwich SE28 .. 3 C6
Golden Plover Cl. E16 .... 1 A7
Golden Sq. TN30 .... 183 B8
Golden Wood Cl. ME5 .... 77 D8
Goldfinch Ave. ME20 .... 75 A2
Goldfinch Cl. Orpington BR6 .. 52 A5
Goldfinch Cl.
Paddock Wood TN12 .... 136 A5
Goldfinch Rd. SE28 .... 2 D3
Goldie Leigh Hospl. SE2 ...... 7 C8
Golding Cl. ME20 .... 75 C1
Golding Gdns. TN12 .... 120 A6
Golding Rd. TN13 .... 84 C5
Goldings. TN12 .... 135 E5
Goldings The. ME8 .... 63 C8
Goldmark House. SE3 .... 5 B4
Goldsel Rd. BR8 .... 39 E5
Goldsmid Rd. TN9 .... 133 C8
Goldsmid St. SE18 .... 2 E1
Goldsmith. RM17 .... 11 F8
Goldsmith Rd. ME8 .... 63 E5
Goldsmith's Bottom. TN14 ... 98 E2
Goldstone Wlk. ME5 .... 62 A1
Goldsworth Dr. ME2 .... 33 A1
Goldthorne Cl. ME14 .... 92 C5
Goldwing Cl. E16 .... 1 A7
Golf Links Ave. DA11 .... 30 B3
Golf Rd. BR1 .... 37 A6
Golford Rd. TN17 .... 169 F4
Gollogly Terr. [9] SE7 .... 1 C1
Goodall Cl. ME8 .... 63 E5
Goodbury Rd. TN15 .... 70 B6
Gooding House. [4] SE7 .... 1 C1
Goodley Stock Rd. TN16 & TN8 . 96 B6
Goodmead Rd. BR6 .... 38 A2
Goods Hill. TN30 .... 182 D8
Goods Station Rd. TN1 ...... 149 B4
Goodtrees La. TN8 .... 145 B2
Goodwin Dr. Maidstone ME14 .. 92 B8
Goodwin Dr. Sidcup DA14 ..... 24 D6
Goodwin Rd. ME3 .... 33 B7
Goodwins The. TN2 .... 148 F1
Goodwood Cl. High Halstow ME23 17 E4
Goodwood Cl. Maidstone ME15 107 F6
Goodwood Cres. DA12 .... 30 C2
Goodworth Rd. TN15 .... 71 F3
Goosander Way. SE18 & SE28 ... 2 D3
Goose Cl. ME5 .... 62 A7
Goose Green Cl. BR5 .... 38 A7
Goose Sq. [8] E6 .... 1 F7
Gooseneck La. TN27 .... 141 C5
Gordon Ct. ME17 .... 106 E3
Gordon Cty Jun Sch. ME2 ..... 47 A8
Gordon House. SE12 .... 22 A8
Gordon Pl. DA11 .... 13 C1
Gordon Prim Sch. SE9 .... 5 F3
Gordon Rd. Chatham ME4 ..... 48 B2
Gordon Rd. Dartford DA1 ..... 26 D8
Gordon Rd. Erith DA17 .... 4 C2
Gordon Rd. Gillingham ME7 ... 48 E5
Gordon Rd.
Gillingham,Brompton ME4 ... 48 A7
Gordon Rd. Hoo St Werburgh ME3 34 D5
Gordon Rd. Northfleet DA11 ... 29 E8
Gordon Rd. Rochester ME2 .... 47 A8
Gordon Rd.
Royal Tunbridge Wells TN4 .. 149 C7
Gordon Rd. Sevenoaks TN13 ... 84 B3
Gordon Rd. Sidcup DA15 .... 6 E2
Gordon Terr. ME1 .... 47 C4
Gordon Way. BR1 .... 36 A8
Gore Cotts. DA2 .... 27 C4
Gore Court Rd. ME15 .... 107 F5
Gore Farm Cotts. DA2 .... 27 C5
Gore Green Rd. ME3 .... 32 E7
Gore La. TN17 .... 153 E4
Gore Rd. Dartford DA2 .... 27 D6
Gore Rd. Silver Street ME9 ... 80 F5
Gorham Cl. ME6 .... 74 F7
Gorham Dr. Maidstone ME15 ... 93 A1
Gorham Dr. Tonbridge TN9 ... 133 E8
Gorman Rd. SE18 .... 1 F2
Gorringe Ave. DA4 .... 41 D7
Gorse Ave. ME5 .... 61 F5
Gorse Cl. E16 .... 1 A7
Gorse Cres. ME20 .... 90 D8
Gorse Rd. Orpington BR5 ..... 53 A8
Gorse Rd. Rochester ME2 ..... 46 F8
Gorse Rd.
Royal Tunbridge Wells TN2 .. 149 B8
Gorse Way. DA3 .... 43 A4
Gorse Wood Rd. Hartley DA3 .. 43 A5
Gorse Wood Rd. New Barn DA3 . 43 A6
Goss Hill. BR8 .... 26 C2
Gossage Rd. SE18 .... 2 D1
Gosshill Rd. BR7 .... 37 A7
Gossington Cl. BR7 .... 23 B4
Gothic Cl. DA1 .... 26 D5
Goudhurst Cl. ME16 .... 91 E4
Goudhurst & Kilndown
CE Prim Sch. TN17 .... 167 E8
Goudhurst Rd. Gillingham ME8 . 49 B3
Goudhurst Rd.
Horsmonden TN12 .... 153 B5

Goudhurst Rd.
Knox Bridge TN12 & TN17 ... 155 C6
Goudhurst Rd.
Wilsley Pound TN17 .... 169 D8
Gouge Ave. DA11 .... 29 E7
Gould Rd. ME5 .... 62 B3
Gouldhurst Rd. TN12 .... 138 B5
Gourock Rd. SE9 .... 6 A2
Gover Hill. TN11 .... 102 E6
Grace Ave. Bexley DA7 .... 7 F5
Grace Ave. Maidstone ME16 ... 91 C6
Grace Cl. SE9 .... 22 D5
Gracious La. TN13 .... 99 B5
Gracious Lane Bridge. TN13 ... 99 A6
Gracious Lane End. TN14 ..... 98 F5
Grafton Ave. ME1 .... 61 E8
Graham Ct. BR1 .... 22 B1
Graham House. SE18 .... 6 B7
Graham Rd. DA7 .... 8 A3
Grain Rd. Gillingham ME8 .... 63 C3
Grain Rd. Grain ME3 .... 20 D3
Grainey Field. ME9 .... 64 E4
Grainger Wlk. TN10 .... 117 E6
Gram Sch for Girls Wilmington.
DA2 .... 26 B5
Grampian Cl. Orpington BR6 ... 37 F3
Grampian Cl.
Royal Tunbridge Wells TN2 .. 149 D5
Grampian Way. ME13 .... 93 A1
Granada House. [6] ME15 ..... 92 A4
Granada St. [7] ME15 .... 92 A4
Granary. TN12 .... 136 B6
Granary Cl. Gillingham ME8 ... 49 F1
Granary Cl. Maidstone ME14 .. 92 E5
Granby House. [14] SE18 .... 1 F2
Granby Rd. Eltham SE9 .... 22 B5
Granby Rd. Northfleet DA11 ... 12 D1
Granby Rd. Woolwich SE18 ..... 2 B3
Grand Depot Rd. SE18 .... 2 A1
Grandshire Gdns. ME3 .... 34 E6
Grandshore La. TN17 .... 156 B5
Grange Cl. Edenbridge TN8 ... 112 C1
Grange Cl. Leybourne ME19 ... 74 C2
Grange Cl. Sidcup DA15 ...... 24 A5
Grange Cl. Westerham TN16 ... 81 C1
Grange Cotts. TN11 .... 101 D5
Grange Cres. Erith SE28 .... 3 C7
Grange Cres. St Michaels TN30 173 A3
Grange Dr. Chislehurst BR7 ... 22 F2
Grange Dr. Pratt's Bottom BR6 . 52 C2
Grange Gdns. SN4 .... 148 D4
Grange Hill. Chatham ME4 .... 48 B3
Grange Hill. Plaxtol TN15 .... 101 E8
Grange House. Erith DA8 .... 9 A5
Grange House. Gravesend DA11 30 A8
Grange House. Maidstone ME16 91 A2
Grange La. Hartley DA3 .... 43 B2
Grange La. Maidstone ME15 ... 77 A1
Grange Rd. Gillingham ME7 ... 49 B5
Grange Rd. Gravesend DA11 ... 30 A8
Grange Rd. Grays RM17 .... 12 B8
Grange Rd. Orpington BR6 .... 51 C8
Grange Rd. Platt TN15 .... 87 C7
Grange Rd. Rochester ME2 .... 47 B7
Grange Rd. Rusthall TN4 ..... 148 D4
Grange Rd. Sevenoaks TN13 ... 99 A8
Grange Rd. St Michaels TN30 . 172 F3
Grange The. East Malling ME19 . 90 A7
Grange The. South Darenth DA4 . 41 D8
Grange The. West Kingsdown
TN15 .... 55 F2
Grange The. Westerham TN16 .. 81 C1
Grange Way. Erith DA8 .... 9 B7
Grange Way. Hartley ME3 ..... 42 F3
Grange Way. Rochester ME1 ... 47 C3
Grangehill Pl. SE9 .... 5 F4
Grangehill Rd. SE9 .... 5 F3
Grangeways Cl. DA11 .... 29 F4
Grangewood. DA5 .... 24 F7
Granite St. SE18 .... 2 F1
Grant Cl. ME7 .... 49 B1
Grant's Cotts. ME17 .... 111 B5
Granton Rd. DA14 .... 24 C2
Granville Ct. TN13 .... 84 A3
Granville Mews. DA14 .... 24 A4
Granville Rd. Bexley DA16 ..... 7 C4
Granville Rd. Gillingham ME7 . 48 E5
Granville Rd. Gravesend DA11 . 29 F7
Granville Rd. Maidstone ME14 . 92 A6
Granville Rd.
Royal Tunbridge Wells TN1 .. 149 C5
Granville Rd. Sevenoaks TN13 . 84 A3
Granville Rd. Sidcup DA14 .... 24 B4
Granville Rd. Westerham TN16 . 81 C1
Granville Sch The. TN13 ..... 84 A4
Grapple Rd. ME17 .... 92 A7
Grasdene Rd. SE18 & SE2 ...... 7 A7
Grasmere Ave. BR6 .... 51 B7
Grasmere Gdns. BR6 .... 51 B7
Grasmere Rd. Bexley DA7 ...... 8 C5
Grasmere Rd. Orpington BR6 .. 51 B7
Grassington Rd. DA14 .... 24 A4
Grasslands. ME17 .... 108 E4
Grasmere. ME20 .... 74 F2
Grassy Glade. ME7 .... 63 B6
Grassy La. TN13 .... 99 B8
Gravel Hill. DA6 .... 8 B2
Gravel Hill Cl. DA5 .... 8 B1
Gravel Hill Prim Sch. DA6 ..... 8 B3
Gravel Pit Way. BR6 .... 38 A1
Gravel Rd. Keston Mark BR2 .. 50 E8
Gravel Rd. Sutton at Hone DA4 . 27 B1
Gravel Wlk. ME1 .... 47 C5
Gravelly Bottom Rd. ME17 .. 109 B2
Gravelly Ways. TN12 .... 120 D5
Gravelwood Cl. BR7 .... 23 C5
Graveney Cl. ME3 .... 33 C7

Graveney Rd. ME15 .... 107 F7
Graves Est. DA16 .... 7 B5
Gravesend Gram Sch for Boys.
DA12 .... 30 D8
Gravesend Gram Sch for Girls.
Gravesend DA11 .... 30 A7
Gravesend Gram Sch for Girls.
Gravesend DA11 .... 30 A8
Gravesend & North Kent Hospl.
DA11 .... 13 A1
Gravesend Rd.
Gadshill ME2 & ME3 & DA12 . 32 C2
Gravesend Rd. Rochester ME2 . 46 F8
Gravesend Rd. Shorne DA12 ... 31 B5
Gravesend Rd. Vigo Village TN15 72 D6
Gravesend Sta. DA11 .... 13 B1
Gravesham Ct. [8] DA11 ...... 30 B8
Grayland Cl. BR1 .... 36 D8
Graylands. RM17 .... 11 E8
Grayne Ave. ME3 .... 21 B5
Grays Farm Prim Sch. BR5 ... 38 B8
Grays Farm Production Village.
BR5 .... 38 B8
Grays Farm Rd. BR5 .... 38 B8
Grays Rd. TN14 & TN16 ...... 81 D7
Grays Sh Ctr. RM17 .... 12 A8
Grays Sta. RM17 .... 12 A8
Grazeley Cl. DA6 .... 8 C2
Great Basin Rd. ME12 .... 21 F2
Great Bounds Dr. TN4 ...... 132 E3
Great Browns Rd. TN4 ...... 149 C8
Great Courtlands. TN3 ...... 148 A3
Great Elms. TN11 .... 102 E1
Great Elms Rd. BR2 .... 36 C5
Great Footway. TN3 .... 147 F3
Great Hall Arc. [3] TN1 ..... 149 B3
Great Harry Dr. SE9 .... 23 A5
Great Ivy Mill Cotts. ME15 .. 106 F4
Great Lines. ME7 .... 48 B5
Great Lodge Cotts. TN2 ..... 133 E2
Great Maytham Hall. TN17 .. 181 F2
Great Oak. TN19 .... 184 A3
Great Queen St. DA1 .... 9 F1
Great South Ave. ME4 .... 48 A1
Great Thrift. BR5 .... 37 C5
Greatness La. TN14 .... 84 C6
Greatness Rd. TN13 & TN14 .. 84 C6
Greatwood. BR7 .... 23 A1
Grebe Apartments. [13] ME15 . 107 E5
Grebe Cl. ME3 .... 19 C4
Grebe Ct. ME20 .... 74 F1
Grecian Rd. TN1 .... 149 B2
Grecian St. ME14 .... 92 A6
Green Acres. ME14 .... 23 F4
Green Bank Cl. ME7 .... 63 A5
Green Cl. ME1 .... 47 D8
Green Court Rd. BR8 .... 39 D3
Green Farm Cl. BR6 .... 51 F5
Green Farm La. DA12 .... 31 E5
Green Gdns. BR6 .... 51 E7
Green Hedges. TN30 .... 183 B8
Green Hill. Maidstone ME15 .. 93 B1
Green Hill. Woolwich SE18 ..... 1 F1
Green Hill La. ME17 .... 110 D1
Green La.
Boughton Monchelsea ME17 . 107 C3
Green La. Cliffe ME3 .... 16 B6
Green La. Collier Street TN12 . 137 E8
Green La. Devil's Den ME17 .. 124 B4
Green La. East End TN17 ..... 171 C6
Green La. Eltham BR7 & SE9 .. 23 B5
Green La. Four Elms TN8 ..... 113 C7
Green La. Grain ME3 .... 21 B5
Green La. Langley Heath ME17 108 C3
Green La. Meopham Station DA13 44 B2
Green La. Platt's Heath ME17 . 110 F2
Green La. Smarden TN27 ..... 143 A1
Green La. Stockbury ME9 ..... 64 F1
Green La. Trottiscliffe ME19 .. 73 A5
Green La. Withyham TN26 ... 159 F3
Green La The. TN11 .... 115 F1
Green Lands. DA13 .... 44 D4
Green Lane Bsns Pk. SE9 ..... 23 A6
Green Lane Cotts.
Collier Street TN12 .... 121 D1
Green Lane Cotts.
Langley Heath ME17 .... 108 C3
Green Lawns. [8] SE18 .... 2 B2
Green Pl. DA1 .... 8 E2
Green Rd. TN12 .... 153 A6
Green Sands. ME14 .... 77 C8
Green Sq. TN5 .... 174 F5
Green St. ME7 .... 48 C5
Green Street Green Prim Sch.
BR6 .... 51 F4
Green Street Green Rd.
DA1 & DA2 .... 27 D4
Green The.
Bexley,Bexley Heath DA7 .... 8 A6
Green The.
Bexley,Falconwood DA16 ..... 6 E3
Green The. East Farleigh ME15 . 106 B7
Green The. Hayes BR2 .... 36 A2
Green The. Langton Green TN3 . 147 E3
Green The. Lenham TN11 ..... 115 F1
Green The. Lewisham BR1 ..... 22 A5
Green The. Sevenoaks TN13 ... 84 B7
Green The. Sidcup DA14 ...... 24 A4
Green The. St Paul's Cray BR5 . 24 B1
Green The. Westerham TN16 ... 81 C1
Green Vale. DA6 .... 7 D2
Green View Ave. TN1 .... 116 A1
Green Way. Bromley BR2 ..... 36 E3
Green Way. Eltham SE9 .... 5 D2
Green Way. Hartley DA3 ...... 42 E4
Green Way. Maidstone ME16 .. 91 B3
Green Way.
Royal Tunbridge Wells TN2 .. 149 E8

Green Wlk. DA1 .... 8 F3
Green's Cotts. ME15 .... 106 A4
Greenacre. DA1 .... 26 D6
Greenacre Cl. Chatham ME5 .. 62 A5
Greenacre Cl. Swanley BR8 ... 39 E5
Greenacre Sch. ME5 .... 61 F5
Greenacres. SE9 .... 6 A1
Greenacres. BR6 .... 51 C6
Greenacres Prim Sch & Language
Impairment Unit. SE9 ...... 23 A6
Greenbank. ME5 .... 62 B8
Greenbank Lodge. [2] BR7 .... 37 A8
Greenbanks. DA1 .... 26 E6
Greenbay Rd. SE7 .... 5 D7
Greenborough Cl. ME15 .... 107 E6
Greencourt Rd. BR5 .... 37 E4
Greencroft Cl. E16 .... 1 D8
Greendale Wlk. [4] DA11 ..... 29 E5
Greenfield. TN8 .... 112 D1
Greenfield Cl. Eccles ME20 ... 76 A6
Greenfield Cl. Rusthall TN4 .. 148 C5
Greenfield Cotts. ME14 ...... 77 C3
Greenfield Gdns. BR5 .... 37 D2
Greenfield Rd. Gillingham ME7 . 48 D6
Greenfield Rd.
Joyden's Wood DA2 .... 25 D3
Greenfields. ME3 .... 33 D3
Greenfields Cl. ME3 .... 33 D3
Greenfinches. Gillingham ME7 . 62 F6
Greenfinches. New Barn DA3 .. 43 B6
Greenfrith Dr. TN10 .... 117 B6
Greenhill Cts. SE7 .... 1 F1
Greenhill La. TN27 .... 143 F7
Greenhill Rd. Northfleet DA11 . 12 D1
Greenhill Rd. Otford TN14 ... 69 C5
Greenhill Terr. SE18 .... 1 F1
Greenhithe. [3] ME15 .... 92 A3
Greenhithe Cl. SE9 .... 23 E8
Greenhithe Sta. DA9 .... 11 A2
Greenholm Rd. SE9 .... 6 B2
Greening St. SE2 .... 3 C2
Greenlands. TN15 .... 87 C7
Greenlands Rd. TN15 .... 85 B8
Greenlaw St. SE18 .... 2 A3
Greenleas. TN2 .... 150 C6
Greenleigh Ave. BR5 .... 38 B5
Greens End. SE18 .... 2 A2
Greensand Rd. ME15 .... 93 A2
Greenshields Ind Est. E16 ..... 1 B5
Greenside. High Halden TN26 . 173 C4
Greenside. Maidstone ME15 .. 92 B3
Greenside. Sidcup DA5 .... 24 E7
Greenside. Swanley BR8 ...... 39 D7
Greenslade Prim Sch. SE18 ... 6 D8
Greentrees Ave. TN10 ...... 117 F5
Greenvale Gdns. ME8 .... 49 B2
Greenvale Rd. SE9 .... 6 A3
Greenview Cres. TN11 ...... 116 E4
Greenview Wlk. ME8 .... 49 A4
Greenway. Chatham ME5 ..... 61 D6
Greenway. Chislehurst BR7 ... 23 B3
Greenway. Cranbrook TN17 .. 169 B4
Greenway Court Farm Cotts.
ME17 .... 95 A1
Greenway Court Rd. ME17 ... 95 A1
Greenway La. ME17 .... 110 A7
Greenway The. TN15 .... 38 B3
Greenways. Maidstone ME14 . 92 F5
Greenways. New Barn DA3 ... 43 D6
Greenways The. TN12 ...... 135 F5
Greenwich Cl. Chatham ME5 . 62 B4
Greenwich Cl. Maidstone ME16 91 D4
Greenwich Com Coll. SE9 ..... 5 E1
Greenwich Cres. E6 .... 1 F8
Greenwich Educ Tuition Ctr
(Foxhill Ctr). SE18 .... 6 B8
Greenwich Ind Est. SE7 .... 1 B2
Greenwood Cl.
Orpington BR5 & BR6 .... 37 E3
Greenwood Cl. Sidcup DA15 .. 24 A6
Greenwood House. [8] RM17 . 12 B8
Greenwood Pl. TN15 .... 72 A2
Greenwood Rd. DA5 .... 25 D4
Greenwood Sch. SE18 .... 6 E6
Greenwood Way. TN3 .... 83 F2
Greggs Wood Rd. TN1 & TN2 . 149 E7
Gregor Mews. SE3 .... 5 A7
Gregory Cl. ME8 .... 63 E4
Gregory Cres. SE9 .... 22 D8
Gregory House. SE3 .... 5 B5
Grenada Rd. SE7 .... 5 C7
Grenadier St. E16 .... 2 A5
Grenadier Cl. DA13 .... 58 A8
Grenville Cl. DA13 .... 58 A8
Gresham Ave. DA3 .... 42 F4
Gresham Cl. DA5 .... 7 F1
Gresham Rd. Coxheath ME17 . 106 D2
Gresham Rd. Hartley DA3 .... 42 F5
Gresham Rd. Newham E16 ..... 1 B7
Gresswell Cl. DA14 .... 24 A5
Grey Wethers. ME14 .... 76 E4
Greybury La. TN8 .... 128 B3
Greyfriars Cl. ME16 .... 91 D5
Greyhound Way. DA1 .... 8 E1
Greys Park Cl. BR2 .... 50 D5
Greystone The. ME14 .... 92 B3
Greystones Cl. TN14 & TN15 . 69 E2
Greystones Rd. ME15 .... 93 A2
Gribble Bridge La. TN27 .... 172 B5
Grieves Rd. DA11 .... 29 F5
Grieveson House. ME4 .... 48 A4
Griffin Manor Sch. SE18 ...... 6 E6
Griffin Manor Way. SE28 ...... 2 F1
Griffin Rd. SE18 .... 2 D1
Griffin Way. SE9 .... 22 E7
Griffin Wlk. DA9 .... 10 F2
Griffiths House. [2] SE18 ...... 6 B8
Grigg La. TN27 .... 142 C7
Grigg's Cross. BR5 .... 38 D3

Griggs Way. TN15 .... 87 A7
Grinling House. [6] SE18 ...... 2 A2
Grizedale Cl. DA16 .... 61 D8
Gromenfield. TN3 .... 161 C7
Groombridge Cl. DA16 .... 7 A2
Groombridge Hill. TN3 ..... 147 D1
Groombridge Place. TN3 .... 161 C8
Groombridge Rd. TN3 ...... 147 A1
Groombridge Sq. [13] ME15 . 107 F6
Grosmont Rd. SE18 .... 2 F1
Grosvenor Ave. ME1 & ME4 .. 47 E3
Grosvenor Bridge. TN1 & TN4 149 B5
Grosvenor Cres. DA1 .... 9 D2
Grosvenor Pk. TN1 & TN4 ... 149 A4
Grosvenor Rd. Bexley DA6 .... 7 E2
Grosvenor Rd. Erith DA17 ..... 8 A8
Grosvenor Rd. Gillingham ME7 . 49 A1
Grosvenor Rd.
Orpington BR5 & BR6 .... 37 E3
Grosvenor Rd.
Royal Tunbridge Wells TN1 . 149 A4
Grosvenor Sq. DA3 .... 42 E6
Grosvenor Wlk. TN1 .... 149 A4
Grove Ave. TN1 .... 149 A2
Grove Cl. BR2 .... 50 A8
Grove Cotts. TN30 .... 183 B6
Grove Green Rd. ME14 .... 92 F5
Grove Hill Gdns. TN1 .... 149 B2
Grove Hill Rd. TN1 & TN2 ... 149 B3
Grove Market Pl. SE9 .... 5 F1
Grove Park Rd. SE12 & SE9 ... 22 D6
Grove Park Sta. SE12 .... 22 B5
Grove Rd. Bexley DA7 .... 8 C3
Grove Rd. Chatham ME4 ..... 48 B2
Grove Rd. [8] Erith DA17 ...... 7 F8
Grove Rd. Gillingham ME7 .... 49 A6
Grove Rd. Grays RM17 .... 12 C8
Grove Rd. Maidstone ME15 .. 107 C7
Grove Rd. Northfleet DA11 ... 12 B2
Grove Rd. Penshurst TN11 & TN8 130 E2
Grove Rd. Rochester ME2 .... 47 B8
Grove Rd. Seal TN15 .... 85 B5
Grove Rd. Sevenoaks TN13 & TN14 84 C6
Grove Rd. Upper Halling ME2 . 59 C5
Grove The. Bexley DA6 .... 7 D3
Grove The. Gravesend DA11 .. 30 B8
Grove The. Maidstone ME14 .. 93 A3
Grove The. Pembury TN2 .... 150 D8
Grove The. Sidcup DA14 ..... 24 E4
Grove The. Swanley BR8 ..... 39 F6
Grove The. Swanscombe DA10 . 11 F2
Grove The. West Kingsdown TN15 55 F1
Grove Vale. BR7 .... 23 A2
Grove Wood Cotts. TN11 ... 100 A1
Grovebury Cl. DA8 .... 8 D8
Grovebury Ct. DA6 .... 8 B2
Grovebury Rd. SE2 .... 3 B4
Grovehurst La. TN12 .... 153 C5
Grovelands. ME17 .... 111 E5
Grovelands Rd. BR5 .... 24 A1
Grovelands Way. RM17 ...... 11 F8
Grover St. [3] TN1 .... 149 B4
Groves The. ME7 .... 74 F7
Grovewood Dr. ME14 .... 92 E4
Guardian Cl. ME8 .... 49 C1
Guardian Ind Est. TN12 .... 138 C7
Guestwick. TN10 .... 117 F5
Guibal Rd. SE12 .... 22 B7
Guild Rd. Erith DA8 .... 8 F7
Guild Rd. Greenwich SE7 ...... 5 D8
Guildford Gdns. ME2 .... 46 C6
Guildford Rd. Newham E6 ..... 1 F7
Guildford Rd. [7]
Royal Tunbridge Wells
TN1 & TN2 .... 149 B3
Gullands. ME17 .... 108 E4
Gulliver Rd. DA15 .... 23 E6
Gumley Rd. RM16 .... 11 E8
Gumping Rd. BR5 .... 51 C8
Gun Hill. RM18 .... 13 D8
Gun La. Horsmonden TN12 .. 153 A6
Gun La. Rochester ME2 ...... 47 B7
Gundulph Rd. Bromley BR2 .. 36 C6
Gundulph Rd.
Chatham ME1 & ME4 .... 47 E4
Gundulph Sq. ME1 .... 47 C6
Gunfleet Cl. DA12 .... 30 E8
Gunlands. TN12 .... 153 A6
Gunn Rd. DA10 .... 11 E1
Gunner La. SE18 .... 2 A1
Gunning St. SE18 .... 2 E2
Gunnis Cl. ME8 .... 63 D4
Gurdon Rd. SE7 .... 1 A1
Guston Rd. ME14 .... 92 C6
Guy Barnett Gr. SE3 .... 5 A4
Gwillim Cl. DA15 .... 7 A2
Gwynn Rd. DA11 .... 29 C6
Gybbon Rise. TN12 .... 139 E3
Gybbons Rd. TN17 .... 181 F3

Ha-Ha Rd. SE18 & SE7 .... 5 F8
Hackney Rd. ME16 .... 91 C2
Hadden Rd. SE28 .... 2 E3
Haddon Gr. DA15 .... 24 A8
Haddon Rd. BR5 .... 38 C4
Hadleigh Ct. ME7 .... 63 B3
Hadleigh Wlk. [1] E6 .... 1 E7
Hadley Cl. DA13 .... 58 B8
Hadley Ct. TN4 .... 148 F6
Hadley Gdns. ME17 .... 94 E2
Hadley House. BR5 .... 37 F7
Hadley Rd. DA17 .... 3 F2
Hadlow Coll of Agriculture &
Horticulture. TN11 .... 118 D8

Hadlow Cty Prim Sch. TN11 ... 118 E8
Hadlow Pk. TN11 .... 102 E1
Hadlow Rd. Bexley DA16 .... 7 C7
Hadlow Rd. Maidstone ME14 ... 92 C5
Hadlow Rd. Sidcup DA14 .... 24 A4
Hadlow Rd. Tonbridge TN9 ..... 117 D3
Hadlow Rd.
  Tonbridge,Higham Wood TN10 .. 118 A5
Hadlow Stair Rd. TN10 .... 117 F4
Hadlow Way. DA13 .... 29 E1
Haffenden Cl. TN12 .... 138 D6
Haffenden Rd. TN30 .... 173 B1
Haig Ave. Chatham ME1 .... 47 D1
Haig Ave. Chatham,Luton ME4 ... 48 A2
Haig Ave. Gillingham ME7 .... 48 E4
Haig Ct. BR7 .... 23 B3
Haig Gdns. DA12 .... 30 C8
Haig Villas. ME3 .... 34 A5
Hailey Rd. DA18 .... 4 A4
Haileybury Rd. BR6 .... 52 A6
Hailstone Cl. TN11 .... 118 E8
Haimo Prim Sch. SE9 .... 5 D2
Haimo Rd. SE9 .... 5 D2
Hainault St. SE9 .... 23 B7
Halcot Ave. DA6 .... 8 C2
Haldane Gdns. DA11 .... 29 C7
Haldane Rd. SE28 .... 3 D6
Halden Cl. ME15 .... 107 F6
Halden La. TN17 .... 181 F6
Hale Cl. BR6 .... 51 C6
Hale Cotts. DA9 .... 11 C2
Hale Ct. TN12 .... 120 A7
Hale La. TN14 .... 68 F2
Hale Oak Rd.
  Hall's Green TN14 & TN8 ...... 114 E4
Hale Oak Rd.
  Sevenoaks Weald TN14 .... 99 B1
Hale Rd. ME3 .... 33 C7
Hale St. TN12 .... 120 A7
Hales Cl. TN30 .... 183 B8
Hales Ct. TN30 .... 183 B8
Haleys Pl. ME1 .... 76 A8
Half Moon La. TN11 .... 116 D6
Halfpence La. DA12 .... 45 B7
Halfpenny Cl. ME16 .... 91 A2
Halfway St. DA15 .... 23 E7
Halifax Cl. ME5 .... 62 B6
Halifield Dr. DA17 .... 3 E3
Hall Hill. TN15 .... 85 C4
Hall Place Cres. DA1 & DA5 ...... 8 D2
Hall Rd. Aylesford ME20 .... 75 F1
Hall Rd. Chatham ME5 .... 62 C3
Hall Rd. Dartford DA1 .... 9 F3
Hall Rd.
  Northfleet,Pepper Hill
  DA11 & DA13 .... 29 C5
Hall Rd.
  Northfleet,Wombwell Park DA11 .. 29 D6
Hall Rd. St Mary Hoo ME3 .... 18 C6
Hall Rd. Wouldham ME1 .... 60 C3
Hall The. SE3 .... 5 A4
Hall View. SE9 .... 22 D6
Hall's Grove Rd. TN2 .... 149 D2
Hall's Hole Rd. TN2 .... 149 E4
Hallam Cl. BR7 .... 22 F3
Hallford Way. DA1 .... 9 C2
Hallgate. SE3 .... 5 A4
Halling Cty Prim Sch. ME2 .... 59 F5
Halling Sta. ME2 .... 60 A5
Halls Cotts. TN5 .... 174 F5
Hallsfield Rd. ME5 .... 61 D2
Hallwards. TN12 .... 139 F2
Hallwood Cl. ME8 .... 63 D5
Hallwood House. ME5 .... 62 C2
Hallywell Cres. E6 .... 1 F8
Halons Rd. SE9 .... 23 A8
Halsbrook Rd. SE3 .... 5 D4
Halstead Cty Prim Sch. TN14 .... 67 F7
Halstead La. TN14 .... 67 E5
Halstead Place Sch. TN14 .... 67 E8
Halstead Rd. DA8 .... 8 E6
Halstead Wlk. ME16 .... 91 C7
Halstow Cl. ME15 .... 107 B6
Halstow Prim Sch. SE10 .... 1 A1
Halstow Rd. SE10 & SE3 .... 1 A1
Halt Robin La. DA17 .... 4 B2
Halt Robin Rd. Erith DA17 .... 4 A2
Halt Robin Rd. Erith DA17 .... 4 B2
Ham La. Gillingham ME5 .... 62 E3
Ham La. Lenham ME17 .... 111 C5
Ham River Hill. ME3 .... 33 A6
Ham Shades Cl. DA15 .... 24 A5
Hamble Rd. TN10 .... 117 B5
Hambledon Rd. ME16 .... 91 B3
Hambledown Rd. SE9 .... 23 E8
Hambro Ave. BR2 .... 36 A1
Hamelin Rd. ME7 .... 62 F8
Hamerton Rd. DA11 .... 12 B2
Hamilton Ct. TN4 .... 149 A5
Hamilton House.
  Coxheath ME17 .... 106 C3
Hamilton House.
  Royal Tunbridge Wells TN4 ... 149 A4
Hamilton Rd. Bexley DA7 .... 7 E5
Hamilton Rd. Gillingham ME7 .... 48 D7
Hamilton Rd. Sidcup DA15 .... 24 A4
Hamilton Wlk. DA8 .... 8 F7
Hamlea Cl. SE12 .... 5 A2
Hamlet House. Eltham SE9 .... 6 A2
Hamlet House. Erith DA8 .... 8 E7
Hamlin Rd. TN13 .... 83 E6
Hamlyn Ct. TN13 .... 83 E6
Hammelton Rd. BR1 .... 36 A8
Hammerwood Pk. RH19 .... 144 C2

Hammond Way. SE28 .... 3 B6
Hammonds. TN18 .... 179 A2
Hammonds Sq. ME6 .... 75 A8
Hamond Hill. ME4 .... 47 E4
Hampden Way. ME19 .... 88 F3
Hampshire Cl. ME5 .... 62 C7
Hampshire Dr. ME15 .... 107 C8
Hampson Way. ME14 .... 93 A4
Hampstead Cl. SE28 .... 3 B5
Hampstead La. ME18 .... 104 C1
Hampton Cl. ME5 .... 62 A5
Hampton Cotts. TN14 .... 67 F4
Hampton Cres. DA12 .... 30 E6
Hampton House. DA7 .... 8 B5
Hampton Rd. ME14 .... 92 C6
Hamptons Rd. TN11 .... 102 B5
Hamwick Gn. ME5 .... 62 C1
Hanameel St. E16 .... 1 B5
Hanbury Cl. ME18 .... 104 E7
Hanbury Wlk. DA5 .... 25 E5
Handel Cres. RM18 .... 13 A7
Handel Wlk. ME15 .... 117 E6
Hands Wlk. E16 .... 1 A7
Hang Grove Hill. BR6 .... 66 B6
Hangmans Cnr. BR7 .... 37 B8
Hanmer Way. TN12 .... 139 E2
Hanover Ave. E16 .... 1 A5
Hanover Cl. ME14 .... 92 B5
Hanover Dr. Chislehurst BR7 ..... 23 C4
Hanover Dr. Gillingham ME8 ..... 63 C4
Hanover Gn. ME20 .... 74 F3
Hanover Pl. ME3 .... 34 F8
Hanover Rd. Coxheath ME17 .... 106 C3
Hanover Rd.
  Royal Tunbridge Wells TN1 ... 149 A4
Hanover Way. DA7 .... 7 D4
Hansol Rd. DA6 .... 7 E2
Hansom Terr. BR1 .... 36 B8
Hanway. ME8 .... 49 A2
Harbex Cl. DA5 .... 25 B8
Harbledown Manor. ME8 .... 49 B3
Harbledown Pl. BR5 .... 38 C5
Harborough Ave. DA15 .... 23 F8
Harbour The. ME17 .... 124 E5
Harbourland Cl. ME14 .... 92 B8
Harbourne La. TN26 & TN30 ... 173 E5
Harcourt Ave. DA5 & DA15 ..... 24 C8
Harcourt Gdns. ME8 .... 63 E4
Harcourt Rd. DA6 & DA7 .... 7 E3
Harden Ct. SE7 .... 1 E2
Harden Rd. DA11 .... 29 F6
Hardens Manorway. SE18 .... 1 D1
Hardie Cl. ME19 .... 74 F1
Harding House. SE18 .... 1 F2
Harding Rd. DA7 .... 7 F5
Hardinge Ave. TN4 .... 132 E3
Hardinge St. SE18 .... 2 C3
Hardman Rd. SE7 .... 1 B1
Hardres Terr. BR5 .... 52 D8
Hards Town. ME4 .... 48 A4
Hardwick Cres. DA2 .... 10 B1
Hardwick Ct. DA8 .... 8 D8
Hardwick House. ME15 .... 107 E8
Hardwick Rd. TN11 .... 116 E6
Hardy Ave. DA11 .... 29 E6
Hardy Cl. ME5 .... 62 B6
Hardy Gr. DA1 .... 10 A3
Hardy Rd. SE3 .... 5 A8
Hardy St. ME14 .... 92 A6
Hare St. Chatham ME4 .... 48 B3
Hare St. Woolwich SE18 .... 2 A3
Harebell Cl. Chatham ME5 .... 61 F4
Harebell Cl. Maidstone ME14 .... 92 E5
Harebell Dr. E6 .... 2 A8
Haredale Cl. ME1 .... 61 D7
Harefield Rd. DA14 .... 24 D5
Harenc Sch Trust. DA14 .... 24 C3
Harescroft. TN2 .... 162 F7
Harfst Way. BR8 .... 39 C8
Hargate Cl. TN2 .... 162 F8
Hargood Rd. SE3 .... 5 C6
Harland Ave. DA15 .... 23 E6
Harland Rd. SE12 .... 22 A7
Harlands Gr. BR6 .... 51 B6
Harlech Cl. ME2 .... 32 F1
Harlequin House. DA18 .... 3 E3
Harley Gdns. BR6 .... 51 E6
Harleyford. BR1 .... 36 C8
Harlington Rd. DA7 .... 7 E4
Harman Ave. DA11 .... 30 B3
Harman Ct. ME5 .... 62 B3
Harman Dr. DA15 .... 6 F1
Harmer Ct. TN4 .... 133 A2
Harmer Rd. DA10 .... 11 F1
Harmer St. DA11 .... 13 C1
Harmers Way. TN27 .... 127 F3
Harmony St. TN4 .... 148 D4
Harness Rd. SE28 .... 3 A4
Harold Ave. Erith DA17 .... 3 F1
Harold Ave. Gillingham ME7 ..... 48 A4
Harold Gibbons Ct. SE7 .... 5 C8
Harold Rd. Cuxton ME2 .... 46 C3
Harold Rd. Hawley DA2 .... 26 F4
Harp Farm Rd. ME14 .... 77 C6
Harper Rd. E6 .... 1 F7
Harper La. ME14 .... 77 F1
Harpswood. ME17 .... 94 F1
Harptree Dr. ME5 .... 61 F5
Harraden Rd. SE3 .... 5 C6
Harrier Mews. SE28 .... 2 D4
Harrier Way. E6 .... 1 F8
Harries Rd. TN1 & TN2 .... 149 E7
Harrietsham Sta. ME17 .... 110 D6
Harrington Way. SE18 .... 1 D3
Harris Cl. DA11 .... 29 F5
Harris Rd. DA7 .... 7 F6

Harrison Dr. ME23 .... 17 E4
Harrison Rd. TN15 .... 86 F7
Harrison Way. TN13 .... 84 A5
Harrow Cl. TN8 .... 112 D3
Harrow Ct. Chatham ME5 .... 62 C4
Harrow Ct. Stockbury ME9 .... 79 D8
Harrow Gdns. BR6 .... 52 B6
Harrow Manor Way. SE2 .... 3 C3
Harrow Rd. Gillingham ME7 ..... 62 F6
Harrow Rd. Knockholt Pound TN14 62 E4
Harrow Way. ME14 .... 92 E5
Harrowby Gdns. DA11 .... 29 E6
Hart Dyke Cres. BR8 .... 39 D6
Hart Dyke Rd. Orpington BR5 .... 38 C1
Hart Dyke Rd. Swanley BR8 ...... 39 D6
Hart Shaw. DA3 .... 43 B7
Hart St. ME16 .... 91 F3
Hart St Commercial Ctr. ME16 .. 91 F3
Hartfield Cl. TN10 .... 117 C5
Hartfield Cres. BR4 .... 50 A7
Hartfield Pl. DA11 .... 29 D8
Hartfield Rd. Hayes BR4 .... 50 A6
Hartfield Rd. Stick Hill TN8 ... 129 A4
Hartford Rd. DA5 .... 8 A1
Hartford Wlk. DA17 .... 4 A1
Harting Rd. SE9 .... 22 E5
Hartington Cl. BR6 .... 51 C5
Hartington Rd. E16 .... 1 B7
Hartington St. ME4 .... 48 A3
Hartlake Rd. TN11 .... 118 D3
Hartlands Cl. DA5 .... 7 F1
Hartley Bottom Rd. DA3 .... 43 C2
Hartley Cl. Bromley BR1 .... 36 F7
Hartley Cl. Maidstone ME15 .... 107 F6
Hartley Court Gdns. TN17 ...... 169 A3
Hartley Cty Prim Sch. DA3 ...... 42 E3
Hartley Hill. DA3 .... 43 A1
Hartley Rd. Bexley DA16 .... 7 C7
Hartley Rd. Hartley TN17 ...... 169 A3
Hartley Rd. Longfield DA3 .... 42 E7
Hartley Rd. Westerham TN16 .... 81 D2
Hartlip Endowed CE Prim Sch.
  ME9 .... 64 D5
Hartlip Hill. ME9 .... 64 F7
Hartmann Rd. E16 .... 1 E5
Hartnokes. TN18 .... 179 A2
Hartnup St. ME16 .... 91 C2
Harton Cl. BR1 .... 36 D8
Hartpiece Cl. ME8 .... 49 F2
Hartshill Rd. DA11 .... 29 F6
Hartsland Rd. TN13 .... 84 C4
Hartslock Dr. SE2 .... 3 D4
Hartsmead Rd. SE9 .... 22 F6
Hartville Rd. SE18 .... 2 E1
Harty Ave. ME8 .... 63 C3
Harvard Ct. SE9 .... 6 A1
Harvel Ave. ME2 .... 46 F7
Harvel Cl. BR5 & BR7 .... 38 A6
Harvel Cres. SE2 .... 3 D1
Harvel La. DA13 .... 58 B2
Harvel Rd. DA13 .... 73 A8
Harvel St. DA13 .... 58 C3
Harvest Bank Rd. BR4 .... 50 A7
Harvest Rd. TN10 .... 117 D6
Harvest Ridge. ME19 .... 74 D2
Harvest Way. BR8 .... 39 D2
Harvesters Cl. ME8 .... 63 E7
Harvesters Way. ME14 .... 92 D4
Harvey Gdns. SE7 .... 1 C1
Harvey Point. E16 .... 1 A8
Harvey Rd. ME8 .... 63 E8
Harvill Rd. DA14 .... 24 E3
Harwood Ave. BR1 .... 36 B7
Harwood Ct. RM17 .... 12 C8
Haslam Est. ME15 .... 107 F5
Haslemere Rd. DA7 .... 8 A5
Hasler Cl. SE28 .... 3 C6
Hasletts Cl. TN4 .... 149 B6
Haslewood Cl. TN27 .... 143 B2
Hassendean Rd. SE3 & SE7 .... 5 B7
Hassock Wood. BR2 .... 50 E6
Hassop Wlk. SE9 .... 22 E4
Haste Hill Cl. ME17 .... 107 B3
Haste Hill Rd. ME17 .... 107 B3
Hasted Cl. DA9 .... 11 C1
Hasted Rd. Greenwich SE7 .... 1 D1
Hasted Rd. Newington ME9 ...... 65 B7
Hasteds. ME17 .... 94 D2
Hastings Cl. ME16 .... 11 E8
Hastings House. SE18 .... 1 F2
Hastings Rd.
  Kipping's Cross TN12 .... 150 F5
Hastings Rd. Maidstone ME15 .... 92 B3
Hastings Rd.
  Newenden TN17 & TN18 .... 187 C6
Hastings Rd. Pembury TN2 ...... 150 D6
Hastings Rd. The Moor TN18 ... 184 F6
Hastings St. SE18 .... 2 C3
Hatch Rd. ME5 .... 61 E1
Hatches La. TN11 & TN12 ...... 119 D6
Hatfield Cl. SE3 .... 5 A7
Hatfield Rd. ME2 .... 47 A8
Hatham Green La. TN15 .... 56 D1
Hathaway Cl. BR2 .... 36 F1
Hathaway Ct. Gillingham ME8 ... 63 D8
Hathaway Ct. Rochester ME1 .... 47 B5
Hatherall Rd. ME14 .... 92 B6
Hatherley Cres. DA14 .... 24 A6
Hatherley Rd. DA14 .... 24 A5
Hathern Gdns. SE9 .... 23 A4
Hatmill La. TN12 .... 152 A7
Hattersfield Cl. DA17 .... 3 F2
Hatton Cl. Northfleet DA11 ..... 29 E5
Hatton Cl. Woolwich SE18 .... 6 D7
Hatton Ct. BR7 .... 22 F1
Hatton Rd. ME5 .... 62 C3

Havant Wlk. ME15 .... 107 F6
Havelock Rd. Bromley BR2 .... 36 C5
Havelock Rd. Dartford DA1 .... 9 B1
Havelock Rd. Erith DA17 .... 3 F2
Havelock Rd. Gravesend DA11 .... 29 F7
Havelock Rd. Tonbridge TN9 ... 117 B2
Havelock St. Chislehurst SE9 .... 22 F5
Haven Cl. Istead Rise DA13 ...... 43 F8
Haven Cl. Rochester ME1 .... 47 C2
Haven Cl. Sidcup DA14 .... 24 C2
Haven Cl. Swanley BR8 .... 39 F7
Haven Hill. ME3 .... 33 C5
Haven Lodge. SE18 .... 2 B2
Haven Way. ME4 .... 34 B1
Havengore Ave. DA12 .... 30 E8
Haverstock Ct. BR5 .... 38 B7
Haverthwaite Rd. BR6 .... 51 D7
Havisham Cl. ME1 .... 47 D2
Havisham Rd. DA12 .... 31 A7
Havock La. ME14 .... 91 F4
Hawbeck Rd. ME8 .... 63 C3
Hawden Cl. TN11 .... 116 F4
Hawden La. TN11 .... 116 F4
Hawden Rd. TN9 .... 117 B2
Hawes Rd. BR1 .... 36 B8
Hawfield Bank. BR6 .... 52 D7
Hawkenbury Cl. TN2 .... 149 D2
Hawkenbury Mead. TN2 .... 149 D1
Hawkenbury Rd.
  Hawkenbury TN12 .... 140 C6
Hawkenbury Rd.
  Royal Tunbridge Wells TN2 & TN3 149 C1
Hawkes Cl. RM17 .... 12 B8
Hawkes Rd. ME20 .... 75 F5
Hawkhurst CE Prim Sch.
  Hawkhurst TN18 .... 178 F2
Hawkhurst CE Prim Sch.
  The Moor TN18 .... 184 F8
Hawkhurst Cottage Hospl.
  TN18 .... 178 D2
Hawkhurst Rd.
  Flimwell TN18 & TN19 & TN5 . 177 E2
Hawkhurst Rd. Gillingham ME8 .. 49 B3
Hawkhurst Rd.
  Hartley TN17 & TN18 .... 178 F7
Hawkinge Wlk. BR5 .... 38 B6
Hawkins Ave. DA12 .... 30 C4
Hawkins Cl. ME4 .... 48 A6
Hawksmoor Cl. Newham E6 .... 1 E7
Hawksmoor Cl. Woolwich SE18 ... 2 E1
Hawksmoor Prim Sch. SE28 .... 3 B6
Hawkwell Cotts. TN2 .... 134 F2
Hawkwood. ME16 .... 91 B5
Hawkwood Cl. ME1 .... 47 D5
Hawkwood La. BR7 .... 37 C8
Hawley Cl. ME16 .... 91 E4
Hawley Rd. DA1,DA2&DA4 .... 27 A4
Hawley Terr. DA2 .... 27 A4
Hawley Vale. DA2 .... 27 A4
Hawser Rd. ME1 .... 47 C1
Hawstead La. BR6 .... 52 F5
Hawthorn Cl. Edenbridge TN8 .. 112 C2
Hawthorn Cl. Gravesend DA12 ... 30 C4
Hawthorn Cl. Orpington BR5 ..... 37 D3
Hawthorn House. ME5 .... 61 F5
Hawthorn La. TN13 .... 83 F5
Hawthorn Pl. DA8 .... 4 C1
Hawthorn Rd. Bexley DA6 .... 7 F3
Hawthorn Rd. Dartford DA1 ...... 26 D7
Hawthorn Rd. Rochester ME2 .... 46 E6
Hawthorn Terr. DA15 .... 6 F2
Hawthorn Wlk.
  Royal Tunbridge Wells TN2 ... 149 E8
Hawthorn Wlk. Tonbridge TN10 . 117 C7
Hawthorndene Cl. BR2 .... 50 A8
Hawthorndene Rd. BR2 .... 50 A8
Hawthorne Ave. ME8 .... 49 C2
Hawthorne Cl. BR1 .... 36 F6
Hawthorne Rd. BR1 .... 36 F6
Hawthorns. Chatham ME5 .... 61 F1
Hawthorns. Hartley DA3 .... 42 F5
Hawthorns The. ME20 .... 75 E1
Haxted Rd. BR1 .... 36 B8
Hay's Mead. DA13 .... 44 F3
Hayday Rd. E16 .... 1 A8
Haydens Cl. BR5 .... 38 C3
Haydens Mews. TN9 .... 117 C3
Haydens The. TN9 .... 117 C3
Hayes Cl. Hayes BR2 .... 50 A8
Hayes Cl. Higham ME3 .... 32 C3
Hayes Cl. West Thurrock RM16 ... 11 C8
Hayes Garden. BR2 .... 36 A1
Hayes La. Hayes BR2 .... 36 A1
Hayes La. Stockbury ME9 .... 79 F6
Hayes Prim Sch. BR2 .... 36 B1
Hayes Rd. Hayes BR2 .... 36 A5
Hayes Rd. Stone DA2 .... 27 E8
Hayes Sch. BR2 .... 36 B1
Hayes Sta. BR2 .... 36 A1
Hayes Terr. DA12 .... 31 E3
Hayes Wood Ave. BR2 .... 36 B1
Hayesbrook Sch. TN9 .... 133 A8
Hayesden La. TN11 & TN3 & TN4 132 B5
Hayesford Park Dr. BR2 .... 36 A4
Hayfield. ME19 .... 74 E2
Hayfield Rd. BR5 .... 38 A4
Hayfields. ME5 .... 62 D2
Hayle Mill Cotts. ME15 .... 106 F8
Hayle Mill Rd. ME15 .... 106 F8
Hayle Rd. ME15 .... 92 A3
Hayley Cl. ME2 .... 46 C2
Hayman Wlk. ME20 .... 75 F6
Haymans Hill. TN12 .... 153 C7
Haymen St. ME4 .... 47 E3
Haynes Cl. DA11 .... 29 F5
Hayrick Cl. ME14 .... 92 E5

Hays Rd. ME6 .... 74 F6
Haysden Ctry Pk. TN11 .... 132 D8
Haywain Cl. Maidstone ME14 .... 91 E8
Haywain Cl. Paddock Wood TN12 136 A5
Hayward Ave. ME2 .... 47 B8
Hayward Cl. DA1 .... 8 D2
Hayward Dr. DA1 .... 26 F6
Hayward Rd. BR2 .... 36 D5
Haywood Rise. BR6 .... 51 E5
Hazel Ave. Hoo St Werburgh ME3 34 E3
Hazel Ave. Maidstone ME16 ..... 91 C5
Hazel Cotts. TN14 .... 68 A6
Hazel Dr. DA8 .... 9 B6
Hazel End. BR8 .... 39 E4
Hazel Gr. Chatham ME5 .... 62 B8
Hazel Gr. Orpington BR6 .... 51 B8
Hazel Rd. Dartford DA1 .... 26 D6
Hazel Rd. Erith DA8 .... 9 A6
Hazel Shaw. TN11 .... 117 D7
Hazel Street Rd. ME9 .... 80 A4
Hazel Wlk. BR2 .... 37 A3
Hazelbank. TN3 .... 147 F3
Hazelden Cl. TN15 .... 56 A2
Hazeldene Rd. DA16 .... 7 C5
Hazelmere Rd. BR5 .... 37 D5
Hazelmere Way. BR2 .... 36 A3
Hazels The. ME8 .... 63 B5
Hazelwood Cl. TN2 .... 149 E8
Hazelwood Cotts. TN5 .... 176 D1
Hazelwood Dr. ME16 .... 91 B4
Hazelwood Rd. TN14 .... 66 D8
Hazlemere Dr. ME7 .... 49 A5
Hazlitt Cl. SE28 .... 3 C5
Hazlitt Dr. ME16 .... 91 D5
Head Race The. ME15 .... 91 D2
Headcorn Cty Prim Sch. TN27 . 141 C5
Headcorn Rd. Bromley BR1 ...... 22 A3
Headcorn Rd. Gillingham ME8 ... 49 B4
Headcorn Rd. Platt's Heath
  ME17 .... 110 F1
Headcorn Rd.
  Smarden Bell TN27 .... 142 C3
Headcorn Rd. Standen TN27 ... 158 A5
Headcorn Rd. Staplehurst TN12 140 B4
Headcorn Rd. The Harbour
  ME17 .... 124 E4
Headcorn Rd. Ulcombe ME17 ... 125 F5
Headcorn Sta. TN27 .... 141 D4
Headingley Rd. ME16 .... 91 B6
Headley Ct. TN8 .... 112 C2
Headley House. BR5 .... 38 B7
Healy Dr. BR6 .... 51 F6
Heansill La. TN18 .... 184 E8
Hearns Cl. BR5 .... 38 C5
Hearns Rd. BR5 .... 38 C5
Hearns Rise. BR5 .... 38 D5
Heartenoak Rd. TN18 .... 179 B3
Heath Ave. DA7 .... 7 D8
Heath Cl. Orpington BR5 .... 38 C3
Heath Cl. Swanley BR8 .... 39 E7
Heath Gdns. DA1 .... 26 C7
Heath Gr. ME16 .... 91 A2
Heath House. DA15 .... 23 F4
Heath La. Dartford DA1 .... 26 C7
Heath La.
  Dartford,Dartford Heath DA1 .. 26 B7
Heath Park Dr. BR1 .... 36 E6
Heath Rd. Coldblow DA5 .... 25 C7
Heath Rd. Coxheath ME17 ...... 106 C3
Heath Rd. Crayford DA1 .... 8 F1
Heath Rd. Langley Heath ME17 . 108 C4
Heath Rd. Maidstone ME16 ...... 90 F3
Heath Rise. BR5 .... 37 C2
Heath Side. DA1 .... 26 D8
Heath Terr. TN27 .... 153 A6
Heath The. ME19 .... 89 F5
Heath View Dr. SE2 .... 7 D8
Heath Villas. SE18 .... 2 F1
Heath Way. DA7 & DA8 .... 8 D6
Heathclose Ave. DA1 .... 26 B6
Heathclose Rd. DA1 .... 26 B7
Heathcote Cl. ME20 .... 75 F2
Heathdene Dr. DA17 .... 4 B2
Heathend Rd. DA5 .... 25 E7
Heather Cl. Chatham ME5 .... 61 F4
Heather Cl. Newham E6 .... 2 A7
Heather Dr. Dartford DA1 .... 26 A8
Heather Dr. Maidstone ME15 .... 92 B2
Heather Dr. St Michaels TN30 . 173 B3
Heather End. BR8 .... 39 D5
Heather Rd. SE12 .... 22 A7
Heather Wlk. TN10 .... 117 B6
Heatherbank. Chislehurst BR7 ... 37 A7
Heatherbank. Eltham SE9 .... 5 F5
Heatherbank Cl. DA1 .... 8 E1
Heatherside Rd. DA14 .... 24 C5
Heatherwood Cl. ME17 .... 109 E2
Heathfield. Chislehurst BR7 ..... 23 C2
Heathfield. Langley Heath ME17 108 E4
Heathfield Ave. Chatham ME5 ... 62 B7
Heathfield Cl. Keston BR2 .... 50 C5
Heathfield Cl. Maidstone ME14 .. 92 B7
Heathfield Cl. Newham E6 .... 1 D8
Heathfield Ct. DA14 .... 24 B3
Heathfield La. BR7 .... 23 C2
Heathfield Rd. Bexley DA6 .... 7 F2
Heathfield Rd. Keston BR2 ...... 50 D5
Heathfield Rd. Maidstone ME14 . 92 C2
Heathfield Rd. Sevenoaks TN13 . 83 F5
Heathfield Terr. Swanley BR8 ... 39 D7
Heathfield Terr. Woolwich SE18 .. 6 F8
Heathfields. TN2 .... 149 D4
Heathlands Rise. DA1 .... 9 B1
Heathlee Rd. DA1 .... 8 E1
Heathley End. BR7 .... 23 C2
Heathorn St. ME14 .... 92 B5

Heathside Ave. Bexley DA7 .... 7 E5
Heathside Ave. Coxheath ME17 106 C4
Heathview. TN4 .... 132 F2
Heathview Ave. DA1 .... 8 E1
Heathview Cres. DA1 .... 26 B7
Heathway. SE3 .... 5 A7
Heathwood Gdns. Swanley BR8 . 39 C7
Heathwood Rd. Woolwich SE7 .. 1 E1
Heathwood Wlk. DA5 .... 25 E7
Heaverham Rd. TN15 .... 70 C2
Heavitree Cl. SE18 .... 2 D1
Heavitree Rd. SE18 .... 2 D1
Hector St. SE18 .... 2 E2
Hectorage Rd. TN9 .... 133 D8
Hedge Place Rd. DA9 .... 11 A1
Hedgerow The. ME14 .... 92 E5
Hedgerows The. DA11 .... 29 E6
Hedges The. ME14 .... 92 A7
Hedley Ave. RM16 .... 11 C8
Hedley St. ME14 .... 92 A5
Heights The. SE7 .... 1 C1
Helen Allison Sch The. DA13 .... 44 A2
Helen Cl. DA1 .... 26 B8
Helen Keller Ct. TN10 .... 117 D4
Helen St. SE18 .... 2 B2
Helverswood. TN14 .... 53 A2
Hemmings Cl. DA14 .... 24 B6
Hempstead Cty Jun Sch. ME7 .. 63 A5
Hempstead Cty Prim Sch. ME7 63 A5
Hempstead Rd. Gillingham ME7 .. 63 A5
Hempstead Rd. Gillingham ME7 .. 63 B6
Hempstead Valley Dr. ME7 .... 63 A4
Hempstead Valley Sh Ctr. ME7 63 A3
Hemsted Rd. DA8 .... 8 E7
Henbane Cl. ME14 .... 92 E5
Henderson Dr. DA1 .... 10 A3
Hendley Dr. TN17 .... 169 C5
Hendry House. ME3 .... 33 F6
Hendy Rd. ME6 .... 75 B8
Henfield Cl. DA5 .... 8 A1
Hengist Rd. Eltham SE12 .... 22 B8
Hengist Rd. Erith DA8 .... 8 C7
Hengrove Ct. DA5 .... 24 E7
Henham Gdns. TN12 .... 120 A6
Henhurst Hill. DA13 .... 44 D8
Henhurst Rd. Gravesend DA13 .. 30 E1
Henhurst Rd. Henhurst DA12 ... 44 E8
Heniker La. TN17 .... 125 A4
Henley Bsns Pk. ME2 .... 47 D7
Henley Cl. Chatham ME5 .... 62 A6
Henley Cl. Gillingham ME8 ...... 63 D8
Henley Cl.
  Royal Tunbridge Wells TN2 .. 149 C4
Henley Deane. DA11 .... 29 E4
Henley Fields. Maidstone ME14 .. 92 E6
Henley Fields. St Michaels TN30 173 B2
Henley Meadows. TN30 .... 173 A2
Henley Rd. Newham E16 .... 1 F4
Henley Rd. Paddock Wood TN12 136 A7
Henley St. DA13 .... 44 F3
Henley View. TN30 .... 173 B2
Henniker Cotts. TN17 .... 169 A3
Henry Cooper Way. SE12 .... 22 D4
Henry St. Bromley BR1 .... 36 B8
Henry St. Chatham ME4 .... 48 B3
Henry St. Grays RM17 .... 12 C8
Henson Cl. BR6 .... 51 B8
Henville Rd. BR1 .... 36 B8
Henwick Prim Sch. SE9 .... 5 E4
Henwick Rd. SE9 .... 5 E4
Henwood Green Rd.
  TN12 & TN2 .... 150 E6
Henwoods Cres. TN2 .... 150 D6
Henwoods Mount. TN2 .... 150 E6
Herald Wlk. DA1 .... 9 F2
Herbert Pl. SE18 .... 6 B8
Herbert Rd. Bexley DA7 .... 7 E5
Herbert Rd. Bromley BR2 .... 36 E4
Herbert Rd. Chatham ME4 .... 48 A3
Herbert Rd. Gillingham ME8 .... 63 E8
Herbert Rd. Hextable BR8 .... 26 B2
Herbert Rd. Swanscombe DA10 .. 11 F1
Herbert Rd. Woolwich SE18 ..... 6 B8
Herdsdown. ME3 .... 34 D5
Hereford Cl. ME8 .... 49 D2
Hereford House. SE18 .... 1 F2
Hereford Rd. ME15 .... 107 D7
Heritage Dr. ME7 .... 48 F1
Heritage Hill. BR2 .... 50 C5
Heritage Rd. ME5 .... 62 A6
Heritage The. BR6 .... 38 A2
Herman Terr. ME4 .... 48 A3
Hermitage La. ME16 .... 90 F5
Hermitage La. Detling ME14 .... 78 B4
Hermitage La.
  Maidstone ME16 & ME20 ..... 90 F6
Hermitage La.
  Rabbit's Cross ME17 .... 123 E6
Hermitage Rd. ME3 .... 32 E4
Hermitage The. BR6 .... 38 A2
Herne Rd. ME8 .... 49 C2
Hero Wlk. ME1 .... 61 C7
Heron Apartments. 3 ME15 .. 107 F5
Heron Cl. TN8 .... 112 C3
Heron Cotts. TN18 .... 187 D3
Heron Cres. DA14 .... 23 E4
Heron Ct. BR2 .... 36 C5
Heron Hill. DA17 .... 3 F2
Heron Hill La. DA13 .... 58 A4
Heron Rd. ME20 .... 74 F1
Heron Way. Chatham ME5 .... 62 B7
Heron Way. Lower Stoke ME3 .. 19 C4
Heronden Rd. ME15 .... 107 F4
Herongate Rd. BR8 .... 25 E2
Herons Way. TN2 .... 150 E8
Heronsgate Prim Sch. SE28 .... 2 D3
Herringham Rd. SE7 .... 1 C3
Herts Cres. ME15 .... 106 F3
Hervey Rd. SE3 & SE7 .... 5 B6

Hesketh Ave. DA2 .... 27 B7
Heskett Pk. TN2 .... 150 E6
Hever Ave. TN15 .... 55 E4
Hever CE Prim Sch. TN8 .... 129 D6
Hever Castle. TN8 .... 129 D7
Hever Cl. ME15 .... 107 F6
Hever Court Rd. DA12 .... 30 D2
Hever Croft. Eltham SE9 .... 23 A4
Hever Croft. Rochester ME2 .. 46 F5
Hever Gdns. Bromley BR1 .... 37 A7
Hever Gdns. Maidstone ME16 .. 91 E3
Hever Hotel & Golf Club. TN8 113 D1
Hever House. ME2 .... 33 C1
Hever Rd. Hever TN8 .... 129 C1
Hever Rd. West Kingsdown TN15 .. 55 E4
Hever Road Cotts. TN8 .... 113 C2
Hever Sta. TN8 .... 129 B6
Hever Wood Rd. TN15 .... 55 E4
Heverham Rd. SE18 .... 2 E2
Heversham Rd. DA7 .... 8 A6
Hewett House. 7 SE18 .... 52 A1
Hewett Pl. BR8 .... 39 D5
Hewitt Cl. ME7 .... 48 F6
Hewitts Rd. BR6 & TN14 .... 52 F3
Hextable Cl. ME16 .... 91 D7
Hextable Cty Inf Sch. BR8 ..... 25 F2
Hextable Cty Jun Sch. BR8 .... 25 F2
Hextable Sch. BR8 .... 39 F8
Hibbs Cl. BR8 .... 39 D7
Hibernia Dr. DA12 .... 30 F5
Hibernia Point. 11 SE2 .... 3 D4
Hickin Cl. SE7 .... 1 D2
Hickman Cl. E16 .... 1 D8
Hickory Dell. ME7 .... 63 A5
Hide. E6 .... 2 A7
Higgins' La. ME4 .... 47 F5
High Banks. Loose ME15 ...... 106 F5
High Banks. Rochester ME1 ... 47 D2
High Beeches. Orpington BR6 .. 52 A4
High Beeches.
  Royal Tunbridge Wells TN2 .. 149 D6
High Beeches. Sidcup DA14 .... 24 E3
High Broom Ind Pk. TN4 ...... 149 C8
High Brooms Rd. TN4 .... 149 C7
High Brooms Sta. TN1 .... 149 C7
High Croft Cotts. BR8 .... 40 A5
High Cross Rd. TN15 .... 86 B1
High Dewar Rd. ME8 .... 64 A8
High Elms. ME8 .... 49 E1
High Elms Public Golf Course.
  BR6 .... 51 D3
High Elms Rd. BR6 .... 51 C2
High Firs. BR8 .... 39 E5
High Firs Cty Prim Sch. BR8 .. 39 F5
High Gr. Bromley BR1 .... 36 D8
High Gr. Woolwich SE18 .... 6 D6
High Halden Parochial
  CE Prim Sch. TN26 .... 173 E7
High Halden Rd. TN27 .... 158 C2
High Halstow Cty Prim Sch.
  ME23 .... 17 E3
High Hilden Cl. TN11 .... 117 A4
High House La. TN11 .... 102 C2
High Meads Rd. E16 .... 1 D7
High Oak Hill. ME9 .... 65 D8
High Point. SE9 .... 23 B5
High Rd. DA2 .... 26 C5
High Ridge. TN17 .... 167 E8
High Rocks. TN3 .... 148 B1
High Rocks La. TN3 & TN4 .... 148 C1
High St. Aylesford ME20 .... 75 F3
High St. Bean DA2 .... 28 B5
High St. Bidborough TN4 ...... 132 C3
High St. Biddenden TN27 ...... 157 F1
High St. Borough Green TN15 .. 86 F7
High St. Brasted TN16 & TN16 .. 82 C3
High St. Brenchley TN12 .... 152 B8
High St. Bromley BR1 .... 36 A7
High St. Chatham ME4 .... 47 E4
High St. Chatham ME4 .... 48 A4
High St. Cowden TN8 .... 145 B5
High St. Cranbrook TN17 ..... 169 C4
High St. Dartford DA1 .... 9 F1
High St. Downe BR6 .... 66 A8
High St. East Malling ME19 .... 90 A6
High St. Edenbridge TN8 ...... 112 C1
High St. Eynsford DA4 .... 54 E8
High St. Farningham DA4 .... 40 F2
High St. Flimwell TN5 .... 177 C3
High St. Frant TN3 .... 163 C4
High St. Gillingham ME7 .... 48 B6
High St. Gillingham ME7 .... 48 C5
High St. Gillingham,Brompton ME4 48 A6
High St. Gillingham,Rainham ME8 . 63 F8
High St. Goudhurst TN17 ..... 167 E8
High St. Grain ME3 .... 21 B6
High St. Gravesend DA11 .... 13 B1
High St. 8 Grays RM17 .... 12 A8
High St. Hadlow TN11 .... 118 E8
High St. Halling ME2 .... 60 A4
High St. Headcorn ME17 ...... 141 C5
High St. Kemsing TN15 .... 70 B2
High St. High Street TN18 .... 178 E2
High St. Lamberhurst TN3 .... 166 B5
High St. Leigh TN11 .... 115 F1
High St. Lenham ME17 .... 111 D5
High St. Maidstone ME14 .... 91 F4
High St. Marden TN12 .... 138 D6
High St. Newington ME9 .... 65 C6
High St. Northfleet DA11 .... 12 C1
High St. Orpington BR6 .... 38 A1
High St.
  Orpington,Farnborough BR6 .. 51 C5
High St.
  Orpington,Green Street Green BR6 51 F4
High St.
  Orpington,St Mary Cray BR5 .. 38 C4
High St. Otford TN14 .... 69 A3

High St. Pembury TN2 .... 150 C6
High St. Penshurst TN11 .... 131 B4
High St. Rochester ME2 .... 47 B7
High St. Rochester ME1 .... 47 C6
High St. Rolvenden ME4 .... 47 E4
High St. Rolvenden TN17 ...... 181 E4
High St.
  Royal Tunbridge Wells TN1 .. 149 A2
High St. Seal TN15 .... 84 F6
High St. Sevenoaks,Chipstead
  TN13 .... 84 C2
High St.
  Sevenoaks,Chipstead
  TN13 .... 83 C5
High St. Shoreham TN14 .... 53 F1
High St. Sidcup DA14 .... 24 A4
High St. Smarden TN27 .... 143 A1
High St. Snodland ME6 .... 75 A8
High St. Staplehurst TN12 .... 139 F3
High St. Sutton Valence ME17 .. 124 E7
High St. Swanley BR8 .... 39 F5
High St. Swanscombe DA10 .... 11 F2
High St.
  Swanscombe,Greenhithe DA9 .. 11 B3
High St. Tenterden TN30 ...... 183 A7
High St. Ticehurst TN5 .... 176 C1
High St. Tonbridge TN9 .... 117 C2
High St. Upper Upton ME2 ..... 33 F1
High St. Wadhurst TN5 .... 174 F4
High St. West Malling ME19 ... 89 C8
High St. Westerham TN16 ...... 96 C8
High St. Wouldham ME1 .... 60 C5
High St. Wrotham TN15 .... 72 A3
High St. Yalding ME18 .... 104 F1
High Tor Cl. BR1 .... 22 B1
High View. ME3 .... 32 C4
High Woods La. TN2 .... 150 B3
Higham Cl. ME15 .... 91 E2
Higham Cty Prim Sch. ME3 .... 32 C5
Higham Gdns. TN13 .... 117 F5
Higham La. TN10 .... 117 F6
Higham Rd. Cliffe ME3 .... 16 A4
Higham Rd. Rochester ME3 .... 33 D3
Higham School Rd. TN10 ..... 117 E6
Higham Sta. ME3 .... 32 D6
Higham View. ME14 .... 76 E4
Highbanks Cl. DA16 .... 7 B7
Highberry. ME19 .... 74 E2
Highbrook Rd. SE3 .... 5 D4
Highbury La. TN30 .... 183 A7
Highcombe. SE7 .... 5 B8
Highcombe Cl. SE9 .... 22 E7
Highcroft Gn. ME15 .... 107 F4
Highcross Rd. DA13 .... 28 D2
Highdown Cotts. TN17 .... 166 F3
Highfield Ave. Erith DA8 .... 8 F8
Highfield Ave. Orpington BR6 .. 51 F5
Highfield Cl. Gillingham ME8 .. 63 D7
Highfield Cl. Hawkhurst TN18 .. 179 A1
Highfield Cl. Pembury TN2 .... 150 D6
Highfield Cotts. ME8 .... 26 B2
Highfield Rd. Bexley DA6 .... 7 F2
Highfield Rd. Bromley BR1 ..... 36 E5
Highfield Rd. Dartford DA1 .... 26 D8
Highfield Rd. Gillingham ME8 .. 63 D7
Highfield Rd. Kemsing TN14 ... 69 F3
Highfield Rd.
  Royal Tunbridge Wells TN4 .. 149 C7
Highfield Rd N. DA1 .... 9 D1
Highfield Rd S. DA1 .... 26 D7
Highfields. TN8 .... 112 C4
Highgate Ct. 8 TN18 .... 178 F2
Highgate Hill. TN18 .... 178 F1
Highgrove. TN2 .... 163 A8
Highgrove Cl. BR7 .... 36 E8
Highgrove Rd. ME5 .... 62 A5
Highland Rd. Badgers Mount
  TN14 .... 68 B8
Highland Rd. Bexley DA6 .... 8 A3
Highland Rd. Maidstone ME15 .. 107 E6
Highlands Cl. ME2 .... 46 D5
Highlands Hill. BR8 .... 40 A8
Highlands Pk. TN15 .... 84 E6
Highlands Rd. BR5 .... 38 C2
Highmead. SE18 .... 6 F7
Highridge. ME7 .... 48 F1
Highridge Cl. ME14 .... 92 F5
Highstead Cres. DA8 .... 8 E7
Highview. Vigo Village DA13 .... 73 B8
Highview. Woolwich SE18 .... 6 B7
Highview Cl. ME15 .... 107 A8
Highview Dr. ME5 .... 61 D5
Highview Rd. DA14 .... 24 B4
Highway Prim Sch. BR6 .... 52 C5
Highway The. BR6 .... 52 C5
Highwood Cl. BR6 .... 51 C8
Highwood Dr. BR6 .... 51 C8
Highwoods Cl. ME3 .... 32 C4
Hilary Cl. DA7 .... 8 C6
Hilary Gdns. ME1 .... 46 F1
Hilbert Cl. TN2 .... 149 C5
Hilborough Way. BR6 .... 51 D5
Hilda May Ave. BR8 .... 39 E7
Hilda Rd. ME4 .... 48 A3
Hilda Vale Cl. BR6 .... 51 A6
Hilda Vale Rd. BR6 .... 51 B6
Hilden Ave. TN11 .... 116 F4
Hilden Dr. DA8 .... 9 B7
Hilden Grange Sch. TN10 ..... 117 B4
Hilden Oaks Sch. TN10 .... 117 B3
Hilden Park Rd. TN11 .... 116 F4
Hildenborough CE Prim Sch.
  TN11 .... 116 D6
Hildenborough Cres. ME16 ... 91 C7
Hildenborough Rd. Leigh TN11 116 A3
Hildenborough Rd.
  Shipbourne TN11 & TN15 .. 100 A4
Hildenborough Sta. TN11 .... 116 B6

Hilders Cl. TN8 .... 112 B4
Hilders La. TN8 .... 112 B4
Hill Brow. Bromley BR1 .... 36 D8
Hill Brow. Crayford DA1 .... 8 F1
Hill Brow. Maidstone ME14 .... 93 A5
Hill Chase. ME5 .... 61 E3
Hill Cl. Chislehurst BR7 .... 23 B3
Hill Cl. Istead Rise DA13 .... 29 E1
Hill Cres. Coldblow DA5 .... 25 C7
Hill Cres. Lenham ME17 .... 111 D5
Hill Crest
  Royal Tunbridge Wells TN4 .. 149 B8
Hill Crest. Sevenoaks TN13 .... 84 A5
Hill Crest. Sidcup DA15 .... 24 B8
Hill Cl. ME3 .... 33 F4
Hill End. Orpington BR6 .... 51 F8
Hill End. Woolwich SE18 .... 6 A6
Hill Farm Ave. ME2 .... 32 F1
Hill Farm Cl. ME23 .... 17 E3
Hill Green Rd. ME9 .... 79 D8
Hill House Rd. DA2 .... 27 C8
Hill Rd. Dartford DA1 .... 26 E6
Hill Rd. Rochester ME1 .... 47 A2
Hill Rd. Wouldham ME1 .... 60 F5
Hill Rise. DA2 .... 27 E3
Hill Sch The. TN16 .... 81 B4
Hill Shaw. DA3 .... 42 F3
Hill St. TN1 .... 149 B5
Hill The. Cranbrook TN17 .... 169 D4
Hill The. Northfleet DA11 ...... 12 C1
Hill Top. TN17 .... 154 E5
Hill Top Cotts. ME17 .... 106 E2
Hill View. Basted TN15 .... 86 F4
Hill View. Borough Green TN15 .. 87 A7
Hill View Cl. TN15 .... 87 A7
Hill View Dr. DA16 .... 6 E5
Hill View Rd.
  Hildenborough TN11 .... 116 F5
Hill View Rd. New Barn DA3 ... 43 B6
Hill View Rd. Orpington BR6 ... 51 F8
Hill View Rd. Rusthall TN4 ... 148 C4
Hill View Way. ME5 .... 61 C5
Hill's Terr. ME4 .... 47 F3
Hillary Ave. DA11 .... 29 E5
Hillary Cl. SE9 .... 22 E6
Hillary Rd. ME14 .... 92 A7
Hillbert Rd. TN1 & TN2 .... 149 C5
Hillborough Ave. TN13 & TN15 .. 84 D5
Hillborough Gr. ME5 .... 62 A3
Hillbury Gdns. TN5 .... 176 D1
Hillcrest. TN8 .... 113 B5
Hillcrest Ave. RM16 .... 11 A8
Hillcrest Dr. Cuxton ME2 .... 46 C2
Hillcrest Dr.
  Royal Tunbridge Wells TN1 .. 149 D7
Hillcrest Rd. Dartwscombe DA9 .. 11 A2
Hillcrest Rd. Bromley BR1 ..... 22 A4
Hillcrest Rd. Chatham ME4 .... 47 F2
Hillcrest Rd. Dartford DA1 .... 25 F8
Hillcrest Rd. Marlpit Hill TN8 .. 112 C4
Hillcrest Rd. Orpington BR6 .. 52 A8
Hillcroft Rd. E6 .... 2 B8
Hillden Shaw. ME15 .... 107 A8
Hilldown Lodge. BR6 .... 52 B8
Hilldrop Rd. BR1 .... 22 B2
Hillfield Rd. TN13 .... 83 E7
Hillfield Villas. TN26 .... 173 F6
Hillgarth. TN11 .... 149 A8
Hillingdon Ave. TN13 .... 84 D6
Hillingdon Rd. Bexley DA7 ...... 8 C4
Hillingdon Rd. Gravesend DA11 .. 30 B6
Hillingdon Rise. TN13 .... 84 D5
Hillreach. SE18 & SE7 .... 1 F1
Hills La. TN15 .... 70 C7
Hillsgrove Cl. ME2 .... 46 D5
Hillsgrove Prim Sch. DA16 ...... 7 C7
Hillshaw Cres. ME2 .... 46 B5
Hillside. Erith DA17 .... 4 C2
Hillside. Farningham DA4 .... 40 F2
Hillside. Lane End DA2 .... 27 E3
Hillside. Tonbridge TN9 .... 133 A7
Hillside Ave. Gravesend DA12 .. 30 D6
Hillside Ave. Rochester ME2 .. 47 B8
Hillside Cotts. TN5 .... 175 B8
Hillside Ct. 1 Rochester ME2 .. 47 A7
Hillside Ct. Swanley BR8 .... 40 A5
Hillside Ct. Wateringbury ME18 . 104 E7
Hillside Dr. DA12 .... 30 D6
Hillside La. BR2 .... 50 A8
Hillside Rd. Chatham ME4 ...... 48 A4
Hillside Rd. Crayford DA1 .... 9 A1
Hillside Rd. Kemsing TN14 ..... 69 F2
Hillside Rd. Sevenoaks TN13 .. 84 D4
Hillside The. BR6 .... 52 B2
Hilltop. Tonbridge TN9 .... 133 B7
Hilltop. West Farleigh ME15 .. 105 D3
Hilltop Gdns. Dartford DA1 ..... 9 F2
Hilltop Gdns. Orpington BR6 .. 51 E8
Hilltop Prim Sch. ME2 .... 33 C1
Hilltop Rd. West Thurrock RM16 . 11 B8
Hillview Cres. BR6 .... 37 F1
Hillview Rd. BR7 & SE9 .... 23 A4
Hillview Sch for Girls. TN9 ... 133 C8
Hillydeal Rd. TN14 .... 69 C4
Hillyfield Cl. ME2 .... 32 F1
Hillyfields Cty Jun Sch. ME7 .. 48 E6
Hilton Rd. ME2 .... 33 B7
Hind Cres. DA8 .... 8 D7
Hines Terr. ME5 .... 48 C1
Hinksden Rd. TN17 & TN18 ... 179 F3
Hinksey Path. SE2 .... 3 D3
Hinstock Rd. SE18 .... 6 C7
Hinton Cl. SE9 .... 22 E7
Hinton Cres. ME7 .... 63 A6
Hitchen Hatch La. TN13 .... 84 B4
Hither Chantlers. TN3 .... 148 A2

Hive La. DA11 .... 12 B2
Hive The. DA11 .... 12 B1
Hoath Cl. ME7 .... 63 B7
Hoath La. ME8 .... 63 B7
Hoath Meadow. TN12 .... 153 A6
Hoath Way. ME7 & ME8 .... 63 B5
Hobart Rd. RM18 .... 13 A6
Hoblands End. BR7 .... 23 E2
Hockenden La. BR5 & BR8 .... 39 B7
Hockers Cl. ME14 .... 93 A8
Hockers La. ME14 .... 93 A7
Hoddesdon Rd. DA17 .... 4 A1
Hodgkins Cl. SE28 .... 3 D6
Hodgson Cres. ME6 .... 60 A1
Hodsoll St. BR5 .... 38 D4
Hodsoll St. TN15 .... 57 D1
Hodson Cres. BR5 .... 38 D3
Hog Hill. ME14 .... 93 B5
Hog La. DA11 .... 29 D5
Hogarth Cl. E16 .... 1 D8
Hogbarn La. ME17 .... 95 F2
Hogben Cl. ME3 .... 33 B7
Hoghole La. TN15 .... 165 F2
Hognore La. TN15 .... 72 D6
Hogtrough Hill. TN16 & TN14 .. 82 A5
Holbeach Gdns. DA15 .... 6 F1
Holborn La. ME4 .... 47 F5
Holborn Rd. E13 .... 1 B8
Holborough Rd. ME6 .... 60 A1
Holbrook House. BR7 .... 37 D8
Holbrook La. BR7 .... 23 D1
Holbrook Way. BR2 .... 36 F4
Holburne Cl. SE3 .... 5 C6
Holburne Gdns. SE3 .... 5 D6
Holburne Rd. SE3 .... 5 D6
Holcombe Rd. Chatham ME4 .. 47 F2
Holcombe Rd. Rochester ME1 .. 47 C3
Holcote Cl. DA17 .... 3 E3
Holden Cnr. TN4 .... 132 F1
Holden Park Rd. TN4 .... 149 A8
Holden Rd. TN4 .... 132 F1
Holder Cl. ME5 .... 62 C6
Holding St. ME8 .... 49 F1
Hole La. TN8 .... 112 A6
Holford St. 1 TN9 .... 117 B1
Holgate St. SE7 .... 1 D3
Holland House. ME1 .... 47 D5
Holland Rd. Chatham ME5 ..... 61 E4
Holland Rd. Maidstone ME14 .. 92 B5
Hollands Cl. DA12 .... 31 E3
Hollies Ave. DA15 .... 23 F7
Hollies The. DA12 .... 30 D2
Holligrave Rd. BR1 .... 36 A8
Hollin Cl. TN4 .... 148 F4
Hollingbourne Ave. DA7 .... 7 F6
Hollingbourne Cty Prim Sch.
  ME17 .... 94 E2
Hollingbourne Hill. ME17 ..... 94 F4
Hollingbourne Rd. ME8 .... 49 C2
Hollingbourne Sta. ME17 ..... 94 C3
Hollingbourne Tower. 4 BR5 . 38 B7
Hollington Ct. BR7 .... 23 B2
Hollingworth Rd.
  Orpington BR2 & BR5 .... 37 B2
Hollingworth Rd.
  Park Wood ME15 .... 107 F5
Hollingworth Way. TN16 .... 81 D1
Hollow La. Hartlip ME9 .... 64 E5
Hollow La. Snodland ME6 ...... 74 F6
Hollow Trees Dr. TN11 .... 116 A1
Holly Bank. TN12 .... 152 B8
Holly Bush La. TN13 .... 84 C3
Holly Cl. Chatham ME5 .... 62 C8
Holly Cl. Gillingham ME7 ...... 48 E6
Holly Cotts. ME7 .... 112 B2
Holly Ct. DA14 .... 24 B4
Holly Farm Rd. ME15 .... 108 C6
Holly Hill. DA13 .... 58 F3
Holly Hill Rd. DA17 .... 4 B1
Holly Rd. Dartford DA1 .... 26 D7
Holly Rd. Orpington BR6 .... 52 A8
Holly Rd. Rochester,Strood ME2 .. 46 E5
Holly Rd. Rochester,Wainscott
  ME2 .... 33 D2
Holly Tree Cl. ME17 .... 109 E2
Hollybrake Cl. BR7 .... 23 D1
Hollybush Cl. TN13 .... 84 C3
Hollybush Ct. TN13 .... 84 C3
Hollybush La. BR6 .... 53 A4
Hollybush Rd. DA12 .... 30 C6
Hollycroft. ME2 .... 46 C2
Hollydale Dr. BR2 .... 50 F7
Hollydene Rd. TN5 .... 174 F6
Hollyshaw Ct. TN2 .... 149 C2
Hollytree Ave. BR8 .... 39 E7
Hollytree Dr. ME3 .... 32 B3
Hollywood La. Knockmill ME17 .. 70 F8
Hollywood La. Rochester ME2 .. 33 C2
Hollywood Manor. TN15 .... 70 F7
Hollywood Way. DA8 .... 9 B6
Holm Ct. SE12 .... 22 B5
Holm Mill La. ME17 .... 110 B6
Holmbury Manor. 6 DA14 ..... 24 A4
Holmbury Pk. BR7 .... 22 E1
Holmcroft Way. BR2 .... 36 F4
Holmdale Rd. BR7 .... 23 C3
Holmdene Ct. BR1 .... 36 E6
Holmes Ct. ME19 .... 74 E1
Holmesdale Cl. Durgates TN5 .. 174 E5
Holmesdale Cl. Loose ME15 .. 106 B3
Holmesdale Com Sch. ME6 ... 74 F7
Holmesdale Hill. DA4 .... 41 C8
Holmesdale Rd. Bexley DA16 ... 7 D5
Holmesdale Rd. Sevenoaks TN13 84 C4
Holmesdale Rd.
  South Darenth DA4 .... 41 C8

Holmesdale Sch (Farm Annex).
ME6 .... 74 F6
Holmewood House. TN3 .. 148 A2
Holmewood Rd. TN4 .... 149 C7
Holmewood Ridge. TN3 ... 147 F3
Holmhurst Cl. TN4 .... 148 F4
Holmhurst Rd. DA17 .... 4 B1
Holmleigh Ave. DA1 .... 9 C2
Holmoaks. Gillingham ME8 .. 49 E2
Holmoaks. Maidstone ME14 .. 92 C5
Holmsdale Gr. DA1 & DA7 .... 8 E4
Holmside. ME7 .... 48 E3
Holmwood Cotts. BR6 .... 52 C1
Holmwood Ct. DA14 .... 23 F3
Holstein Way. DA18 .... 3 E3
Holt Cl. SE28 .... 3 C6
Holt Rd. E16 .... 1 E5
Holt Wood Ave. ME20 .... 90 E8
Holtwood Cl. ME8 .... 63 D6
Holtye Cres. ME15 .... 92 B2
Holtye Golf Club. TN8 .... 144 F3
Holtye Rd. RH19 .... 144 A3
Holwood Park Ave. BR2 & BR6 .. 50 F6
Holy Family RC Prim Sch. SE9 ... 5 C3
Holy Family RC Prim Sch The.
ME15 .... 107 F4
Holy Innocents RC Prim Sch.
BR6 .... 51 F7
Holy Trinity CE Prim Sch.
Dartford DA1 .... 9 C2
Holy Trinity CE Prim Sch.
Dartford DA1 .... 9 D1
Holy Trinity Coll & Prep Sch.
BR1 .... 36 C8
Holy Trinity Lamorbey
CE Prim Sch. DA15 .... 24 A7
Holyhead Cl. E6 .... 1 F8
Holyoake Terr. TN13 .... 84 A3
Holywell Cl. SE3 .... 5 A8
Home Farm Cl. TN11 .... 116 A3
Home Farm Cotts. BR5 ...... 38 D8
Home Farm Ct. TN3 .... 163 C4
Home Farm La. Royal Tunbridge Wells
TN11 & TN2 .... 133 F1
Home Farm La.
Royal Tunbridge Wells TN2 .. 149 E8
Home Gdns. DA1 .... 9 E1
Home Hill. BR8 .... 25 F1
Home Lea. ME9 .... 51 F5
Home Mead Cl. DA11 .... 30 B8
Homedean Rd. TN13 .... 83 C4
Homefield Cl. St Paul's Cray BR5 .. 38 B5
Homefield Cl. Swanley BR8 .. 39 F6
Homefield Rd. Bromley BR1 .. 36 C8
Homefield Rd. Sevenoaks TN13 .. 83 E5
Homefield Rise. BR6 .... 38 A1
Homemead. Gravesend DA11 .. 30 B8
Homemead. Swanscombe DA9 .. 11 B1
Homemead Rd. BR2 .... 36 F4
Homer Cl. DA7 .... 8 C6
Homesdale Rd.
Bromley BR1 & BR2 .... 36 C6
Homesdale Rd.
Orpington BR5 & BR6 .... 37 E2
Homestead Rd. Marlpit Hill TN8 .. 112 B5
Homestead Rd. Orpington BR6 .. 52 B4
Homestead The. Crayford DA1 .. 8 E2
Homestead The. Dartford DA1 .. 9 C1
Homestead The.
Groombridge TN3 .... 161 C7
Homevale Cotts. TN14 .... 67 E4
Homewards Rd. ME3 .... 19 B8
Homewood Cotts. DA12 .... 31 E1
Homewood Cres. BR7 .... 23 E2
Homewood Rd.
Langton Green TN3 .... 147 F3
Homewood Rd. Tenterden TN30 .. 173 B1
Homewood Sch. TN30 ...... 173 B1
Homoepathic Hospl. TN1 .. 149 A3
Honduras Terr. ME14 .... 92 A7
Hone St. ME2 .... 47 B8
Honey Bee Glade. ME8 .... 63 E6
Honey Cl. ME7 .... 63 A5
Honey La. ME15 .... 108 B6
Honeybourne Way. BR5 ..... 37 D1
Honeycrock Hill. ME9 .... 79 F8
Honeyden Rd. DA14 .... 24 E2
Honeypot Cl. ME2 .... 47 B8
Honeypot La. Hodsoll Street TN15 .. 57 D2
Honeypot La. Noah's Ark TN15 .. 85 C8
Honeysuckle Cl. Chatham ME5 .. 61 E4
Honeysuckle Cl. Gillingham ME7 .. 62 F4
Honeysuckle Cl. SE12 .... 22 A8
Honiton Rd. DA16 .... 6 F5
Honywood Rd. ME17 .... 111 C4
Hoo Comm Rd. ME3 .... 34 A4
Hoo Rd. ME2 & ME3 .... 33 D3
Hoo St Werburgh Cty Prim Sch.
ME3 .... 34 D5
Hoo St Werburgh Mid Sch.
ME3 .... 34 C5
Hood Ave. BR5 .... 38 B4
Hook Cl. ME5 .... 61 E5
Hook Farm Rd. BR2 .... 36 D4
Hook Green Ct. DA13 .... 44 A4
Hook Green La. DA2 .... 25 F5
Hook Green Rd. DA13 .... 28 F1
Hook Hill. TN5 .... 176 A6
Hook La. Bexley DA16 .... 7 A4
Hook La. Harrietsham ME17 .. 110 C6
Hook Lane Prim Sch. DA16 .... 7 A4
Hook Rd. ME6 .... 74 F8
Hook St. ME17 .... 127 F8
Hookfields. DA11 .... 29 E5

Hookstead. TN26 .... 173 C7
Hookwood Cotts. TN14 ...... 67 C8
Hookwood Rd. BR6 & TN14 .. 67 C7
Hooper Rd. E16 .... 1 A7
Hooper's Pl. ME1 .... 47 C4
Hooper's Rd. ME1 .... 47 C4
Hoopers La. ME3 .... 18 F5
Hoopers Rd. TN15 .... 84 C1
Hoopers Yd. TN13 .... 84 C1
Hop Pocket Cl. TN17 .... 170 A8
Hop Pocket La. TN12 .... 135 F7
Hope Ave. TN11 .... 102 E1
Hope Cl. SE12 .... 22 B5
Hope Cotts. DA2 .... 28 B6
Hope Rd. DA10 .... 11 F1
Hope St. Chatham ME4 ...... 48 A3
Hope St. Maidstone ME14 .. 91 F6
Hope Terr. ME3 .... 32 D7
Hopedale Rd. SE7 .... 5 B8
Hopehouse La. TN17 & TN18 .. 186 E7
Hopes Gr. TN26 .... 173 D9
Hopewell Dr. Chatham ME5 .. 62 C8
Hopewell Dr. Gravesend DA12 .. 30 F3
Hopgarden Cl. TN8 .... 112 D3
Hopgarden La. TN13 .... 99 A8
Hopgarden Oast. ME18 .... 104 F1
Hopgarden Rd. TN10 .... 117 D6
Hopkins Cnr. ME15 .... 105 D7
Hopton Cl. BR2 .... 36 B1
Hopton Rd. SE18 .... 2 C3
Hopwood Gdns. TN4 .... 149 A6
Horizon Cl. TN4 .... 149 B8
Horley Cl. DA6 .... 8 A2
Horley Rd. SE9 .... 22 E4
Horn La. SE10 .... 1 A2
Horn Park Cl. SE12 .... 5 B2
Horn Park La. SE12 .... 5 B1
Horn Park Prim Sch. SE12 .. 22 B8
Horn Yd. DA11 .... 13 B1
Horn's Oak Rd. DA13 .... 58 B6
Hornbeam Ave. Chatham ME5 .. 62 B2
Hornbeam Ave.
Royal Tunbridge Wells TN2 .. 133 D1
Hornbeam Cl. Larkfield ME20 .. 75 B2
Hornbeam Cl. Putlands TN12 .. 135 F5
Hornbeam House. DA15 ... 24 A5
Hornbeam La. DA7 .... 8 C5
Hornbeams. DA13 .... 73 B8
Hornbeam Way. BR2 .... 37 A3
Horncastle Cl. SE12 .... 22 A8
Horncastle Rd. SE12 .... 22 A8
Horne House. SE18 .... 5 E6
Hornetts Cl. BR8 .... 39 D2
Hornfair Rd. SE7 .... 5 D7
Hornfield Cotts. DA13 .... 58 C3
Horning Cl. SE9 .... 22 E4
Horns La. ME18 .... 88 D1
Horns Lodge La. TN11 ..... 117 A8
Horns Rd. TN18 .... 184 D8
Horsa Rd. Eltham SE12 ...... 22 C8
Horsa Rd. Erith DA8 .... 8 C7
Horse Leaze. E6 .... 2 A7
Horsecroft Cl. BR6 .... 38 B1
Horsegrove Ave. TN5 ...... 176 F1
Horsell Rd. BR5 .... 38 B8
Horseshoe Cl. Gillingham ME7 .. 62 F5
Horseshoe Cl. Maidstone ME14 .. 92 E5
Horseshoes La. ME17 ...... 108 E4
Horsewash La. ME1 .... 47 C6
Horsfeld Gdns. SE9 .... 5 E2
Horsfeld Rd. SE9 .... 5 D2
Horsfield Cl. DA2 .... 27 C8
Horsham Rd. DA6 .... 8 A2
Horsley Rd. Bromley BR1 ... 36 B8
Horsley Rd. Rochester ME1 .. 47 B4
Horsmonden Cl. BR6 .... 37 F2
Horsmonden Cty Prim Sch.
TN12 .... 153 A6
Horsmonden Rd. TN12 .... 152 D6
Horsted Ave. ME4 .... 47 E1
Horsted Cty Inf Sch. ME4 .. 61 D5
Horsted Cty Jun Sch. ME5 .. 61 D5
Horsted Way. ME1 .... 61 D7
Horton Downs. ME15 .... 92 A3
Horton Kirby CE Prim Sch. DA4 .. 41 C6
Horton Pl. TN16 .... 81 D1
Horton Rd. DA4 .... 41 C6
Horton Tower. BR5 .... 38 C5
Horton Way. DA4 .... 40 F2
Hortons Way. TN16 .... 81 D1
Horwood Cl. ME1 .... 61 B8
Hoselands View. DA3 .... 42 E5
Hoser Ave. SE12 .... 22 A6
Hosey Common La. TN16 .. 96 F5
Hosey Common Rd. TN16 & TN8 .. 96 F5
Hosey Hill. TN16 .... 96 E8
Hoskin's Cl. E16 .... 1 C7
Hospital La. ME1 .... 47 C4
Hospital Rd. Hollingbourne ME17 .. 109 E8
Hospital Rd. Sevenoaks TN13 .. 84 C6
Hotel Rd. ME8 .... 49 A2
Hotham Cl. Sutton at Hone DA4 .. 27 B1
Hotham Cl. Swanley Village BR8 .. 40 B8
Hothfield Rd. ME8 .... 49 F1
Hottsfield. DA3 .... 42 E6
Hougham House. BR5 .... 38 D1
Houghton Ave. ME7 .... 63 B3
Houselands Rd. TN9 .... 117 B2
Hove Cl. RM17 .... 12 A8
Hovendens. TN17 .... 170 A8
Hoveton St. SE28 .... 3 C7
How Green La. TN8 .... 113 C2
Howard Ave. Rochester ME1 .. 47 D3
Howard Ave. Sidcup DA5 ... 24 C8
Howard Dr. ME16 .... 91 B5
Howard Gdns. TN2 .... 149 A1
Howard Rd. Bromley BR1 .. 22 A1
Howard Rd. Dartford DA1 .. 10 A1
Howard Rd. East Malling ME19 .. 89 F8

Howard Sch The. ME8 .... 63 D8
Howarth Rd. SE2 .... 3 A2
Howbury La. DA8 .... 9 A5
Howbury Rd. DA1 & DA8 ..... 9 A5
Howbury Wlk. ME8 .... 63 D4
Howden Cl. SE28 .... 3 D6
Howells Cl. TN15 .... 55 E4
Howes Cotts. TN14 .... 184 F8
Howick Cl. ME20 .... 90 F8
Howland Rd. TN12 .... 138 E6
Howlsmere Cl. ME2 .... 60 B3
Hubbard's Rd. TN3 & TN14 .. 99 B4
Hubbard's La. ME15 .... 107 A3
Hubble Dr. ME15 .... 107 E7
Huckleberry Cl. ME5 .... 62 B3
Hudson Cl. ME8 .... 49 C1
Hudson Pl. SE18 .... 2 C1
Hudson Rd. DA7 .... 7 F6
Hugh Christie Tech Coll The.
TN10 .... 117 D6
Hughes Dr. ME2 .... 33 D2
Hulseood Cl. DA2 .... 26 B5
Hulsons Ct. TN18 .... 179 A2
Humber Cres. ME2 .... 46 F7
Humber House. ME15 ...... 107 E8
Humber Rd. Dartford DA1 .... 9 D2
Humber Rd. Greenwich SE10 .. 1 A1
Humber Rd. Greenwich SE3 .... 5 A8
Humboldt Cl. SE8 .... 63 D6
Hume Cl. ME8 .... 49 C1
Hume Rd. ME2 .... 33 C1
Humphreys. TN12 .... 151 F6
Hundred of Hoo Sch. ME3 .. 34 C5
Hungershall Pk. TN4 .... 148 E2
Hunsdon Dr. TN13 .... 84 B4
Hunstanton Cl. ME8 .... 63 E3
Hunt Rd. Northfleet ME3 .... 29 F5
Hunt Rd. Tonbridge TN10 .. 117 E6
Hunt St. Nettlestead ME18 .. 104 F5
Hunt St. West Farleigh
ME15 & ME18 .... 105 B5
Hunter's Gr. BR6 .... 51 C6
Hunters Cl. DA5 .... 25 E5
Hunters Ct. ME7 .... 48 C7
Hunters Lodge. DA15 .... 24 A5
Hunters Way. Gillingham ME7 .. 48 E1
Hunters Way.
Royal Tunbridge Wells TN2 .. 148 F1
Hunters Way W. ME5 & ME7 .. 48 E1
Hunters Wlk. TN14 .... 67 E5
Huntersfield Cl. ME5 .... 62 C1
Huntington Wlk. ME15 .... 107 E7
Huntingfield Rd. DA13 ...... 44 A2
Huntington Cl. TN17 .... 169 D4
Huntington Rd. ME17 ...... 106 B3
Huntley Ave. DA11 .... 12 C1
Huntley Mill Rd. TN5 .... 176 E3
Huntleys Pk. TN4 .... 148 F5
Hunton CE Prim Sch. ME15 .. 121 D7
Hunton Hill. ME15 .... 105 F1
Hunton House. ME4 .... 38 C4
Hunton Rd. TN12 .... 122 A3
Hunts Cl. SE3 .... 5 A5
Hunts Farm Cl. TN15 .... 87 A1
Hunts Mede Cl. BR7 .... 22 F1
Huntsman La. Maidstone ME14 .. 92 B4
Huntsman La.
Wrotham Heath TN15 .... 72 C1
Huntsman's Cnr. ME4 .... 61 B8
Huntsmans Cl. ME4 .... 47 E1
Huntsmoor House. BR5 ..... 38 B5
Hurlfield. DA2 .... 26 C5
Hurlingham Rd. DA7 .... 7 F7
Huron Cl. BR6 .... 51 F4
Hurricane Rd. ME19 .... 88 F3
Hurst Cl. Chatham ME5 ...... 61 E6
Hurst Cl. Staplehurst TN12 .. 139 F4
Hurst Cl. Tenterden TN30 .. 182 F7
Hurst Farm Rd. TN14 .... 99 B3
Hurst Green CE Sch. TN19 .. 184 A4
Hurst Hill. ME5 .... 61 E2
Hurst House. SE2 .... 3 D1
Hurst La. Erith SE2 .... 7 D8
Hurst La. Sevenoaks Weald TN14 .. 99 B2
Hurst Pl. Gillingham ME8 .... 63 F8
Hurst Prim Sch. DA5 .... 24 D7
Hurst Rd. Erith DA8 .... 8 C7
Hurst Rd. Sidcup DA5 .... 24 D7
Hurst Springs. DA5 .... 24 E7
Hurst The. Crouch ME18 ... 102 D7
Hurst The.
Royal Tunbridge Wells TN2 .. 149 E7
Hurst Way. Maidstone ME16 .. 90 F2
Hurst Way. Sevenoaks TN13 .. 99 C8
Hurstbourne Cotts. DA5 .... 25 B8
Hurstfield. ME16 .... 36 A4
Hurstings The. ME16 .... 91 D2
Hurstmere Sch. DA15 .... 24 C7
Hurstwood. ME5 .... 61 E4
Hurstwood Ave. Erith DA7 & DA8 .. 8 E6
Hurstwood Ave. Sidcup DA5 .. 24 E7
Hurstwood Dr. BR1 .... 36 F6
Hurstwood La. TN4 .... 148 F3
Hurstwood Pk. TN4 .... 148 F3
Hurstwood Rd. Bredhurst ME7 .. 63 B1
Hurstwood Rd. Detling ME14 .. 78 B7
Husheath Hill. TN17 .... 154 F6
Husseywell Cres. BR2 .... 36 A1
Hutsford Cl. ME8 .... 63 D5
Hutson Terr. RM16 .... 10 D8
Huxley Cl. ME15 .... 107 D4
Huxley House. SE2 .... 3 D1
Huxley Rd. DA16 .... 6 F4
Hyacinth Rd. ME2 .... 46 E6
Hybrid Cl. ME1 .... 47 D1
Hyde Dr. BR5 .... 38 B5

Hyde Rd. Bexley DA7 .... 7 F5
Hyde Rd. Maidstone ME16 .. 91 D6
Hyde's Orch. TN27 .... 141 E5
Hylton St. SE18 .... 2 F1
Hyperion Dr. ME2 .... 32 F1
Hythe Ave. DA7 .... 7 F7
Hythe Cl. Orpington BR5 .... 38 C5
Hythe Cl.
Royal Tunbridge Wells TN4 .. 133 A1
Hythe St. DA1 .... 9 E1

Ickleton Rd. SE9 .... 22 E4
Icough St. SE3 .... 5 B7
Iddenden Cotts. TN18 ...... 178 D2
Ide Hill CE Prim Sch. TN14 .. 97 F4
Ide Hill Rd. TN14 .... 97 F2
Iden Cres. TN12 .... 139 F2
Iden Rd. ME2 .... 33 C1
Idenwood Cl. ME8 .... 63 D6
Idleigh Court Rd. DA3 & DA13 .. 57 C8
Ifield Cl. ME15 .... 107 F7
Ifield Cotts. TN12 .... 31 C2
Ifield Sch. DA12 .... 30 C3
Ifield Way. DA12 .... 30 D2
Ightham By-Pass. TN15 ..... 86 C7
Ightham Cotts. DA2 .... 28 B6
Ightham Cty Prim Sch. TN15 .. 86 B6
Ightham Mote (NT). TN15 .. 101 A7
Ightham Rd. Erith DA8 .... 8 A7
Ightham Rd.
Shipbourne TN11 & TN15 .. 101 C5
Ilkley Rd. E16 .... 1 C8
Illustrious Cl. ME5 .... 62 A6
Imber Ct. ME5 .... 6 A1
Impala Gdns. TN4 .... 149 B6
Imperial Bsns Pk. DA11 .... 12 F1
Imperial Dr. DA12 .... 30 F3
Imperial Rd. ME7 .... 48 C3
Imperial Ret Pk. DA1 .... 13 A1
Imperial Way. BR7 & SE9 .. 23 C5
Impton La. ME5 .... 62 A1
Inca Dr. SE9 .... 23 B8
Indus Rd. SE7 .... 5 C7
Ingle Rd. ME4 .... 47 F2
Ingleby Way. BR7 .... 23 A3
Ingleden Park Rd. TN30 ... 173 C1
Ingledew Rd. SE18 .... 2 D1
Ingleside Gr. SE3 .... 5 A8
Ingleside Gr. SE3 .... 5 A8
Ingleton Ave. DA16 .... 7 A2
Inglewood. Chislehurst BR7 .. 23 D2
Inglewood. Swanley BR8 ... 39 E7
Inglewood Copse. BR1 ...... 36 F7
Inglewood Rd. DA7 .... 8 D3
Ingoldsby Rd. DA12 .... 30 F7
Ingram Rd. Dartford DA1 ... 26 E7
Ingram Rd. Gillingham ME7 .. 48 E6
Ingress Gdns. DA9 & DA10 .. 11 D2
Ingress Terr. DA13 .... 28 F4
Inigo Jones Rd. SE7 .... 5 E7
Institute Rd. ME4 .... 48 A4
Instone Rd. DA1 .... 26 D8
Inverary Pl. SE18 .... 6 D8
Inverine Rd. SE7 .... 1 B1
Invermore Pl. SE18 .... 2 C2
Inverness House. ME15 ... 107 E7
Invicta Cl. BR7 .... 23 A3
Invicta Gram Sch for Girls.
ME14 .... 92 C4
Invicta Inf Sch. SE3 .... 5 A7
Invicta Rd. Dartford DA2 .... 10 B1
Invicta Rd. Greenwich SE3 & SE7 .. 5 A8
Invicta Villas. ME14 .... 93 C4
Iona Cl. ME5 .... 62 D1
Iona Rd. ME15 .... 107 A7
Ireland Cl. E6 .... 1 F8
Irene Rd. BR6 .... 37 F2
Iris Ave. DA5 .... 7 E1
Iris Cl. ME5 .... 77 A8
Iris Cres. DA7 .... 7 F8
Iron Mill La. DA1 .... 8 F3
Iron Mill Pl. DA1 .... 8 F3
Ironside Cl. ME5 .... 62 A8
Ironstones. TN3 .... 148 B3
Irvine Rd. ME3 .... 32 B3
Irvine Way. BR6 .... 37 F2
Irving House. TN1 .... 149 B5
Irving Wlk. BR8 .... 39 D7
Irving Wlk. DA10 .... 28 E8
Irwin Ave. SE18 .... 6 E7
Isabella Dr. BR6 .... 51 C6
Isla Rd. SE18 .... 6 C8
Islehurst Cl. BR7 .... 37 A8
Ismays Rd. TN15 .... 86 C3
Istead Rise. DA13 .... 29 F1
Istead Rise Cty Prim Sch. DA13 .. 43 E8
Ivedon Rd. DA16 .... 7 C6
Ivens Way. ME17 .... 110 D6
Iverhurst Cl. DA6 .... 7 D2
Iversgate Cl. ME8 .... 49 A3
Ives Rd. TN9 .... 116 F1
Ivor St. SE9 .... 23 B7
Ivorydown. BR1 .... 22 A4
Ivy Bower Cl. DA9 .... 11 B2
Ivy Cl. Dartford DA2 .... 27 A8
Ivy Cl. Gravesend DA12 ..... 30 D5
Ivy Cl. Kingswood ME17 ... 109 D2
Ivy House La. TN13 .... 68 E2
Ivy La. TN14 .... 67 E3
Ivy Rd. E16 .... 1 A7
Ivy St. ME8 .... 63 F8
Ivy Villas. DA9 .... 11 A2
Ivybridge Ct. BR7 .... 37 A8
Izane Rd. DA6 .... 7 F3

Jack Lobley Cty Prim Sch.
RM18 .... 12 F6
Jackass La. BR2 .... 50 C4
Jacklin Cl. ME5 .... 61 F2

Jackson Ave. ME1 .... 61 E8
Jackson Cl. Gillingham ME8 .. 49 C1
Jackson Cl. Stone DA9 .... 11 A2
Jackson Rd. BR2 .... 50 F8
Jackson St. SE18 .... 6 A8
Jackson Way. TN17 .... 171 C3
Jacksons La. TN30 .... 183 A7
Jacob House. DA14 .... 3 D4
Jacob's La. ME3 .... 35 B6
Jade Cl. E16 .... 1 D7
Jaffray Rd. BR2 .... 36 D5
Jaggard Way. TN12 .... 139 E3
Jagger Cl. DA2 .... 27 C8
Jago Cl. SE18 .... 6 C8
Jail La. TN16 .... 66 A3
Jamaica Terr. ME14 .... 92 A7
James Newman Ct. SE9 ..... 23 A5
James Rd. Cuxton ME2 ...... 46 C2
James Rd. Dartford DA1 ..... 26 A8
James St. Chatham ME4 ..... 47 F4
James St. Gillingham ME7 .. 48 C6
James St. Maidstone ME14 .. 92 A5
James St. Rochester ME1 ... 47 C4
James Whatman Way. ME14 .. 91 F5
Janet Ct. DA7 .... 8 A3
Japonica Cl. ME5 .... 62 C2
Jaquets Dr. DA5 .... 25 A6
Jarrah Cotts. RM16 .... 10 D8
Jarrett Ave. ME2 .... 33 C2
Jarvis La. TN17 .... 154 B3
Jarvis Pl. TN30 .... 173 B3
Jashada House. SE18 .... 2 A1
Jasmine Cl. Chatham ME5 .. 61 F4
Jasmine Cl. East Malling ME19 .. 89 F8
Jasmine Cl. Orpington BR6 .. 51 B8
Jasmine Cotts. TN3 .... 161 C7
Jasmine Rd. ME19 .... 89 F8
Jason Wlk. SE9 .... 23 A4
Jasper Ave. ME1 .... 47 D2
Jasper Rd. E16 .... 1 D7
Javelin Rd. ME19 .... 88 F3
Jay Gdns. BR7 .... 22 F4
Jefferson Dr. ME8 .... 49 C1
Jefferson Wlk. SE18 .... 6 A8
Jeffery St. ME7 .... 48 C6
Jeffrey Cl. TN12 .... 139 E4
Jeffrey Row. SE12 .... 5 B2
Jeffrey St. ME14 .... 92 A5
Jeken Rd. SE9 .... 5 C3
Jellicoe Ave. DA12 .... 30 C5
Jellicoe Ave W. DA12 .... 30 C5
Jenkins' Dale. ME4 .... 47 F3
Jenkins Dr. ME15 .... 107 F5
Jenner House. DA17 .... 4 A3
Jenner Rd. ME1 .... 47 C4
Jenner Way. ME20 .... 75 F6
Jennifer Ct. ME3 .... 34 F5
Jenningtree Rd. DA8 .... 9 B7
Jenningtree Way. DA17 .... 4 C4
Jenton Ave. DA7 .... 7 E5
Jerome Rd. ME20 .... 74 F4
Jersey Dr. BR5 .... 37 D3
Jersey Rd. Newham E16 .... 1 C7
Jersey Rd. Rochester ME2 .. 47 A8
Jeskyns Rd. DA12 .... 44 E6
Jessamine Pl. DA2 .... 27 C8
Jessamine Terr. BR8 .... 39 C8
Jessup Cl. SE18 .... 2 C2
Jetty Rd. Kingsnorth ME3 ... 35 D7
Jetty Rd. Sheerness ME12 .. 21 F3
Jetty Wlk. RM17 .... 12 A8
Jevington Way. SE12 .... 22 B7
Jewell Gr. TN12 .... 138 D5
Jeyes Rd. ME7 .... 48 C4
Jezreels Rd. ME7 .... 48 D3
Jim Bradley Cl. SE18 .... 2 A1
Jiniwin Rd. ME1 .... 61 D7
Joan Cres. SE9 .... 22 D8
Jockey La. TN17 .... 169 C5
Johannesburg House. ME15 .. 107 E7
John Hunt Ct. SE9 .... 22 E6
John Mayne CE Prim Sch.
TN27 .... 157 F1
John Newton Ct. TN16 .... 7 B4
John Spare Ct. TN4 .... 149 A6
John St. Grays RM17 .... 12 C8
John St. Maidstone ME14 .. 92 A6
John St. Rochester ME1 ..... 47 C4
John St. R Tunbridge Wells TN4 .. 149 A4
John Wilson St. SE18 .... 2 A2
John's Rd. DA13 .... 43 F4
Johns Cl. DA3 .... 42 F4
Johnson Ave. ME7 .... 48 C7
Johnson Cl. DA11 .... 29 D5
Johnson Rd. BR2 .... 36 D4
Johnsons Ave. TN14 .... 53 B1
Johnsons Way. DA9 .... 11 C1
Joiners Ct. ME4 .... 48 B2
Jonas Dr. TN5 .... 174 E5
Jonas La. TN5 .... 174 E5
Jones Rd. E13 .... 1 B8
Jordan Cl. ME15 .... 107 E5
Joy Rd. DA12 .... 30 C7
Joyce Cl. TN17 .... 169 C5
Joyce Dawson Way. SE28 ... 3 A6
Joyce Green Hospl. DA1 ...... 9 F5
Joyce Green La. Dartford DA1 .. 9 E5
Joyce Green La.
Dartford, Temple Hill DA1 ... 9 F4
Joyce Green Wlk. DA1 .... 9 F3
Joyce Page Cl. SE7 .... 5 E7
Joyden's Wood Rd. DA5 .... 25 E5
Joydens Wood Cty Jun Sch.
DA5 .... 25 E4
Joydens Wood Cty Inf Sch.
DA5 .... 25 E4
Jubilee Ctry Pk. BR2 .... 37 B4
Jubilee Cl. DA9 .... 11 C1

Jubilee Cnr. ME17 .... 125 E3
Jubilee Cres. Gravesend DA12 .. 30 E6
Jubilee Cres. Ightham TN15 ... 86 C6
Jubilee Cl. DA1 .... 26 D8
Jubilee Field. SE28 .... 3 C6
Jubilee Prim Sch. SE28 .... 3 C6
Jubilee Rd. Maypole BR6 .... 53 A4
Jubilee Rd. West Thurrock RM16 .. 11 B8
Jubilee Rise. TN15 .... 84 F6
Jubilee Terr. ME7 .... 48 C6
Jubilee Way. DA14 .... 24 A6
Judd Rd. TN9 .... 133 B7
Judd Sch The. TN9 .... 133 A8
Judeth Gdns. DA12 .... 30 E3
Judkins Cl. ME5 .... 62 C6
Juglans Rd. BR6 .... 38 A1
Julian Rd. BR6 .... 52 A4
Julians Cl. TN13 .... 99 A8
Julians Way. TN13 .... 99 A8
Junction Rd.
  Bodiam TN18 & TN32 .... 185 A3
Junction Rd. Dartford DA1 ...... 9 D1
Junction Rd. Gillingham ME7 .... 48 D4
Juniper Cl. Chatham ME5 .... 62 A4
Juniper Cl.
  Royal Tunbridge Wells TN2 ... 113 D1
Juniper La. E6 .... 1 E8
Juniper Wlk. BR8 .... 39 D7
Jury St. DA11 .... 13 B1
Jutland Cl. ME3 .... 19 D7
Jutland House. SE7 .... 1 E2

Kale Rd. DA18 .... 3 E4
Kashgar Rd. SE18 .... 2 F2
Kashmir Rd. SE7 .... 5 D7
Katherine Cl. ME5 .... 62 B2
Katherine Gdns. SE9 .... 5 D3
Katherine Rd. TN8 .... 128 C8
Katie Rance Ct. SE18 .... 1 F2
Kay St. DA16 .... 7 B6
Keary Rd. DA18 .... 28 F8
Keats Gdns. RM18 .... 13 B5
Keats House. DA1 .... 8 E2
Keats Rd. Bexley DA16 .... 6 F6
Keats Rd. Erith DA17 .... 4 C3
Keats Rd. Lunsford ME20 ...... 74 F3
Kechill Gdns. BR2 .... 36 A2
Kedleston Dr. BR1 .... 37 F4
Keeble Cl. SE18 .... 6 B8
Keedonwood Rd. BR1 .... 22 A3
Keefe Cl. ME5 .... 61 D1
Keel Gdns. TN4 .... 148 E8
Keeling Rd. SE9 .... 5 D2
Keemor Cl. SE18 .... 6 A7
Keep The. SE3 .... 5 A5
Keightley Dr. SE9 .... 23 C7
Keir Hardy House. DA17 .... 4 A3
Keith Ave. DA4 .... 27 B2
Keith Sutton House. SE9 .... 23 C6
Kelbrook Rd. SE3 & SE9 .... 5 E4
Kelchers La. TN11 .... 118 F5
Kelham House. SE18 .... 6 B8
Kellaway Rd. Chatham ME5 ..... 62 A2
Kellaway Rd. Greenwich SE3 .... 5 D5
Kellner Rd. SE28 .... 2 F3
Kelly Dr. ME7 .... 48 C7
Kelly House. ME1 .... 61 C7
Kelsall Cl. SE3 .... 5 B5
Kelsey Rd. BR5 .... 38 B7
Kelso Dr. DA12 .... 30 F4
Kelvin Cl. TN10 .... 117 D7
Kelvin House. DA17 .... 4 A3
Kelvin Par. SE9 .... 37 E1
Kelvin Rd. Bexley DA16 .... 7 A4
Kelvin Rd. Tilbury RM18 .... 13 A5
Kemble Cl. TN2 .... 149 E7
Kemble Dr. BR2 .... 50 E7
Kemnal Rd. BR7 .... 23 D3
Kemnal Tech Coll. BR5 .... 24 B7
Kemnal Warren. BR7 .... 23 D2
Kemp Cl. ME5 .... 61 E4
Kempley Ct. RM17 .... 12 D8
Kempt St. SE18 .... 6 A8
Kempton Cl. Chatham ME5 ...... 62 C2
Kempton Cl. Erith DA8 .... 8 C8
Kemsing Cl. DA5 .... 24 E8
Kemsing Cty Prim Sch. TN15 ... 70 A2
Kemsing Rd. Greenwich SE10 .... 1 A1
Kemsing Rd. Wrotham TN15 .... 71 C3
Kemsing Sta. TN15 .... 85 D8
Kemsley Rd. Northfleet DA11 ... 29 F4
Kemsley Cl. Swanscombe DA9 ... 11 B1
Kemsley Street Rd. ME14 .... 63 C1
Kendal Dr. TN9 .... 117 C2
Kendal Pk. TN4 .... 148 E5
Kendal Way. ME8 .... 63 D8
Kendall Ct. DA15 .... 24 A5
Kendall Lodge. BR1 .... 36 B8
Kendon Bsns Pk. ME2 .... 47 C8
Kenia Wlk. DA12 .... 30 F5
Kenilworth Dr. ME8 .... 63 D6
Kenilworth Gdns. Gillingham
  ME8 .... 63 D7
Kenilworth Gdns. Woolwich SE18 . 6 B5
Kenilworth House. ME16 .... 91 B2
Kenilworth Rd. BR5 .... 37 C3
Kenley Cl. Sidcup DA5 .... 25 A8
Kenley Cl. St Paul's Cray BR7 ... 37 E6
Kenley House. BR5 .... 38 B7
Kenmere Rd. DA16 .... 7 C5
Kennard St. E16 .... 1 F5
Kennedy Cl. BR5 .... 37 D1
Kennedy Gdns. TN13 .... 84 D5
Kennedy House. TN17 .... 180 E6
Kennel Barn Rd. ME9 .... 80 C5
Kennet Ct. BR8 .... 39 E6
Kennet Rd. Crayford DA1 .... 9 A4

Kennet Rd. Tonbridge TN10 .... 117 C5
Kennett Ct. BR5 .... 38 D1
Kennington Cl. Gillingham ME8 .. 49 B4
Kennington Cl. Maidstone ME15 107 F7
Kensington Ct. RM17 .... 12 C8
Kensington House. ME16 .... 91 A2
Kent Ave. Bexley DA16 .... 6 F2
Kent Ave. Maidstone ME15 ..... 92 C1
Kent Cl. Chatham ME1 .... 61 C8
Kent Cl. Orpington BR6 .... 51 E4
Kent Cl. Paddock Wood TN12 .. 136 A6
Kent Coll. TN2 .... 134 D3
Kent County Opthalmic
  & Aural Hospl. ME14 .... 92 A4
Kent County Show Gd. ME14 ... 78 C3
Kent & East Sussex Rly. TN17 . 188 D5
Kent Hatch Rd. TN8 & RH8 .... 96 B4
Kent House. TN18 .... 179 A2
Kent Inst of Art & Design.
  Chatham ME4 .... 47 E4
Kent Inst of Art & Design.
  Maidstone ME16 .... 91 C3
Kent Kraft Ind Est. DA11 ...... 11 F2
Kent Music Sch. ME15 .... 133 B8
Kent Rd. Dartford DA1 .... 9 E1
Kent Rd. Gravesend DA11 ...... 30 A7
Kent Rd. Grays RM17 .... 12 C8
Kent Rd. Halling ME2 .... 60 A6
Kent Rd. Longfield DA3 .... 42 D7
Kent Rd. Orpington BR5 .... 38 B3
Kent Rd. R Tunbridge Wells TN4 149 A6
Kent Rd. Snodland ME6 .... 75 A6
Kent St. ME18 .... 88 E2
Kent & Sussex Hospl. TN4 .... 149 A4
Kent Terr. Lower Higham ME3 .. 32 D7
Kent Terr. Meopham Green DA13 58 A7
Kentish Gdns. TN2 .... 162 E8
Kentish Rd. DA17 .... 4 A2
Kentish Way. BR1 & BR2 ...... 36 B6
Kentmere Rd. SE18 .... 2 E2
Kenward Ct. TN11 .... 118 E8
Kenward Rd. Eltham SE9 .... 5 D2
Kenward Rd. Maidstone ME16 .. 91 C5
Kenward Rd. Yalding ME18 .... 104 C2
Kenwood Ave. Chatham ME5 .... 62 A4
Kenwood Ave. New Barn DA3 ... 43 C6
Kenwyn Rd. DA1 .... 9 D2
Kenya Rd. SE7 .... 5 D7
Kenya Terr. ME14 .... 92 A7
Kenyon Wlk. ME8 .... 63 B3
Kerry Cl. E16 .... 1 B7
Kersey Rd. SE9 .... 22 E4
Kesteven Cl. ME2 .... 60 B5
Kestlake Rd. DA5 .... 7 C1
Kestner Ind Est. DA9 .... 11 A3
Keston Ave. BR2 .... 50 C5
Keston CE Prim Sch. BR2 ...... 50 D5
Keston Cl. DA16 .... 7 C7
Keston Ct. DA5 .... 24 F8
Keston Gdns. BR2 .... 50 C6
Keston Park Cl. BR2 .... 50 F7
Kestrel Ave. E6 .... 1 E8
Kestrel Cl. TN8 .... 112 D3
Kestrel House. ME7 .... 48 B6
Kestrel Rd. ME5 .... 62 C2
Keswick Cl. TN9 .... 117 C2
Keswick Dr. ME16 .... 91 B5
Keswick Rd. Bexley DA7 .... 8 A6
Keswick Rd. Orpington BR6 .... 38 A2
Ketridge La. ME19 .... 89 D2
Kettle La. ME15 .... 105 E6
Kettlewell Ct. BR8 .... 39 F7
Kevington Cl. BR5 .... 37 F5
Kevington Dr. BR5 & BR7 ...... 37 F5
Kevington Prim Sch. BR5 ...... 38 D4
Kewlands. ME14 .... 92 C6
Keycol Hill. ME9 .... 65 F5
Keycol Hospl. ME9 .... 65 E6
Keyes Ave. ME4 .... 47 F2
Keyes Gdns. TN9 .... 132 F7
Keyes Rd. DA1 .... 10 A3
Keynes Ct. SE28 .... 3 B6
Keynsham Gdns. SE9 .... 5 E2
Keynsham Rd. SE9 .... 5 E2
Keyworth Cl. ME8 .... 64 B1
Khartoum Rd. Chatham ME4 .... 47 F5
Khartoum Rd. Gillingham ME4 .. 48 A6
Khyber Rd. ME4 & ME7 .... 48 B7
Kibbles La. TN4 .... 148 E8
Kidbrooke Gdns. SE3 .... 5 A6
Kidbrooke Gr. SE3 .... 5 B6
Kidbrooke La. SE9 .... 5 E3
Kidbrooke Park Cl. SE3 .... 5 B6
Kidbrooke Park Prim Sch. SE3 .. 5 C6
Kidbrooke Park Rd. SE3, 9 & 12 . 5 B4
Kidbrooke Sch. SE3 .... 5 D5
Kidbrooke Sta. SE3 .... 5 B5
Kidbrooke Way. SE3 .... 5 B5
Kidd Pl. SE7 .... 1 E1
Kiddens. BR8 .... 39 B7
Kildare Rd. E16 .... 1 A8
Killewarren Way. BR5 .... 38 C3
Killick Cl. TN13 .... 83 E6
Killick Rd. ME3 .... 34 D5
Killicks Cotts. ME18 .... 120 F8
Kiln Barn Rd.
  ME16 & ME19 & ME20 ...... 90 C7
Kiln Field. TN30 .... 183 C7
Kiln La. TN11 .... 115 F1
Kiln Way. TN12 .... 136 A5
Kildown. DA12 .... 30 D2
Kildown Cl. ME16 .... 91 C7
Kilnfields. BR6 .... 53 A4
Kilnwood. TN14 .... 67 F6
Kimber House. SE18 .... 6 B8
Kimberley Dr. DA14 .... 24 D6
Kimberley Rd. ME7 .... 48 D3
Kimberidge Gdns. SE9 .... 22 E4

Kimmeridge Rd. SE9 .... 22 E4
Kincraig. BR7 .... 37 A8
Kincraig Dr. TN13 .... 84 B4
Kinder Cl. SE28 .... 3 D6
King and Queen Cl. SE9 .... 22 E4
King Arthur's Dr. ME2 .... 33 A1
King Edward Rd. DA1 .... 9 D1
King Edward Rd. Chatham ME4 .. 47 F2
King Edward Rd. Gillingham ME7 48 F6
King Edward Rd. Maidstone ME15 91 E6
King Edward Rd. Rochester ME1 47 C5
King Edward Rd. Stone DA9 .... 11 A2
King George Ave. E16 .... 1 D7
King George Rd. ME5 .... 61 E4
King George V Hill. TN1 ...... 149 C5
King George V Memorial Houses.
  ME8 .... 49 C2
King Harolds Way. DA7 .... 7 E7
King Henry Mews. BR6 .... 51 F5
King Hill. ME19 .... 89 A5
King John's Wlk. SE9 .... 5 E1
King St. Chatham ME4 .... 48 A4
King St. Gillingham ME7 .... 48 C6
King St. Gravesend DA11 ...... 13 B1
King St. Maidstone ME14 & ME15 . 92 A4
King St. Rochester ME1 .... 47 C5
King St. West Malling ME19 .... 89 C8
King William Rd. ME7 .... 48 C7
King's Ave. ME1 .... 47 C3
King's Bastion. ME7 .... 48 A5
King's Cotts. SE18 .... 104 D6
King's Highway. SE18 & SE2 .... 6 F8
King's Orch. Eltham SE9 .... 5 E1
King's Orch. Rochester ME1 .... 47 C5
King's Rd. Chatham ME5 .... 48 D1
King's Rd. Tunbridge TN9 .... 133 D7
King's Sch. ME1 .... 47 C5
King's Standing Ind Est. TN2 . 133 F2
Kingfisher Apartments.
  ME15 .... 107 E5
Kingfisher Cl. Erith SE28 ...... 3 C6
Kingfisher Cl. St Paul's Cray BR5 38 D5
Kingfisher Cl. TN15 .... 55 E3
Kingfisher Dr. ME5 .... 62 C7
Kingfisher Drive Cty Prim Sch.
  ME5 .... 62 B7
Kingfisher Pl. DA4 .... 41 C7
Kingfisher Rd. ME20 .... 75 A2
Kingfisher St. E6 .... 1 E8
Kings Acre. ME15 .... 93 A1
Kings Ave. BR1 .... 22 A2
Kings Cl. DA8 .... 8 E3
Kings Cotts. Leeds ME17 ..... 108 F6
Kings Cotts. Wilsley Green TN17 169 D6
Kings Ct. TN12 .... 153 A6
Kings Dr. DA12 .... 30 D6
Kings Farm Cty Prim Sch. DA12 30 C3
Kings Hill Ave. ME19 .... 89 A4
Kings La. TN12 .... 137 C2
Kings Pk. TN2 .... 149 D3
Kings Rd. Headcorn TN27 .... 141 C5
Kings Rd. Orpington BR6 ...... 51 F6
Kings Standing Way. TN3 .... 133 F1
Kings Toll Rd. TN12 & TN2 ... 151 A6
Kings Wlk. RM17 .... 12 A8
Kingsand Rd. SE12 .... 22 A6
Kingsdale Cl. Chatham ME5 .... 62 A7
Kingsdale Cl. Swanscombe DA10 11 E1
Kingsdale Rd. SE18 .... 6 E8
Kingsdown Cl. Gillingham ME7 .. 63 B4
Kingsdown Cl. Gravesend DA12 . 30 F7
Kingsdown Cl. Maidstone ME16 . 91 E4
Kingsdown Way. BR2 .... 36 A3
Kingsfield House. ME9 .... 22 D5
Kingsfield Cl. TN15 .... 55 E3
Kingsfingfield Rd. TN15 .... 55 E2
Kingsland Gr. TN27 .... 141 D5
Kingsland La. TN27 .... 127 E1
Kingsley Ave. DA1 .... 10 A2
Kingsley Ct. Bexley DA6 .... 7 E2
Kingsley Ct. Wadhurst TN5 ... 175 A4
Kingsley Ct. Woolwich SE28 ... 3 C5
Kingsley Mews. BR7 .... 23 B2
Kingsley Rd. Maidstone ME15 .. 92 A3
Kingsley Rd. Orpington BR6 .... 51 F3
Kingsley Wood Dr. SE9 .... 22 F5
Kingsman Par. SE18 .... 1 F2
Kingsman St. SE18 .... 1 F2
Kingsmead Cl. DA15 .... 24 A6
Kingsmere. BR7 .... 36 E8
Kingsnorth Cl. BR8 .... 39 C3
Kingsnorth Rd. ME8 .... 49 C4
Kingsridge Gdns. DA1 .... 9 D1
Kingston Cres. ME5 .... 62 C4
Kingston Ct. DA11 .... 12 B1
Kingston Dr. ME15 .... 107 A8
Kingsway. Chatham ME5 .... 48 D1
Kingsway. Gillingham ME7 ..... 48 E8
Kingsway. Orpington BR5 ...... 37 D4
Kingswood Ave. Chatham ME4 .. 47 F2
Kingswood Ave. Erith DA7 ..... 3 F2
Kingswood Ave. Swanley BR8 ... 39 F6
Kingswood Cl. Dartford DA1 .... 9 C1
Kingswood Cl. Orpington BR6 .. 37 D2
Kingswood Cl.
  Royal Tunbridge Wells TN2 .. 149 C3
Kingswood Cty Prim Sch.
  ME17 .... 109 E2
Kimmeridge Gdns. SE9 .... 22 E4

Kingswood Rd. Gillingham ME7 .. 48 D6
Kingswood Rd.
  Kit's Coty ME1 & ME20 ..... 76 D3
Kingswood Rd.
  Royal Tunbridge Wells TN2 . 149 C3
Kingswood Rd. Sevenoaks TN13 83 E7
Kinlet Rd. SE18 .... 6 C6
Kinnings Row. TN9 .... 117 C2
Kinross Cl. ME5 .... 62 B7
Kinveachy Gdns. SE7 .... 1 E1
Kipling Ave. RM18 .... 13 C6
Kipling Dr. ME20 .... 74 F4
Kipling Rd. Bexley DA7 .... 7 E6
Kipling Rd. Dartford DA1 ...... 10 B2
Kippington Cl. TN13 .... 83 F3
Kippington Dr. SE9 .... 22 D7
Kippington Rd. TN13 .... 84 A2
Kirby Cl. TN17 .... 169 D4
Kirby Henry Mews. BR6 .... 51 F5
Kirby Rd. Chattenden ME3 ..... 33 F5
Kirby Rd. Dartford DA2 .... 27 D8
Kirk La. SE18 .... 6 C8
Kirkcourt. TN13 .... 84 A4
Kirkdale Cl. ME5 .... 62 D1
Kirkdale Cotts. ME5 .... 106 F5
Kirkdale Rd. Maidstone ME15 . 106 F5
Kirkdale Rd.
  Royal Tunbridge Wells TN1 . 149 B4
Kirkham Rd. E6 .... 1 E7
Kirklands. SE18 .... 6 E8
Kirkins Cl. TN12 .... 153 A6
Kirkland Cl. DA15 .... 6 E1
Kirkman Cl. TN12 .... 139 E3
Kirkside Rd. SE3 .... 5 A8
Kit Hill Ave. ME5 .... 61 E3
Kit's Coty House. ME20 .... 76 C6
Kitchener Ave. Chatham ME4 ... 48 A1
Kitchener Ave. Gravesend DA12 . 30 C5
Kitchener Cotts. ME3 .... 19 C4
Kitchener Rd. Chattenden ME3 . 33 F4
Kitchener Rd. Rochester ME2 .. 47 A8
Knatts La. TN15 .... 70 E8
Knatts Valley Rd. TN15 .... 55 D1
Knave Wood Rd. TN14 .... 69 E2
Knaves Acre. ME8 .... 247 D5
Knavesacre Ct. ME8 .... 63 D5
Knee Hill. SE2 .... 3 C1
Knee Hill Cres. SE2 .... 3 C1
Knight Ave. ME7 .... 48 D7
Knight Rd. Rochester ME2 ..... 47 A6
Knight Rd. Tonbridge TN10 ... 117 E6
Knight's Ct. DA8 .... 8 F7
Knight's Ridge. TN2 .... 150 D7
Knight's Way. TN27 .... 141 D6
Knighton Rd. TN14 .... 68 F2
Knightrider Ct. ME15 .... 92 A3
Knightrider St. ME15 .... 92 A3
Knights Cl. Hoo St Werburgh ME3 34 E5
Knights Cl. Pembury TN2 ..... 150 D7
Knights Croft. DA3 .... 56 F7
Knights Manor Way. DA1 .... 9 F1
Knights Pk. ME2 .... 47 A6
Knights Rd. Hoo St Werburgh ME3 34 D5
Knights Rd. Newham E16 ...... 1 A4
Knights Ridge. BR6 .... 52 B5
Knightsbridge Cl. TN4 .... 148 F5
Knightsbridge Mews. BR7 ..... 22 F1
Knock Mill La. TN15 .... 71 A5
Knockhall Chase. DA9 .... 11 C2
Knockhall Cty Prim Sch. DA9 .. 11 C2
Knockhall Rd. DA9 .... 11 C2
Knockholt CE Prim Sch. TN14 . 67 B2
Knockholt Rd. Eltham SE9 ...... 5 D2
Knockholt Rd. Halstead TN14 .. 67 F6
Knockholt Sta. TN14 .... 52 E2
Knockhurst Ct. TN30 .... 173 C1
Knockwood Rd. TN30 .... 173 C1
Knole. TN15 .... 84 D1
Knole Cl. TN13 .... 99 B2
Knole Gate. DA15 .... 23 E5
Knole La. TN13 & TN15 .... 84 C1
Knole Park Golf Course. TN15 . 84 D3
Knole Rd. Chatham ME5 .... 62 C3
Knole Rd. Dartford DA1 .... 26 B8
Knole Rd. Sevenoaks TN13 .... 84 D4
Knole The. Eltham SE9 .... 23 A4
Knole The. Istead Rise DA13 ... 29 E1
Knole Way. TN13 .... 84 C2
Knoll Rd. Sidcup DA14 .... 24 B4
Knoll Rd. Stone,Old Bexley DA5 .. 8 A1
Knoll Rise. BR6 .... 37 F1
Knoll The. BR2 .... 36 A1
Knotley Hall Cotts. TN11 .... 115 A2
Knott Ct. TN14 .... 91 F6
Knotts Pl. TN13 .... 84 A3
Knowle Ave. DA7 .... 7 F7
Knowle Cl. TN3 .... 147 F3
Knowle Cotts. TN3 .... 163 E1
Knowle La. TN11 .... 136 C3
Knowle Rd. Castle Hill TN12 . 136 D3
Knowle Rd. Keston Mark BR2 ... 50 E8
Knowle Rd. Maidstone ME14 ... 92 B6
Knowle Rd. Wouldham ME1 ..... 60 D4
Knowles Gdns. TN27 .... 141 D5
Knowles Wlk. TN12 .... 139 F3
Knowlton Gdns. ME8 .... 91 B2
Knowlton Gn. BR2 .... 36 A4
Knowsley Way. TN11 .... 116 D6
Knox Ct. TN15 .... 84 F6
Kydbrook Cl. BR5 .... 37 C2
Kyetop Wlk. ME8 .... 63 D6
Kynaston Rd. Bromley BR1 .... 22 A3
Kynaston Rd. Orpington BR5 ... 38 B2

La Tourne Gdns. BR6 .... 51 C7
Labour-in-Vain Rd. TN15 ...... 71 E5
Laburnham Pl. SE9 .... 6 A2
Laburnum Ave. Dartford DA1 ... 26 D7

Laburnum Ave. Swanley BR8 .... 39 D6
Laburnum Ct. TN1 .... 149 C7
Laburnum Dr. ME20 .... 75 A2
Laburnum Gr. DA11 .... 29 D8
Laburnum Rd. ME2 .... 46 E5
Laburnum Way. BR2 .... 37 B2
Lacebark Cl. DA15 .... 23 F8
Lacey Cl. ME17 .... 108 E4
Laceys La. ME17 .... 122 C7
Ladbrooke Cres. DA14 .... 24 D5
Laddingford CE Prim Sch.
  ME18 .... 120 E4
Laddingford Farm Ind Est.
  ME18 .... 120 D4
Ladds Cnr. ME7 .... 49 B5
Ladds La. ME6 .... 60 A2
Ladds Way. BR8 .... 39 D5
Ladham Rd. TN17 .... 154 A2
Ladies Mile. TN3 .... 160 D4
Lady Amherst's Dr. TN14 ..... 98 A4
Lady Boswell's CE Prim Sch.
  TN15 .... 84 C2
Lady Oak La.
  TN17 & TN18 & TN5 ...... 177 C7
Lady Vane Cl. TN11 .... 101 C5
Ladyclose Ave. ME3 .... 33 A7
Ladycroft Gdns. BR6 .... 51 C5
Ladycroft Way. BR6 .... 51 C5
Ladyfern Cl. TN2 .... 149 C4
Ladyfields. Chatham ME5 ..... 62 C2
Ladyfields. Northfleet DA11 ... 29 F4
Ladysmith Rd. SE9 .... 6 A1
Ladywell House. BR5 .... 38 B7
Ladywood Ave. BR5 .... 37 E4
Ladywood Rd. Cuxton ME2 .... 46 B2
Ladywood Rd. Lane End DA2 ... 27 E3
Lagonda Way. DA1 .... 9 C3
Lagoon Rd. BR5 .... 38 B4
Lake Ave. BR1 .... 22 A2
Lake Dr. ME3 .... 32 C6
Lake Rd. Ditton ME20 .... 90 E8
Lake Rd.
  Royal Tunbridge Wells TN4 . 148 E4
Lake View Rd. TN13 .... 84 A4
Lakedale Rd. SE18 .... 2 E1
Lakelands. Harrietsham ME17 . 110 E6
Lakelands. Maidstone ME15 ... 107 A7
Laker Rd. ME1 .... 61 C6
Lakes Rd. BR2 .... 50 C5
Lakeside.
  Royal Tunbridge Wells TN2 . 149 E6
Lakeside. Snodland ME6 ...... 74 F6
Lakeside Ave. SE28 .... 3 A5
Lakeside Cl. Bough Beech TN8 . 113 F4
Lakeside Cl. Sidcup DA15 ...... 7 C2
Lakeside Dr. BR2 .... 50 E7
Lakeside Pk. ME2 .... 47 E7
Lakeswood Rd. BR5 .... 37 C3
Lakeview Cl. ME6 .... 75 A6
Lakeview Rd. DA16 .... 7 B3
Lakewood Dr. ME8 .... 63 C6
Lamb Cl. RM18 .... 13 C5
Lamb's Cross. ME17 .... 124 A5
Lambard House. ME14 .... 92 A5
Lambarde Ave. SE9 .... 23 A4
Lambarde Cl. ME2 .... 60 A4
Lambarde Dr. TN13 .... 84 A5
Lambarde Rd. TN13 .... 84 A5
Lambardes. DA3 .... 56 F7
Lamberhurst CE Prim Sch.
  TN3 .... 166 B6
Lamberhurst Cl. BR5 .... 38 D1
Lamberhurst Gn. ME8 .... 49 B3
Lamberhurst Golf Course. TN3 166 C5
Lamberhurst Rd.
  Horsmonden TN12 & TN3 ... 152 E3
Lamberhurst Rd. Maidstone
  ME16 .... 91 B7
Lambersart Cl. TN2 & TN4 ... 113 D1
Lambert Ct. DA8 .... 8 C8
Lambert Mews. ME6 .... 75 A8
Lambert Rd. E16 .... 1 B7
Lambert's Yd. TN9 .... 117 B1
Lamberts Rd. TN1 & TN2 .... 149 D8
Lambeth Cl. ME5 .... 62 B4
Lambourn Dr. ME18 & ME19 ... 89 A2
Lambourn Way. Chatham ME5 .. 62 C2
Lambourn Way.
  Royal Tunbridge Wells TN2 . 149 D1
Lambourne Pl. SE3 .... 5 B6
Lambourne Rd. ME15 .... 92 F2
Lambs Bank. TN9 .... 133 B7
Lambscroft Ave. SE12 & SE9 ... 22 D5
Lambsfrith Gr. ME7 .... 63 B3
Lamorbey Cl. DA15 .... 23 F6
Lamorna Ave. DA12 .... 30 D6
Lamorna Cl. BR6 .... 38 A2
Lampington Row. TN3 .... 147 E3
Lamplighters Cl. Dartford DA1 .. 9 F1
Lamplighters Cl. Gillingham ME7 62 F5
Lamport Cl. SE18 .... 1 F2
Lamson Rd. RM13 .... 4 F8
Lancashire Rd. ME15 .... 107 E7
Lancaster Ct. Gillingham ME8 ... 63 F7
Lancaster Ct. Gravesend DA12 .. 30 C5
Lancaster Way. ME19 .... 88 F3
Lance Croft. DA3 .... 56 F8
Lancelot Ave. ME2 .... 46 E7
Lancelot Cl. ME2 .... 46 E6
Lancelot Ct. ME2 .... 52 B8
Lancelot Rd. DA16 .... 7 A4
Lances Cl. DA13 .... 44 A2
Lancet La. ME15 .... 107 A6
Lancey Cl. SE7 .... 1 E2

Lancing Rd. BR6 .... **52** B8
Land Way. ME3 .... **32** D5
Landale Gdns. DA1 .... **26** C8
Landor Ct. ME7 .... **63** A3
Landseer Ave. DA11 .... **29** D5
Landseer Cl. TN10 .... **117** E6
Landstead Rd. SE18 .... **6** D7
Landway. TN15 .... **84** F7
Landway The.
  Borough Green TN15 .... **86** F7
Landway The. Kemsing TN15 ... **70** A2
Landway The. Maidstone ME14 ... **93** A4
Landway The. St Paul's Cray BR5 **38** C6
Lane End. DA7 .... **8** B4
Lane The. SE3 .... **5** A4
Lanes Ave. DA11 .... **30** A5
Laneside. BR7 .... **23** C3
Langafel CE (VC) Prim Sch.
  DA3 .... **43** A6
Langafel Cl. DA3 .... **42** E7
Langbrook Rd. SE3 .... **5** D5
Langdale Cl. Gillingham ME8 ... **49** D1
Langdale Cl. Orpington BR6 ..... **51** B7
Langdale Cres. DA7 .... **8** A6
Langdale Rise. ME1 .... **91** C5
Langdale Wlk. **5** DA11 .... **29** E5
Langdon Rd. Bromley BR2 ...... **36** B6
Langdon Rd. Rochester ME1 .... **47** C4
Langdon Shaw. DA14 .... **23** F3
Langford Pl. DA14 .... **24** A5
Langham Gr. ME16 .... **91** C4
Langholm Rd. TN3 .... **147** F3
Langlands Dr. DA2 .... **27** E3
Langley Gdns. BR5 .... **37** B3
Langley House. BR1 .... **22** B1
Langley Rd. DA16 .... **7** C8
Langmore Ct. DA7 .... **7** D4
Langton Cl. ME14 .... **92** C5
Langton Green Cty Prim Sch.
  TN3 .... **147** E4
Langton Rd. Rusthall TN3 & TN4 **148** C3
Langton Rd. Speldhurst TN3 .... **148** A7
Langton Ridge. TN3 .... **148** B3
Langton Way. SE3 .... **5** B7
Langworth Cl. DA2 .... **26** C5
Lankester Parker Rd. ME1 .... **61** C6
Lannoy Rd. SE9 .... **23** C7
Lanridge Rd. SE2 .... **3** D3
Lansbury Cres. DA1 .... **10** A2
Lansbury Ct. **4** SE28 .... **3** B6
Lansbury Gdns. RM18 .... **13** A6
Lansbury House. **5** DA17 .... **3** F1
Lansdown Rd. Northfleet DA11 ... **29** F7
Lansdown Rd. Sidcup DA14 ..... **24** B5
Lansdown Rd. Tilbury RM18 .... **12** F5
Lansdowne Ave. Bexley DA7 ..... **7** D7
Lansdowne Ave.
  Maidstone ME15 .... **107** C6
Lansdowne Ave. Orpington BR6 ... **37** B1
Lansdowne Ct. **2** ME4 .... **47** F4
Lansdowne La. SE7 .... **1** D1
Lansdowne Mews. SE7 .... **1** D1
Lansdowne Prim Sch. RM18 ... **12** F5
Lansdowne Rd. Bromley BR1 ..... **22** B1
Lansdowne Rd. Chatham ME4 ... **47** E2
Lansdowne Rd. Royal Tunbridge Wells
  TN1 & TN2 .... **149** B4
Lansdowne Rd. Sevenoaks TN13 **84** D5
Lansdowne Rd. Tonbridge TN9 . **117** B2
Lansdowne Sq. Northfleet DA11 . **12** F1
Lansdowne Sq. **8**
  Royal Tunbridge Wells TN1 .. **149** B4
Lapins La. ME18 .... **88** F2
Lapis Cl. DA12 .... **31** B7
Lapwing Cl. DA8 .... **9** B7
Lapwing Rd. ME3 .... **21** B5
Lapwings. DA3 .... **43** B6
Lapwings The. DA12 .... **30** D6
Lapworth Cl. BR6 .... **52** C8
Larch Cl. ME20 .... **75** B2
Larch Cres. Hoo St Werburgh ME3 **34** E3
Larch Cres. Tonbridge TN10 ... **117** C6
Larch Dene. BR6 .... **51** A8
Larch Gr. Paddock Wood TN12 ... **135** F6
Larch Gr. Sidcup DA15 .... **23** F7
Larch Rd. DA1 .... **26** D7
Larch Way. BR2 .... **37** A2
Larch Wlk. BR8 .... **39** D7
Larch Wood Cl. ME5 .... **62** D1
Larchcroft. ME5 .... **62** A4
Larches The. ME3 .... **32** C3
Larchwood Rd. SE9 .... **23** B6
Larkfield. TN12 .... **135** A7
Larkfield Ave. ME7 .... **48** E4
Larkfield Brookfield Cty Prim Schs.
  ME20 .... **75** A2
Larkfield Cl. Hayes BR2 .... **50** A8
Larkfield Cl. Larkfield ME20 .... **75** A1
Larkfield Rd. Larkfield ME20 ... **75** B1
Larkfield Rd. Sevenoaks TN13 ... **83** C4
Larkfield Rd. Sidcup DA14 .... **23** F5
Larkfield Trad Est. ME20 .... **75** B5
Larkfields. DA11 .... **29** E5
Larkin Cl. ME2 .... **33** B2
Larks Field. DA3 .... **42** F5
Larkspur Cl. East Malling ME19 . **75** A1
Larkspur Cl. **4** Newham E16 ..... **1** E8
Larkspur Cl. Orpington BR6 ...... **52** C7
Larkspur Rd. Chatham ME5 ..... **61** E4
Larkspur Rd. East Malling ME19 . **74** F1
Larkstore Pk. TN12 .... **139** E5
Larkswood Cl. DA8 .... **9** A6
Larkwell La. DA3 .... **42** F5
Larner Rd. DA8 .... **8** E7

Laser Quay. ME2 .... **47** D6
Lashenden Air Warfare Mus.
  TN27 .... **142** A2
Lassa Rd. SE9 .... **5** F2
Latham Cl. E6 .... **1** E7
Latham Rd. DA6 .... **8** A2
Latimer Pl. **3** ME7 .... **48** C7
Latona Dr. DA12 .... **30** F3
Latymers. TN11 .... **131** B4
Launcelot Prim Sch. BR1 .... **22** A4
Launcelot Rd. BR1 & SE12 ...... **22** A4
Launder Way. ME15 .... **91** E2
Laura Dr. BR8 .... **26** A1
Laurel Ave. DA12 .... **30** C6
Laurel Bank.
  Royal Tunbridge Wells TN4 .. **149** B8
Laurel Bank. Wadhurst TN5 .... **175** A4
Laurel Cl. Dartford DA1 .... **26** C7
Laurel Cl. Sidcup DA14 .... **24** A5
Laurel Gr. Gillingham ME7 ...... **48** C7
Laurel Rd.
  Royal Tunbridge Wells TN1 .. **149** D7
Laurel Way. TN1 .... **149** D7
Laurel Wlk. ME8 .... **63** E6
Laurels The. Bromley BR2 .... **36** A5
Laurels The. **8**
  Bromley,Widmore BR1 .... **36** B8
Laurels The. Maidstone ME16 .. **91** C2
Laurels The. New Barn DA3 ..... **43** D6
Laurels The. Wilmington DA2 ... **26** C5
Laurie Gray Ave. ME5 .... **61** D1
Lavenda Cl. ME7 .... **63** A4
Lavender Cl. Bromley BR2 .... **36** E3
Lavender Cl. **1** Chatham ME5 ... **61** E4
Lavender Cl. East Malling ME19 . **89** F8
Lavender Gdns. TN5 .... **176** E1
Lavender Hill. Swanley BR8 ..... **39** D6
Lavender Hill. Tonbridge TN9 ... **133** C8
Lavender Rd. ME19 .... **89** F8
Lavender Sq. **6** TN18 .... **179** A2
Lavenders Rd. ME19 .... **89** C6
Lavernock Rd. DA7 .... **8** A5
Laverstoke Rd. ME16 .... **91** C8
Lavidge Rd. SE9 .... **22** F6
Lavinia Rd. **1** DA1 .... **9** F1
Lavisham House. BR1 .... **22** B3
Lawford Gdns. DA1 .... **9** C2
Lawn Cl. Bromley BR1 .... **22** B1
Lawn Cl. Chatham ME4 .... **48** B2
Lawn Cl. Swanley BR8 .... **39** C7
Lawn Cl. Tenterden TN30 .... **182** F7
Lawn Cty Prim Sch. DA11 ...... **12** C1
Lawn Pk. TN13 .... **99** B8
Lawn Rd. Northfleet DA11 .... **12** C1
Lawn Rd. Tonbridge TN9 .... **133** B8
Lawns Cres. RM17 .... **12** D8
Lawns The. Brenchley TN12 .... **152** B8
Lawns The. Sidcup DA14 .... **24** B4
Lawrance Sq. DA11 .... **29** F5
Lawrence Cl. ME15 .... **107** A7
Lawrence Dr. DA12 .... **45** A5
Lawrence Gdns. RM18 .... **13** B7
Lawrence Hill Gdns. DA1 .... **9** C1
Lawrence Hill Rd. DA1 .... **9** C1
Lawrence Rd. Erith DA8 .... **8** B7
Lawrence Rd. Hayes BR4 .... **50** A6
Lawrence Rd. Tonbridge TN10 . **117** C6
Lawrence St. ME7 .... **48** C5
Lawson Cl. E16 .... **1** C8
Lawson Gdns. DA1 .... **9** D3
Lawson House. **1** SE18 .... **6** A8
Lawson Rd. DA1 .... **9** D3
Laxey Rd. BR6 .... **51** F4
Laxey The. ME15 .... **91** E1
Laxton Cl. ME15 .... **92** F3
Laxton Dr. ME17 .... **108** A1
Laxton Gdns. TN12 .... **135** E7
Layfield House. **1** SE10 .... **1** A1
Layfield Rd. ME7 .... **48** F7
Layhams Rd. BR2 .... **50** A3
Laymarsh Cl. DA17 .... **3** F3
Layzell Wlk. SE9 .... **22** D7
Le May Ave. SE12 .... **22** B5
Le Temple Rd. TN12 .... **136** B6
Lea Ct. ME14 .... **47** E1
Lea Rd. TN13 .... **99** C8
Lea Vale. DA1 & DA7 .... **8** D3
Leafield La. DA14 .... **24** F5
Leafy Glade. ME8 .... **63** B6
Leafy Gr. BR2 .... **50** C5
Leafy La. DA13 .... **58** A3
Leafy Oak Rd. SE12 .... **22** C5
Lealands Ave. TN11 .... **116** A1
Lealands Cl. TN3 .... **161** C6
Leamington Ave. Bromley BR1 ... **22** C3
Leamington Ave. Orpington BR6 **51** E2
Leamington Cl. BR1 .... **22** C3
Leamouth Rd. E6 .... **1** E8
Leander Dr. DA12 .... **30** F4
Leander Rd. ME1 .... **61** C7
Learoyd Gdns. E6 .... **2** A6
Leas Dale. SE9 .... **23** A5
Leas Gn. BR7 .... **23** F2
Leas The. Turner's Green TN5 ... **175** A6
Leas The. Woolwich SE18 .... **6** B6
Leatherbottle Gn. DA18 .... **3** F3
Leaves Green Rd. BR2 .... **50** D1
Lebrun Sq. SE3 .... **5** B4
Leckwith Ave. DA17 .... **7** E8
Leclair House. SE3 .... **5** B4
Leconfield Cl. TN9 .... **132** F7
Leda Rd. SE18 .... **1** F3
Lee Gn. BR5 .... **38** A4
Lee Green Rd. ME3 .... **33** D4
Lee Rd. ME6 .... **75** D4
Lee Sta. SE12 .... **5** A1
Leechcroft Ave. Sidcup DA15 .... **6** F2

Leechcroft Ave. Swanley BR8 ... **39** F6
Leeds & Broomfield CE Prim Sch.
  ME17 .... **109** A7
Leeds Castle. ME17 .... **109** D7
Leeds Cl. BR6 .... **52** D8
Leeds House. ME2 .... **33** C1
Leeds Rd. ME17 .... **108** E3
Leeds Sq. ME8 .... **49** B3
Lees Rd. ME18 .... **120** E7
Leesons Hill. BR5 & BR7 .... **38** A6
Leesons Prim Sch. BR5 .... **38** B6
Leesons Way. BR5 .... **37** F7
Leet Cl. ME7 .... **48** E6
Leeward Rd. ME1 .... **47** C1
Leewood Cl. SE12 .... **5** A1
Leewood Pl. BR8 .... **39** D5
Legatt Rd. SE9 .... **5** D2
Legge La. ME19 .... **74** D6
Leggs' La. TN3 .... **147** E5
Leghorn Rd. SE18 .... **2** D1
Leicester Dr. TN2 .... **162** E8
Leicester Rd. Maidstone ME15 . **107** D7
Leicester Rd. Tilbury RM18 ...... **12** F6
Leigh Ave. ME15 .... **107** B6
Leigh City Tech Coll The. DA1 . **27** A7
Leigh Cty Prim Sch. TN11 ..... **115** F1
Leigh Green Ind Est. TN30 .... **183** E6
Leigh Halt. TN11 .... **115** F1
Leigh Pl. DA16 .... **7** A5
Leigh Rd. Gravesend DA11 ...... **30** B6
Leigh Rd. Powder Mills TN11 ... **116** D3
Leigh Terr. **2** St Paul's Cray BR5 **38** B6
Leigh Terr. Teston ME18 .... **90** A1
Leighton Cl. TN4 .... **149** A7
Leighton Gdns. ME16 .... **13** A7
Leila Parnell Pl. **14** SE7 .... **5** C8
Leith Hill. BR5 .... **38** A8
Leith Hill Gn. BR5 .... **38** A8
Leith Park Rd. DA11 & DA12 .... **30** B7
Lelland House. **8** SE7 .... **1** E2
Lemonwell Ct. SE9 .... **6** C2
Lemonwell Dr. SE9 .... **6** C2
Len Clifton House. **13** SE18 ...... **1** F2
Len Valley Wlk. ME15 .... **92** F1
Lenderyou Ct. DA1 .... **26** E8
Lendon Rd. TN15 .... **86** F6
Leneda Dr. TN2 .... **162** E8
Leney Rd. ME18 .... **104** E7
Lenfield Ave. ME14 .... **92** B4
Lenham Cty Prim Sch. ME17 ... **111** C5
Lenham Heath Rd. ME17 .... **111** C2
Lenham Rd. Lenham ME17 .... **111** E5
Lenham House. **13**
  Orpington BR5 .... **38** D1
Lenham Rd.
  Broadstone TN27 & ME17 ... **126** D3
Lenham Rd. Erith DA7 .... **7** F8
Lenham Rd.
  Fairbourne Heath ME17 ..... **110** C1
Lenham Rd. Headcorn TN27 ... **141** E6
Lenham Sta. ME17 .... **111** C4
Lenham Way. ME8 .... **49** A3
Lennard Rd. Keston Mark BR2 ... **36** F1
Lennard Rd. Sevenoaks TN13 ... **83** E7
Lennox Ave. DA11 .... **13** A1
Lennox House. **6** DA17 .... **4** A3
Lennox Rd. DA11 .... **29** F8
Lennox Rd E. DA11 .... **30** A8
Lenor Cl. DA6 .... **7** E3
Lensbury Way. SE2 .... **3** D3
Lenside Dr. ME15 .... **93** A2
Lenton St. SE18 .... **2** D2
Leonard Ave. Otford TN14 ...... **69** B3
Leonard Ave. Swanscombe DA10 **28** E8
Leonard Cl. ME16 .... **91** B6
Leonard Judge House. DA2 .... **27** E3
Leonard Robbins Path. **3** SE28 . **3** B6
Leonard St. E16 .... **1** E5
Leopold Rd. **2** ME4 .... **48** A3
Lesley Cl. Istead Rise DA13 ...... **43** F8
Lesley Cl. Sidcup DA5 .... **25** B8
Lesley Cl. Swanley BR8 .... **39** D6
Lesley Tew Ct. TN10 .... **117** C5
Leslie Cres. TN30 .... **173** B2
Leslie Pl. ME16 .... **91** E5
Leslie Rd. Gillingham ME7 ...... **48** D7
Leslie Rd. Newham E16 .... **1** B7
Leslie Smith Sq. **7** SE18 .... **6** A8
Lesnes Abbey (remains of). SE2 . **3** C2
Lesney Park Prim Sch. DA8 ...... **8** D8
Lesney Park Rd. DA8 .... **8** D8
Lesney Pk. DA8 .... **8** D8
Lessness Ave. DA7 .... **7** D7
Lessness Heath Prim Sch. DA17 . **4** A1
Lessness Pk. DA17 .... **4** A1
Lessness Rd. **11** DA17 .... **4** A1
Lested La. ME17 .... **108** B2
Lester Rd. ME4 .... **48** A3
Lestock House. SE3 .... **5** D6
Letchford Ave. ME4 .... **47** F1
Letchworth Cl. BR2 .... **36** A4
Letchworth Dr. BR2 .... **36** A4
Letter Box La. TN13 .... **99** C6
Leverholme Gdns. SE9 .... **23** A4
Levett Cl. ME3 .... **21** B6
Levetts La. TN32 .... **185** D1
Lewes Cl. RM17 .... **12** A8
Lewes Rd. BR1 .... **36** D7
Lewin Rd. DA6 .... **7** E3
Lewing Cl. BR6 .... **37** E1
Lewis Ave. ME8 .... **49** B2
Lewis Court Dr. ME17 .... **107** C3
Lewis Cl. DA11 .... **29** F6
Lewis King House. BR1 .... **22** B1
Lewis Rd. Bexley DA16 .... **7** C4
Lewis Rd. Istead Rise DA13 .... **43** F8

Lewis Rd. Sidcup DA14 .... **24** C5
Lewis Rd. Swanscombe DA10 ... **11** E1
Lewisham Rd. TN11 .... **116** F6
Leybourne CE (VA) Prim Sch.
  ME19 .... **74** E2
Leybourne Cl. Chatham ME5 ... **62** A2
Leybourne Cl. Hayes BR2 .... **36** A3
Leybourne Dell. TN17 .... **180** E6
Leybourne Rd. ME2 .... **46** F8
Leybourne Way. ME20 .... **74** F4
Leybridge Ct. SE12 .... **5** A2
Leyburn House. SE18 .... **5** E7
Leycroft Gdns. DA8 .... **9** B6
Leydenhatch La. BR8 .... **39** D8
Leyes Rd. E16 .... **1** D7
Leyhill Cl. BR8 .... **39** E4
Leyland Rd. SE12 .... **5** A2
Leysdown Ave. DA7 .... **8** C3
Leysdown Rd. SE9 .... **22** F6
Leyton Ave. ME7 .... **48** E1
Leyton Cross. DA2 .... **26** A6
Leyton Cross Rd. DA2 .... **25** F5
Leywood Rd. DA13 .... **58** D3
Lezayre Rd. BR6 .... **51** F4
Libya Terr. **6** ME14 .... **92** A7
Lichdale Cl. **7** BR6 .... **51** F6
Lichfield Cl. ME8 .... **49** D2
Liddon Rd. BR1 .... **36** D6
Lidsing Rd. ME14 .... **77** E6
Lidwells La. TN17 .... **153** E1
Lieth Park Rd. DA12 .... **30** C7
Liffler Rd. SE18 .... **2** E1
Lightfoot Gn. TN18 .... **178** E3
Lila Pl. BR8 .... **39** E5
Lilac Cres. ME2 .... **46** E6
Lilac Gdns. BR8 .... **39** D6
Lilac Pl. DA13 .... **44** B2
Lilac Rd. ME2 .... **46** E5
Lilburne Gdns. SE9 .... **5** E2
Lilburne Rd. SE9 .... **5** E2
Lilian Barker Cl. SE12 .... **5** A2
Lilk Hill. ME14 .... **93** C3
Lillechurch Rd. ME3 .... **32** F7
Lillesden Cotts. TN18 .... **184** E8
Lillieburn. ME19 .... **74** D2
Limavady House. **18** SE18 .... **2** A2
Lime Ave. DA11 .... **29** D8
Lime Cl. Bromley BR1 .... **36** E5
Lime Cl. Frant TN3 .... **163** B3
Lime Cl. Marden TN12 .... **138** C6
Lime Cotts. TN12 .... **139** F3
Lime Cres. ME19 .... **90** A7
Lime Ct. ME8 .... **63** C3
Lime Gr. Orpington BR6 .... **51** B8
Lime Gr. Sidcup DA15 .... **6** F1
Lime Hill Rd. TN1 .... **149** A4
Lime Kiln Dr. SE7 .... **5** B8
Lime Pit La. TN14 .... **68** C2
Lime Row. DA18 .... **3** F3
Lime Tree Cl. TN9 .... **117** C2
Lime Tree Wlk. TN13 .... **84** B2
Limepits Cross. ME9 .... **65** F3
Limes Cl. TN30 .... **183** C8
Limes Gr. TN18 .... **178** F5
Limes The. DA7 .... **51** B5
Limes The. Edenbridge TN8 .... **112** C1
Limes The. Frittenden TN17 ... **156** E6
Limes The. Keston Mark BR2 ... **50** E8
Limes The. Lenham ME17 ...... **111** D5
Limetree Cl. ME5 .... **62** B8
Limetree Terr. ME17 .... **111** E6
Limewood Rd. DA8 .... **8** C7
Linchmere Rd. SE12 .... **22** A8
Lincln Cl. DA8 .... **8** E7
Lincoln Cl. DA8 .... **46** D6
Lincoln Cl. SE12 .... **22** C5
Lincoln Green Rd. BR5 .... **37** F4
Lincoln Rd. Erith DA8 .... **8** F4
Lincoln Rd. Sidcup DA14 .... **24** B3
Lincoln Rd. Maidstone ME15 ... **107** D8
Lincolnshire Terr. DA2 .... **27** D4
Lincon Rd. ME7 .... **48** D7
Linden Ave. ME17 .... **106** C7
Linden Chase Rd. TN13 .... **84** B5
Linden Cl. Orpington BR6 .... **52** A5
Linden Cl. Paddock Wood TN12 . **136** A6
Linden Cl. Purfleet RM16 .... **10** C8
Linden Cl.
  Royal Tunbridge Wells TN2 .. **149** A2
Linden Ct. Sidcup DA14 .... **23** E4
Linden Ct. Tonbridge TN10 .... **117** B7
Linden Gdns. ME2 .... **33** D3
Linden House. **5** ME5 .... **61** F4
Linden Park Rd. TN2 .... **149** A2
Linden Rd. Coxheath ME17 .... **106** C4
Linden Rd. Gillingham ME7 ..... **48** E5
Linden Sq. TN13 .... **83** E5
Lindenfield. BR7 .... **37** B7
Lindens The. ME20 .... **75** E1
Lindisfarne Cl. DA12 .... **30** E6
Lindridge La. TN12 .... **139** C5
Lindsay House. **2** SE18 .... **2** A2
Lindsey Cl. BR1 .... **36** E6
Lindwood Cl. **8** E6 .... **1** E8
Lineacre Cl. ME8 .... **63** D6
Lines Terr. ME4 .... **48** A4
Ling Rd. Erith DA8 .... **8** C8
Ling Rd. Newham E16 .... **1** A8
Lingey Cl. DA15 .... **23** F6
Lingfield Ave. DA12 .... **27** C6
Lingfield Cres. SE9 .... **6** D3
Lingfield Rd. Borough Green TN15 **87** B7
Lingfield Rd. Edenbridge TN8 . **128** A8
Lingfield Rd. Gravesend DA12 ... **30** B6
Lingley Dr. ME2 .... **33** C2
Lingwood. DA7 .... **8** B5

Link Hill La. TN27 .... **127** B11
Link The. Eltham SE9 .... **23** A5
Link The. New Ash Green DA3 ... **56** F8
Link Way. Bromley BR2 .... **36** E2
Link Way.
  Royal Tunbridge Wells TN2 .. **149** E8
Linkden Cotts. TN18 .... **186** E5
Links The. Addington ME19 .... **73** E2
Links The. Chatham ME5 .... **62** B8
Links View. Dartford DA1 .... **26** C7
Links View. Woolwich SE18 ...... **6** B6
Linkway. ME20 .... **75** C1
Linley Cl. RM18 .... **14** D7
Linnet Ave. TN12 .... **136** A5
Linnet Cl. SE28 .... **3** C6
Linslade Rd. BR6 .... **52** A4
Linsted Ct. SE9 & DA15 .... **6** E1
Linton Cl. Bexley DA16 .... **7** B6
Linton Cl. **2** Greenwich SE7 .... **1** C1
Linton Dann Cl. ME3 .... **34** D6
Linton Gdns. E6 .... **1** E7
Linton Gore. ME17 .... **106** D3
Linton Hill. TN12 .... **122** F6
Linton Hospl. ME17 .... **106** C2
Linton Mead Prim Sch. SE28 .... **3** B6
Linton Rd. ME15 .... **106** F4
Lintorn Symonds Rd. ME3 ...... **33** F5
Linwood Ave. ME2 .... **46** E8
Lion Rd. Bexley DA6 .... **7** F3
Lion Rd. Newham E6 .... **1** F8
Lionel Gdns. SE9 .... **5** D2
Lionel Oxley House. **5** RM17 ... **12** B8
Lionel Rd. Eltham SE9 .... **5** D2
Lionel Rd. Tonbridge TN9 ..... **133** A8
Lions Cl. SE12 .... **22** D5
Liphook Way. ME16 .... **91** C8
Lipscombe Rd. TN2 .... **149** D6
Lipton Cl. SE28 .... **3** C6
Liptraps La. TN1 & TN2 .... **149** D7
Liscard Cl. BR7 .... **23** C2
Liskeard Gdns. SE3 .... **5** A6
Lisle Cl. DA12 .... **31** B6
Lismore Cl. ME15 .... **107** A7
Lister Cl. ME19 .... **89** F8
Lister House. SE2 .... **3** D1
Lister Rd. RM18 .... **13** A5
Lister Wlk. SE28 .... **3** D6
Listmas Rd. ME4 .... **48** B3
Little Alley. TN8 .... **128** B5
Little Bayham Cotts. TN3 .... **164** F4
Little Birches. DA15 .... **23** E6
Little Boundes Cl. TN4 .... **132** F3
Little Browns La. TN8 .... **112** A4
Little Buckland Ave. ME16 ..... **91** D6
Little Cl. ME16 .... **91** D2
Little Footway. TN3 .... **147** F3
Little Heath. SE7 .... **1** E1
Little Heath Rd. DA7 .... **7** F7
Little Hill. TN30 .... **173** B2
Little Iridge Farm Cotts. TN19 . **184** C1
Little Job's Cross. TN17 .... **181** F1
Little John Ave. ME5 .... **61** F2
Little Julians Hill. TN13 .... **99** B8
Little Kit's Coty House. ME20 ... **76** C5
Little Mallett. TN3 .... **147** F3
Little Market Row. ME19 .... **74** E2
Little Mount Sion. TN1 .... **149** A2
Little Oakham Ct. ME3 .... **19** C4
Little Orch. ME17 .... **106** D3
Little Oxley. ME20 .... **74** E2
Little Pk. TN5 .... **174** E5
Little Queen St. DA1 .... **26** F8
Little Redlands. BR1 .... **36** E7
Little Sheephurst Cotts. TN12 . **137** E5
Little Thrift. BR5 .... **37** C5
Little Wood. TN13 .... **84** D5
Littlebourne Ave. ME8 .... **49** B4
Littlebourne Rd. ME14 .... **92** C6
Littlebrook Manor Way. DA1 ... **10** A2
Littlecombe. SE7 .... **5** B8
Littlecourt Rd. TN13 .... **84** A3
Littlecroft. Eltham SE9 .... **6** A4
Littlecroft. Istead Rise DA13 ... **29** E1
Littledale. Darenth DA2 .... **27** C5
Littledale. Woolwich SE2 .... **7** A8
Littlefield. TN11 .... **118** E8
Littlejohn Rd. BR5 .... **38** B4
Littlemede. SE9 .... **22** F5
Littlemore Rd. SE2 .... **3** A4
Livesey St. ME18 .... **90** A1
Livingstone Circ. ME7 .... **48** D5
Livingstone Gdns. DA12 .... **30** D3
Livingstone Hospl. DA1 .... **26** E8
Livingstone Rd. Gillingham ME7 . **48** E5
Livingstone Rd. Gravesend DA12 **30** D3
Livingstone Wlk. **4** ME15 ..... **107** F5
Lizban St. SE3 .... **5** B7
Llanover Rd. SE18 .... **6** A7
Lloyd House. **10** SE18 .... **1** F2
Lloyds Gn. TN30 .... **189** D4
Loaland Bsns Ctr. ME2 .... **47** D8
Loam Ct. DA1 .... **26** E7
Loampits Cl. TN9 .... **117** D3
Lobelia Cl. Gillingham ME7 ..... **48** E6
Lobelia Cl. **5** Newham E6 .... **1** E8
Locarno Ave. ME8 .... **49** A2
Lochat Rd. ME3 .... **33** E6
Lochmere Cl. DA8 .... **8** B8
Lock La. ME14 & ME16 .... **76** D1
Lock St. ME7 .... **48** C5
Lock's Yd. TN15 .... **84** C2
Locksley Dr. BR5 .... **38** A3
Lockington Cl. TN9 .... **132** F7
Lockington Gr. ME1 .... **47** C5
Locknut Cotts. DA13 .... **57** E2
Lockside. TN9 .... **117** C2
Locksley Cl. ME5 .... **61** E2

Lockswood. ME16 91 D7
Lockyer Rd. RM16 10 C8
Lockyers Hill. DA13 58 F5
Lodden Ct. 15 BR5 38 D1
Loddington La. ME17 123 A8
Loder Cl. ME17 111 B5
Lodge Ave. DA1 9 C1
Lodge Cl. Orpington BR6 38 B1
Lodge Cl. Wateringbury ME18 104 D8
Lodge Cres. BR6 38 B1
Lodge Ct. DA12 31 E2
Lodge Gdns. ME17 125 F6
Lodge Hill. DA16 7 B7
Lodge Hill La. ME3 33 F7
Lodge La. Cobham DA12 45 B5
Lodge La. Sidcup DA5 7 D1
Lodge La. Westerham TN16 96 C8
Lodge Oak La. TN9 133 D8
Lodge Rd. Bromley BR1 22 C1
Lodge Rd. Maidstone ME14 92 D5
Lodge Rd. Staplehurst TN12 139 E5
Lodge Rd. Tonbridge TN9 117 B2
Lodgewood Cotts. TN8 113 D2
Logs Hill. BR1 & BR7 36 E8
Logs Hill Cl. BR7 36 E8
Lomaria Ct. TN2 149 C4
Lomas La. TN18 186 F5
Lombard St. DA4 41 C5
Lombard Trad Est. SE7 1 B2
Lombard Wall. SE7 1 B2
Lombardy Cl. ME7 63 A6
Lombardy Dr. ME14 92 C5
London City Airport. E16 1 E5
London Golf Course. TN15 56 D4
London Ind Pk The. E6 2 A8
London La. Bromley BR1 22 A1
London La.
Cranbrook Common TN17 156 A2
London Rd. Addington ME19 73 D2
London Rd. Bidborough TN4 132 F3
London Rd. Bromley BR1 36 A8
London Rd. Crayford DA1 8 D2
London Rd. Ditton ME20 75 C1
London Rd. Farningham DA4 40 D3
London Rd. Flimwell TN5 177 D3
London Rd. Gillingham ME8 49 C1
London Rd. Grays RM17 & RM16 11 E8
London Rd.
Hartlip Hill ME8 & ME9 64 D7
London Rd. Hurst Green TN19 184 A3
London Rd. Knockholt Pound TN14 67 E4
London Rd. Maidstone ME16 91 C6
London Rd. Maypole BR6 & TN14 52 F2
London Rd. Newington ME9 65 A6
London Rd. Northfleet DA11 12 E1
London Rd. Rochester ME2 47 A7
London Rd.
Royal Tunbridge Wells,Mount Sion
TN1 & TN2 & TN4 149 A3
London Rd. Sevenoaks TN13 84 B2
London Rd.
Sevenoaks,Dunton Green TN13 83 E7
London Rd. Shepham Heath TN14 68 C6
London Rd. Swanley BR8 39 E6
London Rd.
Swanley,White Oak BR8 39 D7
London Rd. Swanscombe DA9 11 C2
London Rd. Tilbury RM18 13 B5
London Rd.
Tonbridge TN10 & TN11 117 B3
London Rd. Twitton TN13 & TN14 68 D1
London Rd.Watt's Cross
TN11 & TN13 & TN15 116 B7
London Rd. West Kingsdown TN15 56 A1
London Rd. Westerham TN16 81 D3
London Rd. Wrotham TN15 72 B3
London Rd. Wrotham Heath TN15 72 F1
London Rd E. ME20 90 F8
London Road Purfleet. RM16 10 C8
London Road West Thurrock.
RM16 11 A8
Londonderry Par. DA8 8 D7
Lonewood Way. TN11 102 F2
Long Acre. BR5 & BR6 52 D8
Long Barn Rd. TN14 99 B2
Long Catlis Rd. ME8 63 D4
Long La. Bexley DA7 7 E6
Long La. Rabbit's Cross ME17 123 D5
Long Mark Rd. 5 E16 1 D8
Long Mead Cty Prim Sch.
TN10 117 B5
Long Mead Way. TN10 117 B4
Long Meads. TN3 & TN4 148 B4
Long Mill La. Crouch TN15 87 B3
Long Mill La. Platt TN15 87 C7
Long Rede La. ME16 90 F3
Long Slip. TN3 148 A3
Long Wlk. SE18 6 B8
Longbury Cl. BR5 38 B6
Longbury Dr. BR5 38 B7
Longcroft. SE9 23 A5
Longdon Wood. BR2 50 E6
Longfellow Rd. ME7 48 C3
Longfield. TN30 183 A6
Longfield Ave.
High Halstow ME23 17 E4
Longfield Ave. New Barn DA3 43 D7
Longfield Pl. ME15 107 C8
Longfield Rd.
Meopham Station DA13 43 E3
Longfield Rd.Royal Tunbridge Wells
TN1 & TN2 & TN11 133 E1
Longfield Sta. DA3 42 E6
Longfields Dr. ME14 93 A5
Longford Cl. ME8 64 A8
Longford Ct. ME8 64 A8
Longham Copse. ME15 92 F1
Longhill Ave. ME7 48 B3
Longhurst Dr. ME5 61 F2
Longlands Ct. DA15 23 F5
Longlands Park Cres. DA15 23 E6
Longlands Prim Sch. DA15 23 E5
Longlands Rd. DA15 23 F5
Longleat Villas. 3 DA6 7 E3
Longleigh La. SE2 7 C8
Longley Rd. Gillingham ME8 49 F1
Longley Rd. Rochester ME1 47 C4
Longmarsh View. DA4 41 B8
Longmead. BR7 37 A7
Longmead Dr. DA14 24 D6
Longmeadow Rd. DA15 23 E7
Longparish Cl. ME15 107 F6
Longreach Rd. DA8 9 B7
Longshaw Rd. ME15 107 F5
Longspring Wood. TN13 99 A6
Longten's Cotts. DA12 31 E6
Longtown Ct. 7 DA2 10 B1
Longview Way. TN1 149 D7
Longwalk. DA13 43 E8
Longwood. ME5 62 B1
Longworth Cl. SE28 3 D7
Lonsdale Cl. SE12 & SE9 22 D5
Lonsdale Cres. DA2 27 C7
Lonsdale Dr. ME8 63 E7
Lonsdale Gdns. TN1 & TN2 149 A3
Lonsdale Rd. DA7 7 F5
Loop Rd. BR7 23 C2
Loose Cty Prim Sch. ME15 107 A6
Loose Rd. ME15 107 A7
Loraine Ct. BR7 23 B3
Lord Chatham's Ride. TN14 67 D2
Lord Roberts Terr. SE18 2 A1
Lord Romney's Hill. ME14 92 F3
Lord St. Gravesend DA11 30 B8
Lord St. Newham E16 1 E5
Lord Warwick St. SE18 1 F3
Lords Wood Cl. ME5 62 B2
Lords Wood La. ME5 62 B3
Lordswood Cl. DA2 27 E4
Lordswood Cty Prim Sch. ME5 62 B3
Lordswood Ind Est. ME5 77 C8
Lorenden Pk. TN18 178 F1
Lorimar Bsns Ctr. RM13 4 E8
Lorton Cl. DA12 30 E6
Lossenham La. TN18 187 D3
Louisville Ave. ME7 48 D4
Louvain Rd. DA2 27 E8
Lovage App. E6 1 E8
Love La. East End TN27 142 B5
Love La. East Tilbury RM18 14 C8
Love La. Rochester ME1 47 C5
Love La. Sidcup DA5 8 A1
Love La. Wateringbury ME18 104 D7
Love La. Woolwich SE18 2 B2
Lovel Ave. DA16 7 A5
Lovelace Ave. BR2 37 A3
Lovelace Cl. Gillingham ME8 63 D4
Lovelace Cl.
West Kingsdown TN15 55 E4
Lovelace Gn. SE9 5 F4
Lover's La. DA9 11 D3
Lovers La. TN17 153 F1
Lovibonds Ave. BR6 51 B7
Low Cl. DA9 11 A2
Low Meadow. ME2 60 B5
Low Street La. RM18 13 F8
Lowe Ave. E16 1 A8
Lower Bell La. ME20 75 B2
Lower Boxley Rd. 8 ME14 92 A5
Lower Camden. BR7 36 F8
Lower Church Hill. DA9 10 E2
Lower Croft. BR8 39 F5
Lower East Rd. ME4 48 B8
Lower Fant Rd. ME16 91 D2
Lower Farm Rd. ME17 123 D5
Lower Gn. TN11 115 F1
Lower Gravel Rd. BR2 36 F1
Lower Green Rd. Pembury TN2 150 D7
Lower Green Rd.
Rusthall TN3 & TN4 148 C6
Lower Hartlip Rd. ME9 64 E5
Lower Haysden La.
TN11 & TN4 & TN9 132 D8
Lower Hazelhurst. TN5 176 A4
Lower High St. TN5 175 A4
Lower Higham Rd. DA12 31 B7
Lower Park Rd. DA17 4 A2
Lower Platts. TN5 176 F1
Lower Rainham Rd. ME7 49 D5
Lower Range Rd. DA12 30 E8
Lower Rd. Erith DA8 4 D2
Lower Rd. Erith,Belvedere DA17 4 B3
Lower Rd. Hextable BR8 26 B1
Lower Rd.
Lower Higham DA12 & ME3 32 B6
Lower Rd. Maidstone ME15 92 B3
Lower Rd. Northfleet DA11 12 A3
Lower Rd. Orpington BR5 & BR6 38 B3
Lower Rd. Sutton Valence ME17 124 E7
Lower Rd. Tilbury RM18 13 A3
Lower Rd. West Farleigh ME15 105 D7
Lower Rochester Rd. ME3 32 E6
Lower St. Leeds ME17 109 A7
Lower St. Stocks Green TN11 115 F5
Lower Station Rd. DA1 8 E1
Lower Stone St. ME15 92 A3
Lower Tovil. ME15 91 E2
Lower Twydall La. ME7 & ME8 49 C4
Lower Warren Rd. ME5 & ME14 76 E6
Lower Woodlands Rd. ME7 49 A6
Lowfield St. DA1 26 E8
Lownds Ct. BR1 36 A7
Loxwood Cl. BR5 & BR6 52 D8
Lubbock Cl. ME15 107 E5
Lubbock Ct. BR7 22 F1
Lubbock Rd. BR7 22 F1
Lubbock Wlk. ME8 63 D5
Lucas Rd. ME6 74 E7
Lucerne Ct. 5 DA18 3 E3
Lucerne Rd. BR6 37 F1
Lucerne St. ME14 92 A5
Lucknow Rd. TN12 136 A8
Lucknow St. SE18 6 E7
Lucks Hill. ME19 89 D8
Lucks La. Paddock Wood TN12 136 B8
Lucks La. Rabbit's Cross ME17 123 F6
Lucks Way. TN12 138 B6
Luddenham Cl. ME14 92 C6
Luddesdon Rd. DA8 8 A7
Luddesdown House. 5 BR5 38 C4
Luddesdown Rd. DA13 45 A2
Ludham Cl. SE28 3 C7
Ludlow Cl. BR2 36 A6
Luffield Rd. SE2 3 B3
Luffman Rd. SE12 22 B5
Lughorse La. ME15 & ME18 105 C1
Lugilina Dr. TN8 128 C8
Lullingstone Ave. BR8 39 F6
Lullingstone Castle. DA4 54 B5
Lullingstone Cl. Gillingham ME7 63 B3
Lullingstone Cl.
St Paul's Cray BR5 24 B1
Lullingstone Cres. BR5 24 B1
Lullingstone La. DA4 54 C8
Lullingstone Pk. DA4 53 F6
Lullingstone Rd. 3 Erith DA17 7 F8
Lullingstone Rd. Maidstone ME16 91 C7
Lulworth Rd. Bexley DA16 6 F5
Lulworth Rd. Chislehurst SE9 22 E6
Lumley Cl. DA17 4 A1
Lumsden Terr. ME4 47 E4
Lunedale Rd. DA2 27 C7
Lunsford Cty Prim Sch. ME20 75 A2
Lunsford La. ME20 74 F2
Lupton Cl. SE12 22 B4
Lurkins Rise. TN17 167 D7
Lushington Rd. ME14 91 E7
Lusted Rd. TN13 83 E7
Luton Cty Inf Sch. ME5 48 C2
Luton Cty Jun Sch. ME4 48 C2
Luton High St. ME5 48 C2
Luton Rd. Chatham ME4 48 B2
Luton Rd. Sidcup DA14 24 C5
Luxfield Rd. SE9 22 E7
Luxon Rd. DA13 58 E4
Luxted Rd. BR6 66 A6
Lyall Way. ME8 63 E4
Lych Gate Rd. BR6 38 A1
Lychfield Dr. ME2 47 A8
Lydd Cl. DA15 23 E5
Lydd Rd. Chatham ME5 62 B5
Lydd Rd. Erith DA7 7 F7
Lydden Ct. SE9 6 E1
Lydens La. TN8 128 F6
Lydford Ct. 6 DA2 10 B1
Lydia Cotts. 2 DA11 30 B8
Lydia Rd. DA8 8 F8
Lydstep Rd. BR7 23 A4
Lyford St. SE18 & SE7 1 E2
Lyle Cl. ME2 47 B8
Lyle Ct. ME16 91 C5
Lyle Pk. TN13 84 B4
Lymden La. TN5 176 A1
Lyme Farm Rd. SE12 & SE3 5 B3
Lyme Rd. DA16 7 B6
Lyminge Cl. Gillingham ME8 49 C2
Lyminge Cl. Sidcup DA14 23 F4
Lymington Cl. 2 E6 1 F8
Lymington Ct. ME15 107 F4
Lyndean Ind Est. SE2 3 C3
Lynden Way. BR8 39 D6
Lyndhurst. BR7 23 B2
Lyndhurst Ave. ME8 63 C7
Lyndhurst Cl. Bexley DA7 8 B4
Lyndhurst Cl. Orpington BR6 51 B6
Lyndhurst Dr. TN13 83 E3
Lyndhurst Rd. Bexley DA7 8 B4
Lyndhurst Rd. Maidstone ME15 107 C8
Lyndhurst Way. DA13 43 F8
Lyndon Ave. DA15 6 F2
Lyndon Rd. DA17 4 A2
Lynette Ave. ME2 33 A1
Lyngs Cl. ME18 120 F8
Lynmead Cl. TN8 112 B4
Lynmere Rd. DA16 7 B5
Lynmouth Rise. BR5 38 B5
Lynne Cl. 7 BR6 51 F4
Lynors Ave. ME2 33 A1
Lynstead Cl. BR1 36 C7
Lynstead House. ME16 91 A1
Lynsted Cl. DA6 8 B2
Lynsted Gdns. SE9 5 D4
Lynsted Rd. ME8 49 B3
Lynton Ave. BR5 38 B5
Lynton Dr. ME5 62 B3
Lynton Rd. DA11 30 A7
Lynton Rd S. DA11 30 A7
Lynwood. TN3 161 C6
Lynwood Gr. BR6 37 E1
Lyons Cres. TN9 117 C2
Lyoth Rd. BR5 51 C8
Lysander Rd. ME19 88 F3
Lysander Way. BR6 51 C7
Lytchet Rd. BR1 22 B1
Lytton Strachy Path. 8 SE28 3 B6
Lyveden Rd. SE3 5 B7

Mabbett House. 2 SE18 6 A8
Mabel Cotts. DA3 43 A6
Mabel Rd. BR8 26 A2
Mabledon Rd. TN9 133 A8
Macallister House. 8 SE18 6 B8
Macaulay Cl. ME20 75 A4
Macaulay Way. 2 SE28 3 B5
Macbean St. SE18 2 B3
Macdonald Ct. TN12 136 A6
Macdonald Rd. ME7 48 D6
Mace Ct. RM17 12 E8
Mace Farm Cotts. TN14 66 E6
Mace La. TN14 66 D6
Macgregor Rd. E16 1 C8
Mackenders Cl. ME20 76 A6
Mackenders Gn. ME20 76 A6
Mackenders La. ME20 76 A6
Mackenzie Way. DA12 30 D2
Maclean House. 9 SE18 1 F2
Macleod House. SE18 5 E6
Macmillan Gdns. 3 DA1 10 A3
Macoma Rd. SE18 6 D8
Macoma Terr. SE18 6 D8
Mada Rd. BR6 51 B7
Madan Rd. TN16 81 E2
Madden Ave. ME5 61 E5
Madden Cl. DA10 11 E1
Maddocks Cl. DA14 24 E3
Madeira Pk. TN1 149 B2
Madginford Cl. ME15 93 A2
Madginford Park Cty Inf Sch.
ME15 93 A2
Madginford Park Cty Jun Sch.
ME15 93 A2
Madginford Rd. ME15 92 F2
Madison Cres. DA7 7 C7
Madison Gdns. DA7 7 C7
Madison Way. TN13 83 F4
Madras House. 2 ME15 107 E5
Mafeking Rd. ME5 61 F3
Magdalen Cl. ME7 63 A4
Magdelan Gr. BR6 52 B6
Magnolia Ave. ME8 63 B5
Magnolia Cl. TN9 133 C7
Magpie Bottom. TN14 & TN15 69 E6
Magpie Cl. ME20 75 A1
Magpie Gn. 3 TN8 112 D3
Magpie Hall Cl. BR2 36 E3
Magpie Hall La. BR2 36 F3
Magpie Hall Rd. ME4 48 A2
Magpie La. ME9 & ME14 63 F1
Magwitch Cl. ME1 47 B4
Maida Rd. Chatham ME4 48 B2
Maida Rd. Erith DA17 4 A3
Maida Vale Rd. DA1 9 A2
Maiden Erlegh Ave. DA5 24 E7
Maiden La. DA1 9 A3
Maidstone Barracks Sta. ME16 91 E5
Maidstone East Sta. ME14 91 F5
Maidstone Gram Sch. ME15 92 B2
Maidstone Gram Sch for Girls.
ME16 91 E5
Maidstone Hospl The. ME16 91 A4
Maidstone Ind Ctr. ME14 91 F5
Maidstone Mus & Art Gallery.
ME14 91 F5
Maidstone Rd. Chatham ME4 47 F2
Maidstone Rd.
Chatham,Walderslade ME5 61 D4
Maidstone Rd.
Chestnut Street ME9 65 D4
Maidstone Rd.
Colt's Hill TN12 & TN2 135 B4
Maidstone Rd. Five Wents ME17 108 E2
Maidstone Rd. Gillingham ME8 63 C6
Maidstone Rd.
Gillingham,Bredhurst ME7 63 B2
Maidstone Rd.
Goose Green TN11 103 C3
Maidstone Rd. Grays RM17 12 A8
Maidstone Rd. Headcorn TN27 141 B7
Maidstone Rd. Lenham ME17 111 D5
Maidstone Rd. Lower Green TN2 134 E1
Maidstone Rd. Matfield TN12 151 C6
Maidstone Rd.
Nettlestead Green ME18 104 C3
Maidstone Rd.
Paddock Wood TN12 136 A8
Maidstone Rd. Platt TN15 87 C7
Maidstone Rd. Rochester ME1 47 C3
Maidstone Rd. Ruxley DA14 24 F1
Maidstone Rd. Sevenoaks TN13 83 E5
Maidstone Rd. Sidcup DA14 24 D2
Maidstone Rd. Staplehurst TN12 139 E7
Maidstone Rd.
Styants Bottom TN15 85 C5
Maidstone Rd. Swanley BR8 39 B8
Maidstone Rd.
Underling Green TN12 122 F2
Maidstone Rd.
Yewtree Green TN12 137 C3
Maidstone St Francis Sch.
ME14 92 A5
Maidstone West Sta. ME16 91 F3
Mailyns The. ME8 63 D7
Main Gate Rd. Chatham ME4 47 F7
Main Gate Rd. Chatham ME4 48 A8
Main Rd. Chattenden ME3 33 F4
Main Rd. Crockenhill BR8 39 D3
Main Rd. Farningham DA4 40 F3
Main Rd. Hextable BR8 39 F8
Main Rd. Hoo St Werburgh ME3 34 C5
Main Rd. Kingsnorth ME3 35 D7
Main Rd. Knockholt TN14 67 C3
Main Rd. Longfield DA3 42 E7
Main Rd. Marlpit Hill TN8 112 B6
Main Rd. Sidcup DA14 & DA15 23 E5
Main Rd. South Street TN16 81 A7
Main Rd. St Paul's Cray BR5 38 C7
Main Rd. Sundridge TN14 82 E3
Main Rd. Sutton at Hone DA4 27 B1
Main Road Gorse Hill. DA4 55 D7
Mainridge Rd. BR7 & SE9 23 A4
Maison Des Fleurs. ME16 91 C2
Majendie Rd. SE18 2 D1
Major York's Rd. TN4 148 F2
Malden Dr. ME14 92 A8
Mall The. 6 Bexley DA6 8 A3
Mall The. 4 Bromley BR1 36 A6
Mallard Apartments. 12
ME15 107 E5
Mallard Cl. DA1 9 F2
Mallard Path. SE28 2 D3
Mallard Way. Lower Stoke ME3 19 C4
Mallard Way. Marlpit Hill TN8 112 C3
Mallard Wlk. Larkfield ME20 74 F2
Mallard Wlk. Sidcup DA14 24 C2
Mallards Way. ME15 93 A1
Malling Rd. Kent Street ME18 88 F2
Malling Rd. Lunsford ME20 74 F5
Malling Rd. Snodland ME6 75 A7
Malling Rd. Teston ME18 90 A1
Malling Sch The. ME19 89 F7
Malling Terr. ME16 91 C4
Mallingdene Cl. ME3 33 B8
Mallings Dr. ME14 93 C4
Mallings La. ME14 93 C4
Mallow Cl. DA11 29 E4
Mallow Ct. RM17 12 D8
Mallow Way. 1 ME5 61 F4
Mallows The. ME14 91 E7
Mallys Pl. DA4 41 C8
Malmaynes Hall Rd. ME3 18 D3
Malory Sch. BR1 22 A4
Malt House La. TN30 183 A7
Malta Ave. ME5 62 A7
Malta Rd. RM18 12 F5
Malta Terr. 5 ME14 92 A7
Maltby Cl. BR6 38 A1
Malthouse Cl. ME17 111 D5
Malthouse Hill. ME15 106 F4
Malthouse La. DA12 31 E3
Malthouse Rd. TN15 56 F2
Malthus Path. 7 SE28 3 C5
Maltings Cl. TN11 118 E8
Maltings Ent Ctr The. DA12 30 F7
Maltings The. Gillingham ME8 64 A8
Maltings The. Gravesend DA11 13 A1
Maltings The. Maidstone ME14 92 E5
Maltings The. Orpington BR6 37 F1
Maltings The.
The Quarries ME17 107 B4
Malton Mews. SE18 6 E8
Malton St. SE18 6 E8
Malton Way. TN2 149 F7
Malus Cl. ME5 62 B1
Malvern Ave. DA7 7 E7
Malvern House. DA11 12 D1
Malvern Rd. Gillingham ME7 48 E3
Malvern Rd. Orpington BR6 52 B6
Malvina Ave. DA12 30 C6
Malyons Rd. BR8 25 F1
Mamignot Cl. ME14 93 A5
Manchester Cl. ME5 62 C6
Mandela Rd. E16 1 A7
Mandeville Cl. 1 SE3 5 A7
Mandeville Ct. 1 ME14 92 A5
Manford Ind Est. DA8 9 B8
Mangold Way. 4 DA18 3 E3
Mangravet Ave. ME15 107 C7
Manister Rd. SE2 3 A3
Manitoba Gdns. 6 BR6 51 F4
Mann Sq. TN9 133 D7
Manning Ct. 3 SE28 3 B5
Manning Rd. BR5 38 D4
Manningham House. ME19 90 A6
Mannock Rd. DA1 9 F4
Manor Cl. Chalk DA12 31 B6
Manor Cl. Crayford DA1 8 E3
Manor Cl. Erith SE28 3 C7
Manor Cl. Heath Side DA2 26 A5
Manor Cl. Maidstone ME14 93 B3
Manor Cl.
Royal Tunbridge Wells TN4 148 E3
Manor Cotts. Lamberhurst TN3 166 B5
Manor Cotts. Langley ME17 108 C5
Manor Ct. Gillingham ME7 49 C4
Manor Ct. Maidstone ME14 93 B3
Manor Ct. Sole Street DA13 44 D4
Manor Cty Inf Sch. RM18 13 B7
Manor Dr. DA3 43 A3
Manor Farm Cotts. TN15 86 A6
Manor Field. DA12 31 E3
Manor Forstal. DA3 56 F7
Manor Gdns. ME5 61 F4
Manor Gr. TN10 117 C3
Manor House. 8 ME7 48 A6
Manor House Dr. ME16 91 D3
Manor House Gdns. TN8 112 C1
Manor La. Fawkham Green DA3 42 C2
Manor La. Hartley DA3 43 A3
Manor La. Rochester ME1 46 F3
Manor Park Ctry Pk. ME19 89 B7
Manor Park Rd. BR7 37 D8
Manor Pk. Chislehurst BR7 37 D8
Manor Pk. Erith DA8 9 A8
Manor Pk.
Royal Tunbridge Wells TN4 148 E3
Manor Pl. BR7 37 D7
Manor Rd. Chatham ME4 47 F4
Manor Rd. Crayford DA1 8 E3
Manor Rd. Edenbridge TN8 112 B1
Manor Rd. Erith DA8 9 B8
Manor Rd. 19 Gravesend DA11 13 B1
Manor Rd. Grays RM17 12 C8
Manor Rd. Longfield Hill DA3 43 C4
Manor Rd.
Royal Tunbridge Wells TN4 132 E1
Manor Rd. Rusthall TN4 148 C4
Manor Rd. Sidcup DA15 24 A5

Manor Rd. Sidcup,Old Bexley DA5 25 B7
Manor Rd. Sole Street DA13 .... 44 D4
Manor Rd. Sundridge TN14 .... 82 D3
Manor Rd. Swanscombe DA10 ..... 28 E8
Manor Rd. Tilbury RM18 .... 13 A5
Manor Rd. West Thurrock RM16 ... 11 C8
Manor Rise. ME14 .... 93 B3
Manor Road Cty Inf Sch. DA10 ... 28 E8
Manor St. ME7 .... 48 A6
Manor Way. Bexley DA7 .... 8 D4
Manor Way. Bromley BR2 .... 36 E3
Manor Way. Grays RM17 .... 12 B7
Manor Way. Grays RM17 .... 12 D7
Manor Way. Greenwich SE3 .... 5 A3
Manor Way. Northfleet DA11 .... 12 A3
Manor Way. Orpington BR5 .... 37 C5
Manor Way. Rainham RM13 .... 4 E8
Manor Way. Sidcup DA15 .... 25 A7
Manor Way. Swanscombe DA10 ... 11 E3
Manor Way Bsns Ctr. RM9 .... 4 D8
Manorbrook. SE12 & SE3 .... 5 A3
Manordene Rd. SE28 .... 3 D7
Manorfields Cl. BR7 .... 37 F6
Manorside Cl. SE2 .... 3 D2
Manse Ct. DA14 .... 24 C3
Manse Par. BR8 .... 40 A5
Manse Way. BR8 .... 40 A5
Mansel Dr. ME1 .... 47 A2
Mansergh Cl. SE18 .... 5 E7
Mansfield Cl. BR5 .... 38 D3
Mansfield Rd. ME8 .... 25 F2
Mansfield Wlk. ME16 .... 91 E2
Mansion House Cl. TN27 .... 158 A2
Mansion Row. ME7 .... 48 A6
Manthorpe Rd. SE18 .... 2 C1
Manton Rd. SE2 .... 3 A2
Manwarings The. TN12 .... 153 A6
Manwood St. E16 .... 1 F5
Maple Ave. Gillingham ME7 .... 48 E6
Maple Ave. Maidstone ME16 ...... 91 C6
Maple Cl. Larkfield ME20 .... 75 A2
Maple Cl. Orpington BR5 .... 37 D4
Maple Cl.
  Royal Tunbridge Wells TN2 .... 149 A1
Maple Cres. DA15 .... 7 A1
Maple Cl. Newham E6 .... 2 A8
Maple Ct. Stone DA2 .... 27 E8
Maple Leaf Dr. DA15 .... 23 F7
Maple Rd. Dartford DA1 .... 26 C7
Maple Rd. Gravesend DA12 .... 30 C4
Maple Rd. Grays RM17 .... 12 C8
Maple Rd. Hoo St Werburgh ME3 . 34 E3
Maple Rd. Rochester ME2 .... 46 F6
Maplecroft Cl. E6 .... 1 E7
Mapledene. BR7 .... 23 C3
Maples The. DA3 .... 43 B6
Maplescombe La. DA4 .... 55 B6
Maplesden Cl. ME16 .... 90 F3
Maplesden Noakes Sch The.
  ME16 .... 91 E6
Mapleton. TN8 .... 113 A7
Mapleton Cl. BR2 .... 36 A3
Mapleton Rd. TN16 & TN8 .... 96 E3
Maplin House. SE2 .... 3 D4
Maplin Rd. E16 .... 1 B7
Maplins Cl. ME8 .... 49 F1
Mar House. SE7 .... 5 C8
Maran Way. DA18 .... 3 D3
Marathon Paddock. ME7 .... 48 D4
Marble House. SE18 .... 2 F1
Marbrook Ct. SE12 .... 22 C5
Marcellina Way. BR6 .... 51 F7
Marconi Rd. DA11 .... 29 D5
Marcet Rd. DA1 .... 9 C2
Marcus Rd. DA1 .... 26 A8
Marden Ave. BR2 .... 36 A3
Marden Cres. DA5 .... 8 C2
Marden Cty Prim Sch. TN12 .. 138 B5
Marden Rd. Rochester ME2 .... 33 C1
Marden Rd. Staplehurst TN12 .. 139 C5
Marden Sta. TN12 .... 138 C6
Marechal Niel Ave. DA15 .... 23 D5
Marechal Niel Par. DA15 .... 23 D5
Margaret Gardner Dr. SE9 ...... 22 F6
Margaret Rd. DA5 .... 7 D1
Margate Cl. ME7 .... 48 E6
Margetts La. ME1 .... 60 D1
Margetts Pl. ME2 .... 34 A3
Marian Sq. TN12 .... 139 F4
Marina Cl. BR2 .... 36 A6
Marina Dr. Bexley DA16 .... 6 E5
Marina Dr. Dartford DA1 .... 27 A7
Marina Dr. Northfleet DA11 ...... 12 F1
Marine Dr. Hoo St Werburgh ME3 34 E3
Marine Dr. Woolwich SE18 .... 1 F2
Marine View. ME4 .... 34 B1
Mariners Cl. DA9 .... 11 B3
Mariners Wlk. DA8 .... 8 F8
Marion Cl. BR7 .... 62 A2
Marion Cres. Maidstone ME15 .. 107 B8
Marion Cres. Orpington BR5 ..... 38 B4
Maritime Cl. Rochester ME2 ..... 47 D8
Maritime Cl. Swanscombe DA9 .. 11 B2
Maritime Ind Est. SE7 .... 1 B2
Maritime Way. ME4 .... 48 A8
Marjorie McClure Sch. BR7 ... 37 C8
Mark Cl. Bexley DA7 .... 7 E6
Mark Cl. Keston BR2 .... 50 E6
Mark La. DA12 .... 13 E1
Mark Way. BR8 .... 40 A4
Market Alley. DA11 .... 13 B1
Market Bldgs. ME14 .... 91 F4
Market Colonnade. ME14 .... 91 F4
Market Meadow. BR5 .... 38 C5

Market Pl. Bexley DA7 .... 8 A3
Market Pl. Dartford DA1 .... 26 E8
Market Pl. ME14
Market Pl.
  Royal Tunbridge Wells TN2 .... 149 A2
Market Pl. Tilbury RM18 .... 13 A5
Market Sq. Bromley BR1 .... 36 A7
Market Sq.
  Royal Tunbridge Wells TN2 .... 149 B4
Market Sq. Westerham TN16 ...... 81 D1
Market St. Dartford DA1 .... 26 E8
Market St. Maidstone ME14 ...... 91 F4
Market St. ME13
Market St.
  Royal Tunbridge Wells TN2 .... 149 A2
Market St. Staplehurst TN12 .... 139 F5
Market St. Woolwich SE18 .... 2 A1
Market Way. TN16 .... 81 D1
Marks Sq. DA11 .... 29 F4
Marlborough Cl. Orpington BR6 . 37 F3
Marlborough Cl.
  Royal Tunbridge Wells TN4 ... 148 E4
Marlborough Cres. TN13 .... 83 E3
Marlborough Cl. TN16 .... 81 C1
Marlborough House. BR6 .... 63 F8
Marlborough House Sch.
  TN18 .... 178 E2
Marlborough La. SE7 .... 5 C7
Marlborough Park Ave. DA15 ... 24 A7
Marlborough Rd. Bexley DA7 ...... 7 D4
Marlborough Rd. Bromley BR2 .. 36 C5
Marlborough Rd. Dartford DA1 ... 9 C1
Marlborough Rd. Gillingham ME7 48 B5
Marlborough Rd. Woolwich SE18 . 2 C3
Marlborough Sch. DA15 .... 24 A8
Marle Place Rd. TN12 .... 152 C4
Marley House. DA8 .... 8 F5
Marley Ave. DA7 .... 7 D8
Marley La. TN27 .... 142 C3
Marley Rd. Harrietsham ME17 .. 110 F6
Marley Rd. Hoo St Werburgh ME3 34 D6
Marley Way. ME1 .... 47 C2
Marlhurst. TN8 .... 112 B4
Marling Way. DA12 .... 30 E3
Marlings Cl. BR7 .... 37 E5
Marlings Park Ave. BR7 .... 37 E6
Marlow Copse. ME5 .... 61 F1
Marlowe Cl. BR7 .... 23 D2
Marlowe Gdns. SE9 .... 6 A1
Marlowe Rd. ME20 .... 75 A3
Marlowes The. DA1 .... 8 D3
Marlpit Cl. TN8 .... 112 C4
Marlpit Cotts. ME17 .... 107 E2
Marlpit Gdns. TN5 .... 176 E1
Marlpit The. TN5 .... 174 E5
Marlwood Cl. DA15 .... 23 E6
Marmadon Rd. SE18 & SE2 .... 2 F2
Marne Ave. DA16 .... 7 A4
Marquis Dr. ME7 .... 63 B3
Marrabon Cl. DA15 .... 24 A7
Marram Ct. RM17 .... 12 E8
Marriott Rd. DA1 .... 27 A8
Marsden Way. BR6 .... 51 F6
Marsh Cres. ME23 .... 17 E4
Marsh Green Rd. TN8 .... 128 C5
Marsh La. ME3 .... 16 B6
Marsh Quarter La. TN18 .... 186 C3
Marsh Rd. ME2 .... 60 B5
Marsh St. Dartford DA1 .... 10 A5
Marsh St. Rochester ME2 .... 47 B7
Marsh Way. New Hythe ME20 .... 75 A4
Marsh Way. Rainham RM9 .... 4 D8
Marshall Gdns. TN11 .... 102 E1
Marshall Path. SE28 .... 3 B6
Marshall Rd. ME8 .... 63 C8
Marshalls Gr. SE18 .... 1 E2
Marshalls Land. TN30 .... 173 A3
Marsham Cl. BR7 .... 23 B3
Marsham Cres. ME17 .... 108 B1
Marsham St. ME14 .... 92 A4
Marsham Way. ME7 .... 60 A5
Marshbrook Cl. SE3 .... 5 D4
Marshland View. ME3 .... 19 C5
Marston Cl. ME5 .... 61 E3
Marston Ct. DA14 .... 23 F4
Marston Dr. ME14 .... 92 C5
Marston House. RM17 .... 12 A8
Marston Wlk. ME5 .... 61 E3
Martens Ave. DA7 .... 8 C3
Martens Cl. DA7 .... 8 C3
Martham Cl. SE28 .... 3 D6
Martin Bowes Rd. SE9 .... 5 F4
Martin Cl. DA7 .... 8 C3
Martin Dene. DA6 .... 7 F2
Martin Dr. DA2 .... 10 C1
Martin Hardie Way. TN10 .... 117 E5
Martin House. DA11 .... 29 F6
Martin Rd. Rochester ME2 .... 47 B8
Martin Rd. Wilmington DA2 ...... 26 C5
Martin Rise. DA6 .... 7 F2
Martin Sq. ME20 .... 75 A2
Martin's Shaw. TN13 .... 83 C5
Martindale Ave. Newham E16 ..... 1 A6
Martindale Ave. Orpington BR6 . 52 A5
Martins Cl. Lower Higham ME3 .. 32 D6
Martins Cl. St Paul's Cray BR5 .. 38 D6
Martins Cl. Tenterden TN30 .... 183 C8
Martins La. TN12 .... 103 E2
Martyn House. SE2 .... 7 D8
Marvels Cl. SE12 .... 22 B6
Marvels Ct. SE12 .... 22 C5
Marvels Lane Prim Sch. SE12 . 22 B7
Marvillion Ct. TN12 .... 119 F6
Marwin House. SE18 .... 6 B8
Marwell. TN16 .... 81 B1
Marwood Cl. DA16 .... 7 B4
Mary Burrows Gdns. TN15 .... 70 B2
Mary Day's. TN7 .... 167 E2
Mary Lawrenson Pl. SE3 .... 5 A7
Mary Macarthur House. DA17 ... 4 A3

Mary Magdalene House.
  TN9 .... 133 B8
Mary Rose Hall. E6 .... 1 F8
Marybank. SE18 .... 1 F2
Maryfield Cl. DA5 .... 25 E5
Maryland Ct. ME8 .... 63 E5
Maryland Dr. ME16 .... 90 F2
Maryland Rd. TN2 .... 149 D1
Maryon Ct. BR5 .... 38 B5
Maryon Gr. SE7 .... 1 E2
Maryon Rd. SE7 .... 1 E2
Maryville. ME8 .... 6 F5
Mascall's Court La. TN12 .... 136 B4
Mascall's Court Rd. TN12 ...... 136 A4
Mascalls Ct. SE7 .... 5 C8
Mascalls Pk. TN12 .... 135 F5
Mascalls Rd. SE7 .... 5 C8
Mascalls Sch. TN12 .... 136 A4
Masefield Cl. DA8 .... 8 F6
Masefield Dr. ME3 .... 33 B8
Masefield Rd. Dartford DA1 ...... 10 B2
Masefield Rd. Lunsford ME20 ... 74 F4
Masefield Rd. Northfleet DA11 .. 29 D5
Masefield View. BR6 .... 51 C7
Masefield Way. TN9 .... 132 F7
Masham House. SE18 .... 3 D4
Mason Cl. DA7 .... 8 B4
Masons Hill. Bromley BR2 .... 36 B5
Masons Hill. Woolwich SE18 .... 2 B2
Master Gunners' Pl. SE18 .... 5 E7
Masters La. ME19 .... 74 B5
Masthead Cl. DA9 .... 10 C3
Matchless Dr. SE18 .... 6 A7
Mate Hall Villas. ME14 .... 93 C4
Matfield Cl. BR2 .... 36 A4
Matfield Cres. ME14 .... 92 C5
Matfield Rd. DA17 .... 8 A8
Matilda Cl. ME7 .... 63 B8
Matrix Bsns Ctr. DA1 .... 9 E2
Matterdale Gdns. ME16 .... 90 E2
Matthews La. TN11 .... 102 F4
Mattinson Pl. ME9 .... 95 F7
Matts Hill Rd. ME9 .... 63 E2
Maud Cashmore Way. SE18 .... 1 F3
Maude Rd. BR8 .... 26 A2
Maudslay Rd. SE9 .... 5 F4
Maundene Cty Prim Sch. ME5 .. 62 B5
Maunders Cl. ME5 .... 62 C8
Mavelstone Cl. BR1 .... 36 E8
Mavelstone Rd. BR1 .... 36 E8
Mavis Wlk. E6 .... 1 E8
Maxey Rd. SE18 .... 2 C2
Maxim Rd. Crayford DA1 .... 8 E2
Maxim Rd. Erith DA8 .... 4 E2
Maximfeldt Rd. DA8 .... 4 E1
Maximilian Dr. ME2 .... 60 B4
Maxton Cl. ME14 .... 92 F5
Maxwell Dr. ME16 .... 91 B6
Maxwell Gdns. BR6 .... 51 F7
Maxwell House. Chislehurst BR7 23 B1
Maxwell House.
  Woolwich SE18 .... 6 B8
Maxwell Rd. Bexley DA7 .... 7 A4
Maxwell Rd. Gillingham ME7 .... 48 A6
May Ave. Northfleet DA11 .... 29 F7
May Ave. Orpington BR5 .... 38 B4
May Avenue Est. DA11 .... 29 F7
May Ct. RM17 .... 12 E8
May Pl. DA13 .... 44 B4
May Rd. Gillingham ME7 .... 48 C4
May Rd. Hawley DA2 .... 26 F4
May Rd. Rochester ME1 .... 47 C3
May St. Cuxton ME2 .... 46 B2
May St. Snodland ME6 .... 75 B8
May Terr. ME4 .... 48 A7
May Wynne House. E16 .... 1 B7
Maybury Ave. DA2 .... 27 C7
Maybury Cl. BR5 .... 37 B4
Maycotts La. TN12 .... 135 D1
Mayday Gdns. SE3 .... 5 E5
Mayerne Rd. SE9 .... 5 F2
Mayes Cl. BR8 .... 40 A5
Mayeswood Rd. SE12 .... 22 C4
Mayfair. ME2 .... 47 C8
Mayfair Ave. Bexley DA16 .... 7 D6
Mayfair Ave. Maidstone ME15 .. 107 A8
Mayfair Rd. DA1 .... 9 D2
Mayfield. Bexley DA7 .... 7 F4
Mayfield. Swanscombe DA10 ..... 11 E1
Mayfield Ave. BR6 .... 37 F2
Mayfield Cl. Chatham ME5 .... 62 A1
Mayfield Cl. Gillingham ME8 .... 49 E2
Mayfield La. TN5 .... 174 D4
Mayfield Pk. TN5 .... 174 E5
Mayfield Rd. Bromley BR1 .... 36 E4
Mayfield Rd. Erith DA17 .... 4 C2
Mayfield Rd. Northfleet DA11 ... 29 E8
Mayfield Rd.
  Royal Tunbridge Wells TN4 ... 148 F4
Mayfield Villas. DA14 .... 24 C2
Mayford Rd. ME5 .... 62 D2
Mayhill Rd. SE7 .... 5 B8
Maylam Cl. TN10 .... 117 C4
Maylands Dr. DA14 .... 24 D5
Maynard Cl. DA8 .... 8 F7
Maynard House. SE18 .... 2 E2
Maynard Pl. ME5 .... 48 D2
Maynard's Sq. TN12 .... 135 E1
Maynards. TN12 .... 138 C5
Mayor's Pl. TN30 .... 183 A7
Mayors La. DA2 .... 26 C3
Mayplace Ave. DA1 .... 9 A3
Mayplace La. Woolwich SE18 ...... 6 B7
Mayplace La. Woolwich SE18 ...... 6 B7
Mayplace Prim Sch. DA7 .... 8 D3
Mayplace Rd E. DA7 .... 8 C4
Mayplace Rd W. DA7 .... 8 A3

Maypole Cotts. BR6 .... 53 A4
Maypole Cres. DA8 .... 9 D8
Maypole Cty Prim Sch. DA5 ..... 25 E6
Maypole La. TN17 .... 167 F8
Maypole Rd. Gravesend DA12 ... 30 F7
Maypole Rd. Maypole BR6 .... 52 F4
Maytham Bglws. TN17 .... 182 A1
Maytham Rd. TN17 .... 182 A1
Mayweed Ave. ME5 .... 61 E4
Mc Call Cres. SE7 .... 1 E1
Mc Kenzie Rd. ME8 .... 62 A3
Mc Dowall Cl. E16 .... 1 A8
McAlpine Cres. ME15 .... 106 F3
McAuley Cl. SE9 .... 6 A2
McCabe Cl. TN12 .... 139 E2
McCudden Rd. DA1 .... 9 F4
McCudden Row. ME4 .... 48 A6
McDermott Rd. TN15 .... 86 F7
McKenzie Cl. ME20 .... 90 F8
McLeod Rd. SE2 .... 3 B2
McMillan Cl. DA12 .... 30 C4
Mead Cl. BR8 .... 40 A4
Mead Cres. DA1 .... 26 D7
Mead Rd. Chislehurst BR7 .... 23 C2
Mead Rd. Dartford DA1 .... 26 D7
Mead Rd. Edenbridge TN8 .... 128 D7
Mead Rd. Gravesend DA11 .... 30 B6
Mead Road Inf Sch. BR7 .... 23 C2
Mead The. Leybourne ME19 ...... 74 E2
Mead The. New Ash Green DA3 .. 56 E8
Mead The.
  Royal Tunbridge Wells TN2 ... 149 C2
Mead Wall. ME3 .... 15 F8
Mead Way. BR2 .... 36 A3
Meades Cl. TN12 .... 138 B6
Meadfield Rd. DA13 .... 58 A8
Meadow Bank. Leigh TN11 ...... 115 F1
Meadow Bank.
  West Malling ME19 .... 89 C3
Meadow Bank Cl. TN15 .... 55 F2
Meadow Cl. Bexley DA6 .... 7 F2
Meadow Cl. Chatham ME5 .... 61 F5
Meadow Cl. Chislehurst BR7 .... 23 B3
Meadow Cl. Sevenoaks TN13 .... 84 A4
Meadow Cl. Upper Halling ME2 .. 59 E4
Meadow Cres. ME12
Meadow Croft. BR1 .... 36 F6
Meadow Ct. TN15 .... 71 F3
Meadow Hill. BR6 .... TN1 & TN2 149 B3
Meadow La. Marlpit Hill TN8 ... 112 B4
Meadow La. Vigo Village DA13 .. 58 A1
Meadow Rd. Gravesend DA11 ... 30 A6
Meadow Rd. Groombridge TN3 . 161 C2
Meadow Rd. Northfleet DA11 ... 29 C7
Meadow Rd.
  Royal Tunbridge Wells TN1 ... 149 A4
Meadow Rd.Royal Tunbridge Wells,
  Southborough TN4 .... 132 F1
Meadow Rd. Rusthall TN4 .... 148 C4
Meadow Rd. Tonbridge TN9 .... 133 B8
Meadow The. Pembury TN2 .... 150 E8
Meadow View. DA15 .... 24 B8
Meadow View Cotts.
  Hurst Green TN19 .... 184 A3
Meadow View Cotts.
  Laddingford ME18 .... 120 E5
Meadow View Rd. ME17 .... 107 B3
Meadow Way. Dartford DA2 ..... 27 C8
Meadow Way. Marden TN12 ... 138 E6
Meadow Way. Orpington BR6 ... 51 A7
Meadow Wlk. Snodland ME6 .... 74 F7
Meadow Wlk. Wilmington DA2 .. 26 C4
Meadowbank Rd. ME4 .... 48 A4
Meadowdown. ME14 .... 92 E4
Meadowdown Cl. ME7 .... 63 A4
Meadowlands. TN15 .... 84 F7
Meadows. TN7 .... 170 D1
Meadows Ct. DA14 .... 24 B2
Meadows Sch (Barnados).
  TN4 .... 132 F2
Meadows The. Biddenden TN27 157 F2
Meadows The. Halstead TN14 ... 67 F6
Meadows The. Maidstone ME15 . 91 E2
Meadows The. Orpington BR6 ... 52 C4
Meadowside. Dartford DA2 ...... 26 E7
Meadowside. Eltham SE9 .... 5 C3
Meadowside Cotts. TN5 .... 176 F1
Meadowsweet Cl. E16 .... 1 D8
Meadowview. BR5 .... 38 C6
Meadowview Rd. DA5 .... 7 F1
Meads The. TN17 .... 168 F1
Meadside Wlk. ME5 .... 61 F6
Meadway. Halstead TN14 .... 67 F6
Meadway. Hildenborough TN11 . 116 E5
Meadway The. Pembury TN2 .... 52 B4
Meadway The. Sevenoaks TN13 . 83 F5
Meath Cl. BR5 .... 38 B4
Medbury Rd. DA12 .... 30 F7
Mede House. BR1 .... 22 B3
Medebourne Cl. SE3 .... 5 A4
Medhurst Cres. DA12 .... 30 F6
Medhurst Gdns. DA12 .... 30 F6
Medick Ct. RM17 .... 12 E8
Medina House. SE18 .... 6 C7
Medina Rd. Ditton ME20 .... 75 C1
Medina Rd. Tonbridge TN10 .. 117 C6
Medlar Gr. ME7 .... 63 A4
Medlar House. DA15 .... 24 A5
Medlar Rd. RM17 .... 12 E8
Medlars The. Maidstone ME14 .. 92 D6
Medlars The.
  Meopham Station DA13 .... 44 A3
Medway Ave. High Halstow ME23 17 F4
Medway Ave. Yalding ME18 .... 104 F1
Medway Com Coll. ME4 .... 48 A1
Medway Cotts. TN17 .... 180 D3

Medway Ct. BR5 .... 38 D1
Medway Ent Ctr. ME2 .... 47 D6
Medway Gdns. ME4 .... 47 F7
Medway Heritage Ctr. ME4 ...... 47 F5
Medway Hospl. ME7 .... 48 B4
Medway House. ME15 .... 107 D8
Medway Meadows. TN12 .... 120 A6
Medway Rd. Crayford DA1 .... 9 A4
Medway Rd. Gillingham ME7 .... 48 C7
Medway Rd.
  Gillingham,Rainham ME8 .... 49 F1
Medway Service Area. ME8 ...... 63 F3
Medway St. Chatham ME4 .... 47 F5
Medway St. Maidstone ME14 ... 91 F4
Medway Trad Est. ME16 .... 91 F3
Medway View.
  Barnes Street TN11 .... 119 A5
Medway Villas. ME4 .... 106 B7
Medway Wharf Rd. TN9 .... 117 C1
Meerbrook Rd. SE3 & SE9 .... 5 C4
Meeson's La. RM17 .... 11 F8
Meeting House La. ME4 .... 47 F4
Megby Cl. ME8 .... 63 D6
Megrims Hill. TN18 .... 186 A6
Meirs Court Rd. ME8 .... 63 E6
Melanda Cl. BR7 .... 22 F3
Melanie Cl. DA7 .... 7 E6
Melba Gdns. RM18 .... 13 A4
Melbourne Cl. BR6 .... 37 E2
Melbourne Cl. DA11 .... 13 B1
Melbourne Rd. Chatham ME4 ... 48 A3
Melbourne Rd. Tilbury RM18 .... 12 E6
Melbury Cl. BR7 .... 22 F2
Meldrum Cl. BR5 .... 38 C3
Melford Dr. ME16 .... 91 C4
Melliker La. DA13 .... 44 A3
Melling St. SE18 .... 6 E8
Mellish Ind Est. E16 .... 1 D3
Mells Cres. SE9 .... 22 F4
Melody Cl. ME8 .... 63 C4
Melrose Cl. Lewisham SE12 .... 22 B7
Melrose Cl. Maidstone ME15 .. 107 A7
Melrose Cres. BR6 .... 51 D5
Melthorpe Gdns. SE3 .... 5 E6
Melville Cl. ME4 .... 48 A3
Melville Rd. Maidstone ME15 ... 92 A3
Melville Rd. Sidcup DA14 .... 24 C6
Memess Path. SE18 .... 6 A8
Memorial Hospl. SE18 .... 6 A5
Mendip Rd. DA7 .... 8 F5
Mendip Wlk. TN2 .... 149 D5
Mennie House. SE18 .... 5 F6
Meon St. BR5 .... 38 D1
Meopham Cty Prim Sch. DA13 .. 44 A2
Meopham Sch. DA13 .... 58 A4
Meopham Sta. DA13 .... 44 A4
Mera Dr. DA7 .... 8 A3
Merbury Rd. SE28 .... 2 E4
Merbury St. SE18 .... 2 B3
Mercer Dr. ME17 .... 110 F6
Mercer St. TN1 .... 149 B5
Mercer Way. ME17 .... 108 B1
Mercers. Hawkhurst TN18 ..... 179 A1
Mercers. Langton Green TN3 ... 148 A3
Mercers Cl. TN12 .... 135 E6
Merchant Pl. TN12 .... 138 C5
Merchland Rd. SE9 .... 23 C7
Mercury Cl. ME1 .... 47 A3
Mere Cl. BR6 .... 51 B8
Meresborough Cotts. ME8 .... 63 F5
Meresborough La. ME8 & ME9 .. 64 B5
Meresborough Rd. ME8 .... 64 A7
Mereside. BR6 .... 51 A8
Merewood Cl. BR1 .... 37 A7
Merewood Rd. DA7 .... 8 C5
Mereworth Cl. ME8 .... 49 A3
Mereworth Cty Prim Sch.
  ME18 .... 103 C8
Mereworth Dr. SE18 .... 6 C7
Mereworth House. ME2 .... 33 C1
Mereworth Rd.
  Royal Tunbridge Wells TN4 ... 149 A6
Meriden Cl. BR1 .... 22 D1
Meridian Pk. ME2 .... 47 E6
Meridian Rd. SE7 .... 5 D7
Meridian Trad Est. SE7 .... 1 B2
Merifield Rd. SE9 .... 5 C3
Merino Pl. DA15 .... 7 A2
Merivale Gr. ME5 .... 62 B4
Merlewood. TN13 .... 84 B4
Merlewood Dr. BR7 .... 36 F8
Merlin Ave. ME20 .... 74 F2
Merlin Cl. TN10 .... 117 E4
Merlin Gdns. BR1 .... 22 A5
Merlin Prim Sch. BR1 .... 22 A5
Merlin Rd. DA16 .... 7 A3
Merlin Rd N. DA16 .... 7 A3
Mermaid Cl. ME5 .... 62 A6
Mermerus Gdns. DA12 .... 30 F4
Merrals Wood Rd. ME2 .... 46 D5
Merrilees Rd. DA15 .... 23 E8
Merriman Rd. SE3 .... 5 C6
Merriments La. TN18 & TN19 .. 184 D5
Merrion Cl. TN4 .... 149 B7
Merrion Cl. TN4 .... 149 B7
Merry Boys Rd. ME3 .... 33 B8
Merrydown Way. BR7 .... 36 F8
Merryfield. SE3 .... 5 A5
Merryfield Ct. TN9 .... 133 B8
Merryfield House. SE12 .... 22 C5
Merryfields. ME2 .... 33 A1
Merryweather Cl. DA1 .... 9 F1
Mersey Rd. TN10 .... 117 B5

Merton Ave. DA3 .... 42 F5
Merton Cl. ME5 .... 62 C5
Merton Court Prep Sch. DA14 .. 24 C4
Merton Ct. DA16 .... 7 B5
Merton Gdns. BR5 .... 37 B4
Mervyn Ave. BR7 & SE9 .... 23 C6
Mervyn Stockwood House. SE9 23 C6
Mesne Way. TN14 .... 68 F7
Messent Rd. SE9 .... 5 D2
Messeter Pl. SE9 .... 6 A1
Meteor Rd. ME19 .... 88 F3
Methuen Rd. Bexley DA6 .... 7 F3
Methuen Rd. Erith DA17 .... 4 B2
Metro Ctr The. BR5 .... 38 B3
Mews The. Longfield DA3 .... 42 E6
Mews The. Maidstone ME16 .... 91 E5
Mews The. Pembury TN2 .... 150 C6
Mews The. Rochester ME2 ...... 46 F7
Mews The. 5
  Royal Tunbridge Wells TN1 .. 149 B3
Mews The. Sevenoaks TN13 .... 84 A3
Meyer Rd. DA8 .... 8 D8
Micawber Cl. ME5 .... 62 A1
Michael Gdns. DA12 .... 30 E3
Michael Marshall House. SE9 .. 23 C6
Michael Tetley Hall
  (Nursery Trng Coll,
  Dr Barnardo's Home). TN2 .. 149 D6
Michaels La. DA3 .... 56 C8
Michele Cotts. ME3 .... 32 C6
Micklefield Wadhurst Sch.
  TN5 .... 174 C4
Mickleham Cl. ME8 .... 38 A7
Mickleham Rd. BR5 .... 38 A7
Mid Comp Cotts. TN15 .... 87 E6
Mid Kent Coll (City Way Ctr).
  ME1 .... 47 E4
Mid Kent Coll of H & F Ed.
  Chatham ME1 & ME4 .... 61 E6
Mid Kent Coll of H & F Ed.
  Maidstone ME16 .... 91 E3
Mid Kent Coll of H & F Ed.
  Maidstone,Cherry Orchard ME16 . 91 C3
Mid Kent Golf Course. DA11 ... 30 B5
Mid Kent Sch for Girls. ME14 .. 92 A5
Mid Kent Sh Ctr The. ME16 .... 91 F2
Middle Field. TN2 .... 150 E8
Middle Garth. TN17 .... 169 D4
Middle La. TN15 .... 84 F6
Middle Mill Rd. ME19 .... 89 F7
Middle Park Ave. SE9 .... 22 E8
Middle Park Inf & Jun Sch.
  SE9 .... 22 D8
Middle Rd. TN3 .... 164 A5
Middle Row. 6 ME15 .... 91 F4
Middle St. 5 ME4 .... 48 A6
Middle Wlk. TN2 .... 149 E8
Middlefields. ME8 .... 64 A8
Middleham Ct. 12 DA2 .... 10 B1
Middlesex Rd. ME15 .... 107 D7
Middleton Ave. DA14 .... 24 C3
Middleton Cl. ME8 .... 63 E4
Middleton Ct. BR1 .... 22 B1
Middlings Rise. TN13 .... 83 F1
Middlings The. TN13 .... 83 F2
Middlings Wood. TN13 .... 84 A2
Midfield Ave. Bexley DA7 .... 8 C4
Midfield Ave. Hextable BR8 .... 26 B2
Midfield Prim Sch. BR5 .... 24 A1
Midfield Way. BR5 .... 38 B8
Midhurst Cl. ME15 .... 92 A3
Midhurst Hill. DA6 .... 8 A2
Midley Cl. ME16 .... 91 C7
Midsummer Ct. SE12 .... 5 A3
Midsummer Rd. ME6 .... 74 E8
Midway The. TN4 .... 148 D2
Midwinter Cl. 3 DA16 .... 7 A4
Miers Court Cty Prim Sch. ME8 63 F7
Mierscourt Cl. ME8 .... 64 A8
Mierscourt Rd. ME8 .... 63 E6
Mike Spring Ct. DA12 .... 30 F4
Milburn Rd. ME7 .... 48 C7
Mildmay Pl. TN14 .... 68 F8
Mildred Cl. DA1 .... 10 A1
Mildred Rd. DA8 .... 4 E1
Mile La. TN17 .... 168 B8
Mile Oak Rd. TN12 .... 136 C3
Mile Stone Rd. DA2 .... 10 B1
Milebush La. TN12 .... 122 E1
Miles Pl. ME1 .... 47 D3
Milestone Sch. DA2 .... 10 B1
Milford Cl. Erith SE2 .... 7 E8
Milford Cl. Maidstone ME16 ... 91 D5
Military Rd. ME4 .... 47 F5
Milk House Cotts. TN17 .... 170 A8
Milk St. Bromley BR1 .... 22 B2
Milk St. Newham E16 .... 2 B5
Mill Bank. TN27 .... 141 C6
Mill Brook Rd. BR5 .... 38 C5
Mill Cl. Lenham ME17 .... 111 C4
Mill Cl. Rochester ME2 .... 33 B1
Mill Cotts. ME8 .... 105 B6
Mill Cres. TN9 .... 117 C2
Mill Ct. Sutton at Hone DA4 ... 41 C7
Mill Ct. 14 Woolwich SE28 .... 3 B6
Mill Hall Bsns Est The. ME20 .. 75 D2
Mill Hall Rd. New Hythe ME20 . 75 C2
Mill Hall Rd. New Hythe ME20 . 75 C3
Mill Hill. TN8 .... 128 D7
Mill Hill La. DA12 .... 31 D3
Mill House Cl. DA4 .... 41 A4
Mill La. Benover ME18 .... 121 A7
Mill La. Biddenden Green TN27 143 D2
Mill La. Chatham,Bluebell Hill ME5 61 D1
Mill La. Chatham,Luton ME5 ... 48 C1
Mill La. Coxheath ME17 .... 106 D4
Mill La. Eynsford DA4 .... 40 E1
Mill La. Farthing Street BR6 .... 51 B1
Mill La. Frittenden TN12 & TN17 156 D8
Mill La. Hartlip Hill ME9 .... 64 E6
Mill La. Ightham TN15 .... 86 D5
Mill La. Maidstone ME14 .... 91 E6
Mill La. Sevenoaks TN13 & TN14 . 84 D6
Mill La. Shoreham TN14 .... 53 F1
Mill La. Sissinghurst TN17 .... 169 F8
Mill La. Snodland ME6 .... 75 B8
Mill La. Tenterden TN30 .... 173 B1
Mill La. Tonbridge TN9 .... 117 C2
Mill La. Wateringbury ME18 .. 104 D7
Mill La.
  Watt's Cross TN11 & TN15 .. 100 C2
Mill La. West Thurrock RM16 .. 11 D8
Mill La. Westerham TN16 .... 96 C8
Mill La. Woolwich SE18 .... 2 A1
Mill La. Yewtree Green TN12 . 137 B1
Mill Pl. Chislehurst BR7 .... 37 B8
Mill Pl. Crayford DA1 .... 9 A3
Mill Pond Cl. TN13 .... 84 D6
Mill Pond Rd. DA1 .... 9 E1
Mill Rd. Erith DA8 .... 8 C7
Mill Rd. Gillingham ME7 .... 48 C6
Mill Rd. Hawley DA2 .... 26 F4
Mill Rd. Newham E16 .... 1 B5
Mill Rd. Northfleet DA11 .... 29 E8
Mill Rd. Purfleet RM16 .... 10 B8
Mill Rd. Rochester ME2 .... 47 B8
Mill Rd. Sevenoaks TN15 .... 83 E6
Mill St. Iden Green TN17 & TN18 180 C3
Mill St. Loose ME15 .... 106 F5
Mill St. Maidstone ME15 .... 91 F4
Mill St. Mill Street ME19 .... 89 F7
Mill St. Snodland ME6 .... 75 B8
Mill St. Westerham TN16 .... 96 D8
Mill Stone Cl. DA4 .... 41 C7
Mill Vale. BR2 .... 36 A7
Mill View. TN11 .... 102 D1
Mill Wlk. ME16 .... 91 A3
Millais Pl. RM18 .... 13 A7
Millbank Way. SE9 .... 5 A2
Millbro. BR8 .... 40 A8
Millbrook. ME19 .... 74 D1
Millbrook Ave. DA16 .... 6 D3
Millbrook Cl. ME15 .... 91 F1
Millbrook Cotts. BR5 .... 38 B5
Millcroft Rd. ME3 .... 16 B4
Miller Ct. DA7 .... 8 B4
Miller Rd. DA12 .... 31 A6
Miller Way. ME2 .... 33 D2
Millers Cotts. TN11 .... 134 C6
Millers Wharf. ME15 .... 91 E2
Millers Wlk. DA13 .... 58 A7
Millfield. High Halden TN26 ... 173 D7
Millfield. New Ash Green DA3 .. 56 E8
Millfield Dr. DA11 .... 29 E6
Millfield La. DA3 .... 56 E8
Millfield Rd. TN15 .... 55 D4
Millfields. ME5 .... 62 D2
Millfields Cl. BR5 .... 38 B5
Millfields Cotts. BR5 .... 38 B5
Millfordhope Rd. ME2 .... 46 C7
Millhall. ME20 .... 75 E2
Millhouse La. ME19 .... 73 D3
Millman Ct. SE3 .... 5 B7
Millpond Cl. ME2 .... 47 B8
Millpond La. TN27 & TN30 .... 172 D2
Mills Cres. TN15 .... 84 F8
Mills Rd. ME20 .... 90 E8
Mills Terr. ME4 .... 48 A3
Millside Ind Est. DA1 .... 9 D3
Millstock Terr. ME15 .... 91 E2
Millstone Mews. DA4 .... 41 C8
Millstream Cl. TN3 .... 146 D2
Millward Wlk. 14 SE18 .... 6 A8
Millwood Rd. BR5 .... 38 C6
Milne Gdns. SE9 .... 5 E2
Milne House. 15 SE18 .... 1 F2
Milner Rd. ME7 .... 48 D7
Milroy Ave. DA11 .... 29 E6
Milstead Cl. ME14 .... 92 C5
Milsted Rd. ME8 .... 49 C3
Milton Ave. Badgers Mount TN14 53 B1
Milton Ave. Cliffe Woods ME3 .. 33 B8
Milton Ave. Gravesend DA12 ... 30 C7
Milton Ct. DA12 .... 30 C6
Milton Dr. TN1 & TN2 .... 149 D7
Milton Gdns. Tilbury RM18 .... 13 B6
Milton Gdns. Tonbridge TN9 . 132 F7
Milton Hall Rd. DA12 .... 30 D7
Milton House. DA1 .... 8 E2
Milton Lodge. 3 DA14 .... 24 A4
Milton Pl. DA12 .... 13 C1
Milton Rd. Bexley DA16 .... 6 F6
Milton Rd. Erith DA17 .... 4 A2
Milton Rd. Gillingham ME7 ..... 48 C3
Milton Rd. Gravesend DA12 .... 30 D7
Milton Rd. Sevenoaks TN13 .... 83 E6
Milton Rd. Swanscombe DA10 . 11 E1
Milton St. Maidstone ME16 ..... 91 C2
Milton St. Swanscombe DA10 . 11 D1
Milverton Way. SE9 .... 23 A4
Mimosa Cl. BR6 .... 52 C8
Mincers Cl. ME5 .... 62 C2
Mineral St. SE18 .... 2 E1
Minerva Cl. DA14 .... 23 E4
Minerva Rd. ME2 .... 47 A8
Ministry Way. SE9 .... 22 F6
Minshaw Ct. DA14 .... 23 F4
Minster Rd. Bromley BR1 .... 22 B2
Minster Rd. Gillingham ME8 .... 49 C3
Minters Orch. TN15 .... 87 B7
Miranda House. 5 DA17 .... 4 A1
Mirfield St. SE7 .... 1 D3
Miriam Ct. DA14 .... 24 B4
Miriam Rd. SE18 .... 2 E1
Mirror Path. SE12 .... 22 C5
Miskin Cotts. ME3 .... 16 B6
Miskin Rd. Dartford DA1 .... 26 D8
Miskin Rd. Hoo St Werburgh ME3 34 E5
Miskin Way. DA12 .... 30 D2
Mitchell Ave. Chatham ME4 .... 47 F2
Mitchell Ave. Northfleet DA11 .. 29 D6
Mitchell Cl. Dartford DA1 .... 26 E6
Mitchell Cl. Erith DA17 .... 4 C3
Mitchell Cl. Lenham ME17 .... 111 C5
Mitchell Cl. Woolwich SE2 .... 3 C2
Mitchell Rd. Bromley BR1 .... 36 A8
Mitchell Rd. Orpington BR6 .... 51 F6
Mitchell Wlk. Newham E16 .... 1 F8
Mitchell Wlk. Swanscombe DA10 28 E8
Mitchem Cl. TN15 .... 55 E3
Mitre Cl. 5 Erith DA17 .... 4 A2
Mitre Ct. Tonbridge TN9 .... 117 C2
Mitre Rd. ME1 .... 47 B4
Moat Cl. BR6 .... 51 F4
Moat Croft. DA16 .... 7 C4
Moat Ct. Eltham SE9 .... 5 F1
Moat Ct. Sidcup DA15 .... 23 F5
Moat Farm. TN2 .... 163 A7
Moat Farm Rd. ME14 .... 18 D6
Moat La. Cowden TN8 .... 145 E7
Moat La. Erith DA8 .... 9 A6
Moat Rd. TN27 .... 141 B5
Moatbridge Sch. SE9 .... 5 D1
Mockbeggar La. TN17 & TN27 . 171 C4
Model Farm Cl. SE9 .... 22 E5
Modest Cnr. TN4 .... 132 E1
Moira Ct. SE9 .... 5 F3
Molash Rd. BR5 .... 38 C6
Molehill Copse Cty Prim Sch.
  ME15 .... 107 D7
Moles Mead. TN8 .... 112 C2
Molescroft. SE9 .... 23 C5
Molescroft Way. TN9 .... 132 F7
Mollison Rise. DA12 .... 30 E3
Molyneux Almshouses. TN4 .. 148 B4
Molyneux Ct. TN4 .... 148 F4
Molyneux Park Rd. TN4 .... 148 F4
Monarch Cl. Chatham ME5 ..... 62 A6
Monarch Cl. Hayes BR4 .... 50 A6
Monarch Cl. Tilbury RM18 ...... 13 B5
Monarch Dr. E16 .... 1 F8
Monarch Rd. 8 DA17 .... 4 A3
Monckton's Ave. ME14 .... 91 F7
Monckton's Dr. ME14 .... 91 E7
Moncktons La. ME14 .... 91 F7
Moncrieff Cl. 4 E6 .... 1 E7
Moncrif Cl. ME14 .... 93 B4
Monds Cotts. TN14 .... 82 E3
Monica James House. 12
  DA14 .... 24 A5
Monk Dr. E16 .... 1 A6
Monk St. SE18 .... 2 A2
Monkdown. ME15 .... 93 A1
Monkreed Villas. DA3 .... 43 D4
Monks Cl. SE2 .... 3 D2
Monks Orch. DA1 .... 26 D6
Monks Way. BR5 .... 37 D1
Monks Wlk. Southfleet DA13 ... 29 A2
Monks Wlk. 5 Tonbridge TN9 . 133 B8
Monkton Rd. Bexley DA16 .... 7 A5
Monkton Rd. Borough Green TN15 86 F7
Monkwood Cl. ME1 .... 61 B8
Monmouth Cl. Bexley DA16 ..... 7 A3
Monmouth Cl. Gillingham ME8 . 49 D2
Mons Way. BR2 .... 36 E3
Monson Rd. TN1 .... 149 B4
Monson Way. 5 TN1 .... 149 B4
Montacute Gdns. TN2 .... 148 F2
Montacute Rd. TN2 .... 149 A1
Montague Cl. BR8 .... 39 F5
Montague Terr. 1 BR2 .... 36 A5
Montagu Rd. DA15 .... 6 F1
Montbelle Prim Sch. SE9 .... 23 B5
Montbelle Rd. SE9 .... 23 B5
Montbretia Cl. BR5 .... 38 C5
Montcalm Cl. BR2 .... 36 A3
Montcalm Rd. SE7 .... 5 D7
Monteith Rd. TN3 .... 148 A3
Monterey Cl. DA5 .... 25 C6
Montfort Cl. Chatham ME5 ..... 61 F2
Montfort Rd. Kemsing TN14 .... 69 E2
Montfort Rd. Rochester ME2 ... 47 A8
Montgomery Ave. ME5 .... 62 A7
Montgomery Cl. DA15 .... 6 F1
Montgomery Rd. Gillingham ME7 48 C3
Montgomery Rd.
  Royal Tunbridge Wells TN4 . 149 B7
Montgomery Rd.
  South Darenth DA4 .... 41 D8
Montpelier Ave. DA5 .... 24 D8
Montpelier Gate. ME16 .... 91 B5
Montreal Rd. Sevenoaks TN13 .. 83 E4
Montreal Rd. Tilbury RM18 ..... 13 A5
Montrose Ave. Bexley DA16 ..... 6 E4
Montrose Ave. Chatham ME5 ... 62 A7
Montrose Ave. Sidcup DA15 .... 24 A8
Montrose Cl. DA16 .... 6 E4
Monypenny. TN17 .... 181 D3
Moon Ct. SE12 .... 5 A3
Moon's La. TN8 .... 128 A1
Moonstone Dr. ME5 .... 62 B2
Moor Hill. TN8 .... 184 F8
Moor La. TN8 .... 128 A4
Moor Park Cl. ME8 .... 64 A8
Moor Rd The. TN14 .... 84 C7
Moor St. ME8 .... 64 B8
Moor The. TN18 .... 184 F8
Moorcroft Gdns. BR1 .... 36 E4
Moorden La. TN11 .... 115 A1
Moordown. SE18 .... 6 B6
Moore Ave. Grays RM16 .... 11 E8
Moore Ave. Tilbury RM18 .... 13 B5
Moore Rd. DA10 .... 11 E1
Moore St. ME15 .... 47 A8
Moorfield Rd. BR6 .... 38 A2
Moorhead Way. SE3 .... 5 B4
Moorhouse Rd. RH8 .... 96 A6
Mooring Rd. ME1 .... 47 D1
Moorings The. E16 .... 1 C8
Moorside Rd. BR1 .... 22 A4
Morants Court Cross. TN14 ..... 68 C1
Morants Court Rd. TN13 & TN14 83 C8
Morden Cl. ME14 .... 92 B4
Morden Rd. SE3 .... 5 A5
Morden Road Mews. SE3 .... 5 A5
Morden St. ME1 .... 47 C4
More Park RC Prim Sch. ME19 89 D8
Morel Ct. TN13 .... 84 B5
Morella Wlk. ME17 .... 111 C5
Morello Cl. BR8 .... 39 D5
Morement Rd. ME3 .... 34 D6
Moreton Almhouses. TN16 ...... 81 D1
Moreton Ct. DA1 .... 8 E4
Morewood Cl. TN13 .... 83 F4
Morgan Dr. DA2 .... 27 E8
Morgan Rd. BR1 .... 22 A1
Morgan St. E16 .... 1 A8
Morhen Cl. ME6 .... 74 E7
Morland Ave. DA1 .... 9 B2
Morland Dr. Lamberhurst TN3 . 166 B5
Morland Dr. Rochester ME2 .... 33 A1
Morley Cl. ME8 .... 51 B8
Morley Dr. TN12 .... 153 A6
Morley Rd. Chislehurst BR7 ..... 37 C8
Morley Rd. Tonbridge TN9 .... 117 D1
Morley's Rd. TN14 .... 99 D2
Morne Cotts. TN14 .... 68 F8
Morning Cross Cotts. ME3 ...... 16 B4
Mornington Ave. BR1 .... 36 D6
Mornington Ct. DA5 .... 25 D7
Morris Cl. East Malling ME19 ... 74 F1
Morris Cl. Orpington BR6 .... 51 F7
Morris Gdns. DA1 .... 10 A2
Morry La. ME17 .... 125 D7
Morstan Gdns. SE9 .... 22 F4
Mortimer Rd. Erith DA8 .... 8 D8
Mortimer Rd. Orpington BR6 .. 38 A1
Mortimers Ave. ME3 .... 33 A8
Mortlake Rd. E16 .... 1 B7
Morton Cl. BR8 .... 39 E7
Morvale Cl. DA17 .... 3 F2
Mosquito Rd. ME19 .... 88 F3
Mossbank. ME5 .... 62 A3
Mossdown Cl. DA17 .... 4 A2
Mosslea Rd. Bromley BR2 .... 36 D4
Mosslea Rd. Orpington BR6 .... 51 C7
Mossy Glade. ME8 .... 63 E6
Mostyn Rd. ME14 .... 92 C4
Mosul Way. BR2 .... 36 E3
Mosyer Dr. BR5 & BR6 .... 52 D8
Mote Ave. ME15 .... 92 B3
Mote Pk. ME15 .... 92 A3
Mote Rd. Ivy Hatch TN15 & TN11 101 C4
Mote Rd. Maidstone ME15 ...... 92 A3
Mote The. DA3 .... 56 F8
Motherwell Way. RM16 .... 11 A8
Mottingham Ct. SE9 .... 22 F7
Mottingham Gdns. SE9 .... 22 D7
Mottingham La. Eltham SE12 .. 22 C8
Mottingham La.
  Lewisham SE12 & SE9 .... 22 C7
Mottingham Prim Sch. SE9 ..... 22 D7
Mottingham Rd. SE9 .... 22 F7
Mottingham Sta. SE9 .... 22 F7
Mottisfont Rd. SE2 .... 3 B2
Mouat Ct. ME5 .... 62 A3
Moultain Hill. BR8 .... 40 A5
Mound The. SE9 .... 23 A5
Mount Ave. ME18 .... 105 A1
Mount Cl. Bromley BR1 .... 36 E8
Mount Cl. Sevenoaks TN13 ..... 83 F4
Mount Culver Ave. DA14 .... 24 D2
Mount Dr. Bexley DA6 .... 7 E2
Mount Dr. Maidstone ME14 .... 93 B4
Mount Edgcumbe Rd. TN4 .... 149 A3
Mount Ephraim. TN1 & TN4 .. 149 A4
Mount Ephraim Ct. TN4 .... 148 F4
Mount Ephraim Rd. TN1 ...... 149 A4
Mount Harry Rd. TN13 .... 84 B4
Mount La. Hartlip ME9 .... 64 D4
Mount La. Maidstone ME14 .... 93 B4
Mount Lodge. ME1 .... 47 B2
Mount Pleasant. Aylesford ME20 76 A3
Mount Pleasant. Gillingham ME4 48 B3
Mount Pleasant.
  Hildenborough TN11 .... 116 D6
Mount Pleasant.
  Hook Green TN3 .... 165 E6
Mount Pleasant. Ide Hill TN14 .. 97 F4
Mount Pleasant.
  Paddock Wood TN12 .... 135 F6
Mount Pleasant.
  Sparrow's Green TN5 .... 174 E5
Mount Pleasant.
  Tenterden TN30 .... 183 C8
Mount Pleasant. The Moor TN18 184 F8
Mount Pleasant Ave. 2 TN2 .. 149 B3
Mount Pleasant Ct. TN11 ..... 116 D6
Mount Pleasant Dr. ME4 .... 93 A5
Mount Pleasant La. TN3 .... 166 A6
Mount Pleasant Rd. Dartford DA1 9 F1
Mount Pleasant Rd.
  R Tunbridge Wells TN1 & TN2 . 149 A3
Mount Pleasant Rd.
  Sevenoaks Weald TN14 .... 99 D3
Mount Pleasant Terr. ME17 ... 110 F2
Mount Pleasant Wlk. DA5 .... 8 C2
Mount Rd. Bexley DA6 .... 7 E2
Mount Rd. Chatham ME4 .... 47 F3
Mount Rd. Crayford DA1 .... 8 F1
Mount Rd. Rochester ME1 .... 47 B2
Mount Sion. TN1 .... 149 A2
Mount The. DA6 .... 8 B2
Mountain Cl. TN15 .... 71 F3
Mountbatten Ave. Chatham ME5 62 A7
Mountbatten Ave. Higham ME3 . 32 C4
Mountbatten Cl. SE18 .... 6 E8
Mountfield. TN15 .... 87 A7
Mountfield Cl. DA13 .... 57 F2
Mountfield Ct. 4 TN1 .... 149 B3
Mountfield Gdns. TN2 .... 149 B3
Mountfield Pk. TN9 .... 133 C8
Mountfield Rd. TN2 .... 149 B3
Mountfield Way. 1 BR5 .... 38 C5
Mounthurst Rd. BR2 .... 36 A2
Mountjoy Cl. SE2 .... 3 B4
Mounts Hill. TN17 .... 180 B7
Mounts La. TN17 .... 182 A3
Mounts Rd. DA9 .... 11 B1
Mountsfield Cl. ME16 .... 91 D5
Mountview Rd. BR6 .... 38 A2
Moyle Cl. ME8 .... 63 D4
Mozart St. ME4 .... 47 E3
Muir Rd. ME15 .... 92 A2
Muir St. E16 .... 1 E5
Mulberton Ct. BR7 .... 23 D2
Mulberry Cl. Gillingham ME7 .. 63 A4
Mulberry Cl. Greenwich SE7 ..... 5 D8
Mulberry Cl. Meopham Sta DA13 44 B3
Mulberry Cl.
  Royal Tunbridge Wells TN2 . 133 D1
Mulberry Rd. DA11 .... 29 E4
Mulberry Way. DA17 .... 4 C4
Mulgrave House. 20 SE18 .... 1 F2
Mulgrave Prim Sch. SE18 .... 2 A2
Mullein Ct. 6 RM17 .... 12 D8
Mullender Ct. DA12 .... 31 A7
Muller House. SE18 .... 2 A1
Multon Rd. TN15 .... 55 E4
Munday Bois Cotts. TN27 ..... 143 F8
Munday Bois Rd. TN27 .... 127 E1
Munday Rd. E16 .... 1 A6
Munday Works Est. TN9 .... 117 C1
Munford Dr. DA10 .... 28 E8
Mungeam House. ME1 .... 47 C4
Mungo Park Rd. DA12 .... 30 D3
Mungo Park Way. BR5 .... 38 D2
Munn's La. ME9 .... 64 E6
Munnery Way. BR6 .... 51 B8
Murchison Ave. DA5 .... 24 E7
Murrain Dr. ME15 .... 93 A1
Murray Ave. BR1 .... 36 B7
Murray Bsns Ctr. BR5 .... 38 B6
Murray House. 21 SE18 .... 1 F2
Murray Rd. Rochester ME2 ..... 47 C8
Murray Rd. St Paul's Cray BR5 . 38 B6
Murray Sq. E16 .... 1 B6
Murton-Neale Cl. 3 TN18 ...... 179 A2
Muscovy House. DA18 .... 3 E4
Museum of Kent Rural Life.
  ME14 .... 76 D1
Museum St. ME1 .... 47 C5
Musket La. Eyhorne Street ME17 . 94 B2
Musket La. Silver Hill ME17 .... 94 A2
Mussenden La. DA3 & DA4 ..... 41 E3
Mustang Rd. ME19 .... 88 F3
Mycenae Rd. SE3 .... 5 A8
Mynn Cres. ME14 .... 93 A4
Myra St. SE2 .... 3 A2
Myrtle Alley. SE18 .... 2 A3
Myrtle Cl. DA8 .... 8 E6
Myrtle Cres. ME5 .... 61 F5
Myrtle Pl. DA2 .... 27 D8
Myrtle Rd. DA1 .... 26 D6
Myrtledene Rd. SE2 .... 3 A1

Nadine St. SE7 .... 1 C1
Nag's Head La. Bexley DA16 ..... 7 B4
Nag's Head La. Chatham ME1 .. 47 D4
Nagpur House. 4 ME15 .... 107 E5
Nairn Ct. TN15 .... 12 F5
Nansen Rd. DA12 .... 30 D4
Napier Ct. Lewisham SE12 ...... 22 B5
Napier Ct. Maidstone ME14 .... 91 F7
Napier Ct. Newham E16 .... 1 C8
Napier Rd. Bromley BR2 .... 36 B5
Napier Rd. Erith DA17 .... 3 F2
Napier Rd. Gillingham ME7 ..... 48 D4
Napier Rd. Northfleet DA11 ..... 29 F7
Napier Rd.
  Royal Tunbridge Wells TN2 . 149 D2
Napoleon Dr. TN12 .... 138 D5
Napoleon Wlk. ME17 .... 111 C5
Napwood Ct. ME8 .... 63 D6
Nares Rd. ME8 .... 63 D4
Narrow Way. BR2 .... 36 E3
Naseby Ct. DA14 .... 23 F4
Nash Bank. DA13 .... 43 F7
Nash Cl. ME5 .... 62 C2
Nash Croft. DA11 .... 29 E4
Nash Gn. BR1 .... 22 A2
Nash La. BR2 .... 50 A4
Nash St. DA13 .... 44 A7
Nashenden Farm La. ME1 .... 61 A8
Nashenden La. ME1 .... 46 F1
Nassau Path. 6 SE28 .... 3 C5
Natal Rd. ME4 .... 48 A3
Nathan Way. SE28 & SE18 .... 2 E1
National Sea Trng Coll. DA12 ... 14 A4
Naylor's Cotts. ME7 .... 63 B1
Neal Rd. TN15 .... 55 E5
Neale St. ME4 .... 47 F2
Neath Ct. 2 ME15 .... 107 E8
Neatscourt Rd. E16 .... 1 D8
Neills Rd. TN3 .... 165 D2
Nellington Ct. TN4 .... 148 B4
Nellington Rd. TN3 & TN4 .... 148 B4

Nelson Ave. TN9 .... 117 A1
Nelson House. **5**
  Park Wood ME15 .... 107 F5
Nelson House. Swanscombe DA9 11 D2
Nelson Mandela Rd. SE3 .... 5 C4
Nelson Pl. DA14 .... 24 A4
Nelson Rd. Bromley BR2 .... 36 C5
Nelson Rd. Dartford DA1 .... 9 C1
Nelson Rd. Erith DA17 .... 3 F1
Nelson Rd. Gillingham ME7 ...... 48 D4
Nelson Rd. Northfleet DA11 ...... 29 F6
Nelson Rd.
  Royal Tunbridge Wells TN2 ... 149 D2
Nelson Rd. Sidcup DA14 .... 24 A4
Nelson Rd. Wouldham ME1 ...... 60 C5
Nelson Terr. ME5 .... 48 C1
Nepicar La. TN15 .... 72 D3
Neptune Bsns Pk. ME2 .... 47 E7
Neptune Ct. ME2 .... 47 E7
Neptune Wlk. DA8 .... 4 D2
Nesbit Rd. SE9 .... 5 D3
Nesbitt House. DA6 .... 8 B2
Ness Rd. DA8 .... 9 D8
Nestor Ct. ME18 .... 105 A8
Nethercombe House. **4** SE3 .. 5 A8
Nethewode Ct. DA17 .... 4 B3
Netley Cl. ME14 .... 92 D6
Nettlestead La. ME18 .... 104 A6
Nevill Ct. ME19 .... 74 C1
Nevill Gate. TN2 .... 149 B1
Nevill Golf Course. TN2 & TN3 163 D7
Nevill Lodge. TN2 .... 149 C4
Nevill Pk. TN4 .... 148 E3
Nevill Pl. ME6 .... 75 A7
Nevill Rd. ME6 .... 75 A7
Nevill Ridge. TN4 .... 148 D3
Nevill St. TN1 & TN2 .... 149 A2
Nevill Terr. TN2 .... 148 F2
Neville Cl. Maidstone ME14 ..... 92 B8
Neville Cl. Sidcup DA15 .... 23 F4
Neville Rd. ME4 .... 47 E2
New Ash Green Cty Prim Sch.
  DA3 .... 56 F8
New Ash Jun & Inf Sch. DA3 ... 42 F1
New Barn Rd. BR8 .... 39 E8
New Barn Rd.
  Hawkenbury ME17 .... 124 C2
New Barn Rd.
  Northfleet Green DA13 .... 29 C3
New Barn Rd. Swanley BR8 ..... 39 F8
New Barn St. E13 .... 1 B8
New Barns Rd. ME14 .... 92 A8
New Bassetts Cotts. TN12 ..... 153 B5
New Beacon Sch The. TN13 .... 99 A8
New Cotts. Bean DA2 .... 28 B5
New Cotts. Shipbourne TN11 ... 101 D5
New Cotts. Shorne DA12 .... 31 E5
New Covenant Pl. ME1 .... 47 D4
New Cut. **2** TN9 .... 117 C2
New Cut. Chatham ME4 .... 47 F4
New Cut. Dean Street ME15 .... 106 D7
New Cut Rd. ME14 .... 92 D5
New Delhi House. **5** ME15 ... 107 E5
New Eltham Sta. SE9 .... 23 C7
New England Rd. TN4 .... 149 A4
New Farm Ave. BR2 .... 36 A5
New Hall Farm La. ME3 .... 19 B6
New House La. DA11 .... 30 A6
New Hythe La. ME20 .... 75 B3
New Hythe Sta. ME20 .... 75 C4
New Inn Cotts. ME15 .... 106 C7
New Lydenburg Commercial Est.
  E16 .... 1 C3
New Lydenburg St. SE7 .... 1 C3
New Mill Rd. BR5 .... 38 C8
New Pond Rd. TN17 .... 180 D6
New Pound La. ME18 .... 88 C1
New Rd. Bexley DA16 .... 7 B5
New Rd. Burham ME1 .... 60 F1
New Rd. Chatham ME1 .... 47 D4
New Rd. Chatham ME4 .... 47 F4
New Rd. Cliffe ME3 .... 16 A4
New Rd. Cranbrook TN17 ...... 169 B4
New Rd. Ditton ME19 & ME20 .. 75 C1
New Rd. East Malling ME19 ..... 90 A3
New Rd. Egerton TN27 .... 127 F3
New Rd. Erith SE2 .... 3 D1
New Rd. Gravesend DA11 .... 13 B1
New Rd. Grays RM17 .... 12 A8
New Rd. Grays RM17 .... 12 B8
New Rd. Headcorn TN27 ...... 141 D5
New Rd. Hextable BR8 .... 25 F1
New Rd. Langley ME17 .... 108 C5
New Rd. Meopham Station DA13 43 F4
New Rd. Orpington BR6 .... 38 A2
New Rd. Paddock Wood TN12 .. 136 A6
New Rd. Saint's Hill TN11 ..... 131 A1
New Rd. South Darenth DA4 .... 41 D7
New Rd. Sundridge TN14 .... 82 E2
New Rd. Swanley BR8 .... 39 F6
New Road Ave. ME4 .... 47 F4
New Road Cty Prim Sch. ME4 .. 48 A3
New Road Hill. BR2 & BR6 ..... 50 F2
New St. Chatham ME4 .... 47 E3
New St. New Street TN15 .... 57 D4
New St. Westerham TN16 .... 96 C8
New Street Hill. BR1 .... 22 C3
New Street Rd. DA13 & TN15 ... 57 C6
New Strs. ME4 .... 47 F6
New Swan Yd. **7** DA11 .... 13 B1
New Villas. ME15 .... 106 C7
New Wharf Rd. TN9 .... 117 B1
New Wlk. TN15 .... 71 F3
New Years La. BR6 & TN14 ..... 67 A5
Newark Ct. **1** ME2 .... 47 B7

Newark Knok. E6 .... 2 A8
Newark Yd. ME2 .... 47 B7
Newbarn La. TN14 & TN16 ..... 66 C2
Newbery Rd. DA8 .... 8 F6
Newborough Ct. TN10 .... 117 C6
Newbury Ave. ME16 .... 91 C6
Newbury Cl. ME3 .... 33 B8
Newbury Cotts. TN5 .... 175 B8
Newbury Ct. DA14 .... 23 F4
Newbury La. TN5 .... 175 C8
Newbury Rd. BR2 .... 36 A6
Newchurch Rd. ME15 .... 92 A1
Newcomen Rd. TN4 .... 149 A5
Newenden Cl. ME14 .... 92 D6
Newenden Cl. ME2 .... 33 C2
Newham Coll of FE
  (Royal Docks Campus). E16 .... 2 C5
Newham St. ME4 .... 48 B3
Newham Way. E13 .... 1 B8
Newhaven Gdns. SE9 .... 5 D3
Newhaven La. **4** E16 .... 1 A8
Newhouse Terr. TN8 .... 112 C3
Newick Cl. DA5 .... 8 B1
Newing Gn. BR1 .... 22 D1
Newington CE Prim Sch. ME9 .. 65 B7
Newington Ct. TN5 .... 176 E1
Newington Ent Ctr. ME9 .... 65 C8
Newington House. **9** BR5 ..... 38 D1
Newington Ind Est. ME9 .... 64 F6
Newington Sta. ME9 .... 65 B6
Newington Wlk. ME14 .... 92 C6
Newitt Rd. ME3 .... 34 E5
Newland Green La. TN27 ...... 143 D8
Newland St. E16 .... 1 F5
Newlands. TN3 .... 148 A3
Newlands Ct. **8** SE9 .... 6 A1
Newlands Rd. DA13 .... 57 F1
Newlands Rise. TN4 .... 149 A6
Newlands Way. TN4 .... 149 B7
Newling Cl. E6 .... 1 F7
Newlyn Cl. **1** ME14 .... 92 A4
Newlyn Dr. TN12 .... 139 F5
Newlyn Rd. DA16 .... 6 F5
Newman Rd. BR1 .... 36 A8
Newman's Rd. DA11 .... 29 F6
Newmarket Gn. SE9 .... 22 D8
Newnham Cl. ME8 .... 49 C2
Newnham Lodge. DA17 .... 4 A1
Newnhams Cl. BR1 .... 36 F6
Newports. BR8 .... 39 D2
Newstead Ave. BR6 .... 51 E8
Newstead Woods Sch for Girls.
  BR6 .... 51 D7
Newton Abbot Rd. DA11 .... 29 F6
Newton Ave. TN10 .... 117 E2
Newton Cl. Chatham ME5 ...... 62 C2
Newton Cl. **1** Maidstone ME16 91 E3
Newton Gdns. TN12 .... 135 F7
Newton Rd. Bexley DA16 .... 7 A4
Newton Rd.
  Royal Tunbridge Wells TN1 ... 149 B4
Newton Rd. Tilbury RM18 ...... 13 A5
Newton Terr. BR2 .... 36 D3
Newton Willows. TN3 .... 161 C7
Newton's Ct. DA9 .... 10 D3
Newtown Cotts. TN12 .... 139 E6
Nichol La. BR1 .... 22 A1
Nicholas Cl. ME16 .... 91 A3
Nicholas Cl. SE28 .... 3 C7
Nicholas Stacey House. **3** SE7 .. 1 B1
Nicholson House. SE18 .... 5 E7
Nickelby Cl. SE28 .... 3 C7
Nicklaus Dr. ME5 .... 61 F3
Nickleby Cl. ME1 .... 47 C2
Nickleby Rd. DA12 .... 31 A7
Nicola Terr. DA7 .... 7 E6
Nicolson Rd. BR5 .... 38 D2
Nicolson Way. TN13 .... 84 D5
Nigeria St. SE7 .... 5 D7
Nightingale Cl. Gillingham ME8 . 63 E6
Nightingale Cl. Larkfield ME20 .. 74 F2
Nightingale Cl. Northfleet DA11 . 29 E4
Nightingale Cnr. BR5 .... 38 D5
Nightingale Gr. **4** DA1 ...... 10 A3
Nightingale House. SE18 .... 2 A1
Nightingale La. Bromley BR1 ... 36 D7
Nightingale La.
  Goathurst Common TN14 ...... 98 B5
Nightingale Pl. SE18 .... 6 B8
Nightingale Prim Sch. SE18 .... 2 B1
Nightingale Rd. Kemsing TN14 . 69 E2
Nightingale Rd. Orpington BR5 . 37 C3
Nightingale Vale. SE18 .... 6 A8
Nightingale Way. Newham E6 ... 1 E8
Nightingale Way. Swanley BR8 .. 39 E6
Nightingales The.
  Royal Tunbridge Wells TN4 .. 149 A5
Nightingales The.
  Sissinghurst TN17 .... 170 F8
Nile Path. **6** SE18 .... 6 A8
Nile Rd. ME7 .... 48 C4
Nine Acres Rd. ME2 .... 46 B3
Nine Acres Sch. SE18 .... 2 D1
Nine Elms Gr. DA11 .... 30 A8
Nineveh La. TN7 & TN18 ...... 179 E6
Ninhams Wood. BR6 .... 51 A6
Nita Ct. SE12 .... 22 A7
Nithdale Rd. SE18 .... 6 C7
Nizels La. TN11 .... 115 F8
No 1 St. SE18 .... 2 B3
No 2 St. SE18 .... 2 B3
Noah's Ark. TN15 .... 70 B1
Noble Tree Cross. TN11 ...... 116 B6
Noble Tree Rd. TN11 .... 116 B6
Nook The. ME18 .... 104 F2
Norah La. ME3 .... 32 B3
Nordenfeldt Rd. DA8 .... 4 D1

Nore Cl. ME7 .... 48 E1
Norfield Rd. DA2 & DA5 .... 25 D3
Norfolk Cl. Chatham ME5 ...... 62 C3
Norfolk Cl. Dartford DA1 ...... 10 A1
Norfolk Cl. Gillingham ME8 .... 49 D2
Norfolk Cres. DA15 .... 23 E8
Norfolk Gdns. DA7 .... 7 F6
Norfolk Pl. DA16 .... 7 A5
Norfolk Rd. Gravesend DA12 ... 30 D8
Norfolk Rd. Maidstone ME15 .. 107 C8
Norfolk Rd.
  Royal Tunbridge Wells TN1 .. 149 B2
Norfolk Rd. Tonbridge TN9 ... 117 A1
Norham Ct. **11** DA2 .... 10 B1
Norlands Cres. BR7 .... 37 B8
Norman Cl. Gillingham ME8 .... 63 B5
Norman Cl. Kemsing TN14 ..... 69 D2
Norman Cl. Maidstone ME14 ... 92 B6
Norman Cl. Orpington BR6 ..... 51 C7
Norman Ct. TN8 .... 112 B2
Norman Rd. Dartford DA1 ...... 26 E7
Norman Rd. Erith DA17 .... 4 B3
Norman Rd. Erith DA17 .... 4 B5
Norman Rd. New Town ME19 ... 89 B8
Norman Rd.
  Royal Tunbridge Wells TN1 .. 149 B5
Norman Rd. Snodland ME6 ..... 75 A6
Norman Rise. TN17 .... 169 D4
Norman St. TN14 .... 97 F5
Norman Villas. **4** TN18 .... 178 F2
Normandy Prim Sch. DA7 .... 8 D6
Normandy Terr. E16 .... 1 B7
Normandy Way. DA7 & DA8 ...... 8 E6
Normanhurst Ave. DA16 .... 7 D6
Normanhurst Rd.
  Borough Green TN15 .... 87 A7
Normanhurst Rd.
  St Paul's Cray BR5 .... 38 B7
Normans Cl. DA11 .... 30 A8
Norreys Rd. ME8 .... 63 E7
Norrington Rd. ME15 .... 107 B6
Norris Way. DA1 .... 8 F4
Norstead Gdns. TN4 .... 149 B7
Norsted La. BR6 .... 67 B8
North Ash Rd. DA3 .... 56 F7
North Bank Cl. ME2 .... 46 F5
North Basin One Rd. ME4 ..... 34 A1
North Beckton Prim Sch. E6 .... 1 F8
North Borough Cty Jun Sch.
  ME14 .... 92 A6
North Cl. DA6 .... 7 D3
North Cray Prim Schs. DA14 ... 24 E2
North Cray Rd.
  North Cray DA5 & DA14 ...... 25 A6
North Cray Rd. Sidcup DA14 ... 24 E4
North Cres. ME17 .... 106 D4
North Dane Way. ME5 .... 62 C4
North Down. TN12 .... 139 E4
North Downs Bsns Pk. TN14 ... 68 C3
North Downs Terr. ME19 ...... 73 A5
North End La. BR6 .... 51 E6
North End La. BR6 .... 51 B2
North End Trad Est. DA8 .... 8 E6
North Farm La.
  Royal Tunbridge Wells TN2 .. 133 E2
North Farm La.
  Royal Tunbridge Wells
  TN1 & TN2 .... 149 D8
North Farm Rd. TN1 & TN4 ... 149 C8
North Folly Rd. ME15 .... 105 F3
North Glade. DA5 .... 24 F7
North Hill Rd. TN18 .... 178 C1
North Kent Ave. DA11 .... 12 C1
North Lockside Rd. ME4 .... 48 D8
North Meadow. ME19 .... 88 D7
North Pasley Rd. ME4 .... 48 B7
North Pk. SE9 .... 6 A1
North Pole La. BR2 .... 50 A4
North Pole Rd.
  ME16 & ME18 & ME19 ...... 90 C2
North Pondside Rd. ME4 ...... 48 A8
North Rd. Bromley BR1 .... 36 B8
North Rd. Cliffe ME3 .... 16 B6
North Rd. Dartford DA1 .... 9 A1
North Rd. Erith DA17 .... 4 B7
North Rd. Gillingham ME4 & ME7 . 48 A7
North Rd. Goudhurst TN17 ... 153 E1
North Rd. Woolwich SE18 .... 2 E2
North Riding. DA3 .... 43 D6
North Side Three Rd. ME4 ..... 48 C8
North St. Bexley DA7 .... 8 A3
North St. Biddenden TN27 .... 158 A2
North St. Bromley BR1 .... 36 A8
North St. Cowden TN8 .... 145 A6
North St. Dartford DA1 .... 26 D8
North St. Gravesend DA11 ..... 30 B8
North St. Headcorn TN27 .... 141 C5
North St. Maidstone ME16 ..... 90 F2
North St. Rochester ME2 ...... 47 B7
North St.
  Royal Tunbridge Wells TN2 .. 149 C3
North St. Sutton Valence ME17 124 E8
North Terr. ME4 .... 33 F6
North View. ME15 .... 92 B1
North View Ave. RM18 .... 13 A6
North View Cotts. ME15 ...... 106 C7
North View Rd. TN13 .... 84 C6
North Way. ME14 .... 92 B7
North West Kent Coll of Tech.
  DA12 .... 30 F7
North Woolwich Rd. E16 .... 1 B5
North Woolwich Rdbt. E16 ...... 1 E5
North Woolwich Sta. E16 .... 2 A4
Northall Rd. DA7 .... 8 C5
Northbourne. BR2 .... 36 A2
Northbourne Rd. ME8 .... 49 B4
Northcote Rd. Gravesend DA11 . 29 F7
Northcote Rd. Rochester ME2 .. 47 A7

Northcote Rd. Sidcup DA14 .... 23 E4
Northcote Rd. **2** Tonbridge TN9 117 B1
Northcourt Cty Prim Sch. DA12 30 E7
Northdown. ME9 .... 79 D8
Northdown Cl. Maidstone ME14 . 92 B7
Northdown Cl.
  Paddock Wood TN12 .... 135 F6
Northdown Rd. Bexley DA16 ..... 7 C5
Northdown Rd. Kemsing TN14 .. 69 E2
Northdown Rd. Longfield DA3 .. 42 E7
Northdown View. ME17 .... 110 F5
Northend Prim Sch. DA8 .... 8 F6
Northend Rd. DA8 .... 8 F6
Northfield. DA3 .... 42 F6
Northfield Ave. BR5 .... 38 C3
Northfield Cl. BR1 & BR7 ...... 36 E8
Northfields. Maidstone ME16 ... 90 F2
Northfields. Speldhurst TN3 ... 148 A8
Northfleet Cl. ME14 .... 92 C5
Northfleet Ind Est. DA11 ...... 11 F3
Northfleet Sch for Boys. DA11 . 29 D7
Northfleet Sch for Girls. DA11 . 29 C6
Northfleet Sta. DA11 .... 12 B1
Northgate. ME1 .... 47 C6
Northgrove Rd. **9** TN18 .... 178 F2
Northiam Sta. TN31 .... 187 C2
Northlands Ave. BR6 .... 51 E6
Northlands Cotts. TN32 ...... 185 C1
Northleigh Cl. ME15 .... 107 A6
Northolme Rise. BR6 .... 51 E8
Northover. BR1 .... 22 A4
Northpoint Bsns Est. ME2 ..... 47 D8
Northridge Rd. DA12 .... 30 C5
Northside Rd. BR1 .... 36 A8
Northumberland Ave.
  Bexley DA16 .... 6 E4
Northumberland Ave.
  Gillingham ME8 .... 49 E1
Northumberland Cl. DA8 .... 8 C7
Northumberland Cl. ME15 .... 107 C1
Northumberland Gdns. BR1 ... 37 A5
Northumberland Heath Inf Sch.
  DA8 .... 8 C7
Northumberland Heath Jun Sch.
  DA8 .... 8 B7
Northumberland Pk. DA8 .... 8 C7
Northumberland Rd.
  Istead Rise DA13 .... 29 F1
Northumberland Rd.
  Maidstone ME15 .... 107 D8
Northumberland Rd. Newham E6 1 E7
Northumberland Way. DA7 & DA8 8 D6
Northview. BR8 .... 39 E7
Northward Hill Nature Reserve.
  ME23 .... 17 E5
Northwood Av. ME23 .... 17 E4
Northwood Pl. DA18 .... 3 F3
Northwood Prim Sch. DA18 ..... 3 F3
Northwood Rd. ME10 .... 117 C6
Norton Cres. TN10 .... 117 B7
Norton Gr. ME5 .... 61 E3
Norton House. **8** SE18 .... 2 A2
Norton Rd. Five Wents ME17 .. 108 D1
Norton Rd.
  Royal Tunbridge Wells TN1 .. 133 A1
Nortons La. TN27 & TN30 .... 172 E5
Nortons Way. TN15 .... 135 B7
Norvic House. DA8 .... 8 F7
Norway Terr. **4** ME14 .... 92 A7
Norwich Ave. TN10 .... 117 D5
Norwich Cl. ME2 .... 46 D6
Norwich Pl. **7** DA6 .... 8 A3
Norwood Cl. ME3 .... 16 B4
Norwood Ct. **6** DA1 .... 10 A3
Norwood La. ME3 .... 44 B3
Notre Dame RC Prim Sch. SE18 . 6 B8
Nottidge Rd. TN4 .... 148 D1
Nottingham Ave.
  Maidstone ME15 .... 107 D8
Nottingham Ave. Newham E16 .. 1 C7
Nottingham Wlk. ME2 .... 46 D6
Novar Cl. BR6 .... 37 F2
Novar Rd. SE9 .... 23 C7
Nower The. TN14 .... 81 F8
Nuffield Hospl. TN2 .... 149 C3
Nugent Ind Pk. BR5 .... 38 C5
Nunnery La. TN1 .... 146 F8
Nunnington Cl. SE9 .... 22 E5
Nursery Ave. DA7 .... 7 F4
Nursery Ave. Maidstone ME16 . 91 B6
Nursery Cl.
  Maidstone, Bearsted ME14 .... 93 B3
Nursery Cl. Dartford DA2 ...... 27 C8
Nursery Cl. Orpington BR6 ..... 38 A2
Nursery Cl. Sevenoaks TN13 ... 84 C5
Nursery Cl. Swanley BR8 .... 39 C7
Nursery Cl. Tonbridge TN10 .. 117 C4
Nursery Cl. Union Street TN5 .. 177 B3
Nursery Gdns. BR7 .... 23 B2
Nursery Pl. TN13 .... 83 D4
Nursery Rd. Ditton ME20 ...... 75 C1
Nursery Rd. Gillingham ME8 ... 63 D8
Nursery Rd.
  Meopham Station DA13 ...... 44 A4
Nursery Rd. Paddock Wood TN12 135 F8
Nursery Rd.
  Royal Tunbridge Wells TN4 .. 149 B8
Nursery The. Erith DA8 .... 8 F7
Nursery The. Westerham TN16 . 96 C8
Nurstead Ave. DA3 .... 43 D6
Nurstead Church La. DA13 ..... 44 A5
Nurstead La. DA3 .... 43 D5
Nurstead Rd. DA8 .... 8 A7
Nut Tree Cl. ME5 .... 52 D7
Nutfield Cl. ME5 .... 62 B8
Nutfield Way. BR6 .... 51 B8
Nutfields. TN15 .... 86 B4

Nuthatch. DA3 .... 43 B7
Nuthatch Gdns. SE28 .... 2 D2
Nutley Cl. ME8 .... 39 F8
Nutmead Cl. DA5 .... 25 C7
Nuttall Ct. BR5 .... 38 B6
Nutwood Cl. ME14 .... 92 C4
Nuxley Rd. DA17 .... 4 A1
NW Kent Coll of Tech. DA1 .... 26 D8
Nyanza St. SE18 .... 6 D8

O'Neill Path. **11** SE18 .... 6 A8
Oak Ave. Gillingham ME7 ...... 48 E6
Oak Ave. Sevenoaks TN13 ..... 99 B7
Oak Cl. Crayford DA1 .... 8 F3
Oak Cl. Hoo St Werburgh ME3 . 34 E3
Oak Cotts. TN8 .... 113 B6
Oak Ct. BR1 .... 36 F7
Oak Dr. Higham ME3 .... 32 B4
Oak Dr. Larkfield ME20 .... 75 B2
Oak End Ct. TN4 .... 133 A2
Oak Farm Gdns. TN27 .... 141 D6
Oak Farm La. TN15 .... 57 E1
Oak Hill Rd. TN13 .... 84 A2
Oak House. **6** Chatham ME5 .. 61 F4
Oak House. Sidcup DA15 .... 24 A5
Oak La. Headcorn TN27 ...... 141 D5
Oak La. Moor Street ME8 & ME9 . 64 D8
Oak La. Sevenoaks TN13 .... 99 A8
Oak Lodge La. TN16 .... 81 D2
Oak Rd.
  Erith, Northumberland Heath DA8 . 8 C7
Oak Rd. Erith, Slade Green DA8 . 9 A5
Oak Rd. Five Oak Green TN12 . 135 B7
Oak Rd. Gravesend DA12 ...... 30 C4
Oak Rd. Grays RM17 .... 12 C8
Oak Rd. Hoo St Werburgh ME3 . 34 E3
Oak Rd. Orpington BR6 .... 52 A3
Oak Rd. Rochester ME2 .... 46 E6
Oak Rd.
  Royal Tunbridge Wells TN1 .. 149 D7
Oak Rd. Stone DA9 .... 10 E1
Oak Rd. Westerham TN16 ...... 81 D2
Oak Terr. **3** TN18 .... 178 F2
Oak Tree Ave. ME15 .... 107 C2
Oak Tree Cl. Marden TN12 ... 138 D5
Oak Tree Cl.
  Royal Tunbridge Wells TN1 .. 149 A1
Oak Tree Gdns. BR1 .... 22 B3
Oak Trees Cty Prim Sch.
  ME15 .... 107 C7
Oak View. TN8 .... 112 B2
Oakapple La. ME16 .... 91 A3
Oakbrook Cl. BR1 & SE12 ..... 22 B4
Oakcroft. SE12 .... 22 B5
Oakdale La. TN8 .... 96 C2
Oakdale Rd. TN4 .... 148 F4
Oakdene Ave. Chislehurst BR7 . 23 A3
Oakdene Ave. Erith DA8 .... 8 C8
Oakdene Rd. Orpington BR5 ... 38 A3
Oakdene Rd. Sevenoaks TN13 .. 84 A5
Oakenden Rd. DA13 .... 44 E1
Oakenholt House. **1** SE2 ..... 3 D4
Oakes Cl. E6 .... 1 F7
Oakfield. Hawkhurst TN18 .... 178 F2
Oakfield. Rolvenden Layne TN17 182 A1
Oakfield Cotts. TN17 .... 180 C4
Oakfield Court Rd. TN2 ...... 149 C3
Oakfield Cty Prim Sch. DA1 ... 26 E6
Oakfield La. Dartford DA1 ..... 26 C6
Oakfield La. Keston BR2 .... 50 D6
Oakfield Park Rd. DA1 .... 26 D6
Oakfield Pl. DA1 .... 26 D6
Oakfield Rd. Marlpit Hill TN8 . 112 B5
Oakfield Rd. Matfield TN12 ... 151 B8
Oakfields. TN13 .... 84 B1
Oakham Dr. BR2 .... 36 A5
Oakhall House. BR5 .... 38 A8
Oakhill Rd. BR6 .... 51 F8
Oakhouse Rd. DA6 .... 8 A2
Oakhurst Ave. DA7 .... 7 E7
Oakhurst Cl. ME5 .... 61 F3
Oakhurst Gdns. DA7 .... 7 E7
Oakland Cl. ME5 .... 61 F3
Oakland Villas. TN3 .... 161 D4
Oaklands. TN17 .... 169 D4
Oaklands Ave. DA15 .... 23 F8
Oaklands Cl. Bexley DA6 .... 7 F2
Oaklands Cl. Orpington BR5 ... 37 E3
Oaklands Cl.
  West Kingsdown TN15 .... 55 E4
Oaklands Cty Prim Sch. ME5 .. 61 F4
Oaklands Rd. Bexley DA6 .... 7 F2
Oaklands Rd. Dartford DA2 ..... 27 C8
Oaklands Rd. Groombridge TN3 161 B6
Oaklands Rd. Hawkhurst TN18 . 179 A1
Oaklands Rd. Northfleet DA11 .. 29 F4
Oaklands Way. TN11 .... 116 F4
Oaklea Rd. TN12 .... 135 F2
Oakleigh Cl. Chatham ME5 .... 61 E2
Oakleigh Cl. Swanley BR8 ..... 39 E6
Oakleigh Gdns. BR6 .... 51 E6
Oakleigh Park Ave. BR7 .... 37 A8
Oakley Cl. **7** Newham E6 ..... 1 E7
Oakley Cl. West Thurrock RM16 11 C8
Oakley Ct. DA1 .... 27 B7
Oakley Dr. Keston Mark BR2 ... 50 E7
Oakley Dr. Sidcup SE9 .... 23 C7
Oakley Pk. DA5 & DA15 .... 24 C8
Oakley Rd. BR2 .... 50 E8
Oakmead. Meopham DA13 ..... 58 A8
Oakmead. Tonbridge TN10 ... 117 C6
Oakmead Ave. BR2 .... 36 A3
Oakmere Rd. SE2 .... 7 A8
Oakmont Pl. BR6 .... 37 D1
Oaks Bsns Village The. ME5 .. 62 C1
Oaks Dene. ME5 .... 61 F4
Oaks Forstal. TN18 .... 186 C5
Oaks Rd. TN30 .... 183 B8

Oaks The. Aylesford ME20 .... 75 E1
Oaks The. Smarden Bell TN27 .... 142 F2
Oaks The. Swanley BR8 .... 39 E7
Oaks The. Woolwich SE18 .... 2 C1
Oakum Ct. ME4 .... 48 B2
Oakway. SE2 .... 6 B1
Oakwood Ave. BR2 .... 36 B6
Oakwood Cl. Chislehurst BR7 .... 23 A2
Oakwood Ct. Dartford DA1 .... 27 B7
Oakwood Ct. Maidstone ME16 .... 91 D3
Oakwood Ct. Swanley BR8 .... 39 C7
Oakwood Dr. Bexley DA7 .... 8 C3
Oakwood Dr. Sevenoaks TN13 .... 84 B4
Oakwood Gdns. BR6 .... 51 C8
Oakwood Hospl. ME16 .... 91 B3
Oakwood Park Gram Sch.
ME16 .... 91 C3
Oakwood Rd. Maidstone ME16 .... 91 D3
Oakwood Rd. Orpington BR6 .... 51 C8
Oakwood Rise. Longfield DA3 .... 42 E6
Oakwood Rise.
Royal Tunbridge Wells TN2 .... 149 E7
Oasis The. BR1 .... 36 C7
Oast Cl. TN1 .... 149 D7
Oast Ct. ME18 .... 104 F1
Oast House Way. BR5 .... 38 B5
Oast La. TN11 .... 117 A4
Oast View. TN12 .... 153 A6
Oast Way. DA3 .... 42 E3
Oastfield Ct. TN15 .... 84 C2
Oasts The. ME14 .... 93 C4
Oastview. ME4 .... 64 A8
Oatfield Cl. TN17 .... 169 C5
Oatfield Dr. TN17 .... 169 C5
Oatfield Rd. BR6 .... 37 F1
Occupation La. SE18 .... 6 B6
Ockham Dr. BR5 .... 24 A1
Ockley La. TN18 .... 179 A3
Ockley Rd. TN18 .... 179 A2
Octavia Ct. ME5 .... 62 B3
Octavia Way. SE28 .... 3 B6
Odeon Ct. E16 .... 1 A8
Odeon Dr. SE9 .... 5 E3
Odiham Dr. ME16 .... 91 C7
Offen's Dr. TN12 .... 139 E3
Offenham Rd. BR7 & SE9 .... 22 F4
Offham Cty Prim Sch. ME19 .... 88 D8
Offham Rd. ME19 .... 89 A7
Officers' Rd. ME4 .... 48 B8
Ogilby St. SE18 .... 1 F2
Okehampton Cres. DA16 .... 7 C6
Okemore Gdns. BR5 .... 38 C5
Old Ashford Rd. ME17 .... 111 E5
Old Barn Cl. Gillingham ME7 .... 62 F6
Old Barn Cl. Kemsing TN15 .... 70 A2
Old Barn Cl. Tonbridge TN9 .... 132 F8
Old Barn Rd. ME19 .... 74 E2
Old Barn Way. DA7 .... 8 D4
Old Bexley CE Prim Sch. DA5 .. 25 A7
Old Bexley CE Sch. DA5 .... 24 F7
Old Bexley La. Dartford DA1 .... 25 F7
Old Bexley La. Maypole DA5 .... 25 E6
Old Carriageway The.
Gillingham ME7 .... 62 F4
Old Carriageway The.
Sevenoaks TN13 .... 83 C5
Old Castle Wlk. ME8 .... 63 D4
Old Chapel Rd. BR8 .... 39 C2
Old Chatham Rd. Kit's Coty ME20 76 D6
Old Chatham Rd.
Maidstone ME14 .... 76 F1
Old Church La. ME18 .... 103 E4
Old Church Rd. Burham ME1 .... 60 C1
Old Church Rd. Matfield TN2 .. 134 D2
Old Church Rd.
Mereworth ME18 .... 103 D5
Old Church Rd. Pembury TN2 .. 150 D8
Old Clem Sq. SE18 .... 6 A8
Old Coach Rd. TN15 .... 71 E5
Old Ctyd The. BR1 .... 36 B8
Old Dartford Rd. DA4 .... 40 F3
Old Dover Rd. SE3 & SE7 .... 5 B7
Old Downs. DA3 .... 42 E4
Old Dr. ME15 .... 106 F6
Old Farm Ave. DA15 .... 23 E6
Old Farm Gdns. BR8 .... 39 F6
Old Farm Rd E. DA15 .... 24 A6
Old Farm Rd W. DA15 .... 23 F6
Old Forge La. ME9 .... 79 F3
Old Forge Way. DA14 .... 24 B4
Old Garden The. TN13 .... 83 D4
Old Gardens Cl. TN2 .... 163 B8
Old Hadlow Rd. TN10 .... 117 F4
Old Ham La. ME17 .... 111 A4
Old Hill. Chislehurst BR7 .... 37 A8
Old Hill. Orpington BR6 .... 51 E4
Old Homesdale Rd. BR2 .... 36 C5
Old House La. TN3 .... 147 D4
Old House Rd. ME9 .... 64 E4
Old Kent Rd. TN12 .... 136 A6
Old La. TN15 .... 86 C4
Old Lain. ME17 .... 110 F6
Old London Rd.
Badgers Mount TN14 .... 53 A1
Old London Rd. Tonbridge TN10 117 C3
Old London Rd. Wrotham TN15 .. 71 F4
Old Loose Hill. ME15 .... 106 F4
Old Maidstone Rd. BR8 & DA14 . 24 F1
Old Manor Dr. DA12 .... 30 C7
Old Manor Way. Bexley DA7 .... 8 D5
Old Manor Way.
Chislehurst BR7 & SE9 .... 22 F3
Old Mill Cl. DA4 .... 40 E1
Old Mill La. ME20 .... 75 B2
Old Mill Rd. Silver Hill ME17 .... 93 F1
Old Mill Rd. Woolwich SE18 .... 6 D8
Old Oast Bsns Ctr The. ME20 .. 76 A1

Old Orch. TN11 .... 115 A3
Old Orch The. ME8 .... 64 A8
Old Orchard La. ME18 .... 74 D1
Old Otford Rd. TN14 .... 69 B1
Old Park Rd. SE2 .... 3 A2
Old Parsonage Ct. ME19 .... 89 C7
Old Pattens La. ME1 .... 47 D2
Old Perry St. Chislehurst BR7 .... 23 E1
Old Perry St. Northfleet DA11 .... 29 E6
Old Polhill. TN14 .... 68 D4
Old Rd. Chatham ME4 .... 47 F4
Old Rd. Crayford DA1 & DA7 .... 8 F1
Old Rd. East Peckham TN12 .... 120 A6
Old Rd. Wateringbury ME18 .... 104 C7
Old Rd E. DA12 .... 30 D7
Old Rd W. DA11 & DA12 .... 30 B7
Old Regent Dr. TN17 .... 181 E4
Old Riding School The. TN3 .... 161 B2
Old School Cl. ME17 .... 111 D4
Old School Cl. Chattenden ME3 .. 33 F4
Old School Ct. Egerton TN27 .... 127 F3
Old School House The. TN8 .... 112 C1
Old School La. ME19 .... 73 F4
Old Soar Rd. TN15 .... 87 C1
Old Station Rd. TN5 .... 174 E6
Old Tannery Cl. TN30 .... 182 F7
Old Terry's Lodge Rd. TN15 .... 71 A4
Old Timber Top Cotts The.
TN13 .... 84 C4
Old Tovil Rd. ME15 .... 92 A2
Old Trafford Cl. ME16 .... 91 B6
Old Tramyard. SE18 .... 2 E2
Old Tree La. ME17 .... 107 D3
Old Wardsdown. TN5 .... 177 B3
Old Watling St. Cuxton ME2 .... 46 B8
Old Watling St. Gravesend DA13 30 A3
Old Wlk The. TN14 .... 69 C2
Old Yews The. DA3 .... 43 B6
Oldborough Manor Com Coll.
ME15 .... 107 B6
Oldbury Cl. Oldbury TN15 .... 86 B5
Oldbury Cl. Orpington BR5 .... 38 D5
Oldbury Cotts. TN15 .... 86 B6
Oldbury La. TN15 .... 86 B6
Oldchurch Ct. ME16 .... 91 E3
Oldfield Cl. Bromley BR1 .... 36 F5
Oldfield Cl. Gillingham ME8 .... 63 D8
Oldfield Cl. Maidstone ME15 .... 92 E1
Oldfield Rd. Bexley DA7 .... 7 E5
Oldfield Rd. Bromley BR1 .... 36 F5
Oleander Cl. ME5 .... 51 D5
Olive Rd. DA1 .... 26 D7
Oliver Cl. Chatham ME4 .... 48 B2
Oliver Cl. West Thurrock RM16 .. 10 F7
Oliver Cres. DA4 .... 40 F2
Oliver Ct. SE18 .... 2 C2
Oliver Gdns. E6 .... 1 E8
Oliver Rd. Staplehurst TN12 .... 139 E4
Oliver Rd. Swanley BR8 .... 39 D6
Oliver Rd. West Thurrock RM16 .. 11 A7
Oliver Twist Cl. ME1 .... 47 B4
Olivers Cotts. ME14 .... 93 C4
Olivers Mill. DA3 .... 56 E8
Olivine Cl. ME5 .... 77 A8
Olliffe Cl. ME5 .... 61 F2
Olron Cres. DA6 .... 7 E2
Olven Rd. SE18 .... 6 C8
Olyffe Ave. DA16 .... 7 A5
Onslow Cres. BR7 .... 37 B8
Onslow Dr. DA14 .... 24 D6
Onslow Rd. ME1 .... 47 D3
Opal Cl. E16 .... 1 D7
Opal Gn. ME5 .... 62 B2
Openshaw Rd. SE2 .... 3 B2
Orache Dr. ME14 .... 92 E5
Orange Court La. BR6 .... 51 A2
Orange Terr. ME1 .... 47 D5
Orangery La. SE9 .... 5 F2
Orbit Cl. ME5 .... 77 A8
Orchard Ave. Aylesford ME20 .... 75 E1
Orchard Ave. Dartford DA1 .... 26 B7
Orchard Ave. Erith DA17 .... 7 F8
Orchard Ave. Gravesend DA11 .. 30 B3
Orchard Ave. Rochester ME2 .... 32 F1
Orchard Bank. ME17 .... 108 B1
Orchard Bsns Ctr.
Maidstone ME16 .... 91 C8
Orchard Bsns Ctr.
Paddock Wood TN12 .... 136 A6
Orchard Bsns Ctr.
Royal Tunbridge Wells TN4 .. 149 D8
Orchard Bsns Ctr.
Tonbridge TN9 .... 117 C1
Orchard Cl. Bexley DA7 .... 7 E6
Orchard Cl. Coxheath ME17 .... 106 C3
Orchard Cl. Edenbridge TN8 .... 112 B2
Orchard Cl. Horsmonden TN12 .. 152 F6
Orchard Cl. Langley Heath ME17 108 E4
Orchard Cl. New Barn DA3 ...... 43 B7
Orchard Cl.
Royal Tunbridge Wells TN1 .... 149 D6
Orchard Cl. Sevenoaks TN14 .... 84 C7
Orchard Cotts. ME16 .... 106 A8
Orchard Cres. TN12 .... 153 A6
Orchard Ct. TN17 .... 180 D6
Orchard Dr. Edenbridge TN8 .... 112 B2
Orchard Dr.
Meopham Station DA13 .... 43 F4
Orchard Dr. Newington ME9 .... 65 A5
Orchard Dr. Tonbridge TN10 .... 117 E5
Orchard Glade. TN27 .... 141 E5
Orchard Gn. BR6 .... 51 E8
Orchard Gr. Larkfield ME20 .... 75 B2
Orchard Gr. Orpington BR6 .... 37 F1
Orchard Gr.
Royal Tunbridge Wells TN1 .. 149 B5
Orchard Hill. DA1 .... 8 E2

Orchard House. DA8 .... 8 F6
Orchard Ind Est. ME15 .... 107 F3
Orchard Pl. Maidstone ME16 .. 91 E3
Orchard Pl. St Paul's Cray BR5 .... 38 C6
Orchard Pl. Sundridge TN14 .... 82 D3
Orchard Rd. Bexley DA16 .... 7 B4
Orchard Rd. Bromley BR1 .... 36 C8
Orchard Rd. East Peckham TN12 120 A6
Orchard Rd. Erith DA17 .... 4 A2
Orchard Rd. Maidstone ME14 .... 92 E4
Orchard Rd. Northfleet DA11 .... 29 C6
Orchard Rd. Orpington BR6 .... 51 B5
Orchard Rd. Otford TN14 .... 68 F3
Orchard Rd. Pratt's Bottom BR6 .. 52 C2
Orchard Rd. Sevenoaks TN13 .... 83 E5
Orchard Rd. Sidcup DA14 .... 23 E4
Orchard Rd. St Michaels TN30 .. 173 A3
Orchard Rd. Swanscombe DA10 .. 11 E2
Orchard Rise. TN3 .... 161 B7
Orchard Rise E. DA15 .... 6 F2
Orchard Rise W. DA15 .... 6 E2
Orchard St. Dartford DA1 .... 9 E1
Orchard St. Gillingham ME8 .... 63 E8
Orchard St. Maidstone ME15 .... 92 A3
Orchard Terr. DA9 .... 10 E2
Orchard The. Maidstone ME14 .. 93 B4
Orchard The. Sevenoaks TN13 .. 83 E6
Orchard The. Swanley BR8 .... 39 D7
Orchard View. TN30 .... 183 C8
Orchard Villas. TN12 .... 122 A4
Orchard Way.
Horsmonden TN12 .... 153 A6
Orchard Way. Kemsing TN15 .... 70 A2
Orchard Way. Snodland ME6 .... 74 F7
Orchard Way. Turnden TN17 .. 169 B4
Orchard Way. Wilmington DA2 .. 26 D5
Orchardlea. DA13 .... 28 F3
Orchards Sh Ctr The. DA1 .... 9 E1
Orchid Cl. Newham E16 .... 1 E8
Orchid Cl. Rochester ME2 .... 46 C6
Orchidhurst. TN2 .... 149 D7
Ordnance Rd. Gravesend DA12 .. 13 C1
Ordnance Rd. Woolwich SE18 .... 6 A8
Ordnance St. ME4 .... 47 E3
Ordnance Terr. ME4 .... 47 E4
Oregon Sq. BR6 .... 37 D1
Oriental Rd. E16 .... 1 D5
Oriole Way. Larkfield ME20 .... 74 F2
Oriole Way. Woolwich SE28 .... 3 B6
Orion Rd. ME1 .... 61 C7
Orissa Rd. SE18 .... 2 E1
Orlestone Gdns. BR6 .... 52 E5
Orlick Rd. DA12 .... 31 B7
Ormesby Cl. SE28 .... 3 D6
Ormiston Rd. SE10 .... 1 A1
Ormond Ave. BR6 .... 51 C8
Ormsby Gn. ME8 .... 63 E3
Ormsby Point. SE18 .... 2 B2
Orpines The. ME18 .... 104 F7
Orpington By-Pass Rd. TN14 .. 53 A2
Orpington Coll. BR6 .... 38 A1
Orpington Hospl. BR6 .... 51 F6
Orpington Rd. BR7 .... 37 E6
Orpington Sta. BR6 .... 51 E8
Orpington Trad Est. BR5 .... 38 C5
Orwell Cl. Lunsford ME20 .... 74 F3
Orwell Cl. Rainham RM9 .... 4 D8
Orwell House. ME15 .... 107 E8
Osberton Rd. SE12 .... 5 A2
Osborne Rd. Erith DA17 .... 7 F8
Osborne Rd. Gillingham ME7 .... 48 C5
Osbourne Rd. DA2 .... 10 B1
Osgood Ave. BR6 .... 51 F5
Osgood Gdns. BR6 .... 51 F5
Osmers Hill. TN5 .... 174 F7
Osmunda Ct. TN2 .... 149 C4
Osney House. SE2 .... 3 D4
Osney Way. DA12 .... 30 F6
Osprey Ave. ME5 & ME7 .... 48 E2
Osprey Cl. E6 .... 1 E8
Osprey Wlk. ME20 .... 74 F1
Ospringe Ct. SE9 .... 6 D1
Osterberg Rd. DA1 .... 9 F3
Osterley Cl. BR5 .... 38 A8
Ostlers Ct. ME2 .... 75 A8
Otford Cl. Bromley BR1 .... 37 A6
Otford Cl. Sidcup DA5 .... 8 B1
Otford Court (St Michael's Sch).
TN14 .... 69 E4
Otford Cty Prim Sch. TN14 .... 69 B3
Otford La. TN14 .... 68 B6
Otford Rd. TN14 .... 84 B7
Otford Sta. TN14 .... 69 C3
Otham La. ME15 .... 93 C2
Otham St. Maidstone ME15 .... 93 C2
Otham St. Otham ME15 .... 108 B7
Otley Rd. E16 .... 1 C7
Otlinge Cl. BR5 .... 38 D5
Ottawa Rd. ME18 .... 13 A5
Otterbourne Pl. ME15 .... 92 E1
Otterden Cl. BR6 .... 51 E6
Otterham Quay La. ME8 .... 64 B8
Otteridge Rd. ME14 .... 93 A3
Ottershaw House. BR5 .... 38 B8
Otway St. ME4 .... 48 A3
Otway Terr. ME4 .... 48 A3
Our Lady of Grace RC Jun Mix Sch.
SE7 .... 5 C8
Our Lady of Hartley RC Prim Sch.
DA3 .... 42 F4
Our Lady of the Rosary
RC Prim Sch. SE9 .... 6 E1
Our Lady's RC Prim Sch. DA1 .... 9 D1
Oval The. New Barn DA3 .... 43 C6
Oval The. Sidcup DA15 .... 24 A8
Ovenden Rd. Chevening TN14 .. 82 D5
Ovenden Rd. Sundridge TN14 .. 82 D6
Over Minnis. DA3 .... 56 F7

Overcliffe. DA11 .... 13 A1
Overcourt Cl. DA15 .... 7 B1
Overdale. TN14 .... 99 B2
Overdale. Eltham SE9 .... 23 D8
Overmead. Swanley BR8 .... 39 E4
Overton Rd. SE2 .... 3 D3
Overy Liberty. DA1 .... 26 E8
Overy St. DA1 .... 9 E1
Owen Cl. East Malling ME19 .... 89 F8
Owen Cl. Woolwich SE28 .... 3 C5
Owenite St. SE2 .... 3 B2
Owens Way. ME7 .... 49 A6
Owletts. DA12 .... 44 F6
Ox Cl. Rainham RM8 .... 173 B2
Ox Lea. TN3 .... 148 A3
Oxenden Wood Rd. BR6 .... 52 C4
Oxenhill Rd. TN14 .... 69 E2
Oxenhoath Rd. TN11 .... 102 D4
Oxfield. TN8 .... 112 D3
Oxford Cl. DA12 .... 30 F6
Oxford Mews. DA15 .... 25 A7
Oxford Rd. Gillingham ME7 .... 48 D3
Oxford Rd. Maidstone ME15 .... 107 D8
Oxford Rd. Sidcup DA14 .... 24 B3
Oxford St. ME4 .... 75 A8
Oxhawth Cres. BR2 .... 37 B3
Oxleas. E6 .... 2 B7
Oxleas Cl. DA16 .... 6 D5
Oxley Shaw La. ME19 & ME20 .. 74 E2
Oyster Catchers Cl. E16 .... 1 B7
Ozolins Way. E16 .... 1 A7

Pacific Rd. E16 .... 1 A7
Packer Pl. ME5 .... 62 A8
Packham Rd. DA11 .... 29 F5
Packhorse Rd. TN13 .... 83 C4
Packmores Rd. SE9 .... 6 E2
Pad's Hill. ME15 .... 92 A4
Paddlesworth Rd. ME6 .... 59 D1
Paddock Cl. Fordcombe TN3 .. 147 B5
Paddock Cl. Greenwich SE3 .... 5 A5
Paddock Cl. Orpington BR6 .... 51 B6
Paddock Cl. Platt TN15 .... 87 C6
Paddock Cl. South Darenth DA4 .. 41 C8
Paddock Rd. DA6 .... 7 E3
Paddock The. Chatham ME4 .... 47 F4
Paddock The. Hadlow TN11 .... 102 E1
Paddock The. Pembury TN2 .. 150 C6
Paddock The. Vigo Village DA13 . 72 F7
Paddock The. Westerham TN16 . 81 C1
Paddock Way. BR7 .... 23 D1
Paddock Wood Cty Prim Sch.
TN12 .... 136 A6
Paddock Wood Sta. TN12 .... 136 A6
Paddocks Cl. BR5 .... 52 D8
Paddocks The. Cowden TN8 .. 145 B7
Paddocks The.
East Peckham TN12 .... 119 E6
Paddocks The. Gillingham ME7 .. 63 A5
Paddocks The. Sevenoaks TN13 . 84 D3
Padsole La. ME15 .... 92 A4
Padstow Manor. ME7 .... 48 C6
Page Cl. DA2 .... 28 C5
Page Cres. DA8 .... 8 F7
Page Heath La. BR1 .... 36 D6
Page Heath Villas. BR1 .... 36 D6
Pageant Cl. RM18 .... 13 C6
Pagehurst Rd. TN12 .... 139 B3
Paget Gdns. BR7 .... 37 B8
Paget Rise. SE18 .... 6 A7
Paget Row. ME7 .... 48 C5
Paget St. ME7 .... 48 C5
Paget Terr. SE18 .... 6 B8
Pagitt St. ME4 .... 47 E3
Paiges Farm Cl. TN14 .... 99 C2
Painters Ash La. DA11 .... 29 D5
Palace Ave. ME15 .... 92 A4
Palace Ct. Chatham ME5 .... 48 D2
Palace Ct. Eltham SE9 .... 5 F1
Palace Gr. BR1 .... 36 B8
Palace Ind Est. ME15 .... 107 F4
Palace Rd. Bromley BR1 .... 36 B8
Palace Rd. Hill Park TN16 .... 81 A6
Palace View. Bromley BR1 .... 36 B6
Palace View. Lewisham SE12 .... 22 A6
Palace Wood Cty Inf Sch. ME16 91 C6
Palace Wood Cty Jun Sch.
ME16 .... 91 C6
Palewell Cl. BR5 .... 38 B7
Pallant Way. BR6 .... 51 A7
Pallet Way. SE18 .... 5 E6
Palm Ave. DA14 .... 24 D2
Palmar Cres. DA7 .... 8 A5
Palmar Rd. Bexley DA7 .... 8 A5
Palmar Rd. Maidstone ME16 .... 91 D6
Palmarsh Cl. BR5 .... 38 D5
Palmeira Rd. DA16 .... 7 D4
Palmer Ave. DA12 .... 30 D4
Palmers Brook. TN11 .... 102 F2
Palmers Green La. TN12 .... 136 D1
Palmers Orch. TN14 .... 68 F8
Palmerston Cres. SE18 .... 6 C8
Palmerston Rd. Chatham ME4 .... 47 F1
Palmerston Rd. Grays RM16 .... 11 D8
Palmerston Rd. Orpington BR6 .. 51 C5
Panbro House. SE18 .... 5 F6
Panfield Rd. SE28 .... 3 A3
Pankhurst Rd. ME3 .... 34 D6
Pannell Rd. ME3 .... 21 A1
Panter's. ME4 .... 25 F1
Pantiles The. Bromley BR1 .... 36 E6
Pantiles The. Erith DA7 .... 7 F7
Pantiles The.
Royal Tunbridge Wells TN2 .. 149 A2
Panton Cl. ME5 .... 62 C4
Pantyles The. TN14 .... 98 B5
Papillons Wlk. SE3 .... 5 A4
Papion Gr. ME5 .... 61 C2

Parade The. Crayford DA1 .... 8 F2
Parade The. Gravesend DA12 .... 30 D6
Parade The. Kemsing TN14 .... 69 E2
Parade The.
Meopham Station DA13 .... 44 A2
Parade The. Staplehurst TN12 .. 139 F3
Parade The. Swanscombe DA10 .. 11 F2
Paradise Cotts. ME9 .... 64 E5
Paradise Pl. SE7 .... 1 E2
Paragon Cl. E16 .... 1 A7
Paragon The. SE3 .... 5 A5
Parham Rd. ME4 .... 47 F2
Parish CE Prim Sch. BR1 .... 22 A1
Parish Gate Dr. DA15 .... 6 E1
Parish Wharf. SE18 & SE7 .... 1 E7
Park App. DA16 .... 7 B3
Park Ave. Bromley BR1 .... 22 A2
Park Ave. Edenbridge TN8 .... 112 B2
Park Ave. Gillingham ME7 .... 48 B3
Park Ave. Gravesend DA12 .... 30 C7
Park Ave. Hildenborough TN11 .. 116 F5
Park Ave. Loose ME17 .... 106 E2
Park Ave. Maidstone ME14 .... 92 B6
Park Ave. Northfleet DA11 .... 29 E7
Park Ave.
Orpington,Goddington BR6 ...... 52 B7
Park Ave.
Orpington,Locksbottom BR6 .... 51 A8
Park Ave. West Thurrock RM16 .. 11 B8
Park Barn Rd. ME17 .... 109 C5
Park Corner Rd. DA13 .... 28 F4
Park Cotts. TN18 .... 179 A2
Park Cres. Chatham ME4 .... 61 F8
Park Cres. Erith DA8 .... 8 D8
Park Crescent Rd. DA8 .... 8 D8
Park Dr. Longfield DA3 .... 42 E6
Park Dr. Woolwich SE7 .... 5 B8
Park Farm Houses. ME19 .... 90 B8
Park Farm Rd. Bromley BR1 .... 36 D8
Park Farm Rd. Ryarsh ME19 .... 73 F5
Park Gdns. DA8 .... 4 D2
Park Gr. Bexley DA7 .... 8 C3
Park Gr. Bromley BR1 .... 36 B8
Park Hill. Bromley BR1 .... 36 B8
Park Hill. Meopham Station DA13 43 F5
Park Hill Rd. TN14 .... 69 E2
Park House. Maidstone ME14 .. 92 B6
Park House. Sevenoaks TN13 .. 84 C5
Park House. Sidcup DA14 .... 24 A3
Park House Gdns. TN4 .... 133 A2
Park La. Cock Street ME17 .... 107 D2
Park La. Gill's Green TN18 .... 178 D7
Park La. Godden Green TN15 .... 85 A4
Park La. Kemsing TN15 .... 70 A1
Park La. Maidstone ME14 .... 91 F7
Park La. Sevenoaks TN13 .... 84 C3
Park La. Swanley Village BR8 .... 40 C7
Park Manor. ME7 .... 48 B5
Park Mead. DA15 .... 7 B1
Park Mews. BR7 .... 23 B2
Park Pl. Gravesend DA12 .... 30 C8
Park Pl. Sevenoaks TN13 .... 83 D4
Park Rd. Addington ME19 .... 73 C3
Park Rd. Bromley BR1 .... 36 B8
Park Rd. Chislehurst BR7 .... 23 B2
Park Rd. Dartford DA1 .... 27 A8
Park Rd. Dunk's Green TN11 .. 102 C5
Park Rd. Gravesend DA11 .... 30 B7
Park Rd. Leybourne ME19 .... 74 D3
Park Rd. Marden Thorn TN12 .. 139 A4
Park Rd. Mereworth ME18 .... 103 F5
Park Rd. Orpington BR5 .... 38 C4
Park Rd. Royal Tunbridge Wells,
Southborough TN4 .... 133 A2
Park Rd. Royal Tunbridge Wells,
St John's TN4 .... 149 B5
Park Rd. Swanley BR8 .... 39 F5
Park Rd. Swanscombe DA10 .... 11 E3
Park Road Ind Est. BR8 .... 39 F6
Park St. TN2 .... 149 C3
Park Terr. Sundridge TN14 .... 82 D3
Park Terr. Swanscombe DA9 .... 11 B2
Park The. DA14 .... 24 A3
Park View. TN15 .... 57 C2
Park View Cl. TN8 .... 112 B2
Park View Ct. ME15 .... 92 E1
Park View Rd. Bexley DA16 .... 7 C4
Park View Rd. Eltham SE9 .... 23 B6
Park Villas. TN11 .... 102 F1
Park Wallis. DA11 .... 12 B2
Park Way. Coxheath ME17 .... 106 D3
Park Way. Maidstone ME15 .... 92 B1
Park Way Cty Prim Sch. ME15 . 92 B1
Park Wood Cty Prim Schs. ME8 63 E5
Park Wood Gn. ME15 .... 63 D5
Park Wood La. TN12 .... 140 C1
Park Wood Par. ME15 .... 107 F5
Park Wood Trad Est. ME15 .... 107 F4
Parkdale Rd. SE18 .... 2 E1
Parker Ave. RM18 .... 13 C4
Parker Cl. Gillingham ME8 .... 63 E5
Parker Cl. Newham E16 .... 1 E5
Parker House. SE18 .... 2 B1
Parker Rd. RM17 .... 11 F8
Parker St. E16 .... 1 E5
Parker's Cnr. ME3 .... 19 C8
Parkfield. Hartley DA3 .... 42 E5
Parkfield. Wilderness TN15 .... 84 F4
Parkfield Rd. ME8 .... 49 F1
Parkfield Way. BR2 .... 36 F4
Parkfields. ME2 .... 46 C7
Parkgate Cotts. BR6 .... 53 C6
Parkgate Rd. BR6 .... 53 C6
Parkhill Rd. Sidcup DA15 .... 23 E5

Parkhill Rd. Sidcup DA5 .... 24 F8
Parkhurst Gdns. **2** DA5 .... 25 A8
Parkhurst Rd. DA5 .... 25 A8
Parkland Cl. TN13 .... 99 D6
Parklands. TN4 .... 148 E8
Parkside. Cliffe Woods ME3 .... 33 B7
Parkside. Halstead TN14 .... 67 F6
Parkside. Sidcup DA14 .... 24 B6
Parkside Ave. Bromley BR1 .... 36 E5
Parkside Ave. Crayford DA1 & DA7 8 E5
Parkside Ave. Tilbury RM18 .... 13 B5
Parkside Cross. DA7 .... 8 E5
Parkside Cl. TN30 .... 182 F7
Parkside Lodge. DA17 .... 4 C1
Parkside Rd. DA17 .... 4 C2
Parkview Ct. DA1 .... 30 A6
Parkway. Erith DA18 .... 3 E3
Parkway. Tonbridge TN10 .... 117 D5
Parkway Prim Sch. DA18 .... 3 E3
Parkwood Cl. TN1 .... 149 C6
Parkwood Hall Sch. BR8 .... 40 B6
Parkwood Rd. DA5 .... 24 F8
Paroma Rd. DA17 .... 4 A3
Parr Ave. ME7 .... 48 D6
Parrock Ave. DA12 .... 30 C7
Parrock Rd. DA12 .... 30 C7
Parrock St. DA11 .... 30 B8
Parrock The. DA12 .... 30 C7
Parrs Head Mews. ME1 .... 47 C6
Parry Ave. E6 .... 1 F7
Parry Pl. SE18 .... 2 B2
Parsonage Ct. TN4 .... 148 B5
Parsonage La. Cold Harbour ME9 65 F8
Parsonage La. Lamberhurst TN3 166 B6
Parsonage La. Rochester ME2 .... 47 C8
Parsonage La. Sidcup DA14 .... 24 F4
Parsonage La.
    Sutton at Hone DA4 .... 27 B2
Parsonage Manorway.
    DA8 & DA17 .... 8 A8
Parsonage Rd. Rusthall TN4 .... 148 B5
Parsonage Rd.
    West Thurrock RM16 .... 11 C8
Parsons La. Heath Side DA2 .... 26 B5
Parsons La. Stansted TN15 .... 56 E1
Partridge Ave. ME20 .... 74 F3
Partridge Cl. **1** E16 .... 1 D8
Partridge Dr. BR6 .... 51 C7
Partridge Gn. SE9 .... 23 A5
Partridge Rd. DA14 .... 23 E4
Partridge Sq. **3** E6 .... 1 E8
Pasley Rd. ME7 .... 48 A7
Pasley Rd E. ME7 .... 48 B7
Pasley Rd W. ME7 .... 48 A7
Passey Pl. SE9 .... 5 F1
Passfield House. SE18 .... 2 D2
Passfield Path. **13** SE28 .... 3 B6
Paston Cres. SE12 .... 22 B8
Patch The. TN13 .... 83 E5
Patience Cotts. TN14 .... 99 B2
Patricia Ct. Bexley SE2 .... 7 B7
Patricia Ct. Chislehurst BR7 .... 37 D8
Patrixbourne Ave. ME8 .... 49 C2
Pattenden Gdns. TN12 .... 120 A7
Pattenden La. TN12 .... 138 C7
Pattens Gdns. ME4 .... 47 E2
Pattens La. ME4 .... 47 E1
Pattens Pl. ME1 .... 47 D2
Patterdale Rd. DA2 .... 27 D7
Patterson Ct. DA1 .... 10 A2
Pattinson Point. **14** E16 .... 1 A8
Pattison Wlk. SE18 .... 2 C1
Paulinus Cl. BR5 .... 38 C6
Pavement The. TN30 .... 173 B3
Pavilion Gdns. TN13 .... 84 C3
Pavilion L Ctr The. BR1 .... 36 A7
Pavilion La. ME14 .... 104 A8
Pavilion The. **5** TN9 .... 117 B1
Paxton Rd. BR1 .... 22 A1
Payne's La. ME15 .... 107 B7
Paynes Cotts. TN13 .... 68 D1
Peace Cotts. ME15 .... 121 D7
Peace St. SE18 .... 6 A8
Peach Croft. DA11 .... 29 E4
Peacock Mews. **7** ME16 .... 91 E4
Peacock St. DA12 .... 30 C8
Pear Tree Ave. ME20 .... 75 D1
Pear Tree Cl. Bexley DA7 .... 8 D6
Pear Tree Cl. Cranbrook TN17 169 D3
Pear Tree Cl. Swanley BR8 .... 39 D7
Pear Tree La. Gillingham ME7 .... 62 E7
Pear Tree La. Maidstone ME15 . 107 B6
Pear Tree Pl. ME15 .... 32 B3
Pear Tree Row. ME17 .... 108 B5
Pear Tree Wlk. ME9 .... 65 A5
Peareswood Rd. DA8 .... 8 F6
Pearl Cl. E6 .... 2 A7
Pearse Pl. TN3 .... 166 B5
Pearson Way. DA1 .... 26 F6
Pearson's Green Rd. TN12 . 136 F3
Pearson's Green Rd. TN12 . 136 F3
Peartree Cotts. ME8 .... 64 B8
Peartree La. ME2 .... 32 A2
Pease Hill. TN15 .... 56 F4
Peasley La. TN17 .... 167 D6
Peat Way. ME3 .... 20 E6
Peatfield Cl. DA15 .... 23 E5
Peckham Cl. ME2 .... 47 C8
Peckham Rd. TN12 .... 119 F6
Peckham House. **6** BR5 .... 38 C1
Peel Rd. BR6 .... 51 C5
Peel St. ME14 .... 92 A5
Peel Yates House. **13** SE7 .... 1 E2
Peens La. ME17 .... 123 C7
Pegasus Ct. DA12 .... 30 C5

Peggotty Cl. ME3 .... 32 B3
Pegley Gdns. SE12 .... 22 A6
Pegwell St. SE18 .... 6 E7
Pelham Cotts. DA5 .... 25 B7
Pelham Prim Sch. DA7 .... 8 A4
Pelham Rd. Bexley DA7 .... 8 A4
Pelham Rd. Gravesend DA11 .... 30 A8
Pelham Rd S. DA11 .... 29 F7
Pelham Terr. DA11 .... 29 F8
Pelican Cl. ME2 .... 46 C6
Pelican Ct. ME18 .... 104 E7
Pell Ct. TN5 .... 175 A6
Pellipar Gdns. SE18 .... 1 F1
Pellipar Rd. SE18 .... 1 F1
Pells La. TN15 .... 71 A7
Pemberton Gdns. BR8 .... 39 E7
Pemberton Sq. ME2 .... 47 C8
Pemble Cl. TN12 .... 135 A7
Pembroke. ME4 .... 48 B8
Pembroke Cl. DA8 .... 4 D2
Pembroke Ct. ME4 .... 48 A4
Pembroke Gdns. ME8 .... 63 E4
Pembroke Pl. DA4 .... 41 B8
Pembroke Rd. Bromley BR1 .... 36 D7
Pembroke Rd. Coxheath ME17 . 106 C3
Pembroke Rd. Erith DA8 .... 4 D2
Pembroke Rd. Newham E6 .... 1 F8
Pembroke Rd. Sevenoaks TN13 .. 84 B2
Pembroke Rd. Tonbridge TN9 .. 117 A1
Pembury Cl. TN2 .... 150 D7
Pembury Cres. DA14 .... 24 E6
Pembury Cty Prim Sch. TN2 . 150 D8
Pembury Gdns. ME16 .... 91 D3
Pembury Gr. TN9 .... 133 C8
Pembury Grange. TN2 .... 150 A6
Pembury Hall Rd. TN11 & TN2 . 134 C3
Pembury Hospl. TN2 .... 150 B7
Pembury Rd. Erith DA7 .... 7 E8
Pembury Rd. Pembury TN11 . 134 A2
Pembury Rd.
    Royal Tunbridge Wells TN2 . 149 E4
Pembury Rd.
    Tonbridge TN11 & TN9 .... 133 D7
Pembury Walks. TN11 & TN2 . 134 C2
Pembury Way. ME8 .... 49 E2
Pen Way. TN10 .... 117 E5
Pencroft Dr. DA1 .... 26 C8
Penda Rd. DA8 .... 8 B7
Pendennis Rd. Orpington BR6 .. 52 C8
Pendennis Rd. Sevenoaks TN13 . 84 B4
Penderel Mews. TN30 .... 183 B8
Pendlebury House. SE18 .... 5 E6
Pendragon Rd. BR1 & SE12 ..... 22 A5
Pendragon Sec Sch. BR1 .... 22 A5
Pendrell St. SE18 .... 6 D8
Pendrill Pl. TN5 .... 174 F5
Penenden. DA3 .... 56 F8
Penenden Ct. ME14 .... 92 B7
Penenden Heath Rd. ME14 .... 92 C7
Penenden St. ME14 .... 92 A6
Penfold Cl. Chatham ME5 .... 62 B7
Penfold Cl. Park Wood ME15 . 107 E5
Penfold Hill. ME17 .... 109 B8
Penfold House. **14** SE18 .... 6 B8
Penfold La. DA5 .... 24 D7
Penfold Way. ME15 .... 106 F6
Penfolds Cl. TN10 .... 117 C5
Penford Gdns. SE9 .... 5 D4
Pengarth Rd. DA5 .... 7 D1
Penguin Cl. ME2 .... 46 D6
Penhall Rd. SE7 .... 1 D2
Penhill Rd. DA5 .... 24 C8
Penhurst Cl. ME14 .... 92 F5
Penlee Cl. TN8 .... 112 C2
Penmon Rd. SE2 .... 3 A3
Penn Gdns. BR7 .... 37 B7
Penn La. DA5 .... 7 E1
Penn Yd. TN2 .... 150 C6
Pennant Rd. ME1 .... 61 C7
Penney Ct. DA1 .... 26 D8
Pennine Way. Erith DA7 .... 8 B4
Pennine Way. Maidstone ME15 .. 93 A1
Pennine Way. Northfleet DA11 .. 29 E5
Pennine Wlk. TN2 .... 149 D5
Pennington Manor. **1** TN4 .. 132 F2
Pennington Pl. TN4 .... 133 B1
Pennington Rd. TN4 .... 133 A1
Pennington Way. SE12 .... 22 B6
Pennyfields. TN17 .... 169 D4
Pennyroyal Ave. E6 .... 2 A7
Penpool La. DA16 .... 7 B4
Penryn Manor. ME7 .... 48 C6
Penshurst Ave. DA15 .... 7 A1
Penshurst CE Prim Sch. TN11 131 A4
Penshurst Cl. Gillingham ME8 .. 49 B2
Penshurst Cl. New Barn DA3 .. 43 D7
Penshurst Cl.
    West Kingsdown TN15 .... 55 E4
Penshurst Enterprise Ctr.
    TN11 .... 131 C4
Penshurst Place. TN11 .... 131 B4
Penshurst Rd. Bexley DA7 .... 7 F6
Penshurst Rd. Penshurst TN11 . 131 C8
Penshurst Rd.
    Poundsbridge TN11 & TN3 . 147 E8
Penshurst Rd.
    Printstile TN11 & TN3 & TN4 . 131 E3
Penshurst Sta. TN11 .... 114 F1
Penshurst Vinyard. TN11 .... 130 F2
Penshurst Way. BR5 .... 38 C5
Penstocks The. ME16 .... 91 D2
Penton House. **3** SE2 .... 3 D4
Penventon Ct. **3** RM18 .... 13 A5
Pepingstraw Cl. ME19 .... 88 D7
Pepper Cl. E6 .... 1 F8
Pepper Hill. DA11 .... 29 C5
Pepy's Way. ME2 .... 46 F8
Pepys Cl. **5** Dartford DA1 .... 10 A3

Pepys Cl. Northfleet DA11 .... 29 D5
Pepys Cl. Tilbury RM18 .... 13 C6
Pepys Cres. E16 .... 1 A5
Pepys Rise. BR6 .... 37 F1
Perch La. TN3 .... 151 D1
Percival Rd. BR6 .... 51 B8
Percy Rd. DA7 .... 7 E5
Percy St. **8** RM17 .... 12 C8
Peregrine Ct. DA16 .... 6 F6
Peregrine Dr. ME18 .... 89 A2
Peridot St. E6 .... 1 E8
Perimeter Rd. ME20 .... 75 C3
Periton Rd. SE9 .... 5 D3
Perkins Cl. ME20 .... 10 F2
Perpins Rd. SE9 .... 6 E1
Perran Cl. DA3 .... 42 F5
Perry Gr. DA1 .... 10 A3
Perry Hall Cl. BR6 .... 38 A2
Perry Hall Prim Sch. BR6 .... 37 F3
Perry Hall Rd. BR6 .... 38 A2
Perry Hill. ME3 .... 16 C1
Perry St. Chatham ME4 .... 47 C1
Perry St. Chislehurst BR7 .... 23 E2
Perry St. Crayford DA1 .... 8 E4
Perry St. Maidstone ME14 .... 91 F6
Perry St. Northfleet DA11 .... 29 E7
Perry Street Gdns. BR7 .... 23 E2
Perryfield St. ME14 .... 91 F6
Perrys La. BR6 & TN14 .... 67 C6
Perth House. **4** RM18 .... 13 A5
Pescot Ave. DA3 .... 43 B6
Pested Bars Rd. ME17 .... 107 D5
Peter St. **5** DA11 .... 30 B8
Peterborough Gdns. ME2 .... 46 C6
Peters Cl. DA16 .... 6 E5
Petersfield. TN2 .... 150 E7
Petersfield Dr. DA13 .... 57 F1
Petersham Dr. BR5 .... 38 A6
Petersham Gdns. BR5 .... 37 F7
Peterstone Rd. SE2 .... 3 B4
Petham Court Cotts. BR8 .... 39 F4
Petham Gn. ME8 .... 49 C2
Petrie House. **3** SE18 .... 6 A8
Pett St. SE7 .... 1 E2
Petten Cl. BR5 .... 38 D1
Petten Gr. BR5 .... 38 D1
Petteridge La. TN12 .... 151 F7
Pettits Row. TN12 .... 137 D8
Pettman Cres. SE18 & SE28 .... 2 D3
Petts Wood Rd. BR5 .... 37 D4
Petts Wood Sta. BR5 .... 37 C4
Petworth Rd. DA6 .... 8 A2
Peverel. DA3 .... 2 A7
Peverel Dr. ME14 .... 93 A5
Peverel Gn. ME8 .... 63 D4
Peverell Ct. **3** DA2 .... 10 B1
Pheasant Cl. ME14 .... 1 B7
Pheasant La. ME15 .... 107 B8
Pheasant Rd. ME4 .... 48 C2
Phelps Cl. TN15 .... 55 E4
Philipot Almshouse. SE9 .... 5 F1
Philipot Path. SE9 .... 5 F1
Philippa Gdns. SE9 .... 5 D2
Phillip Ave. BR8 .... 39 D5
Phillips Cl. DA1 .... 9 B1
Phillips Ct. ME8 .... 49 B2
Philpots La. TN11 .... 115 E6
Philpott's Cross. TN18 .... 178 E2
Phineas Pett Road Rd. SE9 .... 5 E4
Phipps House. **1** SE7 .... 1 B1
Phoenix Cotts. ME18 .... 104 D6
Phoenix Dr. Keston Mark BR2 ... 50 D7
Phoenix Dr. Wateringbury ME18 104 E7
Phoenix Ind Est. ME7 .... 47 D7
Phoenix Pk. ME15 .... 107 F4
Phoenix Pl. DA1 .... 26 D8
Phoenix Rd. ME5 .... 62 B2
Phoenix Yard Cotts. ME18 .... 89 F1
Picardy Manorway. DA17 .... 4 B3
Picardy Rd. DA17 .... 4 A2
Picardy Sch (Beeches Site).
    DA17 .... 4 B2
Picardy St. DA17 .... 4 A3
Piccadilly The. **4** ME4 .... 48 B3
Pickering Ct. **8** DA2 .... 10 B1
Pickering House. **4** SE18 .... 2 A2
Pickering St. ME15 .... 107 B6
Pickford Cl. DA7 .... 7 E5
Pickford La. DA7 .... 7 E5
Pickford Rd. DA7 .... 7 E4
Pickforde La. TN5 .... 176 D1
Pickhill Oast. TN30 .... 183 B4
Pickhurst La. BR2 .... 36 A1
Pickle's Way. ME3 .... 16 A6
Pickmoss La. TN14 .... 69 A3
Pickwick Cres. ME1 .... 47 C3
Pickwick Ct. SE9 .... 22 F7
Pickwick Gdns. DA11 .... 29 C5
Pickwick House. DA11 .... 29 D5
Pickwick Way. BR7 .... 23 C2
Piedmont Rd. SE18 .... 2 D1
Pier Approach Rd. ME7 .... 48 D7
Pier Par. **3** E16 .... 2 A5
Pier Pl. ME2 .... 34 A3
Pier Rd. Erith DA8 .... 8 F8
Pier Rd. Gillingham ME7 .... 48 E7
Pier Rd. Newham E16 .... 2 A4
Pier Rd. Northfleet DA11 .... 12 F1
Pier Rd. Swanscombe DA9 .... 11 B3
Pier Rd Ind Est. ME7 .... 48 D7
Pier Way. SE28 .... 2 D3
Pierce Mill La. TN11 .... 119 C6
Piermont Pl. BR1 .... 36 F7
Pigdown La. TN8 .... 129 D4
Piggott's Cross. TN8 .... 113 D7
Pigsdean Rd. DA13 .... 45 B2
Pike Cl. BR1 .... 22 B3
Pikefields. ME8 .... 49 C2

Pikefish La. TN12 .... 120 F2
Pikey La. ME19 .... 89 E5
Pilgrim's Way. TN15 .... 70 A2
Pilgrims Ct. Dartford DA1 .... 10 A2
Pilgrims Ct. Greenwich SE3 .... 5 A6
Pilgrims Lakes. ME17 .... 110 E6
Pilgrims' Rd. DA10 .... 11 E3
Pilgrims View. Sandling ME2 .... 59 E6
Pilgrims View. Swanscombe DA9 11 C1
Pilgrims Way. Boxley ME14 .... 77 E3
Pilgrims Way.
    Broad Street ME14 & ME17 .. 94 C6
Pilgrims Way. Cuxton ME2 .... 46 C3
Pilgrims Way. Dartford DA1 .... 27 B8
Pilgrims Way. Detling ME14 .... 78 B1
Pilgrims Way. Eccles ME20 .... 76 B6
Pilgrims Way.
    Hollingbourne ME17 .... 94 F3
Pilgrims' Way.
    Kemsing TN15 & TN14 .... 70 C3
Pilgrims Way. Lenham ME17 ... 111 B7
Pilgrims Way.
    Twitton TN13 & TN14 .... 68 E3
Pilgrims Way.
    Upper Halling ME2 & DA13 .. 59 D3
Pilgrims Way. Upper Halling ME2 59 F6
Pilgrims Way. Vigo Village TN15 . 73 B7
Pilgrims Way. Wouldham ME1 .. 60 E3
Pilgrims Way. Wrotham TN15 .. 72 A3
Pilgrims Way. Wrotham TN15 .. 72 C4
Pilgrims Way E. TN14 .... 69 F3
Pilgrims Way W. Otford TN14 .. 68 F3
Pilgrims Way W. Twitton TN13 .. 68 D3
Pilkington Rd. BR6 .... 51 C8
Pillar Box La. TN11 .... 102 D5
Pillar Box Rd. TN15 .... 85 E5
Pilot Rd. ME1 .... 61 C8
Pilots Pl. DA11 .... 13 C1
Pimp's Court Cotts. ME15 .... 106 E6
Pimp's Court Farm Ctr. ME15 106 E6
Pimpernel Cl. ME14 .... 93 B4
Pimpernel Way. ME5 .... 61 E4
Pinchbeck Rd. BR6 .... 51 F4
Pincott Rd. DA5 .... 8 A3
Pincroft Wood. DA3 .... 43 C6
Pine Ave. DA12 .... 30 D7
Pine Cl. Larkfield ME20 .... 75 A2
Pine Cl. Swanley BR8 .... 39 F5
Pine Cotts. ME14 .... 91 E8
Pine Glade. BR6 .... 50 F6
Pine Gr. Edenbridge TN8 .... 112 B2
Pine Gr. Gillingham ME7 .... 63 A5
Pine Gr. Maidstone ME14 .... 92 B6
Pine House. **3** ME5 .... 61 F5
Pine Lodge. ME16 .... 91 C3
Pine Rd. ME2 .... 46 F6
Pine Ridge. TN10 .... 117 B6
Pine Rise. DA13 .... 44 A3
Pine Tree La. TN15 .... 86 A2
Pine View. TN15 .... 87 C7
Pinecrest Gdns. BR6 .... 51 B6
Pinecroft. DA12 .... 7 A7
Pinecroft Wood. DA3 .... 43 C6
Pinehurst. Chislehurst BR7 .... 23 B2
Pinehurst.
    Sevenoaks TN13 & TN14 .... 84 E6
Pinehurst Wlk. **4** BR6 .... 37 D1
Pineneedle La. TN13 .... 84 B4
Pines Rd. BR1 .... 36 E7
Pinesfield La. ME19 .... 73 B6
Pinewood. BR7 .... 23 A2
Pinewood Ave. Sevenoaks TN13 . 84 D6
Pinewood Ave. Sidcup DA15 .... 23 E7
Pinewood Cl. Orpington BR6 .... 37 D1
Pinewood Cl.
    Paddock Wood TN12 .... 135 F6
Pinewood Cl. TN4 .... 133 A1
Pinewood Dr. Chatham ME14 ... 77 D8
Pinewood Dr. Orpington BR6 .... 51 E5
Pinewood Gdns. TN4 .... 133 A1
Pinewood Rd. Bromley BR2 .... 36 A5
Pinewood Rd. Erith SE2 .... 7 D8
Pinewood Rd.
    Royal Tunbridge Wells TN2 . 149 D5
Pinkham. TN12 .... 120 A5
Pinkham Gdns. TN12 .... 120 A6
Pinks Hill. BR8 .... 39 E4
Pinnacle Hill. DA7 .... 8 B3
Pinnacle Hill N. DA7 .... 8 B3
Pinnell Rd. SE9 .... 5 D3
Pinnock La. TN12 .... 139 E1
Pinnock's Ave. DA11 .... 30 B7
Pintail Cl. Grain ME3 .... 21 B6
Pintail Cl. Newham E6 .... 1 E8
Pintails The. ME4 .... 34 B1
Pinto Way. SE3 .... 5 B3
Pinton Hill. TN5 .... 176 B3
Pioneer Way. BR8 .... 39 E6
Piper's Green Rd. TN16 .... 97 B7
Pipers Cl. TN5 .... 175 A4
Pipers La. TN16 .... 97 A8
Pippenhall. SE9 .... 6 B1
Pippin Cl. ME17 .... 106 B2
Pippin Croft. ME7 .... 63 A6
Pippin Rd. TN12 .... 119 F6
Pippin Way. ME18 .... 89 A2
Pippins The. DA13 .... 44 A3
Pirbright Cl. ME5 .... 62 D2
Pirrip Cl. DA12 .... 30 F6
Pit La. TN8 .... 112 C4
Pitfield. DA3 .... 42 F5
Pitfield Cres. SE28 .... 3 A5
Pitfield Dr. DA13 .... 57 F7
Pitfold Rd. SE12 .... 5 A1
Pitt Rd. Langley Heath ME17 ... 109 A2
Pitt Rd. Maidstone ME16 .... 91 B1
Pitt Rd. Orpington BR6 .... 51 C6

Pittlesden. TN30 .... 183 A7
Pittlesden Pl. **1** TN30 .... 183 A7
Pittsmead Ave. BR2 .... 36 A2
Pittswood Cotts. TN11 .... 118 A8
Pix's La. TN17 .... 182 A3
Pixot Hill. TN12 .... 136 B2
Pizien Well Rd. ME18 .... 104 B7
Place Farm Ave. BR5 & BR6 .... 37 D1
Place La. ME9 .... 64 D4
Plain Rd. TN12 .... 138 C4
Plain The. TN17 .... 167 E8
Plains Ave. ME15 .... 92 C1
Plaistow Gr. BR1 .... 22 B1
Plaistow La. BR1 .... 36 C8
Plaistow Sq. ME14 .... 92 C6
Plane Ave. DA11 .... 29 D8
Plane Tree House. SE7 .... 1 D1
Plane Wlk. TN10 .... 117 C7
Plantagenet House. SE18 .... 1 F3
Plantation Dr. BR5 .... 38 D1
Plantation La. ME14 .... 93 A3
Plantation Rd. Erith DA8 .... 9 A5
Plantation Rd. Gillingham ME7 .. 49 A6
Plantation Rd. Hextable BR8 .... 26 A2
Plantation The. SE3 .... 5 A5
Plat The. TN18 .... 112 D1
Platt CE Prim Sch. TN15 .... 87 C7
Platt Comm. TN15 .... 87 C7
Platt House La. TN15 .... 72 C6
Platt Ind Est. TN15 .... 87 C8
Platt The. Frant TN3 .... 163 B1
Platt The. Sutton Valence ME17 . 124 E7
Platt's Heath Cty Prim Sch.
    ME17 .... 110 F2
Platters The. ME18 .... 63 C7
Plaxdale Green Rd. TN15 .... 71 D7
Plaxtol Cl. BR1 .... 36 C8
Plaxtol Cty Prim Sch. TN15 .... 101 C7
Plaxtol La. TN15 .... 101 D8
Plaxtol Rd. DA8 .... 8 A7
Playstool Cl. ME9 .... 65 B6
Playstool Rd. ME9 .... 65 A6
Pleasance Rd. BR5 .... 38 B6
Pleasant Row. **2** ME4 .... 48 A6
Pleasant View. DA8 .... 4 E1
Pleasant View Pl. BR6 .... 51 C5
Pleasaunce Ct. SE9 .... 5 F3
Pleasure House Rd. ME17 .... 125 A8
Plewis House. ME7 .... 48 E7
Plomley Cl. ME8 .... 63 D4
Plough Cotts. ME17 .... 108 E2
Plough Hill. TN15 .... 86 F4
Plough Wents Rd. ME17 .... 108 B2
Plough Wlk. TN8 .... 112 C3
Ploughmans Way. Chatham ME5 62 A1
Ploughmans Way.
    Gillingham ME8 .... 63 E6
Plover Cl. Chatham ME5 .... 62 D1
Plover Cl. Marlpit Hill TN8 .... 112 C3
Plover Rd. ME20 .... 74 F2
Plowenders Cl. ME19 .... 73 D2
Pluckley Cl. ME8 .... 49 C3
Pluckley Rd. TN27 .... 143 D2
Plug La. DA13 .... 58 D5
Plum La. SE18 .... 6 C7
Plum Tree Cotts. TN18 .... 184 E8
Plum Tree Rd. ME9 .... 79 B8
Plumcroft Prim Sch. SE18 .... 6 C8
Plumey Feather Cotts. TN3 .. 160 E3
Plummer La. TN30 .... 182 F6
Plummers Croft. TN13 .... 83 E6
Plumpton Wlk. **9** ME15 .... 107 F6
Plumstead Common Rd. SE18 .. 6 C8
Plumstead High St. SE18 & SE2 .. 2 E2
Plumstead Manor Sch. SE18 .... 6 D8
Plumstead Rd. SE18 & SE28 .... 2 C2
Plumstead Sta. SE18 .... 2 D2
Plumtree Gr. ME7 .... 63 A4
Plumtree Rd.
    Plumtree Green TN27 .... 125 A1
Plumtree Rd.
    Plumtree Green TN27 .... 140 F7
Plumtrees. ME16 .... 91 A2
Plymouth Dr. TN13 & TN15 .... 84 C3
Plymouth Pk. TN15 .... 84 C3
Plymouth Rd. Bromley BR1 .... 36 B8
Plymouth Rd. Newham E16 .... 1 A8
Plympton Cl. **8** DA17 .... 3 E3
Plymstock Rd. DA16 .... 7 C7
Poachers Cl. ME5 .... 62 C5
Pococks Bank. TN8 .... 113 C3
Podkin Wood. ME5 .... 76 F8
Pointer Cl. SE28 .... 3 D7
Pointer Sch The. SE3 .... 5 A7
Pointers Ash Cty Prim Sch.
    DA11 .... 29 D5
Pokes Cott. TN17 .... 166 F2
Polebrook Rd. SE3 .... 5 C4
Polesden Rd. TN2 .... 149 D2
Polhill. TN14 .... 68 C4
Polhill Dr. ME5 .... 61 F2
Police Station Rd. ME19 .... 89 C8
Pollard Cl. E16 .... 1 A6
Pollard Ct. ME14 .... 48 C5
Pollard Wlk. DA14 .... 24 C2
Polley Cl. TN2 .... 150 D7
Pollyhaugh. DA4 .... 54 E7
Pollyhough. DA4 .... 54 E8
Polperro Cl. BR6 .... 37 F3
Polthorne Gr. SE18 .... 2 D2
Polytechnic St. SE18 .... 2 A2
Pond Cl. SE3 .... 5 A5
Pond Farm Cl. Hucking ME17 ... 79 D1
Pond Farm Rd. Oad Street ME9 .. 65 F1
Pond La. TN15 .... 85 E2
Pond Path. ME7 .... 23 B2
Pondfield La. DA12 .... 31 E1
Pondfield Rd. BR6 .... 51 B7

Pondwood Rise. BR6 .... 37 E2
Pontefract Rd. BR1 .... 22 A3
Pontoise Cl. TN13 .... 83 F5
Pook La. TN27 .... 158 D3
Poona Rd. TN1 & TN2 .... 149 B2
Pootings Rd. TN8 .... 112 E7
Pope Dr. TN12 .... 139 E4
Pope House La. TN30 .... 173 B4
Pope Rd. BR2 .... 36 D4
Pope St. ME5 .... 91 C2
Pope Street Ct. SE9 .... 22 F7
Poplar Ave. Gravesend DA12 ...... 30 C4
Poplar Ave. Orpington BR6 ...... 51 B8
Poplar Cl. ME3 .... 34 E3
Poplar Field. TN30 .... 189 D4
Poplar Gr. ME16 .... 91 C5
Poplar Mount. DA17 .... 4 C3
Poplar Pl. SE28 .... 3 C6
Poplar Rd. Rochester ME2 ...... 46 E5
Poplar Rd. Wittersham TN30 ...... 189 D4
Poplar Wlk. DA13 .... 44 B3
Poplars Cl. DA3 .... 43 C6
Poplicans Rd. ME2 .... 46 B3
Poppy Cl. ME7 .... 48 E5
Popular Cl. ME7 .... 46 F5
Porchester Cl. Hartley DA3 ...... 42 F5
Porchester Cl. Maidstone ME15 107 A6
Porchfield Cl. DA12 .... 30 C6
Porcupine Cl. SE9 .... 22 E6
Porrington Cl. BR7 .... 37 A8
Port Ave. DA9 .... 11 B1
Port Cl. Chatham ME5 .... 62 B3
Port Cl. Maidstone ME14 ...... 93 A5
Port Hill. BR6 .... 67 B7
Port Rise. ME4 .... 47 F3
Port Victoria Rd. ME3 ...... 21 C4
Porter Rd. E6 .... 1 F7
Porters Cl. TN12 .... 151 E6
Porters Wlk. ME17 .... 108 E4
Porters Wood. TN12 .... 151 E6
Porteus Cl. DA1 .... 26 D6
Porthkerry Ave. SE6 .... 7 A3
Portland Ave. Gravesend DA12 .. 30 B6
Portland Ave. Sidcup DA15 ...... 7 A1
Portland Cres. SE9 .... 22 E6
Portland Pl. ME6 .... 75 A8
Portland Rd. Bromley BR1 ...... 22 C3
Portland Rd. Chislehurst SE9 .... 22 E6
Portland Rd. Gillingham ME7 .... 48 E6
Portland Rd. Gravesend DA11 .... 30 B7
Portland Rd. Northfleet DA11 .... 12 D1
Portland Rd. Wouldham ME1 ...... 60 C4
Portland St. ME4 .... 48 B2
Portman Cl. Bexley DA7 ...... 7 E4
Portman Cl. Maypole DA5 ...... 25 E7
Portman Pk. TN10 & TN9 ...... 117 C3
Portobello Par. TN15 .... 56 A2
Portsdown Cl. ME16 .... 91 B2
Portsea Rd. RM18 .... 13 C6
Portsmans Cotts. ME19 ...... 89 B5
Portsmouth Cl. ME2 .... 46 D6
Portway Gdns. SE18 .... 5 D7
Portway Rd. ME3 .... 33 B7
Post Barn Rd. ME4 .... 47 F2
Post Office Rd. TN18 .... 178 F2
Postern La. TN9 .... 117 E1
Postley Commercial Ctr. ME15 92 A2
Postley Rd. ME15 .... 92 A1
Postmill Dr. ME10 .... 91 F1
Potash La. TN15 .... 87 C6
Potter's La. TN18 .... 179 A6
Pottery Rd. Coldblow DA5 ...... 25 C6
Pottery Rd. Hoo St Werburgh ME3 34 D5
Potyn House. ME1 .... 47 C4
Poulters Wood. BR2 .... 50 D5
Pound Bank Cl. TN15 .... 55 F2
Pound Cl. BR6 .... 51 D8
Pound Court Dr. BR6 .... 51 D8
Pound Green Ct. DA5 .... 25 A8
Pound House. TN11 .... 118 E8
Pound La. Knockholt Pound TN14 67 D4
Pound La. Sevenoaks TN13 ...... 84 C3
Pound Park Rd. SE7 .... 1 D2
Pound Pl. SE9 .... 6 A1
Pound Rd. TN12 .... 119 F6
Poundfield Rd. TN18 .... 186 B5
Poundsbridge Hill. TN11 & TN3 147 D7
Pounsley Rd. TN13 .... 83 E6
Pout Rd. ME6 .... 74 F7
Poverest Prim Sch. BR5 ...... 38 A4
Poverest Rd. BR5 .... 38 A4
Povey Ave. ME2 .... 33 C2
Powder Mill La. Dartford DA1 .... 26 F6
Powder Mill La. Leigh TN11 ...... 116 B1
Powder Mill La.
  Powder Mills TN11 .... 116 E2
Powder Mill La.
  Royal Tunbridge Wells TN4 .. 149 B8
Powdermill Cl. TN4 .... 149 C8
Powell Cl. ME20 .... 76 A3
Power Ind Est. DA8 .... 9 A6
Powerscroft Rd. DA14 .... 24 C2
Powis St. SE18 .... 2 A3
Powlett Rd. ME2 .... 33 C1
Powster Rd. BR1 .... 22 B3
Powys Cl. DA7 .... 7 D8
Poynder Rd. RM18 .... 13 B6
Poynings Cl. BR6 .... 52 C8
Poyntell Cres. BR7 .... 37 D8
Poyntell Rd. TN12 .... 139 F4
Pragnell Rd. SE12 .... 22 B6
Prall's La. TN12 .... 135 E2
Pratling St. ME20 .... 76 C4
Pratt's Bottom Prim Sch. TN14 67 C8
Premier Par. ME20 .... 75 E1
Prentiss Cl. SE7 .... 1 D2
Prescott Ave. BR5 .... 37 B3

Presentation House. [9] DA11 .. 30 B8
Prestbury Sq. SE9 .... 22 F4
Prestley Dr. TN10 .... 117 E7
Preston Ave. ME7 .... 48 E1
Preston Cl. DA14 .... 23 F4
Preston Dr. DA16 .... 7 D6
Preston Hall Hospl. ME20 ...... 75 F1
Preston House. [1] SE18 ...... 2 A2
Preston Rd. Northfleet DA11 .... 29 E7
Preston Rd. Tonbridge TN9 ...... 117 A1
Prestons Rd. BR2 .... 50 A8
Prestwood Cl. SE18 .... 7 A7
Pretoria House. [4] Erith DA8 .. 8 E7
Pretoria House. [8]
  Park Wood ME15 .... 107 E5
Pretoria Rd. Chatham ME4 ...... 47 F2
Pretoria Rd. Gillingham ME7 .... 48 D3
Prettymans La. TN8 .... 112 F4
Pridmore Rd. ME6 .... 74 F8
Priest's Wlk. DA12 .... 31 A6
Priestfield Rd. ME7 .... 48 E5
Priestfields. ME1 .... 47 B3
Priestlands Park Rd. DA15 ...... 23 F5
Priestley Dr. Lunsford ME20 .... 74 F4
Priestley Dr. Tonbridge TN10 .. 117 E7
Priestwood Rd. DA13 .... 58 C5
Primrose Ave. ME8 .... 63 B5
Primrose Cl. ME1 .... 61 E7
Primrose Dr. ME20 .... 75 D1
Primrose Rd. ME2 .... 59 E5
Primrose Terr. DA12 .... 30 C7
Prince Arthur Rd. ME7 .... 48 B6
Prince Charles Ave.
  Chatham ME5 .... 62 B4
Prince Charles Ave.
  South Darenth DA4 .... 41 D7
Prince Charles House. DA4 ...... 41 D7
Prince Consort Dr. BR7 ...... 37 D8
Prince Henry Rd. SE7 .... 5 D7
Prince Imperial Rd.
  Chislehurst BR7 .... 23 B1
Prince Imperial Rd.
  Woolwich SE18 .... 5 F6
Prince John Rd. SE9 .... 5 E2
Prince Of Wales Rd.
  Greenwich SE3 .... 5 A6
Prince Of Wales Rd. Newham E16 1 C7
Prince Regent La. E16 .... 1 C7
Prince Regent Sta. E16 ...... 1 C6
Prince Rupert Rd. SE9 .... 5 F3
Prince's Plain. BR2 .... 36 E1
Prince's Plain Prim Sch. BR2 .. 36 E2
Prince's St. Rochester ME1 .... 47 C4
Prince's St.
  Royal Tunbridge Wells TN2 .. 149 C3
Princes Ave. Chatham ME5 ...... 62 B5
Princes Ave. Dartford DA2 ...... 27 B7
Princes Ave. Orpington BR5 .... 37 E4
Princes Cl. DA14 .... 24 D5
Princes Rd. Dartford DA1 ...... 26 B7
Princes Rd. Dartford DA1 ...... 26 D7
Princes Rd.
  Dartford,Fleet-Down DA1 & DA2 .. 27 C7
Princes Rd. Gravesend DA12 .... 30 C5
Princes Rd. Hextable BR8 ...... 26 A2
Princes St. Bexley DA7 ...... 7 F4
Princes St. Gravesend DA11 .... 13 B1
Princes St. Maidstone ME14 .... 92 A5
Princes View. DA1 .... 27 A7
Princes Way. ME14 .... 92 A5
Princess Christian's Hospl.
  TN11 .... 100 E2
Princess Margaret Rd. RM18 .. 14 D7
Princess Mary Ave. ME7 ...... 48 B7
Princess Par. BR6 .... 51 A7
Prinys Dr. ME8 .... 63 C4
Priolo Rd. SE7 .... 1 C1
Prior's Way. TN8 .... 145 A6
Priorsdean Cl. ME16 .... 90 E1
Priorsford Ave. BR5 .... 38 B5
Priory Ave. BR5 .... 37 E3
Priory Cl. Bromley BR1 & BR7 .. 36 F8
Priory Cl. Dartford DA1 ...... 9 D1
Priory Cl. East Farleigh ME15 .. 106 B8
Priory Ct. [3] Dartford DA1 .... 9 D1
Priory Cr. Gillingham ME8 ...... 49 A2
Priory Ctr The. DA1 .... 26 E8
Priory Dr. SE2 .... 3 D1
Priory Fields. DA4 .... 54 F8
Priory Gate. [4] ME14 .... 92 A5
Priory Gdns. DA1 .... 9 D2
Priory Gr. Aylesford ME20 ...... 75 D1
Priory Gr. Tonbridge TN9 ...... 133 B8
Priory Hill. DA1 .... 9 D2
Priory House. [3] SE7 .... 5 C8
Priory La. DA4 .... 40 F1
Priory Leas. SE9 .... 22 E7
Priory Mews. DA2 .... 27 C8
Priory Pl. DA1 .... 9 D1
Priory Rd. Dartford DA1 ...... 9 D1
Priory Rd. Dartford DA1 ...... 9 D1
Priory Rd. Gillingham ME8 ...... 49 A2
Priory Rd. Maidstone ME15 .... 92 A3
Priory Rd. Rochester ME2 ...... 47 A6
Priory Rd. Tonbridge TN9 ...... 133 C8
Priory Sch The. BR5 .... 38 C1
Priory St. TN9 .... 133 B8
Priory Way. TN30 .... 183 C7
Priory Wlk. TN9 .... 133 B8
Pristling La. TN12 .... 155 B8
Progress Est The. ME15 ...... 108 A4
Prospect Ave. ME2 .... 47 B8
Prospect Cl. DA17 .... 4 A2
Prospect Cotts.
  Pratt's Bottom BR6 .... 52 C2
Prospect Cotts. The Down TN3 . 166 A3

Prospect Gr. DA12 .... 30 D8
Prospect Pk. TN4 .... 132 F1
Prospect Pl. Bromley BR2 ...... 36 B6
Prospect Pl. Collier Street TN12 121 C2
Prospect Pl. Dartford DA1 ...... 9 E1
Prospect Pl. Gravesend DA12 .. 30 D8
Prospect Pl. Grays RM17 ...... 12 B8
Prospect Pl. Maidstone ME16 .. 91 E3
Prospect Rd.
  Royal Tunbridge Wells
  TN1 & TN2 .... 149 C3
Prospect Rd.Royal Tunbridge Wells,
  Southborough TN4 .... 132 F1
Prospect Rd. Sevenoaks TN13 .. 84 C4
Prospect Row. Chatham ME4 .... 48 A3
Prospect Row. Gillingham ME4 .. 48 A6
Prospect Vale. SE18 & SE7 ...... 1 E2
Prospero House. [6] DA17 ...... 4 A1
Provender Way. ME14 .... 92 E5
Providence Chapel. TN12 ...... 138 C6
Providence Cotts.
  Groombridge TN3 .... 161 C7
Providence Cotts. Higham ME2 . 32 B2
Providence La. ME1 .... 47 C5
Providence Pl. TN27 .... 141 A7
Providence St. DA9 .... 11 A2
Prudhoe Cl. [13] DA2 .... 10 B1
Pudding La. Maidstone ME14 .. 91 F4
Pudding La. Seal TN15 .... 84 F6
Pudding Rd. ME8 .... 63 F8
Puddingcake La. TN17 .... 182 C5
Puddledock La.
  Hextable BR8 & DA2 .... 25 F2
Puddledock La.
  Toy's Hill TN16 & TN8 .... 97 A3
Puffin Rd. ME3 .... 21 B5
Pullington Cotts. TN17 .... 180 E6
Pullman Pl. SE9 .... 5 E2
Pump Cl. ME19 .... 74 D1
Pump La. Gillingham ME8 ...... 49 D2
Pump La. Gillingham ME7 & ME8 . 49 D3
Punch Croft. DA3 .... 56 E7
Purbeck Rd. ME4 .... 47 E2
Purcell Ave. ME10 .... 117 F6
Purfleet By-Pass. RM16 ...... 10 D8
Purland Rd. SE28 & SE18 ...... 2 F4
Purneys Rd. SE9 .... 5 D3
Purrett Rd. SE18 .... 2 F1
Purser Way. ME7 .... 48 C7
Putlands L Ctr. TN12 .... 136 A5
Puttenden Rd. TN11 .... 101 F3
Pym Orch. TN16 .... 82 C3
Pynham Cl. SE2 .... 3 B3
Pyrus Cl. ME5 .... 77 A8

Quadrant The. DA7 .... 7 D7
Quaggy Wlk. SE3 .... 5 A3
Quaker Cl. TN13 .... 84 D4
Quaker Dr. TN17 .... 169 D6
Quaker La. TN17 .... 169 D6
Quaker's Hall La. TN13 .... 84 C5
Quakers Cl. DA3 .... 42 E6
Quantock Rd. DA1 .... 8 E5
Quarries The. ME17 .... 107 C4
Quarry Cotts. TN5 .... 174 D7
Quarry Hill. TN15 .... 84 D4
Quarry Hill Par. [1] TN9 ...... 133 B8
Quarry Hill Rd.
  Borough Green TN15 .... 86 F6
Quarry Hill Rd. Tonbridge TN9 .. 133 B8
Quarry Rd. ME15 .... 92 A2
Quarry Rise. TN9 .... 133 A7
Quarry Sq. ME14 .... 92 A5
Quarry Way. RM16 .... 10 F8
Quarry Wood Ind Est. ME20 .... 90 E8
Quay La. DA9 .... 11 B3
Quay Rd. TN1 .... 149 B5
Quayside. ME4 .... 48 B8
Quebec Ave. TN16 .... 81 D1
Quebec Cotts. [5] TN16 ...... 81 D1
Quebec Rd. RM18 .... 13 A5
Quebec Sq. TN16 .... 81 D1
Queen Anne Ave. BR2 .... 36 A6
Queen Anne Gate. DA7 .... 7 D4
Queen Anne Rd. ME14 .... 92 B4
Queen Borough Gdns. BR7 ...... 23 D2
Queen Elizabeth Military Hospl The.
  SE7 .... 5 E7
Queen Elizabeth Pl. RM18 ...... 13 A3
Queen Elizabeth Sq. ME15 .... 107 D6
Queen Mary's Hospl. DA14 .... 24 A2
Queen Mother Ct The. ME1 .... 47 B4
Queen St. Bexley DA7 .... 7 F4
Queen St. Chatham ME4 ...... 48 A4
Queen St. Erith DA8 .... 8 E8
Queen St. Gravesend DA11 .... 13 B1
Queen St. Queen St TN12 ...... 136 D7
Queen St. Rochester ME1 ...... 47 C4
Queen St. Sandhurst TN18 ...... 186 B5
Queen's Ave. Maidstone ME16 .. 91 D5
Queen's Ave. Snodland ME6 .... 75 A8
Queen's Dr. TN14 .... 84 C7
Queen's Farm Rd. DA12 ...... 31 E7
Queen's Gdns. TN4 .... 149 B6
Queen's Mews. [12] TN18 ...... 179 A2
Queen's Pas. BR7 .... 23 B2
Queen's Rd. Bexley DA16 ...... 7 B5
Queen's Rd. Bromley BR1 ...... 36 A7
Queen's Rd. Chatham ME5 ...... 48 D1
Queen's Rd. Chislehurst BR7 .. 23 B2
Queen's Rd. Gillingham ME7 .... 48 C4
Queen's Rd. Hawkhurst TN18 .. 179 A2
Queen's Rd. Maidstone ME16 .. 91 C4
Queen's Rd.
  Royal Tunbridge Wells TN4 .. 149 B6
Queen's Rd. Snodland ME6 .... 75 A8
Queendown Ave. ME8 .... 63 D5
Queens Cotts. TN5 .... 174 E6
Queens Ct. Edenbridge TN8 .... 112 D1

Queens Ct. [11] Hawkhurst TN18 .. 179 A2
Queens Gate Gdns. BR7 ...... 37 D8
Queens Gdns. DA1 & DA2 ...... 27 B7
Queens Rd. Erith DA8 .... 8 E8
Queens Rd. Gravesend DA12 .. 30 C5
Queens Way. ME14 .... 78 A1
Queenscroft Rd. SE9 .... 5 D1
Queensland House. [2] E16 .. 2 A5
Queensway.
  Allhallows-on-Sea ME3 ...... 19 D9
Queensway. Hayes BR2 & BR4 .. 50 A6
Queensway. Orpington BR5 .... 37 C3
Queensway Rd. Kit's Coty ME2076 D7
Queensway Rd. Sidcup DA15 .. 6 F1
Quern The. ME15 .... 91 E1
Quernmore Cl. BR1 .... 22 A2
Quernmore Rd. BR1 .... 22 A2
Quickrells Ave. ME3 .... 16 B5
Quickthorn Cres. ME5 .... 61 E5
Quiet Nook. BR2 .... 50 D7
Quilter Gdns. BR5 .... 38 C1
Quilter Rd. BR5 .... 38 D1
Quilter St. SE18 .... 2 F1
Quincewood Gdns. TN10 ...... 117 B7
Quinion Cl. ME5 .... 77 A8
Quinnell St. ME8 .... 49 E1
Quixote Cres. ME2 .... 33 B1

Rabbits Rd. DA4 .... 41 E7
Rablus Pl. DA4 .... 40 F3
Racefield Cl. DA12 .... 31 E1
Radfield Way. SE9 .... 23 D8
Radland Rd. E16 .... 1 A7
Radleigh Gdns. ME4 .... 47 E1
Radley House. [13] SE2 ...... 3 D4
Radnor Ave. DA16 .... 7 B2
Radnor Cl. ME7 .... 23 E2
Radnor Cres. SE18 .... 7 A7
Raeburn Ave. DA1 .... 9 B2
Raeburn Cl. TN10 .... 117 E6
Raeburn Pl. DA10 .... 11 E2
Raeburn Rd. DA15 .... 6 E1
Rafford Way. BR1 .... 36 B6
Raggatt Pl. ME15 .... 92 B2
Ragge Way. TN15 .... 84 F7
Raggleswood. BR7 .... 37 A8
Raglan Ct. SE12 .... 5 A2
Raglan Prim Sch. BR2 .... 36 D5
Raglan Rd. Bromley BR2 ...... 36 C5
Raglan Rd. Erith DA17 .... 3 F2
Raglan Rd. Woolwich SE18 .... 2 C1
Ragstone Ct. ME19 .... 90 C8
Ragstone Rd. ME15 .... 93 A2
Railway App. TN9 .... 133 B8
Railway Cotts. Cowden TN8 .... 145 D8
Railway Cotts. Hartley TN17 .... 168 C2
Railway Cotts. Marden TN12 .. 138 D6
Railway Pl. Erith DA17 .... 4 A3
Railway Pl. [10] Gravesend DA11 .. 13 B1
Railway Sidings The. DA13 .... 44 B4
Railway St. Chatham ME4 ...... 47 F4
Railway St. Gillingham ME7 .... 48 D6
Railway St. Northfleet DA11 .... 12 A2
Railway Terr. TN1 .... 81 D1
Rainham Cl. Eltham SE9 ...... 6 E1
Rainham Cl. Maidstone ME15 .. 92 A1
Rainham Mark Gram Sch. ME8 49 D2
Rainham Rd. ME5 & ME7 ...... 48 C3
Rainham Sch for Girls. ME8 .... 63 F8
Rainham Sh Ctr. ME8 .... 63 F8
Rainham Sta. ME8 .... 49 F1
Rainton Rd. SE7 .... 1 A1
Raleigh Cl. Chatham ME5 ...... 62 A6
Raleigh Cl. Erith DA8 .... 8 F8
Raleigh Rd. [6] BR6 .... 51 F5
Ramac Ind Est. SE7 .... 1 B1
Ramac Way. SE7 .... 1 B1
Ramillies Cl. ME5 .... 62 A6
Ramillies Rd. DA15 .... 7 B1
Rammell Mews. TN17 .... 169 D4
Rampion Cl. ME14 .... 92 E5
Ramsden La. TN17 .... 180 F4
Ramsden Prim Sch. BR5 ...... 38 C2
Ramsden Rd. Erith DA8 .... 8 D7
Ramsden Rd.
  Orpington BR5 & BR6 .... 38 B1
Ramslye Rd. TN2 & TN4 ...... 162 E8
Ramus Wood Ave. BR6 .... 51 E5
Rance House. [12] SE7 .... 1 E2
Rancliffe Gdns. SE9 .... 5 E3
Randall Cl. DA8 .... 8 C8
Randall Hill Rd. TN15 .... 71 F3
Randall Rd. ME4 .... 47 E1
Randall St. ME14 .... 91 F6
Randalls Row. ME15 .... 106 F5
Randle's La. BR6 & TN14 ...... 67 D5
Randolph App. E16 .... 1 C7
Randolph Cl. DA7 .... 8 C4
Randolph Cotts. ME2 .... 33 B1
Randolph Rd. Gillingham ME7 .. 48 C4
Randolph Rd. Keston Mark BR2 . 36 F1
Ranelagh Gdns. DA11 .... 29 F8
Range Rd. DA12 .... 30 E8
Rangefield Rd. BR1 .... 22 A3
Rangeworth Pl. DA15 .... 23 F5
Rankine Rd. TN1 .... 149 D7
Ranleigh Gdns. DA7 .... 7 F7
Ranmore Path. BR5 .... 38 A5
Ranscombe Cl. ME2 .... 46 D5
Ranscombe Farm Cotts. ME2 .. 46 C4
Ransom Rd. SE7 .... 1 C1
Ranters La. TN17 .... 167 C2
Ranters Oak. TN17 .... 181 B4
Ranworth Cl. DA7 & DA8 ...... 8 E5
Raphael Ave. RM18 .... 13 B7
Raphael Cl. TN11 .... 116 F2
Raphael Rd. DA12 .... 30 D8

Rare Farm Animals Pk. TN11 .. 100 C2
Rashleigh Way. DA4 .... 41 C5
Ratcliffe Cl. SE12 .... 22 A8
Ratcliffe Highway.
  Hoo St Werburgh ME3 .... 34 C7
Ratcliffe Highway.
  St Mary Hoo ME3 .... 18 D5
Rathmore Rd. Gravesend DA11 .. 30 B8
Rathmore Rd. Greenwich SE7 .. 1 B1
Raven Cl. ME20 .... 75 A1
Ravens Dane Cl. ME15 .... 93 A1
Ravens Knowle. ME1 .... 60 D4
Ravens Way. SE12 & SE3 ...... 5 A8
Ravens Wood Sch for Boys.
  BR2 .... 50 D7
Ravensbourne Coll of Design &
  Communication. BR7 .... 22 F3
Ravensbourne Cl. [23] BR5 .... 38 D1
Ravensbourne Rd.
  Bromley BR1 & BR2 .... 36 A6
Ravensbourne Rd. Crayford DA1 . 9 A4
Ravensbourne Sch. BR2 ...... 36 B4
Ravensbury Rd. BR5 .... 38 A5
Ravenscourt Rd. BR5 .... 38 B7
Ravenscroft Cl. [5] E16 ...... 1 A8
Ravenscroft Cres. SE9 ...... 22 F5
Ravenscroft Rd. E16 .... 1 A8
Ravenshill. BR7 .... 37 B8
Ravensleigh Gdns. BR1 ...... 22 B1
Ravensquay Bsns Ctr. BR5 .... 38 B4
Ravenswood. DA5 .... 24 E7
Ravenswood Ave. Rochester ME2 33 B1
Ravenswood Ave.Royal Tunbridge Wells
  TN1 & TN2 .... 149 D6
Ravensworth Rd. SE9 .... 22 F4
Ravine Gr. SE18 .... 2 E8
Rawdon Rd. ME15 .... 92 A3
Rawlings Cl. [3] BR6 .... 51 F5
Rawsthorne Cl. E16 .... 1 F5
Rayfield Cl. BR2 .... 36 E3
Rayford Cl. DA1 .... 9 C2
Rayleas Cl. SE18 .... 6 B6
Raymer Rd. ME14 .... 92 B8
Raymere Gdns. SE18 .... 6 E7
Raymond Postgate Ct. [5] SE28 . 3 B6
Raynehurst Cty Prim Sch. DA12 30 F1
Rayners Ct. DA11 .... 12 B1
Raynham Villas. TN12 .... 122 A4
Rays Hill. DA4 .... 41 C4
Read Way. DA12 .... 30 E3
Reader's Bridge Rd.
  TN27 & TN30 .... 172 E4
Readscroft Rd. ME8 .... 63 D5
Rebecca Cl. DA14 .... 24 B4
Recreation Ave. ME6 .... 75 A8
Recreation Rd. ME14 .... 92 B6
Recreation Ground Rd. TN30 . 183 B7
Rectory Bsns Ctr. DA14 ...... 24 B4
Rectory Cl. Crayford DA1 ...... 8 E3
Rectory Cl. Sidcup DA14 ...... 24 B4
Rectory Cl. Snodland ME6 ...... 75 A8
Rectory Cl. Wouldham ME1 .... 60 C5
Rectory Dr. TN4 .... 132 D3
Rectory Field Cres. SE7 ...... 5 C7
Rectory Fields. TN17 .... 169 D5
Rectory Grange. ME1 .... 47 C2
Rectory La. Brasted TN16 ...... 82 C3
Rectory La. Harrietsham ME17 .. 110 E5
Rectory La. Ightham TN15 .... 86 C5
Rectory La. Maidstone ME16 .. 91 A1
Rectory La. Sevenoaks TN13 .. 84 C1
Rectory La. Sidcup DA14 ...... 24 C4
Rectory La. Sutton Valence ME17124 C6
Rectory La. Sutton Valence ME17124 F7
Rectory La N. ME19 .... 74 E2
Rectory La S. ME19 .... 74 E1
Rectory Meadow. DA13 ...... 29 A2
Rectory Paddock Sch &
  Research Unit. BR5 .... 38 C7
Rectory Park Rd. TN12 ...... 153 A2
Rectory Pl. SE18 .... 2 A2
Rectory Rd. Cliffe ME3 .... 16 A3
Rectory Rd. [3] Grays RM17 .... 12 D8
Rectory Rd. Keston BR2 ...... 50 D3
Rectory Rd. Low Street RM18 .. 13 D8
Rectory Rd. Ridley TN15 ...... 57 C5
Rectory Rd. Swanscombe DA10 .. 28 E8
Reculver Wlk. Maidstone ME15 107 F6
Reculver Wlk. Maidstone ME15 107 F7
Red Barracks Rd. [4] SE18 .... 1 F2
Red Cedars Rd. BR6 .... 37 E2
Red Hill. Chislehurst BR7 ...... 23 B3
Red Hill. Red Hill ME18 ...... 89 F1
Red Hill Prim Sch. BR7 ...... 23 B3
Red House Gdns. ME18 ...... 104 C7
Red House La. DA6 .... 7 E3
Red Lion Cl. BR5 .... 38 C3
Red Lion La. SE18 .... 6 A6
Red Lion Pl. SE18 .... 6 A6
Red Lodge Cres. DA5 .... 25 E5
Red Lodge Rd. DA5 .... 25 D5
Red Oak. TN18 .... 184 E6
Red Oak Cl. BR6 .... 51 B8
Red Oast Cotts. TN5 .... 177 C3
Red Robin Cotts. ME9 .... 65 B6
Red St. DA13 .... 29 B2
Redbank. ME19 .... 74 E2
Redbridge Cl. ME5 .... 62 C4
Redcliffe La. ME14 .... 92 B7
Reddy Rd. DA8 .... 8 F8
Rede Court Rd. ME2 .... 46 E4
Rede Wood Rd. ME16 .... 90 F3
Redfern Ave. ME7 .... 48 E5
Redgate Dr. BR2 .... 50 B8
Redhill Rd. TN15 .... 56 F6
Redhill Wood. DA3 .... 57 A7

Redland Shaw. ME4 .... 47 E1
Redlands Rd. TN13 .... 83 F3
Redleaf Cl. Erith DA17 .... 8 A8
Redleaf Cl.
  Royal Tunbridge Wells TN2 .. 149 D6
Redmans La. BR6 & TN14 .... 53 E4
Redpoll Way. ME2 .... 3 D3
Redpoll Wlk. TN12 .... 136 A5
Redruth Manor. ME7 .... 48 C6
Redsells Cl. ME15 .... 93 A1
Redstart Cl. E6 .... 1 E8
Redvers Rd. ME4 .... 48 A4
Redwall La. ME15 & ME17 ...... 122 C6
Redwell La. TN15 .... 86 B4
Redwing Cl. ME20 .... 75 A2
Redwing Path. SE28 .... 2 D4
Redwing Rd. ME5 .... 62 B7
Redwings La. TN2 .... 134 E2
Redwood Cl. Chatham ME5 .... 62 B2
Redwood Cl. Sidcup DA15 .... 24 A7
Redwood Cl. DA1 .... 10 A1
Redwood Pk. TN11 & TN12 ..... 135 A5
Reed Ave. BR6 .... 51 E7
Reed Cl. Eltham SE12 .... 5 A2
Reed Cl. Newham E16 .... 1 A8
Reed Court Cotts. TN12 .... 122 A5
Reed St. ME3 .... 16 B6
Reedham Cres. ME3 .... 33 C7
Reeds Cotts. TN17 .... 170 A8
Reeds La. TN11 .... 101 E5
Reeves Cl. TN12 .... 139 E4
Reeves Cres. BR8 .... 39 D6
Reeves Ct. TN3 .... 147 B5
Reeves Rd. SE18 .... 6 B8
Reeves Terr. TN5 .... 176 E1
Reform Rd. ME4 .... 48 B2
Regency Cl. Gillingham ME8 ..... 63 C3
Regency Cl.
  West Kingsdown TN15 .... 55 E4
Regency Hall. [19] TN2 .... 149 A2
Regency Way. DA7 .... 7 E4
Regent Dr. ME15 .... 107 A8
Regent Pl. TN2 .... 149 D3
Regent Rd. ME4 .... 48 C4
Regent Sq. DA17 .... 4 B2
Regent St. TN17 .... 181 E4
Regent's Pl. ME3 .... 5 A5
Regents Ct. [2] DA11 .... 13 B1
Regents Dr. BR2 .... 50 D5
Regina Ct. TN4 .... 148 F4
Reginald Ave. ME8 .... 46 C3
Reginald Rd. ME16 .... 91 E3
Reidhaven Rd. SE18 .... 2 E2
Reigate Rd. BR1 & SE12 .... 22 A5
Reinden Gr. ME15 .... 92 F1
Rembrandt Cl. TN10 .... 117 E6
Rembrandt Dr. DA11 .... 29 E5
Remington Rd. E6 .... 1 E7
Rendlebury House. [17] SE18 ...... 1 F2
Renfrew Cl. E6 .... 2 A6
Rennets Cl. SE9 .... 6 E2
Rennets Wood Rd. SE9 .... 6 E2
Renown Rd. ME5 .... 62 C2
Renshaw Cl. [7] DA17 .... 7 F8
Renton Dr. BR5 .... 38 D2
Repository Rd. SE18 & SE7 .... 1 F1
Repton Rd. BR6 .... 52 A6
Repton Way. ME5 .... 61 F4
Resolution Cl. ME5 .... 62 A6
Resolution Wlk. SE18 .... 1 F3
Restharrow Rd. ME14 .... 92 E4
Restons Cres. SE9 .... 6 E1
Retreat The. Grays RM17 .... 12 B8
Retreat The. Orpington BR6 ...... 52 B4
Revell Rise. SE18 .... 6 A8
Revenge Rd. ME5 .... 77 C8
Reventlow Rd. SE9 .... 23 C7
Reynard Cl. ME1 .... 37 A6
Reynolds Cl. TN10 .... 117 E6
Reynolds Fields. ME3 .... 32 C6
Reynolds La. TN4 .... 148 F6
Reynolds Pl. SE3 .... 5 B7
Rhode St. ME4 .... 48 A4
Rhodes House. ME5 .... 48 C2
Rhodewood Cl. ME15 .... 93 A1
Rhododendron Ave. DA13 .... 58 A2
Ribblesdale Rd. DA2 .... 27 C7
Ribston Cl. BR2 .... 36 F1
Ribston Gdns. TN12 .... 135 F7
Ricardo Path. [5] SE28 .... 3 C5
Rich Ind Est. DA1 .... 8 F2
Richard Cl. SE18 .... 1 E2
Richard St. Chatham ME4 .... 47 F4
Richard St. Rochester ME1 .... 47 C3
Richard's Cl. TN11 .... 114 F2
Richardson Cl. DA9 .... 11 A2
Richardson Rd. TN4 .... 149 A5
Richborough Cl. BR5 .... 38 D5
Richborough Drive. ME2 .... 33 A1
Richings House. BR5 .... 38 A8
Richmer Rd. DA8 .... 9 A7
Richmond Cl. Chatham ME5 ..... 62 B4
Richmond Cl. Upper Upton ME2 .. 33 F1
Richmond Cty Inf Sch. ME7 ..... 48 C6
Richmond Pl. ME7 .... 2 C7
Richmond Rd. Gillingham ME7 .. 48 C7
Richmond Rd. [1] Grays RM17 .. 12 C8
Richmond Way. ME15 .... 107 A8
Richmount Gdns. SE3 .... 5 A4
Rickyard Path. SE9 .... 5 E3
Riddesdale Ave. TN4 .... 149 A6
Riddons Rd. SE12 .... 22 C4
Rideout St. SE18 .... 1 F2
Rider Cl. DA15 .... 6 F1
Ridge Ave. DA1 .... 8 F1

Ridge La. DA13 .... 58 A2
Ridge Meadow Cty Prim Sch.
  ME5 .... 61 F6
Ridge The. Groombridge TN3 .. 161 A6
Ridge The. Orpington BR6 .... 51 D8
Ridge The. Sidcup DA5 .... 24 F8
Ridge Way. Crayford DA1 .... 8 F1
Ridge Way. Marlpit Hill TN8 ... 112 D4
Ridgebrook Rd. SE3 & SE9 .... 5 D4
Ridgecroft Cl. DA5 .... 25 C7
Ridgelands. TN3 .... 132 C4
Ridgeway. Hayes BR2 .... 50 A8
Ridgeway. Hurst Green TN19 .. 184 A3
Ridgeway. Lane End DA2 .... 27 E3
Ridgeway. Pembury TN2 .... 150 D7
Ridgeway. The Moor TN18 ...... 184 E8
Ridgeway Ave. DA12 .... 30 B5
Ridgeway Bglws. DA12 .... 31 F1
Ridgeway Cres. Orpington BR6 .. 51 E7
Ridgeway Cres. Tonbridge TN10 .. 117 C4
Ridgeway Crescent Gdns. BR6 .. 51 E7
Ridgeway Dr. BR1 .... 22 B4
Ridgeway E. DA15 .... 6 F2
Ridgeway The. Chatham ME4 ... 61 E7
Ridgeway The. Gillingham ME7 .. 48 C7
Ridgeway The.
  Shorne Ridgeway DA12 .... 31 E1
Ridgeway The. Tonbridge TN10 .. 117 D4
Ridgeway W. DA15 .... 6 E2
Ridgeway The. TN4 .... 133 B1
Ridgewood. DA3 .... 43 C7
Ridgway. ME16 .... 91 B2
Ridgwell Rd. E16 .... 1 C8
Riding La. TN11 .... 100 D2
Riding Pk. TN11 .... 116 D7
Ridings The.
  Paddock Wood TN12 .... 136 A7
Ridings The.
  Royal Tunbridge Wells TN2 .. 149 F6
Ridley Rd. Bexley DA16 .... 7 B6
Ridley Rd. Bromley BR2 .... 36 A6
Ridley Rd. Rochester ME1 .... 47 C4
Riefield Rd. SE9 .... 6 C2
Riggs Way. TN15 .... 71 F3
Ring Cl. BR1 .... 22 B1
Ringden Ave. TN12 .... 135 F5
Ringer's Rd. BR1 .... 36 A6
Ringle Gn. TN18 .... 186 C5
Ringlestone Cres. ME14 .... 91 F8
Ringlestone Rd. ME17 .... 95 D4
Ringmer Way. BR1 .... 36 F4
Rings Hill. TN11 .... 116 B4
Ringshall Rd. BR5 & BR7 .... 38 A6
Ringwood Ave. BR6 .... 52 C1
Ringwood Cl. ME8 .... 63 D8
Ringwood Rd. ME15 .... 107 C8
Ripley Cl. BR1 .... 36 F4
Ripley Rd. Erith DA17 .... 4 A2
Ripley Rd. Newham E16 .... 1 E7
Ripon Cl. ME15 .... 106 A7
Ripon Rd. SE18 .... 6 B8
Rippersley Rd. DA16 .... 7 A6
Rippolson Rd. SE18 .... 2 F1
Risden La. TN18 .... 185 D7
Rise The. Crayford DA1 .... 8 F3
Rise The. Gillingham ME7 .... 63 A3
Rise The. Gravesend DA12 .... 30 E4
Rise The. Rochester ME1 .... 47 D3
Rise The. Sevenoaks TN13 .... 99 C7
Rise The. Sidcup DA5 .... 24 C8
Risedale Rd. DA7 .... 8 C4
Riseden Rd. TN5 .... 174 C1
Ritch Rd. ME6 .... 74 E8
Ritter St. SE18 .... 6 A8
River Cl. ME15 .... 106 A7
River Cotts. BR5 .... 38 C7
River Ct. TN13 .... 83 E5
River Dr. ME2 .... 46 E7
River Lawn Rd. TN9 .... 117 B1
River St. [3] ME4 .... 48 A6
River View. [7] Dartford DA1 .... 10 A3
River View. Gillingham ME8 ..... 49 D3
River View. Maidstone ME15 .... 91 F2
River Way. ME20 .... 75 B4
River Wlk. TN9 .... 117 B1
Riverdale Est. TN9 .... 133 D8
Riverdale Rd. Erith DA8 .... 4 C1
Riverdale Rd. Sidcup DA5 .... 7 F1
Riverdale Rd. Woolwich SE18 ..... 2 F1
Riverhead Cl. ME16 .... 91 E6
Riverhead Cty Inf Sch. TN13 .... 83 F5
Riverhill. TN13 & TN15 .... 99 E4
Riverhill Cotts. TN15 .... 99 E5
Riverhill House Gdns. TN15 ..... 99 E5
Rivers Wlk. ME17 .... 111 C5
Riversdale. DA11 .... 29 E5
Riverside. Edenbridge TN8 .... 112 C1
Riverside. Eynsford DA4 .... 54 D8
Riverside. Greenwich SE7 .... 1 B3
Riverside Cl. BR5 .... 38 C7
Riverside Cotts. TN14 .... 53 F1
Riverside Ct. [2] BR5 .... 38 C4
Riverside Ctry Pk. ME7 .... 49 D5
Riverside East Rd. ME4 .... 34 C1
Riverside Ind Est. DA1 .... 9 E2
Riverside North Rd. ME4 .... 34 B2
Riverside Rd. DA14 .... 24 E6
Riverside Sch. DA18 .... 3 E4
Riverside Way. DA1 .... 9 E2
Riverside West Rd. ME4 .... 34 A2
Riverston Sch. SE12 .... 5 A2
Riverview Cty Inf Sch. DA12 .... 30 E4
Riverview Cty Jun Sch. DA12 .. 30 E4
Riverview Hts. SE18 .... 6 B7
Riverview Rd. DA9 .... 11 A2
Riverwood Cl. BR7 .... 37 D8

Rixon House. SE18 .... 6 B8
Roach St. ME2 .... 47 A7
Roan Cl. ME2 .... 46 F8
Robert Napier Sch The. ME7 ... 48 E3
Robert St. Newham E16 .... 2 B5
Robert St. Woolwich SE18 .... 2 D2
Roberton Dr. BR1 .... 36 C8
Roberts Cl. Eltham SE9 .... 23 D7
Roberts Cl. [8] Orpington BR5 .. 38 C4
Roberts House. SE18 .... 5 F6
Roberts Orchard Rd. ME16 ...... 90 F3
Roberts Rd. Erith DA17 .... 4 A1
Roberts Rd. Gillingham ME8 ..... 63 E8
Roberts Rd. Snodland ME6 .... 74 F8
Robertson House. SE18 .... 5 F6
Robin Cres. E6 .... 1 D8
Robin Hill Dr. BR7 .... 22 E2
Robin Hood Gn. BR5 .... 38 A4
Robin Hood La. Bexley DA6 .... 7 F2
Robin Hood La. Chatham ME5 .. 61 D1
Robin Hood Lane (Lower). ME5 .. 61 F2
Robin Hood Lane (Upper). ME5 .. 61 E1
Robin House. [5] ME16 .... 91 E4
Robin Way. BR5 .... 38 B6
Robina Cl. DA6 .... 7 D3
Robina Ct. BR8 .... 40 A5
Robinia Ave. DA11 .... 29 D8
Robins Ave. ME17 .... 111 C5
Robins Cl. ME17 .... 111 C4
Robins Cl. Lewisham SE12 .... 22 C5
Robins Ct. Maidstone ME14 ..... 92 B7
Robins Gr. BR4 .... 50 A7
Robinwood Dr. TN15 .... 84 F8
Robson Cl. E6 .... 1 E8
Robson Dr. Aylesford ME20 ..... 75 D2
Robson Dr. Hoo St Werburgh ME3 .. 34 D6
Robyns Croft. [6] DA11 .... 29 E5
Robyns Way. Edenbridge TN8 .. 128 D8
Robyns Way. Sevenoaks TN13 .. 83 F5
Rocfort Rd. ME6 .... 75 A8
Rochdale Rd.
  Royal Tunbridge Wells TN1 .. 149 C6
Rochdale Rd. Woolwich SE2 .... 3 B2
Rochester Airport. ME1 & ME5 .. 61 C6
Rochester Ave. Bromley BR1 .... 36 B7
Rochester Ave. Rochester ME1 .. 47 C4
Rochester Cath. ME1 .... 47 C6
Rochester Cl. [1] ME16 .... 7 B1
Rochester Cres. ME3 .... 34 D6
Rochester Ct. ME7 .... 48 E8
Rochester Dr. DA5 .... 8 A1
Rochester Gram Sch for Girls The.
  ME1 .... 47 C2
Rochester House. [1] ME15 .... 107 D7
Rochester Rd. Burham ME1 ..... 60 E2
Rochester Rd. Chalk DA12 .... 31 B6
Rochester Rd. Chatham ME5 ... 61 C4
Rochester Rd. Dartford DA1 ..... 27 A8
Rochester Rd.
  Pratling Street ME20 .... 76 B4
Rochester Rd. Rochester ME2 ... 46 B4
Rochester Rd. Tonbridge TN10 .. 117 D4
Rochester Rd. Wouldham ME1 .. 60 F7
Rochester St. ME4 .... 47 E3
Rochester St. ME1 .... 47 D3
Rochester Way. Dartford DA1 .. 25 F8
Rochester Way. Eltham SE9 .... 6 B4
Rochester Way.
  Eltham,Kidbrooke SE3 & SE9 .. 5 D4
Rock Ave. ME7 .... 48 C3
Rock Cotts. TN3 .... 163 B1
Rock Farm Cotts. ME18 .... 104 C6
Rock Hill. BR6 .... 53 B4
Rock Hill Rd. TN27 .... 142 E7
Rock Rd. Borough Green TN15 .. 86 F7
Rock Rd. Maidstone ME14 .... 92 A6
Rock Villa Rd. TN1 .... 149 A4
Rockdale. TN13 .... 84 B2
Rockdale Rd. TN13 .... 84 C2
Rockliffe Manor Prim Sch. SE18 .. 6 F8
Rockmount Rd. SE18 & SE2 ...... 2 F1
Rocks Cl. ME19 .... 90 A6
Rocks Hill. TN17 .... 156 A4
Rocks Rd The. ME19 .... 90 B6
Rocky Hill. ME16 .... 91 E4
Rocky Hill Terr. [2] ME16 .... 91 E4
Roding Rd. E6 .... 2 B8
Rodmell Rd. TN1 .... 149 A2
Rodney Ave. TN10 .... 117 E4
Rodney Gdns. BR4 .... 50 A6
Rodway Rd. BR1 .... 36 B8
Roebourne Way. E16 .... 2 A4
Roebuck Rd. ME1 .... 47 C5
Roedean Cl. BR6 .... 52 B6
Roedean Rd. TN1 & TN2 .... 149 A1
Roehampton Cl. DA12 .... 30 E8
Roehampton Dr. BR7 .... 23 C2
Roethorne Gdns. TN30 .... 183 B8
Roffen Rd. ME1 .... 47 C2
Rogers Ct. BR8 .... 40 A5
Rogers Rough Rd. TN17 .... 167 B2
Rogers Wood La. TN15 .... 56 B6
Rogersmead. TN30 .... 183 A7
Rogley Hill. TN27 .... 171 B6
Rogues Hill. TN11 .... 131 C3
Rokesby Cl. DA16 .... 6 D5
Rolinsden Way. BR2 .... 50 D6
Rollesby Way. SE28 .... 3 C7
Rolleston Ave. BR5 .... 37 B3
Rolleston Cl. BR5 .... 37 B2
Rollo Rd. BR8 .... 25 F1
Rolvenden Ave. ME8 .... 49 C3
Rolvenden Cty Prim Sch.
  TN17 .... 181 E3
Rolvenden Gdns. BR1 .... 22 D1
Rolvenden Hill. TN17 & TN30 .. 182 C5
Rolvenden Rd. Rochester ME2 .. 33 C2
Rolvenden Rd. Tenterden TN30 .. 182 E7

Rolvenden Sta. TN30 .... 182 D6
Roman Cl. ME5 .... 61 D1
Roman Hts. ME14 .... 92 C6
Roman Rd. Edenbridge TN8 .... 128 D5
Roman Rd. Northfleet DA11 ..... 29 C5
Roman Rd. Snodland ME6 .... 74 F8
Roman Sq. SE28 .... 3 A5
Roman Villa Rd. DA2 & DA4 ..... 27 C2
Roman Way. Crayford DA1 .... 8 E2
Roman Way. Rochester ME2 ..... 46 F4
Romany Ct. ME5 .... 48 D1
Romany Rd. ME8 .... 49 C2
Romany Rise. BR5 .... 37 C1
Romden Rd.
  Haffenden Quarter TN27 ..... 159 B8
Romden Rd. Romden TN27 .... 143 D1
Romero Sq. SE9 .... 5 C3
Romford Rd. TN2 & TN12 ...... 150 F7
Romney Cl. ME14 .... 93 A3
Romney Dr. BR1 .... 22 D1
Romney Gdns. DA7 .... 7 F6
Romney Pl. ME15 .... 92 A4
Romney Rd. Chatham ME5 .... 62 B5
Romney Rd. Northfleet DA11 ... 29 E5
Romney Rd. Woolwich SE18 ...... 2 C3
Romney Way. ME7 .... 117 C5
Romsey Cl. Orpington BR6 .... 51 C6
Romsey Cl. Rochester ME2 ...... 46 E8
Ronald House. SE9 .... 5 C3
Ronalds Rd. BR1 .... 36 A8
Ronaldstone Rd. DA15 .... 6 E1
Ronfearn Ave. BR5 .... 38 D4
Ronver Rd. SE12 .... 22 A7
Rook La. ME9 .... 65 F6
Rookdean. TN13 .... 83 C5
Rookery Cres. ME3 .... 16 B6
Rookery Ct. ME16 .... 11 A8
Rookery Dr. BR7 .... 37 A8
Rookery Gdns. BR5 .... 38 C4
Rookery Hill. ME6 .... 74 F8
Rookery La. BR2 .... 36 D3
Rookery Rd. BR6 .... 51 A1
Rookery The. RM16 .... 11 A8
Rookery View. [4] RM17 .... 12 D8
Rookesley Rd. BR5 .... 38 D2
Rookley Cl. TN2 .... 149 D2
Rooks Hill. TN15 .... 100 D6
Roopers. TN3 .... 148 A7
Roosevelt Ave. ME5 .... 62 A8
Rope Wlk. ME4 .... 47 F5
Rope Wlk The. TN18 .... 186 B5
Rope Yard Rails. SE18 .... 2 B3
Ropemakers Ct. ME4 .... 48 A1
Roper Cl. ME8 .... 63 C3
Roper St. [1] SE9 .... 6 A1
Roper's Gate. TN2 .... 148 E1
Roper's Green La. ME3 .... 18 B2
Roper's La. ME3 .... 34 F8
Ropery Bsns Est. SE7 .... 1 C2
Ropewalk. TN17 .... 169 C5
Rose Ave. DA12 .... 30 E7
Rose Bruford Coll The. DA15 ... 24 B7
Rose Ct. ME17 .... 106 D1
Rose Dale. BR6 .... 51 B8
Rose Hill Sch. TN4 .... 148 E5
Rose St. Northfleet DA11 .... 12 B1
Rose St. Rochester ME1 .... 47 D3
Rose St. Tonbridge TN9 .... 133 C8
Rose Terr. ME19 .... 88 D7
Rose Villas. BR6 .... 52 C2
Rose Way. SE12 .... 5 A2
Rose Yd. ME14 .... 92 A4
Roseacre Gdns. ME14 .... 93 A4
Roseacre Jun Sch. ME14 .... 93 A4
Roseacre La. ME14 .... 93 A4
Roseacre Rd. DA16 .... 7 B4
Rosebank Wlk. [14] SE7 .... 1 E2
Roseberry Gdns. Dartford DA1 .. 26 C8
Roseberry Gdns. Orpington BR6 .. 51 E7
Rosebery Ave. DA15 .... 23 E8
Rosebery Rd. Chatham ME4 ..... 47 E2
Rosebery Rd. Gillingham ME7 .. 48 D7
Rosebery Rd. Grays RM17 .... 11 E8
Rosecroft Cl. BR5 .... 38 C3
Rosedale Cl. Dartford DA2 .... 27 B8
Rosedale Cl. Woolwich SE2 .... 3 B3
Rosedene Cl. DA1 .... 26 C8
Rosefield. TN13 .... 84 A3
Rosegarth. DA13 .... 43 E8
Rosehill Wlk. TN1 .... 149 A3
Roseholme. ME14 .... 91 D2
Roselare Cl. TN16 .... 81 D1
Roseleigh Ave. ME16 .... 91 C5
Rosemary Cl. [4] ME5 .... 61 F4
Rosemary La. Hodsoll Street TN15 .. 57 D3
Rosemary La. Stonecrouch TN5 .. 177 A5
Rosemary La.
  Swift's Green TN27 .... 142 F5
Rosemary Rd. Bexley DA16 .... 6 F6
Rosemary Rd. East Malling ME19 .. 74 F1
Rosemary Rd. Maidstone ME15 .. 93 A3
Rosemount Cl. ME15 .... 106 F4
Rosemount Dr. BR1 .... 36 F1
Rosenheath Cl. BR6 .... 52 C3
Roseveare Rd. SE12 .... 22 C4
Rosewood. DA2 .... 25 E4
Rosewood Cl. DA14 .... 24 C5
Rosewood Ct. BR1 .... 36 C8
Rosherville CE Prim Sch. DA11 .. 12 E1
Rosherville Way. DA11 .... 12 E1
Roslin Way. BR1 .... 22 A3
Ross Ct. BR7 .... 22 F1
Ross House. SE18 .... 5 E6
Ross Rd. DA1 .... 9 A1
Ross St. ME1 .... 47 D4
Ross Way. SE9 .... 5 E4
Rossdale. TN2 .... 149 D5

Rosse Mews. SE3 .... 5 B6
Rossell Rd. RM18 .... 12 F5
Rossland Cl. DA6 .... 8 B2
Rosslyn Gn. ME16 .... 91 B5
Rother Ct. [24] BR5 .... 38 D1
Rother House. [5] ME15 .... 107 D8
Rother Rd. TN10 .... 117 C5
Rother Vale. ME5 .... 62 C3
Rothermere Cl. TN17 .... 180 E6
Rothesay Ct. SE12 .... 22 B5
Rothley Cl. TN30 .... 183 B8
Rouge La. DA11 .... 30 B7
Roughetts Rd. ME19 .... 73 F3
Roughway La. TN11 .... 102 C7
Round Ash Way. DA3 .... 42 E3
Round Green Cotts. TN17 ..... 154 F4
Round St. DA12 & DA13 .... 44 D5
Roundel Way. TN12 .... 138 D5
Roundhay. ME19 .... 74 E1
Roundhill Rd. TN2 .... 149 D1
Roundlyn Gdns. BR5 .... 38 B5
Roundtable Rd. BR1 .... 22 A5
Roundwell. ME14 .... 93 D3
Roundwood. BR7 .... 37 B7
Routh St. E6 .... 1 F8
Rover Rd. ME5 .... 62 B2
Row The. DA3 .... 56 F8
Rowan Cl. Aylesford ME20 .... 75 E1
Rowan Cl. Longfield DA3 .... 42 D7
Rowan Cl. Meopham Station DA13 .. 44 B3
Rowan Cl. Putlands TN12 ...... 135 F5
Rowan Cres. DA1 .... 26 C7
Rowan House. [4] Chatham ME5 .. 61 F4
Rowan House. Sidcup DA14 ..... 23 F5
Rowan Lea. ME5 .... 48 B1
Rowan Rd. Bexley DA7 .... 7 E4
Rowan Rd. Swanley BR8 .... 39 D6
Rowan Shaw. TN10 .... 117 D6
Rowan Tree Rd. TN2 .... 148 E1
Rowan Wlk. Chatham ME4 ...... 47 E3
Rowan Wlk. Keston Mark BR2 .. 50 E7
Rowanwood Ave. DA15 .... 24 A7
Rowbrocke Cl. ME8 .... 63 D3
Rowdow La. TN14 .... 69 E5
Rowe Pl. ME20 .... 75 F6
Rowfield. [6] TN8 .... 112 D3
Rowhill Cotts. DA2 .... 25 E2
Rowhill Rd. DA2 .... 26 A3
Rowhill Sch. DA2 .... 26 C4
Rowland Ave. ME7 .... 48 E2
Rowland Cl. ME5 .... 48 E1
Rowlatt Cl. DA2 .... 26 C4
Rowlatt Rd. DA2 .... 26 C5
Rowley Ave. DA15 .... 24 B8
Rowley Hill. TN2 .... 134 D1
Rowntree Path. [1] SE28 .... 3 B5
Rowton Rd. SE18 .... 6 C7
Rowzill Rd. BR8 .... 25 F2
Royal Albert Sta. E16 .... 1 E6
Royal Albert Way.
  Newham,Custom House E16 .... 1 E6
Royal Albert Way.
  Newham,Cyprus E6 .... 2 A6
Royal Ave. TN9 .... 133 D8
Royal Blackheath Golf Course.
  SE9 .... 23 A8
Royal Chase. TN4 & TN1 .... 148 F4
Royal Ct. SE9 .... 22 F7
Royal Docks Rd. E6 .... 2 B7
Royal Eagle Cl. ME2 .... 47 E7
Royal Engineers' Rd. ME14 ..... 91 F7
Royal Oak Rd. DA6 .... 8 A3
Royal Par. BR7 .... 23 C1
Royal Parade Mews. BR7 .... 23 C1
Royal Park Prim Sch. DA14 ..... 24 E5
Royal Pier Rd. DA11 .... 13 C1
Royal Rd. Hawley DA2 .... 27 A3
Royal Rd. Newham E16 .... 1 D7
Royal Rd. Sidcup DA14 .... 24 D5
Royal Sovereign Ave. ME7 ...... 48 B7
Royal Star Arc. [5] ME14 .... 91 F4
Royal Tunbridge Wells Bsns Pk.
  TN2 .... 133 D1
Royal Victoria Place Sh Ctr.
  TN2 .... 149 B4
Royal Victoria Sta. E16 .... 1 A6
Royal West Kent Ave. TN10 ... 117 D4
Roydene Rd. SE18 .... 2 E1
Roydon Hall. TN12 .... 103 F3
Roydon Hall Rd. TN12 .... 103 F4
Royston Ct. Crayford DA1 .... 8 F1
Royston Rd. Maidstone ME15 .. 93 A3
Roystons Cl. ME8 .... 49 F2
Royton Ave. ME17 .... 111 D5
Ruck La. TN12 .... 152 E3
Ruckinge Way. ME8 .... 49 C3
Ruddstreet Cl. SE18 .... 2 C2
Rudge Cl. ME5 .... 62 D2
Rudland Rd. DA7 .... 8 B4
Ruegg House. [5] SE18 .... 6 A8
Ruffet Cl. TN2 .... 148 E1
Ruffets Wood. DA12 .... 30 C2
Rugby Cl. ME5 .... 61 F4
Rugby La. ME17 .... 110 F5
Rumptead La. ME17 & ME 9 .... 79 D4
Rumstead Rd. ME9 .... 79 E4
Rumwood Ct. ME17 .... 108 B5
Runciman Cl. BR6 .... 52 C1
Runham La. ME17 .... 110 E3
Running Horse Rndbt The.
  ME20 .... 76 E1
Runnymede Ct. DA2 .... 27 C7
Rural Vale. DA11 .... 29 E8
Ruscombe Cl. TN4 .... 132 F2
Rush Cl. ME5 .... 62 A3
Rushbrook Rd. SE9 .... 23 C6
Rushdean Rd. ME2 .... 46 D5
Rushdene. SE2 .... 3 D3

Rushet Rd. BR5 .... 38 A7
Rushetts. TN3 .... 147 F4
Rushetts Rd. TN15 .... 55 E3
Rushford Cl. TN27 .... 141 D5
Rushgrove St. SE18 .... 1 F2
Rushley Cl. BR2 .... 50 E6
Rushlye Cl. TN3 .... 163 F5
Rushmead Dr. ME15 .... 107 A7
Rushmere Ct. TN15 .... 86 D7
Rushmore Cl. BR1 .... 36 E6
Rushmore Hill. BR6 & TN14 ... 67 D6
Rushymead. TN15 .... 70 A1
Ruskin Ave. DA16 .... 7 A5
Ruskin Cl. ME19 .... 89 F8
Ruskin Ct. SE9 .... 5 F1
Ruskin Dr. Bexley DA16 .... 7 A4
Ruskin Dr. Orpington BR6 ...... 51 E7
Ruskin Gr. Bexley DA16 .... 7 A5
Ruskin Gr. Dartford DA1 .... 10 A2
Ruskin Wlk. BR2 .... 36 F3
Rusland Ave. BR6 .... 51 D7
Russell Cl. Bexley DA7 .... 8 A3
Russell Cl. Crayford DA1 .... 9 A3
Russell Ct. Greenwich SE7 .... 5 C7
Russell Ct. ME4 .... 48 B3
Russell House Sch. TN14 .... 69 C3
Russell Pl. DA4 .... 41 A8
Russell Rd. Gravesend DA12 ... 13 D1
Russell Rd. Kit's Coty ME20 ... 76 D7
Russell Rd. Newham E16 .... 1 B7
Russell Rd. Tilbury RM18 .... 12 F6
Russell Sq. DA3 .... 42 D6
Russell Terr. DA4 .... 41 C5
Russells Ave. ME8 .... 64 A8
Russet Cl. ME2 .... 46 E8
Russet Cl. ME17 .... 106 C3
Russet House. RM17 .... 12 C7
Russet Way. ME4 .... 88 F2
Russets The. Maidstone ME16 ... 91 B5
Russets The.
  Meopham Station DA13 .... 44 A3
Russett Cl. Ditton ME20 .... 90 E8
Russett Cl. Orpington BR6 ...... 52 B5
Russett Rd. TN12 .... 119 F6
Russett Way. BR8 .... 39 D8
Rusthall Grange. TN4 .... 148 D4
Rusthall High St. TN4 .... 148 C4
Rusthall Pk. TN4 .... 148 D4
Rusthall Rd. TN4 .... 148 D4
Rustwick. TN4 .... 148 D4
Ruth House. ME16 .... 91 E5
Rutherford Way. TN10 .... 117 D7
Rutherglen Rd. SE2 .... 7 A8
Ruthin Rd. SE3 .... 5 A8
Rutland Ave. DA15 .... 24 A8
Rutland Cl. Dartford DA1 .... 26 D8
Rutland Cl. Sidcup DA5 .... 24 D7
Rutland Ct. Chislehurst BR7 ... 37 A8
Rutland Ct. Sidcup BR7 .... 23 C6
Rutland Gate. DA17 .... 4 B1
Rutland Pl. ME8 .... 63 C3
Rutland House. SE18 .... 1 F2
Rutland Pl. ME8 .... 63 C3
Rutland Way. Maidstone ME15 ... 107 E8
Rutland Way. Orpington BR5 ... 38 D8
Ruxley Cl. DA14 .... 24 E2
Ruxley Cnr. DA14 .... 24 E2
Ruxley Corner Ind Est. DA14 ... 24 D2
Ruxley Golf Course. BR5 .... 38 D8
Ruxley Manor Prim Sch. SE9 ... 23 A4
Ruxton Cl. BR8 .... 39 E6
Ruxton Ct. BR8 .... 39 E6
Ryan Cl. SE3 .... 5 C3
Ryan Dr. ME15 .... 93 A2
Ryarsh Cres. BR6 .... 51 E6
Ryarsh Cty Prim Sch. ME19 .... 74 A4
Ryarsh La. ME19 .... 74 B1
Ryarsh Rd. ME19 .... 74 B5
Rycaut Cl. ME8 .... 63 D3
Rycroft La. TN14 .... 98 E5
Rydal Cl. TN4 .... 148 E5
Rydal Dr. Bexley DA7 .... 8 A6
Rydal Dr.
  Royal Tunbridge Wells TN4 ... 148 E5
Ryde Cl. ME5 .... 62 B8
Rydens House. SE9 .... 22 C5
Ryder Cl. BR1 .... 22 B3
Ryders. TN3 .... 148 A3
Rydons Cl. SE9 .... 5 E4
Rye Cl. DA5 .... 24 D8
Rye Cres. BR5 .... 38 D1
Rye Field. BR5 .... 38 D1
Rye La. Otford TN14 .... 69 A2
Rye La. Sevenoaks
  TN13 & TN14 .... 83 F7
Rye Rd. TN18 .... 179 B1
Rye Wood Cotts. TN13 .... 83 F7
Ryecourt Cl. ME16 .... 91 E3
Ryecroft. DA12 .... 30 E3
Ryecroft Rd. Orpington BR5 ... 37 D3
Ryecroft Rd. Otford TN14 ...... 69 A3
Ryedale Ct. TN13 .... 83 E6
Ryegrass Cl. ME5 .... 62 C6
Ryelands Cres. SE12 .... 5 C1
Rymers Cl. TN1 .... 149 D7
Rymill St. E16 .... 1 E2
Rysted La. TN16 .... 81 D1

Sabre Ct. ME7 .... 49 A1
Sackville Ave. BR2 .... 36 A1
Sackville Cl. TN13 .... 84 B5
Sackville Rd. DA1 .... 26 E6
Sackville Sch. TN11 .... 116 C6
Sacred Heart Sch. TN5 .... 174 D5
Saddington St. DA12 .... 30 C8
Saddler's Pk. DA4 .... 54 D7
Saddlers Cl. ME14 .... 92 E5
Sadlers Cl. ME5 .... 61 D2

Saffron Way. 🔟 ME5 .... 61 F5
Sage Cl. 🔟 E6 .... 1 F8
Saigasso Cl. E16 .... 1 D7
Sailfield Ct. ME4 .... 47 F7
Sailmakers Ct. ME4 .... 48 B2
SS Peter & Paul RC Prim Sch.
  BR5 .... 37 E7
St Aidan's Way. DA12 .... 30 E5
St Alban's Cl. DA12 .... 30 D5
St Alban's Gdns. DA12 .... 30 D5
St Alban's Rd. DA1 .... 9 F1
St Alban's Rd Cty Sch. DA1 ..... 9 F1
St Albans Cl. ME7 .... 48 E7
St Albans Rd. ME2 .... 46 C6
St Alfege Rd. SE7 .... 5 D8
St Andrew Rd. ME7 .... 48 D7
St Andrew's Cl. ME16 .... 91 A2
St Andrew's Ct. 🔟 BR8 .... 39 E6
St Andrew's Rd. 🔟
  Gravesend DA11 .... 30 B8
St Andrew's Rd. Maidstone ME16 ... 91 A3
St Andrew's Rd. Tilbury RM18 ... 12 F5
St Andrew's Wlk. ME3 .... 19 D8
St Andrews Cl. TN12 .... 136 A6
St Andrews Ct. 🔟
  Gravesend DA11 .... 13 B1
St Andrews Ct.
  Royal Tunbridge Wells TN4 ... 133 A1
St Andrews Dr. BR5 & BR6 ..... 38 B2
St Andrews Mews. 5 A7
St Andrews Park Rd. TN4 ...... 133 A1
St Andrews Rd.
  Paddock Wood TN12 .... 136 A6
St Andrews Rd. Sidcup DA14 ... 24 D5
St Ann's Green La. TN12 ...... 138 F8
St Anne Ct. ME16 .... 91 E4
St Anselm's RC Prim Sch. DA1 ... 10 A2
St Anthony's Ct. BR6 .... 51 B8
St Aubyns Cl. BR6 .... 51 F7
St Aubyns Gdns. BR6 .... 51 F8
St Audrey Ave. DA7 .... 8 A5
St Augustine of Canterbury
  RC Prim Sch. ME8 .... 63 D3
St Augustine's Ave. BR1 & BR2 ... 36 E4
St Augustine's Jun Sch. DA17 ... 3 F2
St Augustine's RC Prim Sch.
  TN4 .... 149 A7
St Augustine's Rd. DA17 .... 3 F2
St Barnabas CE Prim Sch.
  TN1 .... 149 B5
St Barnabas Cl. Gillingham ME7 ... 48 D3
St Barnabas Cl. Maidstone ME16 ... 91 C8
St Barnabas' Cl.
  Royal Tunbridge Wells TN1 ... 149 B5
St Bartholomew's Hospl. ME1 ... 47 E4
St Bartholomew's La. ME1 ...... 47 E4
St Bartholomew's Terr. ME1 ... 47 E4
St Bartholomews RC Prim Sch.
  BR8 .... 39 E6
St Benedict Rd. ME6 .... 74 E8
St Benedict's Ave. DA12 .... 30 E6
St Benedicts RC Prim Sch. ME5 ... 62 C2
St Benets Ct. TN30 .... 183 B8
St Benets Way. TN30 .... 183 B8
St Benjamins Dr. BR6 .... 52 C2
St Bernards Rd. TN10 .... 117 C6
St Blaise Ave. BR1 .... 36 B7
St Botolph Rd. DA11 .... 29 D5
St Botolph's Ave. TN13 .... 84 A3
St Botolph's CE Prim Sch.
  DA11 .... 29 D8
St Botolph's Rd. TN13 .... 84 B3
St Brelade's Ct. TN8 .... 112 A3
St Brides Cl. DA18 .... 3 D4
St Catherine's Hospl. ME1 ..... 47 D4
St Catherine's Sch for Girls.
  DA6 .... 8 B2
St Chad's Dr. DA12 .... 30 E5
St Chad's Rd. RM18 .... 13 A7
St Chad's Sch. RM18 .... 13 A6
St Christopher's (Trng Coll,
  Dr Barnardo's Home). TN2 ... 149 D4
St Clement's Ave. RM16 .... 11 B8
St Clement's House. ME1 ...... 47 D5
St Clement's Rd. RM16 .... 11 C7
St Clements Cl. DA11 .... 29 F5
St Clements Ct. RM17 .... 11 F8
St Clere Hill Rd. TN15 .... 70 F7
St Columba's Cl. DA12 .... 30 E5
St Columba's RC Boys Sch. DA6 ... 8 B2
St David's Bridge. TN17 ...... 169 D4
St David's Cres. DA12 .... 30 E5
St David's Rd. Allhallows ME3 ... 19 D8
St David's Rd. Hextable BR8 ... 25 F1
St David's Rd.
  Royal Tunbridge Wells TN4 ... 149 B6
St Domingo House. SE18 .... 1 F3
St Dunstan's Dr. DA12 .... 30 E5
St Edith's Rd. TN15 .... 70 A2
St Edmund's Cotts. TN15 ...... 56 A2
St Edmund's Ct. TN15 .... 56 A2
St Edmunds Cl. DA18 .... 3 D4
St Edmunds Rd. DA1 .... 10 A3
St Faith's La. ME14 .... 93 B4
St Faith's St. ME14 .... 91 F4
St Fidelis RC Sch. DA8 .... 8 C8
St Fidelis' Rd. DA8 .... 4 D1
St Francis Ave. DA12 .... 30 E4
St Francis Cl. BR6 .... 37 E3
St Francis RC Prim Sch. ME14 ... 92 B7
St Francis' Rd. Erith DA8 .... 4 D2
St Francis Rd. Harvel DA13 ... 58 B3
St Francis Sch. ME14 .... 92 B7
St George's Bickley CE Prim Sch.
  BR1 .... 36 B7
St George's CE Prim Sch. TN15 ... 71 F3
St George's CE Sch. DA11 ...... 30 A6
St George's Cres. DA12 .... 30 D4

St George's Ct. TN15 .... 71 F3
St George's Ctr. DA11 .... 13 B1
St George's Pk. TN2 .... 162 F8
St George's Rd. Gillingham ME7 ... 48 C6
St George's Rd. Sevenoaks TN13 ... 84 B5
St George's Rd. Sidcup DA14 ... 24 D2
St George's Sch. TN2 .... 150 A5
St George's Sq. ME16 .... 91 E3
St George's Wlk. ME3 .... 19 D8
St Georges Mews. 🔟 TN9 ... 133 B8
St Georges Rd. Bromley BR1 ... 36 F6
St Georges Rd. Orpington BR5 ... 37 D3
St Georges Rd. Swanley BR8 ... 39 F5
St Georges Rd W. BR1 .... 36 E7
St Georges Sq. DA3 .... 42 E6
St German's Pl. SE3 .... 5 A6
St Giles Cl. BR6 .... 51 D5
St Gregory's Catholic Comp Sch.
  TN2 .... 149 A7
St Gregory's Cres. DA12 .... 30 E6
St Gregory's Ct. DA12 .... 30 E6
St Helens CE Prim Sch. ME3 ... 16 B5
St Helens La. ME16 .... 105 E8
St Helens Rd. 🔟 DA18 .... 3 D4
St Helier's Ct. ME16 .... 91 B2
St Hilary's Sch. TN13 .... 84 B5
St Hilda's Way. DA12 .... 30 E5
St Hildas. TN15 .... 101 F8
St James' CE Aided Inf Sch.
  TN2 .... 149 C4
St James' CE Jun Sch. TN2 ... 149 C4
St James' CE (VA) Prim Sch. ... 2 C1
St James Cl. East Malling ME19 ... 89 F8
St James Cl. Grain ME3 .... 21 B6
St James Ct. SE3 .... 5 B6
St James' Cty Inf Sch. ME19 ... 89 F8
St James' La. DA2 & DA9 ...... 27 E8
St James Oaks. DA11 .... 30 A8
St James' Pk. TN1 & TN2 .... 149 C5
St James Pl. DA1 .... 9 D1
St James RC Prim Sch. BR5 ... 37 B4
St James' Rd. Grain ME3 .... 21 B7
St James' Rd. Royal Tunbridge Wells
  TN1 & TN2 .... 149 C5
St James Sq. DA3 .... 42 E6
St James Way. DA14 .... 24 E3
St James's Ave. DA11 .... 30 A8
St James's Cl. SE18 .... 2 C1
St James's Ct. TN1 .... 149 B4
St James's Rd. DA11 .... 13 A1
St James's Rd. Sevenoaks TN13 ... 84 B5
St James's Rd. DA11 .... 13 A1
St Joachim's RC Sch. E16 .... 1 C7
St John Fisher Catholic Comp Sch.
  ME4 .... 47 E3
St John Fisher Catholic Sch
  (Lower Sch). ME4 .... 47 F2
St John Fisher RC Prim Sch.
  DA18 .... 3 E3
St John's CE Inf Sch. ME4 ...... 47 E3
St John's CE Prim Sch.
  Royal Tunbridge Wells TN4 ... 149 A5
St John's CE Prim Sch.
  Sevenoaks TN13 .... 84 D4
St John's CE (VA) Prim Sch.
  ME14 .... 92 E4
St John's Cl. ME3 .... 32 C4
St John's Cl. TN13 .... 84 C5
St John's Hill. TN13 & TN14 ... 84 C5
St John's La. DA3 .... 42 F3
St John's Par. DA14 .... 24 B4
St John's Pk. Greenwich SE3 .... 5 A7
St John's Pk.
  Royal Tunbridge Wells TN4 ... 149 A5
St John's RC Prim Sch. DA12 ... 30 E7
St John's RC Sch. DA12 .... 30 D7
St John's Rd. Bexley DA16 .... 7 B4
St John's Rd. Dartford DA2 ... 27 C8
St John's Rd. Erith DA8 .... 4 D1
St John's Rd. Gillingham ME7 ... 48 D3
St John's Rd. Gravesend DA12 ... 30 D8
St John's Rd. Higham ME3 ..... 32 C4
St John's Rd. Newham E16 .... 1 A7
St John's Rd.
  Orpington BR5 & BR6 .... 37 E3
St John's Rd. Royal Tunbridge Wells
  TN1 & TN4 .... 149 A6
St John's Rd. Sevenoaks TN13 ... 84 C5
St John's Rd. Sidcup DA14 ..... 24 B4
St John's Terr. SE18 .... 6 D8
St Johns CE Prim Sch. TN4 ... 149 B7
St Johns Rd. ME3 .... 34 D6
St Johns Way. ME1 .... 47 D4
St Joseph's RC Prim Sch.
  Bromley BR1 .... 22 B1
St Joseph's RC Prim Sch.
  Crayford DA1 .... 8 E3
St Joseph's RC Prim Sch.
  Northfleet DA11 .... 29 D8
St Josephs Cl. BR6 .... 51 F6
St Justin Cl. BR5 .... 38 D6
St Katherine's Cty Prim Sch.
  ME6 .... 74 F7
St Katherine's La. ME6 .... 74 F7
St Katherines Rd. DA18 .... 3 D4
St Keverne Rd. BR7 & SE9 ..... 22 E4
St Kilda Rd. BR6 .... 37 F1
St Laurence Ave. ME16 .... 91 C8
St Laurence Cl. BR5 .... 38 D6
St Laurence Ave. TN4 .... 132 D3
St Leonard St. ME19 .... 89 B7
St Leonards Ave. ME7 .... 48 F2
St Leonards Cl. 🔟 DA16 .... 7 A4
St Leonards Rd. ME16 .... 91 C8
St Leonards Rd. TN3 .... 148 A3
St Leonards Rise. BR6 .... 51 E6
St Luke's Ave. ME14 .... 92 B5
St Luke's Inf Sch. ME14 ...... 149 C7
St Luke's Rd. Maidstone ME14 ... 92 B5

St Luke's Rd.
  Royal Tunbridge Wells TN4 ... 149 B6
St Luke's Way. ME3 .... 19 D8
St Lukes Cl. Lane End DA2 ..... 27 E3
St Lukes Cl. Swanley BR8 ...... 39 D7
St Margaret Clitherow
  RC Prim Sch. Tonbridge TN10 ... 117 B6
St Margaret Clitherow
  RC Prim Sch. Woolwich SE28 .... 3 B5
St Margaret's at Troy Town
  CE Prim Sch. ME1 .... 47 C4
St Margaret's Banks. ME1 ..... 47 D5
St Margaret's CE Inf Sch. ME8 ... 63 E8
St Margaret's CE Prim Sch. SE18 ... 2 C1
St Margaret's Cres. DA12 ...... 30 E5
St Margaret's Ct. ME23 .... 17 E3
St Margaret's Gr. SE18 .... 6 C8
St Margaret's Mews. ME1 ..... 47 C5
St Margaret's Rd.
  Northfleet DA11 .... 29 E7
St Margaret's Rd.
  St Margarets DA2 & DA4 ..... 27 E2
St Margaret's St. ME1 .... 47 C5
St Margaret's Terr. SE18 .... 2 C1
St Margarets Ave. DA15 .... 23 D5
St Margarets Cl. Maidstone ME16 ... 91 E2
St Margarets Cl. Orpington BR6 ... 52 B6
St Margarets Dr. ME8 .... 63 C5
St Margarets Villas. TN12 ... 137 D8
St Mark's Ave. DA11 .... 29 F8
St Mark's CE Prim Sch.
  Bromley BR2 .... 36 A6
St Mark's CE Prim Sch.
  Royal Tunbridge Wells TN4 ... 148 D1
St Mark's Rd. Bromley BR2 ... 36 B6
St Mark's Rd.
  Royal Tunbridge Wells TN2 ... 162 F7
St Marks CE Inf Sch. ME20 ... 75 F6
St Marks Cl. ME20 .... 75 F6
St Marks Ct. ME20 .... 75 F6
St Marks Rd. ME7 .... 48 C5
St Marks Ind Est. E16 .... 1 D5
St Martin's Cl. ME14 .... 78 A1
St Martin's Dr. DA4 .... 54 D7
St Martin's Rd. DA1 .... 9 F1
St Martins Cl. Erith DA18 .... 3 D4
St Martins Cl. Newington ME9 ... 65 C7
St Martins Meadow. TN16 .... 82 C4
St Mary Cray Prim Sch. BR5 ... 38 C3
St Mary Cray Sta. BR5 .... 38 B5
St Mary St. SE18 .... 2 A2
St Mary & St Joseph's Sch.
  DA14 .... 24 A3
St Mary's. ME3 .... 18 D5
St Mary's Abbey. ME19 .... 89 C8
St Mary's CE (VA) Prim Sch.
  BR8 .... 39 E5
St Mary's Church Rd. TN14 .... 82 F2
St Mary's Cl. Gravesend DA12 ... 30 C6
St Mary's Cl. Grays RM17 ...... 12 D8
St Mary's Cl. Laddingford ME18 ... 120 E4
St Mary's Cl. Platt TN15 .... 87 C7
St Mary's Cl. St Paul's Cray BR5 ... 38 C7
St Mary's Cl. Ticehurst TN5 ... 176 D1
St Mary's Cty Prim Sch. ME2 ... 47 B7
St Mary's Dr. TN13 .... 83 E4
St Mary's Gdns. ME7 .... 48 B7
St Mary's La. Speldhurst TN3 ... 148 A8
St Mary's La. Ticehurst TN5 ... 176 D1
St Mary's Pl. Eltham SE9 .... 6 A1
St Mary's Pl. Newington ME9 ... 65 C7
St Mary's RC Prim Sch.
  Eltham SE9 .... 6 A2
St Mary's RC Prim Sch.
  Gillingham ME7 .... 48 D6
St Mary's Rd. Coldblow DA5 ... 25 C7
St Mary's Rd. Gillingham ME7 ... 48 C6
St Mary's Rd. Rochester ME2 ... 47 B7
St Mary's Rd.
  St Mary's Island ME4 .... 34 A2
St Mary's Rd. Stone DA9 ...... 10 E2
St Mary's Rd. Swanley BR8 ... 39 E5
St Mary's Rd. Tonbridge TN9 ... 133 B7
St Mary's View. ME9 .... 65 C7
St Mary's Wlk. ME1 .... 60 F1
St Marys Ct. SE7 .... 5 D7
St Marys Rd. TN15 .... 72 A2
St Marys Way. DA3 .... 42 E6
St Matthew's CE (VC) Inf Sch.
  ME1 .... 47 A2
St Matthew's Cl. ME9 .... 65 C7
St Matthew's High Brooms
  CE (VC) Prim Sch. TN4 .... 149 B8
St Matthew's Way. ME3 .... 19 D8
St Matthews Dr. Bromley BR1 ... 36 F6
St Matthews Dr. Rochester ME1 ... 47 A2
St Merryn Cl. SE18 .... 6 D1
St Michael's CE Inf Sch. ME16 ... 91 E3
St Michael's CE Jun Sch. ME16 ... 91 E3
St Michael's CE Prim Sch.
  TN30 .... 173 A3
St Michael's Cl. Chatham ME4 ... 47 F3
St Michael's Cl. Erith DA18 ...... 3 D4
St Michael's Cl. ME2 .... 47 B8
St Michael's Cty Prim Sch.
  TN7 .... 160 B5
St Michael's East Wickham
  CE GM Prim Sch. DA16 .... 7 C6
St Michael's RC Prim Sch. ME4 ... 47 F3
St Michael's Rd. Bexley DA16 .... 7 B6
St Michael's Rd. Maidstone ME16 ... 91 D3
St Michael's Rd.
  Royal Tunbridge Wells TN4 ... 149 B7
St Michael's Rise. DA16 .... 7 B6
St Michaels Terr. ME2 .... 173 B3
St Michaels Cl. 🔟 Newham E16 ... 1 D8

St Michaels Cl.
  Pratling Street ME14 & ME20 ... 76 C3
St Michaels Cl. TN11 .... 116 E7
St Michaels Dr. TN14 .... 69 E3
St Mildred's Cl. 🔟 TN30 ...... 183 A7
St Mildreds Rd. 🔟 SE12 .... 22 A8
St Nicholas Ct. SE18 .... 2 F1
St Nicholas Dr. TN13 .... 84 C1
St Nicholas Gdns. ME2 .... 46 F8
St Nicholas Rd. SE18 .... 2 F2
St Nicolas La. BR7 .... 36 E8
St Olave's Sch. BR6 .... 52 B7
St Olaves Prep Sch. SE9 ...... 23 B6
St Patrick's Gdns. DA12 .... 30 D5
St Patrick's RC Prim Sch. SE18 ... 2 D2
St Paul's CE Prim Sch. BR8 .... 40 B8
St Paul's Cl. Greenwich SE7 ..... 1 D1
St Paul's Cl. Rochester ME2 ... 46 D5
St Paul's Cl. Swanscombe DA10 ... 28 E8
St Paul's Cray Rd. BR7 .... 37 D8
St Paul's Ct. TN4 .... 148 C4
St Paul's RC Sec Sch. SE2 .... 7 A8
St Paul's Rd. DA8 .... 8 C7
St Paul's Sq. BR2 .... 36 A7
St Paul's St. TN4 .... 148 C4
St Paul's Wood Hill. BR5 & BR7 ... 37 F7
St Paulinus' CE Prim Sch. DA1 ... 8 E3
St Paulinus Ct. DA1 .... 8 E3
St Pauls CE Inf Sch. TN4 ...... 148 B4
St Pauls CE Jun Sch. TN4 ..... 148 B4
St Pauls Cl. TN10 .... 117 D5
St Pauls Cray CE Prim Sch.
  BR5 .... 38 D6
St Pauls Cty Inf Sch. ME14 ... 92 A7
St Peter Chanel RC Prim Sch.
  DA14 .... 24 C3
St Peter St. ME1 .... 47 D4
St Peter's Bridge. ME16 .... 91 F4
St Peter's CE Prim Sch.
  Aylesford ME20 .... 76 A3
St Peter's CE Prim Sch.
  Royal Tunbridge Wells TN2 ... 149 C3
St Peter's Cl. DA10 .... 28 F8
St Peter's Cl. ME19 .... 75 C1
St Peter's Cty Inf Sch. ME1 ... 47 C3
St Peter's Path. ME1 .... 47 D5
St Peter's RC Prim Sch. SE18 ... 2 B2
St Peter's St. TN2 .... 149 C3
St Peters Cl. Chislehurst BR7 ... 23 D1
St Peters Cl. Ditton ME19 ..... 75 B1
St Peters Pl. ME20 .... 75 F6
St Peters Rd. ME19 .... 75 B1
St Peters Row. TN3 .... 147 A5
St Philip's Ave. ME15 .... 92 B2
St Philip's CE Prim Sch. ME15 ... 92 A3
St Philips Ct. TN1 .... 149 D6
St Philomena's Prim Sch. BR5 ... 38 C2
St Quentin Rd. DA16 .... 6 F4
St Ronan's Cl. ME15 .... 107 C7
St Ronan's Sch. TN18 .... 179 D2
St. Saviours Rd. ME15 .... 107 D6
St Simon Stock RC Sch. ME16 ... 91 C4
St Stephen's CE Inf Sch. ME15 ... 91 E2
St Stephen's Cl. ME9 .... 65 C7
St Stephen's Cty Prim Sch.
  TN9 .... 133 D8
St Stephen's RC Prim Sch. DA16 ... 7 A4
St Stephen's Sq. ME15 .... 91 E2
St Stephen's St. TN9 .... 133 B8
St Stephens Ct. TN1 .... 149 B5
St Thomas' Dr. BR5 .... 37 C1
St Thomas More RC Prim Sch.
  Bexley DA7 .... 7 F5
St Thomas More RC Prim Sch.
  Eltham SE9 .... 5 E4
St Thomas More RC Sec Sch.
  SE9 .... 6 A1
St Thomas More Roman Catholic
  Prim Sch. ME4 .... 62 A5
St Thomas of Canterbury
  Cath Prim Sch. ME8 .... 49 B2
St Thomas RC Prim Sch. TN13 ... 84 B2
St Thomas Rd. Erith DA17 .... 4 C4
St Thomas Rd. Newham E16 ...... 1 A7
St Thomas Rd. Northfleet DA11 ... 29 E6
St Thomas's Almshouses. DA11 ... 30 B7
St Thomas's Ave. DA11 .... 30 B7
St Thomas's CE Prim Sch.
  TN3 .... 161 C6
St Thomas's Pl. 🔟 RM17 ...... 12 C8
St Thomas-a-Becket RC Prim Sch.
  SE2 .... 3 A3
St Timothy's Mews. 🔟 BR1 ... 36 B8
St Vincents Ave. DA1 .... 10 A2
St Vincents La. TN15 .... 73 A2
St Vincents RC Prim Sch. SE9 ... 22 E4
St Vincents Rd. DA1 .... 10 A1
St Welcume's Way. ME17 ..... 110 E6
St Werburgh Cres. ME3 .... 34 D5
St Werburgh Pl. ME3 .... 34 D5
St William of Perth RC Prim Sch.
  ME1 .... 47 B2
St William's Way. ME1 .... 47 D2
St Williams Hospl. ME1 .... 47 D2
Saints Hill. TN11 .... 147 A8
Sala House. SE3 .... 5 B3
Salamons Way. RM13 .... 4 E7
Salcote Rd. DA12 .... 30 E3
Salem Pl. DA11 .... 29 D8
Salem St. ME15 .... 92 A3
Salisbury Ave. Gillingham ME8 ... 63 D8
Salisbury Ave. Swanley BR8 ... 40 A5

Salisbury Cl. TN10 .... 117 D5
Salisbury House. **5** ME15 ... 107 D7
Salisbury Mews. BR2 .... 36 E4
Salisbury Rd. Bromley BR2 .... 36 E4
Salisbury Rd. Chatham ME4 .... 48 A3
Salisbury Rd. Dartford DA2 .... 27 C7
Salisbury Rd. Gravesend DA11 .. 29 F7
Salisbury Rd. **2** Grays RM17 .... 12 C8
Salisbury Rd. Kit's Coty ME20 .. 76 D7
Salisbury Rd. Langton Green TN3 147 F3
Salisbury Rd. Maidstone ME14 .. 92 A6
Salisbury Rd.
  Royal Tunbridge Wells TN4 .... 149 C8
Salisbury Rd. Sidcup DA14 .... 25 A7
Salisbury Rd. Tonbridge TN10 .. 117 D4
Salix Rd. RM17 .... 12 D8
Sallows Shaw. DA13 .... 44 C4
Sally Port. ME7 .... 48 A6
Sally Port Gdns. ME7 .... 48 B6
Salmon Rd. DA17 .... 4 A1
Salomons Rd. Newham E13 .... 1 C8
Salomons Rd. Rusthall TN4 .... 148 C4
Salt La. ME3 .... 15 F4
Salt's Ave. ME15 .... 106 F3
Saltash Rd. DA16 .... 7 C6
Salter's Cross. ME18 .... 105 A1
Saltford Cl. DA8 .... 4 E1
Saltings. ME6 .... 75 A7
Saltley Cl. E6 .... 1 E7
Salts La. ME15 .... 107 A4
Saltwood Cl. BR6 .... 52 C6
Saltwood Rd. ME15 .... 91 F1
Sam Bartram Cl. SE7 .... 1 C1
Samara Cl. ME5 .... 62 A1
Samphire Cl. ME14 .... 92 E4
Samphire Rd. RM17 .... 12 E8
Sampson Cl. DA17 .... 3 D3
Samson House. SE18 .... 2 C2
Samuel Cl. SE18 .... 1 E2
Samuel Palmer Ct. BR6 .... 38 A2
Samuel St. E6 .... 1 F2
Sanctuary Cl. DA1 .... 9 D1
Sanctuary Rd. ME8 .... 49 A3
Sanctuary The. DA5 .... 7 D1
Sand La. TN17 .... 156 F4
Sand Rd. TN3 .... 166 A4
Sandalwood House. DA15 ...... 23 F5
Sandbach Pl. SE18 .... 2 C1
Sandbanks Hill. DA2 .... 28 B2
Sandbourne Dr. ME14 .... 76 F1
Sandby Gn. SE9 .... 5 E4
Sandcliff Rd. DA8 .... 4 D1
Sanderling Ct. SE28 .... 3 C6
Sanderson Way. TN9 .... 117 E1
Sandersons Ave. TN14 .... 53 B1
Sanderstead Rd. BR5 .... 38 B3
Sandfield Rd. TN11 .... 147 A7
Sandford Rd. Bexley DA7 & DA6 .... 7 E4
Sandford Rd. Bromley BR2 .... 36 A5
Sandgate Cl. ME8 .... 63 F4
Sandgate Rd. DA16 .... 7 C7
Sandham Point. **10** SE18 ..... 2 B2
Sandhill La. ME3 .... 32 D6
Sandhurst Ave. TN2 .... 150 E6
Sandhurst Cl. Gillingham ME8 .. 49 C3
Sandhurst Cl.
  Royal Tunbridge Wells TN1 ..... 149 C6
Sandhurst Cl.
  Sandhurst TN18 .... 186 A4
Sandhurst Cross. TN12 .... 140 F1
Sandhurst Cty Prim Sch. TN18 186 C1
Sandhurst House. TN2 .... 149 D5
Sandhurst La. TN17 .... 181 B2
Sandhurst Pk. TN1 .... 149 C6
Sandhurst Rd. Bexley DA5 .... 7 D2
Sandhurst Rd. Orpington BR6 .. 52 A6
Sandhurst Rd. Tilbury RM18 .. 13 C5
Sandhurst Rd. Royal Tunbridge Wells
  TN1 & TN2 & TN4 .... 149 D6
Sandilands. TN13 .... 83 D5
Sandling Cty Prim Sch. ME14 .. 92 B8
Sandling La. ME14 .... 92 A8
Sandling Rd. Maidstone ME14 .. 91 F6
Sandling Rd.
  Maidstone,Ringlestone ME14 .... 91 F7
Sandling Rise. SE9 .... 23 A5
Sandown Cl. TN2 .... 149 F6
Sandown Court Com Coll.
  TN2 .... 149 F5
Sandown Dr. ME8 .... 63 D7
Sandown Gr. TN2 .... 149 F6
Sandown Pk. TN2 .... 149 F6
Sandown Rd. Gravesend DA12 .. 30 C2
Sandown Rd. New Town ME19 .. 89 B8
Sandpiper Rd. ME5 .... 62 D2
Sandpiper Way. BR5 .... 38 D6
Sandpipers The. DA12 .... 30 D6
Sandpit Pl. SE7 .... 1 E1
Sandpit Rd. DA1 .... 9 C3
Sandringham Dr. DA16 .... 6 E5
Sandringham House. ME1 ..... 47 B4
Sandringham Rd. Bromley BR1 .. 22 A3
Sandringham Rd. Gillingham ME8 63 E3
Sandrock House. TN2 .... 149 D4
Sandrock Rd. TN2 .... 149 C4
Sandrock Villas. TN18 .... 178 F3
Sandstone Rd. SE12 .... 22 B6
Sandstone Rise. ME14 .... 77 C8
Sandtoft Rd. SE7 .... 5 B8
Sandway Path. **6** BR5 .... 38 C5
Sandway Rd. Orpington BR5 .. 38 C5
Sandway Rd. Sandway ME17 .. 110 F4
Sandy Bank Rd. DA12 .... 30 B7
Sandy Bury. BR6 .... 51 D7

Sandy Dell. ME7 .... 63 A3
Sandy Hill Ave. SE18 .... 2 B1
Sandy Hill La. SE18 .... 2 B2
Sandy Hill Rd. SE18 .... 2 B1
Sandy La. Bean DA13 & DA2 ... 28 D5
Sandy La. Ightham Common TN15 86 B3
Sandy La.
  Maidstone,Harbourland ME14 .. 92 C8
Sandy La.
  Maidstone,Penenden Heath ME14 92 C7
Sandy La.
  Maidstone,Ware Street ME14 .. 93 B5
Sandy La. New Town ME19 .... 74 A1
Sandy La. Orpington BR6 ...... 38 A2
Sandy La. Sevenoaks TN13 .... 84 C4
Sandy La. Snodland ME6 ...... 74 E6
Sandy La. St Paul's Cray BR5 .. 38 D8
Sandy La. Tenterden TN30 .... 183 B1
Sandy La. Tilbury RM17 .... 13 B8
Sandy La. West Thurrock RM16 .. 11 B8
Sandy La. Westerham TN16 .... 81 D2
Sandy La. Wrotham Heath TN15 .. 72 F1
Sandy Mount. ME14 .... 93 B5
Sandy Ridge.
  Borough Green TN15 .... 87 A7
Sandy Ridge. Chislehurst BR7 .. 23 A2
Sandycroft. SE2 .... 7 A8
Sandycroft Rd. ME2 .... 32 F1
Santana House. SE18 .... 6 B7
Santer House. TN18 .... 184 E8
Sapho Pk. DA12 .... 30 F4
Saphora Cl. BR6 .... 51 D5
Sapphire Cl. E6 .... 2 A7
Sara House. **1** DA8 .... 8 E7
Sara Pk. DA12 .... 30 E4
Sara Turnbull House. **2** SE18 .. 1 F2
Saracen Cl. ME7 .... 48 E7
Saracen Fields. ME5 & ME14 .. 77 C8
Sark Wlk. E16 .... 1 B7
Sarsen Hts. ME5 .... 61 F1
Sarsens Cl. DA12 .... 44 F6
Sassoon Cl. ME20 .... 75 A4
Satanita Cl. E16 .... 1 D7
Saunder's Cross. TN14 .... 53 B2
Saunders Cl. DA11 .... 29 E6
Saunders Rd.
  Royal Tunbridge Wells TN4 .... 148 E1
Saunders Rd. Woolwich SE18 .. 2 F1
Saunders St. ME7 .... 48 C6
Saunders Way. Dartford DA1 .. 26 F6
Saunders Way. Woolwich SE28 .. 3 B6
Savage Gdns. E6 .... 1 F7
Savage Rd. ME5 .... 62 B3
Savill House. E16 .... 2 B5
Saville Rd. E16 .... 1 E5
Savoy Rd. DA1 .... 9 D2
Sawyers Cl. ME4 .... 48 B2
Saxby Wood. TN11 .... 115 F1
Saxbys Rd. TN15 .... 85 D5
Saxon Cl. Kings Hill ME18 .... 88 F2
Saxon Cl. Northfleet DA11 .... 29 C5
Saxon Cl. Otford TN14 .... 69 F7
Saxon Cl. Rochester ME2 ...... 32 F1
Saxon Pl. DA14 .... 41 C4
Saxon Rd. Bromley BR1 .... 22 A1
Saxon Rd. Hawley DA2 .... 26 E4
Saxon Wlk. DA14 .... 24 C2
Saxons Dr. ME14 .... 92 B7
Saxton St. ME7 .... 48 C5
Saxville Rd. BR5 .... 38 B6
Sayer Cl. DA9 .... 11 A2
Sayers La. **4** TN30 .... 183 A7
Sayes Court Rd. BR5 .... 38 B5
Scabharbour Rd. TN11 & TN14 .. 99 C1
Scadbury Park Nature Reserve.
  BR7 .... 23 F2
Scads Hill Cl. BR5 & BR6 ...... 37 F3
Scarborough La. ME1 .... 60 D2
Scarlet Cl. BR5 .... 38 B5
Scarlett Cl. ME5 .... 62 C5
Scarsbrook Rd. SE3 .... 5 D4
Schofield Wlk. SE3 .... 5 A7
Scholars Rise. ME2 .... 46 D7
Scholey Cl. ME2 .... 60 B4
School App. TN15 .... 86 F7
School Ave. ME7 .... 48 E4
School Cl. DA13 .... 44 A2
School Cotts. Crockenhill BR8 .. 39 F2
School Cotts. Sidcup DA14 .... 24 C3
School Cres. DA1 .... 8 F3
School Field. TN8 .... 112 C2
School Hill. TN3 .... 166 B6
School House La. TN12 .... 153 E7
School La. Bean DA2 .... 28 C5
School La. Bexley DA16 .... 7 B4
School La. Borden ME9 .... 65 F4
School La. Hadlow TN11 .... 118 E8
School La. Hextable BR8 ...... 26 B1
School La. Higham ME3 .... 32 C5
School La.
  Horton Kirby DA3 & DA4 .... 41 E4
School La. Knockmill TN15 .... 70 F8
School La. Maidstone ME15 ... 92 E1
School La. Newington ME9 .... 65 B7
School La. Platt's Heath ME17 .. 110 F2
School La. Plaxtol TN11 & TN15 .. 101 E6
School La. Seal TN15 .... 84 F6
School La. Sutton Valence ME17 124 E7
School La. Trottiscliffe ME19 .. 73 A5
School La. Vigo Village DA13 .. 58 A2
School La. Wouldham ME1 .... 60 D5
School Rd. Chislehurst BR7 .... 23 C1
School Rd. Gravesend DA12 ... 30 C5
School Rise. TN2 .... 148 F1
School Terr. **6** TN18 .... 178 F2
School Villas. ME18 .... 104 D5
Schoolfield Rd. RM16 .... 11 A8
Schooner Ct. DA9 .... 10 C3

Scilla Ct. **10** RM17 .... 12 D8
Scimitar Cl. ME7 .... 49 A1
Scords La. TN16 .... 97 C4
Scotby Ave. ME5 .... 62 B4
Scotland La. Cobham DA12 .... 44 F6
Scotland La. Cobham DA12 .... 45 A8
Scotney Castle. TN3 .... 166 D3
Scotney House. ME2 .... 33 C1
Scotsdale Cl. BR5 & BR7 ..... 37 E5
Scotsdale Rd. SE12 .... 5 B2
Scott Ave. ME8 .... 64 A8
Scott Cl. ME8 & ME20 .... 90 C8
Scott Cres. DA8 .... 8 F6
Scott House. ME3 .... 3 F1
Scott Rd. Gravesend DA12 .... 30 D3
Scott Rd. Tonbridge TN9 ...... 132 F8
Scott St. ME14 .... 91 F5
Scott Wilkie Prim Sch. E16 ... 1 C7
Scott's Terr. ME4 .... 47 F3
Scotteswood Ave. ME4 .... 47 F2
Scotts Park Prim Sch. BR1 .... 36 C8
Scotts Rd. BR1 .... 22 A1
Scotts Way.
  Royal Tunbridge Wells TN2 .... 162 E8
Scotts Way. Sevenoaks TN13 .. 83 E5
Scoulding Rd. E16 .... 1 A7
Scragged Oak Rd. Detling ME14 78 C5
Scragged Oak Rd. Hucking ME14 79 C1
Scratchers La. TN15 .... 55 E7
Scratton Fields. DA12 .... 44 D4
Scrubbs La. ME16 .... 91 D4
Scudders Hill. DA3 .... 42 C3
Seabrook Rd. TN11 .... 117 A3
Seabrooke Rise. RM17 .... 12 B8
Seacourt Rd. SE2 .... 3 D4
Seaford Ct. ME1 .... 47 B5
Seagull Rd. ME2 .... 46 D6
Seal CE Prim Sch. TN15 .... 84 F7
Seal Dr. TN15 .... 84 C2
Seal Hollow Rd. TN13 & TN15 .. 84 D4
Seal Rd. TN13 & TN14 & TN15 .. 84 C6
Seal St Lawrence CE Prim Sch.
  TN15 .... 85 E3
Sealand Cl. ME1 .... 47 B5
Seamew Ct. ME2 .... 46 C7
Seaton Cl. Bexley DA16 .... 7 C7
Seaton Rd. Dartford DA1 ...... 26 A8
Seaton Rd. Gillingham ME7 .. 48 E3
Seaview. ME3 .... 21 B5
Seaview Rd. ME7 .... 48 A7
Second Ave. Chatham ME4 & ME5 48 C1
Second Ave. Gillingham ME7 .. 48 E3
Second Ave. West Thurrock RM16 11 A8
Secretan Rd. ME1 .... 47 B1
Sedcombe Cl. DA14 .... 24 C4
Sedge Cres. ME5 .... 61 E4
Sedgebrook Rd. SE3 .... 5 D4
Sedgemere Rd. SE2 .... 3 C3
Sedley. DA13 .... 29 A2
Sedley Cl. Aylesford ME20 .... 75 F2
Sedley Cl. Cliffe Woods ME3 .. 33 C7
Sedley Cl. Gillingham ME8 .... 63 C3
Sedley's CE Fst Sch. DA13 .... 29 A3
Sefton Cl. BR5 .... 37 F5
Sefton Rd. BR5 .... 37 F5
Sejant House. **4** RM17 ...... 12 B8
Selah Dr. BR8 .... 39 C8
Selborne Ave. DA5 .... 24 E7
Selborne Rd. DA14 .... 24 B4
Selbourne Cl. DA3 .... 43 D6
Selbourne Rd. ME7 .... 48 D7
Selbourne Wlk. ME5 .... 107 F6
Selby Cl. Chislehurst BR7 .... 23 A2
Selby Cl. **13** Newham E6 .... 1 E8
Selby Rd. Newham E11 .... 1 B8
Selby Rd. Park Wood ME15 ... 107 F4
Selkirk Dr. DA8 .... 8 E6
Sellbourne Pk. TN3 .... 163 C4
Sellinge Gn. ME8 .... 49 C3
Sellwood Ct. DA1 .... 27 B7
Selsey Cres. DA16 .... 7 D6
Selstead Cl. ME8 .... 49 C2
Selwyn Cres. DA16 .... 7 B3
Selwyn Pl. **1** BR5 .... 38 B6
Selwyn Rd. RM18 .... 12 F5
Semple Gdns. ME4 .... 47 E3
Senacre La. ME15 .... 107 E6
Senacre Sq. ME15 .... 107 F7
Senacre Tech Coll. ME15 ...... 107 D6
Senacre Wood Cty Prim Sch.
  ME15 .... 107 F7
Senator Wlk. SE28 .... 2 D3
Sencler House. SE2 .... 7 D8
Senlac Pl. TN3 .... 161 C7
Senlac Rd. SE12 .... 22 B7
Sennen Wlk. SE9 .... 22 E5
Sennocke Ct. TN13 .... 84 B2
Sequoia Gdns. BR6 .... 37 F2
Sermon Rd. BR6 .... 39 C6
Serpentine Ct. TN13 .... 84 D5
Serpentine Rd. TN13 & TN15 .. 84 D4
Serviden Dr. BR1 .... 36 D8
Setford Rd. ME5 .... 62 C6
Settington Ave. ME5 .... 48 C1
Seven Acres. Crockenhill BR8 .. 39 D3
Seven Acres.
  New Ash Green DA3 .... 56 E7
Seven Mile La.
  Herne Pound ME18 .... 88 A3
Seven Mile La.
  Mereworth TN11 & TN12 ...... 103 E3
Seven Mile La.
  Wrotham Heath TN15 .... 87 F7
Seven Wents. TN15 .... 86 A4
Sevenoaks Bsns Ctr. TN14 .... 84 C6
Sevenoaks By-Pass.
  TN13 & TN14 .... 98 F7
Sevenoaks Cty Prim Sch. TN13 84 B5

Sevenoaks Hospl.
  Sevenoaks TN13 .... 84 B2
Sevenoaks Hospl.
  Sevenoaks,St John's TN13 ... 84 C6
Sevenoaks Prep Sch. TN15 ... 85 A1
Sevenoaks Rd.
  Borough Green TN15 .... 86 F7
Sevenoaks Rd.
  Ightham Common TN15 ...... 86 B4
Sevenoaks Rd. Orpington BR6 .. 51 F6
Sevenoaks Rd. Otford TN14 .. 69 B3
Sevenoaks Rd.
  Pratt's Bottom BR6 & TN14 ... 52 C2
Sevenoaks Sch. TN15 .... 84 C1
Sevenoaks Sta. TN13 .... 84 A3
Sevenoaks Way. BR5 .... 38 C7
Sevenoaks Wildfowl Reserve.
  TN14 .... 84 A7
Severn Cl. TN10 .... 117 C5
Severn Rd. ME5 .... 62 C5
Sevington Pk. ME15 .... 106 F6
Sewell Rd. SE28 .... 3 B4
Sextant Pk. ME2 .... 47 E6
Sexton Rd. RM18 .... 12 F6
Seymour Dr. BR2 .... 36 F1
Seymour Rd. **1** Chatham ME4 .. 48 B3
Seymour Rd. Moor Street ME8 .. 64 C8
Seymour Rd. Northfleet DA11 .. 29 F6
Seymour Rd. Tilbury RM18 .... 12 F6
Seymour St. SE18 .... 2 C3
Seymour Wlk. DA10 .... 28 E8
Shacklands Rd. TN14 .... 53 D1
Shackleton Cl. ME5 .... 62 B6
Shades The. ME2 .... 46 C7
Shaftesbury Cl. ME19 .... 74 F1
Shaftesbury Cl. **3** SE28 .... 3 C5
Shaftesbury Dr. ME16 .... 91 C4
Shaftesbury La. DA1 .... 10 B3
Shaftesbury Rd. TN4 .... 149 A5
Shaftsbury Ct. E6 .... 2 A7
Shakespeare Ave. RM18 ...... 13 B6
Shakespeare Farm Rd. ME3 .. 18 F7
Shakespeare House. **1** ME3 . 3 F1
Shakespeare Rd. Bexley DA7 .. 7 F6
Shakespeare Rd. Dartford DA1 .. 10 B3
Shakespeare Rd. Gillingham ME7 48 D5
Shakespeare Rd. Tonbridge TN9 132 F8
Shalder House. ME7 .... 48 D7
Shalford Cl. BR6 .... 51 C6
Shallons Rd. SE9 .... 23 B4
Shambles The. TN13 .... 84 C2
Shamel Bsns Ctr. ME2 .... 47 C7
Shamley Rd. ME5 .... 62 D2
Shamrock Rd. DA12 .... 30 F8
Shandon Cl. TN2 .... 149 C4
Shanklin Cl. ME5 .... 62 C8
Shannon Ct. BR6 .... 38 A2
Sharfleet Dr. ME2 .... 46 B7
Sharland Rd. DA12 .... 30 C6
Sharman Cl. DA14 .... 24 A4
Sharnal La. ME6 .... 75 A7
Sharnal St. ME3 .... 18 A2
Sharnbrooke Cl. DA16 .... 7 C4
Sharon Cres. ME5 .... 61 F4
Sharp Way. DA1 .... 9 F4
Sharp's Field. TN27 .... 141 E5
Sharsted Way. Gillingham ME7 .. 63 A3
Sharsted Way. Maidstone ME14 .. 93 B5
Shaw Cl. Cliffe Woods ME3 ... 33 B8
Shaw Cl. Woolwich SE28 ..... 3 B5
Shaw Cres. ME14 .... 13 B6
Shaw House. **6** Erith DA17 .. 3 F1
Shaw House. **5** Newham E16 .. 2 A5
Shaw The. TN2 .... 149 C2
Shawbrooke Rd. SE9 .... 5 D3
Shawcroft Sch. BR5 .... 38 E4
Shawfield Pk. BR1 .... 36 D7
Shaws Way. ME1 .... 47 C3
Shawstead Rd. ME7 & ME7 ... 62 D5
Sheafe Dr. TN17 .... 169 C5
Sheal's Cres. ME15 .... 92 A2
Sheals Ct. ME15 .... 92 A2
Shearers Cl. ME14 .... 92 E4
Shears Green Cty Inf Sch.
  DA11 .... 29 F5
Shears Green Cty Jun Sch.
  DA11 .... 29 F5
Shearwater. Maidstone ME16 .. 91 B5
Shearwater. New Barn DA3 ... 43 B6
Shearwater Ct. ME2 .... 46 C7
Shearwood Cres. DA1 .... 9 A4
Sheen Rd. BR5 .... 37 F5
Sheepcote La. BR5 & BR8 .... 38 F4
Sheephurst La. TN12 .... 137 E5
Sheerness Harbour Est. ME12 . 21 F3
Sheerwater Rd. E16 .... 1 D8
Sheet Hill. TN15 .... 86 D2
Sheffield Rd. **4** TN4 .... 132 F2
Sheilings The. TN15 .... 84 F7
Shelbury Cl. DA14 .... 24 A5
Shelden Dr. ME8 .... 63 F8
Sheldon Bsns Ctr. ME2 ...... 47 D8
Sheldon Cl. SE12 .... 5 B2
Sheldon Rd. DA7 .... 7 F6
Sheldon Way. ME20 .... 75 B3
Sheldrake Cl. E16 .... 1 F5
Shell Cl. BR2 .... 36 E3
Shellbank La. DA2 .... 28 B4
Shelldrake Cl. ME3 .... 21 B5
Shelley Cl. BR6 .... 51 E7
Shelley Dr. DA16 .... 6 E6
Shelley Pl. RM18 .... 13 B6
Shelley Rd. ME16 .... 91 C2
Shelleys La. TN14 .... 67 A3
Shelton Cl. TN10 .... 117 C5
Shenden Cl. TN13 .... 99 C1
Shenden Way. TN13 & TN15 .. 99 C1

Shenfield House. SE18 .... 5 D7
Shenley Gr. ME14 .... 76 F2
Shenley Rd. DA1 .... 27 A8
Shenstone Sch. DA1 .... 8 D2
Shepherd St. DA11 .... 29 D8
Shepherds Cl. BR6 .... 51 F7
Shepherds Gate. ME7 .... 62 F5
Shepherds Gate Dr. ME14 ... 92 E6
Shepherds Gn. BR7 .... 23 D1
Shepherds La. DA1 .... 26 B8
Shepherds Leas. SE9 .... 6 D3
Shepherds Way.
  Langley Heath ME17 .... 108 E4
Shepherds Way.
  Lower Stoke ME3 .... 19 C4
Shepherds Wlk. TN2 .... 149 D4
Shepherdsgrove La. RH19 .. 144 A4
Shepperton Cl. ME5 .... 62 C4
Shepperton Rd. BR5 .... 37 C3
Sheppey Cl. DA8 .... 9 B7
Sheppey Rd. ME15 .... 107 A7
Sheppey Way. ME12 .... 25 F8
Shepway Cty Inf Sch. ME15 .. 107 E8
Shepway Cty Jun Sch. ME15 .. 107 E8
Sherard Rd. SE9 .... 5 E2
Sheraton Ct. ME5 .... 61 F1
Sherborne Rd. BR5 .... 37 F4
Sherbourne Cl.
  Royal Tunbridge Wells TN2 .... 149 D2
Sherbourne Cl.
  West Kingsdown TN15 .... 55 E4
Sherbourne Dr. ME16 .... 91 B2
Sherbrooke Cl. DA7 .... 8 A3
Sherenden La. TN12 .... 154 D8
Sherenden Pk. TN11 .... 119 A5
Sherenden Rd. TN11 .... 134 D7
Sherfield Rd. RM17 .... 12 B8
Sheridan Cl. Chatham ME5 ... 62 C7
Sheridan Cl. Maidstone ME14 .. 91 E8
Sheridan Cl. Swanley BR8 .... 39 F6
Sheridan Cres. BR7 .... 37 B7
Sheridan Ct. DA1 .... 10 A3
Sheridan Rd. Bexley DA7 .... 7 E4
Sheridan Rd. Erith DA17 ..... 4 A2
Sheriff Dr. ME5 .... 62 A2
Sherington Prim Sch. SE7 ... 5 B8
Sherington Rd. SE7 .... 5 B8
Sherlies Ave. BR6 .... 51 E8
Sherman Cl. ME7 .... 49 B1
Sherman Rd. BR1 .... 36 A8
Shernden La. TN8 .... 128 C4
Shernold Sch. ME16 .... 91 D5
Shernolds. ME15 .... 107 B7
Sherway Cl. TN27 .... 141 E5
Sherway Rd. TN27 .... 142 D6
Sherwin Knight Cty Prim Sch.
  ME2 .... 46 E5
Sherwood Ave. ME5 .... 62 A2
Sherwood Cl. DA5 .... 7 C1
Sherwood House. Chatham ME5 62 A3
Sherwood House. Erith DA8 .. 8 E8
Sherwood Park Ave. BR5 .... 7 B1
Sherwood Park Cty Prim Sch.
  TN2 .... 149 D6
Sherwood Rd. Bexley DA16 .. 6 E4
Sherwood Rd.
  Royal Tunbridge Wells TN2 .... 149 E5
Sherwood Way. TN2 .... 149 D6
Shieldhall St. SE2 .... 3 C2
Shillingheld Cl. ME14 .... 92 F5
Shinecroft. TN14 .... 69 A3
Shingle Barn La. ME15 ...... 105 C3
Shinglewell Rd. DA8 .... 8 A7
Ship La. Chatham ME1 .... 47 E4
Ship La. Sutton at Hone BR8 .. 40 E8
Shipbourne Cty Prim Sch.
  TN11 .... 101 C4
Shipbourne Rd.
  Shipbourne TN11 & TN10 .... 101 D2
Shipbourne Rd. Tonbridge TN10 117 C5
Shipley Cl. ME14 .... 92 A4
Shipley Hills Rd. Meopham DA13 43 E1
Shipman Rd. E16 .... 1 C7
Shipwrights Ave. ME4 .... 48 B2
Shire Ct. SE2 .... 3 D3
Shire La.
  Farthing Street BR6 & BR2 .... 51 C3
Shire La. Orpington BR6 ..... 51 E5
Shirebrook Rd. SE3 .... 5 D4
Shirehall Rd. DA2 .... 26 E4
Shires The. TN12 .... 136 A7
Shirley Ave. Chatham ME5 ... 61 D5
Shirley Ave. Sidcup DA5 ..... 24 C7
Shirley Cl. Chalk DA12 ...... 31 B6
Shirley Cl. Dartford DA1 ..... 9 C3
Shirley Gdns. TN4 .... 148 C5
Shirley Gr. TN4 .... 148 C5
Shirley House Dr. SE7 .... 5 C7
Shirley Rd. DA15 .... 23 E5
Shirley Way. ME5 .... 93 A3
Sholden Gdns. BR5 .... 38 C4
Sholden Rd. ME2 .... 33 C1
Shooters Hill. SE18 .... 6 B6
Shooters Hill Golf Course. SE18 6 C6
Shooters Hill Rd.
  SE18 & SE3 & SE7 .... 5 D6
Shore The. Northfleet DA11 .. 12 C2
Shore The. Northfleet DA11 .. 12 F1
Shoreham Cl. DA5 .... 24 D7
Shoreham Cty Prim Sch. TN14 68 F8
Shoreham House. TN14 ..... 69 A8
Shoreham La.
  Badgers Mount TN14 .... 68 A7
Shoreham La. Maypole BR6 .. 53 A3
Shoreham La. Sevenoaks TN13 83 F4
Shoreham La. St Michaels TN30 173 A3
Shoreham Pl. TN14 .... 69 A7

Shoreham Rd. Otford TN14 .... 69 B5
Shoreham Rd. St Paul's Cray BR5 38 B7
Shoreham Sta. TN14 .... 69 B8
Shoreham Way. BR2 .... 36 A3
Shoreham Wlk. ME15 .... 107 F7
Shorehill La. TN15 .... 69 F4
Shorne CE Prim Sch. DA12 .... 31 E3
Shorne Cl. Orpington BR5 .... 38 D5
Shorne Cl. 3 Sidcup DA15 .... 7 B1
Shorne Ifield Rd. DA12 .... 31 C2
Shorne Wood (Ctry Pk). DA12 .. 31 C1
Shornefield Cl. BR1 .... 37 A6
Short La. Brenchley TN12 .... 152 A6
Short La. Gillingham ME7 .... 49 A6
Short St. 3 ME4 .... 48 B3
Shortlands Cl. DA17 .... 3 F3
Shortlands Gn. ME15 .... 107 F5
Shorts Way. ME1 .... 47 A3
Shortway. SE9 .... 5 E4
Shottenden Rd. ME7 .... 48 D7
Shottery Cl. SE9 .... 22 E5
Showfields Rd. TN2 .... 148 F1
Shrapnel Cl. SE18 .... 5 E7
Shrapnel Rd. SE9 .... 5 F4
Shrewsbury La. SE18 .... 6 B6
Shroffold Rd. BR1 .... 22 A5
Shropshire Terr. 3 ME15 .... 107 E7
Shrubbery Rd. Gravesend DA12 . 30 C7
Shrubbery Rd.
  South Darenth DA4 .... 41 D8
Shrubcote. TN30 .... 183 C7
Shrublands Ct.
  Royal Tunbridge Wells TN2 ...... 149 C4
Shrublands Ct. 1
  Tonbridge TN9 .... 117 C2
Shrubsall Cl. SE9 .... 22 E7
Shrubsole Dr. ME14 .... 76 F3
Shurlock Ave. BR8 .... 39 D7
Shurlock Dr. BR6 .... 51 C6
Shuttle Cl. Biddenden TN27 ...... 158 A2
Shuttle Cl. Sidcup DA15 .... 23 F8
Shuttle Rd. DA1 .... 9 A4
Shuttlemead. DA5 .... 24 F8
Sibley Cl. DA6 .... 7 E2
Sibthorpe Rd. SE12 .... 22 C8
Sidcup By Pass Rd. Sidcup DA14 23 F3
Sidcup By Pass Rd.
  St Paul's Cray BR5 & BR7 .... 24 B1
Sidcup Hill. DA14 .... 24 B3
Sidcup Hill Gdns. DA14 .... 24 C3
Sidcup Hill Prim Sch. DA14 ..... 24 B3
Sidcup Pl. DA14 .... 24 A3
Sidcup Rd. Eltham SE12 & SE9 .... 22 D7
Sidcup Rd. Eltham SE9 .... 22 E7
Sidcup Rd. Eltham BR7 & SE9 ..... 23 B6
Sidcup Sta. SE9 & DA15 .... 24 A6
Sidewood Rd. SE9 .... 23 D7
Sidmouth Ct. DA1 .... 27 B7
Sidmouth Rd. Bexley DA16 .... 7 C7
Sidmouth Rd. Orpington BR5 .... 38 B5
Sidney Cl. TN2 .... 162 F8
Sidney Gdns. SE14 .... 69 C2
Sidney House. SE18 .... 5 F6
Sidney Rd. Gillingham ME7 .... 48 C7
Sidney Rd. Rochester ME1 .... 47 A2
Sidney St. ME16 .... 91 C2
Siebert Rd. SE3 & SE7 .... 5 A8
Siedle House. 9 SE18 .... 6 A8
Siemens Rd. SE18 .... 1 D3
Silchester Ct. ME14 .... 92 C7
Silcroft Rd. DA7 .... 8 A6
Silk Cl. SE12 .... 5 A1
Silver Bank. ME5 .... 62 A6
Silver Birch Ave. DA13 .... 57 F1
Silver Birch Cl. DA2 .... 25 E4
Silver Birches. ME5 .... 62 A3
Silver Cl. TN9 .... 133 B6
Silver Hill. Chatham ME4 .... 47 F3
Silver Hill. Rochester ME1 .... 46 F2
Silver Hill. Silver Hill TN19 .... 184 B1
Silver Hill. Tenterden TN30 .... 173 B1
Silver Hill Gdns. ME4 .... 47 F3
Silver Rd. DA12 .... 30 E6
Silver Spring Cl. DA8 .... 8 B8
Silver St. ME9 .... 80 F5
Silver Tree. ME5 .... 62 B1
Silverdale. Hartley DA3 .... 42 F5
Silverdale. Maidstone ME16 .... 91 A2
Silverdale Dr. Chislehurst SE9 ..... 22 E6
Silverdale Dr. Gillingham ME8 ...... 63 F7
Silverdale La. TN4 .... 149 B6
Silverdale Rd. Bexley DA7 .... 8 B5
Silverdale Rd. Orpington BR5 .... 37 C5
Silverdale Rd.
  Royal Tunbridge Wells TN4 ...... 149 B6
Silverdale Rd. St Paul's Cray BR5 38 A6
Silverden Cotts. TN18 .... 185 F4
Silverhurst Dr. TN10 .... 117 C7
Silverland St. E16 .... 1 F5
Silverspot Cl. SE9 .... 63 F7
Silversted La. TN16 .... 81 D6
Silverstone Ct. 6 ME1 .... 36 C7
Silvertown Sta. SE16 .... 1 C5
Silvertown By-Pass. E16 .... 1 D5
Silvertown Way. E16 .... 1 A5
Silverweed Rd. ME5 .... 61 F4
Silwood Cl. TN2 .... 149 E7
Simmonds Ct. TN4 .... 148 B4
Simmonds Dr. DA3 .... 43 A4
Simmonds La. ME15 .... 108 B6
Simmons Rd. SE18 .... 2 B1
Simnel Rd. SE12 .... 22 B8
Simon Ct. 5 SE28 .... 3 C6
Simone Cl. BR1 .... 36 D8
Simpson Rd. ME6 .... 75 A6
Simpson's Cotts. BR2 .... 50 C7

Simpson's Rd. BR2 .... 36 A6
Sinclair Cl. ME8 .... 63 E5
Sinclair Way. DA2 .... 27 D4
Singapore Dr. ME7 .... 48 B5
Single St. BR6 & TN16 .... 66 B4
Single's Cross. TN14 .... 67 D4
Single's Cross La. TN14 .... 67 C5
Singlewell Cty Prim Sch. DA12 30 D2
Singlewell Rd. DA11 .... 30 B4
Sinkertweazel. TN17 .... 169 E2
Sir David's Pk. TN4 .... 132 E1
Sir Evelyn Rd. ME1 .... 47 A4
Sir John Hawkins Way. ME4 .... 47 F4
Sir Joseph Williamson's
  Mathematical Sch. ME1 .... 47 C1
Sir Martin Bowes House. 15
  SE18 .... 2 A2
Sir Thomas Longley Rd. ME2 .... 47 E6
Sirdar Strand. DA12 .... 30 F3
Siskin Gdns. TN12 .... 136 A5
Siskin Wlk. ME20 .... 74 F2
Sissinghurst Castle. TN17 .... 156 D1
Sissinghurst Cty Prim Sch.
  TN17 .... 170 B8
Sissinghurst Dr. ME16 .... 91 B4
Sissinghurst Rd.
  Biddenden TN27 & TN17 .... 157 C2
Sissinghurst Rd.
  Sissinghurst TN17 .... 170 D8
Sittingbourne Rd.
  Maidstone,Detling ME14 .... 92 E8
Sittingbourne Rd.
  Maidstone,Penenden Heath ME14 92 B6
Siward Rd. BR2 .... 36 C6
Six Bells La. TN13 .... 84 C1
Six Fields Path. TN30 .... 183 A7
Skeet Hill La. BR5 & BR6 .... 52 E8
Skeffington St. SE18 .... 2 C3
Skeynes Rd. TN8 .... 112 B1
Skibbs La. BR5 & BR6 .... 52 E7
Skinner Gdns. TN17 .... 170 A8
Skinner St. Chatham ME4 .... 47 F3
Skinner St. Gillingham ME7 .... 48 C5
Skinner St. Gillingham ME7 .... 48 C6
Skinner Street Cty Prim Sch.
  ME7 .... 48 C6
Skinner's Way. ME17 .... 108 E4
Skinners Cl. ME20 .... 76 A6
Skinners La. ME20 .... 112 D2
Skinners' Sch The. TN4 .... 149 A6
Skippers Cl. DA9 .... 11 B2
Skua Ct. ME2 .... 46 C7
Skye Cl. ME15 .... 107 A5
Slade Cl. ME5 .... 62 B2
Slade Cty Prim Sch. TN9 .... 117 B2
Slade Gdns. DA8 .... 8 F6
Slade Green Inf Sch. DA8 .... 9 A7
Slade Green Jun Sch. DA8 .... 9 A6
Slade Green Rd. DA8 .... 9 A6
Slade Green Sta. DA8 .... 9 A6
Slade The. The Down TN14 .... 166 A3
Slade The. Tonbridge TN9 .... 117 B2
Slade The. Woolwich SE18 .... 6 E8
Sladebrook Rd. SE3 .... 5 D4
Sladedale Rd. SE18 .... 2 E1
Slades Dr. BR7 .... 23 C4
Slaney Rd. TN12 .... 139 F4
Slaters. TN8 .... 113 F2
Slatin Rd. ME2 .... 47 B8
Sleeches Cross. TN3 .... 163 B2
Sleepers Stile Rd. TN5 .... 165 B1
Slicketts Hill. ME4 .... 48 A4
Slip Mill Rd. TN18 .... 178 E2
Slip Rd. ME4 .... 48 A8
Slip The. TN16 .... 81 C1
Slipway Rd. ME12 .... 21 F3
Sloane Gdns. BR6 .... 51 C7
Sloane Sq. DA3 .... 42 E6
Slocum Cl. SE28 .... 3 C6
Small Bridge Cotts. TN17 .... 153 B2
Small Bridge Rd. TN12 & TN17 153 B2
Small Grains. DA3 .... 56 B7
Small Hythe Rd. TN30 .... 183 C3
Small Profits. ME18 .... 105 A4
Smallhythe Rd. TN30 .... 183 A6
Smarden Bsns Est. TN27 .... 158 D7
Smarden Cl. 7 DA17 .... 4 A1
Smarden Cty Prim Sch. TN27 143 A1
Smarden Gr. SE9 .... 22 F4
Smarden Rd. East End TN27 ...... 142 B4
Smarden Rd. Standen TN27 .... 158 B6
Smarts Cotts. ME14 .... 93 C4
Smarts Hill. TN11 .... 131 A1
Smarts Rd. DA12 .... 30 C6
Smith Rd. ME2 .... 62 B3
Smith St. ME2 .... 47 A6
Smith's Hill. ME15 .... 105 C5
Smithers Cl. TN11 .... 102 E1
Smithers Ct. TN12 .... 120 A7
Smithers La. TN12 .... 120 A7
Smithfield Rd. ME3 .... 21 C5
Smithies Rd. SE2 .... 3 B2
Smiths La. TN8 .... 96 C2
Smithy Field. 7 TN8 .... 112 D3
Smugglers Mews. TN18 .... 179 A1
Smugglers Wharf. DA9 .... 11 B2
Smythe Cl. TN14 .... 132 E3
Smythe Rd. DA4 .... 41 A8
Snag La. TN14 .... 66 D7
Snape View. TN5 .... 174 F4
Snelling Ave. DA11 .... 29 F6
Snipe Cl. Erith DA8 .... 9 B7
Snipe Cl. Pembury TN2 .... 150 E8
Snipe Ct. ME2 .... 46 C7
Snoad La. TN12 .... 155 A8
Snodhurst Ave. ME5 .... 61 D8
Snodland CE Prim Sch. ME6 ..... 74 F8
Snodland Rd. ME19 .... 74 D7

Snodland Sta. ME6 .... 75 B8
Snodlands Cl. BR6 .... 51 A1
Snoll Hatch Rd. TN12 .... 119 F5
Snow House. ME7 .... 48 E7
Snowdon Ave. ME14 .... 92 B5
Snowdon Cl. ME5 .... 62 B7
Snowfield. TN13 .... 99 C8
Sole Fields. TN13 .... 99 C8
Sole St. DA12 & DA13 .... 44 D4
Sole Street Sta. DA13 .... 44 D4
Solefield Prep Sch. TN13 .... 99 C8
Solefields Rd. TN13 .... 99 C8
Solent Gdns. ME5 .... 62 B8
Soleoak Dr. TN13 .... 99 C8
Solomon Rd. Gillingham ME8 ...... 49 F1
Solomon Rd. Gillingham ME8 ...... 64 A8
Solomons Rd. ME4 .... 47 F4
Somerden Rd. BR5 .... 38 D2
Somerfield Cl. ME16 .... 91 D5
Somerfield Hospl The. ME16 .. 91 F5
Somerfield La. ME16 .... 91 D4
Somerfield Rd. ME16 .... 91 D4
Somerhill Ave. DA15 .... 24 B8
Somerhill Rd. Bexley DA16 .... 7 B5
Somerhill Rd. Tonbridge TN9 ... 133 D8
Somerset Ave. DA16 .... 6 F3
Somerset Cl. ME5 .... 62 C8
Somerset Rd. Dartford DA1 .... 26 B8
Somerset Rd. Maidstone ME15 . 107 C8
Somerset Rd. Orpington BR6 .... 38 A2
Somerset Rd.
  Royal Tunbridge Wells TN4 ..... 149 A6
Somerset Villas. TN3 .... 161 C7
Somersham Rd. DA7 .... 7 E5
Somertrees Ave. SE12 .... 22 B6
Somerville Gdns. TN4 .... 148 F4
Somerville Rd. DA1 .... 9 F1
Somner Wlk. ME15 .... 107 F4
Soper's La. TN18 .... 178 D4
Sophia La. TN12 .... 151 C5
Sophurst La. TN12 .... 151 D5
Sopurst Wood. TN12 .... 151 D5
Sorrel Cl. SE28 .... 3 A5
Sorrel Ct. 7 RM17 .... 12 D8
Sorrel Gdns. E6 .... 1 E8
Sorrell Cl. 4 TN8 .... 112 D3
Sorrell Rd. ME5 .... 61 F4
Sorrell Way. DA11 .... 29 E4
Sortmill Rd. ME6 .... 75 B7
Sounds Lodge. BR8 .... 39 C3
South Ash Rd. TN15 .... 56 E4
South Ave. ME8 .... 64 A2
South Aylesford Ret Pk. ME20 90 E8
South Bank. Cliffe Woods ME3 ... 16 B2
South Bank. Staplehurst TN12 .. 139 E2
South Bank.
  Sutton Valence ME17 .... 124 E7
South Bank. Westerham TN16 ... 81 D1
South Borough Cty Prim Sch.
  ME15 .... 92 A2
South Bush Cl. ME8 .... 64 B6
South Cl. DA6 .... 7 D3
South Cres. ME17 .... 106 C4
South Dr. BR6 .... 51 E5
South Eastern Rd. ME2 .... 47 C7
South Frith. TN4 .... 133 A6
South Glade. DA5 .... 24 F7
South Gr. TN1 .... 149 A2
South Green La. ME9 .... 79 F6
South Hall Cl. DA4 .... 40 F2
South Hill. BR7 .... 22 F2
South Hill Rd. DA12 .... 30 C7
South Kent Ave. DA11 .... 12 C1
South La. ME7 .... 124 E6
South Molton Rd. E16 .... 1 A7
South Park Bsns Village. ME15 92 A1
South Park Rd. ME15 .... 92 C1
South Pk. TN13 .... 84 B2
South Pondside Rd. ME4 .... 48 A8
South Rd. Erith DA8 .... 8 F7
South Rd. Gillingham ME7 .... 48 A7
South Rd. Gillingham ME4 .... 48 B7
South Rd. Marden TN12 .... 138 E5
South Rise Jun & Inf Sch. SE18 2 D1
South Row. Greenwich SE3 .... 5 A5
South Row. Weller's Town TN8 . 130 D5
South Side Three Rd. ME4 .... 48 C8
South St. Bromley BR1 .... 36 A7
South St. Gravesend DA11 .... 30 B8
South St. Maidstone ME16 .... 90 E1
South St. Meopham Green DA13 . 57 F7
South Street Rd. ME9 .... 79 C7
South Terr. DA4 .... 40 F2
South View. BR1 .... 36 C7
South View Ave. RM18 .... 13 A6
South View Cl. DA5 .... 7 F1
South View Rd.
  Royal Tunbridge Wells TN4 ..... 149 B8
South View Rd.
  Turner's Green TN5 .... 174 F6
South View Rd.
  West Thurrock RM16 .... 11 C8
South View Rd. Wilmington DA2 26 D5
South Wharf Rd. RM17 .... 11 C8
Southborough CE Prim Schs.
  TN4 .... 148 F6
Southborough Ct. TN4 .... 133 A2
Southborough La. BR2 .... 36 F4
Southborough Prim Sch. BR2 .. 37 A4
Southborough Rd. BR1 & BR2 .... 36 E5
Southbourne. BR2 .... 36 A2
Southbourne Gdns. SE12 .... 5 B2
Southbourne Gr. ME5 .... 62 A4
Southcroft Ave. DA16 .... 6 E4
Southcroft Rd. BR6 .... 51 E7
Southdene. TN14 .... 67 D4
Southend Cl. SE9 .... 6 B1
Southend Cres. SE9 .... 6 B1

Southern Pl. BR8 .... 39 D5
Southerden Rd. TN27 .... 126 E1
Southey Way. 1 ME20 .... 74 F4
Southey Wlk. RM18 .... 13 B6
Southfield.
  Royal Tunbridge Wells TN4 ..... 149 A6
Southfield Rd. Speldhurst TN3 . 148 A7
Southfield Rd. St Paul's Cray BR7 38 A6
Southfield Shaw. DA13 .... 58 B1
Southfields. Rochester ME1 .... 47 C3
Southfields. Turner's Green TN5 174 F6
Southfields Rd. TN15 .... 55 F2
Southfields Sch. DA12 .... 30 C3
Southfields Way. TN4 .... 149 B8
Southfleet Ave. DA3 .... 43 B7
Southfleet Rd. Bean DA2 .... 28 C4
Southfleet Rd. 7
  Northfleet DA11 .... 29 F7
Southfleet Rd. Orpington BR6 ..... 51 E6
Southfleet Rd. Swanscombe DA10 29 C7
Southgate. TN4 .... 148 F3
Southgate Rd. TN30 .... 183 C7
Southill Rd. Chatham ME4 .... 47 F3
Southill Rd. Chislehurst BR7 .... 22 F1
Southlake Prim Sch. SE2 .... 3 D4
Southland Ave. BR6 .... 51 E5
Southlands Gr. BR1 .... 36 E6
Southlands Rd. BR1 & BR2 .... 36 E5
Southlees La. ME9 .... 79 F3
Southold Rise. SE9 .... 22 F5
Southover. BR1 .... 22 A3
Southport Rd. SE18 .... 2 D2
Southspring. SE9 .... 23 D8
Southview. BR8 .... 40 A5
Southwark Pl. BR1 .... 36 F6
Southwark Rd. ME2 .... 46 D6
Southway. BR2 .... 36 A2
Southways. ME17 .... 124 E7
Southwell Rd. ME2 .... 46 D6
Southwold Rd. DA5 .... 8 B1
Southwood. ME16 .... 90 F2
Southwood Ave. TN4 .... 149 A6
Southwood Cl. BR1 .... 36 F5
Southwood House. SE9 .... 23 B6
Southwood Rd. Eltham SE9 .... 23 B6
Southwood Rd. Rusthall TN4 .... 148 B5
Southwood Rd. Woolwich SE28 .... 3 B5
Sovereign Bvd. Gillingham ME7 .. 48 F2
Sovereign Bvd.
  Gillingham,Twydall ME8 .... 49 A2
Sovereign Ct. Bromley BR2 .... 36 A5
Sovereign Ct. Sutton at Hone DA4 41 B8
Sovereign House. SE18 .... 1 F3
Sovereign Way. TN9 .... 117 C1
Sovereigns The. ME16 .... 91 D4
Sovereigns Way. TN12 .... 138 C6
Sowerby Cl. SE9 .... 5 F2
Spa Golf Course. TN4 .... 148 E3
Spa Ind Est. TN2 .... 149 E8
Spade La. ME8 & ME9 .... 64 C6
Sparepenny La. DA4 .... 40 E1
Sparkeswood Ave. TN17 .... 181 F3
Sparkeswood Cl. TN17 .... 181 F3
Sparrow Dr. BR5 .... 37 D1
Sparrow's Farm L Ctr. SE9 .... 23 C8
Sparrows Green Rd. TN5 .... 174 F5
Sparrows La. SE9 .... 23 C7
Spearhead Rd. ME14 .... 91 F7
Spearman St. SE18 .... 6 A8
Spectrum Bsns Ctr. ME2 .... 47 E8
Spectrum Bsns Est. ME15 .... 107 F4
Speedgate Hill. DA3 .... 56 A8
Speedwell Ave. ME5 .... 61 F4
Speedwell Cl. Gillingham ME7 .... 48 E5
Speedwell Cl. Maidstone ME14 .. 92 E5
Speedwell Cl. 5
  Marlpit Hill TN8 .... 112 D3
Speedwell Ct. RM17 .... 12 E7
Spekehill. SE9 .... 22 F5
Spekes Rd. ME7 .... 48 C6
Speldhurst CE Prim Sch. TN3 148 A7
Speldhurst Ct. ME16 .... 91 D4
Speldhurst Hill. TN3 .... 148 B8
Speldhurst Rd.
  Langton Green TN3 .... 147 F4
Speldhurst Rd. Royal Tunbridge Wells
  TN3 & TN4 .... 148 F4
Spelmonden Rd. TN12 & TN17 . 152 F2
Spencer Cl. Chatham ME5 .... 62 A5
Spencer Cl. Orpington BR6 .... 51 E8
Spencer Ct. 5 BR6 .... 51 C5
Spencer Flats. ME5 .... 62 B8
Spencer Mews. 6 TN1 .... 149 A2
Spencer St. DA11 .... 30 A8
Spencer Way. ME15 .... 107 E7
Spencer Wlk. ME8 .... 13 B5
Spencer's Mews. 4 TN1 .... 149 B4
Spenlow Dr. ME5 .... 77 A8
Spenny La. TN12 .... 137 B7
Speranza St. SE18 .... 2 F1
Speyside. TN10 .... 117 B5
Spielman Rd. DA1 .... 9 F3
Spiers The. ME7 .... 49 C5
Spillway The. ME15 .... 91 D2
Spindle Glade. ME14 .... 92 C5
Spindle House. 8 DA15 .... 24 A5
Spindles. ME8 .... 13 A7
Spindlewood Cl. ME5 .... 62 B3
Spinel Cl. SE18 .... 2 F1
Spinnaker Ct. 3 ME1 .... 47 C1
Spinners Acre Cty Jun Sch.
  ME5 .... 62 C1
Spinners Cl. TN27 .... 158 A2
Spinners Wents. TN15 .... 102 D8
Spinney Oak. BR1 .... 36 E7
Spinney The. Chatham ME5 .... 62 B1
Spinney The. Maidstone ME15 .... 92 B2

Spinney The. Sidcup DA14 .... 24 E3
Spinney The. Swanley BR8 .... 39 E7
Spinney The. Tonbridge TN9 .... 133 A2
Spinney Way. TN14 .... 66 D8
Spinneys The. BR1 .... 36 F7
Spire Cl. DA12 .... 30 B7
Spires The. Dartford DA1 .... 26 D6
Spires The. Maidstone ME16 .... 91 D4
Spires The. Rochester ME2 .... 46 D5
Spital St. DA1 .... 9 D1
Spitfire Cl. ME5 .... 62 B6
Spitfire Rd. ME19 .... 88 F3
Spode La. TN8 .... 145 A7
Sponden La. Field Green TN18 .. 185 F8
Sponden La. Sandhurst TN18 ... 186 A7
Spongs La. TN17 .... 156 A1
Sportsfield. ME14 .... 92 B5
Sportsmans Cotts. ME19 .... 89 A5
Spot La. ME15 .... 93 A2
Spout La. Brenchley TN12 .... 152 C5
Spout La. Crockham Hill TN8 ...... 96 C1
Spray Hill. TN3 .... 166 B4
Spray St. SE18 .... 2 B2
Sprig The. ME14 .... 93 A4
Spring Cross. DA3 .... 57 A7
Spring Gdns. Orpington BR6 .... 52 B4
Spring Gdns. Rusthall TN4 .... 148 B4
Spring Gr. DA12 .... 30 B7
Spring Head Rd. TN15 .... 69 F2
Spring Hill. TN11 & TN3 .... 147 A2
Spring La. Bidborough TN4 .... 132 D3
Spring La. Oldbury TN15 .... 86 B5
Spring Lodge. 3 BR5 .... 38 C4
Spring Shaw Rd. BR5 .... 38 A8
Spring Vale. Bexley DA7 .... 8 B3
Spring Vale. Dartford DA1 .... 26 D8
Spring Vale. Maidstone ME16 ...... 91 E4
Spring Vale. Swanscombe DA9 .... 11 C1
Spring Vale Cl. BR8 .... 39 F8
Spring Vale N. DA1 .... 26 D8
Spring Vale S. DA1 .... 26 D8
Springcroft. DA3 .... 43 A4
Springdale Cotts. ME3 .... 33 A3
Springett Almshouses. TN18 .. 184 F1
Springett Cl. ME20 .... 75 F6
Springett Way. ME17 .... 106 D3
Springfield Ave. Maidstone ME14 91 F7
Springfield Ave.
  St Michaels TN30 .... 173 C2
Springfield Ave. Swanley BR8 ..... 39 F5
Springfield Cotts. ME15 .... 152 F5
Springfield Gdns. BR1 .... 36 F5
Springfield Gr. SE7 .... 5 C8
Springfield Ind Est. TN18 .... 178 F3
Springfield Rd.
  Bexley,Bexleyheath DA7 .... 8 B3
Springfield Rd.
  Bexley,Welling DA16 .... 7 B4
Springfield Rd. Bromley BR1 .... 36 F5
Springfield Rd. Edenbridge TN8 112 B1
Springfield Rd. Gillingham ME7 .. 48 E6
Springfield Rd.
  Groombridge TN3 .... 161 C7
Springfield Rd. Lunsford ME20 ... 74 F4
Springfield Rd.
  Royal Tunbridge Wells TN4 ..... 132 F1
Springfield Way. BR5 .... 38 C6
Springfield Wlk. 3 BR6 .... 37 D1
Springfields. TN5 .... 176 E1
Springhead. TN2 .... 149 D5
Springhead Ent Pk. DA1 .... 29 C7
Springhead Rd. Erith DA8 .... 8 F8
Springhead Rd. Northfleet DA11 29 C7
Springrove Cotts. TN12 .... 138 B5
Springshaw Cl. TN13 .... 83 D4
Springvale. ME8 .... 63 C6
Springvale Ct. Eltham SE12 .... 5 A3
Springvale Ct. Northfleet DA11 ... 29 C6
Springview Apartments. TN1 149 D6
Springwater Cl. SE18 .... 6 A6
Springwell Rd. TN9 .... 133 B8
Springwood Cl. ME16 .... 91 A3
Springwood Rd. ME16 .... 91 A3
Spruce Cl. ME20 .... 75 B2
Sprucedale Cl. BR8 .... 39 E7
Spur Rd. BR6 .... 52 A8
Spurgeons Cotts. ME17 .... 106 E2
Spurrell Ave. DA2 & DA5 .... 25 C4
Spurway. ME14 .... 93 A4
Square Hill. ME15 .... 92 B4
Square Hill Rd. ME14 & ME15 .... 92 B4
Square The. Cowden TN8 .... 145 B6
Square The. Hadlow TN11 .... 118 E8
Square The. Hunton ME15 .... 121 D7
Square The. Leigh TN11 .... 115 F1
Square The. Lenham ME17 .... 111 D5
Square The. Swanley BR8 .... 39 D6
Square The. Wadhurst TN5 .... 175 A4
Squerryes Court. TN16 .... 96 C7
Squerryes Mede. TN16 .... 96 C8
Squires Cl. ME2 .... 46 B7
Squires Field. BR8 .... 39 F8
Squires House. 3 SE18 .... 6 B8
Squires Way. DA2 .... 25 D4
Squires Wood Dr. BR7 .... 22 F1
Squirrel Way. TN2 .... 149 E5
Stable Cl. ME5 .... 62 C5
Stabledene Way. TN2 .... 150 D6
Stables End. BR6 .... 51 C7
Stace Cl. TN30 .... 183 C8
Stacey Cl. DA12 .... 30 E3
Stacey Rd. TN11 .... 117 A4
Staceys St. ME14 .... 91 F5
Stack La. DA3 .... 42 F4
Stack Rd. DA4 .... 41 D5

Stacklands Cl. TN15 ... 55 E4
Stadium Rd. SE18 & SE7 ... 5 F8
Stadium Way. DA1 ... 8 E2
Staffa Rd. ME15 ... 107 A7
Stafford Cl. DA9 ... 10 F2
Stafford Rd. Royal Tunbridge Wells TN2 ... 149 E4
Stafford Rd. Sidcup DA14 ... 23 E4
Stafford Rd. Tonbridge TN9 ... 117 B2
Stafford St. ME7 ... 48 C5
Stafford Way. TN13 ... 99 C8
Stag Rd. Chatham ME5 ... 62 B5
Stag Rd. Royal Tunbridge Wells TN2 ... 149 D8
Stainer House. SE9 ... 5 C3
Stainer Rd. TN10 ... 117 F6
Staines Wlk. DA14 ... 24 C2
Stainmore Cl. BR7 ... 37 D8
Stair Rd. TN10 ... 117 F4
Stairfoot La. TN13 ... 83 C5
Stake La. ME2 ... 60 A6
Staleys Rd. TN15 ... 86 F7
Stalham Ct. ME7 ... 63 B4
Stalin Ave. ME5 ... 62 B8
Stalisfield Pl. BR6 ... 51 A1
Stampers The. ME15 ... 91 D2
Stan La. ME18 ... 103 A7
Stanam Rd. TN2 ... 150 E6
Stanbridge Rd. TN8 ... 112 B2
Stanbrook Rd. Northfleet DA11 ... 29 F8
Stanbrook Rd. Woolwich SE2 ... 3 B4
Standard Ind Est. E16 ... 1 F4
Standard Rd. Bexley DA6 ... 7 E3
Standard Rd. Erith DA17 ... 4 A1
Standard Rd. Farthing Street BR6 51 A1
Standen Cl. ME8 ... 63 E4
Standen St. Iden Green TN17 & TN18 ... 180 D2
Standen St. Royal Tunbridge Wells TN4 ... 149 A5
Standings Cross. TN12 ... 135 E1
Standish House. SE3 ... 5 B3
Stane Way. SE18 ... 5 E7
Stanford Dr. ME16 ... 91 C3
Stanford La. TN11 & TN12 ... 103 C2
Stanford Way. ME2 ... 46 C2
Stangate Rd. Birling ME19 ... 74 B8
Stangate Rd. Rochester ME2 ... 46 C7
Stangrove Rd. TN8 ... 112 C1
Stanham Pl. DA1 ... 9 A3
Stanham Rd. DA1 ... 9 C2
Stanhill Cotts. DA2 ... 25 D2
Stanhope Ave. BR2 ... 36 A1
Stanhope Cl. ME14 ... 91 E7
Stanhope Rd. Bexley DA7 ... 7 E5
Stanhope Rd. Rochester ME2 ... 47 A7
Stanhope Rd. Royal Tunbridge Wells TN1 ... 149 C5
Stanhope Rd. Sidcup DA15 ... 24 A4
Stanhope Rd. Swanscombe DA10 ... 11 F1
Stanhope Way. TN13 ... 83 D5
Stanley Cl. Staplehurst TN12 ... 139 E4
Stanley Cl. Stone DA9 ... 10 E2
Stanley Cotts. DA2 ... 27 E3
Stanley Cres. DA12 ... 30 D3
Stanley Rd. Bromley BR2 ... 36 C5
Stanley Rd. Chatham ME5 ... 62 C6
Stanley Rd. Gillingham ME7 ... 48 C6
Stanley Rd. Grays RM17 ... 12 B8
Stanley Rd. Marden TN12 ... 138 D5
Stanley Rd. Orpington BR6 ... 37 F1
Stanley Rd. Royal Tunbridge Wells TN1 ... 149 B5
Stanley Rd. Sidcup DA14 ... 24 A5
Stanley Rd. Swanscombe DA10 ... 11 F1
Stanley Way. BR5 ... 38 B4
Stanmore Rd. DA17 ... 4 C2
Stansfeld Rd. E6 ... 1 D7
Stansted CE Prim Sch. TN15 ... 56 F1
Stansted Cl. ME16 ... 91 D7
Stansted Cres. DA5 ... 24 D7
Stansted Hill. TN15 ... 57 A1
Stansted La. TN15 ... 56 C1
Stanton Cl. BR5 ... 38 C2
Stanton Ct. 5 DA15 ... 24 A5
Staple Cl. DA5 ... 25 D5
Staple Dr. TN12 ... 139 F4
Stapleford Ct. TN13 ... 83 F4
Staplehurst Cty Prim Sch. TN12 ... 139 E3
Staplehurst House. BR5 ... 38 C4
Staplehurst Rd. Bogden TN12 ... 123 C2
Staplehurst Rd. Gillingham ME8 . 49 B3
Staplehurst Rd. Sinkhurst Green TN12 & TN17 ... 140 D1
Staplehurst Sta. TN12 ... 139 E5
Staplers Ct. ME14 ... 92 B8
Stapleton Rd. Erith DA7 ... 7 F8
Stapleton Rd. Orpington BR6 ... 51 F7
Stapley Rd. DA17 ... 4 A1
Star Bsns Ctr. RM9 ... 4 D8
Star Hill. Crayford DA1 ... 8 E2
Star Hill. Rochester ME1 ... 47 D5
Star Hill Rd. TN14 ... 68 A2
Star La. Gillingham ME7 ... 63 A7
Star La. St Paul's Cray BR5 ... 38 E5
Star Mill Ct. ME5 ... 48 D2
Star Mill La. ME5 ... 48 D2
Starboard Ave. DA9 ... 11 B1
Starling Cl. DA3 ... 43 B6
Starnes Ct. 5 ME14 ... 92 A5
Starr Cotts. TN12 ... 121 C2
Starts Cl. BR6 ... 51 A7
Starts Hill Ave. BR6 ... 51 B6
Starts Hill Rd. BR6 ... 51 B6
Starvecrow Cl. TN11 ... 117 D8
State Farm Ave. BR6 ... 51 C6
Station App. Bexley,Barnehurst DA7 ... 8 C5
Station App. Bexley,Bexleyheath DA7 ... 7 E5
Station App. Bexley,Welling DA16 .. 7 A5
Station App. Chislehurst BR7 ... 37 A7
Station App. Chislehurst,Elmstead BR7 ... 22 E2
Station App. Dartford DA1 ... 9 E1
Station App. Edenbridge TN8 ... 112 C2
Station App. Grays RM17 ... 12 A8
Station App. Greenwich SE3 ... 5 B4
Station App. Halling ME2 ... 60 A5
Station App. Hayes BR2 ... 36 A1
Station App. Maidstone ME16 ... 91 F3
Station App. Orpington BR6 ... 51 F8
Station App. Orpington,Chelsfield BR6 ... 52 B5
Station App. Paddock Wood TN12 ... 136 A7
Station App. St Paul's Cray BR5 .. 38 B5
Station App. Staplehurst TN12 .. 139 E5
Station App. Swanley BR8 ... 39 E5
Station Approach Rd. RM18 ... 13 A3
Station Cotts. Gill's Green TN18 178 F5
Station Cotts. Horsmonden TN12 153 B5
Station Cres. SE3 ... 1 A1
Station Ct. TN15 ... 86 F7
Station Hill. Chiddingstone Causeway TN11 .. 114 F1
Station Hill. Chiddingstone Causeway TN11 .. 131 A8
Station Hill. Hayes BR2 ... 50 A8
Station Rd. Aylesford ME20 ... 75 E2
Station Rd. Betsham DA13 ... 29 A4
Station Rd. Bexley DA7 ... 7 E4
Station Rd. Borough Green TN15 . 86 F7
Station Rd. Brasted TN16 ... 82 B4
Station Rd. Bromley BR1 ... 36 A8
Station Rd. Cliffe ME3 ... 16 B3
Station Rd. Crayford DA1 ... 8 F1
Station Rd. Cuxton ME2 ... 46 C2
Station Rd. East Farleigh ME15 .. 106 A7
Station Rd. East Tilbury RM18 ... 14 B7
Station Rd. Edenbridge TN8 ... 112 C2
Station Rd. Erith DA17 ... 4 A3
Station Rd. Eynsford DA4 ... 54 D7
Station Rd. Gillingham ME8 ... 49 F1
Station Rd. Goudhurst TN17 ... 167 C7
Station Rd. Groombridge TN3 ... 161 C7
Station Rd. Halstead TN14 ... 67 F8
Station Rd. Harrietsham ME17 . 110 D6
Station Rd. Headcorn TN27 ... 141 D5
Station Rd. Hurst Green TN19 ... 184 A3
Station Rd. Longfield DA3 ... 42 E6
Station Rd. Maidstone ME14 ... 91 F5
Station Rd. Meopham Station DA13 ... 44 A4
Station Rd. Nettlestead Green ME18 ... 104 C1
Station Rd. Newington ME9 ... 65 B6
Station Rd. Northfleet DA11 ... 12 B1
Station Rd. Northiam TN31 ... 187 C1
Station Rd. Orpington BR6 ... 51 F8
Station Rd. Otford TN14 ... 69 C3
Station Rd. Paddock Wood TN12 135 F7
Station Rd. Rochester ME2 ... 47 C7
Station Rd. Rockrobin TN5 ... 174 C6
Station Rd. Sevenoaks TN13 ... 83 E7
Station Rd. Shoreham TN14 ... 69 A7
Station Rd. Sidcup DA14 & DA15 . 24 A5
Station Rd. St Paul's Cray BR5 ... 38 C5
Station Rd. Staplehurst TN12 ... 139 F5
Station Rd. Sutton at Hone DA4 ... 41 B7
Station Rd. Swanley BR8 ... 39 E5
Station Rd. Swanscombe DA9 ... 11 A2
Station Rd. Tenterden TN30 ... 183 A7
Station Rd. Withyham TN7 ... 160 B5
Station Rd N. DA17 ... 4 B3
Station Sq. BR5 ... 37 C4
Station St. E16 ... 2 B5
Steadman Cl. ME3 ... 32 C6
Stede Hill. ME17 ... 95 F3
Stedman Cl. DA5 ... 25 E5
Steele Ave. DA9 ... 11 A2
Steele St. ME2 ... 47 A8
Steele's La. DA13 ... 58 A6
Steep Cl. BR6 ... 51 F4
Steerforth Cl. ME1 ... 47 C2
Steers Pl. TN11 ... 102 E2
Stella Cl. TN12 ... 138 D5
Stelling Rd. DA8 ... 8 D7
Stephen Cl. BR6 ... 51 F7
Stephen Rd. DA7 ... 8 C4
Stephen's Rd. TN4 ... 149 B6
Stephenson Ave. RM18 ... 13 A6
Stephenson House. SE2 ... 3 D1
Stepneyford La. TN17 ... 181 C7
Steps Hill Rd. ME9 ... 79 D6
Sterling Ave. ME16 ... 91 C5
Sterling House. SE3 ... 5 B3
Sterndale Rd. DA1 ... 26 F8
Stevanne Ct. 1 DA17 ... 4 A1
Stevedale Rd. DA16 ... 7 C5
Stevens Cl. Joyden's Wood DA5 .. 25 D4
Stevens Cl. Lane End DA2 ... 27 E3
Stevens Cl. Maidstone ME15 ... 91 F3
Stevens Cl. Snodland ME6 ... 75 A8
Stevens Rd. ME20 ... 75 F6
Stevenson Cl. DA8 ... 9 B7
Stevenson Way. ME20 ... 74 F4
Stewart Cl. BR7 ... 23 B4
Stewart House. ME3 ... 33 F6
Stewart Rd. TN4 ... 149 C7
Steyning Gr. SE9 ... 22 F4
Steynton Ave. DA5 ... 24 D6
Stickens La. ME19 ... 89 E7
Stickfast La. TN27 ... 125 D3
Stickland Rd. 2 DA17 ... 4 A2
Stilebridge La. Underling Green TN12 ... 122 E3
Stilebridge La. Underling Green ME17 ... 123 A5
Stiles Cl. Bromley BR2 ... 36 F3
Stiles Cl. Erith DA8 ... 4 B1
Still La. TN4 ... 132 F2
Stirling Cl. Gillingham ME8 ... 63 E4
Stirling Cl. Rochester ME1 ... 47 A3
Stirling Dr. BR6 ... 52 B5
Stirling House. 5 SE18 ... 2 B1
Stisted Way. TN27 ... 127 F3
Stock La. DA2 ... 26 C4
Stockbury Dr. ME16 ... 91 D7
Stockbury House. 7 BR5 ... 38 D1
Stockenbury. TN12 ... 119 F6
Stockett La. ME15 ... 106 D6
Stockfield. 1 TN8 ... 112 D3
Stockland Green Rd. TN3 ... 148 B8
Stocks Green Cty Prim Sch. TN11 ... 116 E5
Stocks Green Rd. TN11 ... 116 C5
Stocks Rd. TN30 ... 189 F3
Stockton Cl. ME14 ... 92 B8
Stockwell Cl. BR1 ... 36 B7
Stofield Gdns. SE9 ... 22 D5
Stoke Cty Prim Sch. ME3 ... 19 C5
Stoke Rd. Allhallows ME3 ... 19 C7
Stoke Rd. Hoo St Werburgh ME3 . 34 F6
Stoke Rd. Kingsnorth ME3 ... 35 C8
Stoke Rd. Stoke ME3 ... 18 E1
Stone CE Prim Sch. DA2 ... 27 E8
Stone Cotts. TN3 ... 165 F4
Stone Court La. TN2 ... 150 E8
Stone Cross Rd. TN5 ... 175 A4
Stone Crossing Halt. DA9 ... 10 E2
Stone Ct. DA8 ... 4 F1
Stone Hill Rd. TN27 ... 127 F2
Stone House Hospl. DA2 ... 10 C1
Stone Lodge Farm Park. DA2 .. 10 D1
Stone Pit La. TN18 ... 186 E5
Stone Place Rd. DA9 ... 10 E2
Stone Rd. BR2 ... 36 A5
Stone Row. TN3 ... 147 B5
Stone Row Cotts. TN3 ... 147 D1
Stone St. Cranbrook TN17 ... 169 D5
Stone St. Gravesend DA11 ... 13 B1
Stone St. Royal Tunbridge Wells TN1 ... 149 B4
Stone Street Rd. TN15 ... 85 E2
Stone Wood. DA2 ... 28 C5
Stoneacre Cl. ME8 ... 63 D5
Stoneacre La. ME15 ... 108 B7
Stoneacre (NT). ME15 ... 108 B7
Stonebridge Green Rd. TN27 . 127 F4
Stonebridge Rd. DA11 ... 12 B2
Stonechat Sq. 6 E6 ... 1 E8
Stonecroft. DA13 ... 73 A8
Stonecroft Rd. DA8 ... 8 C7
Stonecross Lea. ME5 ... 48 C1
Stonefield Cl. DA7 ... 8 A4
Stonefield Way. SE7 ... 5 D7
Stonegate Cl. BR5 ... 38 C6
Stonegate Rd. TN5 ... 175 C1
Stonehorse La. ME3 ... 33 A2
Stonehouse Cnr. RM16 ... 10 E8
Stonehouse La. Pratt's Bottom BR6 & TN14 ... 52 E1
Stonehouse La. Purfleet RM16 ... 10 E8
Stonehouse Rd. BR6 ... 52 D1
Stoneings La. TN14 ... 81 F8
Stoneness Rd. RM16 ... 11 C7
Stones Cross Rd. BR8 ... 39 C4
Stonestile Rd. TN27 ... 141 A7
Stonewall. E6 ... 2 A8
Stonewall Park Rd. TN3 ... 147 F3
Stonewood Rd. DA8 ... 4 E1
Stoney Alley. SE18 ... 6 A5
Stoney Bank. ME7 ... 48 F1
Stony Cnr. DA3 ... 43 E6
Stony La. ME5 ... 61 C5
Stonyfield. TN8 ... 112 D3
Stopford Rd. ME7 ... 48 D4
Store Rd. E16 ... 2 A4
Storehouse Wharf. ME12 ... 21 F3
Storey Prim Sch. E16 ... 2 B5
Storey St. E16 ... 2 A4
Stornaway Strand. DA12 ... 30 F4
Stour Cl. Keston BR2 ... 50 C6
Stour Cl. Rochester ME2 ... 46 F7
Stour Cl. Tonbridge TN10 ... 117 B5
Stour Ct. 22 BR5 ... 38 D1
Stour House. 4 ME15 ... 107 D8
Stour Rd. DA1 ... 9 A4
Stowe Rd. BR6 ... 52 B6
Stowting Rd. BR6 ... 51 E6
Strait Rd. E6 ... 1 F6
Strand Approach Rd. ME7 ... 48 E7
Strand Cl. DA13 ... 44 A3
Strandfield Cl. SE18 ... 2 E1
Stratfield House. SE12 ... 22 A6
Stratford Ave. ME8 ... 63 D8
Stratford House Ave. BR1 ... 36 E6
Stratford La. ME8 ... 63 F8
Stratford Rd. ME19 ... 89 A8
Stratford St. TN1 ... 149 C5
Strathaven Rd. SE12 ... 5 B1
Strathaven Par. SE3 ... 5 A7
Stratheden Rd. SE3 ... 5 A7
Stratton Cl. DA7 ... 7 E4
Stratton Rd. DA7 ... 7 E4
Stratton Terr. TN16 ... 96 C8
Straw Mill Hill. ME15 ... 91 E1
Strawberry Cl. TN2 ... 162 E7
Strawberry Fields. BR8 ... 39 E7
Strawberry Vale. TN9 ... 117 C1
Stream La. TN18 ... 185 A7
Stream Lane Cotts. TN18 ... 185 A7
Stream Pit La. TN18 ... 186 B6
Stream Side. TN10 ... 117 D6
Stream The. ME19 ... 75 C1
Stream Way. DA17 ... 8 A8
Streamdale. SE2 ... 7 B8
Streamside. ME19 ... 75 B1
Streamside Cl. BR2 ... 36 A5
Streatfield. TN8 ... 112 D1
Street End Rd. ME5 ... 48 B1
Street Farm Cotts. ME3 ... 34 F6
Street The. Ash TN15 ... 56 E5
Street The. Benenden TN17 ... 180 D6
Street The. Boxley ME14 ... 77 C3
Street The. Bredhurst ME7 ... 63 B1
Street The. Cobham DA12 ... 44 F6
Street The. Detling ME14 ... 78 A1
Street The. Egerton TN27 ... 127 F3
Street The. Fenn Street ME3 ... 18 A3
Street The. Hartlip ME9 ... 64 D5
Street The. High Halstow ME23 ... 17 E3
Street The. Horton Kirby DA4 ... 41 C5
Street The. Ightham TN15 ... 86 D6
Street The. Maidstone ME14 ... 93 C4
Street The. Meopham DA13 ... 44 A1
Street The. Mereworth ME18 ... 103 D8
Street The. Plaxtol TN15 ... 101 F7
Street The. Ryarsh ME19 ... 73 F4
Street The. Shorne DA12 ... 31 E3
Street The. Silver Street ME9 ... 80 F5
Street The. Sissinghurst TN17 ... 170 B8
Street The. Teston ME18 ... 105 A7
Street The. Trottiscliffe ME19 ... 73 A5
Street The. Ulcombe ME17 ... 125 F7
Street The. Upper Halling ME2 ... 59 E5
Street The. Wittersham TN30 ... 189 D3
Street The. Wormshill ME9 ... 95 F7
Streetfield. ME17 ... 125 F7
Streetfield Mews. SE3 ... 5 A4
Streetfield Rd. ME8 ... 49 F1
Strettitt Gdns. TN12 ... 119 F5
Strickland Ave. DA1 ... 9 F4
Strickland Way. 4 BR6 ... 51 F6
Strongbow Cres. SE9 ... 5 F2
Strongbow Rd. SE9 ... 5 F2
Strood Sta. ME2 ... 47 C7
Strover St. ME7 ... 48 C7
Strumer Ct. ME18 ... 89 A2
Struttons Ave. DA11 ... 29 F6
Stuart Ave. BR2 ... 36 A1
Stuart Cl. Hextable BR8 ... 26 A1
Stuart Cl. Maidstone ME14 ... 92 C6
Stuart Cl. Royal Tunbridge Wells TN2 ... 162 F8
Stuart Evans Cl. DA16 ... 7 C4
Stuart Mantle Way. DA8 ... 8 E7
Stuart Rd. Bexley DA16 ... 7 B6
Stuart Rd. Gillingham ME7 ... 48 D3
Stuart Rd. Gravesend DA11 ... 13 A1
Stubbs Hill. BR6 & TN14 ... 67 C6
Stubbygrove Cotts. TN3 ... 163 E4
Studland Cl. DA15 ... 23 F5
Studley Cres. DA3 ... 43 C7
Studley Ct. DA14 ... 24 B3
Stumble Hill. TN11 ... 101 C5
Sturdee Ave. ME7 ... 48 E4
Sturdee Cotts. ME3 ... 35 A6
Sturges Field. BR7 ... 23 D2
Sturla Rd. ME4 ... 48 A3
Sturry Way. ME8 ... 49 C2
Styants Bottom Rd. TN15 ... 85 F5
Style Cl. ME8 ... 63 E4
Styles Cl. TN8 ... 113 B5
Styles Cotts. TN8 ... 113 B5
Sudbury. E6 ... 2 A7
Sudbury Cres. BR1 ... 22 A3
Suffolk Ave. ME8 ... 49 F1
Suffolk Rd. Dartford DA1 ... 9 E1
Suffolk Rd. Gravesend DA12 ... 13 D1
Suffolk Rd. Maidstone ME15 ... 107 D8
Suffolk Rd. Sidcup DA14 ... 24 C2
Suffolk Way. TN13 & TN15 ... 84 C2
Sullivan Ave. E16 ... 1 D8
Sullivan Cl. DA1 ... 26 C8
Sullivan Rd. Tilbury RM18 ... 13 A6
Sullivan Rd. Tonbridge TN10 ... 117 E5
Sultan Rd. ME5 ... 62 C2
Summer Cl. TN30 ... 173 C1
Summer Hill. BR7 ... 37 A7
Summerfield. 6 Bromley BR1 ... 36 B8
Summerfield. Winchet Hill TN17 154 B6
Summerfield St. SE12 ... 22 A8
Summerhill. TN27 ... 141 A6
Summerhill Ave. TN4 ... 132 F1
Summerhill Cl. BR6 ... 51 E7
Summerhill Rd. Bogden TN12 .. 123 C1
Summerhill Rd. Dartford DA1 ... 26 D8
Summerhouse Dr. DA2 & DA5 ... 25 D4
Summerlands Lodge. BR6 ... 51 A6
Summerton Way. SE28 ... 3 D7
Summervale Rd. TN2 & TN4 ... 148 E1
Sumner Cl. Orpington BR6 ... 51 C6
Sumner Cl. Rolvenden TN17 ... 181 F3
Sun Ct. DA8 ... 8 F5
Sun Hill. DA3 ... 56 A8
Sun La. Gravesend DA12 ... 30 C6
Sun La. Greenwich SE3 ... 5 B7
Sun Rd. DA10 ... 11 F1
Sun Terr. ME5 ... 62 B4
Sunburst Cl. TN12 ... 138 D5
Sunbury St. SE18 ... 1 F3
Sunderland Cl. ME1 ... 47 A3
Sunderland Dr. ME8 ... 64 A8
Sunderland House. 2 ME7 ... 48 C7
Sundew Ct. 8 RM17 ... 12 D8
Sundorne Rd. SE7 ... 1 C1
Sundridge Ave. Bexley DA16 ... 6 D4
Sundridge Ave. Bromley BR1 & BR7 ... 22 E1
Sundridge & Brasted CE Prim Sch. TN14 ... 82 E2
Sundridge Cl. DA1 ... 10 A1
Sundridge Dr. ME5 ... 62 A4
Sundridge Hill. Cuxton ME2 ... 46 C3
Sundridge Hill. Knockholt TN14 .. 67 C1
Sundridge Hospl. TN14 ... 97 E8
Sundridge La. TN14 ... 67 C2
Sundridge Park Golf Course. BR1 ... 22 C2
Sundridge Park Sta. BR1 ... 22 B1
Sundridge Rd. TN14 ... 83 B8
Sunfields Pl. SE3 ... 5 B7
Sunhill Ct. TN2 ... 150 C6
Sunland Ave. DA6 ... 7 E3
Sunningdale Cl. ME8 ... 63 D6
Sunningdale Ct. ME15 ... 92 B4
Sunningdale Dr. ME8 ... 63 D6
Sunningdale Rd. BR1 & BR2 ... 36 E4
Sunninghill. DA11 ... 29 E6
Sunnybank. TN5 & TN19 ... 177 E3
Sunnydale. BR6 ... 51 A8
Sunnydale Rd. SE12 ... 5 B2
Sunnyfield Rd. BR5 & BR7 ... 38 A6
Sunnyfields Cl. ME8 ... 63 E8
Sunnymead Ave. ME7 ... 48 E5
Sunnyside. TN8 ... 112 B3
Sunnyside Rd. TN4 ... 148 C4
Sunray Ave. BR2 ... 36 F3
Sunrise Ind Pre-Prep Sch. ME17 ... 108 D4
Sunset Cl. DA8 ... 9 B7
Sunset Rd. SE28 ... 3 A5
Superabbey Est. ME20 ... 76 B2
Superior Dr. 4 BR6 ... 51 F4
Surlingham Cl. SE28 ... 3 D6
Surrenden Rd. TN12 ... 139 E3
Surrey Cl. TN2 ... 162 F8
Surrey Rd. ME15 ... 107 D8
Susan Rd. SE3 ... 5 B5
Susan Wood. BR7 ... 37 A8
Sussex Cl. TN2 ... 149 C1
Sussex Dr. ME5 ... 62 A4
Sussex Mews. 10 TN2 ... 149 A2
Sussex Rd. Dartford DA1 ... 27 A8
Sussex Rd. Erith DA8 ... 8 B7
Sussex Rd. Maidstone ME15 ... 107 D8
Sussex Rd. Orpington BR5 ... 38 C3
Sussex Rd. Sidcup DA14 ... 24 B3
Sussex Rd. Tonbridge TN9 ... 133 A8
Sussex Road Cty Prim Sch. TN9 ... 133 A8
Sutcliffe Rd. Bexley DA16 ... 7 C5
Sutcliffe Rd. Woolwich SE18 ... 6 E8
Sutherland Ave. Bexley DA16 ... 6 E3
Sutherland Ave. Orpington BR5 .. 37 F4
Sutherland Cl. DA12 ... 31 B6
Sutherland Gdns. ME8 ... 63 E6
Sutherland House. SE18 ... 5 F6
Sutherland Rd. Erith DA17 ... 4 A3
Sutherland Rd. Royal Tunbridge Wells TN1 & TN2 ... 149 B3
Sutlej Rd. SE7 ... 5 C7
Sutton at Hone CE Prim Sch. DA4 ... 27 A1
Sutton Cl. ME8 ... 64 A8
Sutton Ct. TN12 ... 138 C5
Sutton Forge. TN12 ... 138 D5
Sutton Rd. Langley ME17 ... 108 C5
Sutton Rd. Maidstone ME15 ... 107 D6
Sutton St. ME14 ... 93 D4
Sutton Valence Cty Prim Sch. ME17 ... 124 E7
Sutton Valence Sch. ME17 ... 124 E7
Swadelands Cl. ME17 ... 111 C5
Swadelands Sch. ME17 ... 111 C5
Swaffield Rd. TN13 ... 84 C5
Swain Cl. ME2 ... 46 F8
Swain Rd. Gillingham ME8 ... 63 B6
Swain Rd. St Michaels TN30 ... 173 D3
Swaisland Rd. DA1 ... 9 B1
Swaislands Dr. DA1 ... 8 F2
Swale House. 1 ME15 ... 107 E7
Swale Rd. Crayford DA1 ... 9 A3
Swale Rd. Rochester ME2 ... 46 C7
Swaledale Rd. DA2 ... 27 C7
Swallow Cl. Erith DA7 ... 8 E6
Swallow Cl. Stone DA9 ... 10 F2
Swallow Ct. 3 SE12 ... 22 A8
Swallow Dr. TN2 ... 149 F6
Swallow House. 4 ME16 ... 91 E4
Swallow Rd. ME20 ... 74 F2
Swallow Rise. ME5 ... 62 A5
Swallow St. E6 ... 1 E8
Swallowfield Rd. SE7 ... 1 B1
Swallowfields. 2 DA11 ... 29 E5
Swan Apartments. 10 ME15 ... 107 E5
Swan App. E6 ... 1 E8
Swan Bsns Pk. DA1 ... 9 C3
Swan Cl. BR5 ... 38 A6
Swan Cotts. TN30 ... 189 D4
Swan La. Brandfold TN17 ... 153 F3
Swan La. Dartford DA1 ... 25 F8
Swan La. Marlpit Hill TN8 ... 112 C4
Swan Rd. SE18 ... 1 D3
Swan Ridge. TN8 ... 112 D4
Swan St. West Malling ME19 ... 89 C8
Swan St. Wittersham TN30 ... 189 C3
Swanbridge Rd. DA7 ... 8 B6
Swanland Dr. TN9 ... 132 F7
Swanley Ctr. BR8 ... 39 E6
Swanley La. BR8 ... 39 F6
Swanley Rd. DA16 ... 7 C6
Swanley Sch. BR8 ... 39 E6
Swanley Sta. BR8 ... 39 D5

Swanley Village Rd. BR8 .... 40 B8
Swanmead Way. TN9 .... 117 D2
Swanscombe Bsns Ctr. DA10 ... 11 E2
Swanscombe Cty Inf Sch. DA10 28 F8
Swanscombe House. **1** BR5 ... 38 B7
Swanscombe St. DA10 .... 11 F1
Swanscombe Sta. DA10 .... 11 F2
Swanton Rd. Erith DA8 .... 8 B7
Swanton Rd. Swanton ME18 ... 103 A8
Swanzy Rd. TN14 .... 84 C7
Sward Rd. BR5 .... 38 A3
Swattenden La. TN17 .... 169 B1
Swaylands Rd. DA17 .... 8 A8
Sweeps Hill Cl. TN2 .... 150 D7
Sweeps La. BR5 .... 38 D5
Sweetings La. TN3 & TN5 ... 165 D1
Sweets La. ME19 .... 90 A4
Swetenham Wlk. SE18 .... 2 C1
Sweyn Pl. SE3 .... 5 A5
Sweyne Cty Prim Jun Sch The.
    DA10 .... 28 F8
Sweyne Rd. DA10 .... 11 E1
Swift Cl. ME20 .... 75 A2
Swift Cres. ME5 .... 62 C6
Swift House. **6** ME16 .... 91 E4
Swift's Ct. ME5 .... 85 A6
Swifts View. TN17 .... 169 D6
Swiller's La. DA12 .... 31 E3
Swinburne Gdns. RM18 .... 13 B5
Swingate Ave. ME3 .... 16 B6
Swingate Cl. ME5 .... 62 B2
Swingate Cty Inf Sch. ME5 ... 62 C1
Swingate La. SE18 .... 6 E7
Swinton Ave. ME3 .... 33 F5
Swires Shaw. BR2 .... 50 D6
Swithland Gdns. SE9 .... 23 A4
Sycamor Ct. DA8 .... 4 D1
Sycamore Ave. DA15 .... 6 F1
Sycamore Cl. Eltham SE9 ... 22 E6
Sycamore Cl. Gravesend DA12 ... 30 D8
Sycamore Cl. Tilbury RM18 ... 13 A5
Sycamore Cotts. TN2 .... 150 C6
Sycamore Cres. ME16 .... 91 C5
Sycamore Ct. DA2 .... 27 E8
Sycamore Dr. Aylesford ME20 ... 75 E1
Sycamore Dr. Swanley BR8 ... 39 E7
Sycamore Gdns. TN12 .... 135 F5
Sycamore Lodge. ME5 .... 52 A8
Sycamore Rd. Dartford DA1 ... 26 D7
Sycamore Rd. Rochester ME2 ... 46 E5
Sychem La. TN11 & TN12 ... 135 A6
Sychem Pl. TN12 .... 135 A7
Sydney Rd. Bexley DA6 .... 7 D3
Sydney Rd. Chatham ME4 ... 48 A3
Sydney Rd. Erith SE2 .... 3 D3
Sydney Rd. Sidcup DA14 ... 23 E4
Sydney Rd. Tilbury RM18 ... 13 A5
Sydney St. SE18 .... 2 C3
Sydney Terr. TN18 .... 178 F3
Sylewood Cl. ME1 .... 61 B8
Sylvan Glade. ME5 .... 77 A8
Sylvan Rd. ME8 .... 63 C8
Sylvan Wlk. BR1 .... 36 F6
Sylvester Ave. BR7 .... 22 F2
Sylvestre Cl. ME2 .... 60 A4
Sylvestres. TN13 .... 83 E6
Symonds Cl. TN15 .... 55 E5
Symonds La. ME18 .... 120 F6
Symonds Rd. ME3 .... 16 A4
Symons Ave. ME4 .... 48 A2
Syon Lodge. **9** SE12 .... 22 A8
Syringa Ct. **9** RM17 .... 12 D8

Tabor Ct. TN12 .... 153 A6
Tadburn Gn. ME5 .... 62 B4
Taddington Wood La. ME5 ... 61 E2
Tadley Cl. ME7 .... 48 F6
Tail Race The. ME15 .... 91 E2
Tainter Rd. TN11 .... 102 E1
Talbot Pk. TN2 .... 149 D5
Talbot Rd. Maidstone ME16 ... 91 C6
Talbot Rd. The Moor TN18 ... 184 F8
Tall Trees Cl. ME17 .... 109 D2
Tallents Cl. DA4 .... 27 B1
Tallis Cl. E16 .... 1 B7
Tallis Gr. SE7 .... 5 B8
Tamar Dr. ME2 .... 46 F7
Tamar House. **4** ME15 .... 107 E8
Tamar Rd. TN10 .... 117 B5
Tamar St. SE7 .... 1 E3
Tamarind Cl. ME7 .... 63 A4
Tamesis Strand. DA12 .... 30 E3
Tan Yard La. DA5 .... 25 A8
Tandridge Dr. BR5 & BR6 ... 37 D1
Tandridge Pl. **2** BR6 .... 37 D1
Tangier La. TN3 .... 163 B6
Tangleberry Cl. BR1 .... 36 F5
Tanglewood Cl. ME8 .... 63 C6
Tanglewood Ct. BR5 .... 38 C6
Tangmere Cl. ME7 .... 48 F5
Tanker Hill. ME8 .... 63 D6
Tanners Mead. TN8 .... 112 C1
Tannery Rd. TN9 .... 117 C1
Tansy Cl. E6 .... 2 A7
Tanyard. Rolvenden TN17 ... 181 E4
Tanyard. Sandhurst TN18 ... 186 B5
Tanyard Cotts. DA12 .... 31 E1
Tanyard Hill. DA12 .... 31 E2
Tanyard La. TN4 .... 132 F1
Tanyard The. TN17 .... 169 D4
Tapsell's La. TN5 .... 174 D5
Tarbutts. TN17 .... 169 D4
Target Bsns Ctr. ME15 .... 107 F4
Tarling Cl. DA14 .... 24 B5
Tarnwood Pk. SE9 .... 22 F7
Tasker Cl. ME15 .... 93 B3
Tasman Wlk. E16 .... 1 D7
Tasmania House. RM18 .... 13 A6

Tate Rd. E16 .... 1 F5
Tates. TN18 .... 179 A1
Tates Orch. DA3 .... 42 F3
Tatler Cl. ME5 .... 62 D2
Tatsfield Cl. ME8 .... 49 A2
Tatsfield La. TN16 .... 81 A6
Tattenhall Cl. Bexley DA7 ... 8 D5
Tattlebury La. TN11 .... 153 F1
Tattlebury Rd. TN27 .... 141 C8
Taunton Cl. Bexley DA7 ... 8 A4
Taunton Cl. Maidstone ME15 ... 107 F6
Taunton Rd. DA11 .... 12 A2
Taunton Vale. DA12 .... 30 D5
Tavern Cl. TN15 .... 86 F7
Tavern Cotts. TN15 .... 85 A3
Taverners Rd. ME8 .... 63 E7
Tavistock Cl. Chatham ME5 ... 61 F1
Tavistock Cl. Gillingham ME8 ... 63 E7
Tavistock Rd. Bexley DA16 ... 7 F6
Tavistock Rd. **2** Bromley BR2 ... 36 A5
Tavy Bridge. SE2 .... 3 C4
Tawney Rd. SE28 .... 3 B6
Tay Cl. ME5 .... 62 B5
Taylor Cl. **3** BR6 .... 51 F6
Taylor Rd. ME6 .... 74 F8
Taylor St. TN4 .... 149 A8
Tea Garden La. TN3 & TN4 ... 148 C2
Teal Cl. Grain ME3 .... 21 B5
Teal Cl. Newham E16 .... 1 D8
Teapot La. ME20 .... 75 E1
Teasaucer Hill. ME15 .... 106 F8
Teasel Cl. ME14 .... 92 F4
Teasel Rd. ME5 .... 61 F4
Teasels. TN27 .... 158 A1
Tebbs Way. TN15 .... 86 C3
Ted Williams Ct. **6** SE18 ... 1 F2
Tedder Ave. ME5 .... 62 A7
Tedder Rd. TN4 .... 149 B7
Tees House. **9** ME15 .... 107 E7
Teesdale Rd. DA2 .... 27 C7
Teeswater Ct. SE2 .... 3 D3
Teignmouth Rd. DA16 .... 7 C5
Telegraph Hill. ME3 .... 32 C3
Telemann Sq. SE3 .... 5 B4
Telford House. **2** Erith DA17 ... 4 A3
Telford House. **1**
    Maidstone ME14 .... 92 A6
Telford Rd. BR7 .... 23 D6
Tellson Ave. SE18 .... 5 E8
Telscombe Cl. BR6 .... 51 E8
Telston La. TN13 & TN14 ... 68 F2
Tempest Rd. ME19 .... 88 F3
Templar Dr. Erith SE28 .... 3 D7
Templar Dr. Gravesend DA11 ... 30 A3
Templars Ct. **11** TN8 .... 112 D3
Temple Cl. SE28 .... 2 C3
Temple Gdns. ME2 .... 47 A6
Temple Hill. DA1 .... 9 F2
Temple Hill Cty Prim Inf Sch.
    DA1 .... 10 A2
Temple Hill Cty Prim Jun Sch.
    DA1 .... 10 A2
Temple Hill Sq. DA1 .... 9 F2
Temple Rd. ME2 .... 33 B2
Temple Way. DA1 .... 74 F1
Templemore. DA14 .... 24 B3
Tenby Rd. DA14 .... 7 D6
Tenney House. RM17 .... 12 B7
Tennyson Ave. ME3 .... 33 B7
Tennyson Cl. DA16 .... 6 F6
Tennyson House. **2** DA17 ... 3 F1
Tennyson Rd. Dartford DA1 ... 10 A2
Tennyson Rd. Gillingham ME7 ... 48 C3
Tennyson Rd. Northfleet DA11 ... 29 D5
Tennyson Wlk. Tilbury RM18 ... 13 B5
Tensing Ave. DA11 .... 29 E5
Tenterden CE Jun Sch. TN30 ... 183 B7
Tenterden Cl. SE9 .... 22 F4
Tenterden Cty Inf Sch. TN30 ... 183 B7
Tenterden Rd. Biddenden TN27 172 B7
Tenterden Rd. Chatham ME5 ... 62 B5
Tenterden Rd. Parkgate TN27 ... 171 F4
Tenterden Rd. Strood TN17 ... 182 A5
Tenterden Town Sta. TN30 ... 183 A8
Tenzing Ct. SE9 .... 22 E6
Terence Cl. Chatham ME4 ... 48 A2
Terence Cl. Gravesend DA12 ... 30 F6
Terence Ct. **6** DA17 .... 7 F8
Terminus Rd. ME16 .... 91 A2
Tern Cres. ME2 .... 46 C6
Terrace Rd. ME16 .... 91 E3
Terrace The. DA1 .... 13 B1
Terrace The. Chatham ME4 ... 47 F7
Terrace The. **22** Gravesend DA11 13 B1
Terrace The. Gravesend DA11 ... 13 C1
Terrace The. Rochester ME1 ... 47 C5
Terrace The. Sevenoaks TN13 ... 83 D5
Terraces The. DA2 .... 27 C8
Terry Wlk. ME20 .... 74 E2
Terry's Lodge Rd. TN15 .... 71 C6
Teston House. ME18 .... 105 A7
Teston La. ME15 & ME18 ... 105 C7
Teston Rd. Kings Hill ME19 ... 89 B5
Teston Rd. Offham TN15 & ME19 ... 88 C7
Teston Rd. Red Hill ME19 ... 89 E2
Teston Rd.
    St Leonard's Street ME19 ... 89 A6
Tetty Way. BR1 & BR2 .... 36 A7
Teviot Cl. DA16 .... 7 B6
Tewson Rd. SE18 .... 2 E1
Teynham Gn. Gillingham ME8 ... 49 A4
Teynham Gn. Hayes BR2 .... 36 A4
Teynham House. SE9 .... 6 D1

Thackeray Ave. RM18 .... 13 B6
Thackeray Rd. ME20 .... 74 F3
Thames Ave. Gillingham ME8 ... 63 E8
Thames Ave. High Halstow ME23 ... 17 E4
Thames Barrier Visitor Ctr. SE18 1 A3
Thames Gate. DA1 .... 10 A3
Thames House. **3** ME15 .... 107 D8
Thames Rd. Crayford DA1 .... 9 A4
Thames Rd. Grays RM17 .... 12 B7
Thames Rd. Newham E16 .... 1 D5
Thames Rd. Tonbridge TN10 ... 117 C5
Thames Road Ind Est. E16 .... 1 D5
Thames Terr. ME3 .... 16 B6
Thames View. ME3 .... 33 C7
Thames View Cotts. ME3 .... 32 D3
Thames View Cty Inf Sch. ME8 49 D2
Thames View Cty Prim Sch (Jun).
    ME8 .... 49 D2
Thames Way. Gravesend DA12 ... 13 A1
Thames Way. Northfleet DA11 ... 29 E7
Thamesbank Pl. SE28 .... 3 C5
Thameside Ind Est. E16 .... 1 D4
Thameside Cty Jun Sch. RM17 12 C8
Thamesmere Dr. SE28 .... 3 A6
Thamesview Sch. DA12 .... 30 F5
Thanet Dr. BR2 .... 50 D7
Thanet House. **6** DA11 .... 29 F7
Thanet Rd. Erith DA8 .... 8 E7
Thanet Rd. Sidcup DA5 .... 25 A8
Thanington Ct. SE9 .... 6 E1
Thatch Barn Rd. TN27 .... 141 D6
Thatcher Ct. DA1 .... 26 D8
Thatcher Rd. TN12 .... 139 E4
Thatchers La. ME5 .... 16 B5
Thatchers The. ME16 .... 91 B5
Thaxted Rd. SE9 .... 23 C6
Theatre Sq. **5** TN30 .... 183 A7
Thelma Cl. DA12 .... 30 F3
Thelma Gdns. SE18 .... 5 E6
Theobalds. TN18 .... 178 F2
Theobalds Cl. TN15 .... 70 A1
Theodore Cl. TN2 .... 149 E7
Theodore Pl. ME7 .... 48 C5
Thicketts. TN13 .... 84 C4
Third Ave. Chatham ME4 & ME5 ... 48 C1
Third Ave. Gillingham ME7 ... 48 F4
Third Ave. West Thurrock RM16 ... 11 A8
Third St. TN3 .... 147 F3
Thirlmere Cl. Gillingham ME7 ... 49 A5
Thirlmere Cl. Rochester ME1 ... 33 C1
Thirlmere Rd. Bexley DA7 ... 8 C6
Thirlmere Rd.
    Royal Tunbridge Wells TN4 ... 148 E5
Thirza Rd. DA1 .... 9 F1
Thistle Ct. DA1 .... 27 B7
Thistle Rd. DA12 .... 30 E8
Thistlebank. ME5 .... 62 A3
Thistlebrook. SE2 .... 3 C4
Thistledown. Gravesend DA12 ... 30 D2
Thistledown. Maidstone ME14 ... 92 F4
Thistledown Cl. ME7 .... 63 A4
Thistlemead. BR7 .... 37 B7
Thomas Aveling Sch The. ME1 61 C8
Thomas Cotts. DA13 .... 29 B1
Thomas Dinwiddy Rd. SE12 ... 22 B6
Thomas Dr. DA12 .... 30 D6
Thomas St. Rochester ME1 ... 47 C3
Thomas St.
    Royal Tunbridge Wells TN4 ... 149 A5
Thomas St. Woolwich SE18 ... 2 B2
Thomas Tallis Sch. SE3 .... 5 B4
Thomas Wyatt Way. TN15 ... 71 F3
Thompson Cl. ME8 .... 64 A8
Thomson Cl. ME6 .... 60 A1
Thong La. Basted TN15 .... 86 F5
Thong La. Thong DA12 .... 31 A2
Thorn Cl. Bromley BR2 .... 37 A3
Thorn Cl. Chatham ME5 .... 61 D1
Thorn Rd. TN12 .... 138 E4
Thorn's Meadow. TN16 .... 82 C4
Thorndale Cl. ME5 .... 61 D4
Thorndike Ct. TN17 .... 188 A8
Thorndon La. TN17 .... 182 A1
Thorndike Ct. ME4 .... 61 F8
Thorndon Cl. BR5 .... 37 F7
Thorndon Rd. BR5 .... 37 F7
Thorndyke Way. TN15 .... 71 F3
Thorne Cl. Erith DA8 .... 8 B8
Thorne Cl. Newham E16 .... 1 A7
Thornet Wood Rd. BR1 .... 37 A6
Thorney Croft Cl. ME17 ... 109 D2
Thornfield Gdns. TN2 .... 149 F5
Thornham Rd. ME8 .... 49 C3
Thornhill Ave. SE18 .... 6 E7
Thornhill Pl. ME14 .... 92 A6
Thornton Rd. Bromley BR1 ... 22 A3
Thornton Rd. Erith DA17 ... 4 B2
Thorntree Inf Sch. SE7 .... 1 B1
Thorntree Rd. SE7 .... 1 D1
Thorold Rd. ME4 .... 48 B3
Thorpe Ave. TN10 .... 117 C5
Thorpe Cl. BR6 .... 51 E8
Thorpe Wlk. ME8 .... 63 D3
Thorpe Works. TN4 .... 148 F8
Thrale Way. ME8 .... 63 E4
Three Corners. DA7 .... 8 B5
Three Elm La. TN10 & TN11 ... 118 D5
Three Gates Rd. DA3 .... 42 A2
Three Oaks La. TN15 .... 174 D7
Thresher Field. TN8 .... 130 A6
Threshers Dr. ME14 .... 92 E5
Thrift The. DA2 .... 28 C5
Throckmorten Rd. E16 .... 1 B7
Throwley Cl. SE2 .... 3 C3
Thrushes Cl. ME5 .... 62 B7
Thunderer Rd. RM9 .... 3 F8
Thurnham CE Inf Sch. ME14 ... 93 A4
Thurnham House. **5** BR5 ... 38 D1

Thurnham La. ME14 .... 93 C6
Thurrock Bsns Ctr. RM16 ... 10 F8
Thurrock Ent Ctr. RM17 .... 12 A8
Thurrock Park Way. RM17 ... 12 C7
Thursland Rd. DA14 .... 24 E3
Thursley Rd. SE9 .... 22 F5
Thurston Dr. ME2 .... 46 D7
Thurstone Ct. ME14 .... 91 F6
Thwaite Cl. DA8 .... 8 C8
Thyer Cl. BR6 .... 51 C6
Tibbs Court La. TN12 .... 152 A7
Ticehurst Cl. BR5 .... 24 A1
Tichborne Cl. ME16 .... 91 C6
Tickford Cl. SE2 .... 3 C4
Tidal Basin Rd. E16 .... 1 A6
Tidebrook Ct. **4** BR5 .... 38 C5
Tideway The. ME1 .... 61 C8
Tidford Rd. DA16 .... 6 F5
Tiger La. BR2 .... 36 B5
Tilbrook Rd. SE3 & SE9 .... 5 D4
Tilbury Cl. BR5 .... 38 B7
Tilbury Gdns. RM18 .... 13 A3
Tilbury Manor Cty Jun Sch.
    RM18 .... 13 B7
Tilbury Town Sta. RM18 ... 12 F5
Tilden Cl. TN26 .... 173 D3
Tilden Gill Rd. TN30 .... 183 C7
Tilden La. TN12 .... 122 C3
Tilden Rd. TN27 .... 125 E2
Tile Farm Rd. BR6 .... 51 D7
Tile Fields. ME17 .... 94 D2
Tile Kiln La. Coldblow DA5 ... 25 C6
Tile Kiln La.
    Joyden's Wood DA2 & DA5 ... 25 F5
Tilebarn Cnr. TN10 .... 117 E4
Tilehurst Point. **2** SE2 .... 3 C4
Tilghman Way. ME6 .... 60 B1
Till Ave. DA4 .... 40 F2
Tillingbourne Gn. BR5 .... 38 A5
Tilmans Mead. DA4 .... 41 A2
Tilsden La. TN17 .... 169 E3
Tilt Yard App. SE9 .... 5 F1
Tilton Rd. TN15 .... 86 F7
Timber Bank. DA13 .... 72 F8
Timber Cl. BR7 .... 37 A7
Timber Tops. ME14 .... 77 D8
Timberbank. ME5 .... 62 A6
Timbercroft Jun Sch. SE18 ... 6 E7
Timbercroft La. SE18 .... 6 E7
Timothy Cl. DA6 .... 7 E3
Timothy House. DA18 .... 3 E4
Tinker Pot La. TN15 .... 70 D6
Tinkermill Rise. TN15 .... 70 C5
Tinkers La. TN5 .... 176 E3
Tintagel Gdns. ME2 .... 46 F7
Tintagel Manor. ME7 .... 48 C6
Tintagel Rd. BR5 .... 38 C1
Tintern Rd. ME16 .... 91 D7
Tippens Cl. TN17 .... 169 D4
Titan Rd. RM17 .... 12 B8
Titchfield Cl. **5** ME15 .... 107 F6
Titchfield Rd. ME15 .... 107 F6
Tithe Wlk. ME17 .... 111 D5
Titmuss Ave. SE28 .... 3 B6
Tiverton Dr. SE9 .... 23 C7
Tivoli Gdns. Gravesend DA11 ... 30 B7
Tivoli Gdns. **11** Woolwich SE7 ... 1 E2
Tobruk Way. ME5 .... 61 F6
Toby Gdns. TN11 .... 118 E8
Toddington Cres. ME5 .... 61 D1
Tolcairn Ct. **2** DA17 .... 4 A1
Tolgate La. ME2 .... 47 B7
Tolgate Way. ME14 .... 76 E4
Tolhurst Rd. ME14 .... 135 A7
Tollgate Pl. TN27 .... 141 E5
Tollgate Rd. Dartford DA2 ... 27 D8
Tollgate Rd. Newham E6 .... 1 E8
Tolsey Mead. TN15 .... 87 A8
Tom Coombs Cl. SE9 .... 5 E3
Tom Cribb Rd. SE18 & SE28 ... 2 D3
Tom Joyce Cl. ME8 .... 74 F7
Tomlin Cl. Snodland ME6 ... 75 A8
Tomlin Cl. Staplehurst TN12 ... 139 E4
Tonbridge By-Pass.
    Stocks Green TN11 & TN9 & TN4 &
    TN14 & TN15 .... 116 B5
Tonbridge By-Pass.
    Tonbridge TN11 & TN4 .... 133 C6
Tonbridge Chambers. **3** TN9 133 B8
Tonbridge Cottage Hospl.
    TN11 .... 133 C6
Tonbridge Ct. ME16 .... 91 D3
Tonbridge Gram Sch for Girls.
    TN9 .... 133 C7
Tonbridge House. ME2 .... 33 C1
Tonbridge Rd.
    Hadlow TN10 & TN11 .... 118 C7
Tonbridge Rd.
    Hildenborough TN11 .... 116 E5
Tonbridge Rd.
    Ightham Common TN15 ... 86 C3
Tonbridge Rd.
    Little Mill TN11 & TN12 .... 119 D4
Tonbridge Rd. Maidstone ME16 ... 90 E1
Tonbridge Rd. Royal Tunbridge Wells
    TN2 & TN11 .... 150 A7
Tonbridge Rd.
    Wateringbury ME18 .... 104 C8
Tonbridge Sch. TN10 .... 117 B3
Tonbridge Sta. TN9 .... 117 B1
Tong La. TN12 .... 152 B2
Tong Rd. TN12 .... 152 A4
Tongswood Dr. TN18 .... 179 C1
Tooley St. DA11 .... 29 D8
Top Dartford Rd. BR8 .... 26 A2
Topcliffe Dr. BR6 .... 51 D6

Topley St. SE9 .... 5 D3
Tor Rd. DA16 .... 7 C6
Torbay Rd. TN12 .... 120 B5
Tormount Rd. SE18 .... 6 E8
Toronto Rd. Gillingham ME7 ... 48 E4
Toronto Rd. Tilbury RM18 ... 13 A5
Torrens Wlk. DA12 .... 30 E3
Torrington Cl. ME18 .... 103 D8
Torver Way. BR6 .... 51 D7
Totnes Rd. DA16 .... 7 C7
Tovil Gn. ME15 .... 91 E2
Tovil Green Bsns Pk. ME15 ... 91 E1
Tovil Hill. ME15 .... 91 E2
Tovil Rd. ME15 .... 91 F2
Tower Cl. Gravesend DA12 ... 30 E3
Tower Cl. Orpington BR6 ... 51 F7
Tower Croft. DA4 .... 54 E8
Tower Gdns. ME14 .... 93 B4
Tower Hill. ME19 .... 88 D7
Tower Ind Est. TN15 .... 71 D5
Tower La. ME14 .... 93 B4
Tower Rd. Bexley DA7 .... 8 A3
Tower Rd. Dartford DA1 .... 9 C1
Tower Rd. Erith DA17 .... 4 C2
Tower Rd. Orpington BR6 ... 51 F7
Tower View. ME19 .... 89 B5
Towers Wood. DA4 .... 41 D8
Town Acres. TN10 & TN9 ... 117 C4
Town Hill. Lamberhurst TN3 ... 166 A4
Town Hill. West Malling ME19 ... 74 C1
Town Hill Cl. ME19 .... 74 C1
Town Lock House. **3** TN9 ... 117 C2
Town Meadow. TN17 .... 169 D4
Town Pier. **4** DA11 .... 13 B1
Town Rd. ME3 .... 33 A6
Town Sq. DA8 .... 8 E8
Town Station Cotts. TN8 ... 112 D1
Towncourt Cres. BR5 .... 37 D5
Towncourt La. BR5 .... 37 D5
Townfield Cnr. DA12 .... 30 D7
Townland Cl. TN27 .... 158 A2
Townlands Rd. TN5 .... 174 F4
Townley Gram Sch for Girls.
    DA5 .... 7 F1
Townley Rd. DA6 .... 7 F2
Townsend Rd. Snodland ME6 ... 74 F8
Townsend Rd. Woolwich SE18 ... 2 B3
Townshead Cl. DA14 .... 24 C2
Townshend House. **19** SE18 ... 1 F2
Townshend Rd. BR7 .... 23 B3
Toy's Hill. TN16 & TN8 .... 97 C3
Toynbec Ct. BR7 .... 23 B4
Tracies The. ME9 .... 65 C6
Trader Rd. E6 .... 2 B7
Tradescant Dr. DA13 .... 44 B3
Trafalgar Rd. Dartford DA1 ... 26 E6
Trafalgar Rd. Gravesend DA11 ... 30 A8
Trafalgar Rd. Wouldham ME1 ... 60 C4
Trafalgar St. ME7 .... 48 C5
Tranquil Rise. DA8 .... 4 E1
Transfesa Rd. TN12 .... 136 A7
Transmere Ct. BR5 .... 37 C3
Transmere Rd. BR5 .... 37 C3
Transom House. **2** ME1 .... 47 C1
Trapfield Cl. ME14 .... 93 C4
Trapfield La. ME14 .... 93 C4
Trapham Rd. ME16 .... 91 D5
Travers Gdns. ME9 .... 80 F5
Travertine Rd. ME5 .... 62 B1
Trebble Rd. DA10 .... 11 E1
Trebilco Cl. TN1 .... 149 D7
Tredegar Rd. DA2 .... 26 A5
Tredwell Cl. BR2 .... 36 E5
Tree La. TN15 .... 101 E8
Tree Rd. E16 .... 1 C7
Treetops. Gravesend DA12 ... 30 B4
Treetops. Tonbridge TN9 ... 133 B7
Treetops Cl. SE2 .... 3 E1
Treewall Gdns. BR1 .... 22 B4
Trefoil House. Erith DA18 ... 3 E4
Trefoil House. Grays RM17 ... 12 B7
Trelawn Cres. ME5 .... 62 B2
Trellyn Cl. ME16 .... 90 F2
Trench Rd. TN10 .... 117 C6
Trent House. **2** ME15 .... 107 E7
Trent Rd. ME5 .... 62 B5
Trentham Dr. BR5 .... 38 A5
Trenton Cl. ME16 .... 91 B7
Trevale Rd. ME1 .... 47 B1
Trevelyan Cl. DA1 .... 9 F3
Trevereux Hill. RH8 .... 96 A3
Trevino Dr. ME5 .... 61 F2
Trevithick Dr. DA1 .... 9 F3
Trevor Cl. BR2 .... 36 A2
Trevor Dr. ME16 .... 91 C5
Trewin Cl. ME20 .... 75 D2
Trewsbury House. **2** SE2 ... 3 D4
Triangle Cl. E16 .... 1 C8
Trident Cl. ME2 .... 47 D7
Trinity Cl. Keston Mark BR2 ... 36 E1
Trinity Cl.
    Royal Tunbridge Wells TN2 ... 149 C4
Trinity Ct. Aylesford ME20 ... 76 A3
Trinity Ct. Dartford DA1 .... 27 B7
Trinity Ct. Eltham SE9 .... 6 B1
Trinity Pl. DA6 .... 7 F3
Trinity Rd. Gillingham ME7 ... 48 E4
Trinity Rd. Gravesend DA12 ... 30 C8
Trinity Sch, Belvedere. DA17 ... 4 C2
Trinity St. **12** E16 .... 1 A8
Tristan Gdns. TN4 .... 148 D4
Triumph Rd. E6 .... 1 F7
Trivett Cl. DA9 .... 11 A2
Trolling Down Hill. DA2 ... 27 C6
Troodos Hill. ME14 .... 91 F8

Trosley Ave. DA11 .... 30 B6
Trosley Ctry Pk. ME19 ...... 73 A7
Trosley Rd. DA17 .... 8 A8
Trottiscliffe CE Prim Sch.
ME19 .... 73 A5
Trottiscliffe Rd. ME19 ...... 73 D3
Trotts La. TN16 .... 96 C8
Trotwood Cl. ME5 .... 77 A8
Troughton Rd. SE7 .... 1 B1
Troutbeck House. ME19 ...... 75 C1
Troy Ct. 5 SE18 .... 2 B2
Troys Mead. ME17 .... 94 D2
Trubridge Rd. ME3 .... 34 E5
Truro Cl. ME8 .... 49 D3
Truro Rd. DA12 .... 30 D5
Truro Rd. TN10 .... 117 D5
Trusedale Rd. E6 .... 1 F7
Trycewell La. TN15 .... 86 D6
Tuam Rd. SE18 .... 6 D8
Tubbenden Cl. BR6 .... 51 E7
Tubbenden Dr. BR6 .... 51 D6
Tubbenden Inf & Jun Sch. BR6 51 D6
Tubbenden La. BR6 .... 51 E7
Tubbenden La S. BR6 .... 51 D5
Tubs Hill. TN13 .... 84 B3
Tubs Hill Par. TN13 .... 84 A3
Tudeley La. Tonbridge TN9 .. 133 D7
Tudeley La. Tudeley TN11 & TN9 134 B8
Tudor Ave. ME8 .... 92 B6
Tudor Cl. Bromley BR7 ...... 36 F8
Tudor Cl. Dartford DA1 ...... 9 B1
Tudor Cl. Northfleet DA11 ... 29 E7
Tudor Cres. TN14 .... 69 D3
Tudor Ct. Crockenhill BR8 .... 39 C2
Tudor Ct. R Tunbridge Wells TN2 148 E1
Tudor Ct. Sidcup DA14 ...... 24 A5
Tudor Dr. ME3 .... 69 C3
Tudor Gr. Chattenden ME3 .. 33 F4
Tudor Gr. Gillingham ME8 ... 63 F8
Tudor Par. SE9 .... 5 E3
Tudor Way. BR5 .... 37 D3
Tudor Wlk. DA5 .... 7 E1
Tudway Rd. SE3 & SE9 .... 5 C3
Tufa Cl. ME5 .... 62 B1
Tuff Cotts. ME3 .... 19 C3
Tuffield House. 9 SE18 ...... 2 A2
Tufnail Rd. DA1 .... 9 F1
Tufton Rd. ME8 .... 49 F1
Tufton St. ME14 .... 92 A4
Tugboat St. SE28 .... 2 E4
Tugmutton Cl. BR6 .... 51 B6
Tulip Cl. 5 E6 .... 1 F8
Tulip Tree Cl. TN9 .... 133 B8
Tumblefield Est. TN15 ...... 71 F8
Tumblefield Rd. TN15 ...... 71 E7
Tumblers Hill. ME17 .... 124 F7
Tunbridge Wells Golf Club.
TN4 .... 148 E3
Tunbridge Wells
Gram Sch for Boys. TN4 ... 149 A7
Tunbridge Wells
Gram Sch for Girls. TN4 ... 149 A6
Tunbridge Wells Ind Hospl The.
TN3 .... 147 B3
Tunbury Ave. Chatham ME5 .. 61 F1
Tunbury Ave. Chatham ME5 .. 61 F2
Tunbury Ave S. ME5 .... 61 F1
Tunbury Cty Prim Sch. ME5 .. 61 F1
Tunnan Leys. E6 .... 2 A7
Tunnel Ave. SE10 .... 1 A1
Tunnel Est. RM16 .... 10 F8
Tunnel Rd. TN1 .... 149 B4
Tunstall Cl. BR6 .... 51 E6
Tunstock Way. DA17 .... 3 E3
Tupman Rd. ME1 .... 47 B4
Turgis Cl. ME17 .... 108 E4
Turks Hall Pl. ME2 .... 59 E5
Turley Cotts. SE3 .... 148 A8
Turnberry Way. BR6 .... 37 D1
Turnbull Cl. DA2 .... 27 E8
Turnden Rd. TN17 .... 169 A3
Turner Ave. TN17 .... 169 D3
Turner Cl. DA1 .... 9 C2
Turner House. DA12 .... 30 C6
Turner Rd. Bean DA2 .... 28 B5
Turner Rd. Tonbridge TN10 . 117 E5
Turner St. ME3 .... 16 B5
Turners Ave. TN30 .... 183 B8
Turners Gdns. TN13 .... 99 C7
Turners Green Rd. TN5 .... 174 F6
Turners Green Rd. TN5 .... 174 F6
Turnpike Cl. DA6 .... 7 D3
Turnpike Dr. BR6 .... 52 D2
Turnpike La. RM18 .... 13 D8
Turnstone. DA13 .... 43 A7
Turnstone Rd. ME5 .... 62 C1
Turnstones The. DA12 ...... 30 D6
Turpin La. DA8 .... 9 A8
Turpington Cl. BR2 .... 36 E2
Turpington La. BR2 .... 36 E3
Turton House. 5 SE18 .... 6 B8
Tuscan Dr. ME5 .... 62 C1
Tuscan Rd. SE18 .... 2 D1
Tutsham Way. TN12 .... 135 F6
Tuxford Rd. TN4 .... 148 B5
Tweed Rd. TN10 .... 117 C5
Tweedy Rd. BR1 .... 36 A8
Twigg Cl. DA8 .... 8 E7
Twisden Rd. ME19 .... 89 F8
Twiss House. 6 SE18 .... 2 B1
Twistleton Ct. DA1 .... 9 D1
Twitton La. TN14 .... 68 E3
Twitton Meadows. TN14 .... 68 E3
Two Gates Hill. ME3 .... 32 F5
Twydall Cty Inf Sch. ME8 ... 49 B2

Twydall Cty Prim Jun Sch. ME8 49 B2
Twydall Gn. ME8 .... 49 B3
Twydall La. ME8 .... 49 B2
Twyford Ct. ME14 .... 92 D6
Twyford Rd. TN11 .... 102 E1
Twysden Cotts. TN18 ..... 186 A4
Tydeman Rd. ME15 .... 92 F2
Tye La. BR6 .... 51 C5
Tyehurst Cl. SE2 .... 3 E1
Tyland La. ME14 .... 76 F3
Tyler Cl. ME19 .... 89 F8
Tyler Dr. ME8 .... 63 E4
Tyler Gr. DA1 .... 9 F3
Tylers Green Rd. BR8 ...... 39 C2
Tylney Rd. BR1 .... 36 D7
Tyndall Rd. DA16 .... 6 F4
Tyne Cl. ME5 .... 62 C5
Tyne House. 10 ME15 ...... 107 E7
Tyne Rd. TN10 .... 117 B5
Tynedale Cl. DA2 .... 27 D7
Tynemouth Rd. ME15 ...... 92 F2
Typhoon Rd. ME19 .... 88 F3
Tyron Way. DA14 .... 23 F3
Tyrrell Ave. DA16 .... 7 B2
Tyrrells Hall Cl. RM17 ..... 12 D8

Uckfield La. TN8 .... 129 D4
Ufton Cl. ME15 .... 92 E1
Ulcombe CE Prim Sch. ME17 125 F6
Ulcombe Hill. ME17 .... 109 F1
Ulcombe Rd. Headcorn TN27 141 C6
Ulcombe Rd.
Langley Heath ME17 ..... 108 E3
Underdown Ave. ME4 ...... 47 F1
Underhill Jun Sch. ME17 ... 124 C7
Underlyn Ind Est. TN12 ... 122 F2
Underlyn La. TN12 .... 122 D1
Underriver House Rd.
TN11 & TN15 .... 100 D5
Underwood. ME19 .... 88 D7
Underwood Cl. ME15 ...... 91 F2
Underwood The. SE9 ...... 22 F6
Unicorn Wlk. DA9 .... 10 F2
Unicumes La. ME16 .... 91 C2
Union Pk. ME15 .... 107 F4
Union Rd. BR2 .... 36 D4
Union Sq. 18 TN2 .... 149 A2
Union St. Chatham ME4 .... 48 A3
Union St. Maidstone ME14 .. 92 A5
Union St. Rochester ME1 ... 47 C5
Union St. Union Street TN5 . 177 B3
Unity Way. SE18 .... 1 D3
Univ of Greenwich. SE18 .... 2 A2
Univ of Greenwich
Avery Hill Campus. SE9 .... 6 C1
Univ of Greenwich Avery Hill
Campus Southwood Site. SE9 23 D8
Univ of Greenwich
(Dartford Campus). DA1 .. 26 C6
Univ of Greenwich
(Riverside House Annexe).
SE18 .... 2 A3
Univ of Greenwich
(Southwold Site). SE9 ..... 6 C2
University Gdns. DA5 ...... 24 E8
University Pl. ME15 .... 8 C7
University Way. DA1 .... 9 E4
Unwin Cl. ME20 .... 76 A3
Upbury Manor High Sch. ME7 48 B4
Upbury Way. ME4 .... 48 A4
Upchat Rd. ME2 & ME3 ... 33 F3
Updale Rd. DA14 .... 23 F4
Upland Inf Sch. DA7 .... 7 F4
Upland Jun Sch. DA7 .... 7 F4
Uplands Cl. Rochester ME2 .. 46 D6
Uplands Cl. Sevenoaks TN13 . 83 F4
Uplands Com Coll. TN5 ... 175 A4
Uplands Rd. BR6 .... 38 B1
Uplands Way. TN13 .... 83 F4
Upnor Castle. ME2 .... 33 F2
Upnor Rd. Rochester ME2 .. 47 D8
Upnor Rd. Upper Upton ME2 .. 33 E2
Upper Abbey Rd. DA17 ...... 4 A2
Upper Austin Lodge Rd. DA4 .. 54 D4
Upper Ave. DA13 .... 43 E8
Upper Barn Hill. ME15 .... 105 E3
Upper Britton Pl. ME7 ..... 48 B5
Upper Bush Rd. ME2 .... 45 F2
Upper Church Hill. DA9 .... 10 F2
Upper Cumberland Wlk. TN1 . 149 B1
Upper Dunstan Rd. TN4 ... 149 B6
Upper East Rd. ME4 .... 48 B8
Upper Fant Rd. ME16 ...... 91 D2
Upper Green La. TN11 .... 101 D5
Upper Green Rd. TN11 .... 101 D5
Upper Grosvenor Rd.
TN1 & TN4 .... 149 B6
Upper Grove Rd. DA17 ...... 4 A1
Upper Haysden La. TN4 & TN9 132 E6
Upper Holly Hill Rd. DA17 .... 4 B1
Upper Hunton Hill. ME15 .. 106 A3
Upper Luton Rd. ME4 & ME5 .. 48 C2
Upper Mill. ME18 .... 104 D8
Upper Nellington. TN3 .... 148 B4
Upper Park Rd. Bromley BR1 .. 36 C8
Upper Park Rd. Erith DA17 .. 4 B2
Upper Platts. TN5 .... 176 F1
Upper Profit. TN3 .... 148 A3
Upper Rd. ME15 .... 92 B2
Upper Sheridan Rd. DA17 .... 4 A2
Upper Spring La. TN15 ..... 86 B5
Upper St. Hollingbourne ME17 94 E3
Upper St. Leeds ME17 .... 108 F5
Upper St. Rusthall TN4 ... 148 D4
Upper Stephens. TN3 ..... 148 A3
Upper Stone St. ME15 ..... 92 A3
Upper Street N. DA3 .... 56 F8

Upper Street S. DA3 .... 56 F8
Upper Wickham La. DA16 ... 7 B6
Upperton Rd. DA14 .... 23 F3
Upton Cl. DA5 .... 7 F1
Upton Day Hospl. DA6 ...... 7 E3
Upton Prim Sch. DA6 .... 7 F2
Upton Quarry. TN3 .... 147 F3
Upton Rd. Bexley DA6 ...... 7 E2
Upton Rd. Woolwich SE18 ... 6 C8
Upton Rd S. DA6 .... 7 F1
Upton Villas. 4 DA6 .... 7 E3
Uptons. TN27 .... 141 C6
Upwood Rd. SE12 .... 5 A1
Uridge Cres. TN10 .... 117 C4
Uridge Rd. TN10 .... 117 C4
Urquhart Cl. ME5 .... 62 A5
Ursula Lodge. DA14 .... 24 B3
Usborne Cl. TN12 .... 139 E3

Vale Ave. Royal Tunbridge Wells,
Mount Sion TN1 .... 149 A3
Vale Ave. Royal Tunbridge Wells,
Southborough TN4 .... 132 F1
Vale Cl. ME1 .... 51 A6
Vale Cotts. ME9 .... 80 A8
Vale Ct. TN4 .... 133 A2
Vale Dr. ME5 .... 61 E6
Vale Rd. Bromley BR1 & BR7 .. 37 A7
Vale Rd. Dartford DA1 ..... 26 B7
Vale Rd. Hawkhurst TN18 .. 178 F3
Vale Rd. Loose ME15 ..... 106 E4
Vale Rd. Northfleet DA11 ... 29 E7
Vale Rd. Royal Tunbridge Wells,
Mount Sion TN1 .... 149 A3
Vale Rd. Royal Tunbridge Wells,
Southborough TN4 .... 132 F1
Vale Rd. Tonbridge TN9 ... 117 D1
Vale Rd. Tonbridge TN9 ... 133 C8
Vale Rise. TN9 .... 133 E8
Valence House. ME15 ..... 107 C7
Valence Rd. DA8 .... 8 D7
Valence Sch. TN16 .... 81 F1
Valence View. TN17 ...... 156 E7
Valentine Ave. DA5 .... 24 E7
Valentine Cl. ME7 .... 49 A1
Valentine Rd. ME15 ...... 107 E7
Valerian Cl. ME5 .... 61 E4
Valiant House. 5 SE7 .... 1 C1
Valiant Rd. ME5 .... 62 C2
Valiant Way. E6 .... 1 F8
Valley (Charlton Athletic FC) The.
SE7 .... 1 C1
Valley Cl. DA1 .... 8 F1
Valley Dr.
Gravesend,Riverview Park DA12 .. 30 D4
Valley Dr.
Gravesend,Singlewell DA12 .. 30 E1
Valley Dr. Maidstone ME15 . 106 E5
Valley Dr. Sevenoaks TN13 .. 84 B1
Valley Forge Cl. TN10 .... 117 F4
Valley Gdns. DA9 .... 11 B1
Valley Gr. SE7 .... 1 C1
Valley L Ctr. SE9 .... 23 C8
Valley Rd. Crayford DA1 ..... 8 F1
Valley Rd. Erith DA8 .... 4 D2
Valley Rd. Fawkham Green DA3 .. 42 C2
Valley Rd. Gillingham ME7 .. 48 E4
Valley Rd. Rusthall TN4 ... 148 D4
Valley Rd. St Paul's Cray BR5 .. 38 B8
Valley Rise. ME5 .... 61 F1
Valley The. ME17 .... 106 D3
Valley View.
Royal Tunbridge Wells TN4 . 133 A2
Valley View. Swanscombe DA9 .. 11 B1
Valley View Rd. ME1 .... 47 B1
Valley View Terr. DA4 ..... 40 F1
Valleyside. SE7 .... 1 D1
Valliers Wood Rd. DA15 .... 23 E7
Vambery Rd. SE18 .... 6 C8
Vandome Cl. E16 .... 1 B7
Vange Cottage Mews. ME1 .. 47 B4
Vanity La. ME17 .... 106 D1
Vanoc Gdns. BR1 .... 22 A4
Vanquisher Wlk. DA12 ..... 30 F5
Varley Rd. E16 .... 1 B7
Varnes St. ME20 .... 75 F6
Vaughan Ave. TN10 ...... 117 E6
Vaughan Rd. DA16 .... 6 F5
Vauxhall Cl. DA11 .... 29 F8
Vauxhall Gdns. TN9 ...... 133 C7
Vauxhall La.
Bidborough TN11 & TN4 ... 133 A6
Vauxhall La.
Tonbridge TN11 & TN9 ... 133 D6
Vauxhall Pl. DA1 .... 26 E8
Vauxhall Rd. TN4 .... 133 A6
Veitchil Barn. ME14 ...... 39 F8
Veles Rd. ME6 .... 74 F8
Venmead Cl. 4 DA17 .... 4 A2
Venners Cl. DA7 .... 8 E5
Ventnor Cl. ME5 .... 62 C8
Venture Cl. DA5 .... 24 E8
Venture Ct. 5 SE12 .... 22 A8
Venus Rd. SE18 .... 1 F3
Verdun Rd. SE18 & SE2 ..... 7 A8
Vermont Rd. TN4 .... 148 C4
Vernham Rd. SE18 .... 6 C8
Vernon Cl. St Paul's Cray BR5 . 38 B6
Vernon Cl. West Kingsdown TN15 55 F2

Vernon Rd.
Royal Tunbridge Wells TN1 . 149 C6
Vernon Rd. Swanscombe DA10 .. 11 F1
Veroan Rd. DA7 .... 7 E5
Verona Gdns. DA12 .... 30 E4
Verona House. DA8 .... 8 F7
Vert House. RM17 .... 12 C7
Vesper Ct. TN27 .... 143 A1
Vestry Cotts. DA3 .... 43 C5
Vestry Rd. TN14 .... 84 C8
Via Romana. DA12 .... 31 B7
Viaduct Terr. DA4 .... 41 C7
Vicarage Ave. SE3 .... 5 A7
Vicarage Cl. Aylesford ME20 .. 75 F3
Vicarage Cl. Erith DA8 .... 8 C8
Vicarage Cl. Halling ME2 .... 60 A5
Vicarage Cl. Stoke ME3 ..... 19 A3
Vicarage Ct. Chalk DA12 ... 31 A7
Vicarage Ct. Newington ME9 .. 65 B7
Vicarage Dr. DA11 .... 12 C1
Vicarage Hill. TN1 .... 81 D1
Vicarage La. Chalk DA12 .... 31 A6
Vicarage La. East Farleigh ME15 106 B6
Vicarage La.
Hoo St Werburgh ME3 ..... 34 E4
Vicarage La. Sevenoaks TN13 .. 83 D8
Vicarage Pk. SE18 .... 2 C1
Vicarage Rd. Coldblow DA5 .. 25 B7
Vicarage Rd. Gillingham ME7 . 48 C5
Vicarage Rd. Halling ME2 ... 59 F5
Vicarage Rd. Rochester ME2 . 47 B8
Vicarage Rd.
Royal Tunbridge Wells TN4 . 132 F2
Vicarage Rd. Woolwich SE18 . 2 C1
Vicarage Rd. Walling ME18 . 105 A1
Vicarage Row. ME3 .... 32 C4
Vicarage Sq. RM17 .... 12 A8
Vicarage Way. TN19 ...... 184 A3
Vicary Way. ME16 .... 91 D5
Vickers Rd. DA8 .... 4 D1
Victor Mills Cotts. BR8 ..... 25 A1
Victoria Ave. 3 DA11 ...... 30 B8
Victoria Bsns Ctr. DA16 ..... 7 B5
Victoria Cl. Chatham ME5 ... 61 E3
Victoria Cl. Edenbridge TN8 . 128 C8
Victoria Cotts. Cranbrook TN17 169 D5
Victoria Cotts. Edenbridge TN8 . 128 C8
Victoria Dock Rd. E16 .... 1 B6
Victoria Dr. Kings Hill ME18 . 88 F1
Victoria Dr. South Darenth DA4 . 41 D7
Victoria Hill Rd. BR8 .... 40 A8
Victoria Ind Pk. DA1 .... 9 E2
Victoria Rd. Bexley DA6 ..... 8 A3
Victoria Rd. Bromley BR2 ... 36 D4
Victoria Rd. Chatham,Luton ME4 . 48 B2
Victoria Rd.
Chatham,Walderslade ME5 .. 61 E3
Victoria Rd. Chislehurst BR7 .. 23 A3
Victoria Rd. Dartford DA1 ... 9 E2
Victoria Rd. Edenbridge TN8 . 128 C8
Victoria Rd. Erith DA8 .... 8 E8
Victoria Rd. Golden Green TN11 118 F6
Victoria Rd. Gravesend DA11 . 29 F7
Victoria Rd.
Royal Tunbridge Wells TN1 . 149 B4
Victoria Rd. Royal Tunbridge Wells,
Modest Corner TN4 ...... 132 E1
Victoria Rd. Sevenoaks TN13 . 84 B2
Victoria Rd. Sidcup DA15 ... 24 A5
Victoria St. Eccles ME20 .... 75 F6
Victoria St. Erith DA8 .... 3 F1
Victoria St. Gillingham ME7 .. 48 D6
Victoria St. Maidstone ME16 . 91 E3
Victoria St. Rochester ME2 .. 47 B7
Victoria St.
Rochester,Troy Town ME1 .. 47 A5
Victoria Terr. ME1 .... 47 A2
Victoria Way. SE7 .... 1 B1
Victoria Wharf. DA1 .... 9 E2
Victory Cotts. TN14 .... 99 C2
Victory Pk. ME2 .... 47 E7
Vidal Manor. ME7 .... 48 C5
Vidgeon Ave. ME3 .... 34 D6
View Rd. ME3 .... 33 B7
View The. SE2 .... 3 E1
Viewfield Rd. DA5 .... 24 C7
Viewland Rd. SE18 .... 2 F1
Viewlands Ave. TN16 ...... 81 F7
Viewpoint Ct. DA3 .... 42 F5
Vigilant Way. DA12 .... 30 F3
Vigo Cty Prim Sch. DA13 .... 73 A8
Vigo Rd. TN15 .... 72 C7
Viking Gdns. E6 .... 1 E8
Viking House. 3 SE7 .... 1 C1
Viking Rd. DA11 .... 29 C5
Viking Way. Erith DA8 & DA17 . 4 C3
Viking Way.
West Kingsdown TN15 .... 55 E5
Villa Cl. DA12 .... 31 B6
Villa Ct. DA1 .... 26 E6
Villa Rd. ME3 .... 32 B3
Villacourt Rd. SE18 & SE2 ... 7 A8
Village Green Rd. DA1 .... 9 A3
Village The. SE7 .... 5 D8
Villas Rd. SE18 .... 2 C1
Vincent Cl. Bromley BR2 .... 36 B5
Vincent Cl. Sidcup DA15 .... 23 E7
Vincent Rd. Kit's Coty ME20 . 76 C7
Vincent Rd. Woolwich SE18 .. 2 B2
Vincent St. 8 E16 .... 1 A7
Vine Ave. TN13 .... 84 B3
Vine Court Rd. TN13 ...... 84 C4
Vine Ct. ME18 .... 104 D8
Vine Lodge Ct. TN13 ...... 84 B3
Vine Rd. BR6 .... 51 F4
Vine The. TN13 .... 84 C3
Vine Wlk. TN12 .... 139 E3

Vineries The. ME7 .... 48 E5
Vines La. Rochester ME1 .... 47 C5
Vines La. Watt's Cross TN11 . 100 C1
Viney's Gdns. TN30 ...... 173 C1
Vineyard La. TN5 .... 176 C2
Vinson Cl. BR6 .... 38 A1
Vinters Rd. ME14 .... 92 B4
Vinters Sch for Boys. ME14 .. 92 C4
Vintners Way. ME14 .... 92 E4
Viola Ave. SE2 .... 3 B1
Violet Cl. ME5 .... 77 A8
VIP Trad Est. SE7 .... 1 C2
Virginia Rd. ME7 .... 48 C7
Virginia Wlk. DA12 .... 30 E2
Viscount Dr. E6 .... 1 F8
Vista The. SE9 .... 22 E8
Vixen Cl. ME5 .... 62 C6
Voce Rd. SE18 .... 6 D7
Volante Way. DA12 .... 30 E4
Vulcan Cl. ME5 .... 62 B7
Vyne The. DA7 .... 8 B4
Vyvyan Cotts. TN17 ...... 180 C3
Vyvyon House. SE18 .... 6 A6

Wadard Terr. BR8 .... 40 C4
Wade Ave. BR5 .... 38 D2
Wade Rd. E16 .... 1 C7
Wadeville Cl. DA17 .... 4 A1
Wadhurst Bsns Pk. TN5 ... 174 B7
Wadhurst CE Prim Sch. TN5 . 174 F5
Wadhurst Par. TN5 ...... 174 F4
Wadhurst Sta. TN5 .... 174 C6
Wadlands Rd. ME3 .... 16 B5
Waghorn Rd. ME6 .... 75 A8
Waghorn St. ME4 .... 48 B3
Wagon La. TN12 .... 120 C1
Wagoners Cl. ME14 .... 92 E4
Waid Cl. DA1 .... 9 F1
Wainscott Cty Prim Sch. ME2 . 33 D2
Wainscott Rd. ME2 .... 33 D2
Wainscott Wlk. ME2 ...... 33 D3
Waite Davies Rd. 6 SE12 ... 22 A8
Wake Rd. ME1 .... 61 C8
Wakefield Cl. ME2 .... 46 D6
Wakefield Rd. DA9 .... 11 C2
Wakehurst Cl. ME17 ..... 106 B3
Wakeleys Cotts. ME8 ...... 64 B8
Wakerly Cl. 6 E6 .... 1 F7
Waldair Ct. E16 .... 2 B4
Waldeck Rd. DA1 .... 10 A1
Waldegrave Rd. BR1 ...... 36 F5
Walden Ave. BR7 .... 22 F4
Walden Cl. DA17 .... 3 F1
Walden Rd. BR7 .... 22 F2
Waldenhurst Rd. BR5 ...... 38 D2
Waldens Cl. BR5 .... 38 D2
Waldens Rd. BR5 .... 38 E3
Waldens The. ME17 ...... 109 E2
Walderslade Cty Prim Sch.ME5 62 A3
Walderslade Girls Sch. ME5 .. 61 F5
Walderslade Rd. ME5 ...... 61 F6
Walderslade Woods.
Chatham ME5 .... 61 E2
Walderslade Woods.
Chatham ME5 & ME14 .... 77 B8
Waldo Ind Est. BR1 .... 36 D6
Waldo Rd. BR1 .... 36 D6
Waldrist Way. DA18 .... 3 F4
Waldron Dr. ME15 .... 106 F6
Walk The. ME17 .... 109 E2
Walkden Rd. BR7 .... 23 A3
Walker Cl. Crayford DA1 ..... 8 F4
Walker Cl. Woolwich SE18 ... 2 C2
Walkhurst Cotts. TN17 ... 180 F7
Walkhurst Rd. TN17 ..... 180 F7
Walkley Rd. DA1 .... 9 B2
Walks The. TN3 .... 161 C8
Wall Cl. ME3 .... 34 D7
Wallace Cl. Erith SE28 ...... 3 D6
Wallace Cl.
Royal Tunbridge Wells TN2 . 163 A8
Wallace Gdns. DA10 .... 11 E1
Wallace Rd. ME1 .... 61 E8
Wallace Terr. TN15 .... 56 E4
Waller Hill. TN17 .... 156 B5
Wallers. TN3 .... 148 A8
Wallhouse Rd. DA8 .... 9 C7
Wallis Ave. ME15 .... 107 E5
Wallis Cl. DA2 .... 25 F5
Wallis Field. TN3 .... 161 B6
Walmer Cl. BR6 .... 51 D6
Walmer Ct. 3 ME14 .... 92 A5
Walmer House. ME2 .... 33 C1
Walmer Terr. SE18 .... 2 D2
Walmers Ave. ME3 .... 32 A4
Walnut Cl. Chatham ME5 ... 62 B8
Walnut Cl. Paddock Wood TN12 . 136 A4
Walnut Cl. Yalding ME18 .. 104 F1
Walnut Hill Rd. DA3 & DA13 . 43 E6
Walnut Tree Ave. Dartford DA1 . 26 E6
Walnut Tree Ave.
Loose Hill ME15 .... 107 A5
Walnut Tree Cl. BR7 ...... 37 C8
Walnut Tree Ct. ME20 .... 75 B1
Walnut Tree La. ME15 .... 107 A5
Walnut Tree Rd. DA8 .... 4 E1
Walnut Tree Way. DA13 ... 44 B3
Walnut Way.
R Tunbridge Wells TN2 & TN4 . 113 D1
Walnut Way. Swanley BR8 .. 39 D7
Walnuts Rd. BR6 .... 38 B1
Walnuts The. BR6 .... 38 A1
Walpole Cl. ME19 .... 74 F1
Walpole Pl. 3 SE18 .... 2 B2
Walpole Rd. BR2 .... 36 D4
Walsham Cl. SE28 .... 3 D6
Walsham Rd. ME5 .... 61 F1
Walshaw House. 2 ME14 ... 92 A6

Walsingham Cl. ME8 .... 63 D3
Walsingham House. **3** ME14 ... 92 A6
Walsingham Pk. BR7 .... 37 D7
Walsingham Rd. BR5 .... 38 B8
Walsingham Wlk. DA17 .... 8 A8
Walter Burke Ave. ME1 .... 60 C5
Walter's Farm Rd. TN9 .... 117 C1
Walters Green Rd. TN11 & TN3 146 F6
Walters Rd. ME3 .... 34 E6
Walters Yd. BR1 .... 36 A7
Waltham Ct. Dartford DA1 .... 9 A1
Waltham Cl. Orpington BR5 .... 38 D1
Waltham Rd. ME8 .... 49 C3
Walthamstow Hall. TN13 .... 84 C4
Walthamstow Hall Jun Sch.
TN13 .... 84 C4
Walton Rd. Sidcup DA14 .... 24 C5
Walton Rd. Tonbridge TN10 ..... 117 F6
Walwyn Ave. BR1 .... 36 D6
Wanden La. TN27 .... 143 C8
Wansbury Way. BR8 .... 40 A5
Wanstead Cl. BR1 .... 36 C7
Wanstead Rd. BR1 .... 36 C7
Wansunt Rd. DA5 .... 25 C7
Warblers Cl. ME2 .... 47 A7
Ward Cl. Durgates TN5 .... 174 C5
Ward Cl. Erith DA8 .... 8 D8
Ward's La. TN5 .... 175 E4
Warde's. ME18 .... 104 F2
Warden Cl. ME16 .... 91 C4
Warden Mill Cl. ME18 .... 104 E7
Warden Rd. ME1 .... 47 C2
Wardens Field Cl. **2** BR6 ...... 51 F4
Wardona Ct. DA10 .... 11 F1
Wardwell La. ME9 .... 65 C8
Ware St. ME14 .... 93 A5
Warepoint Dr. SE28 .... 2 D4
Warham Rd. TN14 .... 69 B3
Waring Cl. BR6 .... 51 F4
Waring Dr. BR6 .... 52 A4
Waring Rd. DA14 .... 24 C2
Warland Rd.
West Kingsdown TN15 .... 55 F2
Warland Rd. Woolwich SE18 ..... 6 F7
Warmlake. ME17 .... 108 F1
Warmlake Est. ME17 .... 108 E1
Warmlake Rd. ME17 .... 108 C1
Warne Pl. **4** DA15 .... 7 B1
Warner St. ME4 .... 47 F3
Warnett Ct. ME6 .... 60 A1
Warnford Gdns. ME15 .... 107 A8
Warnford Rd. ME6 .... 51 F5
Warren Ave. BR6 .... 51 F5
Warren Cl. DA6 .... 8 A2
Warren Cotts. TN11 .... 131 A3
Warren Ct. TN15 .... 84 C3
Warren Dr. BR6 .... 52 B5
Warren Farm La. TN3 .... 162 B4
Warren Gdns. BR6 .... 52 A5
Warren La. Hartlip ME9 .... 64 C3
Warren La. Woolwich SE18 ...... 2 B3
Warren Rd. Bexley DA6 .... 8 A2
Warren Rd. Dartford DA1 .... 26 E5
Warren Rd. Hayes BR2 .... 50 A8
Warren Rd.
Kit's Coty ME5 & ME20 .... 76 D7
Warren Rd.
Lower Bush DA12 & DA13 ..... 45 D3
Warren Rd. Orpington BR6 ...... 52 A7
Warren Rd. Sidcup DA14 .... 24 C5
Warren Rd. Southfleet DA13 .... 29 B3
Warren Ridge. TN3 .... 163 C3
Warren The. Gravesend DA12 ... 30 D4
Warren The. Penshurst TN11 .. 131 A4
Warren The. Ticehurst TN5 ... 176 E1
Warren View. 31 E2
Warren Wlk. **1** SE7 .... 5 C8
Warren Wood Cl. BR2 .... 50 A8
Warren Wood Cty Prim Sch.
ME1 .... 61 C8
Warren Wood Rd. ME1 .... 61 C7
Warrens The. DA3 .... 42 F3
Warrington Rd. TN12 .... 136 A6
Warrior Ave. DA12 .... 30 C4
Warspite Rd. SE18 & SE7 .... 1 E3
Warwall. E6 .... 2 B6
Warwick Cl. Orpington BR6 ...... 52 A7
Warwick Cl. Sidcup DA5 .... 24 F8
Warwick Cres. ME1 .... 46 F2
Warwick Gdns. DA13 .... 58 A8
Warwick Pk. TN1 & TN2 .... 149 B1
Warwick Pl. Maidstone ME16 ... 91 E3
Warwick Pl. Northfleet DA11 ... 12 B2
Warwick Rd. Bexley DA16 .... 7 C4
Warwick Rd. **4**
Royal Tunbridge Wells TN1 .. 149 A2
Warwick Rd. Sidcup DA14 .... 24 B3
Warwick Terr. SE18 .... 6 E7
Washneys Rd. BR6 & TN14 ..... 67 B6
Washwell La. TN5 .... 174 F3
Wassall La. TN17 .... 187 E7
Wat Tyler Way. ME15 .... 92 A4
Watchgate. DA2 .... 27 E3
Water La. Four Elms TN8 .... 179 B4
Water La. Harrietsham ME17 .. 110 B5
Water La.
Headcorn TN17 & TN27 .... 141 A4
Water La. Kingswood ME17 .... 109 F3
Water La. **4** Maidstone ME15 .. 92 A4
Water La.
Maidstone,Bearsted ME14 ..... 93 E6
Water La. Shoreham TN14 .... 68 F6
Water La. Smarden Bell TN27 . 142 F2
Water La. West Malling ME19 .. 89 C8
Water Mill Way. DA4 .... 41 B7
Water Slippe. TN11 .... 102 D1

Watercress Cl. TN14 .... 84 C7
Watercress Dr. TN14 .... 84 C7
Watercroft Rd. TN14 .... 52 F1
Waterdale Rd. SE2 .... 7 A8
Waterdales. DA11 .... 29 D7
Waterdown Rd. TN4 .... 148 C1
Waterfield. TN2 .... 163 A7
Waterfield Cl. Erith DA17 .... 4 A3
Waterfield Cl. Woolwich SE28 ... 3 B5
Waterfield Sch. SE28 .... 3 A5
Waterfrets Cotts. TN3 .... 147 F5
Watergate House. **5** DA12 ...... 30 C8
Waterhead Cl. DA8 .... 8 E7
Waterhouse Cl. E16 .... 1 D8
Wateringbury CE Prim Sch.
ME18 .... 104 E6
Wateringbury Cl. BR5 .... 38 B7
Wateringbury Rd. ME19 .... 89 F3
Wateringbury Sta. ME18 .... 104 E6
Waterlakes. TN8 .... 128 C8
Waterloo Pl. Cranbrook TN17 .. 169 D5
Waterloo Pl. Tonbridge TN9 ... 133 B8
Waterloo Rd. Cranbrook TN17 . 169 D6
Waterloo Rd. Gillingham ME7 .. 48 C4
Waterloo St. **1** Gravesend DA12 30 C8
Waterloo St. Maidstone ME15 ... 92 A3
Waterlow Rd. Maidstone ME14 .. 92 A6
Waterlow Rd. Vigo Village DA13 . 72 F7
Waterman's La. TN12 .... 136 B3
Watermeadow Cl. ME7 .... 62 F6
Watermill Cl. Maidstone ME15 .. 91 B5
Watermill Cl. Rochester ME2 .... 47 C8
Waters Cotts. TN5 .... 175 A4
Waters Edge. ME15 .... 91 F2
Waters Pl. ME7 .... 63 A6
Waterside. DA1 .... 8 F2
Waterside Cl. SE20 .... 74 E2
Waterside La. ME7 .... 48 F7
Waterside Mews. ME18 .... 104 D6
Watersmeet Way. SE28 .... 3 D7
Waterton Ave. DA12 .... 30 E8
Watery La. Heaverham TN15 .... 85 D7
Watery La. Sidcup DA14 .... 24 B2
Watford Rd. E16 .... 1 A8
Watkins Cl. TN12 .... 139 E5
Watling Ave. ME5 .... 48 D2
Watling House. **10** SE18 .... 6 A8
Watling St. Bexley DA6 & DA7 ... 8 C3
Watling St. Chatham ME5 & ME7 . 48 D2
Watling St. Dartford DA1 & DA2 . 27 C8
Watling St. Gillingham ME5 & ME7 48 D2
Watling St. Gravesend DA11 .... 30 B3
Watling St. Gravesend DA11 .... 30 C2
Watling St.
Northfleet DA11 & DA13 ...... 29 C5
Watling St. Rochester ME2 ...... 46 D7
Watson Ave. ME5 .... 61 D5
Watson Rd. RM16 .... 11 A6
Watt's Cross Rd. TN11 .... 116 B6
Watt's La. BR7 .... 37 C8
Watts' Ave. ME1 .... 47 C4
Watts Cl. Snodland ME6 .... 75 B8
Watts Cl. Wadhurst TN5 .... 174 F4
Watts' St. ME4 .... 47 E3
Wavell Dr. DA15 .... 6 E1
Waveney House. **7** ME15 ..... 107 E8
Waveney Rd. TN10 .... 117 B5
Waverley Cl. Bromley BR2 .... 36 D4
Waverley Cl. Chatham ME5 ...... 62 D2
Waverley Cl. Coxheath ME17 .. 106 C3
Waverley Cres. SE18 .... 2 D1
Waverley Dr. TN2 .... 149 F6
Waverley Gdns. E6 .... 1 E1
Waverley Rd. SE18 .... 2 D1
Wayfield Cty Prim Sch. ME5 ... 62 A7
Wayfield Link. SE9 .... 6 D1
Wayfield Rd. ME5 .... 62 A7
Waylands. BR8 .... 39 F5
Waylands Cl. TN14 .... 67 E4
Wayne Cl. BR6 .... 51 F7
Wayne Ct. ME2 .... 33 D2
Wayside. TN30 .... 173 B2
Wayside Ave. TN30 .... 173 B3
Wayside Dr. TN8 .... 112 D3
Wayside Flats. TN30 .... 173 B2
Wayside Gr. BR7 & SE9 .... 22 F4
Wayville Rd. DA1 .... 27 B8
Weald Cl. Istead Rise DA13 .... 29 E1
Weald Cl. Keston Mark BR2 ..... 50 E8
Weald Cl. Maidstone ME15 .... 107 C6
Weald Cl. Sevenoaks Weald TN14 99 C2
Weald Ct. TN11 .... 116 D6
Weald Cty Prim Sch. TN14 ..... 99 B2
Weald of Kent
Gram Sch for Girls The. TN9 133 C7
Weald Rd. TN13 .... 99 B7
Weald The. BR7 .... 22 F2
Weald View. Castle Hill TN12 .. 136 E1
Weald View. Frittenden TN17 . 156 E6
Weald View. Turner's Green TN5 174 F6
Weald View Rd. TN9 .... 133 F7
Wealden Ave. TN30 .... 173 B1
Wealden Cl. TN11 .... 116 E5
Wealden Ct. **5** ME4 .... 48 B3
Wealden Pl. TN13 .... 84 D6
Wealden Way. ME20 .... 90 E7
Wealdon View. TN17 .... 167 E8
Weardale Ave. DA2 .... 27 C7
Weare Rd. TN4 .... 149 C8
Weatherly Cl. ME1 .... 47 C4
Weathersfield Ct. SE9 .... 5 F1
Weaver Cl. E16 .... 2 B6
Weaver's Orch. DA13 .... 29 A2
Weavering Cl. ME2 .... 33 B2
Weavering Cotts. ME14 .... 92 E3
Weavering St. ME14 .... 92 F4
Weavers Cl. Gravesend DA11 ... 30 A7

Weavers Cl. Staplehurst TN12 . 139 F4
Weavers Cotts. TN17 .... 167 E8
Weavers La. TN14 .... 84 C6
Weavers The. Biddenden TN27 . 158 A1
Weavers The. Maidstone ME16 .. 91 B5
Webb Cl. ME3 .... 34 D6
Webb Ct. **6** SE28 .... 3 B6
Webb's Meadow. TN15 .... 84 C2
Webber Cl. DA8 .... 9 B7
Webster Rd. ME8 .... 49 F1
Wedgewood Cl. ME16 .... 91 B5
Wedgewood Ct. DA5 .... 24 F8
Wedgewood Dr. ME5 .... 62 A7
Weeds Wood Rd. ME5 .... 61 F4
Week St. ME14 .... 92 A4
Weeks La. TN27 .... 158 A5
Weigall Rd. SE12 & SE3 .... 5 A3
Weinhouse Cl. TN8 .... 112 D3
Weir Rd. DA5 .... 25 B8
Weird Wood. DA3 .... 43 C6
Welbeck Ave. Bromley BR1 ...... 22 B4
Welbeck Ave.
Royal Tunbridge Wells TN4 .. 149 C8
Welbeck Ave. Sidcup DA15 ..... 24 A7
Welcombe Cl. ME8 .... 63 D8
Weld Cl. TN12 .... 139 F4
Well Cl. TN11 .... 115 F1
Well Field. DA3 .... 42 F5
Well Hall Par. SE9 .... 5 F3
Well Hall Rd. Eltham SE9 .... 5 F2
Well Hall Rd. Eltham SE18 & SE9 . 5 F5
Well Hill. ME3 .... 53 B5
Well Hill La. BR6 .... 53 B4
Well Penn Rd. ME3 .... 16 C3
Well Rd. Maidstone ME14 .... 92 A5
Well Rd. Wrotham ME14 .... 69 C3
Well St. Loose ME15 & ME17 .. 106 E4
Well St. Well Street ME19 .... 89 E6
Wellan Cl. DA16 .... 7 B2
Welland House. **8** ME15 ...... 107 E8
Welland Rd. TN10 .... 117 B4
Wellands Cl. BR1 .... 36 F7
Wellbrook Rd. BR6 .... 51 A6
Wellcome Ave. DA1 .... 9 E3
Weller Ave. ME1 .... 47 D2
Weller Pl. BR6 .... 66 A8
Weller Rd. TN4 .... 148 C4
Wellers Cl. TN16 .... 96 C8
Wellesley Cl. **8** SE7 .... 1 C1
Welling High St. DA16 .... 7 A4
Welling Sch. DA16 .... 7 B6
Welling Sta. DA16 .... 7 A5
Welling Way. DA16 .... 6 D4
Wellingfield Ct. **1** DA16 .... 7 A4
Wellington Ave. Sidcup DA15 ... 7 A1
Wellington Ave. Woolwich SE18 . 2 C3
Wellington Cotts.
Gill's Green TN18 .... 178 E4
Wellington Cotts.
Meopham Green DA13 .... 58 A7
Wellington Gdns. SE7 .... 1 C1
Wellington House. **6** ME15 ... 107 E5
Wellington Par. DA15 .... 7 A2
Wellington Pl. Maidstone ME14 . 91 F6
Wellington Pl.
Sparrow's Green TN5 .... 174 F5
Wellington Rd. Bexley DA5 ...... 7 D2
Wellington Rd. Bromley BR2 ... 36 C5
Wellington Rd. Dartford DA1 .... 9 C1
Wellington Rd. Erith DA17 .... 3 F1
Wellington Rd. Gillingham ME7 . 48 C4
Wellington Rd. Orpington BR5 .. 38 C3
Wellington Rd. Tilbury RM18 ... 13 A5
Wellington St. Gravesend DA12 . 30 C8
Wellington St. Woolwich SE18 ... 2 A2
Wellington Way. ME19 .... 88 F3
Wellingtonia Way. TN8 .... 112 C2
Wellmeade Dr. TN13 .... 99 B8
Wells Cl.
Royal Tunbridge Wells TN1 .. 149 A3
Wells Cl. Tenterden TN30 ...... 183 B8
Wells Cl. Tonbridge TN10 & TN9 117 C4
Wells Cotts. ME18 .... 104 C2
Wells House. BR1 .... 22 B3
Wells Rd. Bromley BR1 .... 36 F7
Wells Rd. Rochester ME2 .... 46 D5
Wellsmoor Gdns. BR1 .... 37 A6
Welton Cl. TN9 .... 132 F7
Welton Rd. SE18 .... 6 E7
Wemmick Cl. ME1 .... 61 D7
Wendover Cl. ME2 .... 60 B5
Wendover Ct. BR2 .... 36 B6
Wendover Rd. Bromley BR1 & BR2 36 B6
Wendover Rd. Eltham SE9 .... 5 D8
Wendover Way. Bexley DA16 ..... 7 A3
Wendover Way. Orpington BR6 . 38 A3
Wensley Cl. SE9 .... 5 F1
Wents Wood. ME14 .... 92 F5
Wentworth Cl. Gravesend DA11 . 30 A3
Wentworth Cl. Hayes BR2 .... 50 A8
Wentworth Cl. Orpington BR6 .. 51 E5
Wentworth Cty Prim Sch. DA1 26 A8
Wentworth Dr. Cliffe Woods ME3 33 B8
Wentworth Dr. Dartford DA1 ..... 9 A1
Wentworth Dr. Gillingham ME8 . 63 E7
Wenvoe Ave. DA7 .... 8 B5
Wernbrook St. SE18 .... 6 C8
Wesley Ave. E16 .... 1 A5
Wesley Cl. Maidstone ME16 ..... 90 F3
Wesley Cl. St Paul's Cray BR5 ... 38 B7
Wessex Dr. DA8 .... 8 E6
West App. BR5 .... 37 C4
West Borough Cty Prim Sch.
ME16 .... 91 B3
West Brow. BR7 .... 23 B3
West Common Rd. BR2 .... 50 B7
West Crescent Rd. DA11 .... 13 C1
West Cross. TN30 .... 182 F7

West Cross Gdns. TN30 .... 182 F7
West Dr. Chartway Street ME17 . 125 D7
West Dr. Chatham ME5 .... 61 D5
West End. Brasted TN16 .... 82 B2
West End. Kemsing TN15 .... 70 A2
West End. Marden TN12 .... 138 C5
West Hallowes. SE9 .... 22 E7
West Heath Cl. DA1 .... 8 F1
West Heath La. TN13 .... 99 B7
West Heath Rd. Crayford DA1 ... 8 F1
West Heath Rd. Erith SE2 .... 7 D8
West Heath Sch. TN13 .... 99 B6
West High Sch for Boys. DA1 .. 26 C8
West High Sch for Girls. DA1 .. 26 D8
West Hill. DA1 .... 9 D1
West Hill Cty Prim Jun Sch. DA1 9 C1
West Hill Dr. DA1 .... 9 C1
West Hill Hospl. DA1 .... 9 D1
West Hill Rise. DA1 .... 9 D1
West Holme. DA8 .... 8 C6
West Kent Ave. DA11 .... 12 C1
West Kent Coll. TN9 .... 133 A7
West Kent Coll of FE. TN4 .... 149 A7
West Kingsdown CE Jun Sch.
TN15 .... 56 A2
West Kingsdown Cty Inf Sch.
TN15 .... 56 A2
West Kingsdown Ind Est. TN15 55 F2
West La. ME3 .... 21 A6
West Lodge Sch. DA14 .... 24 A5
West Malling CE Prim Sch.
ME19 .... 89 B8
West Malling Ind Pk. ME19 ..... 89 C7
West Malling Sta. ME19 .... 89 D8
West Mill. DA11 .... 12 F1
West Mill Rd. ME20 .... 75 C4
West Park Ave. TN4 .... 132 F1
West Park Rd. ME15 .... 92 B2
West Pk. SE9 .... 22 E7
West Rd. Gillingham ME4 .... 48 A7
West Rd. Goudhurst TN17 ..... 167 E8
West Shaw. DA3 .... 42 D7
West St. Bexley DA7 .... 7 F4
West St. Bromley BR1 .... 36 A7
West St. Erith DA8 .... 4 E1
West St. Gillingham ME7 .... 48 D6
West St. Gravesend DA11 .... 13 B1
West St. Grays RM17 .... 12 A8
West St. Harrietsham ME17 ... 110 C6
West St. Hunton ME15 .... 121 D7
West St. Rochester ME2 .... 33 B1
West St. West Malling ME19 ... 89 B8
West St. Woodside Green ME17 . 111 E8
West St. Wrotham TN15 .... 71 F3
West Terr. DA15 .... 23 E7
West Thurrock Cty Prim Sch.
RM16 .... 11 A8
West Thurrock Way. RM16 ..... 11 B8
West View Hospl. TN30 .... 182 E6
West View Rd. Crockenhill BR8 . 39 D3
West View Rd. Dartford DA1 ..... 9 F1
West View Rd. Swanley BR8 .... 40 A5
West Way. BR5 .... 37 D4
West Wlk. BR5 .... 91 B3
West Wood Rd. ME9 .... 79 B8
West Woodside. DA5 .... 24 E7
Westbere House. BR5 .... 38 C4
Westbourne Rd. DA7 .... 7 E7
Westbrook Ct. SE3 .... 5 B6
Westbrook Dr. BR5 .... 38 D1
Westbrook Rd. SE3 .... 5 B6
Westbrook Terr. TN2 .... 149 D1
Westbrooke Cl. ME4 .... 48 A2
Westbrooke Cres. DA16 .... 7 C4
Westbrooke Rd. Bexley DA16 .... 7 C4
Westbrooke Rd. Sidcup DA15 .. 23 D6
Westbrooke Sch. DA16 .... 7 C4
Westbury Rd. BR1 .... 36 D8
Westbury Terr. TN16 .... 96 C8
Westcombe Hill. SE3 & SE10 .... 5 A8
Westcombe Park Rd. SE3 .... 5 A7
Westcombe Park Sta. SE3 .... 1 A1
Westcott Ave. DA11 .... 30 A5
Westcott Cl. BR1 .... 36 D8
Westcourt Cty Prim Sch. DA12 30 E6
Westcourt Rd. ME4 .... 48 A6
Westdale Rd. SE18 .... 6 B8
Westdean Ave. SE12 .... 22 C7
Wested Farm Cotts. BR8 .... 39 F2
Wested La. Swanley BR8 .... 40 A3
Wested La. Swanley BR8 .... 40 A4
Westerdale. **3** SE10 .... 1 A1
Westergate Rd. Erith SE2 .... 7 E8
Westergate Rd. Rochester ME2 . 32 F1
Westerham Cl. ME8 .... 49 B3
Westerham Dr. DA15 .... 7 B1
Westerham Hill. TN16 .... 81 B5
Westerham Rd. Brasted TN16 .. 82 A2
Westerham Rd. Keston BR2 .... 50 D4
Westerham Rd.
Sevenoaks TN13 & TN14 ..... 83 C4
Westerham Rd. Westerham TN16 96 A4
Westerhill Rd. ME17 .... 106 C1
Westerland Rd. ME2 .... 23 C2
Western Ave. **7** TN18 .... 178 F2
Western Cross Cl. DA9 .... 11 C1
Western Gateway. E16 .... 1 A6
Western Rd. Borough Green TN15 86 F7
Western Rd. Hawkhurst TN18 . 178 F2
Western Rd. Maidstone ME16 .. 91 C2
Western Rd.
Royal Tunbridge Wells TN1 .. 149 C5
Western Rd. Royal Tunbridge Wells,
Southborough TN4 .... 133 A1
Western Rd. Turner's Green TN5 174 F6
Western Way. SE28 .... 2 E4
Westfield. New Ash Green DA3 . 56 F6

Westfield. **1** Orpington BR6 ..... 51 C5
Westfield. Sevenoaks TN13 ..... 84 C5
Westfield Bsns Ctr. ME2 .... 47 C7
Westfield Cl. DA12 .... 30 C2
Westfield Cotts. Cudham TN14 . 66 D3
Westfield Cotts.
West Kingsdown TN15 .... 55 F4
Westfield House. TN30 .... 182 F7
Westfield Rd. DA7 .... 8 C4
Westfield Sole Rd. ME14 .... 77 D8
Westfield St. SE18 .... 1 D3
Westfield Terr. TN17 .... 168 F1
Westgate Ct. SE12 .... 22 A7
Westgate Cty Prim Sch. DA1 .. 26 D8
Westgate Rd. DA1 .... 9 D1
Westharold. BR8 .... 39 D6
Westhill Cl. DA11 .... 30 B7
Westholme. ME3 .... 37 F2
Westhorne Ave. SE12 & SE9 ..... 5 C2
Westhurst Dr. BR7 .... 23 B3
Westland House. **1** E16 .... 2 A5
Westland Lodge. **1** BR1 .... 36 C7
Westleigh Dr. BR1 .... 36 E8
Westmarsh Cl. ME15 .... 107 F7
Westmead. ME20 .... 75 C4
Westminster Ind Est. E16 .... 1 D3
Westmoor St. SE7 .... 1 D3
Westmoreland Ave. DA16 .... 6 E3
Westmoreland Pl. **5** BR1 .... 36 A6
Westmoreland Rd. BR2 .... 36 A5
Westmorland Cl. ME15 .... 107 E7
Westmorland Gn. ME15 .... 107 E7
Westmorland Rd. Bromley BR2 . 36 A5
Westmorland Rd.
Maidstone ME15 .... 107 E7
Westmount Ave. ME4 .... 47 F3
Westmount Rd. SE9 .... 6 A3
Weston Ave. RM16 .... 10 F8
Weston Rd. ME2 .... 47 A8
Westport Rd. E13 .... 1 B8
Westree Rd. ME16 .... 91 E3
Westrise. TN9 .... 133 A7
Westway. Coxheath ME17 ..... 106 C3
Westway. Pembury TN2 .... 150 D7
Westways. Marlpit Hill TN8 ... 112 C2
Westways. Westerham TN16 ... 81 C5
Westwell Cl. BR5 .... 38 D1
Westwell Ct. TN30 .... 182 F7
Westwell House. TN30 .... 182 F7
Westwood Cl. BR1 .... 36 D6
Westwood Inf Sch. DA16 .... 6 E3
Westwood Jun Sch. DA16 .... 6 E3
Westwood La. DA16 .... 6 F4
Westwood Rd.
East Peckham TN12 .... 119 E6
Westwood Rd. Maidstone ME15 107 A7
Westwood Rd. Newham E16 ...... 1 B5
Westwood Rd. Rusthall TN4 ... 148 C5
Westwood Rd. Westwood DA13 . 28 E2
Westwood Tech Coll. DA16 .... 6 E3
Westwood Way. TN13 .... 83 F5
Wetheral Dr. ME5 .... 62 B4
Wey Cl. ME5 .... 62 C5
Weybridge Cl. ME5 .... 62 C4
Weyhill Cl. ME14 .... 92 C6
Weyman Rd. SE3 & SE7 .... 5 C6
Weymouth Cl. E6 .... 2 B7
Wharf La. ME3 .... 16 B6
Wharf Rd. Gillingham ME7 ...... 48 C2
Wharf Rd. Gravesend DA12 .... 13 E1
Wharf Rd. Grays RM17 .... 11 F8
Wharf Rd. Maidstone ME15 .... 91 E2
Wharfedale Rd. DA2 .... 27 C7
Wharncliffe. DA9 .... 11 B1
Wharton Rd. BR1 .... 36 B8
Whatman Cl. ME14 .... 92 C6
Wheatcroft Gr. ME8 .... 63 F7
Wheatear Way. ME5 .... 62 B7
Wheatfield. ME19 .... 74 E1
Wheatfield Cl. TN17 .... 169 C5
Wheatfield Dr. TN17 .... 169 C5
Wheatfield Lea. TN17 .... 169 C5
Wheatfield Way. TN17 .... 169 C5
Wheatfields. Chatham ME5 ..... 62 D2
Wheatfields. Maidstone ME14 .. 92 D4
Wheatfields. Newham E6 .... 2 B7
Wheatley Cl. DA9 .... 11 A2
Wheatley Terrace Rd. DA8 .... 8 F8
Wheatsheaf Cl. ME15 .... 107 B8
Wheatsheaf Hill. Ide Hill TN14 . 97 F4
Wheatsheaf Hill. Maypole TN14 . 52 F2
Wheatsheaf Way. TN10 .... 117 D6
Wheelbarrow Park Est. TN12 . 138 B7
Wheeler St. Headcorn TN27 .. 141 E5
Wheeler St. Maidstone ME14 .. 92 A5
Wheeler's La. ME17 .... 122 E7
Wheelers The. ME8 .... 63 B6
Whenman Ave. DA5 .... 25 C5
Whernside Cl. SE28 .... 3 C6
Whetsted Rd.
Five Oak Green TN12 .... 135 C8
Whetsted Rd. Whetsted TN12 . 119 F1
Whetstone Rd. SE3 .... 5 D6
Whiffen's Ave. ME4 .... 47 F5
Whiffen's Ave W. ME4 .... 47 F5
Whimbrel Cl. SE28 .... 3 C6
Whimbrel Gn. ME20 .... 74 F2
Whimbrel Wlk. ME5 .... 62 C1
Whinchat Rd. SE18 & SE28 .... 2 D3
Whinfell Way. DA12 .... 30 F4
Whinyates Rd. SE9 .... 5 E4
Whippendell Cl. BR5 .... 38 B8
Whippendell Way. BR5 .... 38 B7
Whistler Rd. TN10 .... 117 D6
Whitby Cl. DA9 .... 11 A2

Whitby Rd. SE18 .... 1 F2
Whitchurch Cl. ME16 .... 91 E4
Whitcombe Cl. ME5 .... 62 C3
White Ave. DA11 .... 29 F5
White Bear Pas. **3** TN1 & TN4 149 A2
White Cottage Rd. TN10 .... 117 D6
White Hart Cl. TN13 .... 99 C7
White Hart Par. TN13 .... 83 E5
White Hart Rd. Orpington BR6 ..... 38 A2
White Hart Rd. Woolwich SE18 ...... 2 E2
White Hart Wood. TN13 .... 99 C6
White Hill Rd. ME14 .... 63 D1
White Horse Hill. BR7 & SE9 .... 23 A4
White Horse La. Harvel DA13 ...... 58 C2
White Horse La.
  Otham Hole ME15 .... 108 A6
White Horse Rd. DA13 .... 58 E1
White House La. TN14 .... 98 F5
White House Rd. TN14 .... 98 F5
White Lodge. TN1 .... 149 C4
White Lodge Cl. TN13 .... 84 B4
White Oak Cl. **10** TN9 .... 133 B8
White Oak Cty Inf Sch. BR8 .... 39 E7
White Oak Cty Prim Sch. BR8 .... 39 E7
White Oak Gdns. DA15 .... 23 F8
White Oak Sq. **3** BR8 .... 39 E6
White Post. Four Elms TN8 .... 113 A6
White Post. Hollingbourne ME17 . 95 B5
White Post Cnr. TN11 .... 101 F5
White Post Hill. DA4 .... 41 A2
White Post La. DA13 .... 44 B5
White Rd. ME4 .... 48 A2
White Rock Ct. ME16 .... 91 E3
White Rock Pl. **5** ME16 .... 91 E3
White's La. TN13 .... 179 B2
White's Meadow. BR1 .... 37 A5
Whitebeam Ave. BR2 .... 37 A3
Whitebeam Dr. ME17 .... 106 B3
Whitebine Gdns. TN12 .... 120 A6
Whitecroft. BR8 .... 39 E7
Whitefield Cl. BR5 .... 38 C6
Whitefield Rd. TN4 .... 149 A6
Whitefriars. TN13 .... 99 A8
Whitegate Cl. TN4 .... 149 A8
Whitegates Ave. TN15 .... 55 E4
Whitegates La. TN5 .... 174 D8
Whitehall Dr. ME17 .... 109 D3
Whitehall La. Erith DA8 .... 8 F5
Whitehall La. Grays RM17 .... 12 C8
Whitehall Rd. Broad Street ME14 94 A6
Whitehall Rd. Bromley BR2 .... 36 D5
Whitehaven Cl. BR2 .... 36 A5
Whitehead Cl. DA2 .... 26 C5
Whiteheads La. ME14 .... 93 B4
Whitehill. TN15 .... 72 B3
Whitehill Cty Inf Sch. DA12 .... 30 C5
Whitehill Cty Jun Sch. DA12 ...... 30 C5
Whitehill La. DA12 .... 30 D5
Whitehill Par. DA12 .... 30 D5
Whitehill Rd. Crayford DA1 .... 9 A2
Whitehill Rd. Gravesend DA12 ..... 30 C6
Whitehill Rd.
  Longfield,Whitehill DA13 .... 42 D8
Whitehill Rd. Meopham DA13 ...... 58 B7
Whitehorse Hill. ME4 .... 48 B3
Whitehouse Cl. ME3 .... 34 E4
Whitehouse Cres. ME1 .... 76 A8
Whitelake Rd. TN10 .... 117 C5
Whiteleaves Rise. ME2 .... 46 B3
Whitelimes. TN18 .... 178 D8
Whiteoak Cl. **1** ME8 .... 39 E6
Whitepost La.
  Culverstone Green DA13 .... 57 F2
Whitepost La. Vigo Village DA13 . 73 A8
Whites Cl. DA9 .... 11 C1
Whitewall Ctr. ME2 .... 47 D8
Whitewall Rd. ME2 .... 47 D7
Whitewall Way. ME2 .... 47 D7
Whitewebbs Way. BR5 .... 37 F8
Whitfield Rd. DA7 .... 7 F7
Whitings Way. E6 .... 2 A8
Whitmore St. ME16 .... 91 D2
Whittaker St. ME4 .... 48 A4
Whitworth Rd. SE18 .... 6 A7
Whybourne Crest. TN2 .... 149 D1
Whyman Ave. ME4 .... 48 A1
Wichling Cl. BR5 .... 38 D1
Wicken House. ME16 .... 91 E4
Wickenden Rd. TN13 .... 84 C5
Wickets The. TN14 .... 99 C2
Wickham Common Prim Sch.
  BR4 .... 50 A6
Wickham Ct. DA16 .... 6 E5
Wickham Field. TN14 .... 68 F3
Wickham Gdns. TN14 .... 148 D5
Wickham La. SE2 & SE18 .... 7 A8
Wickham Pl. ME17 .... 111 D5
Wickham St. Bexley DA16 .... 7 A6
Wickham St. Rochester ME1 .... 47 D3
Wickhams Way. DA3 .... 42 F4
Wickhurst Rd. TN14 .... 98 F3
Wicks Cl. SE12 .... 22 D4
Wicksteed Cl. DA5 .... 25 D5
Widbury Cl. TN3 .... 147 F2
Widecombe Rd. SE9 .... 22 E5
Widgeon Cl. E16 .... 1 B7
Widgeon Path. SE28 .... 2 D3
Widgeon Rd. ME2 .... 46 D6
Widmore Lodge Rd. BR1 .... 36 C7
Widmore Rd. BR1 .... 36 C7
Wierton Hill. ME17 .... 123 D7
Wierton La. ME17 .... 107 E1

Wierton Rd. ME17 .... 123 E8
Wigmore Rd. Gillingham ME8 ...... 63 B4
Wigmore Rd. Gillingham ME8 ...... 63 B5
Wilberforce Ct. **2** SE28 .... 3 C5
Wilberforce Rd. ME17 .... 106 D3
Wilberforce Way. DA12 .... 30 D3
Wilde Cl. RM18 .... 13 C5
Wilde Rd. DA8 .... 8 B7
Wilderness Rd. BR7 .... 23 B1
Wilderness Sch for Boys The.
  TN15 .... 84 E6
Wildernesse Ave. TN15 .... 84 E6
Wildernesse Golf Course. TN15 85 A4
Wildernesse Mount. TN13 .... 84 D5
Wildfell Cl. ME14 .... 77 C8
Wildman Cl. ME8 .... 63 D3
Wildwood Cl. Kingswood ME17 . 109 E2
Wildwood Cl. **1** Lewisham SE12 22 A8
Wildwood Glade. ME8 .... 63 B4
Wilford House. **3** SE18 .... 2 B1
Wilfred St. **20** DA11 .... 13 B1
Wilkinson Cl. Dartford DA1 .... 9 F3
Wilkinson Cl. **1** Dartford DA1 ..... 10 A3
Wilkinson Rd. E16 .... 1 C7
Wilks Ave. DA1 .... 26 F6
Will Adams Ct. ME7 .... 48 C6
Will Adams Way. ME7 .... 48 F1
Will Crooks Gdns. SE9 .... 5 D3
Will Thorne Pav The. E16 .... 1 E7
Willenhall Rd. SE18 .... 2 B1
Willersley Ave. Orpington BR6 ..... 51 D7
Willersley Ave. Sidcup DA15 .... 23 F7
Willersley Cl. DA15 .... 23 F7
Willesley Gdns. TN17 .... 169 D6
Willett Cl. BR5 .... 37 E3
Willett Way. BR5 & BR6 .... 37 E3
Willetts Cotts. TN3 .... 146 C4
Willetts La. TN3 .... 146 C4
William Baker House. ME20 .... 90 F8
William Barefoot Dr. SE9 .... 23 A5
William House. **4** DA11 .... 30 B8
William Judge Cl. TN30 .... 183 D7
William Luck Cl. TN12 .... 119 E6
William Rd. ME2 .... 46 C2
William Smith House. **10** DA17 ... 4 A3
William St. Gravesend DA11 .... 30 B8
William St. Grays RM17 .... 12 C8
William St.
  Royal Tunbridge Wells TN4 ...... 149 A5
Willington Gn. ME15 .... 107 E2
Willington St. ME15 .... 92 F2
Willis House. ME1 .... 47 C4
Willis Rd. DA8 .... 4 D2
Willoughby Way. SE7 .... 1 B2
Willow Ave. Hoo St Werburgh
  ME3 .... 34 E3
Willow Ave. Sidcup DA15 .... 7 A1
Willow Ave. Swanley BR8 .... 39 F5
Willow Cl. Bromley BR2 .... 36 F4
Willow Cl. Orpington BR5 .... 38 B2
Willow Cl. Sidcup DA5 .... 7 F1
Willow Cres.
  Five Oak Green TN12 .... 135 B7
Willow Cres. Staplehurst TN12 .. 139 F5
Willow Gr. BR7 .... 23 B2
Willow House. **2** ME5 .... 61 F5
Willow La. TN12 .... 136 E6
Willow Lea. TN10 .... 117 C7
Willow Pk. TN14 .... 68 F2
Willow Rd. Dartford DA1 .... 26 C7
Willow Rd. Erith DA8 .... 9 A6
Willow Rd. Larkfield ME20 .... 74 F3
Willow Rd. Rochester ME2 .... 46 E6
Willow Rise. ME15 .... 92 F1
Willow Terr. DA4 .... 54 E8
Willow Tree Ct. DA14 .... 23 F3
Willow Tree Rd. TN2 .... 148 F1
Willow Tree Wlk. BR1 .... 36 B8
Willow Vale. BR7 .... 23 B2
Willow Way. ME15 .... 92 B3
Willow Wents. ME18 .... 88 D1
Willow Wlk.
  Culverstone Green DA13 .... 57 F3
Willow Wlk. Orpington BR6 .... 51 B7
Willow Wlk.
  Royal Tunbridge Wells TN2 ...... 149 E8
Willow Wood Rd. DA13 .... 57 F2
Willowbank Dr. ME23 .... 17 E4
Willowby Gdns. ME8 .... 63 E4
Willowmead. ME20 .... 74 E2
Willows The. Gillingham ME8 ...... 49 E2
Willows The. Grays RM17 .... 12 D8
Willows The. Newington ME9 ...... 65 B6
Willowside. ME6 .... 60 A1
Willrose Cres. SE2 .... 3 B1
Willys Cotts. TN8 .... 96 C2
Wilman Rd. TN4 .... 149 B7
Wilmar Way. TN15 .... 84 F7
Wilmecote Ct. ME8 .... 63 D8
Wilmington Ave. BR6 .... 52 C8
Wilmington Court Rd. DA2 .... 26 A6
Wilmington Gram Sch for Boys.
  DA2 .... 26 B5
Wilmington Hall Sch. DA2 .... 26 B5
Wilmington Prim Sch. DA2 .... 26 B5
Wilmington Way. ME8 .... 49 B2
Wilmot Rd. DA1 .... 9 B2
Wilmount St. SE18 .... 2 B2
Wilson Ave. ME1 .... 61 E7
Wilson Cl. Hildenborough TN11 . 116 E5
Wilson Cl. Maidstone ME15 ...... 107 E7
Wilson House. **2** SE7 .... 5 C8
Wilson Rd. TN10 .... 117 C5
Wilsons La. ME15 .... 106 A5
Wilsons Way. DA13 .... 57 F3
Wilton Dr. ME19 .... 90 B8
Wilton Rd. SE2 .... 3 C1
Wiltshire Cl. Chatham ME5 .... 62 C8

Wiltshire Cl. Dartford DA2 .... 27 D8
Wiltshire Rd. BR6 .... 38 A2
Wiltshire Way. Maidstone ME15 107 E8
Wiltshire Way.
  Royal Tunbridge Wells TN1 ...... 149 D7
Wimborne. DA14 .... 24 B4
Wimborne Ave. BR5 & BR7 .... 37 F6
Wimborne Dr. ME8 .... 63 D6
Wimpole Cl. BR2 .... 36 C5
Winch Cl. TN17 .... 169 D3
Winch's Garth. TN12 .... 139 F5
Winchcomb Gdns. SE9 .... 5 D4
Winchelsea Ave. DA7 .... 7 F7
Winchelsea Rd. ME5 .... 62 B5
Winchester Ave. ME5 .... 61 F4
Winchester Cl. **11** E6 .... 1 F7
Winchester Cres. DA12 .... 30 D5
Winchester Gr. TN13 .... 84 B4
Winchester House.
  Greenwich SE18 .... 5 D7
Winchester House. **4**
  Maidstone ME15 .... 107 D7
Winchester Pl. **7** ME14 .... 92 A5
Winchester Rd. Bexley DA16 .... 7 D5
Winchester Rd.
  Hawkhurst TN18 .... 179 A2
Winchester Rd. Orpington BR6 ... 52 C6
Winchester Rd. Tonbridge TN10 117 D5
Winchester Way. ME8 .... 64 A8
Wincliff Rd. TN9 .... 133 B8
Wincrofts Dr. SE9 .... 6 D3
Windermere Cl. Dartford DA1 ..... 26 B7
Windermere Cl. Orpington BR6 ... 51 B7
Windermere Dr. ME8 .... 63 D7
Windermere Rd. DA7 .... 8 C5
Windhover Way. DA12 .... 30 E4
Windmill Cl. ME7 .... 48 C4
Windmill Cotts. Lower Stoke ME3 19 C5
Windmill Cotts.
  Wilsley Green TN17 .... 169 D6
Windmill Ct.
  Boughton Monchelsea ME17 ... 107 B3
Windmill Ct.
  Royal Tunbridge Wells TN2 ...... 149 C3
Windmill Dr. BR2 .... 50 C6
Windmill Hill. Hill Top TN12 .... 136 B1
Windmill Hill. Platt TN15 .... 87 D7
Windmill Hill. Pye Corner ME17 126 B7
Windmill Hts. ME14 .... 93 B4
Windmill La. Cousley Wood TN5 175 C8
Windmill La. Durgates TN5 .... 174 E4
Windmill La.
  Wrotham Heath TN15 .... 87 E8
Windmill La E. ME19 .... 89 C6
Windmill La W. ME19 .... 89 A6
Windmill Pk. TN15 .... 87 E7
Windmill Rd. Gillingham ME7 ..... 48 C4
Windmill Rd. Sevenoaks TN13 .... 99 B6
Windmill Row.
  Sevenoaks Weald TN14 .... 99 B2
Windmill St. Gravesend DA11 ..... 30 B7
Windmill St. Rochester ME2 .... 33 B1
Windmill St.
  Royal Tunbridge Wells TN2 ...... 149 C3
Windrush Prim Sch. SE28 .... 3 B5
Windsor Ave. ME4 .... 47 F2
Windsor Cl. Chislehurst BR7 .... 23 B3
Windsor Cl. Maidstone ME14 ...... 92 B6
Windsor Ct. ME1 .... 36 E6
Windsor Dr. Dartford DA1 .... 9 A1
Windsor Dr. Orpington BR6 .... 52 A4
Windsor Rd. Bexley DA16 .... 7 E3
Windsor Rd. Gillingham ME7 .... 48 D5
Windsor Rd. Gravesend DA12 ..... 30 B4
Windward Rd. ME1 .... 47 C1
Windy Ridge. BR1 .... 36 E8
Windyridge. ME7 .... 48 E1
Winfield La. TN15 .... 86 E3
Wingate Rd. DA14 .... 24 C2
Wingfield Prim Sch. SE3 .... 5 B4
Wingfield Rd. DA11 .... 30 B8
Wingham Cl. Gillingham ME8 ...... 49 C3
Wingham Cl. Maidstone ME15 ... 107 F7
Wingrove Dr. Maidstone ME14 ... 92 E5
Wingrove Dr. Rochester ME2 ...... 47 C8
Winifred Rd. Dartford DA1 .... 9 B2
Winifred Rd. Erith DA8 .... 4 E1
Winifred Rd. Maidstone ME15 ..... 92 F3
Winifred St. E16 .... 1 F5
Winn Common Rd. SE18 .... 6 E3
Winn Rd. SE12 & SE9 .... 22 B7
Winnipeg Dr. **3** BR6 .... 51 F4
Winser Rd. TN17 .... 182 A1
Winsor Prim Sch. E6 .... 2 A7
Winsor Terr. E6 .... 2 A8
Winston Cl. DA9 .... 10 F1
Winston Ct. **7** BR1 .... 36 B8
Winston Dr. ME2 .... 33 D2
Winston Rd. ME2 .... 46 D5
Winstone Scott Ave. TN3 .... 147 E4
Winterborne Ave. BR6 .... 51 D7
Winterfield La. ME19 .... 89 E8
Wintergreen Cl. **7** E6 .... 1 E8
Winters Croft. DA12 .... 30 D2
Winton Cl. BR8 .... 39 E5
Winton Rd. BR6 .... 51 B6
Wirral Wood Cl. BR7 .... 23 A2
Wirrals The. ME5 .... 62 A4
Wise's La. TN15 .... 56 E2
Wiseacre. TN3 .... 166 A3
Wishart Rd. SE3 .... 5 D5
Wisley Rd. BR5 .... 24 B1
Wistaria Cl. BR6 .... 51 B8
Wisteria Gdns. BR8 .... 39 D7
Witches La. TN13 .... 83 D4
Witham Way. ME2 .... 46 D7
Withens Cl. BR5 .... 38 C5

Witherston Way. SE9 .... 23 A5
Withyham Rd. TN3 .... 161 A6
Wittersham CE (VA) Prim Sch.
  TN30 .... 189 D2
Wittersham Cl. ME5 .... 62 B5
Wittersham House. **2** BR5 .... 38 D1
Wittersham Rd.
  Potman's Heath TN17 & TN30 . 188 D4
Wittersham TN30 .... 189 C5
Wittersham Road Sta. TN17 .... 188 D6
Wixom House. SE9 .... 5 C3
Wodehouse Cl. ME20 .... 74 F4
Woldham Pl. BR2 .... 36 C5
Woldham Rd. BR2 .... 36 C5
Wolds Dr. BR6 .... 51 A6
Wolfe Cl. BR2 .... 36 A3
Wolfe Cres. SE7 .... 1 D1
Wolfe Rd. ME16 .... 91 B2
Wollaston Cl. ME8 .... 63 D3
Wolseley Rd. TN4 .... 149 C7
Wolsey Ct. SE9 .... 5 F1
Wolsey Mews. BR6 .... 51 F5
Wolsley Cl. DA1 .... 8 E2
Wolvercote Rd. SE2 .... 3 D4
Wombwell Gdns. DA11 .... 29 E6
Wood Cl. Ditton ME20 .... 90 E8
Wood Cl. Joyden's Wood DA5 ..... 25 E5
Wood Dr. Chislehurst BR7 .... 22 E2
Wood La. East End TN17 .... 171 C3
Wood La. Lane End DA2 .... 27 F4
Wood Lodge Gdns. BR1 .... 22 E1
Wood Lodge Grange. TN13 .... 84 C5
Wood Point. **10** E16 .... 1 A8
Wood Ride. BR5 .... 37 E5
Wood St. Cuxton ME2 .... 46 B2
Wood St. Gillingham ME7 .... 48 A6
Wood St. Newham E16 .... 1 B6
Wood St.
  Royal Tunbridge Wells TN1 ...... 149 B4
Wood St. Swanley Village BR8 .... 40 D8
Wood View Cl. TN15 .... 55 E3
Wood Way. BR6 .... 51 A8
Woodberry Gr. DA5 .... 25 D5
Woodbine Rd. DA15 .... 23 E7
Woodbridge Dr. ME15 .... 91 F1
Woodbrook Rd. SE2 .... 7 B8
Woodbury Cl. TN4 .... 149 A5
Woodbury La. TN30 .... 183 A7
Woodbury Park Gdns. TN4 .... 149 B5
Woodbury Park Rd. TN4 .... 149 B5
Woodbury Rd. Chatham ME5 ...... 61 F1
Woodbury Rd. Hawkhurst TN18 179 A2
Woodchurch Cl. Sidcup DA14 .... 23 D5
Woodchurch Cres. ME8 .... 49 C2
Woodchurch Ct. **1** BR5 .... 38 C4
Woodchurch Dr. BR1 .... 22 D1
Woodchurch House. ME8 .... 49 C2
Woodchurch Rd. TN30 .... 183 D8
Woodclyffe Dr. BR7 .... 37 A7
Woodcock La.
  Grafty Green ME17 .... 126 E5
Woodcock La. Iden Green TN17 180 E3
Woodcocks. E16 .... 1 D8
Woodcote Dr. BR6 .... 37 D2
Woodcote Wlk. DA15 .... 24 A7
Woodcroft. SE9 .... 22 F5
Woodcut. ME4 .... 92 A8
Woodfall Dr. DA1 .... 8 F3
Woodfalls Inst. ME18 .... 120 D6
Woodfield Ave.
  Hildenborough TN11 .... 116 E5
Woodfield Rd. TN9 .... 133 B8
Woodfield Way. ME5 .... 33 E4
Woodfields. TN13 .... 83 D4
Woodford House. **13** SE18 .... 6 B8
Woodford Rd. ME16 .... 91 B2
Woodgate La. ME9 .... 65 C2
Woodgate Rd. ME19 .... 73 D4
Woodgate Way. TN9 .... 133 E7
Woodgers Gr. BR8 .... 39 F7
Woodget Cl. E6 .... 1 E8
Woodhatch Cl. E6 .... 1 E8
Woodhayes. BR7 .... 23 B2
Woodhead Dr. BR6 .... 51 E8
Woodhill. SE18 & SE7 .... 1 E2
Woodhill Prim Sch. SE18 .... 1 E2
Woodhurst. ME5 .... 61 D4
Woodhurst Ave. BR5 .... 37 C3
Woodhurst Cl. ME2 .... 46 B2
Woodhurst Rd. SE2 .... 3 A2
Woodington Cl. SE9 .... 6 A1
Woodknoll Dr. BR7 .... 36 F8
Woodland Cl. New Barn DA3 ...... 43 C6
Woodland Cl. New Town ME19 ... 89 A8
Woodland Cl.
  Royal Tunbridge Wells TN4 ...... 149 C7
Woodland Dr. TN8 .... 112 D3
Woodland Rd. TN4 .... 149 C7
Woodland Rise. TN15 .... 84 E4
Woodland Terr. SE7 .... 1 E2
Woodland View. TN30 .... 189 C4
Woodland Way.
  Bidborough TN4 .... 132 D3
Woodland Way. Erith SE2 .... 3 D2
Woodland Way. Maidstone ME14 92 B7
Woodland Way. Orpington BR5 ... 37 C4
Woodlands. Chatham ME5 .... 62 A2
Woodlands. Coxheath ME17 ..... 106 B3

Woodlands. Paddock Wood TN12 135 F7
Woodlands. Romford TN2 .... 150 F7
Woodlands.
  Royal Tunbridge Wells TN4 ..... 133 A2
Woodlands. Swanley BR8 .... 39 E6
Woodlands. Wilsley Green TN17 169 D6
Woodlands Ave. Sidcup DA15 ..... 23 E7
Woodlands Ave. Snodland ME6 ... 74 F8
Woodlands Cl. Bromley BR1 .... 36 F7
Woodlands Cl. Maidstone ME14 . 92 B7
Woodlands Cl. Swanley BR8 .... 39 F7
Woodlands Cl. Teston ME18 ..... 105 E4
Woodlands Cty Jun Sch. TN10 117 E6
Woodlands Cty Prim Sch. ME7 48 F4
Woodlands High Sch. ME7 .... 48 F4
Woodlands La. DA12 .... 31 E1
Woodlands Manor Golf Course.
  TN15 .... 70 D6
Woodlands Pk. DA5 .... 25 D4
Woodlands Rd. Bexley DA7 .... 7 E4
Woodlands Rd. Bromley BR1 ...... 36 F7
Woodlands Rd. Ditton ME20 .... 90 D8
Woodlands Rd. Gillingham ME7 .. 48 F4
Woodlands Rd. Orpington BR6 ... 52 A4
Woodlands Rd. Tonbridge TN9 . 133 A2
Woodlands Rise. BR8 .... 39 F7
Woodlands Terr. BR8 .... 39 B3
Woodlands The. BR6 .... 52 B4
Woodlands View. TN14 .... 53 A1
Woodleas. ME16 .... 90 F2
Woodman Par. **4** E16 .... 2 A5
Woodman St. E16 .... 2 A5
Woodmere. SE9 .... 22 F7
Woodmount. BR8 .... 39 D2
Woodpecker Cl. **2** TN8 .... 112 D3
Woodpecker Glade. ME8 .... 63 D6
Woodpecker Rd. Larkfield ME20 74 F1
Woodpecker Rd. Woolwich SE28 3 C6
Woodrow. SE18 .... 1 F2
Woods Green Cotts. TN5 .... 174 F7
Woodsgate Way. TN2 .... 150 B6
Woodside. Gillingham ME8 .... 63 C6
Woodside. Vigo Village DA13 ...... 72 F8
Woodside Ave. BR7 .... 23 C3
Woodside Cl. Crayford DA1 & DA7 8 D3
Woodside Cl. Pembury TN2 .... 150 E6
Woodside Cres. DA15 .... 23 E5
Woodside Ct. DA2 .... 25 E4
Woodside Gn. ME3 .... 33 B7
Woodside La. DA5 .... 7 D1
Woodside Rd. Bromley BR1 .... 36 E4
Woodside Rd. Crayford DA7 .... 8 D3
Woodside Rd. Maidstone ME15 107 C7
Woodside Rd. Pembury TN2 ...... 150 E6
Woodside Rd. Rusthall TN4 ...... 148 D4
Woodside Rd. Sevenoaks TN13 ... 84 B4
Woodside Rd. Sidcup DA15 .... 23 E5
Woodside Rd. Sundridge TN14 ... 82 E3
Woodside Rd. Tonbridge TN9 .... 133 B7
Woodside Sch. DA7 .... 8 D3
Woodstock Cl. DA5 .... 24 F7
Woodstock Ct. SE12 .... 5 A1
Woodstock Rd. ME2 .... 47 A7
Woodvale Ct. BR1 .... 36 B7
Woodview Cl. BR6 .... 51 C8
Woodview Cres. TN11 .... 116 F5
Woodview Cty Prim Sch. DA3 .. 43 A6
Woodville Rise. ME2 .... 32 F1
Woodville. SE3 .... 5 B6
Woodville Cl. SE12 .... 5 A2
Woodville Gr. **2** DA16 .... 7 A4
Woodville Pl. DA11 .... 30 B8
Woodville Rd. ME15 .... 92 A2
Woodville St. **16** SE7 .... 1 E2
Woodward Terr. DA9 .... 10 E1
Woodyates Rd. Lewisham SE12 ... 5 A1
Woodyates Rd. Lewisham SE12 .. 22 B8
Woolacombe Rd. SE3 .... 5 C5
Woolaston Cl. ME15 .... 91 F1
Wooldeys Rd. ME8 .... 49 F2
Woolf Cl. SE28 .... 3 B5
Woolf Wlk. RM18 .... 13 C5
Woollett Cl. DA1 .... 9 A3
Woollett St. ME14 .... 92 A5
Woolley Cl. TN4 .... 132 F1
Woolley Rd. Maidstone ME15 ... 107 F7
Woolley Rd.
  Royal Tunbridge Wells TN4 ..... 132 F1
Woolpack Cnr. TN27 .... 172 A7
Woolwich Arsenal Sta. SE18 .... 2 B1
Woolwich Church St. SE18 & SE7 1 E3
Woolwich Cl. ME5 .... 62 A7
Woolwich Coll. SE18 .... 2 B2
Woolwich Coll (Charlton). SE7 . 1 D2
Woolwich Comm. Woolwich SE18 6 A7
Woolwich Comm. Woolwich SE18 6 A8
Woolwich Dockyard Ind Est.
  SE18 .... 1 E3
Woolwich Dockyard Sta. SE18 .. 1 F2
Woolwich Manor Way.
  Newham,Beckton E6 .... 2 A7
Woolwich Manor Way.
  Newham,North Woolwich E16 .... 2 B5
Woolwich Manorway. E16 .... 2 B4
Woolwich Poly Sch.
  .... 2 B1
Woolwich Poly Sch .
  Woolwich SE18 .... 2 B3
Woolwich Rd. Bexley DA7 .... 8 A4
Woolwich Rd. Erith SE2 .... 3 E1
Woolwich Rd.
  Greenwich SE10 & SE7 .... 1 C2
Wootton Gn. ME8 .... 49 D3

Wootton House. SE9 .... 6 D1
Wopsle Cl. ME1 .... 61 D7
Worcester Ave. ME18 & ME19 .... 89 A2
Worcester Cl. Istead Rise DA13 .. 29 F1
Worcester Cl. Rochester ME2 ..... 46 E8
Worcester Cl. Swanscombe DA9 . 11 B3
Worcester Rd. ME15 .... 107 D7
Wordsworth Cl. Chatham ME5 .... 62 C7
Wordsworth Cl. Tilbury RM18 ..... 13 C5
Wordsworth House. 15 SE18 .... 6 A8
Wordsworth Rd. Bexley DA16 ...... 6 E6
Wordsworth Rd.
    Maidstone ME14 .... 92 B7
Wordsworth Way.
    Dartford DA1 .... 10 A3
Wordsworth Way.
    Lunsford ME20 .... 75 A4
Workhouse La. ME15 .... 106 C4
Workhouse Rd.
    Chartway Street ME17 .... 125 A8
Workhouse Rd. Ryarsh ME19 ..... 73 F4
Worlds End La. BR6 .... 52 B3
Wormdale Hill. ME9 .... 65 B3
Wormdale Rd. ME9 .... 65 B4
Worsenden. TN27 .... 157 E1
Worships Hill. TN13 .... 83 E4
Worth Cl. BR6 .... 51 E6
Wotton Cl. ME15 .... 107 E5
Wotton Gn. BR5 .... 38 D5
Wouldham CE Prim Sch. ME1 . 60 C5
Wouldham Rd. Grays RM16 .... 11 E8
Wouldham Rd.
    Rochester ME1 .... 46 E1
Wouldham Terr. 3 BR5 .... 38 B6
Wrangleden Cl. ME15 .... 107 E5
Wrangleden Rd. ME15 .... 107 E5
Wrangling La. DA13 .... 58 F3
Wratham Road Cty Prim Sch.
    DA11 .... 30 B8
Wrekin Rd. SE18 .... 6 C7

Wren Cl. Larkfield ME20 .... 74 F1
Wren Cl. St Paul's Cray BR5 .... 38 D6
Wren Ind Est. ME15 .... 107 F4
Wren Path. SE28 .... 2 D4
Wren Rd. DA14 .... 24 C5
Wren Way. ME5 .... 62 B6
Wren Wlk. RM18 .... 13 B7
Wrens Croft. DA11 .... 29 E4
Wrens Rd. ME9 .... 80 F6
Wricklemarsh Rd.
    Greenwich SE3 .... 5 B6
Wricklemarsh Rd.
    Greenwich SE3 .... 5 D6
Wright Cl. Gillingham ME8 .... 49 C2
Wright Cl. Swanscombe DA10 ... 11 D1
Wrights Cl. TN30 .... 183 A8
Wrot & Hill Ct. DA4 .... 41 B8
Wrotham Hill Rd. TN15 .... 72 A6
Wrotham Rd. Bexley DA16 .... 7 C6
Wrotham Rd.
    Borough Green TN15 .... 87 A8
Wrotham Rd.
    Culverstone Green DA13 .... 57 E2
Wrotham Rd.
    Gravesend DA11 & DA13 ..... 30 A4
Wrotham Rd.
    Meopham Station DA13 ...... 44 A3
Wrotham Sch. TN15 .... 72 A1
Wrotham Water La. ME19 .... 72 E5
Wrotham Water Rd. TN15 .... 72 E4
Wrottesley Rd. SE18 .... 6 C8
Wroxham Rd. SE28 .... 3 D6
Wulfred Way. TN15 .... 70 B1
Wyatt Cl. TN15 .... 86 F7
Wyatt House. 2 ME2 .... 47 A7
Wyatt Pl. ME2 .... 47 A7
Wyatt Rd. DA1 .... 8 F4
Wyatt St. ME14 .... 92 A4
Wyborne Prim Sch. SE9 .... 23 B7
Wybourne Rise. TN2 .... 163 B8

Wybournes La. ME23 .... 17 C3
Wycliffe Cl. DA16 .... 6 F6
Wycliffe House. 5 DA11 .... 29 F7
Wycliffe Row. DA11 .... 29 F7
Wycombe Ct. SE3 .... 5 A7
Wydeville Manor Rd. SE12 ...... 22 B4
Wye Cl. BR6 .... 37 F2
Wye Rd. Borough Green TN15 ... 87 A8
Wye Rd. Gravesend DA12 .... 30 D6
Wye Rd. Tonbridge TN10 .... 117 C5
Wyfold House. 10 SE2 .... 3 D4
Wyke Manor Rd. ME14 .... 92 A4
Wykeham Cl. DA12 .... 30 E2
Wykeham Cotts. ME17 .... 106 F2
Wykeham Gr. ME17 .... 109 A7
Wykeham St. ME2 .... 47 B8
Wyles Rd. ME4 .... 47 E2
Wyles St. ME7 .... 48 C7
Wylie House. ME3 .... 33 B6
Wylie Rd. ME3 .... 34 D6
Wyncham Ave. DA15 .... 23 E7
Wyncroft Cl. BR1 .... 36 F6
Wyndam Rd. ME4 .... 47 E2
Wyndcliff Rd. SE3 & SE7 .... 5 B8
Wyndham Ave. TN11 .... 115 F1
Wyndham Cl. Leigh TN11 .... 115 F1
Wyndham Cl. Orpington BR6 ..... 37 C1
Wynford Gr. BR5 .... 38 B6
Wynford Pl. DA17 .... 8 A8
Wynford Way. SE9 .... 22 F5
Wynn's Ave. DA15 .... 7 A2
Wytchlings The. ME17 .... 109 D2
Wythens Wlk. SE9 .... 6 B1
Wytherling Cl. ME14 .... 92 F5
Wythes Cl. BR1 .... 36 F7
Wythes Rd. E16 .... 1 E5
Wythfield Rd. SE9 .... 5 F1
Wyvern Cl. Dartford DA1 .... 26 C8
Wyvern Cl. Orpington BR6 .... 52 B7
Wyvern Cl. Snodland ME6 .... 75 A7

Wyvern House. 3 RM17 .... 12 B8
Wyvill Cl. ME8 .... 63 E5

Yalding Cl. Orpington BR5 .... 38 D5
Yalding Cl. Rochester ME2 .... 33 B1
Yalding Hill. ME18 .... 105 A3
Yalding Prim Sch. ME18 .... 105 A1
Yalding Sta. ME18 .... 104 D1
Yantlet Dr. ME2 .... 46 C7
Yardley Cl. TN9 .... 117 D3
Yardley Park Rd. TN9 .... 117 D3
Yarnton Way. DA17 & DA18 .... 3 E4
Yarrow Cres. E6 .... 1 E8
Yarrow La. ME14 .... 92 F5
Yarrow Rd. ME5 .... 61 F4
Yateley St. SE18 & SE7 .... 1 D3
Yaugher La. ME9 .... 64 C3
Yelsted La. Chatham ME14 ...... 77 D7
Yelsted La. Yelsted ME9 .... 64 A1
Yelsted Rd. ME9 .... 79 A7
Yeoman Ct. ME14 .... 93 B3
Yeoman Dr. ME7 .... 48 F1
Yeoman Gdns. TN12 .... 135 F6
Yeoman La. ME14 .... 93 B4
Yeoman Way. ME15 .... 93 A2
Yeoman's Meadows. TN13 ..... 84 A1
Yeovil Cl. BR6 .... 51 E8
Yester Dr. BR7 .... 22 E1
Yester Pk. BR7 .... 22 F2
Yester Rd. BR7 .... 22 F1
Yew Rd. ME3 .... 34 E3
Yew Tree Cl. Aylesford ME20 .... 75 E1
Yew Tree Cl. Bexley DA16 .... 7 A6
Yew Tree Cl. Chatham ME5 ...... 62 D1
Yew Tree Cl. New Barn DA3 ..... 43 D7
Yew Tree Cl. Sevenoaks TN13 ... 83 D4
Yew Tree Cotts.
    Groombridge TN3 .... 161 F8
Yew Tree Cotts. Halstead TN14 . 67 F7
Yew Tree Cotts. Sandling ME14 . 76 F1

Yew Tree Green Rd. TN12 .... 137 A1
Yew Tree Pl. ME7 .... 63 D1
Yew Tree Rd. TN4 .... 149 B8
Yews The. DA12 .... 30 D7
Yewtree Ind Est. ME20 .... 75 D2
Yolande Gdns. SE9 .... 5 E2
Yopps Gn. TN15 .... 86 E1
York Ave. Chatham ME5 .... 61 F3
York Ave. Gillingham ME7 .... 48 C4
York Ave. Sidcup DA15 .... 23 F6
York Cl. E6 .... 1 F7
York Hill. ME4 .... 48 C2
York Par. TN10 .... 117 C6
York Pl. RM17 .... 12 A8
York Rd. Dartford DA1 .... 26 F8
York Rd. Gravesend DA12 .... 30 C5
York Rd. Maidstone ME15 .... 92 C2
York Rd. Northfleet DA11 .... 29 D8
York Rd. Rochester ME1 .... 47 C3
York Rd.
    Royal Tunbridge Wells TN1 .... 149 A4
York Rd. Tonbridge TN10 .... 117 D5
York Rise. BR6 .... 51 E8
York Road Cty Jun Sch. DA1 .... 26 F8
York Terr. DA8 .... 8 C6
Yorkland Ave. DA16 .... 6 F3
Youens Pl. ME3 .... 32 B3
Young Rd. E16 .... 1 C7

Zambra Way. TN15 .... 84 F7
Zangwill Rd. SE18 & SE3 .... 5 D6
Zealand House. 4 SE7 .... 1 E2
Zelah Rd. BR5 .... 38 C2
Zetland Ave. ME7 .... 48 E2
Zion Pl. DA11 .... 30 B8
Zion St. TN15 .... 84 F6

STREET ATLASES ORDER FORM

All Street Atlases contain Ordnance Survey mapping and provide the perfect solution for the driver who needs comprehensive, detailed regional mapping in a choice of compact and easy-to-use formats. They are indispensable and are ideal for use in the car, the home or the office.

The series is available from all good bookshops or by mail order direct from the publisher. Before placing your order, please check by telephone that the complete range of titles are available. Payment can be made in the following ways:

By phone Phone your order through on our special Credit Card Hotline on **01933 443863** (Fax: **01933 443849**). Speak to our customer service team during office hours (9am to 5pm) or leave a message on the answering machine, quoting your full credit card number plus expiry date and your full name and address.

By post Simply fill out the order form (you may photocopy it) and send it to: **Philip's Direct, 27 Sanders Road, Wellingborough, Northants** NN8 4NL.

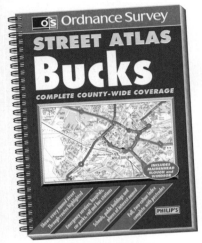

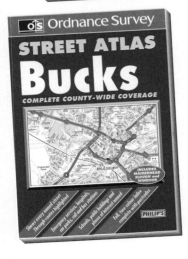

COLOUR EDITIONS

	HARDBACK	SPIRAL	POCKET	£ Total
	Quantity @ £10.99 each	Quantity @ £8.99 each	Quantity @ £4.99 each	£ Total
BERKSHIRE	☐ 0 540 06170 0	☐ 0 540 06172 7	☐ 0 540 06173 5	➤ ☐
MERSEYSIDE	☐ 0 540 06480 7	☐ 0 540 06481 5	☐ 0 540 06482 3	➤ ☐
	Quantity @ £12.99 each	Quantity @ £8.99 each	Quantity @ £4.99 each	£ Total
SURREY	☐ 0 540 06435 1	☐ 0 540 06436 X	☐ 0 540 06438 6	➤ ☐
	Quantity @ £12.99 each	Quantity @ £9.99 each	Quantity @ £4.99 each	£ Total
BUCKINGHAMSHIRE	☐ 0 540 07466 7	☐ 0 540 07467 5	☐ 0 540 07468 3	➤ ☐
DURHAM	☐ 0 540 06365 7	☐ 0 540 06366 5	☐ 0 540 06367 3	➤ ☐
HERTFORDSHIRE	☐ 0 540 06174 3	☐ 0 540 06175 1	☐ 0 540 06176 X	➤ ☐
EAST KENT	☐ 0 540 07483 7	☐ 0 540 07276 1	☐ 0 540 07287 7	➤ ☐
WEST KENT	☐ 0 540 07366 0	☐ 0 540 07367 9	☐ 0 540 07369 5	➤ ☐
EAST SUSSEX	☐ 0 540 07306 7	☐ 0 540 07307 5	☐ 0 540 07312 1	➤ ☐
WEST SUSSEX	☐ 0 540 07319 9	☐ 0 540 07323 7	☐ 0 540 07327 X	➤ ☐
TYNE AND WEAR	☐ 0 540 06370 3	☐ 0 540 06371 1	☐ 0 540 06372 X	➤ ☐
SOUTH YORKSHIRE	☐ 0 540 06330 4	☐ 0 540 06331 2	☐ 0 540 06332 0	➤ ☐
	Quantity @ £12.99 each	Quantity @ £9.99 each	Quantity @ £5.50 each	£ Total
GREATER MANCHESTER	☐ 0 540 06485 8	☐ 0 540 06486 6	☐ 0 540 06487 4	➤ ☐
	Quantity @ £12.99 each	Quantity @ £9.99 each	Quantity @ £5.99 each	£ Total
NORTH HAMPSHIRE	☐ 0 540 07471 3	☐ 0 540 07472 1	☐ 0 540 07473 X	➤ ☐
SOUTH HAMPSHIRE	☐ 0 540 07476 4	☐ 0 540 07477 2	☐ 0 540 07478 0	➤ ☐

ORDNANCE SURVEY

COLOUR EDITIONS

	HARDBACK	SPIRAL	POCKET	£ Total
	Quantity @ £12.99 each	Quantity @ £9.99 each	Quantity @ £5.99 each	
OXFORDSHIRE	☐ 0 540 07512 4	☐ 0 540 07513 2	☐ 0 540 07514 0	➤ ☐
WEST YORKSHIRE	☐ 0 540 06329 0	☐ 0 540 06327 4	☐ 0 540 06328 2	➤ ☐
	Quantity @ £14.99 each	Quantity @ £9.99 each	Quantity @ £5.99 each	£ Total
LANCASHIRE	☐ 0 540 06440 8	☐ 0 540 06441 6	☐ 0 540 06443 2	➤ ☐

BLACK AND WHITE EDITIONS

	HARDBACK	SOFTBACK	POCKET	£ Total
	Quantity @ £10.99 each			
WARWICKSHIRE	☐ 0 540 05642 1	—	—	➤ ☐
	Quantity @ £12.99 each	Quantity @ £9.99 each	Quantity @ £4.99 each	£ Total
BRISTOL AND AVON	☐ 0 540 06140 9	☐ 0 540 06141 7	☐ 0 540 06142 5	➤ ☐
CARDIFF, SWANSEA & GLAMORGAN	☐ 0 540 06186 7	☐ 0 540 06187 5	☐ 0 540 06207 3	➤ ☐
CHESHIRE	☐ 0 540 06143 3	☐ 0 540 06144 1	☐ 0 540 06145 X	➤ ☐
DERBYSHIRE	—	☐ 0 540 06138 7	☐ 0 540 06139 5	➤ ☐
EDINBURGH & East Central Scotland	☐ 0 540 06180 8	☐ 0 540 06181 6	☐ 0 540 06182 4	➤ ☐
EAST ESSEX	☐ 0 540 05848 3	☐ 0 540 05866 1	☐ 0 540 05850 5	➤ ☐
WEST ESSEX	☐ 0 540 05849 1	☐ 0 540 05867 X	☐ 0 540 05851 3	➤ ☐
NOTTINGHAMSHIRE	—	☐ 0 540 05859 9	☐ 0 540 05860 2	➤ ☐
STAFFORDSHIRE	☐ 0 540 06134 4	☐ 0 540 06135 2	☐ 0 540 06136 0	➤ ☐
	Quantity @ £12.99 each	Quantity @ £9.99 each	Quantity @ £5.99 each	£ Total
GLASGOW & West Central Scotland	☐ 0 540 06183 2	☐ 0 540 06184 0	☐ 0 540 06185 9	➤ ☐

Post to: **Philip's Direct,**
27 Sanders Road,
Wellingborough, Northants,
NN8 4NL

◆ Free postage and packing

◆ All available titles will normally be dispatched within 5 working days of receipt of order but please allow up to 28 days for delivery

◆ Please tick this box if you do not wish your name to be used by other carefully selected organisations that may wish to send you information about other products and services

Registered Office: 25 Victoria Street, London SW1H 0EX.

Registered in England number: 3396524

I enclose a cheque / postal order, for a **total** of ☐
made payable to *Reed Book Services*, or please debit my

☐ Access ☐ American Express ☐ Visa ☐ Diners

account by ☐

Account no
☐☐☐☐ ☐☐☐☐ ☐☐☐☐ ☐☐☐☐

Expiry date ☐☐ ☐☐

Signature...

Name...

Address...

....

....

....POSTCODE

STREET ATLASES ORDER FORM